MW00397979

2024 NHL DRAFT BLACK BOOK
PROSPECT SCOUTING REPORTS & DRAFT RANKINGS

BY HOCKEYPROSPECT.COM

© 2024

INFORMATION

THE RANKINGS

Much like years past we will be following the same system for our rankings that we included since the 2020 NHL Draft Black Books. Rather than rank 217 players the way we did years ago, we want our list we include in this book to be the same as the rankings we show to NHL teams. The ranking closely reflects the rankings format of NHL teams. To give you an idea of what we're talking about, we got some feedback from some teams. The feedback spans data from numerous draft years.

List Length

NHL team draft lists vary in length by the team and by year, but in general the average team had anywhere from 85 players ranked (not including goalies)) to 120 players ranked. Teams also mentioned that in the average draft year, any player ranked in the 70+ range on their list begins to have much less chance of actually being drafted. We know of at least one team that didn't reach the 60th player on their list in draft a few years ago.

Our draft list length will be at least 90 players each year.

Actual Draft Examples

To give you an idea of where a player is ranked and where that player might actually be drafted, we asked a few teams for some actual examples of where they had a player ranked on their list and where that player was selected by them on draft day. These examples are from multiple teams and range as far as 12 years.

- *Example 1 - Player Ranking was 29th on team list and was drafted 50th overall.*
- *Example 2 Player Ranking was 40th on team list and was drafted 59th overall.*
- *Example 3 Player Ranking was 30th on team list and was drafted 47th overall.*
- *Example 4 Player Ranking was 33rd on team list and was drafted 56th overall.*
- *Example 5 Player Ranking was 57th on team list and was drafted 93rd overall.*
- *Example 6 Player Ranking was 43rd on team list and was drafted 65th overall.*
- *Example 7 Player Ranking was 68th on team list and was drafted 144th overall.*
- *Example 8 Player Ranking was 11th on team list and was drafted 25th overall.*
- *Example 9 Player Ranking was 53rd on team list and was drafted 155th overall.*

As you can see from these examples, a player who is listed #40 on our list does not equate to being the player we would select if we had the 40th pick in the draft.

Here is an example going back to the 1st round in 2018 using our own list:

Let's assume we were picking 9th overall in the New York Rangers spot. Although we had Kravtsov (NYR actual selection)ranked very high at 6th overall, we had Noah Dobson ranked one spot higher at 5th overall. Dobson would've been our selection in the Rangers 9th spot and also in the Edmonton Oilers 10th spot (Oilers selected Evan Bouchard and we had Dobson ranked 5th and Bouchard ranked 10th) We would have obviously been quite happy to get our 5th ranked prospect at 10th overall.

In our **2024 NHL Draft Black Book** our list will once gain be the same format as an average NHL team's list*. If you see a player ranked by us, it tells you we would be willing to draft him.

NHL team's will make some adjustments during the draft based on live draft results. As an example, if they draft a goalie they might scratch all the other goalies off their list.

*Sometimes teams have side lists. Some examples include small players lists or players with off ice concerns being listed separately As mentioned earlier, teams we've spoken to over the years use separate lists for goalies.

	PLAYER	TEAM	LEAGUE	HEIGHT	WEIGHT	POS	GRADE
NR	SANDLER, ADAM	NEW JERSEY	NAHL	5' 09"	185	LC	**NI**
NHLCS	CEILING	FLOOR	HOCKEY SENSE	COMPETE	SKILL	SKATE	MISC
NA-145	5	5	4	9	5	4	5

The sample player table above shows a fake players details and our ratings, ranking and grade. **NR** indicates **"Not Ranked"** so he did not make our draft list. If he had made our list, a ranking number would replace the "NR". NHLCS is NHL Central Scouting

NI indicates a **"No Interest"** grade for us. Other options are, "A" "B" "C" and "C+"

THE RATINGS (THE GRADES ARE BASED ON A 3 TO 9 SCALE ALSO USED BY AN NHL TEAM.)

CEILING	FLOOR	HOCKEY SENSE	COMPETE	SKILL	SKATING	MISC.
THIS IS A GRADE TO ASSIST IN SHOWING HOW WE PROJECT A PLAYERS CEILING	THIS IS A GRADE TO ASSIST IN SHOWING HOW WE PROJECT A PLAYERS FLOOR	DECISION MAKING	WORK ETHIC	SHOT POWER	QUICKNESS	HEIGHT
		ANTICIPATION	ATTACK THE NET	SHOT RELEASE	SPEED	WEIGHT
		PLAYMAKING/VISION	CONSISTENCY	SHOT ACCURACY	BALANCE	STRENGTH
		DECEPTION	FIRST ON PUCKS	PUCK PROTECTION	MOBILITY	ENDURANCE
A HIGH GRADE (9) WOULD SHOW THAT WE FEEL THE PLAYER HAS A VERY HIGH CEILING. A LOW GRADE (3) WOULD SHOW THE OPPOSITE	A HIGH GRADE (9) WOULD SHOW THAT WE FEEL THE PLAYER HAS A VERY HIGH FLOOR. A LOW GRADE (3) WOULD SHOW THE OPPOSITE	PROCESSING SPEED	BACKCHECK	PASSING	MECHANICS	ATHLETICISM
		CREATIVITY	SHOT BLOCKING	STICKHANDLING	BACKWARDS	MISC
		SPATIAL AWARENESS	PLAYING INSIDE	SCORING ABILITY		
		TEMPO	TOUGHNESS			
RATED ON 3-9 SCALE	RATED ON 3-9 SCALE	RATED ON 3-9 SCALE	RATED ON 3-9 SCALE	RATED ON 3-9 SCALE	RATED ON 3-9 SCALE	RATED ON 3-9 SCALE

We've included some areas we scout. There is no magical formula. We won't dock a defenseman for not attacking the net.

3 -Poor, **4**- Below Average, **5** Average, **6** Good, **7** Very Good, **8** Excellent, **9** Elite

The "Average" grade is based on the player against his fellow draft eligibles in his current draft class. The grades simply give you an idea of where we see a player rate in several key aspects that we evaluate. There are obviously several tiers within a grade. Not all "6" skaters are created equal etc. We will take into account a players age and physical maturity when grading skating as an example. If we felt like a 2002 birth was closer to his ceiling, he might get the same grade as a player who isn't quite at his level yet, but we project that it will get better. **NOTE: WE DO NOT** add up the five grades for any type of score. There are other factors that can carry weight for where a player ranks on our list, including off ice factors , level of competition, current team, next team, coaching etc…

THE TRAITS BELOW ARE FACTORED INTO OUR RATINGS FOR GOALIES AND DEFENSEMAN.

DEFENSEMAN SPECIFIC	GOALIE SPECIFIC
PUCK RETRIEVAL	ANGLES & POSITIONING
GAP CONTROL	NET PRESENCE
QUARTERBACKING (POWER PLAY)	POISE, CONFIDENCE, BIG IN NET.
DEFENDING	LATERAL MOVEMENT
FIRST PASS	RECOVERY
	REBOUND CONTROL
	GLOVE
	MENTAL TOUGHNESS
	PLAYING THE PUCK
	OVERALL QUICKNESS

NEW SINCE OUR 2023 NHL DRAFT BLACK BOOK: CEILING AND FLOOR GRADES

New to our player profile table in is the addition of **ceiling** and **floor** grades. Scouts will often discuss players' ceilings and floors. A scout saying that he projects a player to have both a high ceiling, and high floor, is best case scenario. This would mean that a scout thinks the player has plenty of potential in his game, but also a high floor, meaning that the player has already reached a high threshold of talent that would project to being a safer bet to play in the NHL.

In simplest of terms, Connor McDavid would've received our highest (9) rating for both our ceiling and floor grades. Incredible talent and potential and already playing at a very high level at draft time which obviously also made him an incredibly talent and a safe player to select.

These grades can lead to discussions about "Boom or Bust" players. A high ceiling (9) rating with a low floor (3) rating is an example of a player who may shine in the NHL in the future or conversely never be able to make or remain in the NHL.

Another example might be a player with a higher floor grade than ceiling grade. This could be a player we feel confident will play in the NHL but might not have as high a ceiling if he makes it. So you could potentially see a player with a Ceiling grade of say 6 (Good) and a floor grade of 8 (Excellent). This could perhaps be.a forward who might have a lower offensive ceiling in the NHL but we feel has a very good chance to play in the NHL in that role.

DRAFT GRADES

We also include a draft grade in the player profiles. We use these draft grades as a sorting tool.

As a real life example, an NHL's teams Director of Scouting will look to his area scouts grades in the various leagues to assist in his scheduling. The scout is not going to make a trip cross country to go see one player with a "C" grade on a team. The scout would seek out "A" and "B" graded players in a certain area. This gives them an idea of which players and how many players he would be watching during the course of the trip. The scout might see three "A" players two "B" players and 5 "C" players (who are included in the games with A's and B's). It obviously varies on each trip. As the season moves along, the number of players with draft grades drops. We use A.B.C,C+ Watch (Watch List) and NI (No Interest).

A Round 1

B Rounds 2-3

C Rounds 4-7

C+ Closer to round 4 than round 7

Not all the players we rate with a draftable grade will make our list. We will have several "C" rated players who don't crack our final list. Any players who we have rated with draft-able grades who don't get drafted would start the next season as watch list players. Note that actual NHL teams will be inviting some of their top rated players who went undrafted to their camps.

A common question:

Q: Why don't you have 32 "A"rated players when there are 32 players selected in the first round?

A: Because not all draft classes have 32 players that Scouts deem worthy of giving a 1st round grade.

In speaking to several NHL Scouts for the draft, the majority have told us they have between 17-20 "A" rated prospects this year. More than one scout had less than 17 players with a 1st round "A"grade.

SOME EXPLANATIONS

Tempo: We included tempo under hockey sense. We are referring to a player controlling the speed with which he moves throughout a shift or at times more specifically during an individual rush. An example would be a player changing speeds to open a lane. For example, Cole Perfetti was excellent at changing his speed to open lanes.

Processing Speed: This is referring to the speed in which a player is able to process the play around him. We assess how quickly he can process the situation in order to move on to the next step, which is to make a good decision.

The "MISC." Category: This is a category to allow us rate a player's physical stature, athleticism and endurance. **Toughness is included under the compete category** and would include a player's willingness to take the body.

NHL DRAFT LIST

HOCKEYPROSPECT.COM 2024 NHL DRAFT LIST

RANK	LAST	FIRST	TEAM	LEAGUE	POS	HEIGHT	WEIGHT
1	Celebrini	Macklin	Boston University	HOCKEY EAST	LC	5'11.75"	197
2	Lindstrom	Cayden	Medicine Hat	WHL	LC	6'03"	213
3	Buium	Zeev	University of Denver	NCHC	LD	6'00"	186
4	Demidov	Ivan	SKA St. Petersburg Jr	RUSSIA-JR	LW/RW	5'11"	181
5	Silayev	Anton	Torpedo Nizhny Novgorod	RUSSIA	LD	6'07"	211
6	Sennecke	Beckett	Oshawa	OHL	RW	6'02.75"	175
7	Iginla	Tij	Kelowna	WHL	LW	6'00"	191
8	Dickinson	Sam	London	OHL	LD	6'02.75"	203
9	Parekh	Zayne	Saginaw	OHL	RD	6'00.25"	178
10	Levshunov	Artyom	Michigan State	BIG 10	RD	6'01.75"	205
11	Catton	Berkly	Spokane	WHL	LC	5'10.25"	175
12	Luchanko	Jett	Guelph	OHL	RC	5'11"	187
13	Helenius	Konsta	Jukurit	FINLAND	C/RW	5'11"	189
14	Yakemchuk	Carter	Calgary	WHL	RD	6'02.75"	202
15	Greentree	Liam	Windsor	OHL	LW	6'02.5"	215
16	Brandsegg-Nygard	Michael	Mora	SWEDEN-2	RW	6'00.75"	207
17	Jiricek	Adam	Plzen	CZECHIA	RD	6'02.5"	178
18	Chernyshov	Igor	Dynamo Moscow	RUSSIA	LW	6'02"	192
19	Eiserman	Cole	USA U18	NTDP	LW	5'11.75"	197
20	Parascak	Terik	Prince George	WHL	RW	5'11.75"	179
21	Beaudoin	Cole	Barrie	OHL	LC	6'02"	210
22	Miettinen	Julius	Everett	WHL	LC	6'03"	201
23	Vanacker	Marek	Brantford	OHL	LW	6'00.5"	175
24	Solberg	Stian	Vålerenga	NORWAY	LD	6'01.5"	205
25	Gridin	Matvei	Muskegon	USHL	LW	6'01.5"	189
26	Surin	Yegor	Yaroslavl Jr	RUSSIA-JR	LC/LW	6'01"	192
27	Freij	Alfons	Vaxjo Jr	SWEDEN-JR	LD	6'00.5"	197
28	Basha	Andrew	Medicine Hat	WHL	LW	5'11.25"	187
29	Villeneuve	Nathan	Sudbury	OHL	LC	5'11"	193
30	Boisvert	Sacha	Muskegon	USHL	LC	6'02"	183
31	Pulkkinen	Jesse	JYP	FINLAND	LD	6'06"	219
32	O'Reilly	Sam	London	OHL	RC/RW	6'00.25"	184
33	Muggli	Leon	Zug	SWISS	LD	6'00.5"	177
34	Letourneau	Dean	St.Andrews College	PREP-ONT	RC	6'06.5"	214
35	Sahlin Wallenius	Leo	Vaxjo Jr	SWEDEN-JR	LD	6'00"	180
36	Connelly	Trevor	Tri-City	USHL	LW	6'00.75"	160
37	Badinka	Dominik	Malmo	SWEDEN	RD	6'02.75"	185
38	Brunicke	Harrison	Kamloops	WHL	RD	6'02"	185
39	Artamonov	Nikita	Torpedo Nizhny Novgorod	RUSSIA	RW	5'11"	187
40	Hage	Michael	Chicago	USHL	RC	6'00.5"	190
41	Roberts	Colton	Vancouver	WHL	RD	6'03.75"	204
42	Eriksson	Linus	Djurgardens	SWEDEN-2	LC	6'00"	189
43	Howe	Tanner	Regina	WHL	LW/LC	5'10"	184
44	Battaglia	Jacob	Kingston	OHL	RW	6'00.25"	202
45	He	Kevin	Niagara	OHL	LW	5'11.25"	181
46	Hutson	Cole	USA U18	NTDP	LD	5'10.25"	165
47	Pettersson	Lucas	Modo Jr	SWEDEN-JR	LC	5'11.5"	173
48	Shuravin	Matvei	CSKA Jr	RUSSIA-JR	LD	6'03"	195
49	Masse	Maxim	Chicoutimi	QMJHL	RW	6'02.25	190
50	Hemming	Emil	TPS	FINLAND	RW	6'01.25"	205
51	Ritchie	Ryder	Prince Albert	WHL	RW	6'00.25"	177
52	Elick	Charlie	Brandon	WHL	RD	6'03.25"	202
53	Gill	Spencer	Rimouski	QMJHL	RD	6'03.75"	186
54	Marrelli	Luca	Oshawa	OHL	RD	6'01.5"	185
55	Fernstrom	Melvin	Orebro Jr	SWEDEN-JR	RW	6'00.75"	188

56	Stiga	Teddy	USA U18	NTDP	LW	5'10"	178
57	Traff	Herman	HV71 Jr	SWEDEN-JR	RW	6'02.75"	216
58	Skahan	Will	USA U18	NTDP	LD	6'04"	211
59	Emery	EJ	USA U18	NTDP	RD	6'03.25"	183
60	Walton	Kieron	Sudbury	OHL	LC/LW	6'05.5"	211
61	Wooley	Jared	London	OHL	LD	6'04.5"	207
62	Marques	Miguel	Lethbridge	WHL	RW	5'10.25"	187
63	Danford	Ben	Oshawa	OHL	RD	6'01.5"	191
64	Ziemer	Brodie	USA U18	NTDP	RW	5'11"	196
65	Mustard	John	Waterloo	USHL	LW	6'01"	186
66	Boilard	Raoul	Baie-Comeau	QMJHL	LC	6'01"	189
67	Avramov	Fyodor	Stupino Jr	RUSSIA-JR	LW	6'03"	190
68	Galvas	Tomas	Liberec	CZECHIA	LD	5'10.25"	153
69	Kiviharju	Aron	HIFK	FINLAND	LD	5'09.5"	184
70	Maistrenko	Oleg	CSKA Jr	RUSSIA-JR	RC	6'01"	190
71	Berglund	Jack	Farjestad Jr	SWEDEN-JR	LW	6'03.5"	210
72	Kleber	Adam	Lincoln	USHL	RD	6'05.5"	215
73	Jecho	Adam	Edmonton	WHL	RC	6'05"	201
74	Ruhonen	Heikki	Kiekko-Espoo Jr	FINLAND-JR	LC	6'01"	196
75	Kos	Ondrej	Ilves JR.	FINLAND JR	LC/LW	6'02.5"	176
76	Smith	Tarin	Everett	WHL	LD	6'01.25"	187
77	Caswell	Clarke	Swift Current	WHL	LW	5'10.75"	170
78	Forslund	Charlie	Falu IF	SWEDEN-3	LW/RW	6'03"	212
79	Fransen	Noel	Farjestad Jr	SWEDEN-JR	LD	6'00"	179
80	Koivu	Aatos	TPS Jr	FINLAND-JR	RC	6'00.5"	170
81	Johansson	Loke	AIK Jr	SWEDEN-JR	LD	6'03"	214
82	Kol	Timur	Omskie Jr	RUSSIA-JR	LD	6'03"	198
83	Mateiko	Eriks	Saint John	QMJHL	LW	6'05"	216
84	Poirier	Justin	Baie-Comeau	QMJHL	RW	5'08"	190
85	Satan	Miroslav	Bratislava Jr	SLOVAKIA-JR	LC	6'07"	190
86	Pikkarainen	Kasper	TPS-JR	FINLAND-JR	RW	6'03"	197
87	Holinka	Miroslav	Trinec Jr	CZECHIA-JR	RC/RW	6'01"	187
88	Mews	Henry	Ottawa	OHL	RD	6'00.25"	189
89	Gojsic	Hiroki	Kelowna	WHL	RW	6'03"	198
90	Zether	Simon	Rogle	SWEDEN	RC/RW	6'03"	176
91	De Luca	Tommaso	HC Ambri-Piotta	SWISS	LW	6'00"	187
92	Marchenko	Arseni	Team Belarus U18	BELARUS-JR	RD	6'06"	207
93	Misa	Luke	Mississauga	OHL	LC	5'10"	175
94	Montgomery	Blake	Lincoln	USHL	LW	6'03.25"	180
95	Bernier	Alexis	Baie-Comeau	QMJHL	RD	6'01.25"	197
96	Eliasson	Gabriel	HV71 Jr	SWEDEN-JR	LD	6'06.75"	206
97	Humphreys	Christian	USA U18	NTDP	RC	5'10.5"	170
98	Gustafsson	Viggo	HV71 Jr	SWEDEN-JR	LD	6'02"	187
99	Nieminen	Daniel	Pelicans Jr	FINLAND-JR	LD	5'11.25"	177
100	Plante	Max	USA U18	NTDP	LW	5'11"	177
101	Fibigr	Jakub	Mississauga	OHL	LD	6'00"	171
102	Curran	Maxmilian	Tri-City	WHL	LC	6'03"	185
103	Fischer	Lukas	Sarnia	OHL	LD	6'04"	181
104	Becher	Ondrej	Prince George	WHL	LC	6'01.25"	187
105	Mrsic	Tomas	Medicine Hat	WHL	LC	5'11.25"	170
106	Lavoie	Tomas	Cape Breton	QMJHL	RD	6'03.5"	215
107	Korotky	Matvei	SKA St.Petersburg	RUSSIA-JR	RC	6'01"	198
108	Vesterheim	Petter	Mora IK	SWEDEN-2	LC	5'11"	172
109	Pridham	Jack	West Kelowna	BCHL	RW	6'01"	177
110	Thorpe	Tyler	Vancouver	WHL	RW	6'04"	209
111	Laing	Hunter	Prince George	WHL	RC	6'05"	205
112	Procyszyn	Ethan	North Bay	OHL	RC	6'02.25"	190
113	Solovey	Justin	Muskegon	USHL	LW	6'02"	209

HOCKEYPROSPECT.COM 2024 NHL DRAFT GOALIE LIST

RANK	LAST	FIRST	TEAM	LEAGUE	POS	HEIGHT	WEIGHT
1	Zarubin	Kirill	AKM Tula Jr	RUSSIA-JR	G	6'04"	179
2	Moysevich	Pavel	SKA St.Petersburg	RUSSIA	G	6'04"	187
3	Yegorov	Mikhail	Omaha	USHL	G	6'05"	188
4	Gidlof	Marcus	Leksand Jr	SWEDEN-JR	G	6'06"	212
5	Obvintsev	Timofei	CSKA Jr	RUSSIA-JR	G	6'04"	176
6	Nabokov	Ilya	Magnitogorsk	RUSSIA	G	6'00"	179
7	Saarinen	Kim	HPK Jr	FINLAND-JR	G	6'04.25"	176
8	Yunin	Ivan	Omskie Jr	RUSSIA-JR	G	6'02"	196
9	Leenders	Ryerson	Mississauga	OHL	G	6'00.5"	165
10	George	Carter	Owen Sound	OHL	G	6'01"	194
11	Gardner	Evan	Saskatoon	WHL	G	6'00"	175
12	St.Hilaire	Samuel	Sherbrooke	QMJHL	G	6'02.25"	185
13	Vinni	Eemil	JoKP	FINLAND-2	G	6'02.75"	187
14	Kavan	Jan	HC Kometa Brno	CZE JR	G	6'01"	176

HOCKEYPROSPECT.COM RANKINGS NOTE FROM MARK EDWARDS

When we begin the process of putting our rankings together, **I constantly remind our scouts to rank players as if they are on a contract with an NHL team**. I drive home the point to them that it is much easier to take a chance on a player's ranking if they don't factor in the ramifications it might have on them personally. I remind them that we have NHL staff members who view our rankings and they want us to rank the players as if we are at a table on the draft floor, like they are.

I tell our scouts I don't want to see player rankings where they place some high risk or lesser known player way up their list just so that on the 10% chance that the player "hits", they can proclaim themselves a scouting savant.

I tell our scouts to imagine they are entering the final year of their contact with an NHL team. I tell them to imagine banging the table for a player on the draft floor and then placing their own name on that player's jersey as they watch him in the upcoming season. Would they be proud or scared to have their own name on that player's jersey name bar ?

It's much more difficult for NHL team scouts to make their personal rankings than it is for John Doe throwing his list on social media. The NHL scouts have bills to pay and have kids to send to University. I remind our scouts to imagine that paying their bills is directly tied to how good their rankings look in 4 or 5 years..

When I'm ranking players I ask myself how easily I would sleep after day 1 of the draft if I selected a certain player. I know a huge number of NHL scouts, and I know I will see them back in the rinks in September for the next upcoming draft. I want to be able to look those scouts in the eye knowing that I'm ranking players in spots where I would actually select them if I was on the draft floor with them. **We'll make our share of mistakes like any other scouts, but the NHL scouts and staffers who know me, know that I do my best to simulate the way an actual team makes their lists.**

Draft rankings are much easier to make if the person/people making them have zero to lose if they swing and miss. I feel that HockeyProspect.com has something to lose if we swing and miss. We lose credibility and that is something that matters to me very much.

Mark Edwards
Founder & GM
HockeyProspect.com

PROSPECT PROFILES

NR	PLAYER	TEAM	LEAGUE	HEIGHT	WEIGHT	POS	GRADE
	ANTENEN, ROBIN	ZUG	SWISS JR	6' 01.25"	190	LW	NI

NHLCS	CEILING	FLOOR	HOCKEY SENSE	COMPETE	SKILL	SKATE	MISC
INT-75	5	5	6	5	4	5	6

A reliable forward out of Zug's U20 program in Switzerland, Robin Nico Antenen shows both leadership and intelligence on the ice. In 44 games this season in the U20 Swiss league, Antenen put up 40 points, 20 goals and assists, before getting a cup of coffee in the NL. In the playoffs Antenen added 7 points in 11 games for Zug U20. He showed production as a secondary scoring option both in U20 and internationally for Switzerland.

Offensively, Antenen does not offer much in terms of skill as he is not a primary attacker in any area of the ice. He does not possess high end skills down low or while in motion which takes out his ability to be a volume scorer at a higher level. He is not more or less of a playmaker than he is a goal scorer with a shot that he needs time getting off and average vision. Most of his puck possession comes from the outside and he has trouble breaking into the middle with the puck from the outside in the offensive zone or while entering the zone. This is because his hands, brain and feet are not on the same page which causes him to lose possession at times or skates himself into trouble offensively.

His skating is average with nothing strikingly good or bad. He does not possess the best speed, but he has a decent burst every once in a while, that gets him deep on the forecheck. As he translates to smaller ice it will be difficult for him as he will have trouble with more limited space due to hi lack of speed and skill. If he ramps up his physicality, he could position himself into a lineup as a fourth line forward, however that seems to be his ceiling should he not make improvements to his skill.

When looking at spending a draft pick on Antenen, you will need to look at how correctable his skill set is and at what rate he can improve it. For us, at this stage in his development his skill level and speed make it hard to justify a draft selection with limited potential.

39	PLAYER	TEAM	LEAGUE	HEIGHT	WEIGHT	POS	GRADE
	ARTAMONOV, NIKITA	NIZHNY NOVGOROD	RUS	5' 11"	187	LW	B

NHLCS	CEILING	FLOOR	HOCKEY SENSE	COMPETE	SKILL	SKATE	MISC
INT-19	6	6	7	7	6	7	6

Artamonov spent the past season in the KHL playing for Igor Larionov and Chaika Nizhny Novgorod. He finished the season with 7 goals and 23 points in 54 games, on the same team as Anton Silayev, which is an extremely rare example of two draft-eligible players playing on the same KHL team. He closed his season by helping Chaika's MHL team reach the semifinals in the postseason, collecting 10 points in 11 games along the way.

This was a season with some ups and downs for Artamonov. He was really good in the first half of the season, even becoming the first U18 player in KHL history to record a 4-point game. At that point of the season, he had 13 points in 22 games, but only finished with 10 points in his last 32 games. He had a 14-game scoreless streak in December and January. During his cold streak, his confidence seemed to really be affected, and we had some bad viewings in that stretch where he would be invisible on the ice. One of his calling cards early in the season was his positive energy level, but there were a lot of games during that bad stretch where he didn't bring much energy at all, and his bad puck touches led to his skill level not showing up well, either. As a scout, though, you've got to remember that the KHL is a tough league to play in for an 18-year-old, and it's normal to see a player like Artamonov encounter those ups and downs during the season. He's also not a world-beater in terms of skill. He's a fine player, but he's not a high-end skilled player, either. He did find his game back late in the year, mostly with his stint in the MHL playoffs, a good reminder about his skill level that he couldn't always show in the KHL. We saw Artomonov from the first three months of the season, where his speed, smarts and compete level became factors again.

We project him as a middle-6 forward for the NHL. Earlier this year, we compared him to Artturi Lehkonen of the Colorado Avalanche in that he has similar size, a solid two-way game, his effort level is usually great, and he has above-average hockey sense and skating skills. If everything goes right, he could end up being a very good utility forward in your top-9 that can play on any line because he can keep up speed-wise with everyone and make players around him better. He's got good playmaking skills, he sees the ice well and anticipates the play well to get open to receive passes in top scoring areas. He's also quite useful in his team's transition game thanks to his speed and one-on-one skills. His skill level is not in the legit top-6 realm, but with everything else he brings to the table, similar to Lehkonen, you could play him with top forwards and he won't look out of place. There's a chance he can end up playing on a PP2 in the NHL as well, but with his great sense of anticipation, speed and work ethic, he can be a good penalty killer.

His not being a gifted goal scorer could limit how high he plays in the lineup as well as his production. He has a decent shot, but he'll need to get closer to the net to have success with it at the NHL level, as he won't be a threat from distance. He's a good forechecker with his speed and strong puck-pursuit game. He uses his speed and angling well to pressure opposing defensemen. We like his compete level; he's more annoying with his no-quit and relentless game than someone with a really strong heavy physical presence on the ice.

We don't think Artamonov did enough to crack our top 32, but he's a player we like, and he's a safe bet to play in the NHL if you disregard the Russian factor. We think he could make his way to the NHL to start as a smart, energetic 3rd line player who could see his role expand as he gets more experience in the NHL, similar to what happened to Lehkonen.

67	PLAYER	TEAM	LEAGUE	HEIGHT	WEIGHT	POS	GRADE
	AVRAMOV, FYODOR	STUPINO JR.	RUS JR	6' 03"	190	LW	C
NHLCS	CEILING	FLOOR	HOCKEY SENSE	COMPETE	SKILL	SKATE	MISC
INT-53	6	4	6	8	6	7	7

Avramov is a hard-hitting, quick-strike power forward who uses static posture and hesitation feints before exploding into offensive plays. He played on the worst team in the best conference, the Western Conference Gold Division in the MHL. Kapitan Stupino was the only team from that division that missed the playoffs, yet Avramov led the way on his team, finishing with 44 points in 49 games, including 23 goals. His primary assist rates on his team were also impressive, with 17 of his 21 assists being primary.

One of the most important aspects in determining if a young, raw power forward's game can translate is evaluating if they inherently or instinctively display offensive tendencies that make them more difficult for the opposition to pick up. Avramov always has the option of dictating with his tool-kit and size, yet when he can operate in both aspects of the game, combining power with stealth, it gives him more options.

In Fyodor's case, he has the physical base and size to run through players, yet he generally looks to systematically pick defenses apart by generating plays that lack tells. He doesn't telegraph plays as often as most strong and young power forwards who play a similar style, and that's the critical component to this player.

For example, he's very good at maintaining static posture before exploding into space, generating a speed differential as a result. When setting up his passing plays with his hands, he lulls opposing players into a false sense of security before using his hand activation to explode through the end phase of his playmaking. During pass reception plays, he will momentarily freeze, then off-look his actual option he intends to pass to before transitioning immediately into an explosive pass. His sharper passes are also extremely accurate at times, forming a base that isn't so dissimilar to Chernyshov in terms of making difficult passes look relatively easy.

His shooting mechanics aren't so dissimilar to Michael Cammalleri's. We're not suggesting he's going to score as much at the NHL level as Cammalleri did in his impressive career, but we refer to the way he drops through his shot and his comfort in dropping to a knee. In fact, over half of Avramov's goals this season were a direct result of him dropping through his release point. He also features a soft catch-and-release and displayed the ability to extend his shooting windows to give himself higher percentage shooting options in tight to the net.

Although he's a dual threat, Avramov's hands can let him down at times, specifically when he's attempting to operate with them at full speed or when he has to suddenly handle the puck tighter to his frame. He's a heavier-set player who isn't overtly nimble at this stage in his development, so when he has pucks in tight to his skates, he can have trouble using his footwork in combination with his handling.

He projects to be able to primarily drive around or through players on his backhand or by spinning off of pressure, but not as often through multi-touch handling or lateral drag-and-slip triangle dekes. That said, he can perform double rock-backs and rapidly drag the puck across the body of opposing defensemen when setting his shot up through a screen. We just wish there was better operational handling for making outside-to-inside moves, considering he's a tenacious net-driving player and could take advantage of that kind of skill set if he had it.

He primarily compensates for his handling by doing hesitation half-spins, where he will extend the puck on his stick while using his frame to counteract sticks and protect the puck so that he remains primarily back onto incoming defensemen. This component of his game really highlights how adapted he is to making sure he can still translate his game to the MHL.

Although Avramov is a physically imposing power forward who can turn himself into a freight train to take opposing players out of the play, he's green when it comes to understanding how to use his power to his advantage down low and around the net area. As an example, when he's attempting to spin off pressure and become a back door option, or when he needs to push off of a defender to generate temporary space in a high-danger area so that he can get his shot off in time, he can fail to weight transfer effectively or dynamically use his weight to counteract the opponent's momentum against him. This meant that a lot of potential in-tight setup plays that he should theoretically finish given his talent didn't materialize for him.

One of the better ways to look at Avramov's game as a whole is similar to how we evaluated Jani Nyman's. We think Nyman was the better prospect with more talent at the same age, but they both operated similarly in their initial draft seasons from the perspective that they had a lot of untapped potential, but it wasn't getting realized because they didn't know how to seamlessly transfer between their skill sets. Avramov is talented with an untapped skating base, but his talent, as of right now, is segmented or compartmentalized. He doesn't know how to bring everything together yet, but if he can figure it out, then there's something there to untap.

Avramov plays the game extremely hard, he plays the game the right way, he brings a lot of energy and competitiveness to a lineup, and he was the go-to player for an overwhelmed team this past season. He was matched up against some of the best talent in the MHL and rarely looked out of place. He might not have true top-6 talent, but if he can merge his skills together, then we think there's some potential for a top-9 role, where he can be a versatile, hard-hitting, 200-foot power forward who brings a well-rounded skill set to the ice. Although he's one of the older prospects in this class, we feel he actually has a lot of filling out left to do, and with another uptick in coordination, he can develop correctly.

Our ranking reflects that we see the potential, but we also see a prospect who hasn't put his talent together yet.

"He's the Russian dark horse of this class with Oleg Maistrenko." - HP Scout, Brad Allen

"What you see isn't what you're going to get. He has the potential to become a truly unique power forward that every team wants if he develops well." - HP Scout, Brad Allen

"If Avramov was playing on the program or in the CHL on a solid team, everybody would be talking about this kid." - HP Scout, Brad Allen

37	PLAYER			TEAM	LEAGUE	HEIGHT	WEIGHT	POS	GRADE
	BADINKA, DOMINIK			MALMO	SWE	6' 02.75"	185	RD	B
NHLCS	CEILING	FLOOR	HOCKEY SENSE		COMPETE	SKILL		SKATE	MISC
INT-14	6	6	5		6	5		7	7

Badinka is a late birthday prospect (November 2005) from Czechia who played this past season mostly in the SHL but also in the Swedish junior league with Malmo. The year prior, he played for Jokerit in the junior league in Finland. We have also seen him in some international tournaments, but he was cut from last year's U18 Czechia team and didn't make the cut for this year's World Junior team.

This season, he played 33 games with Malmo (SHL) and performed well when he got the chance to play regular minutes. Even though he didn't produce much (4 points total) he showed some good things that could translate to the NHL. He produced more in junior (13 points in 17 games) but his overall game was not as good as it was in the SHL; we saw some of the poor decision-making appearing more frequently there than it did in the SHL.

The junior league in Sweden is a league where we've noticed less emphasis on structure, which leads to certain players making more questionable plays compared to their performance against professional teams. Simon Edvinsson, during his draft year in 2021, was a perfect example of this. When Badinka played with more structure, he was able to perform a more efficient game, albeit less flashy and risky.

To be fair, we've observed these decision-making errors in Badinka's game over the past two years. His passing game can suffer as a result, which may have also contributed to his being cut from national teams during this time. The question now is, which version is the real Badinka? We've seen both over the past two seasons, but performing well enough at the SHL level in his 18-year-old season is a good sign nevertheless. Consistency remains the big question we have with him when trying to project him for the NHL and also when ranking him.

He's a good-sized right-handed defenseman with solid skating skills. While he possesses decent puck skills, we don't project him as a power-play guy for the NHL due to a lack of playmaking and handling skillsets. The biggest issue we noted with him was the lack of passing accuracy and his overall decision-making under pressure last year. It's tough to project defensemen in the NHL when their first pass can be so inconsistent. For transitional plays, he relies more on his good skating than his passing skills. His passing game did improve in the SHL, but it's still not a strong part of his game. A determining factor in whether or not he will have an NHL career will be his understanding of how to manage risk. He has the tools to play in the NHL; enough skills, skating that is good for his frame, and teams are always on the lookout for right defensemen to add to their squad. Defensively, he has good physicality. With his skating, he can cover a good amount of ice. He can also recover well enough with his skating and reach to get back defensively. However, there's a lack of positional awareness with him at times, and his average hockey sense is demonstrated in some of his decision-making and reads.

"He's a kid I need to watch more. He has some work to do but he's got a good base." - NHL Scout, January 2024

NR	PLAYER	TEAM	LEAGUE	HEIGHT	WEIGHT	POS	GRADE
	BAKER, AUSTIN	USA U-18	NTDP	6' 00"	190	LW	NI

NHLCS	CEILING	FLOOR	HOCKEY SENSE	COMPETE	SKILL	SKATE	MISC
NA-104	5	4	5	5	4	5	5

Austin Baker started the season with a four point effort in game one playing on a line with Cole Eiserman and Christian Humphreys. Baker would have five points before the season was a week old and then ended up with just nine more for the rest of the USHL season. Given how he continued to fall down the lineup, it's looking likely that he'll wait a year on going to Michigan State and instead remain in the USHL with Sioux Falls

Baker owns a heavy shot and that's probably his best quality by a good margin. We like his pull and drag wrist shot motion in transition. He has a decent catch and release shooting technique, that still has more to give on the follow-through portion of the motion. If he works on getting more core rotation worked in, he'll likely be more effective with it. His 10 goal figure in USHL play isn't overly impressive (it also sits on a 33.3% shooting percentage), but given how poor the team was this year, it's not too discouraging. Among the U18 players, outside of goal vacuum Cole Eiserman, only Teddy Stiga (18) and Kamil Bednarik (11) tallied more. More than his shooting technique, Baker really needs to improve his spatial awareness and pace if he is serious about scoring at the next level. He doesn't fight for space enough despite having a good enough frame to do it.

At 6'0", 190 pounds, Baker isn't a crusher but he looks to have good upper body strength. The application of it isn't totally there – part of it seems physical and part of it seems mental. On the physical side, he carries a wide skating base and looks to make it wider when going into contact. He loses his balance in battle situations like this, unless he leads with his upper body/arms first. Naturally, that's not going to work very much in high-traffic shooting situations. Plus, if he can bring the feet closer together more, he'll improve his closing speed and actually end up with more pucks out of these battles. The other part appears just to be a determination or confidence deal. In the rare event that he picks up some space and speeds down the wing with the puck, he almost never challenges a d-man physically, doesn't try to turn the corner on them and drive the net. He'll turn against the grain and buy some time or support, but given his lack of vision and passing acumen, that's generally a rush killer.

His skating base lacks some pop. His wide stance does him no favors in hitting the ignition. The agility, turning, and small area footwork push the skating down a grade as they aren't nearly as good as his top speed. There has been some improvement in his body posture as the year has gone on, which is usually an indication that things are on the way up and that his core strength is on the rise. We'd really like to see him be tougher to play against in defensive situations.

NR	PLAYER	TEAM	LEAGUE	HEIGHT	WEIGHT	POS	GRADE
	BARAN, RICHARD	VICTORIA	BCHL	6' 01"	181	LD	NI

NHLCS	CEILING	FLOOR	HOCKEY SENSE	COMPETE	SKILL	SKATE	MISC
-	5	5	6	5	5	6	6

Baran is a native of Slovakia but has spent the last couple of seasons in North America in preparation for heading the NCAA route. Baran has been a staple on the back end for the Slovakian national teams the last couple years, participating in the Hlinka, U18 and this past year the U20 World Junior team for the Slovaks. Baran had a solid year for Victoria (BCHL) this season, playing primarily in a middle pairing but really saw his game take another step in the playoffs where he had 2 goals and 6 assists in 11 games and logged big minutes for the Grizzlies.

Baran displays solid t all-around skating abilities and does a good job of allowing that to be the staple of his game. Baran has good hockey sense and ability to escape the forechecker and move pucks quickly up the ice from his own zone. In our viewings Baran did a good job identifying where pressure was coming from to determine his next move with the puck, this anticipation allowed him more options with the puck on breakouts. Baran uses his feet to gain zones and showed the ability to leg pucks into the offensive zone and execute clean offensive zone entries. Baran shows excellent vision with the puck and while he certainly has the skating ability to move pucks north, he does a good job making quick reads, combined with crisp tape to tape passing to stretch the ice. In the offensive zone, Baran isn't flashy but he has shown good hands to be able to make good plays under pressure at the offensive blueline to extend plays in the zone. Baran uses good hockey sense in when to hold onto the puck and try to make something happen and when to make the simple play and put the puck back down the wall and live to fight another day. Baran saw a decent amount of power play time this year in the BCHL but we don't see him being a big PP guy at the professional levels. Baran also does an excellent job of getting pucks through to the net area. While Baran certainly looks for opportunities to join the rush or get involved in the play by coming down from the point in the offensive zone. He shows good timing and decision making in this regard and didn't sacrifice the defensive side of the puck and has good effort to get back to his position when he does pick his spots.

Baran attacks the puck defensively really well. He closes down the angle on the puck carrier quickly and limits their options. This goes back to his skating abilities that allow him to be more aggressive without the fear of getting beat with speed on the edge. Baran could play with more jam and energy defensively at times. While he excels at using positioning and timing to defend, around his net and in the corners he needs to continue to work on using his frame and leverage to seal off opponents and win puck battles. Boxing out opponents and tying up sticks in the crease area is another area of his game that Baran will need to continue to improve upon, but those are finer details in his game that will develop over time.

Baran will likely be moving to the USHL next season. He was drafted fairly high in the USHL Phase 2 draft by Des Moines and will be heading to Arizona State after next season.

28	PLAYER		TEAM	LEAGUE	HEIGHT	WEIGHT	POS	GRADE
	BASHA, ANDREW		MEDICINE HAT	WHL	5' 11.25"	187	LW	B
NHLCS	CEILING	FLOOR	HOCKEY SENSE	COMPETE	SKILL		SKATE	MISC
NA-26	7	5	7	6	7		6	5

After being a 5th round pick in the WHL, Basha showed constant improvement throughout his three WHL seasons, going from 14, to 56, to 85 points. His 55 assists and 85 points rank 3rd amongst first year NHL draft eligible players in the WHL. The Tigers' young offensive core of McKenna, Lindstrom, Basha and Mrsic should be one of best offensive firepower in the WHL next season. Basha played some games as a center this season (especially when Lindstrom was injured), but he projects as a winger at the next level.

Basha is a dominant playmaking winger and was one of the best puck carrier and rush forwards in the WHL this season. His overall speed is good, but he's good at acquiring pucks at top speed. He knows when to get moving and sprints on potential change of possession from defense to offense. When his defensemen have clean possession, he loves to swings on the weakside and build speed away from the puck, then sprinting right in the middle ice with good timing to acquire the puck with speed and ready to attack the dangerous ice. Basha is also of the best WHL forwards at getting off the wall. Every time he touches a puck on the wall or outside dots, he looks to attack the inside. His pre-scanning habits, along with his shiftiness and small-area skills allows him to do that. All these aspects make Basha a puck carrier on always seems to enter the offensive zone in control on the rush. On he enters the zone, his poise and skills are on display. His arsenal of options is wide, and he uses many of them. He can invite pressure before passing it to his teammate with more space, he can make quick plays, and his poise and skills allow him to cut laterally to attack the inside and freeze opposing defenders.

In offensive zone play, Basha used many of the same skills described above to generate offense. His wall play is a strength of his game, taking puck from the yellow wall and attacking the inside. He's good at attacking defender nose-to-nose to freeze them, then beat them with a lateral move. His puck skills a strong in tight, and even when he's inside the slot, he loves to be patient, bait defenders and make short passes inside for grade A scoring chances. When's not able to attack inside directly, Basha climbs the wall, allowing his defensemen to activate and his team to create offensive motion. Basha is a pass first forward with a fine shot, but he scored many of his goals around the net with good timing for rebound and puck skills in tight. On the power play, Basha played basically every role this season, depending on what Medicine Hat wanted as a power play set up. In the playoffs, he played mostly the bumper role in the middle one the 1-3-1 on the Tigres' five forwards unit. He did a solid job, using his hockey IQ to play between checks and his small area skills to create with the puck.

Defensively, Basha was trusted by his coaching staff. With his hockey IQ, he's smart in his team systems' and is well positioned. He played on the PK as well. For better efficiency at the next level, Basha will need to improve his pace without the puck and how he pressures the puck. Without the puck offensively, adding more off-the puck play to help his linemates like offensive pick or middle net drive would be a plus for his game as well.

Overall, Basha is a good playmaker who excels on the rush and at getting off the wall to attack the inside. The constant progression in his game is a huge plus. If he can add more pace to his play, his game can take another level.

"Good energy. I like him as a late first rounder." – NHL Scout, December 2023

"I think he's a winger for sure." – NHL Scout, February 2024

"I love Basha's rush game and how he gets off the wall to play inside". – HP Scout, Tim Archambault, February 2024

44	PLAYER	TEAM	LEAGUE	HEIGHT	WEIGHT	POS	GRADE
	BATTAGLIA, JACOB	KINGSTON	OHL	6' 00.25"	202	RW	B

NHLCS	CEILING	FLOOR	HOCKEY SENSE	COMPETE	SKILL	SKATE	MISC
NA-42	7	4	7	6	7	5	6

One of the best development curves in the OHL draft eligible class this season, Jacob Battaglia proved himself to be a reliable and intelligent forward with upside moving forward. After a respectable rookie season, Battaglia posted a strong second year scoring 31 goals and 64 points in 67 games this season for the Kingston Frontenacs. It was the tale of two seasons for both Kingston and Battaglia in the pre-Troy Mann and Post-Troy Mann seasons. The team and Battaglia were on completely different paths before and after the coaching change. Pre-Troy Mann Battaglia had some potential, but found himself waiting for opportunity to come to him. This changed drastically when Kingston brought in Troy Mann and Battaglia found a strong rhythm to his game that suddenly put him on the NHL Draft radar.

Maybe the biggest strength of Battaglia's game is his positioning. It comes in many ways for him, as he can win board battles by winning inside body positioning from defenders by using his stick and frame to knock opponents off the puck and retrieve it himself. His strength in both stick battles and with his still developing frame are assets that NHL teams will love. This showed in the OHL playoffs with his 4 points in 5 games including 3 goals. One of the big improvements for Battaglia throughout the year and as the season wore on, was that he began engaging more. Battaglia is the type of player who can beat you if you're stronger, bigger, older or more skilled as he can and will change how he will beat you depending on the situation. He can beat you just as easily with his strength on his stick as he can with his body positioning and balance. This makes him formidable in the cycle game and a threat to score off plays from down low and in front of the net. When a net front presence is needed, he can and will provide a good screen in front of the net, while also being an option for deflections with good hand-eye ability and can bury rebounds with quick hands in tight or with an intelligent ability to kick the puck to his stick for a stronger scoring chance.

Battaglia's biggest weakness is his skating due to his lack of speed. Battaglia has trouble generating speed with a poor first step and issues accelerating with his crossovers. He will need to improve this to become a threat at the NHL level. He drives from outside to inside and up the middle on the rush well with his balance, and is tough to knock off the puck while in motion. He controls the puck well, but earlier in the year he could lag behind the play at times if he was out of position. As the year progressed, his lack of speed was less noticeable because his positioning greatly improved. He showed us more often that he had the hustle to stay up to speed with faster OHL players in transition and on the rush.

He has the intelligence to read plays and react quickly, especially coming out of his zone, making smart transitional passes that push his teammates up ice and in the neutral zone to create good rush opportunities for his team. In the NHL space is limited and you need the ability to create plays with limited time and space with the strength to be able to hold off opponents and Battaglia has shown his ability to do just that with his intelligent reads and smart and accurate passing.

Intelligent on the forecheck, Battaglia will finish checks and break up passes in the neutral zone with his strong positioning in his coverage. His lack of speed holds him back from causing turnovers deep on the forecheck, however he still plays a patience and mistake free game in coverage, which will help his future team lock up neutral zones and force dump ins.

His skills are more in the passing game from the perimeter than as a rush attacker, but he can power himself to the net in lieu of his ability to be a finesse attacker. Despite this, Battaglia can be creative as a playmaker and create opportunities with behind the back passes and saucer passes five on five and on the power play should he be moved from his typical net front position. He creates a good amount of offense by creating space and finding open space for himself which should continue to translate to the pro-level. As a special teams player, Battaglia creates screens and proves to be a pest in front of the net forcing teams to commit a man to him as he is a danger to make a play in front. If he is pushed outside, this does not hurt his offensive capabilities, as he will use his passing to create cross ice opportunities or take shots from the circle with good power and accuracy.

If the skating improves, it will give him a better chance to be a middle six forward who plays more along the perimeter but has the tools and capabilities to drive the middle for net front rush deflections and play a strong game on the cycle. Players of Battaglia's ilk succeed because of their intelligence, compete and ability to provide highly desired skills that are needed in both the regular season and the playoffs. He has shown that kind of player in the OHL and his final year in the GTHL AAA U16, where he got better and more involved as the season progressed and the games got bigger. That kind of player is coveted by NHL teams who want playoff success.

"I wish his skating was better because he's a pretty smart player and he is skilled." – NHL Scout, December 2023

"Other than the skating he is a pretty solid player." – NHL Scout, May 2024

"He caught my eye recently. He has some talent...pretty skilled player. I wish he played with a little more pace and that doesn't help his skating issues. He really intrigued me with a few high end shifts in a recent game so I'm going to keep an eye on him." – HP Scout, Mark Edwards, November 2023

"He was buried down the Kingston lineup until they made the coaching change. I'm a fan. Skating is just ok but I mentioned to our guys that he kinda reminded me of a poor man's version of Jason Robertson. He is smart and skilled. If he competed slightly harder I'd really move him up my list. He's not lazy but I wish there was a little more pushback. His skating would benefit too. Good hands." – HP Scout, Mark Edwards, March 2024

"Good combine interview feedback." - HP Scout, Mark Edwards, June 2024

21	PLAYER	TEAM	LEAGUE	HEIGHT	WEIGHT	POS	GRADE
	BEAUDOIN, COLE	BARRIE	OHL	6' 02"	210	LC	B

NHLCS	CEILING	FLOOR	HOCKEY SENSE	COMPETE	SKILL	SKATE	MISC
NA-25	6	9	7	9	6	5	7

Beaudoin is a power center who had just under a point per game (62 points in 67 games) with Barrie in the OHL this season. He also played well for Canada at the Hlinka-Gretzky Cup in August and the World U18 Hockey Championship in April. He comes from a hockey family: both his father, Eric (4th round pick of Tampa Bay in 1998) and uncle, Nic (2nd round pick of Colorado in 1995) were drafted in the NHL.

Cole is one of the best power-forwards available in this draft class. He's got a great frame and uses it well to play a physical game. His puck-protection is excellent. He plays the game the right way, which makes him a player coaches will love on their team. He's not a high-end offensive player, but his attention to detail is very good, and his game is built for playoff hockey. He's a smart hockey player whose best offensive asset is his playmaking. He possesses underrated creativity with the puck, showcasing an ability to read the ice and execute effective plays, particularly along the boards or from down low. His poise with the puck, coupled with his frame, enables him to extend plays while protecting the puck, creating opportunities for passing plays to develop. While he has a decent shot, his greatest offensive strength lies in his playmaking abilities.

Meanwhile, he's going to get his own goals around the net. His good net presence creates chaos for tips and rebounds. However, he needs to continue to improve his stickhandling skills to improve his one-on-one game. He can overpower players one-on-one with his strength alone, but if he can add more elusiveness with his hands, it would add even more value to his offensive game. There's really good velocity behind his shot, but he needs to improve the quickness of its release. If he can do that, his shooting skills and overall offensive game will be boosted in value. He was not a big threat with his distance shots this season. He's a player who will make his true mark offensively with his play down low and in front of the net.

The area where he needs the most improvement is his skating. However, we've observed progress since last year, notably since the Hlinka-Gretzky Cup in August. While there's still work to be done, he's moving in the right direction. A dedicated athlete, he is committed to his training regimen, and we're confident that his skating will improve with time. When he's at full speed, he's capable, as demonstrated by his effectiveness on the forecheck and during rushes. Players' development curves are so important when assessing progress from year to year. His ability to beat defenders wide with his speed has improved compared to last year. His skating progression is reminiscent of Boone Jenner's in 2011; while Jenner faced similar concerns, we saw progression during the year and were confident that it wouldn't hinder his NHL potential (going so far as to rank him 12th in our list, and he was chosen 37th in the end). While we're not directly comparing Beaudoin to Jenner, there are similarities in their skating progression during their draft years. While Jenner may have greater talent and goal-scoring ability, Beaudoin has shown superior playmaking skills at the same age.

We mentioned his physical game earlier. He's a force on the forecheck and he loves to finish his hits. He's powerful and a threat for opposing defensemen, making their lives tougher on the ice. He also uses his physicality and great frame to absorb others' physicality. It's one thing to dish out punishment, but he also can take it. He protects the puck very well and is always willing to take a hit to make a play. He's a great team player with a "whatever it takes" mentality that we love.

We're confident NHL teams will have seen the same progression with his skating that we have, and select him in the first round. The rest of his game is just a solid professional package that will translate to the NHL well and have even more value come playoff time. We think of him as a good third-line center in the NHL who can also play on the wing if need be.

"Love his game. Top 25 on my list." NHL Scout, March 2024

"Tight choosing between him and Villeneuve. Both are glue guys." - NHL Scout, April 2024

"He's a warrior." - NHL Scout, May 2024

"I love his game. I think I have him in the right spot now." - NHL Scout, May 2024

Watching Adam Lowry in the playoffs with Winnipeg and how good he was, Beaudoin is not as huge as Lowry but there are some similarities there in what he could bring in the NHL." - HP Scout Jérôme Bérubé, April 2024

"He's a physical specimen off the ice and it translates on the ice." - HP Scout, Brad Allen, May 2024

"Just saw him recently and it might be the best I've ever seen him play. Made some really smart plays and was all over the ice. Not blessed with fantastic skating but I think he might be able to get it to the point where it's not a stopper for him." - HP Scout, Mark Edwards, December 2023

"I've had some people tell me that this kid will kick ass in his NHL Combine interviews. Enough to even move him up lists." - HP Scout, Mark Edwards, January 2024

"It's hard not to love what he brings to the table. He's a gamer who gives huge effort all the time. Feet are a weakness but I'm very confident he'll still play. He kinda reminds me of Boone Jenner. He had sluggish feet too but I loved his game. Much like Boone during his draft year, Cole has improved his skating this season. The weakness in skating is not the only part of Cole's game that remind me of Boone Jenner though. They share a lot of traits including that pure gamer quality. If we had a gamer rating, than Cole would be a 9 rating in that category. - HP Scout, Mark Edwards, February 2024

"High floor. He plays the game the right way. I think he'll get drafted higher than some might think." - HP Scout, Mark Edwards, May 2024

"So I saw today that Cole said that models his game after Boone Jenner. That made me laugh since he reminds me a bit of Jenner." - June 2024

"The combine feedback was really good. Scouts enjoyed interviewing him. Two scouts in particular raved about him." - HP Scout, Mark Edwards, June 2024

104	PLAYER	TEAM	LEAGUE	HEIGHT	WEIGHT	POS	GRADE
	BECHER, ONDREJ	PRINCE GEORGE	WHL	6' 01.25"	187	LC	C
NHLCS	CEILING	FLOOR	HOCKEY SENSE	COMPETE	SKILL	SKATE	MISC
NA-69	6	4	7	5	6	7	4

Playing in his 19 year old season, Becher enters his last chance to get drafted. He had a dominant season with 96 points in 58 games. His 64 assists total and 1.66 pts/game rank 9th in the WHL. It's an impressive jump in production, with only 38 points in 63 games last season. Becher had multiple impressive milestones this season. He started the season on a heater with 27 points in his first 12 games. He finished the season with a 19 games points streak, scoring 42 points in this sequence. He had a 4 goals, 5 points games on march 16 against Victoria, including scoring 3 goals early in the 3rd period in a less than 5 minutes span. He also had a strong world junior championship for the Czech with 10 points in 7 games. He had some clutches moments in the tournament as well. He had an assist in the quarter final game against Team Canada on the game winning goal with less 0:13 left to play in the 3rd period. He had 5 points in a 8-5 victory against Finland in the Bronze medal game, including a 6-on-5 goal with less than 2 minutes left to play to tie the game at 5-5, and an assist on the game winning goal 15 seconds later. He was a top 9 center for the Czech, played on their top PP unit and on the penalty kill. His role in Prince George is similar, playing 2nd line center, top PP unit and on the penalty kill.

Offensively, Becher stands out with his skating and vision. He was one of the best playmakers in the WHL, constantly generating potential primary assist inside scoring areas. In terms of ice location, he's most dangerous in the rush. Becher is really good at acquiring pucks with speed from his own end or the neutral zone to rush the puck with speed. Although he's very fast straight line, but Becher is shifty and owns impressive lateral agility. He's able to attack inside when carrying the puck with lateral weight shift or by cutting laterally with 90 degrees change of direction. This timing of his execution is why he's such a strong playmaker. With good pre-scanning habits and understanding of the ice, he knows when to move the puck right away on his acquisition or when to skate to change the picture and find more options to improve the condition of the puck.

In the offensive zone, Becher's playmaking stands out, using his skating, puck skills and vision to find teammates inside scoring locations. An area where Becher can improve his game is his play without the puck in the offensive zone. Improving his off-puck routes and adding more offensive zone retrievals would give him more puck touches to give him even more opportunities to make plays.

Becher's shot is interesting. As a playmaker first, Becher's looking to pass so his shot quantity isn't that high. His shot from mid-distance needs to improve as well, which would make him more dangerous as a shooter on the rush. His wrist shot in tight in really good. He scored many goals by lifting the puck top net really close from the goaltender or quick top shelf breakaway shot. His one-timer is also really good. He scored multiple one-timer goals, either as F3 weakside on the rush or on Cougars' half-wall on their top power play unit. Prince George PP was dominant, ending the season 2nd in the WHL with 30.1%. Heidt, Becher, Funk, Parascak and Thornton were the five primary players.

Becher is good two-way player with a strong defensive game. As mentioned, he was a primary PK player for Prince George and the Czech. Becher is often on the ice when his team is defending a 6-on-5 against late in the game. In the playoffs against Kelowna, his line with Funk and Valis were trusted to play against the dynamic Kelowna Rocket line of Iginla, Cristall and Szturc. Becher also finished the season with 51.9% on 918 faceoffs. His anticipation, stickwork and skating allow him to intercept plays to transition from defense to offense. He's a good return to defensive zone player with good speed and effort on the tracking. In his own-end, he's positionally sounds. Some areas he needs to improve defensively are his strength in one-on-one battles and his ability to make stops down low as a center.

NR	PLAYER	TEAM	LEAGUE	HEIGHT	WEIGHT	POS	GRADE
	BEDNARIK, KAMIL	USA U-18	NTDP	6' 00.25"	187	LC	C

NHLCS	CEILING	FLOOR	HOCKEY SENSE	COMPETE	SKILL	SKATE	MISC
NA-28	5	4	6	5	5	5	5

Kamil Bednarik spent a lot of time centering noted goal scorer Cole Eiserman this season, which left Bednarik with an opportunity to do a lot of the nitty-gritty detail work without having to worry about getting the puck back a second time. That's probably the right role for him anyhow given his skillset. The former New Jersey Rocket was more or less the same player at the end of the year as he was at the beginning of it. His skating looks to have improved a bit. He still lacks explosiveness and notable small-area footwork. This is a real drawback on the 6-foot centerman, as he's going to need those skating qualities to be an effective battler. Right now, he doesn't have the ability to really lock horns with most player types and calibers…so agile players can shake loose from him, or stronger players can wall him off, or skilled players can work around him. There's a willingness from Bednarik to compete, there's even a burgeoning physical element that crops up in bigger spots, but overall he's not overly effective in battle situations yet. He is positionally sound and safe. Almost to a fault sometimes, as it seems like he could take a calculated risk for a steal, but instead chooses to defend ice first and foremost.

Besides his feet lacking pop, his skill level is a step below that. There is no dynamic element to his game. Even in open ice situations, he's more of a puck pusher than a puck handler. His puck control window is pretty small. Passes and shots fail to jump off of his blade in any situation. There appears to be almost no quick twitch element to him and his physical development arc – while certainly not tapped out – doesn't seem to be notably steep either. Just lacks the natural fluidity that we'd like to see at this point from even a mid-tier prospect. Too often, plays are bobbled because of his below average pass catching ability or his lack of puck protection know-how. Not every player on a scoring line has to be a superstar, but if you're not one – you have to have the tools necessary to keep plays alive. Watching Bednarik try to handle pucks in traffic or watching him work into contested areas shows that he's not equipped with those tools even for the junior level. He fails to create initial faux contact points to pin defenders to their heels, he lacks deceptive maneuverability, and his puck poise drops in congested areas. In a late season game vs. Dubuque, close game, mid-3rd period: Post-faceoff scramble, offensive zone, Bednarik has a clear path to winning the puck and he does. There is pressure on his back. He must be somewhat aware of the pile of bodies in the slot, as he just came from that same pile a stride and a half ago. He is facing away from the Dubuque net, he has two open point men to kick it back to…his body posture is directionally towards them. Bednarik chooses a no-look, spin-around, fadeaway wrister into all five Fighting Saints and one NTDP player. Needless to say, it doesn't get through and the puck is lost. To be a play facilitator inside, the panic threshold needs to be better; the mental processor needs to be sharper. Also, it's tough to find many goals that he scored outside the crease area…shooting from mid-range, even in pristine conditions, is not a recipe for goals from Bednarik.

" Nothing jumps off the page with Bednarik, and the detail work isn't impressive either…I don't see what he can become that would warrant a draft pick." HP Scout, Michael Farkas

71	PLAYER	TEAM	LEAGUE	HEIGHT	WEIGHT	POS	GRADE
	BERGLUND, JACK	FARJESTAD JR.	SWE JR	6' 03.5"	210	LC	C
NHLCS	CEILING	FLOOR	HOCKEY SENSE	COMPETE	SKILL	SKATE	MISC
INT-28	5	5	5	6	5	5	7

Berglund is a good-sized forward from Sweden. With the Farjestad junior team, he had 34 points in 41 games this season. He also played 8 SHL games, scoring one goal. He was a regular on the Swedish U18 national team this season, playing in the November, December, February and April tournaments. His father (Christian) was a second-round pick by the New Jersey Devils in 1998 and played 86 NHL games.

On the national team, Jack mostly played a depth role in the bottom 6, but in the February Five Nations tournament, he also found a way to be a good offensive contributor, scoring 3 goals against Finland in the opening game. Although we don't project him as an offensive player moving forward, he has adequate offensive skills. His strength lies in his ability to win puck battles along the boards and physical game down low, on the forecheck, in puck-protection situations, and around the net, which will be his bread and butter at the NHL level. While not known for a mean streak, he engages physically with his imposing frame, making an impact with his hits.

Most of his offense will come from his play down low and around the net. He can use his strength to win puck battles along the wall, and he's going to score ugly goals on rebounds and tips. His playmaking abilities are underrated, having shown some flashes during the April U18s of quality passing, particularly in transition and down low in the offensive zone. Although he needs to continue working on his skating and explosiveness, his current level is acceptable for his size. His strong work ethic and willingness to sacrifice his body to block shots also make him an asset on the penalty kill.

We think that he has a chance to become a depth forward at the NHL level, he's got the size that NHL teams covet in that role and the physicality to go with it. He has enough skills to survive in the NHL, but we don't see him playing higher in a NHL lineup.

95	PLAYER	TEAM	LEAGUE	HEIGHT	WEIGHT	POS	GRADE
	BERNIER, ALEXIS	BAIE-COMEAU	QMJHL	6' 01.25"	197	RD	C
NHLCS	CEILING	FLOOR	HOCKEY SENSE	COMPETE	SKILL	SKATE	MISC
NA-62	5	4	6	6	5	5	5

Alexis Bernier is a right-handed two-way defenseman who was drafted by the Baie-Comeau Drakkar in the 2nd round (21st overall) of the 2022 QMJHL draft. He has steadily improved over his two seasons in Baie-Comeau and has worked himself into a consistent top 4 role for a Drakkar team that is a top contender to win the QMJHL championship. He finished the regular season with 4 goals and 27 assists in 67 games played.

His skating is one of his areas that need improvement. While his straight-line speed is decent, we feel that his stride is very clunky and heavy which causes his first three strides to be rather sub par. While we find that his crossovers are effective in generating some speed while skating backwards, we also think that he has limited edgework which limits his lateral movements and leads to him getting beat wide while the opposing team is on transitional attack.

His offensive game is decent but not very developed. He is a decent puck mover on the powerplay as he can deliver accurate one touch passes and can send accurate passes in areas where he is not turned too which proves that he made the read before receiving the puck. We find that he does a good job at reading the defense and getting to open ice but not much is generated from this. He does not take shots very often (83 shots in 67 games) and even when he does, he has trouble getting them through.

Defensively, we find that his biggest asset is that he is tough to play against. He can be very tenacious in battles in front of the net and will never miss an occasion to finish his hit on an opposing player. He can deliver solid breakout passes on both his forehand and his backhand and is rarely inaccurate. Sometimes we find that his gap control is a little off. He backs up too far down in the defensive zone before making a move and leaves the opposing attackers with quality chances from the hashmarks.

Bernier does not stand out as a great prospect and does not have an aspect of his game that is particularly good. However, if you think his skating can get better, he could be a solid option in the mid to late rounds. We think that it's possible to project him as a bottom pairing defenseman at the NHL level if everything goes well in development. His compete level and tenacity could convince an organization to take a chance on him.

"This kid is a gamer, I wish he was a better skater though" - HP Scout Jérôme Bérubé, April 2024

NR	PLAYER		TEAM	LEAGUE	HEIGHT	WEIGHT	POS	GRADE
NR	BILIC, MARCO		CUSHING	HIGH-MA	6' 01.75"	175	G	C

NHLCS	CEILING	FLOOR	HOCKEY SENSE	COMPETE	SKILL	SKATE	MISC
NA-14	6	4	5	7	6	6	6

Marco Bilic comes in as the top goalie from prep hockey and follows Hunter Slukynsky who was drafted by the Kings in 2023 as being a bonafide goalie prospect out of high-school. He is our only ranked goalie from the high-school level this season. He was tremendous for Cushing Academy where he looked consistently dominant on a very dominant team.

Bilic isn't a goalie that presents with a calm demeanor, instead there's an intensity and assertiveness to his game. At first we thought he was too busy, but we feel the better term is active. He's active with his blocker and glove, especially on high shots where he's trying to get both arms out-front of the shot to deflect the puck.

His micro-adjustments are some one of the best in this class. He can adjust his position at a better speed than almost any goalie available after misinterpreting the initial shooting or play angle, and that's the critical base of this goalie. The reason it's critical is because his tracking ability is relatively average. When we mean average, we don't mean average for his respective league, at the high school levels it's good, but when evaluating his sense for an NHL projection it comes down to a mid tier range.

He can still read high danger lateral passes off of back hand options and evaluates point blank shooting placement well, it's just the inability to recognize when he can stay standing. The tell is within how often he collapses into his butterfly on either fake shots, or a shot that's from range that's blocked on its way to the net. He's overzealous when it comes to using his butterfly and actively trying to stop a puck that's not going to make it to the net. The more difficulty a goalie has at reading the intentions of a player, the more weight we attribute to their ability to make micro-adjustments to get back out in-front of the play and it's where Bilic excels. We bring this up because in some of our viewings he's had difficulty recognizing when a player transfers a shot into a lateral pass, so to counteract these types of plays Bilic has to move and readjust rapidly to get back into a position to make up for misinterpreting the initial intentions.

He excels at adjustments because he's a gifted and fully coordinated athlete. A lot of younger goalies in this class are more athletically raw and as a result we have to project them with extra weight and subsequent power packed into their frame, but that's not the case here; Bilic already presents as a pro goalie in terms of his athletic ability and within his physical development.

The two stand out athletic traits with Bilic are his reflexes which are bordering elite, and his dexterity when needing to incorporate his upper and lower halves in order to come away with a save. He can move rapidly, maintains proper posture, and has one of the best transitional butterflies in this class. His athleticism and skating can make him appear a bit busy in the net though.

When it comes to his spatial awareness, he maintains his net at an okay level. He can be overactive due to his natural aggression and he can have difficulty recognizing how much room he gives up on his far side. When players are driving from the circles or the goal line and cutting in on him; he overcommits and extends his overlap positioning too far from the center of the net.

Another issue is how often he uses his blocker and glove in combination when attempting to deflect high shots. It's a double-edged sword, in the sense that on the one hand, getting your hands out in-front of the puck on point shots that are high can negate a potential redirect in tight, but on the other, if you mistime it, then it's actually easier for a shot to redirect past you since you aren't sealed. In Bilic's case, he needs to find a better balance of when to time using his active hands when cutting down potential redirects on shots from the point, but it's a skill-set that can be developed with more time and a bit more awareness.

Another issue that can be corrected over time is his instinct to collapse forward through his butterfly movement when pucks hit his chest. Instead of remaining tall in his butterfly, he has a tendency to drop through his butterfly motion and this can put him in a position that leads to high danger rebounds he sometimes can't get to.

We think the most important factor when looking at Marco's long term development is calming down his net presence which we rarely say. He's over assertive and he gains tunnel vision through his intensity on attempting to react to the initial intentions of a forward baring down on him. He needs to remember to factor in the trailing and weak side options and allow the game to come to him a bit more than actively attempting to seek it at the current rate he does. His mentality has worked well for him at the high school level but as he moves up levels and he starts dealing with more skilled and deceptive players, he will have to incorporate a more tactical approach within his reads. If he can develop his situational awareness, and read and react to deception at a better rate then the competitive attributes are present, as well as the physical ones needed to be a solid NHL goalie down the road. Our ranking reflects the difficulties of projecting a goalie from high-school where we had to take into consideration more risk than usual, but there's a lot to like here and there is potential for him to become a 1B split starter if things go well.

"I would be excited to draft Bilic, and I don't think i've said that about a high school goalie in a long time, though admittedly I didn't get to watch Slukynsky until he was already drafted, so maybe he would have been the first one but from what I've seen I think this kid has some upside." - HP Scout, Brad Allen

"I have no problem admitting I might be missing something big in this evaluation due to the quality of competition he was facing. It's already hard evaluating goalies tracking and sense for the position when you're scouting the CHL or a Jr. Euro league. High school is a different beast altogether because there's just not as much talent, and then you have to factor in that he was on an incredibly dominant team and it just makes the evaluation that much harder and more difficult due to lower shot rates." - HP Scout, Brad Allen

NR	PLAYER	TEAM	LEAGUE	HEIGHT	WEIGHT	POS	GRADE
	BLAIS, ALEXANDRE	RIMOUSKI	QMJHL	5' 10"	152	LW	C

NHLCS	CEILING	FLOOR	HOCKEY SENSE	COMPETE	SKILL	SKATE	MISC
NA-81	5	4	6	6	6	6	5

Alexandre Blais is a playmaking left-winger who has also spent some time at center. He was drafted by the Rimouski Oceanic in the 2nd round (25th overall) of the 2021 QMJHL entry draft. He just finished his 2nd full season in the QMJHL as Rimouski's leading scorer with 20 goals and 64 assists for 84 points in 68 games, 20 more points than anyone else on the team.

Blais is a decent skater. What we like about his skating stride is his edgework constantly using his inside edges to move around on the ice and he can make tight turns in the corners to escape with the puck. That being said, he is lacking a bit of high-end separation speed which is crucial for him since he has a smaller stature. His offensive game is all about his great senses and we like his playmaking ability. We like that he can be tactical and will look to beat you in a few different ways. He makes nice crisp passes and is always scanning his surroundings to find the better passing options. His shot could definitely get more powerful as he has a hard time

beating any goaltender from mid to long range and he also needs to learn how to get his shots through from a distance as we noticed that a lot of his shots get blocked.

His defensive game is not very developed. He gets frequently shoved around by bigger players in 1 on 1 battles and struggles to coral pucks in the dirty areas. He has some good hand eye coordination and we saw him bat quite a few pucks out of the air or intercept quite a few passes from his opponents. His playmaking ability help him to find passing lanes while on the breakout. He is not a very physical player and rarely takes the body on opposing players.

Blais has practically willed himself into the draft conversation this year with his performance on the ice. There is definitely stuff to like with his game like his playmaking ability. That being said, with how small he is and his skating not being elite, we think that he could possibly be one of those guys that are really good in juniors but they're offensive skills are easily dealt with at the next level. If he is still available in the later rounds, we could definitely see him being worth a flyer just based on offensive upside alone, but his game will have to grow in a couple different areas for him to be a successful NHL player.

"He reminds me a lot of Alex Barre-Boulet as a small, energetic, playmaker that lacks speed for his size. Barre-Boulet was better at the same age and has not been able to play full time in the NHL" - HP Scout Jérôme Bérubé, January 2024

66	PLAYER	TEAM	LEAGUE	HEIGHT	WEIGHT	POS	GRADE
	BOILARD, RAOUL	BAIE-COMEAU	QMJHL	6' 01"	189	LC	C

NHLCS	CEILING	FLOOR	HOCKEY SENSE	COMPETE	SKILL	SKATE	MISC
NA-51	7	5	7	5	7	6	6

Boilard was in his first season in the QMJHL after playing his 16-year-old season in the BCHL with Salmon Arm and Alberni Valley. He really made an impact on our scouts in the first half of the season, but his play cooled off a bit in the 2nd half. Statistically speaking, he had 34 points in 34 games at the Christmas break and finished with 28 points in his last 34 games. With Baie-Comeau, he played on a stacked team that finished 1st in the league. He would have likely played more minutes on other teams, but he was still a good contributor for the Drakkar, finishing at just under a point per game.

Boilard's top quality is his playmaking. He sees the ice well and can make some great passes on both his forehand and backhand. He's got good poise, and he's a smart player both with and without the puck. There is a good level of creativity in his game. While we don't anticipate him becoming a top-6 player, he does have strong passing skills. He's good at generating offense through his transition play and can also create scoring opportunities from the wall, thanks to his effective puck-protection abilities and willingness to hold onto the puck for an extra second to allow his teammates to find open space in high-scoring areas. His solid frame allows him to protect the puck effectively, further helped by his reach and ability to escape pressure through edgework.

We would like to see him improve his skating. While he does have good edgework and agility, his acceleration and top speed need work. He doesn't have the smoothest stride either; there's some refinement that could be done to improve in that area. He does use his edges well to change directions, and that makes him tough to handle one-on-one in tight spaces, such as along the boards when he has the puck. Some of the best sequences we saw from him this season involved him pivoting away from pressure and protecting the puck from defenders, creating scoring chances. Possibly his best highlight of the season: an early-season goal he scored in Gatineau where that good puck-protection game was on display. He also used some deception along the wall and had a good give-and-go with his brother Jules.

If everything goes right with his development, we project him as a 3rd line center. For that, you need good hockey sense. We mentioned earlier that he's a smart player offensively and has good skills in terms of playmaking and creativity. Away from the puck, we like his anticipation and stick activation to break down plays and create turnovers in the neutral zone. In his zone, he needs to work a bit on his positional game, but we feel that as he gains more experience, his overall defensive game is going to be solid. He barely played on the PK unit this season, but based on his IQ and tools, we think he's going to be good in that department. Look for him to start playing more next season and become a bigger part of Baie-Comeau's penalty kill.

He was strong in the faceoff circle in his rookie season, averaging 57%. With his role expanding and as he continues to face top centers around the league more often, we will see if he can continue to build on that percentage next season, as his minutes were slightly sheltered this year. One thing that made us drop him in our rankings since January is our need to see him compete harder on the ice. There were some games throughout the season against good teams such as Drummondville where he just didn't bring it. We need to see him use his size more, play more on the inside and just be tougher to play against. We didn't see enough of that this season.

We don't project him as a top-6 forward because his hands and shooting were too inconsistent for us this season. We felt that he mishandled the puck too many times while in transition. He did have some good moments in transition, beating players one-on-one, but overall, this area of his game was a letdown too often. The same goes with his shot. He scored some very nice goals from distance and from the left faceoff circle, mostly using his wrist shot. However, he also had moments where his shot didn't look technically sound, and we saw him as having a tougher time translating as a 20+ goal scorer in the NHL. Consistency in those two areas (shooting and hands) was problematic in our eyes this season.

Our initial projection made earlier in the year was higher than it was in the second half; the more we watched him this season, the more we re-evaluated this as having been too high. Having said that, he still has potential to become a 3rd or 4th line center in the NHL if he puts in the work. We want to see him improve his speed and compete level. Sometimes a lack of compete level can be viewed as a player being lazy, but this is not the case here. We want to see more tenacity and urgency out of him that makes him a tougher player to play against, and that should help him improve his overall game–as well as improve his chances of reaching the NHL.

"He is a smart player. Great two way game." – NHL Scout, January 2024

"Plays on the perimeter a lot but I like his smarts. He has upside." – NHL Scout, January 2024

"In my last viewing he wouldn't go to the net. I can't stomach that." – NHL Scout March 2024

"Saw him twice recently, Wasn't bad but I need him to get into the mix more. – NHL Scout, April 2024

"He's ahead of Massé for me now" – NHL Scout (November 2023)

"Too soon to put him ahead of Massé" – NHL Scout (November 2023)

"He didn't meet my expectations in the 2nd half and I had to drop him on my list, I wish he was tougher to play against." – HP Scout Jérôme Bérubé (April 2024)

"I had high hopes when I saw him in the fall but he has kinda flat lined." – HP Scout, Mark Edwards, March 2024

"With Masse struggling he was our top ranked player from the QMJHL in January. He really flatlined in the second half and Masse played better to grab top spot." – HP Scout, Mark Edwards, May 2024

30	PLAYER	TEAM	LEAGUE	HEIGHT	WEIGHT	POS	GRADE
	BOISVERT, SACHA	MUSKEGON	USHL	6' 02"	183	LC	B
NHLCS	CEILING	FLOOR	HOCKEY SENSE	COMPETE	SKILL	SKATE	MISC
NA-16	6	7	5	7	6	5	7

Sacha Boisvert appears to offer a fairly wide array of skills at the junior level, but his progression throughout the year left us wondering about the likelihood of many of his traits translating effectively. His best quality is his scoring ability. He has a terrific wrist shot and he's not afraid to use it. He's among the top volume shooters in the USHL. Boisvert ended up finishing fifth in the USHL in goals during the regular season with 36. However, he was shutout from a goal scoring perspective in the postseason (0+3=3 in 8 GP). Some of that can be attributed to bad luck, but it also winks at some of his flaws as a player that might limit his upside. Just from a pure goal scoring perspective, the diversity in how he scored his goals seemed to shrink as the year went on. His early season goals saw him lower in the slot and competing in traffic more often. As the season wore on, however, many of his goals were outside-in cuts to around the dot line or just inside and punctuated with a shot from the top of the circle. While some of those wrist shots are well placed and really humming, the two primary factors noted are not readily transferrable to the pro game. Goalies aren't giving up long-range wristers usually and, more poignantly, a player crossing the blueline with the puck outside the dot line is rarely afforded the opportunity to get back inside the dots by NHL defensemen. About half of his last 20 goals (including three empty netters, two of which were scored from beyond center ice) were scored in this fashion. Another fair chunk of them were scored from low-angle wrist shots from outside the dots in the lowest layer of the offensive zone. The goal sample in the first half of the season saw goals scored off of net-mouth scrambles, off of contact and through traffic, off sudden change semi-breakaways, etc. In short, the goals became more homogeneous and more on the "junior" side as the year went on. That reads less like a player experimenting and more like a player settling for taking advantage of a bad situation.

This style of play also cut down on our faith in him becoming a dual-threat center. Early in the season, he gave the impression of a player that may be able to carry the puck across multiple lines and distribute it well. Unfortunately, those skills didn't improve as the season continued. In fact, they seemed to worsen. Boisvert has some very good hands and he can take players on 1 on 1. But again, his dekes and 1 on 1 play went from very interesting down to very predictable as we went along. The positive is that Sacha has a really intriguing puck control window – both off his hips and out in front of his body. He uses his reach to put defenders in vulnerable situations and then tries to sashay past them. Categorically, however, these moves are quite similar. They involve a lot of puck exposure and they create a wide target for defenders to hit him in the chest mid-move. In these far-reaching maneuvers, there is no "auto" puck protection mechanism that engages. He doesn't swing a hip around, he doesn't extend a knee to allow him a chance to complete the move with a higher chance of success. Later in the season, defenders took advantage of these points. Boisvert kept going back to the well though and that's a red flag on his adaptive (mental) processing ability. Is he actually evaluating the situation and making a dynamic move to optimize his next position or is he attempting to fit a "pre-programmed" move into a situation and hoping it works? Ultimately, we leaned towards the latter. Which isn't to say he'll be locked into that forever and be a complete bust – but it means that it's worthwhile to question just how steep his technical and mental development arcs really are. His game did not become more robust, and we'd expect to see that from an upper echelon prospect. Worse yet, not only did he not meaningfully add layers to his game, but as his game scaled down, his risk mitigation went down with it. The ways that he found to consistently turn the puck over ended up being the most organic part of his game: trying to exit the zone and losing at his own blue, trying to enter the zone and losing it at that line, trying to make categorically similar dekes, trying to walk off the wall by himself without passing or faking a pass, trying to make a deke from the low angle/lowest layer of the offensive zone across the net line without passing. There was just a lot of immaturity and lacklustre hockey sense on display with his turnovers and even when the dekes succeed, they don't highlight intelligent play. It's reasonable to say that he committed some of the most egregious giveaways of any USHL draft eligible player this year.

It's his playmaking that really breaks down when he's pressured or in traffic. So, when he's deking to get into an area or out of a situation, it's predominantly to setup a wrist shot. It's not to setup a teammate. We saw this often in odd-man rush situations. The amount of 2 on 1, 3 on 2, 4 on 2, etc. situations where he crosses the attack line with the puck and doesn't pass it is concerning. Muskegon might have the best roster in the USHL, so it's not a bad-team situation. The cross net-line pass plays that he made were largely under little or no duress. They also had a pattern of being situations where he walked from outside the dots, back inside, and then all the way to the other side of the ice. Those kinds of plays become pretty scarce in the pros and all the more so with Boisvert's unexciting skating package. We wished there were more one-touch or quick passing plays…a give and go around a defender in the mid- or lower-layer would have been nice. But, again, going back to the adaptive processing for him…when he receives a pass, he needs some time to figure out where he's going on and where the puck is going next. His lack of vision and passing creativity eats into his puck carrying scalability. He isn't an overly smooth puck handler as it is, and it's rockier when he's trying to play at speed. Without a true dynamic element to his game and a limited passing scope, he's not projecting to be much of a threat in the neutral zone.

Boisvert did make an effort comeback defensively in most of our viewings. He wasn't consistent in this regard, both from an effort perspective and a technique perspective…but it's better than nothing. Obviously, the hockey sense concerns that loom large in his playmaking process are the same hockey sense concerns that exist in trying to stop another team from making a play. When he's at his best, he provides an element of physicality and can be a stopper from that regard. Despite his posture, he can connect with some good contact and surprising ability to shift his weight into a hit. Typically with stiffer skaters that lack a good, deep knee bend and three-point flexion, we see a somewhat discordant motion that lacks punch. He's far from a mauler, but it looks like he uses physicality to get himself into games early. That element to his game should help him down the line and we would expect it to improve as he eats into his physical development arc. When he's not able to make a physical play defensively, he has a tendency to be unable to truly be a stopper. Even if he's in the neighbourhood, his mental processor and his skating make it tough for him to create sudden change opportunities. In other words, he can be near a play or near his man, but not quite able to shut it down consistently. His penalty killing left a lot to be desired: it lacks details, it has holes…he almost over-played it at times. Charging out to the point and leaving seam passes behind him, for instance.

At 6'2", 176 pounds, we expect him to grow into his frame – not just from a strength perspective, but also from an improved athleticism perspective. Between his stiff posture and lacklustre balance, there's some awkwardness to his game that hopefully he can wash out by adapting to his frame more. It looks like he struggles to even bear down enough for faceoffs – as is reflected in his faceoff percentage. We're hoping for some better hip mobility too. He lacks the ability to drop his hip level and get off of his center line to drive through turns…as such, he has a wide turning radius with a lot of inefficient hitch steps littered throughout. He gets around the ice fine. It's not pretty, but it's fine. The trouble is absorbing and playing off contact. He can deliver some hits, but he has a hard time rolling off of them depending on his posture. It's disruptive to his process. As mentioned above, he got away from really challenging himself more in traffic.

Though this reads as fairly negative, it's really in relation to what we thought we might have had at the beginning of the year. With athletic improvements – first-step quickness, agility, hip mobility – and some technical advents to his game ("getting corner" on defenders for shooting opportunities, incorporating a puck protection element to his dekes and walks off the wall, getting back to his deflection and low-slot scoring ways, etc.), this can be an NHL player. We lost the confidence in this being a top-six center and feel more that this is a bottom six winger, but there's a fairly clear path for him to get there. He has the requisite skill and frame to do it.

"I love his game but I don't think he's a top six player at the next level. I think he plays though 100%." - NHL Scout, March 2024

"He's a player that I think has enough to fall down an NHL lineup and still hang on. He looks like a 12-18 goal bottom six winger than a legit top-six center down the line." HP Scout, Michael Farkas

"He'll drop the gloves. Tough kid. I like the energy and compete. He'll find away to make it." - HP Scout, Mark Edwards, May 2024

NR	PLAYER	TEAM	LEAGUE	HEIGHT	WEIGHT	POS	GRADE
	BRAUTI, JACK	BARRIE	OHL	5' 11"	159	LD	NI
NHLCS	CEILING	FLOOR	HOCKEY SENSE	COMPETE	SKILL	SKATE	MISC
-	5	4	5	7	5	6	5

Jack Brauti is an off the radar left shot defenseman from the Barrie Colts in the Ontario Hockey League that most wouldn't have had any interest in at the beginning of the season. By the end of the year, he was arguably Barrie's best and most consistent defenseman, especially in the Colts playoff series. In the first half of Brauti's season he posted 3 goals, 5 points, 56 penalty minutes and a -6 while in his second half of the season he put up 6 goals, 16 points, 14 penalty minutes and a -2 while playing on a much weaker team. In the second half he played top minutes against the opponent's top players and even began playing special teams and with this opportunity he improved.

Early in the year Brauti had trouble as a rush defender and in his anticipation to join the rush. As the year progressed, Brauti developed more situational awareness with regards to his aggression. He used this to become more patient as a rush defender and read the play up ice better to not get caught up ice as well as improvements in his gap control keeping players to the outside more consistently. In addition, he reads the play up ice better and chooses to be a high option while his teammates break into the zone. His hockey IQ has grown as a strong pace and one of the best examples of this is in his breakout passes up ice which hit his target and put his teammates in good positions up ice while reading the forecheck and making plays under pressure.

One thing about Brauti that was consistent all year was his aggression and high compete. He never backed down from fights, hits or physical contact of any kind. Was he always on the winning end? No. However, Brauti faired better than his size would have you believe including an early season fight against a Niagara forward with more than 30lbs on him. As the year went on, the physicality did not diminish, it improved in how he utilized it and found himself in position more and not chasing hits or players defensively.

There is still work to be done with rounding out Brauti's game as a whole and despite his improvements he does still need to be more aware in coverage in his own end and when pinching.

Brauti has a solid shot that got better in terms of power as the season went on but with some added strength will improve as he keeps it in a good range for his forwards to get sticks on it. Next season, with more consistent ice time in Barrie's top four will show us if Brauti can continue his trend of improving every year. He is a long-term project, who in the right system and with patience could develop into a fluid skating and aggressive bottom pairing player.

NR	PLAYER	TEAM	LEAGUE	HEIGHT	WEIGHT	POS	GRADE
	BROWN, CHRISTOPHER	SOO	OHL	5' 10"	157	LC	NI
NHLCS	CEILING	FLOOR	HOCKEY SENSE	COMPETE	SKILL	SKATE	MISC
-	5	4	6	5	5	5	6

Christopher Brown is an undersized forward for the Soo Greyhounds in the Ontario Hockey League. Brown put up 31 points in 66 games this past season shuffling between the top and later in the year middle six forward group. Brown was a former first round pick in the OHL Draft.

The defensive awareness was Brown's top attribute this season as he proved to be a reliable penalty killer who broke up passes with his stick and aggressively took away space from opposing puck carriers. We thought his awareness improved as the year progressed but not enough to overlook some of the other aspects of his game such as his stick skills with the puck as he does not have the hands to be an effective rush or cycle attacker as he has trouble generating offense on the whole.

Brown's inability to generate speed hurt his projectability as he can keep pace at the OHL level, but as competition grows stronger, he will struggle to keep pace with higher level and older skaters. In addition to his speed, Brown does not possess the strength to protect the puck or physically challenge players who are stronger at his current level let alone be able to do this at a higher level.

38	PLAYER	TEAM	LEAGUE	HEIGHT	WEIGHT	POS	GRADE
	BRUNICKE, HARRISON	KAMLOOPS	WHL	6' 02.75"	185	RD	B
NHLCS	CEILING	FLOOR	HOCKEY SENSE	COMPETE	SKILL	SKATE	MISC
NA-52	7	5	5	7	7	8	7

Depth defender in his rookie season last year on a contending Kamloops team, the former 3rd round pick in the WHL draft played a big role on rebuilding Kamloops team this season, playing top 4 and in all situations for the Blazers. Brunicke played at the CHL top prospect game and finished 4th in the weave agility with puck in one-ice testing. The 6'3" defenseman represented team Canada at the U18, winning a gold medal. Brunicke suffered an injury on February 19th that held him out for the rest of the WHL season before coming back for the U18.

Brunicke is an athletic defenseman with size and good skating. Offensively, he didn't have a huge season production wise with 21 points (10 goals) in 49 games, but he shows high-end flashes, particularly when in the rush and in the offensive zone. With his effortless skating, Brunicke's always active in the rush off the puck, either as F2 or F3 on the first wave of attack to make the opposing D's back off, or as F4 by timing his route for a 2nd wave passing option. With his skating, he can get back to defend with ease if there is no play available. With the puck, Brunicke is a great puck carrier. He's a smooth skater and deceptive player, as he'll front pressure by going nose-to-nose against them to freeze their angling/feet, then skate around them. He loves to use hip-hip 10-2 skating move to scan the scan, and he owns good puck skills to dangle around defender. His skating, combined with his manipulation skills, allow him to carry with puck with ease and score a few beautiful coast-to-coast goals this season.

In the offensive zone, Brunicke can wall the blueline with ease. Eyes up, scanning the eyes and taking the middle smoothly. He's also an activations machine. Off puck, he uses inside or outside scissors as the strong side defenseman to attack downhill. As D2, he loves to sneak back-door on the weakside when the opposing team inside winger is puck watching. He also really active with the puck. He can walk the line with ease, but he also often activates downhill after low-to-high pass acquisitions. He gets off the blueline, attack the defensive winger nose-to-nose with fake shots to freeze him, then change his route and gets around him. Like when carrying the puck, his puck skills, skating and manipulation allow him to circle around the offensive zone with ease. 10 of his 12 goals this season where below the circles in the offensive zone. His quick passing/vision thought layers of defense and ability to find offensive advantageous plays with the puck less than 1 second on his stick are areas that Brunicke will need to improve to up his points total.

Defensive zone breakout retrievals in an inconsistent part of Brunicke's game with the puck. Positively, he makes some high-end breakout plays when he's able to skate, invite pressure, attracting multiple forecheckers, then making a play to his forwards to create numerical advantage. When he has a forechecker on his back and no time to skate to beat him, his decision making can struggle. Adding even more scanning before his touches, adding more strength and knowing when to eat/bump the puck to your partner when there's no space versus when to skate/make a deceptive play are all things that will help Brunicke improve in these situations.

Defensively, Brunicke is a great rush defender. With no surprise, he's hard to beat one-on-one with his skating, length and compete. He kills play early, skating forward and angling when needed to close play before his own blueline. In his own-end, he uses his tools to close play early. He's not a punishing defenseman physically, but he'll complete hits when needed and box out in front of his net. He plays against top forwards in the WHL, and played a key defensive role at the U18 for team Canada, facing strong competitios and playing on their top PK unit.

Brunicke is a fascinating prospect to evaluate. He has high upside with his athleticism, skating, size, manipulation habilities and puck skills, but the the offensive production isn't there yet. As good as he is at holding the puck and that's obviously a huge positive in his game, he'll also need to be able to create out of quick puck touches, like on the breakout or at the offensive bleuline, as he'll obviously have way less time and space at the NHL level. Brunicke needs to figure out what will translate and what will not at the next level, but there's huge upside in transition game and some good upside offensively as well. Defensively, with how he can kill plays early, his game is projectable at the next level and should be a good defender with his tools.

"Need to see him more because I can't figure him out." – NHL Scout, March 2024

"His game needs a lot refinement, but high-upside if a team develops him well. Love his manipulation skills with the puck and how he can kill plays early when defending the rush". HP Scout, Tim Archambault, May 2024

3	PLAYER	TEAM	LEAGUE	HEIGHT	WEIGHT	POS	GRADE
	BUIUM, ZEEV	DENVER	NCHC	6' 00"	186	LD	A

NHLCS	CEILING	FLOOR	HOCKEY SENSE	COMPETE	SKILL	SKATE	MISC
NA-4	8	8	9	7	7	6	6

Zeev Buium is a dynamic two-hundred-foot defenseman, with fantastic hockey sense. Buium chose the college route for his draft season and it was the right decision as he helped Denver to a national championship, while finishing with an outstanding 50 points in 42 games, including 11 goals. Buium also won gold at the U20's, where he finished with 5 points in 7 games. His NCAA production puts him in truly elite company. His 1.19 points per game fall into second all time for a first year draft eligible defenseman playing in the NCAA. Only Craig Redmond during the 82-83 season has ever out-produced Buium and considering the scoring rates of the 80's relative to current hockey, it paints a picture of a special prospect who had a special season.

With Buium it starts with his ability to process to game. He is able to dynamically evaluate the right play at the right time, regardless of how fast the game is being played, even while under pressure. Players with elite adaptive processors can adjust rapidly to a chaotic situation, they can speed the game up past an opposing team's comfort level, and they can operate at a higher rate of speed than most other prospects. It is the single separating quality for Zeev, relative to the other top end defenders in this class, with the only other defender coming close being Zayne Parekh. It's also a big reason why we have Buium ranked ahead of Levshunov even though Levshunov is the bigger defender.

What makes Buium unique though is that his pre-set processing ability and understanding of how to see unfolding plays in advance is right there with his ability to adapt on the fly. What this means is that when he needs to think two or three steps ahead he can, and when he's blindsided by a play, he can fall back on his split second read and react, adapting to any situation.

That's essentially the base of his hockey sense, and it's why his game should seamlessly translate despite having a good but not great tool-kit.

Speaking to his tool-kit, he's physically strong, sturdy, and coordinated, but his skating probably falls into the solid but unspectacular category. Buium has limited use of his multi-directional crossovers. What this looks like on the ice is that he can fail to keep his hips forward and inadvertently skate over the top of himself, shortening his stride length. This reduces how efficient a skater he can be, which matters considering the amount of minutes we think he will be logging at the NHL level. It means that he can be susceptible to agile skaters who force him to pivot or reach out with his stick rapidly, since his rate of recovery will be slightly reduced as the result of his improper posture when initiating his crossovers.

The good news is that as he gains strength, and as he continues to develop, his mechanical issues should self correct at least to some degree. It's just with a defenseman who we project in the top of the lineup at his size, you rather not see the issues he does have.

Will his skating ultimately keep him from being able to develop into the potential number one defenseman we envision? The answer is that we don't think so. We wish he skated like Luke Hughes or Josh Morrissey, but his skating means that he's just more likely to need an insulating partner in a playoff series when he's going up against the likes of a Connor McDavid or a Nathan MacKinnon.

He offsets his skating deficiencies by having an excellent sense of when to skate. He rarely gets caught in transition because he understands where to be positioned and when to time his C-cuts through the neutral zone. He understands how to time his lateral crossovers to stay in-front of an opponent who's trying to cut east-west and attack inside. His skating also doesn't keep him from being incredibly difficult to contain at the offensive blueline, and he can still activate into a transitional attack with no issues.

Speaking of attack, Buium has an advanced understanding of how to generate offense. Offensive talent often doesn't shine unless there's confidence, which he has it in spades. He's extremely confident along the line, and can make high-skill plays routinely as the result of his confidence. He knows when he has a defender beat and looks to further penetrate the offensive zone. In transition he recognizes where to position himself to set up for a lateral one timer or how to mask his positioning behind coverage so he can get set up correctly for a drop pass. His spacing and sense of timing compliment his skill well.

When looking further into mechanics regarding his deking ability and his shot, there's a lot to like. Few players in this class understand how to mask their playmaking and shooting placement behind their hands like Zeev. This ties into his ability to adapt his deking on the fly, and re-adjust his lanes depending on the play. Additionally, he can use his hands in-tight to his body and make technical drag moves around opposing players while going near full speed. His ability to stay in motion from the line, in combination with his fast hands, gives him a multi-dimensional approach to breaking down opposing players that's uncommon. His hands work in combination with his wrist-shot. He can rapidly change his shooting angle thanks to the dexterity in his wrists.

He's also a multi-dimensional puck mover, never needing to rely on one skill in order to get the job done. If an opponent closes distance on him in a straight line, he can use his hands and agility to side step them. If an opponent is coming in on a proper angle, he can use his deception to slow the player down, giving him more time to find his next option. He's an equal parts breakout machine and offensive threat.

He's already a capable defender who is very tenacious. He doesn't give space unless he's physically over-matched, he leans heavy along the boards, and he's willing to deliver a stand up hit if the play calls for it. He doesn't get drowned out, and he uses his recognition abilities in advance to correctly interpret who he needs to cover while anticipating the position of his opponents in advance.

Defense won't be the strongest area of Buium's game and it won't be the reason that he's selected, but smaller defenseman need to have considerable push-back and he has it. He's an incredibly well rounded defenseman who brings almost everything to the table. We wish he was bigger but you can say that about literally every defender that's under 6 '2".

We think he falls into the category of a defenseman who plays defense less often than a lot of other players because of how gifted he is at generating breakouts and offense. He might not end up the best defender in a class that's full of exceptionally talented defenseman, but a lot of them have more variables you have to take into consideration on draft day, or have red flags that give you pause that Buium doesn't have. These are the reasons he's our top defender on our board.

" My top D in this draft." NHL Scout, November 2023

" So hard to find guys like him...he'll go top three in this draft." - NHL Scout, November 2023

" If his skating was better I'd have him as my top Dman - he's still my third Dman." - NHL Scout, November 2023

" Great hockey sense, thinks the game really well and has some offense in his game to go along with his ability to defend. Love him." - NHL Scout, November 2023

" Hard to find PP QB's and he can be one. Might be a second paring guy...a number three but on your number one powerplay. I have Silayev ahead of him but Buium is my second Dman." - NHL Scout, November 2023

" If he's your top Dman you could do a lot worse."- NHL Scout, May 2024

" All the tops guys were great interviews (combine) but I really liked Buium." - NHL Scout, June 2024

" He plays like 30 minutes per game at the College level as a freshman and barely ever makes a mistake on the ice." - HP Scout Jérôme Bérubé, April 2024

" Those NCAA playoffs games were huge for me, not only did it make my decision easier to put him above Levshunov but as my top D in the draft" - HP Scout Jérôme Bérubé (April 2024)

" He just put together the best season out of any defender I can remember since I've started doing this and yet I still feel he's under-appreciated." - HP Scout, Brad Allen

" I will be very surprised if he doesn't have a significantly better career than most of the other, if not all the other defenseman in this class. Levshunov can't hold a candle to him from my point of view." - HP Scout, Brad Allen

"Skating is not elite but I really like everything else in his game. Great hockey sense and he can both defend and bring offense to the table." - HP Scout, Mark Edwards, December 2022

"It was really tight ranking my top Dman but Zeev just edged out Silayev. In the end I chose the guy that can do it all." -HP Scout, Mark Edwards, May 2024

NR	PLAYER	TEAM	LEAGUE	HEIGHT	WEIGHT	POS	GRADE
	BURNEVIK, AUSTIN	MADISON	USHL	6' 03.5"	195	RW	NI
NHLCS	CEILING	FLOOR	HOCKEY SENSE	COMPETE	SKILL	SKATE	MISC
NA-113	5	5	5	4	6	3	6

Austin Burnevik went from being a depth forward on the USNTDP in 2022-23, to a 40-goal man in his D+1 year. Second in the league in goals and shots on goal, Burnevik was the primary trigger man on a team that only had one other player eclipse the 20-goal plateau.

That's going to be Austin's calling card if he goes anywhere: his shot. Pucks explode off his blade. His shooting game is primarily centered around being the late man and firing a wrist shot to the far post, but he also boasts impressive catch-and-release shooting and some one-timer upside. His passing game is simple, but generally effective. He slides pucks to the adjacent lane in an accurate fashion. Often times on the rush, he works pucks from one side of his body to the other and uses these little slide or hook passes as the outlet from his puck protection mechanisms.

Unfortunately, the big drawback here is the skating – it has all the makings of being a stopper despite his 6'4", almost 200 pound frame. His edges are okay, but the rest of his skating game is notably poor…especially his first-step (few steps, really) quickness. He almost never does anything with the puck in stride. His shots, passes, any rare noteworthy handles, all come out of the glide primarily. The interesting thing about Burnevik is how he has adapted to his square wheels. For starters, he has a massive pass-catch radius. He can swat pucks down and pull them into him like a lizard's tongue almost. From the pass catch, he employs automatic puck protection mechanisms. This buys him the time and space he needs to not have as many plays die with him as we'd expect. He still turns the puck over if an opponent knows how to play him and he can't counteract a lost puck in any reasonable way, but right now he's making it work. He's far from a worker bee, nor can he play that style – so if a puck is lost in any zone, Burnevik is unlikely to recover it; or if any linemate is expecting him to set a pick in motion, that's probably not going to happen either. His off-the-puck support is average at best and he's not a backchecker. That said, another adaptation to his game against the speed of the USHL is that he sort of throws his frame into passing and, rarer, shooting lanes to knock down pucks.

NR	PLAYER	TEAM	LEAGUE	HEIGHT	WEIGHT	POS	GRADE
	BURROWS, HAGEN	MINNETONKA	HIGH-MN	6' 01.5"	174	RW	NI
NHLCS	CEILING	FLOOR	HOCKEY SENSE	COMPETE	SKILL	SKATE	MISC
NA-68	5	5	6	5	5	6	6

Burrows was part of a nucleus that returned to Minnetonka High School as late 05's seniors instead of moving on to Junior hockey full time. Minnetonka overwhelmed many of their opponents throughout the season and Burrows was a big reason for that where his size and strength was a big advantage at the High School level that allowed him to be effective in playing a power game with the puck. Burrows saw 25 regular season games with Sioux City as well as 8 playoff games where he was a consistent point producer for the Musketeers, scoring 9 goals and 13 assists in 25 regular season games as well as showing decent production in the 8 playoff games as well.

Hagen doesn't display a ton of high-octane offensive talent. He isn't going to blaze past opponents with explosive speed or dangle around numerous opponents with a high-end finishes to beat goaltenders but where Burrows excels offensively is by using his vision, timing, and hockey sense to set up his teammates for scoring chances. We saw him be successful in being a good passer and playmaker, both at the High School and USHL levels this season. He is able to find teammates coming through lanes with speed and get them the puck in stride to create scoring chances. Burrows showed the ability to read the play and find east-west lanes quickly, both in the neutral and offensive zones. Burrows shooting ability still needs to develop a bit to be a big scoring threat at the professional level but he displays the willingness to go to the hard areas in order to find the back of the net. Many of his goals we saw in our viewings came from the slot and net front area where he used his quick hands to get shots off in the crowd and jam pucks past the goalie in scrambles so that part of his offensive game will translate at the upper levels, as he has good size and strength to be effective in that area of the ice. Off the puck, Burrows needs to continue to work on his consistency and his compete. While he did show improvement with his overall effort in the USHL than he did at the high school level, there is still a ways to go in this department to be effective at the professional level.

Burrows is committed to play college hockey at Denver, which is a good fit for him. Denver has done a good job in developing players and getting them ready for the next level. Burrows will likely spend one full season in the USHL next year before heading to Denver.

77	PLAYER	TEAM	LEAGUE	HEIGHT	WEIGHT	POS	GRADE
	CASWELL, CLARKE	SWIFT CURRENT	WHL	5' 10.75"	170	LW	C
NHLCS	CEILING	FLOOR	HOCKEY SENSE	COMPETE	SKILL	SKATE	MISC
NA-77	6	4	8	5	5	5	4

The former 6th overall pick in the bantam draft in one of the players who progressed the most this season amongst this draft class. After scoring 29 points in his rookie season, Caswell had 77 points in 68 games this season. His game found an even better gear in the playoffs, playing left wing on Broncos' top line with Arizona Coyotes 1st round Conor Geekie. This season, Caswell played games as a center, but we project him more as a winger at the next level. As a pass first forward, his 51 assists rank 5th amongst 1st year NHL draft eligible players from the WHL this season.

Caswell is a pass first winger. In the offensive zone with the puck, Caswell does a great job of finding open teammates in the slot to create high-end scoring chances and primary assists. Without the puck in the offensive zone, Caswell does a great job as F3. He covers for his defensemen pinching when needed, and he does a great job of attacking downhill with timing to get open in scoring areas.

In transition, Caswell is excellent at knowing his play before his 1st touch, which allows him to move the puck fast and with purpose. Caswell's wall work as a winger on the breakout is efficient. He pre-scans and can one-touch the puck to his center. When needed, he's able to use body positioning to shield the pressure away, take a step back and exits the zone with the weakside defenseman. On the rush, due to his average skating, Caswell is not a primary puck carrier, which limits some of the offense he can create in transition. When he does enter the zone in control, his playmaking excels. He's patient with the puck, often attracting two defenders before moving the puck to create advantageous numerical situations for his team.

In terms of two-way play, Caswell improved this season. As mentioned, he's responsible as F3 in the offensive zone. He does a fine job of tracking trough the neutral zone and defending in his zone, but it's still an area that will needs work and refinement to be an efficient player at the next level.

Caswell's improvement from his D-1 to the playoffs of his draft season was impressive. With high-end hockey IQ, good puck skills and vision, the offensive upside is real. With improved top speed and some fine tuning in his play without the puck, Caswell's upside can be high.

"Bad skater with a lot of skill." - NHL Scout, March 2024

"Good Junior player. He'll score a ton in junior but he has a stopper with that skating." - NHL Scout, May 2024

"Caswell progressions, overall season and playoffs run make him a really interesting prospect. I love how he improves the condition of the puck with his passing, either with pre-scanning and strong one-touch game, or by inviting pressure to beat two defenders with his pass." -HP Scout, Tim Archambault, April 2024

11	PLAYER	TEAM	LEAGUE	HEIGHT	WEIGHT	POS	GRADE
	CATTON, BERKLY	SPOKANE	WHL	5' 10.25"	175	LC	A

NHLCS	CEILING	FLOOR	HOCKEY SENSE	COMPETE	SKILL	SKATE	MISC
NA-8	8	7	6	6	8	6	5

Berkley Catton is a dynamic scoring center who we think will translate into a winger long-term. He was instrumental in helping Spokane reach the playoffs after producing 116 points, including 54 goals, in 68 regular season games. One of his more staggering stats is just how often he was deployed while playing in all situations. He played an average of over twenty-three minutes per game during the WHL season, with several performances topping the thirty-minute mark. Yet, he was productive right up until the end of the regular season.

Berkley's game has developed as a direct result of his limited frame. What we mean by that is Catton is both slight and light, while also having a narrow build, which he has had to adapt to the rigours of the WHL.

When physically contested, he can lose battles where he can't find an immediate pocket of space to exit from, and he's rarely capable of overpowering a defenseman when driving shoulder-first into them. To compensate for his lack of physical advantages, he's adapted a highly deceptive offensive game built around generating speed differentials in combination with rapid handling plays that momentarily shift his angular momentum, forcing an opposing weight transfer from a defender. This, in turn, gives him direct skating routes closer to the net. This buys him time and space to find a setup option or generate an opening to get off his most translatable quality, which is his shot.

His misdirection starts on the mental side of the game. He lulls opposing players into a false sense of security before jetting and cutting rapidly around them. What this looks like is that he will stay in a glide until he thinks the defenseman has miscalculated the amount of space he has to operate with, then immediately explodes into that space. His top speed isn't exceptional and, mechanically speaking, his open ice and north-south skating isn't dynamic, but he's extremely efficient in his first three steps, which makes him difficult to match.

As a result, if he's in open space, he's rarely relying on his peak speed; he's instead relying on his weight shifts to keep opposing defenses from tracking his entries. Out of the top forwards, he's one of the few who relies less on his base and more on his edgework, weight, and angle shifts. These subconscious calculations allow him to make last-second adjustments as he's initiated on so that he can slip and bypass opposing players. This made him a dangerous zone entry machine, who could drive possession through the neutral zone often.

His ability to differentiate his speed allows him to manipulate the speed that opposing defensemen operate against him, which forms the base for how he adjusts and re-opens his passing and shooting lanes. For example, if he explodes down a wing while simultaneously recognizing that the defenseman covering him is attempting to match him, he will slow back down or rapidly pivot, peel off the pressure, and use his newfound time and space to find a sharp lateral pass. On the same play, as opposed to setting up the lateral pass, he can dynamically shift on a separate angle while using his hands and further try to carve around the defender who has momentarily slowed down so that he can set up his shot off the rush.

Speaking of the rush, Catton is at his best off the rush, and that's because he's a quality distance shooter who has both solid mechanics and a very good understanding of where to place his shot in the allotted time frame needed to get it off his stick on most attempts. His shots can be difficult to read because, unlike Konsta Helenius, for example, who has difficulty rapidly shifting his shooting angle or laterally dragging the puck with his hands, Catton doesn't. He can rapidly handle pucks behind screens and use opposing triangles to mask his shooting placement, making his release more difficult to pick up by opposing goalies. We wouldn't say his shot is the best in the class, but it's his best projectable offensive weapon and is in the top tier range of this class.

The only real concern we had when evaluating his shot this season was how often he was looking to shoot on lower percentage short-side angles after cutting to the net. He does have excellent seam recognition, especially in tight to the net, but there were games where too much of his shot selection was on shooting angles that were simply too low percentage. It isn't so dissimilar to how we evaluated Kent Johnson's shot selection in the NCAA in his initial draft season, but he has since modified it, and we expect the same to happen with Catton's game.

What's less projectable is his playmaking and open ice handling. Although Catton is a gifted technical playmaker at times, his playmaking success rates were surprisingly average to below average, despite having elite primary assist rates. This was a conundrum for us. On the one hand, we have seen Catton execute feathered backhand saucer passes through traffic that also incorporated a level of deception that translates, such as static body posture and off looks. However, on the other hand, Catton turned the puck over a ton through bad playmaking setups in our viewings, especially blind passes that were largely generated below the goal line. Again, he can make beautiful, highly technical passes, but he can also be prone to off-the-mark passes that you wouldn't expect from a player as talented as he is.

His adaptive handling error rates were also surprising in open ice. Now, he is a good puck handler and can make some fantastic multi-touch dekes to bypass opposing triangles while simultaneously pivoting with the puck, but in open ice situations, he would have some difficulty. Part of this can be attributed to his lateral dragging and extension dekes acquiring him to get off his centerline so that he could shorten the duration of time between the initial phase and end phase of his deke. Catton is a good skater in some areas as we've discussed, but he is not a natural athlete, and his biggest weakness as a skater is his inability to properly rotate off his centerline, which directly affected aspects of his handling.

Berkley is dynamic and can score, but he's not a clean or efficient offensive threat at this stage in his development. There was too much zero-sum displayed right through the end of the season. Part of this can be attributed to having free rein in the offensive zone, and we don't mind experimentation; on the contrary, at this stage of his career, we usually welcome it if the player is dynamic enough (we were fans of Nils Hoglander as one of many examples), but this wasn't experimentation.

Instead, this was a junior player who largely played with a junior mentality. For every beautiful flash and dash play that was successful, where he incorporated his skating, handling, and either playmaking or shooting combination, there was another where he would mistime a pass or mistime a handling sequence. He looks to constantly set up blind plays as well, and that's a problem because there was a general lack of instinct in determining the trajectory of his teammates after spinning or off-looking the puck. Heck, even routine passing plays broke down far too often in our viewings.

It reminds us a bit of the issues with Trevor Zegras's game, which has also come to materialize at the NHL level currently. We factored in the general late-game fatigue he would experience occasionally due to the sheer minutes he played, and admittedly he was cleaner in his overall decisions during his playoff round against Prince George, but if you look at our total game count, it was still concerning. We do think he can and will clean up his game when developing into a full-time pro, but we doubt he ever becomes as efficient or as effective as his production suggests.

The last issue we have with Catton's game is that, as stated earlier, we don't feel that he's a reliable 200-foot center. Catton will compete for a puck or defend if he's already in range to do so, but there's too much variance in his overall effort level and willingness to physically initiate play in the defensive zone when he should. He was caught flat-footed or caught lagging behind the play instead of staying ahead of it too often to project as a center.

He also rarely anticipates defensive coverage in advance, and you can tell he's defending for the sake of it, as opposed to thinking it matters. He cherry-picks at times, and his thought process is to create separation in case his teammates generate a turnover instead of naturally supporting them.

Production always needs context, and in the case of Berkley Catton, it doesn't represent the on-ice product. There was a lot more Jekyll and Hyde in his game than we normally feel comfortable with. If Catton can develop more consistency within his thought process in the offensive zone and within his playmaking skill set while continuing to develop his pace so that it's an extra gear higher off the puck, then he can develop into a top-of-the-line-up winger who plays on a top power-play unit that can be trusted. He's built for regular season hockey, and despite our concerns, we do feel he has the potential to score a lot of goals at the NHL level. Our hesitation with the player and our ranking of him come down to the potential for him to get drowned out as the game ramps up in pace and physicality come playoff time.

We know our evaluation looks critical, and in some ways, it is, but our ranking philosophy is that we leave players outside our top-10 if we don't think they are going to be playoff performers. In Berkley's case, we rightfully predicted that he would have difficulty against Prince George in their playoff series, and that made us feel like we have assessed this correctly, despite the backlash we know we're going to receive.

We see a fantastic regular season scorer who will have impressive neutral zone entry rates.

"I like Catton a lot but you can't get carried away ranking him top 10. He has too many limitations." - NHL Scout, April 2024

"I could see him going higher than he should...like I could see him going top six or seven when he's not really a top twelve or thirteen guy." - NHL Scout, May 2024

"Excellent interview. (Combine) - NHL Scout, June 2024

"I really liked his game and his resiliency at the Hlinka tournament" - HP Scout Jérôme Bérubé, August 2023

"Not a center in the NHL" -HP Scout Jérôme Bérubé, January 2024

"The difference between his good and bad games has been wild this year. I had too many bad games to have him in my top-10." - HP Scout Jérôme Bérubé, April 2024

"I saw the stats that Catton is the only player in the 21st century alongside Crosby, Kane & Bedard to get 50 + goals & 115 + points in their draft year. It's impressive, but if you go back one extra year to 1999, Pavel Brendl scored 73 goals & 134 points in his draft year and was a gigantic bust. Not quite as cool of a stat now.." -HP Scout Jérôme Bérubé, May 2024

"I'm the scout on our staff that is highest on Catton but that said, he slid down my list a little bit as well.." - HP Scout, Mark Edwards, May 2024

1	PLAYER	TEAM	LEAGUE	HEIGHT	WEIGHT	POS	GRADE
	CELEBRINI, MACKLIN	BOSTON U	H- EAST	5' 11.75"	197	LC	A

NHLCS	CEILING	FLOOR	HOCKEY SENSE	COMPETE	SKILL	SKATE	MISC
NA-1	9	9	8	8	8	8	7

Macklin Celebrini is a high octane, dynamic, line driving power center. He was the youngest player playing in the NCAA this past season, and it also turned out that he was the best player too. His play awarded him the Hobey Baker award, as he led BU to an NCAA championship, while finishing with 64 points in 38 games, including 32 goals. He also represented Canada at the U20's, where he led Canada in scoring finishing with 8 points in 5 games, including 4 goals.

Celebrini is a special player that's basically the modern age prototype of how you want a center to play hockey. Rarely are dynamic first overall types of talents well rounded off the puck, but in the case of Celebrini, he carries an elite two way-base. There isn't a prospect featured in any draft in recent memory, that's as well rounded and we don't remember the last time we evaluated a player this gifted, who already plays an elite 200-foot game, but that's exactly what a team is getting here.

He's decisive in his own zone, and when he commits, he fully commits. There's no second guessing his initial reading of the play, which allows him more opportunity to react correctly. We love when a dynamic talent is willing to play physically, but the separating quality for any prospect that can hit is the understanding of when to actually initiate one, and that's where Celebrini is truly gifted.

He carries the natural instincts we look for that's needed for puck-on-stick defending as well. Some players are good at timing their poke-checking, or timing their puck-on-stick plays by taking away passing lanes in advance, but Macklin is that rare blend of both. Now couple that with an imposing, powerful frame, that can separate the puck from a player, and it really starts showcasing why we're so excited about his impact on the defensive side of the ice, and why we wanted to initially highlight is since everyone will be talking about his offensive impact, when in reality it's the zone-to-zone impact that makes him truly unique.

Speaking to his physical offensive impact, Celebrini can evade coverage and go undetected into back door areas, but even more impressively, he can erase coverage. On one play, he's staying below the defenses radar – on the next – he's breaking it by using his power game to push and hit the defenseman out of position.

When a defense is initiated on with the aggression Celebrini commits with, it forces more communication, which in turn forces additional positional switches in order to maintain coverage on him. With more position switches and communication, comes a greater likelihood of a defensive error occurring on the ice, the type of defensive errors that Celebrini can then exploit with his vast skill-set.

There's a beautiful mix of power and skill that can dictate the terms of the game in every zone, on any given play, while still being able to systematically break down the defense by out-thinking them with advanced feints and hesitation plays.

It's a skill set that has its own distinguishing traits too. Very few prospects in any class, have the capacity to rapidly shift into a pivot, into the opposite direction they just peeled off of pressure from and then one arm their way with a direct cut to the net, while simultaneously using their frame to throw the opposing defense off balance, before finding a one handed high danger lateral set up. Celebrini not only can do this, he can do it on his backhand.

That's something we have seen Celebrini do consistently and it really speaks to just how diversified he can be. On one sequence, he's exploding through all three zones while making rapid multi directional puck touches that turn several layers of traffic inside out, while pressuring with his speed, and on the next he's over-powering players and strong arming them into bad areas of the ice before initiating another dynamic play.

After he puts himself into high danger positions on the ice as a result of his skating, fakes, and handling skill-set, he can then set up for his shooting and playmaking ability, which we would label as both primary dual threat elements in his game.

When you look at his shot quality as a whole, it forces opposing defenses to over react. These over reactions allow Celebrini to reset his shot through screens, or turn his shot into a potential lane adjusted pass. The sequences presented through his handling phase into his shooting phase are elite, allowing him to modify the trajectory of his plays faster than most opponents can respond. He incorporates his phenomenal shooting mechanics into his lateral playmaking options with ease.

Coordination is significant to every prospect when discussing their shooting ability, but Macklin uses his high end coordination to mask his intentions within his release at a better rate than a lot of other players available in this class. He can remain static within his body mechanics before exploding his back foot, while simultaneously rotating his core and shoulders through his release. He transfers through his lower and upper halves simultaneously on the majority of his releases and this gives him a spring loaded wrist shot, which compliments his dextrous hand activation, giving him a ton of velocity relative to his frame.

Where the outlier lies within his offensive game, is that he can apply those same mechanics when he passes the puck. From the kickback, to the core rotation, to the head and stick fakes - they are all present - when he looks to pass the puck as well. What this means is that opponents have a very difficult time assessing if he's trying to make a pass or if he's going to shoot the puck. It's uncommon for a prospect who keeps such a blistering pace, while having the shot volume that he generates, to have reduced tunnel vision when transitioning at full speed, but Celebrini is fully capable of recognizing when he has a better passing option in-front of him, which prevents him from taking too many low percentage shots.

When his mechanics are incorporated with his seam recognition, understanding of time and space, his ability to find teammates through layered traffic, and his advanced shooting placement, it leaves him with a tremendous amount of offensive versatility.

Celebrini has old school substance, but new school technique out on the ice. He's a special breed of player who has a throwback mentality to the guts and glory days of the game's previous era's, and it's fantastic to watch. We know for some, an on ice mentality of a player is secondary, if not totally pointless to discuss. However, we believe that the mind set of each player is not only vital, but they are the players who ultimately fulfill their projection and his projection is of a franchise altering center.

"The only part of making my list that will be easy is putting Celebrini at number one." - NHL Scout, November 2024

"I have Celebrini at number one and I have no idea who to put at number two. Nobody seems worthy" - NHL Scout, May 2024

"He's basically the ultimate prototype of what a coach would dream up as a first line center. There's nothing missing." - HP Scout, Brad Allen

"I disagree with scouts that think he tops out at around 70 points. I think PPG is very likely and I won't be surprised if he has peak seasons that hit the 100 point mark." - HP Scout, Brad Allen

"I'm getting asked a lot on where he would get drafted last year so I'll answer it here. I think it's likely he would have been taken 2nd overall but would have forced teams to have real conversations about him vs Bedard just due to how much more physically imposing and defensively present he is." - HP Scout, Brad Allen

"Best player in both of Canada's U20 practices and games in camp. Then he flys to Sweden and showed why he is a slam dunk number one overall. I absolutely love his game and love watching him play" - HP Scout, Mark Edwards, January 2024

"I barely spoke to scouts about him because he was such a slam dunk number one that it was almost as if he wasn't part of this draft class." - HP Scout, Mark Edwards, May 2024

NR	PLAYER	TEAM	LEAGUE	HEIGHT	WEIGHT	POS	GRADE
	CHEYNOWSKI, CALLUM	NIAGARA	OHL	6' 01"	190	LD	NI
NHLCS	CEILING	FLOOR	HOCKEY SENSE	COMPETE	SKILL	SKATE	MISC
-	5	5	5	5	5	6	6

Callum Cheynowski is a left-shot defenseman for the Niagara IceDogs who also split time with the Brantford Bulldogs. He put up eleven points in 52 games this past season with both the Bulldogs and IceDogs after being selected in the third round of the OHL draft.

A fluid skater, Cheynowski has good speed, quick strides and he pivots and skates smoothly backwards. He moves quickly around the ice to cover off his teammates who pinch deep and can get back in time to mitigate odd man rushes if he gets caught himself. His edge work and his speed backwards need work, but should he be caught, he can easily catch up to forwards. Defensively he has some issues with positioning and coverage in his own end with some bad reads coming out of his own end. He typically cannot gain inside position on plays and is forced to pin forwards without a good level of strength. When pressured he has trouble making decisions up ice and can turn the puck over in open ice with a slow reaction time. Mentally he is behind the play slightly, however he can make it up with his speed.

He does not have bad size but, the poor strength and lower hockey IQ are big weaknesses in his game at this point in his development. Even if he shoulder checks more and improves his mental game along with his strength, the path to the NHL will be difficult.

18	PLAYER	TEAM	LEAGUE	HEIGHT	WEIGHT	POS	GRADE
	CHERNYSHOV, IGOR	DYNAMO MOSCOW	RUS	6' 02"	192	RW	A
NHLCS	CEILING	FLOOR	HOCKEY SENSE	COMPETE	SKILL	SKATE	MISC
INT-9	7	7	7	7	7	7	7

Igor Chernyshov is a two-way - power-forward - who keeps a very good pace. He played for Dynamo both in the MHL and with the main club in the KHL this past season. Dynamo calling up an 18 year old to play for the majority of the season is extremely rare and it's a testament to how pro ready Chernyshov's game is already. With the MHL club, he produced 28 points in 22 games, including 13 goals. With the KHL team, he was restricted to limited minutes and attempting to adapt to a much higher level of competition which can be seen through his 4 points in 34 games, and zero points in 10 playoff games. Despite his lack of scoring production at the KHL level, there were several games we evaluated throughout the season that showed just how translatable his game is.

Chernyshov's a bigger and more physically developed prospect, and his frame works well in combination with his acute attention to detail off the puck. He's a switch hitter, in the sense that he can cycle between playing styles, going from a primary playmaker one minute, into a driving power forward the next, before falling back and supporting his team properly in the defensive-zone when needed. He blends a very good tool-kit with a mature, in your face brand of hockey.

He's a structured player, who understands that good defense can lead to offensive opportunities. He's a clean pick-pocketer on the backcheck, he knows how to support the breakout on the wing by getting himself in positions where he can seamlessly transition into the neutral zone, and he can stay above the puck in the offensive zone, while cutting down on angles to generate pressure. He rarely cheats on plays, and he understands when lower percentage plays make sense to attempt.

He's not a one plane thinker either. He looks to attack both laterally and in straight lines in transition and his main objective is to force defenses to collapse, so that he can find his playmaking options. On one play, he will manipulate you, on the next he will outwork you, and that's a welcomed mix. He blends the ability to explode past or through opposing players, while recognizing the ebbs and flows of an attack, mixing and matching his speeds relative to the distance of his teammates, when they are positioned either in-front of him or when trailing him.

This can be seen in how he optimizes his attack in transition. He rarely forces low percentage plays, and usually carries the poise to assert himself into high danger areas, obtaining the middle area of the ice. He can use his smooth skating base and adaptive handling to dissect defenses. He's multi-faceted. If he needs to stay strong on pucks, take a hit to make a play, or make direct cuts to help magnetize the defense, so that he can readjust his lanes and find his teammates, he can do just that

There's distinct advantages to Chernyshov's power game, while being a right handed shot and playing primarily on the left-wing. For starters, Chernyshov looks to use attack skating by using sudden punch stops or by downshifting after a burst of speed so he can open up the ice and find his trailing teammates on the weak side or backdoor. Due to his handedness, when he's driving down his proper wing he can set them up on his forehand, instead of having to rely on his backhand when rotating back towards the middle of the ice. If the passing option doesn't open, he can suddenly rotate back to his backhand, protecting the puck by using his frame and shielding with his shoulder to drive parallel into the defender.

Conversely, when he's driving down his off wing, he has the option of laterally dragging the puck while moving from the circles to the slot area, giving him an opportunity to shift his shooting angle, while again simultaneously protecting the puck with his shoulder parallel to the closest defenseman. If he can't find a lateral transitional shooting option, again he has a multitude of other options such as making direct outside-to-inside dekes that have him finishing the end of phase of his moveset on his forehand so he can find short area lateral options or drop the puck back to a direct supporting option.

Taken together what this means, is that regardless of which wing he's driving down, he can protect the puck with his frame while exploiting his move-set away from the closest defender's reach, all while primarily operating on his forehand to set up his passing plays, regardless of which side of the ice he's on. We want our power-forwards and most other forwards optimizing their play so that they can largely operate on their forehand more than their backhand since it's easier to execute high danger passes at a more efficient rate, and Chernyshov does this in spades.

He's a highly skilled and creative playmaker, who can scope out the highest danger passing play, while simultaneously calculating if it's the cleanest. He can recognize backdoor options down the weak side, evaluate the trajectory of drop and trailing passes to teammates without looking at them, and has an advanced cycle game. When he's at his top speed, he can hook passes and feather passes with precision.

When he's mechanically in sync, look out. He can score off of multi-touch lateral drags that are set up through screens, drop through a one timed snap shot in one motion, and rapidly shift his shooting angle through his wrist shot due to his dexterous hands. He can laterally cut before going against the grain and elevating the puck in tight to the net. and he can redirect the puck or finish off an in tight give and go sequence with a soft catch and release. Like the variation in his offensive game in general, it can be applied to just how many different ways he's scored this past season.

From a mental perspective, Chernyshov is an intense competitor who understands how to alter the momentum of a shift. There's a reason that we sometimes use the term – matching the urgency of the play – as opposed to over extending the play, and he rarely over-extends play, while consistently matching the urgency. This made him a physical presence that was difficult to handle.

Power forwards are valued for their ability to drive into the anterior portions of the rink and play a heavy game, but the secondary value is that if they can successfully knock a player down to the ice, then that player can no longer recover in the time frame necessary to defend properly, which in turn grants the power forward additional time and space to work with. Which is what Igor has shown us he can do time and time again.

Advanced, physically developed dual-threat power forwards with dynamic qualities, who happen to be intense competitors are not common in any class. Which is exactly why we value Chernyshov's game as much as we do. He plays a heavy game but can out-skill and out score his opponents as well. He's one of the best 200-foot forwards in this class, and he happens to have one of the highest floor to ceiling ratios, much like Brandsegg Nygard does. These players are coveted during playoff hockey, and Chernyshov is built for the playoffs.

"He's my favourite power-forward in this class after Cayden Lindstrom and Macklin Celebrini, he's the total package." - HP Scout, Brad Allen

"It will be very interesting to evaluate his career relative to Nygard's since they have some similar traits." - HP Scout, Brad Allen

NR	PLAYER	TEAM	LEAGUE	HEIGHT	WEIGHT	POS	GRADE
	CHROMIAK, JAKUB	KINGSTON	OHL	5' 11"	183	RD	C
NHLCS	CEILING	FLOOR	HOCKEY SENSE	COMPETE	SKILL	SKATE	MISC
-	6	5	5	5	6	7	5

Jakub Chromiak is a right-shot offensive defenseman for the Kingston Frontenacs in the OHL. He came over to Kingston in a trade after the Sudbury Wolves brought over Dalibor Dvorsky and had too many import spots making him the odd man out and on his way to Kingston. In Kingston he put up 18 points in 48 games and 19 points with both Sudbury and Kingston on the season.

Chromiak's top attribute is probably his skating ability. He walks the blueline well with the puck on his stick, reading the play well from high up in the offensive zone. He uses his edgework to create opportunities for passes down low or shots from the point. He skates well both with and without the puck on his stick but can struggle at times with awareness.

He has patience at the blueline with the puck and has good puck control and hands at the point but, he can lose space quickly from forwards deep on the forecheck or from high coverage in the offensive zone. His space problem makes it seem like the larger ice surfaces in Europe are a better option for him at a pro-level than the tighter North American ice surfaces, as space only decreases as the competition at the pro-level gets better.

In the defensive zone he is able to break up passes with an active stick. He needs to work on his strength when working against big forwards deep in his zone and in front of his net, in order to be able to find success defending at the next level. On the breakout, he will either make great or poor breakout decisions and his passes are either a great outlet hitting his teammate in stride or he throws away pucks for turnover. As a rush defender he is about 50/50 and can be beat defending against speed or fakes. It also does not help that his pivots forward to backward need improvement which hinders his ability to give himself time to read the rush.

As a whole, Chromiak had some strong flashes this season, but that was where it ended. He is good but nothing is great in his game. He can make plays offensively, especially with the puck on his stick but, on the defensive side of the puck he struggles on the rush and in front of his own net. If he works on these skills he could become a long-term development project, but with his poor defending ability and lack of size he will likely have trouble reaching the NHL level.

NR	PLAYER	TEAM	LEAGUE	HEIGHT	WEIGHT	POS	GRADE
	CIBULKA, TOMAS	CAPE BRETON	QMJHL	6' 00"	170	LD	C
NHLCS	CEILING	FLOOR	HOCKEY SENSE	COMPETE	SKILL	SKATE	MISC
-	5	4	5	5	6	6	5

Cibulka is in his 3rd year of draft eligibility and has made good strides since coming into the QMJHL. Prior to this season, he had not played on a competitive team. Val-d'Or consistently ranked among the bottom three teams in the league during each of the seasons he played there. However, since his trade to Cape Breton, he has had the opportunity to play on a stronger team.

Cibulka started his season on a good note with a standout performance at the U20 Four Nations tournament in August, where he emerged as one of Czechia's top performers. In the QMJHL between Val-d'Or and Cape Breton, he was one of the top-scoring defensemen in the league with 49 points in 55 games, placing him 6th overall in points and 3rd for points per game among defensemen. Some similarities can be made between Cibulka and another Czech-born former QMJHL defenseman who was only drafted in his 3rd year of eligibility: David Spacek. Spacek, drafted in the 5th round of the 2022 NHL Draft by Minnesota, showcased a better hockey IQ compared to Cibulka. However, Cibulka stands out as the better skater between the two. Both players represented Czechia at the World Juniors in their 19-year-old seasons, with Spacek ultimately outperforming Cibulka, making a more significant impact for his team when looking at their respective showings.

Cibulka still stands a chance of hearing his name called at the draft, despite not having a standout performance at the World Juniors like Spacek did. He's a strong skater who can skate pucks out of trouble, out of his zone and into the offensive zone with ease at the QMJHL level. His skating is his best asset, and we would add that his shot quality is his second best. He's got good puck skills, is a good stickhandler and is not afraid to use his skating to help him create offense. However, his hockey IQ and creativity are on the average side. He occasionally struggles to anticipate and execute plays effectively. Instead of reading plays quickly, he'll just get by using his individual and athletic offensive-creation abilities. That works at the junior level, but is a lot less likely to as he moves forward. Defensively, he's average at best when projecting him for the NHL level due to his average size and average physicality. What he lacks in hockey IQ also shows at times with some poor decision-making under pressure in his zone and when retrieving pucks. He could have a better gap and use his stick more efficiently.

With higher hockey IQ and creativity, there would have been more deliberation about his potential and placement on our list. However, based on observations over the past three seasons, we view him as a solid prospect for the professional level, but not necessarily suited for the NHL.

36	PLAYER	TEAM	LEAGUE	HEIGHT	WEIGHT	POS	GRADE
	CONNOLY, TREVOR	TRICITY	USHL	6' 00.75"	160	LW	B

NHLCS	CEILING	FLOOR	HOCKEY SENSE	COMPETE	SKILL	SKATE	MISC
NA-6	7	4	5	6	7	6	4

Trevor Connelly finished second in the USHL in points (78) with a 31 goal, 47 assist stat line in just 52 games. He left the Tri-City Storm (USHL) just before the start of the postseason to join Team USA for the U18 Worlds. Tri-City salvaged a first round series win before succumbing to the eventual champs - Fargo. Meanwhile, Connelly put together a 9-point tournament which might have been highlighted by his Michigan goal in a well-at-hand game against Latvia. Instead, he made a much-publicized and ill-advised high hit on a Canadian player in the middle of the 3rd period of the gold medal game in which the Americans were winning. The proceeding major penalty caused the Americans to unravel and lose. Connelly played with a lot of pace in the tournament and tried to acclimate himself into a group that had largely been together all season – Connelly was the only non-NTDP skater invited to participate – and obviously got overzealous in a big spot.

Connelly is a complicated enough evaluation just focusing on his on-ice product. On the positive side, he's the best 1 on 1 player in the U.S. region by a mile. He can routinely cut through all sorts of defensive players and structures with relative ease. Not only can he use his speed to take defenders wide, but he also has a major east-west component to him that creates all kinds of havoc. Despite just four goals in his first 17 USHL games, he rallied to finish 7th in the circuit with 31. Not only does he have superb hands and a plethora of deceptive maneuvers, he has the pace and skating to go along with it. There's a lot to like about his first-step quickness and overall acceleration package. He has high-end agility with a nimble stride that allows him to change directions in a snap. The skating package accentuates his ability to overtake defenders on a regular basis. Whether it's short, quick misdirection plays or longer moves that stretch a defender's triangle to allow Trevor to sashay by, he has the skating ability to make it happen. He has a "burst, glide, burst" style, so he rarely incorporates starts and stops into his game. To that end, he also doesn't demonstrate much in the way of tempo control, so there aren't a lot of well-timed, sudden turns against the grain to find second wave players, for instance.

Despite his elite puck transporting ability and superlative production rates, it's actually his ability to get points at the NHL level that is one of the biggest of several concerns. First of all, he's not a high end shooter. He's a volume shooter that takes a ton of low quality shots. These shots often came at the expense of much better passing options that he didn't see. A fair amount of his early primary assists were off of rebounds or pucks caroming in off the net-front presence. His playmaking process did evolve a bit over the course of the year, which gives us some hope. One really nice aspect to Connelly's passing is that he understands the value of seam passes and crossing the net line with the puck in the attacking zone. Whether he carries it across the middle himself and throws it to the back post or if he gets an odd-man situation and makes the "finishing" pass, that's a conceptually good trait to have. One advent that became prominent late in the season is his net-swing pass to the slot combination right near the posts. His timing and accuracy with those not only added to the scoresheet, but it also added a transferable skill and process to his playmaking package. Between USHL play and the U18, he picked up eight primary assists on 2 on 1's alone – those are a delicacy at the NHL level, not an every day meal. There's an overwhelming amount of cross-seam passes in his assist sample, it's important to look at the sustainability of those too. We'd like to see a little more head and shoulder feints in Connelly's playmaking process, or some more look-off/fake shot combinations to open up these seams more legitimately – as opposed to just purely being exploitative of bad structure at this level. It seems at least a little bit unlikely that the 6-foot, 156 pound Connelly is going to have as much success entering the zone with the puck and carrying it fully dot to dot in an east-west fashion at higher levels. One key thing that we don't see in his game is a lot of passing zone entries or second wave finds. He has one stretch pass primary assist this season. His zone entry proficiency is almost entirely with his multi-line carrying, not passing players into open space, not area passes, not even a lot of passes to players moving at any sort of high pace. When he does try them, they're often inaccurate or poorly conceived. Now, of course, he's not a center and he won't be…so that might take a bite out of the neutral zone passing sequences a bit. There's definitely concerns about his vision, his passing timing and accuracy on the rush, and his predisposition to (not) passing under pressure in general that makes us wonder about how transferable his playmaking is to the pro level. In a more "controlled' environment where there is less ice to manage and movement to track, like in a power play formation, we think there's bigger upside for his passing game. He could be a very effective piece on the half-wall of a power play or even as a downhill option from the point.

As mentioned, he's a volume shooter. Not only did he lead the league in shots on goal at 240, but he registered at least a shot on goal more per game than almost all the other top 20 shooters in the USHL. At over 4.6 shots per game, only Zam Plante (3.8) and Austin Burnevik (3.7) could hold a candle to Connelly. He had almost a hundred more shots than his next closest teammate, in nine less games. There's the natural positive that he has the puck and he's getting shots through, of course. And while shots are categorically not a bad play, they aren't always optimal. A microcosm of his style in this excerpt from a midseason game versus Fargo:

Late 1st period power play, he's the last guy picking up the puck with speed. It's against a 1-3 forecheck that got stacked on with speed above the puck. Connelly gains the zone and has two very obvious kick out options, one is close to his left and then another backup option on the far side. Connelly decides to try to split two defenders who are a stick length apart. He gets knocked down and loses the puck into the corner. He's able to retrieve and reverse it up the side boards. He eventually gets it back and wheels around the high offensive zone on his backhand…then he just randomly fires a turnaround wrist shot from 40ish feet away that hits off the body of one of his teammates in the slot and it finds a way through Slukynsky. It's all a really unsophisticated sequence but nets a primary assist despite his intent.

If the low angle shots and fadeaway wristers can be converted into something more useful, even if it's just a cycle-starting pass or a give and go with his point man or something to that effect, it might really open up some more scalable aspects to his attack zone game. The trouble is that he shows limited ability to even conceptualize these types of plays. We already touched on how he has trouble passing his teammates into useful space, and going along with that he doesn't set a lot of picks, he doesn't even retrieve a ton of pucks that his teammates lose. He's fast enough to get them, but he just doesn't anticipate what's going to happen next at a high level. It's not even enough to go with a cliché like, "he needs to simplify his game" as there isn't much simpler (conceptually) than skating down the ice and taking a shot. It's more about tempo control and keeping sustainable offense alive in the attack zone. And again, there was some improvement in that regard, but it's still a weakness. And what's more, he's not a sniper. For as much as he shoots, it would be too far to call him a true finisher. Pucks don't exactly explode off his blade quickly. And while there was some improvement, despite his excellent 1 on 1 hands, his array of finishing moves isn't overly threatening. His shot is good, but not great. The shooting mechanics are generally on the money, but it's the inconsistent release point that tends to take some steam out of it. He lets pucks drift pretty far out in front of him, especially on the rush, and as a player that likes to put it under the bar that's going to be ok…but there's still going to need to be better velocity behind it or a more consistent threat to deke his way to a finish. Not a lot of evidence of him shooting intentionally for a rebound either, that would be a nice piece to add if he's going to continue to be a volume shooter.

Obviously we touched on his lacklustre anticipation, so his defensive game is absent of substance. He could up his compete level off the puck and move the needle a bit because of his speed. That's why he's used on the penalty kill in Tri-City is because he's fast. But a lot of pucks get through him and he's not very prolific in puck battle situations yet either. If he smells blood in the water with a d-man mishandling the puck at the point or has him on the backfoot in the NZ, he dogs him pretty good. He can free up some pucks for breakaways like that. Even the details that go into making good body contact aren't there, he commits to the wrong hit point sometimes or goes after the wrong shoulder or wrong side of the puck. Not that he packs heavy punch at his weight right now anyway, but he slides right through or right off his opponents because he doesn't read their path very well. His whole spatial awareness system is pretty wonky. There's no angling to his game, he just goes at where a target used to be. We don't see a lot of redeemable qualities about his on-ice mental game that gives up hope that he'll improve markedly and that really dulls what is otherwise a really intriguing player.

So, it's really complex. We have a 6'0" frame playing in the 150 pound range and really fast. We have a volume shooter, to a fault, that really doesn't have great finishing ability. We have a high assist total on the wing but lacking pro-level vision and playmaking variance. We have negligible anticipation ability and off the puck play. All packed in a really immature game.

There's a few ways this can go: The least likely of which is that he becomes a supreme technical skill master that cleans up his warts and transforms into a much more complete player. Or, he becomes a player that flashes some skill and a highlight reel play here and there, but is ultimately undone by his lacking hockey sense and true purpose.. We're thinking it's probably closer to the latter, so we're going to put him on our list where we would be willing to grab him if he slides into a place where it's tremendous upside value for that spot.

"He's like 155 pounds and plays with blinders on." - NHL Scout, January 2024

"You can't deny that he has plenty of skill. He will still be a high pick." - NHL Scout, January 2024

"I have him just inside my top 20. Too much skill to drop him." - NHL Scout, May 2024

"Not on my list." - NHL Scout, May 2024

"I don't think I saw him hit anyone in any of my viewings." - NHL Scout, May 2024

"He's not on my list." NHL Scout, May 2024

"Doubt we would draft him." - NHL Scout, May 2024

"He plays the game by himself. Reminds me of Josh Ho-Sang in that regard. Not my cup of tea for that and other reasons." - HP Scout, Mark Edwards, November 2023

NR	PLAYER	TEAM	LEAGUE	HEIGHT	WEIGHT	POS	GRADE
	CONNOR, JOE	MUSKEGON	USHL	5'10"	173	LW	NI

NHLCS	CEILING	FLOOR	HOCKEY SENSE	COMPETE	SKILL	SKATE	MISC
NA-118	4	4	5	6	5	5	4

Hard working winger, Joe Connor was passed over in 2023 despite leading Avon Old Farms (USHS) in scoring and finding six points in 12 USHL games. This season – now full time with Muskegon (USHL) – there's less bite to his game but he really racked up the points. He finished 18th in the USHL with a 31+29=60 stat line. He benefited plenty from playing a lot of time with the USHL's leading scorer Matvei Gridin – as Gridin directly factored into just short of half of Connor's points. He proved to be a nice complement to the slower paced Russian. Overall, Connor isn't very skilled in space. That said, he tries to put some pucks into areas that make d-men uncomfortable. He'd have a higher success rate if he was a better skater. He's usually good for one quick stick maneuver to set himself up for a deception...but the skill chaining isn't really there. The 5'10" winger rarely exhibits the ability to get the puck back into the interior once it's outside the dots. Many of his goals could be categorized as "junior goals", but there are some mildly scalable greasy goals in the mix. Even his one finishing move – a shoulder fake, forehand to backhand number – converted a lot of breakaways, but it doesn't have a lot of extension or width to it which will likely limit its effectiveness against pro goalies.

The biggest disappointment here is the skating and size combination. The stride isn't pretty, but he gets around fine. Though, his methodology is to just outwork his stride. So, his constant motion makes him a threat but he can't handle the puck very well at his highest speed. As such, his skating looks better on the forecheck and in other puck pursuit situations. Connor can elicit a fair bit of panic at this level (and a ton at the high school level), but the edge work and small-area footwork will need to improve if he wants to meaningfully compete with better players at higher levels. His mental processor seemed to improve as the year went on, even at his pace of play…that's a good sign for upward trajectory, even if the ceiling is that of a 12th/13th forward. There is nothing terribly noteworthy about his playmaking or passing combination, he got away with a few more hope passes than many other players of his skill level because of what team he was on. This is not a player that can be utilized in carrying pucks across lines. It's a nice boost in recognition that the Northeastern commit was able to play with a top talent and produce, as that's the type of "skill floor" we want to see for a player to ideally become an F1 and/or penalty killing specialist at the next level. He's a long way from that though and at his size, it's not going to be easy.

NR	PLAYER	TEAM	LEAGUE	HEIGHT	WEIGHT	POS	GRADE
	CORMIER, BEN	OWEN SOUND	OHL	6'00"	181	LC	NI
NHLCS	CEILING	FLOOR	HOCKEY SENSE	COMPETE	SKILL	SKATE	MISC
-	5	5	5	7	6	6	5

Ben Cormier is a center for the Owen Sound Attack in the OHL. He under performed on the score sheet this past season after higher expectations as a former first round selection in the OHL Draft producing 24 points and 14 goals in 65 games this season.

The best attribute and highest rated category for Cormier is his compete. He was a good energy player for the Attack this season but struggled to find a consistent role in the top six in a scoring role. His forecheck is strong, he will throw his weight around and he can play a good positional game on the penalty kill however, this is where we start to focus on his other skills and shift Cormier into the "NI" ranking.

He can be beat of loose pucks and be beat physically due to his lack of size. Cormier's offensive game is not the strongest with a shot that struggles with accuracy and not the best passing ability overall. His skating is not bad as he is able to keep up with the play and quickly move up ice but, he can have trouble with his speed with the puck on his stick and in making sharp cuts.

On the whole, his combination of lack of size and lack of overall skill will hurt his chances in making the NHL. Working on his offensive skills will help him become more of a two-dimensional threat as opposed to a high energy penalty killing forward.

NR	PLAYER	TEAM	LEAGUE	HEIGHT	WEIGHT	POS	GRADE
	CRISTOFORO, ANTHONY	WINDSOR	OHL	5'11"	191	RD	NI
NHLCS	CEILING	FLOOR	HOCKEY SENSE	COMPETE	SKILL	SKATE	MISC
NA-194	5	3	5	5	7	6	5

Anthony Cristoforo is a slightly undersized right-shot defenseman playing for the Windsor Spitfires in the OHL. He put up 38 points in 67 games this season, 3 points less in 4 more games than his rookie season. He played top four minutes on a young Spitfires team that relied heavily upon him as the season went on and they traded away key veteran defensemen. After a promising rookie season in Windsor, Cristoforo had a slightly disappointing sophomore season and did not overly impress us as an NHL prospect throughout the year.

As an offensive defenseman, Cristoforo gives his team a threat to create offense from the point. He walks the line well by either skating forwards or by back peddling and scanning for an open forward. Offensively, he loves to pass and shoot from the point with a hard but inaccurate hot that typically misses high and away from potential deflections. Cristoforo's skating is good with strong transitions front to back and strong edgework. He does not have high end speed. His offensive awareness is a strength overall, but the offensive side of his game is not good enough to overlook the defensive side.

Cristoforo's defensive game eroded this past season, and it was already not a strong portion of his game. The struggles are heavily highlighted in his inability to get out of his zone, where he has trouble leading his teammates into good opportunities and even further with his scanning abilities. He is often passing into traffic or to teammates with coverage right on top of them leading to turnovers or broken plays. His coverage in his own end is not consistent or energetic and despite his strong skating ability he sometimes is not able to keep up with the pace because of his lack of compete. This is also true with his rush defence where he has trouble with power moves and with containing players with quick hands. With the defensive issues and poor overall performance defensively, his offensive skill alone is not enough to compensate.

This type of defenseman does not translate to the professional levels very well and as we have seen in previous years, as referenced in an early season article, NHL teams are starting to distance themselves more from drafting smaller defensemen.

He took a step backwards in some aspects of his game and seemed too comfortable at times and we were left wanting more. The offensive talent is unmistakably there, however the defensive side to his game and his zone exits are well below average and his compete level and IQ in the defensive zone is not survivable in the NHL. This may be the result of playing on a last place Windsor team and that needs to be accounted for, but the consistent downwards trajectory.

NR	PLAYER			TEAM		LEAGUE	HEIGHT	WEIGHT	POS	GRADE
	CROSBY, LOGAN			HALIFAX		QMJHL	6' 01.75"	195	RW	NI
NHLCS	CEILING	FLOOR		HOCKEY SENSE		COMPETE	SKILL		SKATE	MISC
NA-169	4	5		5		7	5		6	6

Logan Crosby is a right-wing power forward who was drafted by the Halifax Mooseheads in the 1st round (20th overall) of the 2021 QMJHL entry draft. After two average seasons on a stacked Halifax team, Crosby was looking quite good to start his draft year, but his season was shortened by two different injuries. He was never able to regain his beginning of season form and ended up finishing with 9 goals and 13 assists in 33 regular season games.

Crosby is a decent skater with good straight-line speed when he gets going. We feel that an area of improvement could be his stride as it seems a little heavy and clunky which affects his stop and go abilities and his first three strides do not generate a ton of speed. Crosby is a simple offensive player. Known as more of a north/south guy, he generates the majority of his offense from in tight, where he can be a pain to deal with. He does not possess much of a playmaking flair, he will often choose the dump and chase play while in transition instead of trying to make something happen. We like his ability to protect the puck with his body, he is tough to steal possession from.

On the defensive side of the puck, we like that he is always moving and will give a 2nd and even a 3rd effort on defensive coverage. He never gives up in his pursuit of the puck. He does not seem to make very many errors. We would maybe like to see him use physicality a little more, but he is a fine defensive player.

Constant injuries and not getting quality possessions because he was playing on a stacked team might have hampered his development a little. He's not on our draft list and we think the chances of getting drafted are slim. However, he does have some qualities that could get him drafted as a NHL team could see a guy playing a depth role in the NHL one day if the development goes nicely in the next few years and if he stays injury free.

102	PLAYER	TEAM	LEAGUE	HEIGHT	WEIGHT	POS	GRADE
	CURRAN, MAXMILIAN	TRI-CITY	WHL	6' 03"	185	LC	C
NHLCS	CEILING	FLOOR	HOCKEY SENSE	COMPETE	SKILL	SKATE	MISC
NA-58	5	5	7	5	6	4	8

The 6'4" center from Czechia played his first season in the WHL, registering 32 points in 40 for the Americans. As his 27 assists in 40 shows, Curran is a pass first center. He played in all-situations for his team, mostly running the 1st PP unit from his strong side half-wall and was a primary option on the penalty kill. Curran also represented Czechia at the U18 after the season, playing in a top 6 role.

As mentioned, Curran is a playmaking center who was a driver in transition for his team, even with below average skating. He's smart off puck and supports the play well with greatly timed center routes to acquire the puck in open space at full speed. He gets off the wall and attacks the inside to create confusion and to open more options. Once entering the offensive zone on the rush, Curran does a great job slowing down the play. His patience and puck poise allows his linemates to sprint into open space, and his vision allows him to find them with success.

In the offensive zone, Curran's playmaking abilities come out when he works down low. He establishes body position early, lift his eyes and uses his length to protect the puck and find open teammates inside the slot. Improving his first few steps and adding strength would help him to win more 50/50 battles, and improving his shot would make him more of a dual threat offensively. On the man advantage, he moves the puck well when running the power play from the half-wall.

Defensively, Curran is a smart two-way center. He works hard on the tracking, and shows good awareness with his positioning on the PK and in the defensive zone at 5-on-5. Improving his quickness and strength will help his small aera defending to find another level, like defending one-on-one down low or when boxing out in front of the net.

Overall, Curran has solid offensive upside with his playmaking abilities and puck protection skill. With his size and IQ, his game projects well defensively as a two-way center. Improving his skating will be an important part of his development to find success playing at an higher pace at the next level.

63	PLAYER	TEAM	LEAGUE	HEIGHT	WEIGHT	POS	GRADE
	DANFORD, BEN	OSHAWA	OHL	6' 01.5"	191	RD	C
NHLCS	CEILING	FLOOR	HOCKEY SENSE	COMPETE	SKILL	SKATE	MISC
NA-35	6	5	5	7	5	6	7

A smooth-skating, right-shot presence on Oshawa's blue line, Ben Danford provides high-level leadership and competes while patrolling the blue line. Putting up 33 points in 64 games this season for the Generals, Danford was relied upon for his defensive game and excellence on the penalty kill while being a sturdy second-year leader on a young Generals team.

Danford's ability to kill penalties is one of the best among draft-eligible defenders in this class. His awareness, ability to get the puck out of the zone, and consistent shot-blocking make him a must-have on the ice when a man down. He positions his body well and uses his stick to cut off passing lanes from his side of the ice, jumping onto loose pucks behind his net and deep along the wall. He is constantly aware of where everyone is on the ice and can cover off either side of the ice as a right-shot defender. He can play aggressively and take away space from puck carriers to rush passes, or he can play patiently and clog lanes to keep the puck to the outside. The biggest plus for Danford on the penalty kill is his willingness to get in front of the puck and block shots. Teams have avoided his side of the ice while he is killing penalties, and watching him take away space on his side of the ice, you can see why. His penalty-killing skills are translatable to the NHL, and we could see him becoming a strong defense-first penalty-killing specialist.

On the defensive side of the puck, Danford closes gaps well and can defend against fast opponents. As a rush defender, he is better against speed players than he is against physical players driving to the middle through him. He does defend both well, but as he progresses and plays against stronger and faster players, we are more confident in his abilities against speedier players as opposed to physically dominant forwards because of his backpedaling ability skating backward and his body positioning to box them out. Off the puck in coverage, Danford can close gaps quickly, and for a defender who is not large or one who possesses great strength, he plays well physically along the boards. He has the ability to rub players off the puck and transition it up the ice well, and with the puck on his stick in his own end, he can create space for himself and give himself more time to make decisions because of his backward cuts and smooth backward strides.

In transition with the puck, there are some big mental lapses at times for Danford that really hold him back from taking his projectability from a bottom-pair defender to a second-pair guy. His noted ability to kill penalties might get him a job at the pro level, but it is hard to project him higher because of his inability to see forecheckers on some breakouts and bad turnover habits. There is nothing to hate about his hockey sense, but there is a lot left on the table as well. He is not strong with the puck when rushed and turns the puck over or ices the puck at times from an aggressive forecheck from the opposing team. His first read coming out of his own zone is not the greatest, but when he does connect on his breakout passes, they do lead his teammates into good rush or offensive zone entries. His mental lapses also occur in coverage where he will leave his man or lose his man and have to hustle to get back into position. This happens at the blue line offensively as well, where he hesitates to pinch at times and can get caught at the blue line. Luckily, his skating and hustle are there for him to work hard to get back to help defensively, but it is still something he needs to work on as you cannot get away with that at the pro level.

Offensively, he gets off a strong shot from the point, which finds its way through traffic in front of the net but at the same time is kept at a good height for tips from his men in front. He collects bad passes well and can get off his shot with a good release and power. For a more defensive defenseman, Danford likes to be aggressive and join the rush but is not much of a shooting option. He accelerates quickly with the puck, but it is too quick for his hands to keep up, and he can bobble the puck before he gets the opportunity to make a play. When patient with the puck, whether at the blue line looking for a shot, on breakout passes, or taking shots from the point, Danford is at his best. He does need to put more on his passes at this point in his development, but as he gets stronger, this should not be a concern.

"Playing with Marrelli and honestly he is probably playing more minutes than he is ready to play right now but that is the situation on Oshawa right now. I like him but he's a bit limited...stay at home guy all day long for me." – HP Scout, Mark Edwards, October 2023

91	PLAYER	TEAM	LEAGUE	HEIGHT	WEIGHT	POS	GRADE
	DE LUCA, TOMMASO	HC AMBRÌ-PIOTTA	SWISS	6' 00"	187	LW	C
NHLCS	CEILING	FLOOR	HOCKEY SENSE	COMPETE	SKILL	SKATE	MISC
-	7	4	7	5	7	5	5

De Luca went undrafted last season in his first year of eligibility, which was a surprise for us given his skill set and how much he was an offensive driver for Spokane. It was an eventful season for De Luca. He played his first pro season in

Switzerland for Ambri-Piotta, played 6 playoffs game for their U20 team, represented Italy in the WJC-20 D1B and WC D1A and played in a few U20 international competition. It was a pretty strong first pro season for a U20 player with 20 points in 41 games in the NL.

Du Luca is an offensive driver in transition. With his IQ, vision and puck skills, most of his puck touches and passes find the inside ice to improve the condition of the puck. When carrying the puck, he's agile, skilled and slippery, allowing him to attack the inside and beat defensive players in one-on-one situations. Once he enters the zone, he moves laterally to attack the middle and create defensive confusion, and his vision allows him to create grade-A off the rush.

In the offensive zone, De Luca is all about getting off the wall and attacking the inside. He protects the puck well, creates trap door to cut-back and change direction, then attack the middle, either with his feet and by passing the puck. His skills and agility make him hard to defend down low, and he's a guy who love to attack the inside and doesn't hesitate to drive the net, with and without the puck.

Without the puck, De Luca's game improved playing in a pro league. He was involved, reloading on change of possession. The things he'll need to work on to keep getting better in this area: Adding more strength, making more stops all over the ice, and better awareness in the defensive zone.

De Luca is a highly talented player with great vision who loves to attack the inside, which is a important trait to translate offensive game at the NHL level. If he's not drafted again this season, it wouldn't be a surprise for us to see De Luca become an highly sought after European free agent in the NHL in a few years.

NR	PLAYER	TEAM	LEAGUE	HEIGHT	WEIGHT	POS	GRADE
	DEHLI, MATHIAS	LORENSKOG	NORWAY	6' 02"	185	RC	NI

NHLCS	CEILING	FLOOR	HOCKEY SENSE	COMPETE	SKILL		SKATE	MISC
INT-80	5	4	6	6	5		5	6

Mathias Dehli is an intelligent, two-way center, who has a well rounded skill-set and plays a structured game that allowed him to play in Norway's top pro league the entire season. He finished the year with 8 points in 22 games, including 7 goals, though most of his production occurred at the start of the season. Internationally, he represented Norway at the U18s, where he performed well, registering 6 points in 5 games, with 3 goals.

Dehli is a European player that plays largely a North-American style of game, where he uses his heavier set frame to physically overwhelm opposing players. He's not overly dynamic and there isn't one or two specific areas that he specializes in. Instead, he uses his well rounded skill-set to chip in and do a bit of everything all over the ice.

He can support his defense with his frame, weighing heavy along the boards, helping come up with loose pucks through well-timed cross checks that throw opposing players off of balance, and he can move well enough to transport the puck through the neutral zone. Arguably the most impressive aspect of his curve has come through his playmaking. When he was playing pro hockey, he would play a steam-lined game, which was expected, but it was to a fault. There was very little creativity or advanced play creation; but, further into his season and when he was playing in his own age group, he started showing more impressive playmaking that was backed with his frame.

He started cutting east-west and pivoting back onto defense while identifying trailing options in transition, and he started displaying the ability to use advanced hesitation reverse passes to open up the ice when hitting his teammates in stride. His shooting upside falls a bit under his playmaking but he's scored a couple of impressive goals that have displayed shot quality and his bottom hand activation is decent.

He can threaten from distance, set up his teammates off the cycle and in transition, and he can support his defense but there's limitations within his tool-kit and his translatable skill-set. Most depth options at the NHL level are specialized and he isn't. His hands are average, his skating is roughly average, his playmaking is slightly above average and his shooting is average. It can take him too long in terms of fluidly transferring between different plays and his ability to chain his skill together can be delayed.

There's still an opportunity for him to play as a depth option due to his intelligence and willingness to support, but if he makes it, we think it's very likely in a defensive role. He's one of those prospects that plays the game the right way, but we think falls under the needed talent or specialization to think he can fit in a top-9 role at this time.

"He was on track to match Balcers production in Norway's top league earlier in the season but he got injured and his play fell off. He was better at the U18's, but I don't think there's enough here, but I've also been very wrong." - HP Scout, Brad Allen

NR	PLAYER	TEAM	LEAGUE	HEIGHT	WEIGHT	POS	GRADE
	DESJARDINS, VINCENT	BLAINVILLE	QMJHL	5' 10.25"	155	RC	NI
NHLCS	CEILING	FLOOR	HOCKEY SENSE	COMPETE	SKILL	SKATE	MISC
NA-105	5	4	6	5	6	5	4

Capable of playing both center and the wing, Desjardins progressed well this season with the Armada despite a slow start; 32 of his 47 points came after the Christmas break (plus 7 points in 7 games in the playoffs). He played his 16-year-old season in the QM18AAA with St-Eustache, where he was one of the league's top scorers with 47 points in 39 games. He was 8 days away from being eligible for the 2025 NHL Draft which, making him one of the youngest players eligible for the 2024 NHL Draft.

An average-sized player with good playmaking skills, his vision and creativity are his best assets on the ice. He's a smart and versatile player. At the pro level, we think he'll be a winger due to his lack of size. We like his play on the power play, where he demonstrates creativity from the half-wall, and his playmaking shines the most with added time and space. He has good hands one-on-one, but he'll need to improve his shot (he's currently not a threat with his long-distance shot). He needs to venture in rough areas more often to get his goals, which is even more true as he moves to higher levels. He'll also need to get stronger physically in order to be able to survive playing in traffic. He's only an okay skater for his size, though, and we would like to see him more explosive on the ice even if he has decent agility and edgework.

We feel he shares similarities with other QMJHL players in that he's a good junior player, but not good enough for the NHL (it's worth noting that his second-half surge and young age do pose small doubts about that projection, however). His teammate Jonathan Fauchon faced a similar situation two years ago; he's also a very good QMJHL player, but doesn't have much NHL upside.

4	PLAYER	TEAM	LEAGUE	HEIGHT	WEIGHT	POS	GRADE
	DEMIDOV, IVAN	SKA ST PTBG	RUS JR	5' 11"	181	LW	A
NHLCS	CEILING	FLOOR	HOCKEY SENSE	COMPETE	SKILL	SKATE	MISC
INT-2	8	7	8	7	8	6	6

Demidov has been on our radar since we first saw him at the 2021 Hlinka-Gretzky tournament playing for Russia's U18 team. He was still 15 years old at the time. A dominant player in the MHL over the past two seasons, he was named MVP of the league last year and followed that up by leading his team to the MHL Championship, with 28 points in 17 playoff games this season.

Having started the year in the KHL on a top team, he couldn't get enough ice time and was sent down to the MHL. He hurt his knee in an MHL game at the start of October, missing 6 weeks of action. Although he returned mid-November, he never went back to the KHL. But he went on a tear in the MHL for the rest of the season. After his injury, he played 28 regular season games and recorded a point in 26 of them. From December 17th to February 19th, he had a ridiculous streak of 17 straight games with a point...collecting 44 points in that span. In the playoffs, he had a point in 14 of the 17 games he played in. In one of those games (game #4 of the final), he played only 3 minutes before getting injured. Overall, Demidov had a dominant season, accumulating 88 points in 47 games across both the regular season and postseason. This was expected, as he showcased his dominance the previous year in the league, clinching the MVP title with his 75 points across 51 games in the regular season and playoffs combined.

He belonged in the KHL this year. He could have gotten the Michkov treatment and gone to Sochi or other lower-ranked KHL teams if he couldn't get ideal ice time with SKA. The VHL would have been an option as well (although it's not ideal for player development). He was just too good for the MHL, a league that did not challenge him this season. Demidov's contract ends after 2024-2025, which may have been a reason why he didn't return to the KHL. He's not in the same position as Michkov, who had 3 more years to his contract during his draft year last season.

Demidov has special puck skills and is the best stickhandler in this draft class. He's a highlight-reel machine with his ability to manipulate opponents and make them look silly on the ice. He excels in tight spaces with his elite stickhandling skills. He loves one-on-one confrontations and has never met a player he doesn't think he can beat. When he plays in junior, he sometimes tries too hard to beat everyone on the ice with his quick, skilled hands. However, he has gotten better over time at adopting a more professional approach, even in his short KHL experience where he played a reserved but effective game.

There have been comparisons between him and Trevor Zegras because of his puck skills and creativity on the ice. It's a legit comparison to make, but you shouldn't automatically think that Demidov is the Russian Zegras; a few notable differences include how they play away from the puck and their effort level. Demidov is a much more involved player away from the puck; he can create turnovers in the neutral zone with his great sense of anticipation and stick activation plays. He can be a good forechecker and create turnovers when he puts pressure on opposing defensemen. He gives an honest effort on the backcheck and he's not a liability in his zone. He's a much more complete player than Zegras, if you compare both players at the same age.

Demidov is great when handling the puck in the offensive zone; there's more value in his game there because he's not an explosive skater (which diminishes some of his transition effectiveness). He has great agility and edgework, but his acceleration and explosiveness have not improved much over the past two years. He has to use his edgework a lot to help him be effective, often changing directions and using deceptive head and shoulder fakes to help his skating. He also often uses the 10-2 skating technique when making zone entries on the left side of the ice. This is not very common in the NHL, but we see it from different players like Kirill Kaprizov, Dawson Mercer and prospects like Brandt Clarke and Antonio Stranges. One notable aspect of his frequent use of edges is that it increases the risk of injury due to the fact that he can't protect himself adequately all the time (demonstrated by his two knee injuries in the same season).

His deceptive game is really good, though, and a huge part of his offensive game. It's somewhat similar to William Eklund; Eklund was not a good skater for his size, but his ability to create false information for his opponents was fantastic. There are some similarities there between the two in how they operate on the ice as well, but Demidov's skill level is way higher than Eklund's. You also see it with his play along the wall, where he constantly moves his body to different angles to protect the puck (another layer of his deception game).

Demidov is not a huge player (listed at 5'11", 168 pounds) and it showed in his brief KHL stint this year. He lacks the strength to really perform physically at that level, but he has the right mindset and technique to do well in the future once he's able to add more strength to his frame. When projecting him in the NHL, we would also like to see him improve his explosiveness (to be a bigger factor in transition). He should also play at a higher pace and with added urgency. Although a lot of his game is about puck control, intelligence and poise, he does need to find a better balance to maximize his potential.

Deadly on the power play, he likes to have the puck on his stick with more time and space on the ice. He likes to run the man-advantage from the half-wall on the right side. He has this great creativity and ability to create a play out of nothing, which only high-end thinkers and skilled players can do. He's quite talented at not letting opponents know which plays he's going to execute. He hides his intentions well, even when shooting the puck. He's got that delayed release that can also be used to set up a passing play.

We project him as a 25-30 goal scorer in the NHL due to his deceptive shot and above-average velocity, but he's not a high-end sniper like Michkov was last year. However, he's a more well-rounded player than Michkov. Next to his puck skills, his creativity and playmaking are his best assets, and his overall playmaking abilities are what we see as his top asset in the NHL. He makes the players around him better, and he feels like a center that plays on the wing. He did spend some time at center in the first round of the playoffs, but that didn't last long (his faceoff game was lacking).

Next up in his development is stepping onto the KHL stage, something we're looking forward to seeing next season. If he were to land with SKA, a good team, it would be good for him, but there's a chance he might get lost in the mix, which isn't ideal. He could also get loaned to a team like Sochi and get all the ice time he wants (like Michkov the past two seasons).

That's the risk NHL teams have to take into consideration: how will he be used next season? Michkov ended up going back to Sochi for a second straight year. His stats may look good, but is he developing his two-way game? It's not the best situation for a young player to play in a losing environment for too long. Having said that, Demidov did make the SKA roster out of training camp this past season, unlike Michkov. Also, the fact that he has only one year left on his contract could make things more tolerable for NHL teams. All this to say: they are hoping he's in a good situation in the KHL next season.

"Works hard and super skilled." - NHL Scout, December 2023

"Weak top 10 this year but he's in my top 5." - NHL Scout, January 2024

"Kinda undersized and not really all that quick. I don't have him as high as the lists out there." - NHL Scout, March 2024

"He's second on my list but let's face it, we all have the same 5 or 6 guys in various order." - NHL Scout, April 2024

"He will go second overall and that's who I have second too." - NHL Scout, May 2024

"A bit of a waste this season playing in the MHL again after dominating that league last year" - HP Scout Jérôme Bérubé, February 2024

-It was close with Iginla for me but I went with the more naturally skilled and dynamic player" - HP Scout Jérôme Bérubé, May 2024

"He's a better playmaker than Michkov, but he has the same issues too, primarily with the lack of high-end skating. If he was a high-end skater, then it would make sense to put him top 2, but for us, he isn't." - HP Scout, Brad Allen, May 2024

" I feel that he was stuck between leagues. He was too gifted for the MHL, but not physically developed enough for the KHL, and never played in the VHL." - HP Scout, Brad Allen, May 2024

" He has the best hands I've seen since Stutzle" - HP Scout, Brad Allen, May 2024

" Very tight ranking the guys from 2-8 ish - Demidov was in that group. No argument from me if some scouts have him 2nd and others have him 8th." - HP Scout, Mark Edwards, May 2024

NR	PLAYER	TEAM	LEAGUE	HEIGHT	WEIGHT	POS	GRADE
	DESRUISSEAUX, THOMAS	CHICOUTIMI	QMJHL	5' 10.75"	162	LC	NI
NHLCS	CEILING	FLOOR	HOCKEY SENSE	COMPETE	SKILL	SKATE	MISC
NA-96	5	4	7	5	5	5	4

Desruisseaux is a slight-frame center from the Chicoutimi Saguenéens in the QMJHL. Collecting a total of 60 points in 68 games, he was paired with Maxim Massé often this past season on the top line, in addition to the 1st PP unit of the Saguenéens.

A pass-first type of player, this is an easy conclusion to draw when looking at his stats (with 44 of his 60 points being assists). Desruisseaux has above-average vision and is always looking to feed his teammates the puck in scoring areas. There's good creativity to his game with his smarts and passing skills. He takes advantage of power play situations, with more space and time available to him to create plays for his teammates.

However, his 5-on-5 play, as was the case for Chicoutimi for most of the season, was pretty average. Desruisseaux lacks strength, has a slight frame, and will need to add more mass to his frame to be able to compete at the next level. He's not a good skater for his size either when projecting him for the NHL, which leaves us with some doubts as to how his overall game will translate. Looking at other, similar players, we much prefer Alexandre Blais of Rimouski because he's much more dynamic with his skating in comparison. Desruisseaux is not much of a shooter, and needs to get closer to the net to score goals. When you have a frame like his, not being a threat from long distance can be tough. Long-term, players like him tend to get tired due to constantly having to fight through traffic. He has good hands and decent one-on-one skills, but he needs to find a way to have more impact playing inside hockey.

We see Desruisseaux as a good junior player, one that could end up playing in the ECHL/AHL or Europe at some point during his career, but we don't see a guy we would want to invest a draft pick on, hence why he's not ranked in our list.

8	PLAYER	TEAM	LEAGUE	HEIGHT	WEIGHT	POS	GRADE
	DICKINSON, SAM	LONDON	OHL	6' 02.75"	203	LD	A
NHLCS	CEILING	FLOOR	HOCKEY SENSE	COMPETE	SKILL	SKATE	MISC
NA-7	7	7	7	7	7	8	8

Dickinson has been a key player for the Knights since his 16-year-old season, and was one of this year's top defensemen in the OHL with 70 points in 68 games. He has played a lot of hockey in the past two years: two full OHL seasons with very full postseasons (the Knights lost in the final last year and won it all this year). In total, that's 169 OHL games. Those 39 playoff games also have top-notch value when it comes to experiencing high-pressure hockey. He also played at the U17 Hockey Challenge, the Hlinka-Gretzky Cup and the Memorial Cup all before turning 18. Playing in London for Dale and Mark Hunter is also like the Harvard of hockey development.

He's one of the best skaters from the backend in this draft class, and you could make a case that he's the best. He's incredibly fluid on the ice, with excellent footwork and agility. His skating ability allows him to never be in trouble on the ice, and he can recover quickly from any situation. He's a great athlete overall, using his skating effectively to close gaps quickly, enhancing his ability to defend rushes. Offensively, he's able to jump into plays as a fourth forward at times, thanks to his skating. When pressured by the opposing team's forecheck, he can skate himself out of trouble in his own zone. His skating and athletic ability are his best assets, and when you add his size and frame to the equation, it creates one of the best size/skating combinations in the entire draft.

Offensively we don't consider him a high-end offensive player, but he is still above-average. Depending on the team he goes to, he could get a PP1 role, but what he lacks in elite offensive tools (good, but not great) leads us to believe he would most likely be a PP2 guy on a good team. He's good in transition, can pass the puck at a high level from his zone, is adept at long-stretch passes, and his decision-making is both solid and fast. He can be a threat from the point, using his agility to move laterally at the line to give himself different options or lanes to either pass or shoot. He can score from far away, as his shot is above-average in terms of velocity and release, and he shoots it a lot. He finished 11th in the OHL for shots on goal, 2nd overall for defensemen. His creativity level and puck distribution skills are good, but not great. In our eyes, this will prevent him from being a true PP1 guy in the NHL. But, as mentioned, he has an above-average shot and he's not afraid to use it. He has decent hands as well, which help him both at the line and in transition when rushing the puck through the neutral zone.

Defensively, it's a similar story. We think of him as a very solid defender, but not an elite shutdown defenseman. We like his stick activation when it comes time to remove pucks from opponents, or at least make them uncomfortable when they go to his side of the ice. He covers tons of ice with his reach and is rarely in trouble due to his excellent skating.

He has enough pushback in his game, but he's not an exceptionally tough physical player to compete against. He plays a lot, usually around 25 minutes per game, but we would like to see more urgency in his play in his zone. Earlier in the season, given his size and skating, we thought there might be some comparisons to be made with Jake Sanderson in terms of defensive play. However, the more we watched, the more we saw a gap between Sanderson and Dickinson. We think Sanderson could become an elite defender in the NHL, but we don't see the same level of shutdown ability in Dickinson. The Ottawa Senators defenseman is better with his gap control, is more aggressive with his skating to challenge forwards off the rush, and overall has superior decision-making skills. Dickinson can get too aggressive in his zone at times and can get caught puck-watching,

One aspect about Dickinson that we feel is of particular importance: NHL teams know he's in a great environment with the Knights, who are as good as anyone to produce talent for the NHL. Being coached by Dale Hunter for possibly the next two seasons is going to help Dickinson's stock for the draft. He could be in the NHL either next season, or the year after, but if a team is patient and keeps him in junior with London, they can be more secure in knowing that he will continue to get better, which is not the case for all players.

We always like to find comparable's with prospects, and the one that stands out the most for Dickinson is Noah Hanifin, formerly of the Calgary Flames and now with the Vegas Golden Knights. Throughout the year, we kept feeling that Dickinson at 3rd overall felt too high, which led us to the Hanifin comparison. Hanifin was drafted 5th overall in 2015 by Carolina, and has become a very good defenseman in the NHL, though not necessarily one worthy of a top-5 selection. When you look at Hanifin's skillset, he's a left defenseman like Dickinson with similar size. Both players' best qualities are their skating skills. They are both good but not great offensively and defensively. They both have enough pushback, but neither is overly physical, and both could use more urgency in their defensive game. We feel this comparison fits perfectly for Dickinson.

We debated extensively in the second half of the season about Dickinson's placement in our top 10 and how he compares to other defensemen. For instance, we felt that based on Silayev's freak athleticism and playoff hockey abilities, he might be in a category with him and Buium. The debate was between Dickinson, Levshunov, and Parekh.

When comparing Dickinson to Levshunov, we see Dickinson as the safer prospect, whereas Levshunov, the riskier selection, has more raw potential. A similar story emerges when comparing Dickinson to Parekh: Dickinson feels like a safer pick for us, but Parekh has the higher upside, although his defense is riskier. Versus Buium, both are pretty safe prospects, but we think Buium has more offensive upside and an advantage with his decision-making and hockey IQ.

It's difficult to predict exactly where Dickinson will go in the draft, but he shouldn't have to wait too long. We expect a run on defensemen to happen very quickly after the Celebrini pick.

" My top four Dmen are Dickinson, Parekh, Levshunov and Silayev and it is really tight." - NHL Scout, May 2024

" I've heard Hanifin as the comparison so many times but Dickinson is better. Hanifin plays 23 minutes a night and every situation and is non physical but he's not as skilled as Dickinson, Hanifin is a puck manager and not creative at all. Neither of them can run a powerplay." - NHL Scout, May 2024

"His skill is better than his brain. He makes some passes that are high end skilled passes but not creative passes." - NHL Scout, May 2024

" I have him just ahead of Parekh and Levshunov is next." - NHL Scout, May 2024

" Somebody told me he was better than Pietrangelo at the same age and I don't see that." - NHL Scout, May 2024

" He's Noah Hanifin 2.0 for me, he's a good player and will play for a long time but you probably don't want to draft him in the top 3. Hanifin has had a good career in the NHL but he's not worth a top-3 pick looking back." - HP Scout Jérôme Bérubé

" He's a top 5 skater in this class." - HP Scout, Brad Allen , Oct 2023

" Mark Hunter made a point of raving about Dickinson to me as far as his off ice...couldn't say enough good things about him. The on ice is obvious." - HP Scout, Mark Edwards, March 2024

" Sam kinda makes me think of a poor man's Pietrangelo. Petro was more skilled offensively and smarter at the same age which led to amazing creativity. Dickinson is smart, but he plays a simpler straight ahead game. So for me Petro is easily ahead but Dickinson does remind me of Petro at times because of his maturity and poise at that age." HP Scout, Mark Edwards, March 2024

A few months into last season I wouldn't have thought Dickinson would be as good offensively as he is now. Great player. Tight between him and Zayne but Sam got the nod." - HP Scout, Mark Edwards, June 2024

NR	PLAYER	TEAM	LEAGUE	HEIGHT	WEIGHT	POS	GRADE
	EDWARDS, BRAYDEN	LETHBRIDGE	WHL	6' 00"	186	RC	NI
NHLCS	CEILING	FLOOR	HOCKEY SENSE	COMPETE	SKILL	SKATE	MISC
NA-170	4	5	5	8	5	6	5

In his 2nd year of NHL draft eligibility, Edwards had a strong season with 31 goals and 70 points in 66 games, leading his team in the goals category. As a December 2004 birthday, Edwards played his 19 years old season. He was mostly used as the top line center for the Hurricanes, and played in every situation (PP1, PK, 6-on-5 for and against, etc.).

Offensively, Edwards is a really dynamic player. His transition game makes him an efficient center. He's a strong skater who carry the puck with ease, using linear crossovers to build speed and change direction. Without de puck, he supports his defensemen well on the breakout. He's always in available for a middle breakout, and if the puck goes to his winger, he sprints the dot lane and acquire the puck with speed. Because of these details, Edwards is often able to enter the offensive zone with control of the puck on entries. He loves to attack defensemen with speed on his weakside. He can beat them wide with speed, or change speed by putting the puck in his back pocket. Now a dual threat, he can either shoot the puck or make a seam pass. He's not a player who shoots a lot in quantity, but he has a solid wrist-shot from mid-distance et good puck skills in tight to score around the net. Off the puck, he's good at driving ads F2 on the rush to make the D's back-off and create space for the puck carrier.

In the offensive zone, he hunts pucks with purpose. He's hard in puck pressure, and with his speed, he creates contact fast. With possession in the offensive job, he does a fine job climbing the wall and making plays, and he can also score goal in tight from the inside.

Defensively, Edwards is a strong defensive center. On the tracks, he's always hard and most of the time the first forward back because of his compete and his speed. He plays the right way, stops when he needs to, work hard, support his defensemen down low, and is a strong PK'er. Faceoffs is an area he'll need to improve, finishing the season with a below average 44.9% on 1286 faceoffs.

96	PLAYER			TEAM	LEAGUE	HEIGHT	WEIGHT	POS	GRADE
	ELIASSON, GABRIEL			HV71 JR.	SWE-JR	6' 06.75"	206	LD	C
NHLCS	CEILING	FLOOR		HOCKEY SENSE	COMPETE		SKILL	SKATE	MISC
INT-29	5	3		4	7		3	6	8

Eliasson stands out as one of the largest defensemen eligible for the 2024 NHL Draft, in addition to being among the youngest, born on September 9th. He spent this past season with the HV71 J20 team in the J20 Nationell league, collecting 1 goal, 6 points, and over 100 penalty minutes. He also played internationally at the U18s in various events throughout the season.

Eliasson is easy to find, thanks to his gigantic frame and the way he moves on the ice. Just by reading that sentence, you can easily understand why NHL teams are intrigued by his potential. Every NHL team is looking for big, mobile defensemen who can play a lot of minutes. Eliasson possesses a coveted combination of size and skating. His north-south speed is already very good, although there is room for improvement in his lateral agility and footwork. Considering his size and age, his overall skating ability is already quite promising and provides him an excellent foundation. He also has a lot of physicality, challenging opponents along the wall with regularity, and will happily clear the front of the net. He does, however, take too many penalties because of his aggressiveness. He'll need to learn to play a physical game while minimizing those. At the U18 level, his tendency to take unnecessary penalties led to benchings, highlighting the importance of improving his decision-making on the ice and maintaining more discipline.

His size, skating ability, and physical presence offer him potential to compete in the NHL someday. However, significant improvements in other facets of his game are necessary in order for him to realize this. For example, when defending, he needs to close his gaps faster; he currently offers too much space to puck-carriers despite having tools such as his reach and skating skills to help him close the gap. He needs to trust his skating skills more than what he showed us this season. He also needs to work on improving his overall skill level; his skills are currently below-average. His puck-handling skills and passing accuracy are below-average, limiting his value to his team's transition game. He must make quicker decisions both with and without the puck, as his current processing speed limits his effectiveness. In the defensive zone, he occasionally looks lost, not knowing where to go and turning his back on the play. While he doesn't necessarily need to excel with the puck, improving his skills and hockey sense is crucial to him having a future in the NHL.

As mentioned earlier, he's one of the youngest and rawest players in this draft class. There is potential for growth in Eliasson's game, offering hope to NHL teams that his current level may not be indicative of his potential in 4 or 5 years. That could be a reason why he'll hear his name called, but his pure physical package and skating also help his chances. A long-term project at this point, we still envision teams taking a chance on him. He was drafted 2nd overall in the USHL Draft (Phase 2) by Cedar Rapids, also recently committing to Michigan University in the NCAA.

"One scout called him a Unicorn...yeah ok...he can't play but he's a Unicorn. I like the Unicorns that can play a bit." - NHL Scout, May 2024

"He had some troubles with Spence during the warmup at the U18 (laughs) - practically broke his stick on him. All the scouts were racing to watch warmup because of the entertainment factor." - NHL Scout, May 2024

NR	PLAYER	TEAM	LEAGUE	HEIGHT	WEIGHT	POS	GRADE
	ELLINAS, LUKE	KITCHENER	OHL	6' 02"	198	LW	NI
NHLCS	CEILING	FLOOR	HOCKEY SENSE	COMPETE	SKILL	SKATE	MISC
NA-88	5	4	5	5	6	4	6

Luke Ellinas is a versatile winger for the Kitchener Rangers in the Ontario Hockey League who got of to a slow start to the year but really turned thing on as the year progressed. Ellinas put up 33 points in 67 games in the regular season and followed that up with 8 points in 10 playoff games. After getting traded to Kitchener at the start of the year it was unclear how much ice time Ellinas would get on a Kitchener team that did not lack in young scoring talent or scoring veterans. The bigger Ellinas was expected to be more of a grinding forward but he stepped into a scoring role later in the year as some of Kitchener's scorers ran dry.

Ellinas showed major progression as the season progressed, displaying his strong shot with a quick release in his snapshot that he likes to take deep in the offensive zone. For more of his wrist shots, it takes him more time to load up and they typically wield the same power which he should correct for any chance to score at a greater pace. In terms of processing pace, he could use some work and needs to get better at making decisions with the puck on his stick. Coming out of the zone, Ellinas has some trouble in pass reception which either resets his team or causes a turnover.

His skating is the roughest part of his game with heavy feet and choppy skating mechanics. It has improved from the beginning of the season, but he still has trouble on his feet and is often behind the play. Despite this, he does have a quick stick but will need more hip mobility to be able to make better cuts deep in the offensive zone. On the penalty kill he can be too aggressive which with a slow skating speed he cannot make up for any overcommitment and cannot block shots well because he is too late getting there.

The skating and IQ hurt his projectability as a whole and despite his obvious progression, he still has too many skills under construction to be considered by us at this time. He will need to fix his foot speed first to have a chance moving up the ranks and into the draft conversation.

52	PLAYER	TEAM	LEAGUE	HEIGHT	WEIGHT	POS	GRADE
	ELICK, CHARLIE	BRANDON	WHL	6' 03.25"	202	RD	C+
NHLCS	CEILING	FLOOR	HOCKEY SENSE	COMPETE	SKILL	SKATE	MISC
NA-31	5	5	4	7	4	7	8

The former 3rd overall pick in the WHL bantam draft is accustomed to play big minutes, averaging more than 21 minutes a game on Wheat Kings' top 4 this season. He also played more than 24 minutes in the gold medal game for

Team Canada at the Hlinka Gretzky Cup this past summer. Elick is a big defenseman with great athleticism, as demonstrated by his on-ice testing at the CHL top prospect game, finishing top 4 in 30M forward stride, 30M backwards skate, transition ability, transition ability with puck and 5th best results overall amongst all testers.

Elick's calling card at the next level will be his defense and shutdown abilities. In the defensive zone, he covers a lot of ice and space with his skating, compete and length. He can be physical down low, throwing hits with timing and pinning opposing players along the wall. He does a great out boxing out opposing forwards in front of his net. Elick can improve some details in his zone defending. His stickwork can be a random, as he cen be caught vulnerable defending by swinging too much or by his stick or by having his stick in the air. He'll also need to add some strength, as we often saw him lose some 50/50 race to the puck inside contact plays. With added and some refinement, Elick defensive zone play projects as a strength at the next level.

Without repeating myself, Elick's size, reach, skating and athleticism makes him a strong rush defender who is hard to get around for the opposing team forwards. One of Elick's strength is setting his gap in the offensive zone. If his teams have numbers, he does a great job sitting early or pinching or the opposing team winger. He can throw huge hits in these situations as well. If not, he does a good job gapping up, then retrieving inside dots to keep the puck carrier on the wall. Sometimes, he gets caught defending the rush with too many crossovers and with an over-aggressive stickcheck, which opens the middle ice for the puck carrier. On change of side plays, Elick uses his skating and reach to surf and angling skating forward.

With the puck, I thought Elick's game improved a lot from earlier this season. At the beginning of the season, Elick struggled with breakout puck retrievals under pressure. He lacked the poise to find the next play under high forechecking pressure situations. It improved a lot over the course of the season, but it's still an area Elick will need to work on to have success at the next level. In neutral zone transition with less pressure, Elick moves the puck well. He can make quick plays, or he can use his skating to invite or escape pressure with lateral weight shift to find the next play. Without the puck offensively, Elick activates as the weakside defenseman on the breakout and can join the rush in the right situations.

Most of Elick's production came from his shot in the offensive zone. He has a hard-shot, both his wrist shot or slap shot, and he loves to use it. He shoots often, shooting for open forward's stick or by looking to create rebound in the slot. Elick activates well when needed in the offensive zone to create motion, but he hasn't shown flashes of offensive zone playmaking/passing yet.

There's no doubt that with his athleticism, size, skating, physicality and compete that Elick is a prospect that has great tools to work with for NHL teams. Improving his breakout retrievals under pressure and fine tuning a few defensive details will be the two areas he'll need to focus on to bring his game to another level.

" I think for him to play he will need to somehow develop into a rugged defender and he is anything but that right now." - NHL Scout, December 2023

" Solid and steady. You don't notice him much and that is a compliment." - NHL Scout, December 2023

" He's pretty vanilla. He'll need to develop some bite and nastiness to give himself a chance to play (in the NHL) - NHL Scout, December 2023

" Elick has great tools to work with and to project. He needs to add some details in his game, but these are all things that can improve, so I like his chances.- HP Scout, Tim Archambault, March 2024

"He is what he is and I don't think it's high end so he will need to get better at something to be his defining trait to allow him to play in the NHL." - NHL Scout, April 2024

"I ask myself if he will play in the NHL and my answer is probably not and if he does it will be as a fringe in and out of the lineup guy....and that is probably just because he gets over-drafted." - NHL Scout, May 2024

"I haven't seen him in months but he wasn't good in my early views." - NHL Scout, January 2024

"He's not an overly smart player and he isn't hard to play against." - NHL Scout, January 2024

"I ask myself if he will play in the NHL and my answer is probably not and if he does it will be as a fringe in and out of the lineup guy....and that might just be because he got over-drafted." - HP Scout, Mark Edwards March 2024

"No traits jump out and scream draft me other than the popular 'he's big and a right shot Dman' - that's nice but I need more than that to draft him high." - HP Scout, Mark Edwards, March 2024

"I'm not a big fan. Struggles with pressure and I question the hockey sense. Not overly difficult to play against either. I see third pairing guy at best." - HP Scout, Mark Edwards, May 2024

19	PLAYER		TEAM	LEAGUE	HEIGHT	WEIGHT	POS	GRADE
	EISERMAN, COLE		USA-U18	NTDP	5' 11.75"	197	LW	A
NHLCS	CEILING	FLOOR	HOCKEY SENSE	COMPETE	SKILL		SKATE	MISC
NA-12	8	4	5	5	8		5	5

Eiserman came into the season with a lot of hype following a great first season at the NTDP and was widely regarded as a potential top-5 pick, alongside Ivan Demidov but slightly below Macklin Celebrini. Despite his impressive stats line this season (even surpassing Cole Caufield's record for goals with the program), it was not a smooth journey for him. The season was marked by highs and lows, which ultimately affected his draft stock, causing a slip in rankings. This happens every year, though: some players continue to improve, others don't.

The number one asset of Eiserman's game is (and will always be) his shooting skills. He's the best pure goal scorer in this class. He has all the ingredients to see his shot translate to the next level: high-end velocity, high-end release, a full package that is tough to read for goaltenders. He's also a threat on the power play on the right side of the ice with his great one-timer; he's great at finding soft ice to get open to receive the puck in prime scoring areas. He can also score from different places in the offensive zone with his quick release. He can be successful from the slot area, but needs to show more tenacity and willingness to play inside. He has also demonstrated the ability to score from distances and from the point, preferring to shoot from around both faceoff circles. At the junior level (soon in college), he possesses the skills and smarts to exploit defensive vulnerabilities in one-on-one situations on the rush.

His puck skills enable him to make some of those defenders look foolish, but this is not something we see translating as smoothly to the pro level without improvements to his skating. He's not an explosive skater in transition, which will make it more difficult for him to achieve the same level of success in transitional play. In fact, we prefer him not to be the puck-carrier on his line; a strong, line-driving center who can carry the puck should be the one to open things up for Eiserman offensively. Eiserman's lack of skating limits the effectiveness of his transitional game as a puck-carrier, but we see him more as a complementary scorer than the guy on his line driving the bus. Improvements in explosiveness are necessary for him to become a more impactful presence with his speed and transitional play, as his current skating abilities are something we feel are overrated for a player of his stature.

It's one thing to score goals. If you become too much of a one-dimensional player, NHL teams will soon figure you out. A lot of comparisons with Cole Caufield have been made, but Caufield is the perfect example of a player who made adjustments to his game and became a more complete player in the NHL. Other scorers considered to be high-end in their draft year never made such adjustments, and are now struggling in the NHL (Oliver Wahlstrom is a name that comes to mind).

Some aspects we believe Eiserman has not sufficiently improved upon this year or has shown inconsistency in: compete level, passing game, and play away from the puck. While he has the potential to play the complete game that NHL teams seek, he has struggled this year to put it all together. Despite his above-average passing skills and vision, there were too many times this year that we felt his playmaking contributions were lacking. Whether it was tunnel vision, selfishness, or difficulties finding open teammates in general, his playmaking value was often absent in many games. Having said that, we also saw games where he was quite good in this facet of the game. He would show good poise and deception skills to make nice passes to his teammates off the rush, or from his play along the wall. His compete level manifested similarly; some games saw little energy out of him, no physical involvement whatsoever. During others, he was a force on the forecheck, hitting guys hard (as seen most recently in the semi-final against Slovakia where he threw a terrific open-ice hit).

When Eiserman is fully engaged, his ability to protect the puck down low and along the wall improves. While his offensive zone effort was inconsistent, there were still some positive displays. However, his effort level in the defensive zone was a significant issue, usually absent in our viewings. His tendency to prioritize offense (a common trait for scorers) often resulted in him cheating defensively—leaving the defensive zone early, not moving his feet on backchecks. While no one expects him to excel defensively as a Selke Trophy candidate would, a better commitment to defensive play (showing effort) is essential for his NHL future.

As Eiserman transitions to higher-level leagues (such as the NCAA next season and potentially the pros), he needs to demonstrate more focus and effort away from the puck. Unlike the offensive-focused environment of the NTDP, he won't be able to rely on offensive shortcuts under an NHL coach. In terms of USHL defensive metrics, Eiserman ranked very poorly in categories such as blocked passes (195th), one-on-one battles won (199th), puck retrievals (207th), and stripping pucks from opponents (221st).

When Eiserman manages to bring out the best of his compete level and playmaking, when added to his elite shooting skills, one could easily see a top-10 player in the draft (which is what most saw happening a year ago). The problem was we didn't see him do so consistently this year. His best stretch was the February Five Nations Tournament. At the U18 World Championship in April, he took advantage of a weak schedule to score a lot of goals early on, but his year-long inconsistency replicated itself for the rest of the tournament. The easiest thing for him to do is to score goals, no matter how good or bad he is playing. This will happen often in junior, even college, but won't be as easy after that. All this to say: Eiserman sparked debate in this draft class, but significant areas of his game left us concerned. His playmaking and compete level showed flashes of brilliance but also raised red flags.

As one of the youngest players in this draft class, if he was born 3 weeks later than he was, he would only be eligible for the 2025 NHL Draft. This is not something we can forget; despite being quite physically mature with a strong frame, he is very young. There might be more development time ahead of him that would enable him to make the necessary improvements we alluded to. He's going to a great college program next season, Boston University, under former NHLer Jay Pandolfo (who happens to know a thing or two about playing a complete game, both on or away from the puck). This looks like a good fit if Eiserman wants to add more layers to his game, outside of his shooting abilities.

"He's not a great playmaker but he scores goals better than anyone. He's third on my list right now." – NHL Scout, January 2024

"If someone told me he was going to have an Oliver Wahlstrom type of career I wouldn't be surprised." - NHL Scout, March 2024

"He's on my list after all the guys I really have passion about." -NHL Scout, March 2024

"The release is elite and you can't score that many goals if you are dumb. He has the timing and the feel. I don't think the skating is going to be good in the NHL...not ugly bad but not good." - NHL Scout, March 2024

"Someone told me he's like Owen Tippett but Tippett was fast. Tippett could could really skate." - NHL Scout, March 2024

"Bigger, stronger and faster than Caufield and he broke his record. Nuff said." - NHL Scout, May 2024

"He is what he is right now. He's not getting stronger and he's not getting faster so how high would you draft what he is right now? He's not getting smarter (hockey sense) either." - NHL Scout, May 2024

"People can say what they want but he scores over a goal per game. I have him ranked pretty high." - NHL Scout, May 2024

"I see that he is falling on every list and I don't get it...people don't want goal scorers?" - NHL Scout, May 2024

"Who knows where he goes (in the draft) I ranked him well behind where we are picking." - NHL Scout, May 2024

"So is he Cole Caufield or Oliver Wahlstrom?" - HP Scout Jérôme Bérubé, March 2024

"The best version of Eiserman is when he's playing a physical game and being a dual threat offensively but we didn't see enough of it this year." - HP Scout Jérôme Bérubé, May 2024

"Best case scenario is that he ends up resembling something similar to a fusion between Caufield and Boeser. That's a real good player, but a lot has to go right for him in order to hit that projection." - HP Scout, Brad Allen, May 2024

"Great goal scorer but there isn't a way to sugar coat it. He underwhelmed the large majority of scouts I spoke to. He probably won't slide too far though, because teams want and need goal scorers." - HP Scout, Mark Edwards, May 2024

59	PLAYER	TEAM	LEAGUE	HEIGHT	WEIGHT	POS	GRADE
	EMERY, ERIC	USA-U18	NTDP	6' 03.25"	183	RD	C
NHLCS	CEILING	FLOOR	HOCKEY SENSE	COMPETE	SKILL	SKATE	MISC
NA-39	5	5	5	6	4	8	8

E.J. Emery slotted in with all the other non-Cole Hutson draft eligible d-men on the NTDP this year with a 0+6=6 line in 27 games. A line he would match in seven games at the U18 World Junior Championships, along with a tournament-best plus-15 rating, to cap his season. Clearly, he never turned the corner from an offensive perspective – that's evident on the scoresheet and on the ice. That's the big drawback here is he never had that late season "it's all coming together" push of dominance.

Emery still looks skittish with the puck, his puck poise is very low end, and his retrievals don't give us a lot of confidence. Even with time and space, there's no puckhandling that makes a forechecker hesitate for a second. His passing game is pretty average overall. There's nothing creative about it and even the simpler short and medium passes don't lead teammates into valuable ice. His partner support off of steals or sudden change situations is uninspiring too. Even if he doesn't like to join the rush, at least provide some wide support or some light rotation up the weakside to give your teammates a better chance to get up the ice. On the rush, even if Emery has cover, he'll bail out before the potential pay-off almost every time. His mechanically weak shot is accurately accounted for with his zero goals across 68 USHL, NCAA, and WJC games. For as good of an athlete as he is, there's really no physical reason why he needs to put himself off balance and push the puck with his arms towards the net as often as he does. He could probably improve his shot a great deal if he was vested in the cause mentally and could apply it in-game. But again, the puck poise and confidence in his offensive game is so low that it shows through in the process and the mechanics. His passes rarely have zip on them either.

So, if we can't trust that there's offense coming, the defensive game is going to need to really scalable and really high end. There are elements to his defensive game that are extremely likeable. He's a composed player with a very strong skating base. His range and four-way mobility allow him a lot of positive outs for defending. As such, he's really good at rush defense right now. He can play rush absorption straight up or surf across to stop plays before they really have a chance to get going. That's a big positive in his game. The thing to really watch for is the varied ability in which he defends rushes. In almost all rush absorption situations, Emery turns inside and pokechecks from the hip and then to recover will turn and go with the rush if he fails. That is a very effective strategy and a useful weapon to have in your defensive toolbox. The trouble is: does he have any other weaponry readily available? He doesn't really show it. Why might this be problematic at a higher level? The best rush (attack) players in the world have a fairly simple goal in mind: They want to get defenders to turn their toes to then attack their heels. In order for Emery to pokecheck from the hip, he has to turn his toes. So, if his only strong play is to give up half the battle to strong rush attackers, he's going to get adapted against pretty quickly. At best, that means he'd have to be pushed down the lineup to avoid top-end puck handlers. The other danger here is that in Emery's recovery process on the rush, he's not that difficult to play against consistently. There were minimal flashes of mean but it doesn't look terribly natural. So, we saw some players try to take him outside-in on the rush after a failed pokecheck and Emery allowed them to "get corner" on him a bit more than we'd like to see at the level of competition he was dealing with.

As mentioned, we think the recovery skating and first-step launch will continue to improve – so that will help, but even the best defenders in the world don't get three chances to kill a play. So we'd like some more assurances that his recovery process after a missed pokecheck is going to mitigate the rush.

The in-zone coverage comes with the same positives and negatives. Emery is generally well-positioned, he's not running around chasing hits, and he's calm. There are instances where we've seen him go to the boards and break up a cycle with physicality – and that's great. There is big upside in his walling off and box-out techniques, even if he's not a mauler, his athleticism and skating base grant him that ability and he does it well for his age group. Again though, not the toughest guy to play against and then his inability to facilitate sudden change zone exits might extend shifts unnecessarily. The stick-led defense is definitely a plus. It's a strong poke, it's well timed, and well executed.

So, we have a 6'3" frame with huge athletic upside. He's a better 1-on-1 defender than anything else. E.J. isn't a natural mauler or big hitter despite how he often gaps up in the neutral zone. And the puck skills might actually be a stopper in terms of NHL upside. His decisions with the puck put some caution on the overall hockey sense and mental processor that this player offers as well. Even in lengthy in-zone coverage situations, there are moments when Emery seems to freeze for a couple beats trying to figure out what's happening and even then he doesn't always come away with neutralizing the biggest threat. Emery says he models his game after K'Andre Miller – and there's some stylistic connection there – but Miller was bigger, meaner, and more skilled by a significant degree. There's just not enough obvious upside here to justify taking Emery too high.

"I'll put on the GM hat for a minute. If I need to find a 15-point defensive d-man, I can probably do it in a trade or via free agency a lot easier than finding an impact skill player on an entry-level deal. Absolutely no chance I'd spend a top 50 pick here." HP Scout, Michael Farkas

"My eyes seemed to be pulled to him to constantly see him turning over pucks. Not a fan." – NHL Scout, November 2023

"I think he competes and defends well but he can't move pucks so that keeps you out of the NHL." – NHL Scout, December 2023

"He's a great culture guy." – NHL Scout, March 2024

"Same type of player as Danford in Oshawa. I'll take Danford." – NHL Scout, April 2024

"He couldn't process the game fast enough on bigger international ice so I'm officially done with him." – NHL Scout, May 2024

"When Dmen struggle to retrieve pucks my spidey senses get elevated. It's not a weakness I see get fixed too often. If he plays I think it will be as a third paring guy who gives an honest effort." – HP Scout, Mark Edwards, March 2024

"I'm told that he's staying in Plymouth all summer to train." – HP Scout, Mark Edwards, June 2024

NR	PLAYER	TEAM	LEAGUE	HEIGHT	WEIGHT	POS	GRADE
	EPPERSON, KRISTIAN	USA-U-18	NTDP	5' 11.25"	180	LW	NI
NHLCS	CEILING	FLOOR	HOCKEY SENSE	COMPETE	SKILL	SKATE	MISC
NA-201	4	4	6	7	4	5	4

Energy forward. Kristian Epperson had a tough year and ended up being demoted to the U17 team, leaving him off the U18 Worlds roster. Epperson is a smart player that plays with enthusiasm all over the ice. He has good speed, but his edges and explosiveness are lacking. He doesn't chop the puck up into pieces, even when playing at speed, but he's not a dynamic puck handler by any means. He has good ideas about playmaking, and flashes some creativity in that regard. But, again, the execution of these passes is just off. Especially area and saucer passes, they tend to come out soft and wobbly. Goal sample is all pretty similar: proper arc to the net and a short side wrist shot...even in situations where a cross net line finishing move would probably be the play. He only scored four goals in 32 games at the USHL level this year, so it isn't much to say that his current goal scoring process isn't very scalable to a higher level. That said, he was really driving the net hard later in the year and he made a big mess for defenses and goalies at times – even after the whistle. Epperson developed into a good backchecker and showed some stick lift steal capability, but without a get-away burst, auto puck protection maneuvers, or accurate passing in sudden change situations, this has limited upside. And it's really another microcosm of his game – the lack of skill chaining is evident. He has to focus on each compartmentalized piece in order to execute, right down to accepting passes in a productive way and without a bobble. The University of Michigan commit just doesn't look like a very fluid athlete. He struggles to get off his center line and lean into contact. At 5'11", 180 pounds, he gets spilled quite a bit on the rink.

Epperson needs a chance to reset and get a look higher in a lineup, so he'll likely be in Madison (USHL) next year for that purpose. There are a lot of loose, disconnected elements to his game that are interesting but it's so abstract right now it becomes tough to endorse. He's worth a check-in next season, but not a draft pick now.

42	PLAYER	TEAM	LEAGUE	HEIGHT	WEIGHT	POS	GRADE
	ERIKSSON, LINUS	DJURGARDEN	SWE-2	6' 00"	189	LC	B
NHLCS	CEILING	FLOOR	HOCKEY SENSE	COMPETE	SKILL	SKATE	MISC
INT-10	5	7	7	7	5	7	6

Linus Eriksson is a two way – competitive center, with a high level of hockey sense who plays a pro-style game. He played both at the J20 level and Allsvenskan level for Djurgarden, where he produced 21 points in 25 games at the junior level, and 11 points in 29 games at the pro level during the regular season. He came close to helping Djurdarden qualify for the SHL but they were beaten out in the finals, however he still managed to produce 4 points in 12 games against better quality competition. He also represented Sweden Internationally at the U18's, where he produced 7 points in 7 games, scoring 1 goal.

Eriksson's defining attributes are his center instincts and his skating package. He thinks the game really well at both ends of the ice and he's a player a coach can trust in any situation, due to his supporting skill set. He's a natural center who knows how to be a third option for his defense, but he's also good at recognizing transitional play, while staying above the puck. Due to his hockey sense, it was easy for him to not only adapt to his linemates, but be a driving force in making his teammates better. This allowed him to play up for most of the season at the Allsvenskan level despite being a first year eligible prospect for the draft. In-fact only two forwards managed to play primarily in Allsvenskan coming out of Sweden in their first year of eligibility and that was Michael Brandsegg Nygard and Eriksson. In Nygard's case, it was a testament to his tool-kit and power game, in Eriksson's case, it's a testament to his on ice maturity and attention to detail.

Unlike several other center prospects who are going to have to move to the wing as a result of having a weak skating base, Eriksson isn't one of them. He's agile on his skates, which can be seen when he's extending from a launch or stationary position. A lot of younger players have difficulty simultaneously transferring between their upper and lower halves, but that's not the case with Linus. He features a strong shoulder rotation and knows how to propel himself forward through his initial arm swing, into his deep knee extensions. Even though he's still growing into his frame, his coordination and athleticism is already developed, allowing him to rebalance himself quickly, so that he could still use his skill when getting physically initiated on. He's a multi-directional skater who can side step, pivot sharply, spin off checks, and explode when traveling north south. The projectable skating base, with his overall sense, stands out at a consistent level.

There's a versatility to his game as a result of his base that gets complimented by his overall effort level. He's a hard worker, he plays in the dirty areas, and he's tenacious during plays that require him to use his frame and fight for positioning along the boards. His compete level mixes with his strong level of anticipation, which allows him to recognize options on the defensive side before they are generated, which in turn gives him advanced positioning. He's also good at reading the play in general off the puck, using a smart stick when defending and trying to block passing lanes or using well timed stick-lifts to generate takeaways. There's a maturity found within his defensive and forechecking structure, giving him good value as a player that we think can be used regularly in shorthanded situations at the NHL level.

On the power play, he was more often than not controlling the play from the half wall, where his playmaking abilities were on display. This is a result of having above average passing with good on-ice vision, not only during the powerplay, but at even strength as well.

He can spin off pressure and find teammates in transition through layers, as well as make deceptive look off passes while going at high speed. We've seen him pull off impressive no look, behind the back hook passes to his linemates from below the net area, and he can make lateral weakside passes that can set up his teammates on the powerplay from stationary positions. Although his playmaking is one of his standout qualities, he can sometimes struggle controlling his passing velocity, and he can fail to turn a handling play into a playmaking sequence as fluidly as you would typically see in a player that projects to play in the top-6.

The reason that Eriksson's going to have to use his playmaking at speed, and his deception when generating rush opportunities or when generating transitional zone entries, is due to his hands having inconsistencies. Early in the season, he was having difficulty maintaining puck possession in open ice, let alone tight areas, and that's because of the lack of puck control.

He was using a shorter stick and this gave him difficulty completing even simple, routine passes. There were too many mishandled pucks and too many misfired passes even when pressure was minimal. However, as the season progressed, he did change his stick length and we saw an improvement that allowed us to think he had potential as a depth center that could actually play, instead of one that's skill-set was too limited.

Normally, you wouldn't rate hand speed and puck control at this stage in a prospects development above certain categories in the skill department, such as shooting and playmaking, but hand speed is used to mask specific passing and shooting placement. He is good at shielding the puck and this will help compensate for his hands to a degree but it was definitely a critical point discussed during our final rankings meetings on where to exactly place him on our list.

At the NHL level, defenders close quicker with their gaps, and more chaotic plays happen more often that are unpredictable, just due to the general speed of the game. Eriksson must have a fall back option that isn't simply chipping and chasing, or using manipulation skating to go inside and back outside, as two examples. He must have hands that can protect and contain the puck, so that his natural affinity for driving play through the neutral zone can materialize at the professional level. Even more importantly, he can't mask his passing options as just discussed within his skill chaining, as often as we would like. Which takes away his primary playmaking instincts to a degree.

We took these factors into consideration while still recognizing that he did make improvements after changing up his equipment and after he modified his handling to make it based around shielding pucks as opposed to using it in open-ice as often.

Despite our concerns, there is still potential for Eriksson to improve his puck protection skill-set. He still has more time than most other prospects in this age bracket to improve his hand speed and get more comfortable chaining plays together in succession. Furthermore, he did save some of his better performances for last in both the Allsvenskan playoffs and at the U18's, where he quite frankly made some highly skilled plays that we were surprised to see from him, since he had previously shown little indication throughout the season that they could be made. He is unlikely to ever develop into much of a scorer but his intelligence merges into his scoring, where he can set himself in tight to the net and score gritty and greasy goals.

Linus Eriksson isn't going to be drafted based on his goal scoring upside or due to having a dynamic element. He's not flashy but he's a substance over style center who can adapt to his lineup in any situation. He's the type of player that you win with and he's improved over the course of the season to the degree that we think has a chance to be a specialized shutdown center, who chips in occasionally on offense.

" Low ceiling player who is easy to like but I'm not sure I'd be willing to draft him earlier enough to get him. Mid rounder at earliest for me" - NHL Scout, May 2024

" He made my list. Third rounder." - NHL Scout, May 2024

"Lack of skill always makes it more difficult to crack the NHL because you are often up against 90 point junior players who couldn't stick in the top 9." - NHL Scout, May 2024

"He improved a ton from the beginning of the Allsvenskan playoffs to the U18's. I had a discussion with one of his main development coaches, who told me that they started making him play with a shorter stick and once that happened his passing rates and handling rates definitely improved." – HP Scout, Brad Allen

"Good feedback from Combine his interviews." – HP Scout, Mark Edwards, June 2024

NR	PLAYER	TEAM	LEAGUE	HEIGHT	WEIGHT	POS	GRADE
	FELICIO, WILL	WATERLOO	USHL	5'10"	161	LD	NI

NHLCS	CEILING	FLOOR	HOCKEY SENSE	COMPETE	SKILL	SKATE	MISC
-	6	4	6	6	6	7	3

Will Felicio put together a 10 goal, 29 point campaign in 54 USHL games in 2023-24. He was just off the point lead for first-time draft eligible defenseman in the USHL, a crown which he might have otherwise captured if he wasn't called to participate in the World Jr. A Challenge – where he finished third in defensemen scoring for the tournament.

It's been a tale of two seasons for Felicio in more ways than one. First of all, after falling into a slump, he was traded to Waterloo for John Stout. Secondly, the change in his game from the start of the year to the end is quite noteworthy. He really put the work into playing a more well-rounded game as the year progressed. In short, he was porous defensively in every conceptual way to start the year. Even in ways that smooth skating defensemen usually aren't…with things like rush absorption and speed matching, but he was not good at those either. By the end of the season though, his gaps, rush absorption, line defense, and even physical play had jumped leaps and bounds. He kept his production levels pretty high as well, as he put up 16 points in 31 games with Waterloo alone in the back half. He doesn't play a lot either, closer to 16, 17 minutes a night. That's probably part of the reason he's coming back to the Black Hawks next season, is to try to be a legitimate top pairing defenseman at this level in what will be his third season.

Felicio has a really good skating base. He's nimble, sharp on his edges, and exceptional laterally. His overall lack of strength hinders his explosiveness and long speed still, but he seems very, very low on his physical development arc. He's playing at sub-160 pounds on a 5'10" frame, so he's constantly punching up, even at this level. As mentioned, towards the end of the year, he was stepping up on plays in the neutral zone with body contact. He battled to try to clear his crease – unsuccessfully in almost every occasion, but the effort was there. His overall pace and energy seemed to really perk up in general. He's a good puck handler with enough hand quickness to freeze defenders for enough time for him to move or pass around them. At top speed, sometimes pucks can get away from him a bit. He typically recovers, but in order for this to work, he has to play on a certain rhythm, and those little imperfections can really throw it off. He is a good pass receiver though. He melds the pass reception right into his foot churn, so that will give him a lot of rope at the attack line to go after tight seam plays. He wants the puck a lot and isn't shy about calling for it. He has a weaker shot, as we'd expect, but he still funnels a lot towards the net anyhow. Sometimes we'd like to see a little more creativity in his attack zone passing game, but maybe that will come back when he's more confident in his game remodelling. It's tough to see right now because the size and strength combination is so far from where it needs to be, but there's enough here from a technical perspective that some might give him a late look.

If he didn't improve his defensive game so much, and just kept playing as a fourth forward – a Kirill Koltsov type – this wouldn't be much of a discussion. But now there is some modelling more in the Quinn Hughes mold (obviously, a far far lesser version) and that makes him slightly more palatable. He de-committed from Denver to go to Michigan, but really the extra year in the USHL might be the thing that makes all the difference for this player type. There's still a ways to go, as he's not as quick execution-wise and as technically fluid as we'd like to see from a smaller defenseman.

"He's in the process of remodelling his game, to his credit, so this is a longer term deal. Maybe very, very late I'd give him a look." HP Scout, Michael Farkas

55	PLAYER	TEAM	LEAGUE	HEIGHT	WEIGHT	POS	GRADE
	FERNSTROM, MELVIN	OREBRO JR.	SWE-JR	6' 00.75"	188	RW	C+

NHLCS	CEILING	FLOOR	HOCKEY SENSE	COMPETE	SKILL	SKATE	MISC
INT-23	6	5	7	6	6	5	5

Melvin Fernstrom is a highly intelligent, dual-threat winger who is more than the sum of his parts. He falls into the Tyler Toffoli or Terik Parascak style of player, meaning they rely less on their tools and more on their spatial awareness and sense of timing to put the puck in the back of the net. Fernstrom had a very successful season for Orebro by producing 63 points in 45 games, including 31 goals. His 1.40 points per game mark ranked 2nd for draft eligible forwards that played more than 20 games at the J20 level, in what we would consider an under-the-radar season that featured a strong development curve.

The physical tools can be described as pro average when projecting them, yet the mind that Fernstrom possesses allows him to generate consistently, despite looking limited at first glance. It starts with his timing; his sense of timing both on and off the puck are exceptional. Off the puck, this can be seen when he's attempting to evaluate when and where he can become a backdoor passing option or when he looks to move into open ice in a high danger area such as the slot during low to high sequences. On the puck, his timing relates to his ability to slow down the play so that he can readjust and reconfigure the ice surface, so that his passes can hit his teammates in stride through layers of traffic. If he doesn't like his options when leading the attack over the line, he remains calculated and poised, rarely rushing or forcing plays if there's none there.

His overall hockey IQ in combination with his skills, keeps opponents guessing, and if an opponent is guessing, there's a good chance they are becoming hesitant. Hesitancy can breed indecision on the ice, and that's what Fernstrom is exceptional at taking advantage of.

One sequence at the U18's against Slovakia summarizes a lot of his playmaking game. He had the puck at the right point, feathered a pass to a teammate in the circle which generated a potential give and go play. As he skated into the middle of the ice, the returning pass was intercepted by an opposing defenseman, but Fernstrom had the wherewithal to rapidly stick lift the puck, then immediately made a reverse spinning pass that went through the slot and should have resulted in an easy tap in goal to his teammate in the right circle, that was just whiffed on by his teammate. This type of sequence showcases his playmaking creativity, his adaptive thinking, and his advanced sense of timing when his teammates are streaking into shooting locations, even if he has his back momentarily turned to the play.

Although he's not an overly physically gifted player, he is a decent puck handler who can rapidly pull the puck across the length of his body or use a backhand to forehand and vice versa motion, to keep players from being able to read the precise moment he's passing. His best deking moments have come through using wide A-stances and using extension dekes. He also has shown that he can absorb contact while remaining balanced which is going to be critical for his game, since he's not a separator as a skater and he's not an overly nimble player either. If there was a drawback to his handling, it's that it tends to breakdown when he's at his full speed; because of this, we think it's unlikely that he's going to be plus transitional zone entry player at the NHL level, and he's not a player who's likely to drive possession to the same degree that we have in junior; especially when you factor in his tool-kit.

Fernstrom doesn't need to drive possession though in order to score. This isn't a flashy or dynamic rush player who sets up scoring chances for himself very often, or when projecting him down the line. Instead, he understands where to position himself in order to become a scoring option in each area of the offensive zone. His one-timer was automatic at times from the left circle on the powerplay and he features impressive wheelhouse mechanics that allow him to still fire off bad passes and make them count. He's one of the most gifted redirect specialists in this class when determining the angle to place the puck in tight to the net when he's streaking through the crease area. His snap and wrist-shot mechanics all project to be above average to good at the NHL level, and there's real potential for him to be a scoring threat both at even strength and on the powerplay when projecting him.

He's just more of an in-zone offensive threat, then he is a transitional threat, and that's okay. Not every player needs to be an explosive skater who can score off the rush.

Which brings us to his skating development. Mechanically, Melvin isn't fleet of foot and lacks foot speed out of the gate. Although he isn't overly large, he skates like a larger, heavier set player who has difficulty in his initial take off at times. He can generate gear shifts, but once he shifts down, he doesn't project to be able to create differentials that allow him to blow by opposing forwards. That said, his skating base saw a developmental shift in the sense that towards the second half of the season, he started to understand how to become a better exit option for his team in transition as a result of keeping his feet moving more often and not remaining as stationary as he initially was.

In-fact, that was arguably the biggest area of developmental improvement that we saw from him over the course of the season.

Consistency is usually a byproduct of mental preparation, and in this regard, Fernstrom is already at the NHL level despite his age. We haven't seen this prospect have many unproductive games of hockey. Has he had off shifts occasionally or even tough periods? Sure, but each time we have seen him be a zero-sum player on a given play, he has always found a way to bounce back and become an impact player for his team. Gauging his zero-sum is important because Fernstrom doesn't project to have impressive recovery rates, but he rarely operates by making lower percentage plays, instead playing a mostly clean and efficient style of hockey.

We have been impressed by his willingness to take hits to enter traffic, and dish out hits when closing on players off the puck. He doesn't project to be the most imposing player but he does project to physically hold and that's what matters.

Fernstrom is a rare player-type that carries more risk than prospects that have better tool-kits. He has natural finishing ability and offensive instincts that you can't teach. He also has molded his game around counteracting his own limitations. He's not a play driver, but he is an interesting complement to a line that can set up his teammates and finish off plays with a rare level of timing. He's a technician and we think his subtle skill-set has the potential to translate into a top-9 capacity. In order for our projection to happen, Melvin needs to continue to physically develop so that he can handle physical pressure and he needs to continue to develop additional power so that he doesn't get drowned out in transitional hockey.

"If he doesn't make it, it's because his skating, his pace of play, and overall motor didn't improve enough, but it already was heading in the right direction by the end of the season." - HP Scout, Brad Allen

"He's one of the more underrated players in this class to me and looks like a less talented version of Parascak in some ways. These complimentary sniper types work in the opposite way you typically want, since they don't drive possession and don't transition well with the puck but that doesn't mean they are entirely useless, especially if they can give you 20-25 goals like I think Fernstrom can." - HP Scout, Brad Allen

101	PLAYER	TEAM	LEAGUE	HEIGHT	WEIGHT	POS	GRADE
	FIBIGR, JAKUB	MISSISSAUGA	OHL	6' 00"	171	LD	C
NHLCS	CEILING	FLOOR	HOCKEY SENSE	COMPETE	SKILL	SKATE	MISC
NA-67	6	5	7	6	5	6	5

Jakub Fibigr settled into his game in North America around the midway point in the season and found himself becoming a confident factor with and without the puck on the Mississauga Steelheads blueline. He had a strong offensive output with 43 points in 61 games in he regular season and 4 points in 5 playoff games for the Steelheads while playing in all situations. At the beginning of the season, Fibigr seemed slightly timid and reserved, but fast forward to the end of the year and he developed a confidence defenseman who was not afraid to carry the puck up ice.

After Fibigr settled into the league he established himself as a good rush defender forcing attacking forwards to the outside with good body positioning and staying square to attackers while moving in reverse. He does not often allow play to move to the middle on the rush by using his mentioned body positioning and his stick skills which force defenders to the outside. His strength will need improvement to play a more physical game along the boards and in front of his own net but he does have the frame to be able to fill out. When he does he will have the reach to be able to push players around a bit more and become even better at keeping players to the outside against bigger forwards. As the year went on, Fibigr got chippier during play and would not get pushed around like he did a few times at the beginning of the year. This showed in his more aggressive defending style as the year progressed and even though he was not too physical he did get better at breaking up plays.

On the offensive side of the puck Flbigr will need some rounding out. He quarterbacks Mississauga's power play and has good enough vision to fill the role at the OHL level but moving up to the pro-level, Fibigr does not translate to a powerplay specialist by any means. He tends to take a bit too long to make decisions and find good scoring opportunities, as he is a bit slow on reading the opposing team. His wrist shot release time has improved but still takes too long to load and it does not generate much power once released.

The confidence with the puck grew greatly and was maybe his more noticeable improvement from viewings later in the season. He is a better skater without the puck on his stick than with it, however his tempo up ice was much better and he showed a greater amount of confidence to join the rush. Despite his slower speed and slow starts, he is quick to transition forwards to backwards and has good enough edgework and mobility left to right not to hold him back and does not have trouble closing gaps.

With good situational awareness in all three zones and the ability to know when to be aggressive and when to be conservative, Fibigr does not make many mistakes but also does not take make too many high level plays up ice. With more time on North American ice he should continue his development and become more aware of the space he and his opponents have on both sides of the puck. With his hockey IQ where it is, this should help him bite less defensively and pinch more effectively offensively.

"Overall he's been good in my two early views and I currently have him as a draft." - HP Scout, Mark Edwards, October 2023

103	PLAYER	TEAM	LEAGUE	HEIGHT	WEIGHT	POS	GRADE
	FISCHER, LUKAS	SARNIA	OHL	6' 03"	182	LD	C
NHLCS	CEILING	FLOOR	HOCKEY SENSE	COMPETE	SKILL	SKATE	MISC
NA-45	6	4	4	7	6	6	7

The son of former NHLer Jiri Fischer, Lukas Fischer is a strong stay at home defender for the Sarnia Sting in the Ontario Hockey League. In a full 68 game season for Sarnia, Fischer put up 34 points and 79 penalty minutes for a rebuilding Sarnia team. Fischer often played a ton of minutes that he may not have been ready for, although it showed off some positives in his game

The biggest projectable for Fischer is his size and frame combined with his better than average skating and his strength. Fischer moves well for a bigger man and with some added weight will greatly improve upon his already good strength. Clearing the front of the net and boxing out players on the rush are positives in Fischer's game that we love in combination with his size. Although he is not a fast skater, Fischer makes up for this with a long reach in puck retrievals and in breaking up plays defensively. This also comes in handy on the rush as Fischer, if beat can still use his long stick to poke the puck away from forwards who thought they got the jump on him. He can be beat by forwards with speed, so improving his speed without slowing himself down as he adds weight will be one of his top priorities.

Coming out of the zone is maybe Fischer's biggest weakness. He has trouble scanning and making accurate outlet passes, especially through traffic as he can be rushed by a quick pressing forecheck and pass directly into traffic. He will need to develop better scanning habits and more patience coming out of his zone and use his pivots and edgework to his advantage to create more space for himself in addition to more time for him to make these decisions. We did want to see more progression as the year went along with this but unfortunately this was the same from the beginning to the end of the year for Fischer as he is currently better without the puck on his stick that with it.

In coverage, Fischer is constantly aware of where his man is on the ice and clogs up passing and shooting lane effectively with his size and reach. Along the boards he wins puck battles and pins players effectively giving forwards little breathing room to make plays once he is on them. When covering the front of the net, forwards have a tough time battling with Fischer as he battles and clears the net well with power. We would like to see more bite and aggression for his size but he does have a lot of strength at his disposal while not being close to filled out so we can be a bit patient in hoping he will develop a snarl to his game. When he was at his best this season his coverage and ability to close gaps was strong, the one thing we are cautious about is the consistency of his compete and how this will progress through his junior career.

Fischer does have a lot of good qualities that make him more difficult to pass on in the draft. His hard shot, strong positioning and how he is in good control of his body and stick. This gives us hope that he could develop into a strong stay-at-home defenseman at the NHL level with some improvements to his game. Currently, he is playing a ton of minutes and there are times late in the game where he is making some of these mistakes due to fatigue.

" Big athletic Dman. I like the size and athleticism but I think the weakness is his hockey IQ. Hockey sense is the number one thing we look for so obviously that hurts him. Just a late name for me as of today." - HP Scout, Mark Edwards, December 2023

NR	PLAYER	TEAM	LEAGUE	HEIGHT	WEIGHT	POS	GRADE
	FISHER, JAKE	FARGO	USHL	6' 01.75"	190	LC	NI

NHLCS	CEILING	FLOOR	HOCKEY SENSE	COMPETE	SKILL	SKATE	MISC
NA-97	6	4	7	6	5	4	6

Jake Fisher got a taste of USHL hockey in his first draft-eligible season after an outstanding year for Cretin-Derham Hall in the Minnesota High School circuit. In 2023-24, Fisher put that experience to good use – posting 23 goals and 47 points in 51 games as he helped Fargo to a Clark Cup championship.

Fisher's most scalable trait is his shooting ability. His catch-and release shooting and wrist shot carry some heavy velocity. He shoots to score with his quick release; Jake shows some conceptual understanding of the timing of goalie movements to make the most of his opportunities from mid-range and closer. Despite being a center, Fisher isn't a very creative or confident playmaker. Based on his body language, it almost looks like he second guesses his passes and ends up holding on to pucks for longer than he should or simply resorts to shooting from distance. It's an odd gap in the hockey sense package, because he's otherwise a very intelligent player that supports the play well in all three zones. His defensive game carries a lot of positional integrity to it, but is still lacking from an execution perspective. A big part of the issue there is his lacking athleticism. At 6'2", 190 pounds, Fisher carries an upright, narrow skating stance. His weight transfer into hits is very poor, so he ends up mostly breezing through body contact despite being well positioned to make an impact. This negatively reflects on his ability fight through traffic on the attack as well. It's easy to knock him off his stride with the puck or disrupt his routes without it. It's poor enough where it might end up being a stopper, or at least prevent him from meaningfully holding on to a lower line role at a higher level. He gets around the ice fairly well, despite his skating mechanics – but it really breaks down in traffic. Even his puck handles are still a little too clumsy and he lacks quality puck control. He doesn't have a penchant for 1 on 1 moves.

For a big smart player that can really shoot, it's a shame he has such a lack of fluidity to him because otherwise this would be a certain draft pick. For what he lacks in his transition and setup game, he recovers a lot of pucks in the offensive zone with his smarts. If he can find a way to win physical battles and/or get pucks off the wall and into the middle, he may provide decent value as a late pick despite being an early '05.

78	PLAYER	TEAM	LEAGUE	HEIGHT	WEIGHT	POS	GRADE
	FORSLUND, CHARLIE	FALU	SWE-3	6' 03"	212	LW	C

NHLCS	CEILING	FLOOR	HOCKEY SENSE	COMPETE	SKILL	SKATE	MISC
-	6	4	5	6	6	6	6

Charlie Forslund is a large, sniping winger with one of the better curves out of any prospect this past season. Teams didn't consider him a viable option for the J20 Nationell level and as a result he started his season playing for Falu in J18 region. He dominated there before moving up to the Div1 J20 level where he produced 16 points in 7 games, including 13 goals. As a result of dominating the Div1 level, Falu gave him an opportunity with their main team at the HockeyEttan level and that's where we caught notice of him because he not only held at the HockeyEttan level despite being 17, but actually out-performed fellow prospect Joel Svensson in our viewings, despite being a full calendar year younger. At the HockeyEttan level (third division pro hockey in Sweden), he produced 19 points in 19 games, and during a qualification series he produced another 4 points in 3 games. The majority of his production came in the second half of the season. His production and subsequent growth has forced our hand into breaking him down and finding a spot for him in the ranking.

Forslund's stand out quality is his wrist and snap shot. He's a long player who understands how to extend his lateral drags into sudden angle shifting wrist shots through triangles of opposing defenseman. He understands weight transfers, through loading his inside-leg when extending through his shot, and he has elasticity through his shoulders and core that allow him to rotate further through his release to generate additional torque.. There's a high level of dexterity featured in his wrists which blend into his ability to shift his shooting angle as well. Taken together, his shot quality allows him to threaten from the top of the circles and in and when you factor in his frame and growth potential, it speaks to a prospect who's going to be able to generate consistently heavy shots that are difficult for goalies to manage.

His shot placement and understanding of how to mask his release point, compliments his shooting mechanics. He understands how to fold his hands over and present the opposite side he actually intends to shoot on. Additionally, because defenses have to respect his shot from distance, he has displayed the wherewithal to handle the puck on his backhand, use his length and frame and drive inward, in-tight to the net area before elevating the puck. Forslund projects to score at the pro level from extended range and from around the net area; so there's a lot of range within his scoring, and it's the most enticing aspect of his game.

Another important aspect of his game that's a bit further behind but projects to hold at the NHL level is regarding his skating ability. Despite being a bigger and lankier kid, Charlie has surprisingly good stride depth when skating in open ice and straight lines. Typically, players who are physically raw lack depth, as a result of going off balance if they skate too deep within their stride, but that's not the case here. Forslund is also adequate when moving off his centerline, and has displayed a decent amount of power as well. HIs edgework needs further refinement and he's not an agile skater at this point but we believe these areas of his game have an opportunity to emerge over time.

From a mental perspective, Charlie has advanced routes and a good sense of timing when he needs to skate into space in order to receive passes. We've seen him circle off pressure which temporarily alleviates coverage, before slipping behind coverage, or through coverage. We've seen him come through as the F3 trailer option and recognize when to time coming into heavy traffic for low to high danger passing set-ups, and we've seen him understand proper spacing, so that he doesn't get counteracted on drop pass attempts when setting up his release.

His playmaking lags behind his shooting and skating ability though. He can set up high danger passing plays if he sees his option in-front of him, but he's been far less successful and hitting blind or trailing options. He has a tendency to be overly reliant on his shot quality instead of looking for high danger weakside passing options and he's not a gifted technical playmaker at this time. He can occasionally set up an advanced passing play from below the net area but as of now that's the most dynamic element of his playmaking and we would consider him largely a single threat option at this time.

His 200-foot game is raw like the rest of his game, but he does show the ability to compete and we have seen him win 50/50 puck battles along the boards. He also has surprisingly decent shot blocking rates, so there's a commitment by him to sacrifice his body when the play calls for it. He lacks pace at times but we think that's largely a conditioning issue factoring his age and frame, when going up against developed players at the pro level. Overall, Forslund presents pro size, a pro level shot, functional skating, and a lot of untapped potential, and that's why he's made our list as the only prospect featured from HockeyEttan this year.

"He's one of the hidden gems in this class, and he's getting drafted." - HP Scout, Brad Allen

79	PLAYER	TEAM	LEAGUE	HEIGHT	WEIGHT	POS	GRADE
	FRANSEN, NOEL	FARJESTAD	SWE-JR	6' 00"	179	LD	C

NHLCS	CEILING	FLOOR	HOCKEY SENSE	COMPETE	SKILL	SKATE	MISC
INT-48	6	4	5	5	7	7	5

Fransen is an offensive defenseman from Sweden who had a breakthrough season with Farjestad's J20 team. After only playing 5 games last year, he exploded with 20 goals, 44 points in 45 games this year, which was good for first place in goals and points for a defenseman in the league. He also played 5 games in the SHL and two tournaments (in February and April) with the U19 National Team.

An explosive skater from the back end, he demonstrates good acceleration and top speed. He loves to rush the puck out of his zone and go end to end. This won't be as easy for him to do at the pro level, but in the J20, his good skating skills and athleticism served him well in that department. Thanks to his skating, he can also escape pressure and the forecheck. With him on the ice, his team's transition game is always in good hands. He's good in transition, can make a good first pass, and he's never shy to rush the puck out of his zone.

You don't score 20 goals as a defenseman in any league if you don't have a great shot from the point. Whether it's his slapshot or wrist shot, both have good accuracy and velocity. He's a threat from the point with the puck on his stick because of that great shooting ability, but he's also not trying to shoot 100 mph shots from the point all the time. He does use placement shots quite often as well. He makes good reads when jumping into the play, and he's assertive with the puck on his stick. He's very noticeable on the ice with these skills. We like his lateral movements at the offensive line, which enable him to create different shooting or passing lanes; he's certainly not immobile. However, his decision-making can be inconsistent at times. While he generates offense with his shot, skills, and skating ability, there are occasions when his decision-making falls short. We wish his creativity and overall puck-management were better, because the rest of his tools are exciting.

Defensively is where we have some concerns with this player. He's not bad, but much of it boils down to effort. There's a noticeable lack of consistent effort from him when it comes to defending at a high level. While we've seen occasional physical pushback from him this season, it hasn't been consistent enough to fully convince us or instill enough confidence for us to rank him aggressively on our list. Instead of projecting him as a 2nd round pick, we view him more as a 4th round pick in our evaluation.

The lack of effort in his zone is what might make the difference between Fransen playing in the NHL versus the SHL. He's not a big defenseman, but he's also not small, he's around 6 foot tall with a decent frame. There's no size dilemma here with him, but a lot of it has to do with him focusing more on defending. Too many times we felt he was too passive in his own zone; this won't cut it at the NHL level. He also can get lost in his zone, similar to Zayne Parekh. He does a good job defending against the rush because of his good skating, but in the defensive zone, he can get confused in his coverage. He focuses too much on the puck-carrier and needs to improve on his defensive zone reads. He has the potential to improve in this aspect and prove us wrong, but we're also not expecting him to emerge as a standout offensive talent like Zayne Parekh or Lane Hutson. While he possesses solid offensive tools, they're not exceptional, which explains where he is ranked.

We like Fransen's offensive game and think he'll play a regular role next season in the SHL. Regarding the NHL, however, he's one we're unsure about. He's one of those players we see as potentially excelling in European leagues but may fall just short of NHL calibre. However, it's not out of the realm of possibility… if he makes adjustments to his game. These types of players pose the toughest challenge for us in terms of ranking because with just a few tweaks to his game, he could easily prove us wrong. We consider him a mid-round pick, but it'll be intriguing to see where he ultimately lands.

NR	PLAYER		TEAM	LEAGUE	HEIGHT	WEIGHT	POS	GRADE
	FRASCA, GABRIEL		KINGSTON	OHL	6' 00.25"	175	LC	NI
NHLCS	CEILING	FLOOR	HOCKEY SENSE	COMPETE	SKILL		SKATE	MISC
NA-85	6	4	6	5	6		4	6

Gabriel Frasca is the latest feature of the OHL's "Frasca Brother's" with older brothers Jacob and Jordan completed their OHL careers and his younger brother's Nick, recently drafted to Niagara in the OHL draft. Gianni, a 2011 birth year, waiting in the wings. The middle brother put up 32 points, including 15 goals, in an injury shortened 44 games this season adding a single assist in 5 playoff games for the Kingston Frontenacs.

Frasca's major issue stopping him from being a higher impact OHL player and projectable NHLer is his skating. He has slow straightaway speed up the ice which does not improve with the puck on his stick which hurts his translatability to the pro-level. Frasca's mobility is stiff overall in his upper body and has his stick and elbows close to his body limiting his range of motion especially in tight spaces along the boards while cycling. He skating stance is good while on the cycle and is tough to push off the puck but, he still limits himself with his upper body mobility. As for being pushed around, this only applies to the cycle, when he plays in front of the net, he struggles to plant himself and is easily removed by opposing defenders.

Strong awareness overall is what brings Frasca success on both the score sheet and defensively. He is good positionally in the defensive zone and is able to close gaps on forwards looking for offense in his defensive zone and cuts off lanes in the neutral zone on the back check making sure he has his man. The shot mechanics are not poor but, he does not possess a goal-scorers shot despite his solid goal total. Offensively he does not drive play and relies on his teammates to bring offense on the rush and is not the player you want carrying the puck into the zone.

With Frasca, you get a defensively responsible forward who can kill penalties and be responsible in his own end. The big stopper for Frasca is his skating, which prevents him from making a lot more plays offensively and limits him when projecting for the NHL.

27	PLAYER		TEAM	LEAGUE	HEIGHT	WEIGHT	POS	GRADE
	FREIJ, ALFONS		VAXJO JR	SWE JR	6' 00.5"	197	LD	B
NHLCS	CEILING	FLOOR	HOCKEY SENSE	COMPETE	SKILL		SKATE	MISC
INT-13	7	5	6	5	6		9	6

Alfons Freij is a puck moving, mobile defenseman with untapped offensive and defensive potential. He played this past season for the Vaxjo Lakers in J20, where he produced the second most goals for any first-year draft eligible defenseman playing in J20, with 14 goals and 33 points in 40 games.

The defining feature of Freij's game is his skating ability. We include him in the top tier of skaters in this class and he is arguably the best skating defenseman in this class.

What makes his skating special is how agile he is on his skates, which can be seen when he's extending from a launch or stationary position. A lot of younger players have difficulty simultaneously transferring between their upper and lower halves, but that's not the case with Freij. He features a strong shoulder rotation and knows how to propel himself forward through his initial arm swing, into his deep knee extensions. Even though he's still growing into his frame, his coordination and athleticism is already developed, allowing him to rebalance himself quickly, so that he can still handle pucks when he's getting physically initiated on. He's a multi-directional skater who can perform lateral cutbacks, C-cuts, side steps, sharp pivots, spin offs, and he can explode when traveling north south.

He uses his skating to become an activating machine when carving through the neutral-zone and typically joins the offensive attack as the 4th forward. What's unique or atypical within his game is that he can adaptively process the play at his full speed and it's this quality that works in combination with his offensive skill-set that allows him to generate translatable offense.

Furthermore, his spatial awareness syncs with his explosive open ice skating, which means that he's rarely running himself into traffic or running out of room before he can make a successful offensive play. His spacing is adequate and it allows his teammates to find him in transition on a consistent basis.

When opponents are pressuring him, he can make fast plays under pressure but he can also use body and head feints to throw off the initial layer of defense, so that he can further penetrate either through the neutral zone or when he's pinching in the offensive end.

The second aspect of his puck moving game that needs to be discussed is in regards to his playmaking ability. He's been a very consistent outlet passer on both his backhand and forehand which gives him a significant advantage. He can make tape to tape backhand saucer passes while in motion, no look reverse spinning stretch passes off of pivot, short bank passes, or long sharp stretch passes through layers. When he's activating through the neutral zone, he's capable of controlling the trajectory of his dump ins, allowing for recollection by his teammates to happen before even needing the forecheck.

Most importantly, his decision making behind his playmaking has been good in our viewings. If he can increase his efficiency by making a one touch pass through the neutral zone, he will, but he can also recognize which one of his teammates is most likely to be able to stay in motion so that they can gain the line while evaluating his options. We've seen him evaluate stretch passing options that are available to stationary targets, yet evaluate that the shorter pass to a streaking teammate whose gaining momentum is the safer and better option. There's an impressive amount of maturity featured within his structured passing game, and one that we think can translate successfully to the NHL. Now don't get us wrong, he can occasionally put his teammates in bad positions after receiving transitional exit passes out of his own end, or miss the tape too, but by and large, he's shown a lot of upside with his playmaking ability. We just wish he would display his playmaking upside more often in the offensive zone.

One of his more unique characteristics as a defender and admittedly, it's a characteristic that we wish he would dial back at times, is his tendency to look to over-shoot the puck despite having better playmaking options readily available, depending on the play. It's a characteristic he shared with Elias Salomonsson in his draft season, but like Salomonsson who is a gifted shooter mechanically, so is Freij, so we give him leeway and at least understand why he carries tunnel vision more often than most other defenseman.

There's a translatable combination of rush activation, handling and shooting ability that makes Freij a threat. From a psychological perspective, Alfon's is extremely assertive. He knows he's a better skater than almost any other player on the ice, and he challenges players to try and keep up with him. This is not a passive defenseman, but he also recognizes risk at a high rate when specifically evaluating his offensive transitional play.

Where risk with Freij in a general sense comes into play is on the defensive side of the puck. The spatial awareness and recognition of which skating lane to take when attacking is reduced when it comes to his off puck defensive recognition. He can mentally map the ice in advance when breaking out and exiting the zone, but he has far more difficulty anticipating and mapping potential attacking routes the opposing team is going to take off the rush.

He does have the great defensive equalizer which is his skating, and due to his skating his rate of recovery and retrievals projects to be elite, and we weigh that heavily within his evaluation as a result of his instincts for the position being relatively average. He mismanages his gaps, he can be late to picking up his coverage in chaotic situations around his net area, and he can have difficulty containing or boxing out bigger or stronger opponents. However, we did feel he started showing progress when it came to showing a physical edge at times (although fleeting), that simply wasn't present at the start of the season. He's a one dimensional defender who relies on his length and stick as opposed to playing with an edge and that's arguably his weakest trait as of this writing. That said, if a defenseman is going to have difficulty occasionally defending, they need to make sure that they don't need to defend too often in the first place, and Freij's skill-set lends well to that.

Freij is a fantastic athlete whose skating base alone makes him one of the more interesting defensive prospects in this class. We feel his playmaking is untapped and will eventually get brought out at a better rate when he develops as a pro. We started seeing the necessary ingredients defensively at the end of the season to think that his defense should be able to be passable, so that his puck moving game and goal scoring upside can flourish.

" I would be very surprised if he doesn't play in some capacity, the trick is figuring out exactly what role he's going to have. Does the defense come around enough so that he can insulate a pairing? Does he have enough offensive upside to suggest a powerplay quarterback where he operates similarly to Ryker Evans or Elias Salomonsson who or both more shoot first defenseman, or maybe he ends up a puck mover which I think makes the most sense when evaluating where he is right now." - HP Scout, Brad Allen

" Some of you might be wondering why Freij is far ahead of Wallenius, and it comes down to one major factor for me and that's the tool-kit." - HP Scout, Brad Allen

" His game reminds me of Jonas Brodin's at the same age" - NHL Scout, May 2024

" Ridiculously good skater who started to look better in his own zone as the season progressed." - HP Scout, Mark Edwards, April 2024

NR	PLAYER	TEAM	LEAGUE	HEIGHT	WEIGHT	POS	GRADE
	FRYER, SETH	VICTORIA	WHL	6' 06.5"	197	RD	C
NHLCS	CEILING	FLOOR	HOCKEY SENSE	COMPETE	SKILL	SKATE	MISC
NA-206	5	3	4	5	3	6	7

The 6'7", right-handed defenseman played his 1st season in the WHL this year, after playing his 16 years old season in the VIJHL, a tier-2 Jr. A league in Vancouver.

Fryer owns decent mobility for his size. When he defends the rush, he can be tough to get around because of how he covers ice with his skating and reach. Although he shows decent rush defense habits, like defending inside dots against strong side rush or angling versus change of side rush, he needs to improve some details, particularly the timing of his pivots and his stickwork. In his own-end, Fryer isn't overly physical as he won't get out of position to throw a big hit, but he'll use his size and reach to make stops and immobilize opposing forwards. Fryer had one fight this season, stepping up defending his teammates after a huge hit from the opposing team.

His game with the puck needs a lot of work, especially under pressure. As of now, he relies heavy on his partner to move the puck. If not his partner, chipping the puck north is a play he uses often. His patience with the puck and the accuracy of his passing are areas he'll need to improve. With his decent mobility, he can carry the puck with success when there's open space. At the offensive blueline, Fryer keeps it simple by using D2D passes. He has a decent ability to find shooting lanes with his wrist shot.

In the playoffs, Fryer lacked confidence and had a really limited role for the Royals, playing less than 10 minutes in Royals' four games against Portland. He had a strong stretch of games in late February and early march where he averaged around 20 minutes and played with more confidence. As of right now, Fryer is a long-term project. He's a late bloomer with some tools to work with, with his huge frame and decent mobility, but the rest of his game is raw and needs a lot of work.

68	PLAYER	TEAM	LEAGUE	HEIGHT	WEIGHT	POS	GRADE
	GALVAS, TOMAS	LIBEREC	CZE	5' 10.25"	153	LD	C

NHLCS	CEILING	FLOOR	HOCKEY SENSE	COMPETE	SKILL	SKATE	MISC
INT-33	6	3	6	7	5	8	4

Tomas Galvas is a high energy - modern day - undersized puck moving defenseman who relies on his elusiveness and vision to get the job done. It's a big step up in competition when transitioning from the U20 circuit to Czech Extraliga as a 17-18 year old, yet Galvas never looked out of place from his opening shift in his first game this season.

The reason for having success early and remaining consistent regardless of playing limited minutes when up at the pro level is the result of his assertiveness, his skating agility, and his defensive tenacity. We're going to start with his defense, since that's the pressing area of concern when evaluating his long term outlook.

Undersized defenseman have to be able to read the play well, they have to take hits in order to make plays when they no longer can rely on their elusiveness; they also have to be willing to physically engage even when they're overmatched, and they must have the recovery tools necessary to get back into position. In Galvas's case he checks a lot of boxes.

The most impressive aspect of his defensive ability is to anticipate both transitional and cycle sequences on both the strong side and weak side in advance so that he can rapidly close his gaps or stay above the puck and kill plays before they begin.

On his strong side, he's quick to evaluate not only what the play driver is attempting to do after coming over the defensive line, but where the secondary option that he needs to cover is located as well. This allows him to get in front of and ahead of give and go sequences so that he can intercept them or use his stick and body positioning to counteract them. Which brings us to our next attribute, which is his ability to process information rapidly off the puck. This is exceptionally important for this player, since it allows him to take advantage of his rapid pivoting and turning ability, which allows him to C-cut and close down his gap on proper angles, so that he can control the geography of the rink against opposing wingers. We talk extensively about defenseman mitigating or reducing risk in a lot of our evaluations, and Galvas is more than capable of exactly that.

The hallmark of this player is his scanning ability and spatial awareness, which puts him in proper positions quickly enough so that he's rarely caught behind the play. There's a huge difference between the speed of Junior hockey in Czechia U20 and Extraliga, yet Tomas's ability to keep up was never in doubt after evaluating him. He's rarely rushed and rarely misses coverage. Sometimes though, even when you're smart and have a good stick, you still have to deal with aggressive forwards who can lean on you, and that's where Galvas's evaluation becomes more difficult.

If you're a small defenseman, your margin for error is less than a larger defenseman with more range, which is why a defenseman with size, length, who can also skate are so coveted. They don't need to be as good at anticipating plays or be as spatially aware as a player like Galvas. In some of our viewings, we have seen him have some difficulty with both dynamic, yet agile forwards, as well as forwards with range and size.

There is a susceptibility displayed within his defensive game when opponents are able to gain a step on him and cut around him from the outside since he lacks the range of a typical NHL defender. That said, he's shown that his transitional defense off the rush can hold surprisingly well though. The reason why is that if the opposing players attempted to cut back inside, he was very good at recovering and taking away the middle portion of the ice, which reduced their high danger shot rates.

This is a testament to the mental makeup of Galvas. If he loses a step on an opponent or is initiated on by bigger, fully physically developed men. If an opposing winger attempted to drive him wide while cutting inside, he would drive his shoulder parallel directly into his opponents before slipping back on the inside and fighting to regain the puck, as one of many examples we could give. Time and time again, he showed a high compete level, a never back down attitude that culminated in tenacious and high tempo defensive plays. These types of plays have us believing there's enough fortitude within his psychological foundation to bend, but not break at the NHL level.

Defense isn't ever going to be the strongest area of Galvas's game, but the reason we aren't overly concerned is because for every defensive misplay or chance against that occurs when he's on the ice due to his lack of size, he makes multiple, yet efficient plays that gets the puck moving out of his own end and back into his opponent's end. The name of the modern NHL game is transitional hockey, and that's exactly where Galvas thrives.

It starts with his puck retrievals. His confidence and poise to handle pressure against top competition in small areas of the ice with a limited operating window has been nothing short of exceptional.

Good puck retrievers give themselves multiple exit points, in Galvas's case his fantastic outside edges, high end skating posture, and ability to read and react in tight spaces, has made him very hard to read and pin down behind his goal line or when getting closed on around the boards. Additionally, he's quick to recognize when an opponent is looking to force a dump or when an opponent is attempting a chip play around him. Which in turn, allows him to use his rapid body rotations to reorient himself and get back on the inside so that he can win the majority of loose puck races that he's involved in. He wins races, he can escape when under heavy pressure, but he also can slow down the play by using advanced manipulation with his passing fakes and head fakes. He's not easy to read or get a hold of, and that's' the catalyst for him getting the puck moved up the ice.

The second aspect of his puck moving game that needs to be discussed is in regards to his playmaking ability. We wouldn't label him a dynamic or even exceptional playmaker but he's aware of his skill-set and stays constrained within it. What this means is that he looks to optimize his playmaking and use his agility and speed to shorten the ice so that he can rely more on shorter area playmaking when it's appropriate. That doesn't mean he can't outlet a stretch pass and stretch the length of the ice, he can, but he's not a player whose going to be making passing plays through multiple layers of traffic when advanced saucer passes or by feathering the puck.

Most importantly, his decision making behind his playmaking has been good in our viewings. If he can increase his efficiency by making a one touch processing pass through the neutral zone, he will, but he can also recognize which one of his teammates is most likely to be able to stay in motion so that they can gain the line while evaluating his options. We've seen him evaluate stretch passing options that are available to stationary targets, yet evaluate that the shorter pass to a streaking teammate whose gaining momentum is the safer and better option. There's an impressive amount of maturity featured within his structured passing game, and one that we think can translate successfully to the NHL.

If he's unable to find a passing option, Galvas is more than capable of transitioning through the neutral zone with his impressive on the puck spatial awareness and plus risk assessments; he rarely activates at the wrong time. His success rates are a result of agile stutter steps, quick linear crossover, and rapid lateral cutbacks. Mechanically he's refined, and can spin better than almost any other player in this class.

In-fact, how he largely operates within each zone is by making subtle adjustments to what's available to him while in mid spin. He looks to spin and rapidly re-orient himself to find options. This style of game isn't so dissimilar to Samuel Girard's. Like Girard, he can dissect the first layer from the offensive line, but he's a poor finisher who lacks good shooting mechanics at this time. His top and bottom hand activation are poor and that means he has difficulty generating the necessary torque on his release or elevating the puck rapidly enough. His offense will be generated through his off look playmaking set ups.

Taken together, Galvas presents an impressive puck moving game with considerable risk as a result of his slight frame. However, he does have the necessary tool-kit and mental makeup that gives him a legitimate shot to play meaningful NHL games. We don't think he's a powerplay option, and its going to be difficult for him to remain past a third pairing or sheltered role in a playoff series most likely, which is reflected in our rankings, but we have more time for this player than we initially expected and that's a testament to the fire and mentality on the ice that he possesses.

"He's tiny, but I think there's a legitimate chance that he's one of those rare defensive anomaly's that actually plays meaningful games. I think he's unlikely going to be a big point producer but his retrieval, activation, and exit ability gives him potential for a heavy transition game that a lot of teams want." - HP Scout, Brad Allen

"Zero interest" NHL Scout, May 2024

"He is what...about a buck fifty. Solid player but not for me." - NHL Scout, May 2024

11	PLAYER	TEAM	LEAGUE	HEIGHT	WEIGHT	POS	GRADE
	GARDNER, EVAN	SASKATOON	WHL	6' 00"	175	G	C
NHLCS	CEILING	FLOOR	HOCKEY SENSE	COMPETE	SKILL	SKATE	MISC
NA-7	6	3	7	6	5	7	5

Evan Gardner is a mechanically and technically efficient goalie who shares the same polish and confidence that we saw in Devon Levi at the same age. We want to stress that we don't think Gardner is as dynamic or as talented as Levi, but mentally he shares similarities. This is an impressive goalie who has had an understated season, albeit on a very good Saskatoon team.

Evan Gardner is arguably one of the most efficient goalies out of any of the top end goalies available. He can micro-adjust well, he keeps everything sealed remarkably well when transitioning between save types, and his overall movement is impressive. His skating base rarely puts him in a position where he's off balance or over-committing on a shot. He syncs his skating to the speed of the play. As an example, if a very fast player is cutting rapidly around his net area and he needs to go post to post, he will explode at the velocity needed. This applies to lateral passing plays as well. He takes into consideration the player attacking him and downloads their movement and skating patterns. It's one of the reasons why he can not only survive at the WHL level but also thrive.

Due to Gardner's below average frame, he's had to rely far more on his advanced tracking than most of the other top goalies who are much larger than him that we have ranked. One of the best indicators of advanced tracking is the ability to stay upright without dropping into a butterfly on high danger shots that are through traffic, and this is where you really see Gardner excel. He rarely drops into a butterfly on blocked shots, even if they are tight to the net, and this allows him to take advantage of his skating base, while not having to rely on his recovery rates as often. Taken together, he's almost always square, rarely over-commits on a play, rarely enters a butterfly in advance of the play, and rarely makes the wrong save type.

His impressive attributes tied into his mental approach as well. He was up there with Zarubin, George, and Moysevich in terms of overall consistency rates in the regular season. He rarely had what we would call a bad game, and yes part of that is definitely a byproduct of his dominant team, but there were also many games we evaluated, where he had to be focused and mentally dialled in order to close out the game correctly.

He understands how to remain on balance in a RVH while extending his stick to counteract in tight passing options. He also extends his RVH without transitioning to the opposite post when dealing with players who are skating around the back of his net. This delayed RVH counteracts potential no-look behind the back passing options on his short side. He also knows how to remain centered when dealing with a player who has both short or far side passing options available from below the goal line, and times when he needs to transfer to his post depending on the trajectory of the pass. Essentially, when you look at his play in general down low, he has little in the way of wasted movement and this is a critical component of any goalies game, because if teams are unable to generate heavy minutes against him, then theoretically if he hits the NHL, it will mean that he can have the conditioning necessary where he can maintain a high level of consistency without his energy dipping.

His down low mechanics are advanced. He understands how to take advantage of a paddle down position and use it to take the bottom part of the net away, so that he can be less reliant on his extension rates. He's also fluid at transitioning from a paddle down position into his butterfly and vice versa. In fact, his style of play, when you take it as a whole, is predicated around his ability to transition between these two save types. It's a fascinating and rare style of play.

He carries a unique style that has fluid transitional qualities so that he can counteract his own limitations and setbacks as a player, at least to a degree.

The biggest setback to Evan's game isn't his fault, and that has to do with his overall frame and kicking length. He doesn't have high-end extension rates relative to his frame. That matters a ton, and it's the biggest reservation we have when projecting him, despite having the style he has to counteract it. If he was 6 '3'', with longer legs and better overall extensions then he's moving up our rankings, but he doesn't, and the extension rates and overall size are absolutely critical in his projection, which is why he's ranked further down then his talent would suggest.

Though Gardner is a magnificent tracker at times, he's also one of the stranger goalies in this class, or any class really. Typically smaller goalies who are compact and lack extension rates rely on their depth assessment on an initial shot, and cut down angles aggressively. Furthermore, smaller goalies need to leverage their speed and ability to recover quicker to stay in-front of the puck, but Gardner doesn't fall into these categories.

He plays the position like he's 6 '4'' plus at times, and can fail to cut down on angles to the degree we wish he would. He's actually too contained in his net. This doesn't mean he doesn't assess angles properly, or that he doesn't come out to the top of his paint, but it means he does it less than you would typically want to see for a goalie built like him. There's a balancing act between being efficient and controlled, but then also being aggressive at the right times. Gardner towards the end of the season and into the playoffs, did show some improvements in this area though. So there was growth, but it's still an area that needs to improve.

The above point is highlighted when factoring in how he presents in the net. His stance is going to have to be modified. He doesn't elevate his shoulders, which means he fails at keeping his blocker parallel to the ice, which makes him susceptible to high shots. His hands are set low and he doesn't have active hands relative to a lot of the other goalies in this class. He can fail to remain tall, but a set stance can be heavily modified over time. What we see now, won't show how he presents in the net down the road, so it's an issue, but a correctable one.

There are exactly zero goalies as of this writing that have Gardner's style, combined with his frame that have currently translated. He's undersized, he lacks extension rates, but he plays an efficient, calm, puck absorbing style that's meant largely for a bigger goalie. He can make dynamic saves, but it's not going to be the selling point. He's shown significant adaptation for his weaknesses and he's got a natural quality, despite playing a very unnatural game.

We have him ranked because he's a brilliant tracker and has some advanced technical mechanics. If he can overhaul his depth management and physically develop into a more explosive goaltender, then he still has a chance of developing into a successful NHL goalie. He has the mental consistency and constitution of a calm, cool, and collected starter, but the rest of his game falls a bit behind that, which we took into consideration when ranking him.

"Some kids look unnatural at the position in their initial draft season. It was one of the reasons I didn't think highly of Topias Leinonen. He looked more like an athlete who had recently put on pads, whereas Gardner looks like a kid born for the position but then has to overhaul aspects of his foundation." - HP Scout, Brad Allen

"There are aspects to Evan that are special, then there are aspects that are terrifying." - HP Scout, Brad Allen

"If he was 6'4", he would be one of my first goalies ranked, but he isn't." - HP Scout, Brad Allen -

NR	PLAYER	TEAM	LEAGUE	HEIGHT	WEIGHT	POS	GRADE
	GATTO, SEBASTIAN	LEAMINGTON	OJHL	6' 03"	165	G	C

NHLCS	CEILING	FLOOR	HOCKEY SENSE	COMPETE	SKILL	SKATE	MISC
NA-16	6	3	5	7	7	5	7

Sebastian Gatto is a raw, athletically gifted goalie who showed an impressive curve this past season. At the beginning of the year, we thought he was mechanically rigid and his overall fluidity and transitional save rates were under the minimum threshold for a 6'3' goalie that we typically look for. However, as the season progressed so did Gatto's physical growth and it changed our interpretation of what he could potentially develop into. Gatto finished a successful season with a playoff run that had his team lose in the OJHL Conference finals. Without his consistent effort, they very likely wouldn't have made it as far as they did.

Gatto is green, and he's also playing in a league that can't fully exploit his lack of technique in critical areas yet. What this means is that he wasn't put in a development environment that would force technical improvements on the foundations of his game in some areas. Instead, what we felt happened, was that Gatto grew into his body as the year progressed and that he could get away with a lack of technique through his new-found athleticism, competitive nature, and an impressive level of mental focus.

Where he lags technically is regarding his over-rotation that sometimes occurs after making an initial save, as the result of his edgework needing considerable refinement. Another key area for him to develop is how he integrates into a post on some play-types. When he needs to fall back into a RVH position, he has a tendency to use an overlap position instead. His overlap can leave him susceptible to lateral transfers when he's not aligned properly to push off on an angle that can get him exploding from post-to-post. Additionally, his overlap can leave him susceptible since he can fail to spatially recognize how far he has extended out past his net. We've seen him give up goals that should be routine saves as the result of this. His overlap is similar to Yegor Yegorov's primary issue from last season, though this is largely correctable over-time for most goalies.

Another technical area he needs to shore up is his depth-management. Sometimes he will be over-zealous at cutting the initial shooting angle, that puts him in positions where the shot switches into a lateral high danger pass or a back door pass, and he's too far out to attempt to recover from.

Although he has numerous technical flaws, Gatto presents a very interesting athletic base. For starters, his extension rates are very good. He's the prototypical goalie height, but he's also the length that we look for and he can effortlessly extend into a full split, while still keeping his core and arms elevated. We have beaten up on his technique a bit in this profile, but one area where he's technically strong is when he enters a full split, he can still seal off his blocker and position his glove properly above his pad so that he can simultaneously take up additional room if a puck is elevated, while also remaining sealed.

His athleticism extends to his shoulder rotations as well. When he is either in a butterfly or RVH position, he can fully manipulate his frame and rotate his shoulders upwards to cover shots that are elevated in tight to him. He can get off his centerline in unique positions in a hurry.

Speaking to his butterfly, he can transfer into his butterfly very quickly, and he can explode laterally and cover distance quickly as well. We like that he uses his extensions within his butterfly to present a wider one.

This works in unison with his kicking reflexes which grade above-average to good. It's impressive how much more fluid he really became by the end of the season, relative to the beginning portion.

His sense for the position is decent. He can recognize back-door passing plays in advance, track lateral options through traffic and he can process low to high plays from below his net area rapidly. However, he can over-anticipate the play as well; meaning, he recognizes the highest danger option but then slightly moves into position to take away that option before the developing play has advanced to the player he thinks is the intended target. This extends to his butterfly. He can fall into his butterfly prematurely, putting him in a position to have pucks elevated on him in tight to the net. on a shot placement that he would normally stop with his frame, if he timed the shot better.

Due to his ability to manipulate himself off his centerline; he has natural upside for being able to find a position to track through screens. He combines his tracking with his athleticism to move into space when needing to transfer from a short-side shot behind a screen or far-side shot, depending on the angle. What this means, is that instead of using just his extension rates in his upper and lower-halves, he will primarily stay sealed and then move into the space from the initial angle he set up behind the screen. This is one of his better technical skills that's further ahead than most other areas of his game.

Sebastian surprised us over the course of the season. We had written him off early, only to come back around on him in the second half. His curve was impressive. He reminds us a lot of fellow goalie prospect Hugo Laring in some ways. They're both athletically gifted but are also raw. They are both competitive but sometimes to a fault. By being as aggressive as they are, they can inadvertently take themselves out of plays. Gatto needs to calm his game down on high danger plays in tight to the net and instead, let the game come to him. If he develops a more poised approach and shores up his technical deficiencies then he has a shot at the NHL one day.

"There's three goalies who are the dark horses in this class that I would consider drafting late. Sebastian Gatto, Hugo Laring and Bor Glavic represent real athletes in the net that need a ton of time and work done to modify aspects of their game, but all three have upside. It's going to be very interesting to see which one can take their career the furthest." - HP Scout, Brad Allen

"Before I saw him myself I asked four NHL Scouts their thoughts on him. Three out of four said no draft and the other said maybe a late pick. I had him as a no draft after my first viewing but that has changed. - HP Scout, Mark Edwards, May 2024

10	PLAYER		TEAM	LEAGUE	HEIGHT	WEIGHT	POS	GRADE
	GEORGE, CARTER		OWEN SOUND	OHL	6' 01"	194	G	C
NHLCS	CEILING	FLOOR	HOCKEY SENSE	COMPETE	SKILL		SKATE	MISC
NA-2	6	5	7	7	6		6	5

Carter George reminds us of a smaller Carter Hart and Spencer Knight in a lot of ways. He's compact, technical in his movements and reads the play remarkably well at his age and in this stage of his development. Unlike Evan Gardner,

George was under-fire at a much higher rate and had to routinely stand on his head just to keep his teams in games. At the U18's, he helped Canada win gold. His performance against the U.S. was a perfect example of one of his peak performances, and paints a picture of a goalie with upside.

Although his physical traits are more limited than some of the other goalies in this class, his mental traits are extremely strong and allowed him to carry Owen Sound due to his poise and spatial awareness. He manages his depth consistently, he's calculated within his movements, evaluates the highest percentage angles and he recognizes when he needs to use advanced edgework to get aligned with potential lateral passes, so that he can still play the shot if it comes closer to the net, but also be able to play the lateral one timer set up or catch and release set up. The other noticeable and stand out trait regarding George is how tight he maintains his glove and blocker side, in both a relaxed and set stance.

His blocker side technique is ahead of most other goalies featured in this class. He understands when and how to keep his blocker on the necessary plane to deflect pucks into corners while maintaining proper stick posture and he doesn't punch pucks back into traffic almost at all. His rebound control is advanced for his age on his blocker as a result.

He's also very active with his stick and consistently uses well timed stick deflections to deflect pucks into dead space, or uses his stick when shooters are in tight to him. Not every goalie has the ability to actually time rapid handling plays around the net area, but George does.

One of the more unique aspects of George's set stance is how he holds and maintains his glove. As opposed to having his glove held towards his hip line in a neutral position, he keeps it tucked directly into his midsection bringing it further upwards into his centerline (he's not the only goalie who maintains this glove position in a set stance, but it's less common). George isn't a big goalie, in fact, with the exception of Nabokov, he's the smallest goalie in the draft that is relevant, and so his glove positioning makes him appear very narrow in net at times. Yet, because he keeps it tucked, it allows him to generate dextrous downward motions on his glove-side at an impressive level. Some of the best glove-hand saves we have seen from any goalie this past season, are a direct result of his emphatic, almost Patrick Roy style wind-mill saves where he swings his glove hand down rapidly before rotating back up and through the shot so that he can snare the puck.

Another unique property to his game is how he transitions during lateral one timer set ups at mid range from the circles occasionally. As opposed to entering a butterfly and sliding across or using a T-push off and exploding into his set stance on the other side of his net, he has a tendency to enter a modified VH. It's not so dissimilar to a technique Georgiev used to implement at a more common frequency when he was on the Rangers, before he was traded to Colorado. We've never been big fans of a lateral push off into a VH in general during one timers, but especially if the goalie is smaller. The reason why has to do with being stuck after making an extension through the VH. If anything happens to the puck on its way to the net, then it's much harder for the goalie to generate a reactionary save. It's something that can be modified out of his game over-time as long as physically matures enough, but he was doing it right up until the end of the season, so we thought it was important enough to discuss.

Another interesting adaptation George has implemented, is to make up for a lack of dexterity and high-end kicking reflexes. His reflexes are functional and they project to hold, but we wouldn't grade his kicking reflexes specifically, as anything more than average. This is not to be mistaken for kicking extension rates, which he actually grades well in. He can do a full split comfortably, while remaining tall and he uses that to his advantage often on secondary saves as well. What's interesting is that it can take him longer than a faster, more dextrous goalie to actually enter the full extension.

He's modified his game to compensate for this. As an example, when he's dealing with high danger shots in tighter to the net, or when he's dealing with rapid handling plays near his crease area, where he's expected to use his legs, he will enter a very wide set position that's lower to the ice, which is much wider then his typical set stance that he uses on shots that he's facing him from the middle of the ice and towards the blue-line.

He looks to actively move while maintaining his butterfly position more often than most other goalies, when there's point blank re-directs or short area passes that force him to suddenly shift and react to a new shooting angle. This again, allows him to take the bottom part of the net away without having to rely on his kicking reflexes and lack of dexterity within his hipline, as often as a prototypical goalie would. However, it also makes him more susceptible to redirect and deflection shots, than for a goalie who has better kicking reflexes or a higher degree of dexterity.

When comparing him to Gardner, Gardner also modifies his set stance to compensate. Now, there is a big difference as to why. In Gardner's case, it's to compensate for the lack of full extensions he can generate, while with George it's to compensate for the lack of dexterity in his hip line that takes away his ability to react with a kicking motion in the time frame needed. They are both modifying their set-stance on shots that are tighter to the net, but for completely different reasons.

When you look at this athleticism as a whole, it starts making a lot of sense as to why George operates the way he does. He's not slow relative to his size; he can still move from a RVH position into a sprawling save across the net quickly, and he can make dynamic saves from time-to-time, but we would argue it's about pro-average. He falls well under Devon Levi, Dustin Wolf or Juuse Saros at the same age. If you look at goalies who are very similarly sized to him, Shesterkin grades well ahead of him at the same age, Quick grades way ahead of him at the same age as well. Which means that the mental consistency of George is going to define his career. He doesn't have the same margin of error that a lot of other goalies who are either larger or are more athletically gifted than him have.

Luckily, he's ahead of most other goalies featured in this class from a mental perspective. He can play with ice in his veins, which was obvious at the U18's and in some of his playoff performances, and he rarely lets in bad goals. Even when a bad goal is scored on him, it's almost always from the circles and in, and very rarely the result of a shot from the point or something that should be routine. Part of this can be attributed to his overall concentration levels, which are fantastic when he's operating up to his top level of play. He can remain in a focused state under fire for the entire duration of a game, and relentless shot volume really doesn't seem to phase him, even in some high scoring games that he was a part of.

George features the mental maturity and composure you want in a starting goalie. He was under-fire this season and shined, in-spite of it. He mixes a very good blend of technical ability, with exceptional reads, and an impressive glove-hand. It's always interesting seeing how a goalie compensates for their shortcomings, and in George's case, he's successfully augmented his game so that he isn't as reliant on his athletic deficiencies. George has starting potential, but there is some projectable risk too. There aren't many goalies his size, with his athletic traits that have made it, but as long as he continues to augment and modify his game to compensate, then he certainly looks like he has a better shot than most goalies we have ranked of least.

" I have George as my number one goalie." - NHL Scout, May 2024

" Great junior goalie but we are not touching the small goalies." - NHL Scout May 2024

" I see the good qualities but there is no chance we are taking him. Guys don't even want to mention six foot goalies in our meetings." - NHL Scout, May 2024

" Here's food for thought. How much separation is there between Evan Gardner, Ryerson Leenders and Carter George? George has better extension rates, so I'll take George over Gardner, since I weigh them heavily, but it's not as if George blows him out of the water when breaking down each attribute. On the contrary, I think Gardner is better in some critical areas and I think it's way closer between the two of them than most people realize." - HP Scout, Brad Allen

"There's a Zach Fuchale-like effect happening this season with George. I'm not saying he's a bust and I'm not saying he isn't better at the same age. I had no time for Fuchale because of how inconsistent he actually was despite his win totals, but they're both Canadian, they both underwhelmed in some areas athletically for their size, and they both finished unbelievably strong and that put them on the hype train." - HP Scout, Brad Allen

"I've been very wrong before, and I'll be very wrong again, and hey I'm human just like everybody, so maybe I'm the one missing something here but I was right about Eric Comrie and right so far about Michael DiPietro. I just think George presents more risk than most other people." - HP Scout, Brad Allen

4	PLAYER	TEAM	LEAGUE	HEIGHT	WEIGHT	POS	GRADE
	GIDLOF, MARCUS	LEKSAND	SWE JR	6' 06"	212	G	B
NHLCS	CEILING	FLOOR	HOCKEY SENSE	COMPETE	SKILL	SKATE	MISC
INT-10	7	3	7	6	6	4	7

Marcus Gidlof is the largest goalie we have ranked this season. Some of the comparable goalies size wise to him are Damian Clara, Michael Hrabel, Dennis Hildeby, Ivan Fedotov, Jakub Markstrom, Ben Bishop, Robin Lehner and Nikita Tolopilo. However, we can narrow that down further by identifying where he falls categorically in terms of his athleticism at his size, relative to them. We feel he's closer to Fedotov and Lehner than the others, and that makes our evaluation incredibly difficult. That's a very small list of goalies to draw comparisons from, but like them, he has been a dominant starter in his draft season, while playing for Leksands J20 this past season. 7/3/6/6/6/3/7

Size can have some obvious advantages, several of which Gidlof can exploit. For starters, he takes a ton of the net in his RVH position and unlike most goalies who have to exaggerate their shoulder posture or lift themselves up while crouched temporarily to take away high shots, Gidlof doesn't, he can remain seated and takes up the top corner. Another advantage of him in his RVH is due how broad he is. Typically, shooters look to exploit the far-side angle on goalies who collapse into a RVH when they are driving toward the net, but Gidlof is wide and long, so this makes it a lower percentage option, relative to the other goalies in this draft. Secondly, Gidlof's extension rates are the best in this class as a result of his size. When he needs to sprawl out and take away a shot that's lower to the ice, he can fully extend from one post to the other, covering every down low option.

Another factor is that when Gidlof has cut down an angle successfully or when he's collapsing into his butterfly, there's very little for shooters to look at. When further breaking down his butterfly, typically with a larger goalie, shooters like to exploit the five hole as a result of it being more difficult to collapse at the rate needed to cover it when dealing with high danger five hole shots in tight to the net, but Gidlof has the transitional butterfly needed to hold. Part of that is the result of having a solid technical foundation within his butterfly, but the other attribute which really can be generalized to the rest of his game, is that he has impressive reflexes considering how big he is.

There's a sweet spot though and that sweet spot is dependent on the athletic ability of the goalie, relative to his height. In the case of Gidlof, he's not a Damian Clara, Jakub Markstrom or Nikita Tolopilo style of goalie as an example. They were super athletes who had unbelievable fast twitch and fluidity in their draft eligible seasons, while displaying an abnormal level of coordination within their skating mechanics. This means that when evaluating their long term upside, they made adjustments at the rate a much smaller goalie could, and that's one of the distinguishing factors of a larger goalie making it, to one that doesn't.

In the case of Gidlof, he's a heavier set goalie, his skating base is sloppy, and his micro-adjustment rates are below average. The extension rates are impressive due to his length and he does have power. He's actually knocked the net off of its pegs more than any goalie we can remember, just as a result of trying to slide into his RVH or when he attempts to push off his post, so there's some positives, but the negatives remain.

The biggest issue is when Gidlof needs to adjust on a secondary save or rebound save. When a play breaks down and he needs to quickly adapt and switch his position, the transfer rate is below average to average on most sequences, and that means it's difficult for him to get back in-front of the secondary shot in the time frame necessary. This is especially true on saves that require him to micro-shuffle rapidly across his net or on saves that require a secondary adjustment after already initially pushing off.

So to counteract this, Gidlof has incorporated one of the stranger goalie styles we've seen in recent years. There aren't really any public terms to describe different styles of goalies nowadays. It used to be you were a stand-up goalie, a butterfly goalie, or a hybrid goalie. We can count one NHL goalie that we would refer to as a stand-up goalie and he's a hybrid goalie. You can refer to Obvintsev's profile to find out who that is, since we think he might be the second if he plays, and if his style isn't heavily modified, which admittedly it might be. For the rest of the goalies, everyone's essentially adapted a butterfly style, but we bring this up because Gidlof is a very unique goalie who enters his RVH more than any other goalie we can remember.

This goes back to what we discussed earlier though. He has a specific advantage with how wide he is and how much room he takes up when entering the position, but more importantly it eliminates some of his disadvantages that we also just discussed. If a goalie is entering a RVH position then they aren't relying as heavily on their skating foundation and on their agility.

Let's look at an example together. Say a forward is skating on an angle that sees him cutting wide on Gidlof's defender and he releases a shot at the bottom of one of the circles that's aimed towards the far side in the hopes of generating a rebound that then forces Gidlof to laterally transition. Instead of cutting off the angle by overlapping and remaining square within his set stance, so that he can then transfer into a butterfly, he adapts RVH more often, because it makes it easier on him to be able to laterally push off when needing to transfer across the net in one motion.

Why would he do this? Because Gidlof is at a disadvantage if he chose option one, which was to overlap with his post and rely on his butterfly, since he would then need to rotate his bigger frame and rely more on his skating to quickly re-orient himself and put himself on an angle that then allows the transition. It requires more footwork, and it requires more dexterity. By maintaining the RVH, the very same shot that causes the same rebound would only require a push off from his post and a simultaneous head rotation. it only requires a single motion.

We don't want to give the wrong impression here though. He doesn't use his RVH the entire game, he just does a lot more than any other goalie we have evaluated in recent years. He still moves laterally at a decent rate, it seems he understands his own limitations. We like seeing goalies adapt their games to give themselves advantages dependent on their physical makeup, and that's exactly what we see in the case of Gidlof.

So the question then becomes, can his heavily used RVH style actually hold long term, especially when factoring in how precise NHL shooters are? We don't think so, and that's because NHL shooters are simply too good at picking the right seam, at the right time, on angles he hasn't been exploited on yet. Which means he's going to have to heavily modify his game. The good news is that we think he can get there as long he physically develops.

The primary factor is growth rate. It might come down to his physical growth rate and coordination improvements that are likely to happen as the result of him being such a big kid. He's one of the oldest players in the draft, but he's still just 18 years of age and a mountain of a goalie. If he can develop physically to the point where he doesn't need to rely so heavily on his RVH style of play, then he will be most likely molded and streamlined into a prototypical goalie and therefore becoming less reliant on his RVH. This might be the easiest way for his game to help translate long term but also factors in a variable that's very difficult to project down the road and that's figuring out the end point of his athletic upside.

When evaluating the rest of his skill-set, there's a lot of positives that can be taken from it. We have to weigh his tracking and general reading of the play heavily here considering his size and recovery rate weaknesses. In Gidlof's case, he is consistent at identifying trailer options off of transitional plays, he also recognizes high danger back-door options. Part of this can be attributed to how deep he plays at times due to taking advantage of his enormous frame, and he recognizes during tick-tack-toe setups, where he needs to be in order to get ahead of the play and back out-front of the puck. He's already comfortable looking around screens in both a relaxed and set stance, and his reads on the initial release point or sudden angle shift of a shot are bordering high-end when he's on his game.

Technically speaking, he has very long arms but knows how to position them with a low hands-in-front set stance that keeps him balanced while allowing him a postural advantage where his shoulders are slopped on angle when pucks are in tight on him. He's also surprisingly dextrous within his upper half, especially on his blocker side. The glove has been a bit more hit and miss, but we wouldn't call it a glaring weakness either.

Mentally, Gidlof competes hard, rarely gives up on save attempts despite being at a disadvantage depending on the save type, and shows a lot of poise in tightly contested games.

We like Marcus Gidlof, but he's a very difficult evaluation. There's very few modern day player comps for a massive, blocking style goalie who has adapted such a unique game that's based around his RVH. His growth rate, we think will ultimately determine what he ends up developing into, but admittedly, he showed by the end point of the season, athletic saves that we didn't think were possible when evaluating him earlier on.

Our ranking is based around the risk when looking out how heavily he's going to have to modify his current game, while still being comfortable, and the risk of having to rely so heavily on a growth rate that's very difficult to predict. That said, there is starting potential here and he is a fascinating goalie study for years to come and one we would draft, just not at the top end of what we feel is a deep and under-appreciated class.

"I know a scout who's telling me he's still growing. Sometimes a goalie is too big for his own good. That might be the case here, time will tell." - HP Scout, Brad Allen

"He fits into the last slot of the B range for me. I like him, but it's just so hard to determine his growth rate and how he will ultimately look in 5 years." - HP Scout, Brad Allen

53	PLAYER		TEAM	LEAGUE	HEIGHT	WEIGHT	POS	GRADE
	GILL, SPENCER		RIMOUSKI	QMJHL	6' 03.75"	186	RD	C+
NHLCS	CEILING	FLOOR	HOCKEY SENSE	COMPETE	SKILL		SKATE	MISC
NA-29	6	5	6	5	6		5	6

Spencer Gill is a right-handed two-way defenseman who was selected by the Rimouski Oceanic with the fifth overall pick in the 2022 QMJHL entry draft. He just finished his second season with Rimouski as the highest scoring defenseman on the team, putting up 12 goals and 34 assists in 65 games. While still being a pretty raw prospect and with a young birthday for this draft class, Gill has seen his stock rise in the 2nd half of the season as he finished with 33 points in his last 38 games after getting 18 in his first 32 games which is a notable progression. He also took over and became the go to guy on Rimouski's backend this past season. His older brother Dylan was drafted by Tampa Bay in the 7th round of the 2022 NHL Draft and played the past 4 seasons with Rouyn-Noranda in the QMJHL.

His skating is decent for a bigger player even though he still lacks strength and he's physically immature. While we find that he can be a little heavy on his feet at times and that his edgework might need a little work. That being said, he is pretty quick and can cover a lot of ground with his long stride and his reach. We think when he starts adding more strength to his frame he's going to generate more power into his stride.

Defensively we find that Gill is calm and collected while moving the puck. He does a good job identifying open players while on the breakout and in transition and can deliver accurate passes while in stride. His gap control is good, and we find that he almost never gets overly aggressive on defensive coverage and does a good job at pushing opposing players to the outside. He's not a mean guy to play against but his compete level is fine he's just not overly aggressive physically in front of the net or along the boards.

Offensively we have had some good viewings as well as some bad ones as the year has progressed. We like that on the PP he will choose different approaches and will adapt depending on what the opposing teams PK is giving him. He is able to use little head fakes and such to create some shooting lanes for himself from that QB slot. Improvements in edgework could help him walk the line with more pace and agility. He is not an elite creative offensive player, but he can make the routine plays and can move the puck pretty well in the offensive zone. We also think that he could maybe add a little bit of power on his shot, this will probably come when he adds on a bit more weight, but we think that it would really help him become a threat on the PP. We don't project him as a power play guy for the next level even though his stats in the 2nd half improve.

Gill is a very interesting prospect because he showed a lot of growth as the season went on and seemed to get better with every viewing that we had. He's still raw and has so much more room to improve in all facets of his game which makes his profile an intriguing one for the draft. Because of how reliable he is on the defensive side of the puck and if we project what he could eventually become when he grows into his body, we feel that there is definitely a chance that he could make an NHL roster. Teams at the pro level seem to succeed when they have strong puck-moving defenseman like Gill on their roster. With his combination of size and hockey IQ we think it's a strong possibility that he will hear his name called at some point in the top 4 rounds of the draft.

"Good puck skills. Pretty smart player." – NHL Scout, December 2023

"My issues with him are his skating and he is way too easy to play against." – NHL Scout, April 2024

"I have time for him in the middle rounds." – NHL Scout, May 2024

"I struggled to really like him this year but he's super raw, a 6'04" right defenseman and has a mid-august birthday. He's far from a finished product" – HP Scout Jérôme Bérubé (May 2024)

NR	PLAYER	TEAM	LEAGUE	HEIGHT	WEIGHT	POS	GRADE
	GLAVIC, BOR	HDD JESENICE	SLO JR	6' 04"	192	G	C
NHLCS	CEILING	FLOOR	HOCKEY SENSE	COMPETE	SKILL	SKATE	MISC
-	6	3	5	6	7	5	7

Bor Glavic has left us in a unique position. We've never had to scout or rank a Slovenian goalie who has played in both the Slovenian Jr league and the Slovenian pro league. We've scouted goalies out of the AlpsHL and evaluated goalies playing in lower levels of international competition, but he primarily played in leagues we've never really had to focus on. It's very rare for a 17-year-old goalie to play in the AlpsHL. His last game in the AlpsHL made it apparent as to why; after he let in 3 goals on 6 shots before getting pulled at the beginning of the 2nd, but that game doesn't characterize the consistency he needed just to get called up, and it certainly doesn't characterize the upside.

Glavic is an athletically gifted, reactive, yet raw goaltender who, much like Vladimir Nikitin last season or Arturs Silovs before him, needs a lot of work to potentially play in the show, but he also showed the necessary curve to get a mention. Last season, we watched Glavic in international play, but he looked like a slower, more methodical goalie who lacked the fast twitch, coordination, and power needed at the position.

Fast forward to this past season, and it was apparent that he physically developed. He went from being a slower-moving goalie who couldn't fully extend and take advantage of his length to one that was capable of making lateral-full-extension high-danger saves that required a lot of movement. Not only did his movement and extension rates improve, but so did his reflexes. This meant that he could make point-blank redirect reaction saves that required the opposite half of his body, then the initial direction of the shot intended to travel in. It also meant that he could make more dynamic saves when combining his newfound movement with his fast twitch.

His extensions are very good, but his ability to recover after already being in an extension isn't. He can be susceptible to letting in short area rebound goals after fully extending on the first save, although it's an area that will improve as he continues to physically develop. We think his recovery rates after an extending save top out as roughly average when he becomes a developed adult playing pro hockey.

Typically, Euro goalies who play in lesser junior leagues before transitioning to pro leagues I like the AlpsHL have difficulty tracking through drive-by and set screens, and occasionally just lose the puck due to the amount of congestion in front of them, but Glavic has shown impressive adaptation in his early development. One of the primary reasons for this is how often he manages to keep his head on the same plane throughout his tracking, relative to his body positioning. If he needs to slightly orient and tilt himself while in his set stance to look around a hip-line, he can do it without suddenly moving his head. By keeping his head on a singular plane, it keeps his tracking consistent throughout the release of the shot.

One issue that he needs to correct is his over-reliance on his extensions, since he's a long and tall goalie, as opposed to instinctually or automatically trying to get his frame back out in front of the puck after having to make a sudden transition across his net. We want to see goalies extend, but extend when the shot requires them to; otherwise, we want goalies to make saves look as easy as possible by squaring up functionally, and Glavic can have some difficulty with that. This isn't dissimilar to Silovs in his draft season.

We also mentioned Vladimir Nikitin earlier, and one other similarity Glavic shares with Nikitin is that at the same age, they could just overstep their position and put themselves out of their own net, specifically when they are in a standing overlap position. This made them susceptible to shots that were labeled for the far side of the net and made them susceptible to a shooter capable of faking a shot in tight to the net before rapidly cutting behind the net and trying to tuck it.

One of the main areas of improvement, and it's fundamental to his development, is modifying his skating base so that he physically doesn't get behind the play when dealing with rapid one-touch passing plays that involve multiple players. How he integrates into his post is awkward, but how he transfers to the other is even more awkward. This can be seen in how he transfers from a standing position post-to-post. He often transfers in two motions as opposed to one fluid motion using his edgework, and it means that even though he's not behind the play mentally on swing passing plays, physically he can be. This applies to his T-push offs from a standing position and his lateral transfer rates in his butterfly as well. There's a lot of work to be done with his skating base.

He has a functional butterfly, and his glove hand and blocker hand have both been at least adequate, but we like to be honest in our assessments. Due to the league he was primarily playing in and the international competition he faced, it's extremely difficult to gauge exactly where each element of his game currently is.

The reason we wrote Glavic is because of his curve, starting from last season to the end of this season and his base. He's big, he's athletic, his reflexes are decent, and we think there's enough of a base to mold into potentially a player that has a chance at the NHL one day. Our hesitancy comes from not only the environment he played in but also his sense and anticipation of the play, sometimes failing to keep up with the speed of the game at these lower levels. His anticipation and how he evaluates various high-danger sequences weren't overly consistent when we evaluated past the Slovenian Jr League. The question then becomes, was this a development glitch as a result of him needing additional time to adapt after having success in a bad league, or is it a true stopper? We don't honestly know and we won't know until he either comes over and plays in the CHL or moves up another level full-time overseas. Either way, he's an interesting case study.

"There's uncertainty here around how well he reads the play, due to how slow the leagues he played in are." - HP Scout, Brad Allen

"If he was in the OHL, I think he would fare relatively well and would most likely be a draft as long as he could track the play quickly enough. That said, because of where he played, he might not have had enough eyes on him, but we will see." - HP Scout, Brad Allen

"The version of Bor that I watched in Slovenian U19 hockey, the Slovenian pro league and the U18 level, was a different version than the one I watched in the AlpsHL, at least for the most part. He was more confident and tracked the puck a lot better in those leagues than in the AlpsHL, but he still held at a decent level in the AlpsHL, which at 17-years of age isn't easy to do. In fact, his best performance during the season came against EHC Lustenau in AlpsHL." - HP Scout, Brad Allen

89	PLAYER	TEAM	LEAGUE	HEIGHT	WEIGHT	POS	GRADE
	GOJSIC, HIROKI	KELOWNA	WHL	6' 03"	198	RW	C
NHLCS	CEILING	FLOOR	HOCKEY SENSE	COMPETE	SKILL	SKATE	MISC
NA-63	5	4	5	6	5	6	7

Gojsic played last season in the BCHL on a stacked Penticton team with the Nadeau brothers (Bradley and Josh) and Aydar Sunyev. He didn't get much playing time, but still produced at a decent rate, mostly on their 4th line. This season, he moved to the WHL, joining the Kelowna Rockets. He had a slow start, scoring 4 goals and 9 points in his first 28 games. However, he finished as a point-per-game player for the rest of the season, with 17 goals and 41 points in his last 40 games. In the WHL playoffs, he went scoreless in 11 games, registering only 5 assists. He often played on Tij Iginla's line in the second half of the season, which likely contributed to the improvement in his stats.

Gojsic is large, and his frame projects really well to be a 220 pound power-forward in the future. He has broad, wide shoulders that indicate good possible physical growth. His game projects well to play in the rough areas of the ice, and his play along the wall and in front of the net is solid. At the pro level, we think many of his goals will come from being around the net and in tight. He can screen the goaltender's view, tip pucks, jump on rebounds, and receive passes from teammates at the side of the net. His strength, reach, and frame will help him along the boards to win and maintain possession of the puck with his good puck-protection game. He can also play that power game that translates well to playoff hockey. Over the course of the season, he started showing some pushback in his game, which is encouraging for playing that grinding style at the pro level.

A good skater for his size, his starts could be better, but once he gets going, his speed is quite interesting for a big guy. Any time a player with his size can move like he does, he draws attention from scouts. This adds value to his transitional game and helps him keep pace with his teammates on the ice.

Unfortunately, his biggest weakness also affects his transition game, and not in a good way: his handling skills. This weakens his effectiveness in one-on-one confrontations as well. When a player is one skill away from being a very good prospect, it can be a frustrating thing to see. If Gojsic was a better stickhandler, it would open up things up offensively for him and he would be more than just a net-presence offensive player. With his combination of size and skating, he would be more dangerous off the rush, leading to more shooting opportunities in the offensive zone. His passing game is fine, but nothing too amazing, either. We wish his playmaking from the wall would enable him to create more, because he can extend plays with both his puck-protection game and reach. We love power playmakers (power-forwards that can really pass the puck); unfortunately, this is not what he is. Yes, he can make simple passing plays, but his passing won't be a huge difference-maker on the ice. He has a good shot in terms of velocity (mostly his wrist shot), but he's not a natural goal scorer. We've already mentioned his hands (stickhandling skills) that are lacking a bit, and this decreases some of his value as a goal scorer when projecting him for the NHL.

It's worth noting that this is a player who might be lacking sufficient experience at the junior level. Last year in the BCHL, he was playing around 10 minutes per game, only playing 36 games total. The rawness was evident in his first half of the season, but there was noticeable progress in the second. We think the NHL team that will draft him (most likely in the mid or late rounds) will bet on his progression curve. Their skill coach can get him to improve his stickhandling skills, shooting skills and elevate his passing game to another level.

NR	PLAYER	TEAM	LEAGUE	HEIGHT	WEIGHT	POS	GRADE
	GOLICIC, JAN	GATINEAU	QMJHL	6' 05.25"	188	LD	C
NHLCS	CEILING	FLOOR	HOCKEY SENSE	COMPETE	SKILL	SKATE	MISC
NA-106	5	4	5	5	5	5	7

Golicic is a Slovenian defenseman who played his draft year in the QMJHL with the Gatineau Olympiques. His raw, lanky frame presents a significant amount of projection scouts need to consider. He has considerable physical development ahead of him before he's ready for the professional game. He also had a tough start this year with the Olympiques, who struggled out of the gate. By the end of December he had a -15, and in the 2024 calendar year, he was +11. While this represents quite a big change, it's also a good indication of how much better the Olympiques were after the Christmas break.

Golicic has decent skills for his size in addition to decent footwork and agility, but he'll need to add power to his stride in order to be more explosive on the ice. That could come once he starts filling out his frame to work on his aforementioned lack of strength. His missing explosiveness is on display when forced to use recovery skating in the neutral zone following a turnover, or when he has to change directions quickly while pivoting.

He has decent puck skills, and we prefer his offensive skills to his defensive ones. His ability to move the puck is commendable, and he has demonstrated good passing skills, but there's room for improvement in the velocity of his shot. While we don't project him as a power play guy, his puck distribution skills are respectable. However, he does need to work on his decision-making under pressure. Quick forechecks or retrieving pucks in his own zone can sometimes lead to problematic decision-making.

Defensively, he has a long reach. Combined with his skating skills, he can cover lots of ice. He's been inconsistent with his gap control this season, though. Sometimes it can be really lacking and other times it's on point. He can occasionally lose track of his coverage, unsure of what to do and getting caught puck-watching. One of the biggest issues with his play in his zone is that he's too passive on the ice. We understand that he's still physically raw and that those one-on-one battles will improve with added strength, but overall, we do see a lack of pushback from him. He occasionally throws a decent hit along the boards, but there's no mean streak there. That can become an issue when projecting his overall defensive game for the next level.

Given that we don't foresee his game translating to becoming a power play specialist in the NHL, his defensive skills would need to be exceptional for him to be a big, mobile shutdown defenseman. However, he's far from meeting that standard. It's tough to project him due to his rawness, but we've observed improvement this season. Another significant step in his development within the next year could lead to more clarity regarding his projection. As of now, his rawness and lack of physicality stop us from ranking him aggressively.

NR	PLAYER		TEAM	LEAGUE	HEIGHT	WEIGHT	POS	GRADE
	GRANBERG, DAVID		LULEA JR	SWE JR	6' 01"	185	LC	C
NHLCS	CEILING	FLOOR	HOCKEY SENSE	COMPETE	SKILL		SKATE	MISC
-	5	3	6	5	6		6	6

David Granberg is a two-way, playmaking center with high end technical passing. He had a massive spike in production, going from 5 points in 20 games at the J20 Nationell level in his initial draft season, to 47 points in 40 regular season games this past season. His play gave him more than a cup of coffee with Lulea's main team in the SHL, where he went pointless in 16 games.

There's three mental attributes that come together to form Granberg's attack; which are his poise, his vision, and his timing. These attributes work in unison to open up the entire length of the offensive zone. His mental mapping is high-end and it resulted in some beautiful primary assists that featured feathered saucer passes directly on the tape to his teammates. He can be a creative playmaker as well, using his own triangle to his advantage when needing to pivot or rotate while simultaneously passing a puck to avoid contact.

His playmaking helps give his teammates advanced shooting options more often when he is out on the ice. He has a creative nuance to how he sets up a lot of his offensive plays and that's led to him having impressive transitional rates at the U20 level in some of our viewings.

He's an adaptive thinker and a situational feeler of the game, who rarely counteracts his own playmaking windows by rushing his options. It comes to timing, and an understanding of how to look off his options. He's usually aware of where his teammates are going to skate into space and he is adept at suddenly stopping up to readjust his lanes when under pressure.

There are some very talented players in this draft that generate offensive plays through forced passes and hope passes at times. Meaning, passes that are the result of spinning off of pressure blind. Yet, David has a reduced rate of these attempts, making him a more efficient playmaker in most of our viewings. His handling compliments his playmaking as well, where he can generate quality passing plays at the end phases of his dekes.

His playmaking translation is critical for his game since If he wasn't an advanced playmaker, he would have limited fallback options. We view him more as a single threat player at this stage of his development.

His skating base from a visual perspective and mechanical perspective reminds us a bit of Jett Luchenko's. Granberg doesn't project to be as good a skater and lacks Luchenko's explosive, fast-twitch skating. Despite Granberg being a year older, like Luchenko, there's still a lot of room for to fill out so he can take advantage of his deep stride.

He uses his anticipation off the puck and natural center instincts to position himself relatively well, and we've seen him make some high end defensive reads which have counteracted opponents in tight to the net. He's not the most physical player and he's not going to overwhelm most players, but he has a good sense of when he should try and push on players to throw them off balance during scrums, or during supporting wall plays when he's trying to acquire a puck. That said, he still needs to get functionally stronger so he can fight through checks better than he currently does, and so that he has an increase in his current acceleration out of the gate so that he can separate easier than he currently does.

Granberg put together a quality season, and maybe even you could label it an unexpected one. He became an impact player for Lulea and stood out enough to force our hand into writing him up. There are modern day playmaking elements to his game that should translate. His translation is largely going to come down to his physical growth-rate and how much more consistent he can become at generating his dynamic passing plays. He's more of a spurt offensive performer at this time, but there's an interesting center base to work with here. That said, he's still a long shot, which is reflected in our rankings.

NR	PLAYER	TEAM	LEAGUE	HEIGHT	WEIGHT	POS	GRADE
	GREEN, DAVID	ST. MICHAELS	OJHL	6'01.25"	197	LD	NI
NHLCS	CEILING	FLOOR	HOCKEY SENSE	COMPETE	SKILL	SKATE	MISC
NA-122	5	5	6	5	6	6	6

David Green is a two-way defenseman who is more offensively inclined and put up a good amount of points this season for the St. Michael's Buzzers in the OJHL. Green posted 57 points in 56 games for the Buzzers and added 9 points in 11 playoff games. His strong production was highlighted by good offensive instincts, however despite the production he was underwhelming with his compete level and strength.

As a defender he can be too aggressive at times in coverage and can be inconsistent as a rush defender. On breakouts, he leaves a lot to be desired as he has trouble getting the puck consistently out of his zone and up to his forwards. He does not have great speed to carry the puck out himself and his breakout passes do not often lead his forwards into the offensive zone or give them good potential rush opportunities.

In the offensive zone he makes good decisions with the puck and distributes it well from the point. He is patient from the point and gets off his shot with a smooth release through traffic and uses the aggression that hurts him defensively to his advantage offensively with his ability to create offensive quickly from high to low. He also played well as a puck distributer on the power play and created scoring opportunities with his offensive vision.

Next season Green will have the choice to stay in the OJHL with the Buzzers or move on to the USHL and the Green Bay Gamblers.

15	PLAYER	TEAM	LEAGUE	HEIGHT	WEIGHT	POS	GRADE
	GREENTREE, LIAM	WINDSOR	OHL	6'02.5"	215	LW	A
NHLCS	CEILING	FLOOR	HOCKEY SENSE	COMPETE	SKILL	SKATE	MISC
NA-14	8	5	6	5	8	5	7

Liam Greentree is a dynamic dual-threat, heavy-set winger who plays a finesse style of hockey. He captained an overwhelmed and often overmatched Windsor team, where he led his team in production with 90 points in 64 games, including 36 goals. The way Liam operates is unique, both making him very dangerous and at times very frustrating. We'll do our best to break down the pros and cons of how he operates.

Greentree is one of the most talented players in this class and can seemingly make any play in any given moment. As just some examples, we've watched him rush end-to-end, while bypassing multiple opponents using his handling before backhanding a shot far-side with less than two minutes remaining with his team down to tie a game. We've watched him stop up under pressure after receiving a bad pass in the neutral zone only to effortlessly pivot while simultaneously doing a crossbody drag, which he extended into a weakside backhand saucer pass through layered traffic to his teammate that landed directly on the tape. We've also seen him score explosive goals from distance after using advanced feints at the offensive line to get himself in position at the top of the circles. He's one of only a handful of prospects that you could grade having exceptional handling, shooting and passing ability.

Greentree's deception, coordination, and dexterity translate into his shooting mechanics. He can seamlessly transfer his footwork, through his core rotation, and into his extension. In real time, this makes for a very fast release point and one that's difficult to pick up. Furthermore, he's good at recognizing how to use his hands to manipulate his shooting angle and can time his shot with extended windows when he's delaying his release. He can catch and release in one motion off the rush but he can also generate from stationary positions.

The other differentiating quality in his shot, is his synchronous hand activation. His top hand drives so much force downward through his release, and it's met by his bottom hand which creates a tremendous amount of whip at the upward point of his extension. There's a beautiful blend of coordination and dexterity

He's also one of the more dangerous shooters on his backhand. He can elevate the puck in tight and he generates a lot of torque. This makes him very difficult to read at times, since he has so many options when evaluating when and where to place a shot, since he can rapidly rotate from his forehand to his backhand and vice versa.

His comfort level on his backhand, extends to his playmaking as well. His primary assist rates are very good, and he's actually had some of the most impressive primary assists on his backhand we've seen from any prospect this season. He typically likes to use static, and hesitation off-looks to set up his passing plays and this makes it difficult to recognize his intentions. He can also thread passes with a remarkable level of precision that you typically see in smaller skilled forwards.

Taken together, Greentree has as many offensive options as the very top end players in this class and when you look at his improved skating and size combination, it paints the picture of a prospect that realistically should be close to blue-chip, but we don't think he is. In-fact we think you could make the argument that he's one of the most perplexing and at times frustrating players we've scouted this season. He has all the tools but the tool-box is scattered and jumbled.

It starts with how Greentree fundamentally operates. Elite offensive forwards are efficient and understand when and how to take risk into consideration when generating offensive plays. You typically want to see forwards try low percentage, high danger plays if the play actually calls for it. In Liam's case, although he's gifted on his backhand, he looks to operate on his backhand almost to a fault.

What this means is that when there's a short area, efficient, and safer option on his forehand, instead of taking that option, he will instead extend his handling play, lose the easy option then try a much lower percentage backhand pass through multiple layers of traffic instead. He wants to be a human highlight-reel, and we appreciate his level of talent for being able to pull it off, but you don't want to see him default to what you could call the three-point play. This is something he shared with Trevor Zegras, and it's something that has always bothered us with Zegras, despite us ranking Zegras as high as we did.

Another issue is that he looks to over-handle and extend possession, operating in a vacuum when first receiving a pass in the offensive zone. Again, he is capable of dynamic passing plays and he does have good vision, but his initial phase of attack is largely predicated on the idea of him operating with his own window, as opposed to the windows of space and time that are actually being afforded to him.

This might sound slightly confusing so let's break it down in simpler terms. He rarely rushes his options, instead he consistently over extends them, and through this over extension, he can run himself into bad areas of the ice and take away a far more efficient and safer play as a result. This isn't some sort of once in a while evaluation either. This is a consistent issue on a game to game basis.

We were hoping to see him address this issue over the course of the season. That hasn't happened. He doesn't play with structure and he doesn't understand why a simple and effective play can be the better play on a lot of sequences.

He's not a dumb hockey player though. Dumb hockey players can't generate the advanced and creative offensive plays that he can make and he can react very quickly to incoming pressure. What it means is that he's lacking a system right now that can help make him as functional as he needs to be in order to successfully translate his game. One might argue it's been enabled.

Another issue with Greentree is that despite being a bigger kid with physical advantages, he largely plays the game like he's a smaller forward. We wish he played with power elements so we could refer to him as a hybrid forward but he looks to use open area handling, rarely protecting the puck with his length or with his frame. He doesn't look to use his frame to cut through the hands of opposing players, he rarely uses his frame to drive into opposing players so that he can further enhance his space, and we haven't seen him react correctly to resistance in general. We want to see him dominate physically when the play calls for it, and he doesn't do that nearly enough as of this writing.

Although he's a gifted offensive player, there's a lot of work to be done off the puck as well. He's willing to attempt to defend, he just doesn't know how to do it yet. This can be seen when he's attempting to switch with his defenseman during transitional plays in his own end and when he needs to cover and support down-low. There's a lack of understanding how to stick-lift and press properly, and he doesn't know how to use his frame effectively yet along the walls when trying to get the puck. Which goes back to our above point about playing smaller than his size.

The last trait that has us slightly concerned is his inability to seem dialled in as often as we would like. When he's playing up to his ability, Greentree is an offensive force on the ice, but he has a tendency to play down to his opponents and not dominate or dictate in the way his skills suggest he can. This was evident not only throughout the season but at the U18's, where he underwhelmed.

The offensive ability and the technical skillset is there, the ability to use it seamlessly at a consistent rate through the entirety of the offensive zone isn't. Neither is the 200-foot game.

Liam Greentree is a rare player though. He comes with a good frame, a lethal shot, and advanced handling seen in much smaller players. He's adept at incorporating deception into his attack and the raw elements can be refined over time. In any given sequence, he has that "wow' factor to him, which as a scout, immediately makes you think about his potential down the line.

One of the most difficult aspects of scouting is taking risk into consideration, relative to the upside of the player. In the case of Greentree, he presents some risk. He doesn't play the game the way he needs to right now in order to be an impact player at the NHL level. We think he can get there if his game is refined and he's put in a system which forces him to play the right way more often. Greentree presents as a top-6 forward who can generate a ton of points for a team, but there's a lot of variables to work through in order for that to materialize, which is why he's a bit further down the list than his talent level suggests.

"Plenty of talent but I'm not a fan of his lazy play and his defensive game needs a ton of work." – NHL Scout, November 2023

"Love his skill and offensive instincts." – NHL Scout, November 2023

"Explosiveness isn't good." – NHL Scout, November 2023

"His skating is ok with the exception of his first few steps." – NHL Scout, November 2023

"Skating is confusing. At times it looks sluggish and then another shift he is blowing passed someone winning a puck race." – NHL Scout, December, 2023

"Skating is an obvious weakness but I'm more concerned about how inconsistent his effort level is from game to game." - NHL Scout, December 2023

"His attention to detail in the D-zone is poor. He won't get in a shooting lane either." - NHL Scout, December 2023

"F***. I don't get him. No clue if he will boom or bust." - NHL Scout, December 2023

"He has zero help on that garbage team and still posted all those points. He's a top 15 pick." - NHL Scout, February 2024

"When he wants to play he looks like a top 10 pick but that happens about every fourth viewing for me. In the other games he can look like a mid rounder." - NHL Scout, February 2024

"I had him higher on my list in the first half of the season but dropped him a bit as the second half moved along. He is still in my top 20." - NHL Scout, May 2024

"I have an issue with his work ethic at times." - NHL Scout, May 2024

"I can't figure him out so I keep watching video of him and after each video I ask myself how did he get so many f***ing points?" - NHL Scout, May 2024

"One of the hardest players for me to evaluate based on sheer talent, relative to the bust potential." - HP Scout, Brad Allen

"Looks like he had a good off season. Seems to have improved his skating." HP Scout, Mark Edwards, October 2023

"He's not physical and that bothers me. For me you're not a power forward if you don't play physical." - HP Scout, Mark Edwards, January 2024

"Incredibly talented player. He has some warts in his game but the good news is that those warts are fixable. The difficult part for scouts is knowing if the player will be willing to fix the weaknesses." - HP Scout, Mark Edwards, January 2024

"If there is one player from the OHL that scares me a bit to rank too high it's Greentree. I saw him look like a top 5 pick at times and on other nights he didn't even look like you would want him on your AHL team. There was very little consistency." - HP Scout, Mark Edwards, June 2024

25	PLAYER		TEAM	LEAGUE	HEIGHT	WEIGHT	POS	GRADE
	GRIDIN, MATVEI		MUSKEGON	USHL	6'01.5"	189	LW	B
NHLCS	CEILING	FLOOR	HOCKEY SENSE	COMPETE	SKILL		SKATE	MISC
NA-21	8	3	7	4	8		6	6

Matvei Gridin had a USHL season for the ages. Since the USHL became a Tier I junior league in 2002-03, only two first-year, draft eligible players had put up better numbers than Gridin's 83 point campaign this year (Matt Coronato 85, Taylor Cammarata 93); his 38 goals is the second highest mark behind Coronato's 48 goal season in 2021. Gridin might be the most technically skilled player in the USHL. He has gamebreaking ability from the off wing and he has improved the balance with which he attacks. If nothing else from his game materializes, Gridin's release on his wrist and snap shots might be enough to carry him a large chunk of the way. The puck explodes off his blade consistently. Additionally, Gridin has gotten better at making pre-shot adjustments with his feet to position himself to just catch and release or one-time pucks from any angle. These minor adjustments have allowed him to be more dangerous, as it doesn't allow the defense or goaltenders any time to adjust while he dusts the puck off. He made a nice living for himself at the bottom of the right circle ripping shots short-side high. But he's not a one-trick pony, he has scored a fair variety of goals in many situations this season. Between his release and his understanding of his blade's shooting angles, he's a threat from anywhere inside the house to any part of the net.

As mentioned, the pre-shot adjustments have been a great advent to his scoring process…but even before that, his commitment to weakside rotation plays stands out as a positive. It's easy to question his mental game because of his lack of compete and often that can trick viewers into thinking a player is unintelligent. Really focusing on what his eyes are seeing and what his stimulus is for movement (economical, as it may be) shines a light on his hockey sense and helps to separate it from his low-level competitive spirit. Matvei has markedly improved his feel for weakside rotation plays, both as a finisher and a passer. His playmaking game has improved a good deal from where it was at the beginning of the season. There are less "hope" passes and much more intentionality to his attack zone passing game – better timing, better accuracy. His off the puck movement puts him in position for some high quality shooting opportunities. That said, this movement does tend to be towards the outer boundaries of the house. Things like slash support or dives to the far post are not readily part of his scoring or setup process.

The huge shadow that's cast upon Gridin is his low compete level. He generally plays to the beat of his own drummer. Though there has been some minor flashes in this regard as the season has gone along, it's still a glaring issue. Naturally, this bald spot shows up most obviously in his defensive game. A recent example is in game 2 of the Eastern Conference Final vs. Dubuque. With Muskegon down 3-0 early in the 2nd period, Gridin is coming down to pick up the weak side guy at the far post who is all alone (so there is recognition of the play that is supposed to be made). All the Lumberjacks are on the strong side and they're a bit discombobulated. The Dubuque player on the far post gets the pass and initial shot away and the goalie makes a terrific save. The puck comes back to that same player while the goalie is in a scramble…the player brings the puck to his forehand (towards the interior of the rink)…and Gridin, just now getting to him, goes to the outside/backhand side of the shooter and then just cruises around behind the net as Dubuque makes it 4-0. This disinterest is littered throughout his game: he rarely will stop on anything, even if it's a loose puck for offensive purposes…he's very unlikely to put the brakes on to go back and get it; he generally forechecks from the boards/outside back into the interior; he routinely flies the zone even if it doesn't appear the Lumberjacks are likely to recover the puck in their own zone; he pops up fairly randomly in his weak-side winger role and in their neutral zone forecheck formation; etc. He does penalty kill sometimes, but even that feels like a situation where it's more for the chance at a breakaway than anything else fundamentally advantageous.

His skating is another aspect of his game that can be tough to read because of his lack of effort. He has a short stride and his lack of extension seems to be killing his top speed. He has looked quicker and more agile in the second half of the year – a little bit stronger overall too. He's listed at 6'1", 182 pounds right now and doesn't look quite as thin or wobbly as he did in the first couple weeks of the season. The bloodlines are decent as well, his father was an Olympic cross-country skier. There's a decent stride hidden in there – in game 1 of the playoffs vs. Green Bay he beat everyone from his own zone on a shorthanded breakaway, got stopped by the goalie, retrieved the puck in the corner, and wheeled a dime to the trailer for a very important 3rd period goal. But playing fast and being fast doesn't just happen, of course, a player has to want to play fast. Right now, there's some pop, some quality edge work, and even a decent glide, but until he's more engaged in what he's doing, the speed will remain a question mark.

One area where he's really smooth is his puckhandling, he's a dangerous 1 on 1 player. His pass catching radius and ability to skill chain make him a threat off the rush. While he is elusive enough to beat the first forechecker with regularity, he's not as effective starting a rush. It's better if he's in motion, especially coming up the weakside. The success and conversion of a zone entry with that method is far more promising than him kicking it off. He doesn't have the same expansive puck control window as teammate Sacha Boisvert, but he's much more dynamic than Boisvert and much less prone to getting blown up in the process. Gridin has improved his ability to look off shots and turn them into cross net-line passes, which is a huge piece to add towards making him a truly balanced attacker instead of just a pure, mid-range sniper. His passing game is far from perfect though, and is very much still in its developmental phase. We'd like to see more puck poise in traffic. Sometimes in congested areas, he'll unnecessarily rush a puck out the door into a worse situation or with a degree of inaccuracy that kills the momentum of the play. Is he willing to truly cycle the puck along the boards and be patient enough to let a play like that develop? Even that's a little unclear at this point and might be part of the next wave of playmaking to improve upon. But not only is that a playmaking piece, but it's also about being competitive for the puck. There was an early season game where the puck was in the corner, and the opposing defender lost his stick in his own defensive corner. The defender resorted to kicking the puck up the wall, then up the side boards, and Gridin is just watching him do this. He didn't make a play to force that defender to make a mistake or panic or – most likely – give the puck away to a stick-enabled Gridin. That "edge" (liberally applied) needs to get from 0 to 1 to make this all work.

If the compete gets from 3ish to 5ish, there's a lot of technical skill, there's deception, there's going to be an NHL caliber shot, there's going to be cross-ice playmaking exploits, on a projectable skating framework. Gridin can absolutely be an impact NHL winger if he buys into the notion.

"Ridiculous talent. Not sure about his effort level though. It's kinda spotty." NHL Scout, October 2023

"In a draft class where so many players have potentially fatal flaws, Gridin is a player that has all the tools. He's producing at an insane rate and he barely breaks a sweat. If he starts trying even a little bit, he's a big steal..." HP Scout, Michael Farkas

"His hockey sense and his skill are going to get him to another level." – NHL Scout, December 2023

"I think Arthur Kaliyev competed harder than Gridin." – NHL Scout, March 2024

"My fave Russian. He is really good." – NHL Scout, March 2024

"If you take him in the right spot and have good culture he could end up being a steal." – NHL Scout, March 2024

"I love him. One of the smartest players in the whole draft class and high end skill. I'd have bad body language too if I made the plays that he does and they died after they left my stick. Wait until he gets some talent around him and see what he does." – NHL Scout, March 2024

"Not hard to evaluate...has all the talent in the world but when you watch him you wonder if he will ever play. Too talented not to draft him at some point but some team will take him way before I will." – NHL Scout, March 2024

"That kid's got some talent but he does infuriate me with his lack of compete and body language on the ice. He's one of those guys that I might regret not putting him higher on my list in a few years though" – HP Scout Jérôme Bérube, April 2024

"I only spoke to one scout who didn't at least note his low effort level or poor body language along with his high end skill. A lot are scared off a bit despite the ridiculous talent." – HP Scout, Mark Edwards, March 2024

"Very long discussions about him in our final meetings. One of our scouts has him as an 'A' player and is willing to draft him inside the top 20 despite the inconsistent work ethic, the rest of us pushed him down our list a bit more. Tough player to rank because he's a really high end talent but body language and compete were issues." – HP Scout, Mark Edwards, May 2024

"Told scouts (combine) he was pissed off he had to go to the USHL because he always wanted to play in the CHL. So it might get interesting to see where he plays next season." – HP Scout, Mark Edwards, June 2024

"Good interview reports from the combine so that's nice to hear." – HP Scout, Mark Edwards, June 2024

NR	PLAYER	TEAM	LEAGUE	HEIGHT	WEIGHT	POS	GRADE
	GROENEWOLD, ELLIOTT	CEDAR RAPIDS	USHL	6'01.5"	200	LD	C

NHLCS	CEILING	FLOOR	HOCKEY SENSE	COMPETE	SKILL	SKATE	MISC
NA-66	5	5	6	6	3	7	7

Physical, defensive defenseman. Elliott Groenewold isn't a big point producer, as evidenced by his 5+11=16 line in his first 57 USHL games. But on a team that had no full time defensemen in plus territory, Groenewold's minus-1 rating on a team that really struggled, especially down the stretch, isn't terrible. Keeping the puck out of his own net is where the 6'2", 200 pound rearguard's strength lies. His frame sits on an excellent skating base. He has a powerful, fluid stride, razor sharp edges, and wonderful lateral mobility. From a standing start, he can generate enough power to leave a leveraged F1 in his wake at times. Really good stride extension and hip mobility. To help with his combative nature, he also has really good balance and overall hockey strength. One of the rarer traits for defensive players (forwards or defensemen) to have so early in their careers is this "defensive viscosity" – the ability to really stick to their opponent while disrupting their path and disabling their hands – and Groenewold shows signs of having it already. He's rangy, physical, and has a strong stick defensively. He's upper tier in terms of box outs and walling off. He's really tough to play against in the lowest layer of his defensive zone, but generally doesn't run around chasing violence. There are a couple instances where players have snuck behind him while he's a little puck-focused out-high, but it's not an epidemic.

His puck skills, on the other hand, are very low-end. He just isn't a good puck handler and despite his ability to sort of separate the top half of his body from the lower half, he's not a consistently good pass receiver – typically the aforementioned "separation" or independent rotation allow for seamless pass acceptance opportunities, but that's not the case here. Pucks leak into his triangle on pass-catch situations and it causes a re-adjustment and his eyes have to go down, it pours cold water on a play too often. We've seen him use his wheels to push down the wall on a pinch, but the conversion of those plays was limited by his poor vision and subpar passing ability. Some of his passes really poked holes in his hockey sense as the year wore on. Some were so telegraphed that it's tough to explain them away as "technical experimentation" or something categorically similar. The numbers don't really bear it out, but he actually prefers to put pucks on net from the point rather than even making simple hi-lo passes. The shot is not threatening even from mid-range. So overall, this is not going to be a point producer certainly, but if he can get his breakout passing up to a certain level, there's enough defensive gumption to play. He's off to Quinnipiac which produced a similar but smaller version of this player with Connor Clifton.

98	PLAYER	TEAM	LEAGUE	HEIGHT	WEIGHT	POS	GRADE
	GUSTAFSSON, VIGGO	HV71 JR.	SWE JR	6' 02"	187	LD	C

NHLCS	CEILING	FLOOR	HOCKEY SENSE	COMPETE	SKILL	SKATE	MISC
INT-72	5	4	5	6	5	6	6

Gustafsson is one of the youngest players in this draft class (born September 11th, 2006) and played the last season with HV71 in the Swedish junior league. He also played in various international tournaments but missed the Hlinka-Gretzky tournament in August due to injury.

He made some good progress this year with passing skills and decision-making. In the first half of the season, some of his decisions were problematic, but he did clean this up a bit in the 2nd half. Now he's moving pucks out of his zone faster, and has cut down on bad passes and turnovers. Also, his hands have improved (or should we say, his puck confidence has). He's a lot more comfortable handling pucks, and he's not afraid to try to beat players one-on-one with his hands in his zone, in transition or the offensive zone. He has a lot more confidence, which is a good sign for the future if he keeps improving. However, we don't project him as a PP1 guy. If he keeps improving his puck game, there's some chance he could find his way to PP2, but at this point, it's not a bet we would make. Considering his age in this draft class and the fact that he has a lot of development ahead, it's not something impossible, either.

He's a good skater who still needs to add more explosiveness to his stride, but it's smooth with his good agility and footwork. He started using his skating more and more to create some offense in the 2nd half of the season. There are some good deception skills to his game when retrieving pucks, and with his newly-improved stickhandling skills, we saw some good uses of his edges when manipulating defenders trying to counter him.

When defending, he can cover a good amount of ice with his lateral agility and reach. He also has a good gap and can defend well against the rush (most of the time, as real high-end skaters can expose and exploit his lack of explosiveness). He has good size, can play a physical game in his zone, and there is some pushback to his game.

At 5 days away from being 2025 draft-eligible, he has plenty of time to continue to improve his skills and get physically stronger. We already saw some good improvement in the 2nd half of the season that gives us some good hope for the future. That is a positive sign and one reason you could see a team use a selection on him: his age and the untapped potential that he has.

40	PLAYER		TEAM	LEAGUE	HEIGHT	WEIGHT	POS	GRADE
	HAGE, MICHAEL		CHICAGO	USHL	6' 00.5"	190	RC	B
NHLCS	CEILING	FLOOR	HOCKEY SENSE	COMPETE	SKILL		SKATE	MISC
NA-10	7	4	5	5	7		7	5

Puck carrying forward. Michael Hage rebounded after a slow start – in part, due to returning from a serious injury that ended his 2022-23 season and sadly, due to a family tragedy. He finished fourth in the USHL in points with 75 in 54 games. Unlike in recent years, this Chicago Steel team was basically a one-line show (with Mick Thompson and Charlie Major) and Hage was the biggest help to the Steel sneaking into the last playoff spot.

Hage uses a strong combination of puckhandling, skating, and deception to make him one of the best multi-line puck carriers in the USHL. One really unique aspect to Hage's game is his overall window of control. He has a wide skating base, he has a fairly wide puck control window, and boasts one of the largest pass-catch windows (maybe the largest) in the U.S. region. This creates a real problem, particularly for less rangy defensemen. It makes Hage tough to pin down when he's moving at speed. Despite perhaps below average playmaking vision, he doesn't take a ton of heavy contact. Also, despite his propensity for multi-line puck carries, there's a lot of waste that comes along with this. Naturally, not every rush opportunity generates a scoring chance but it's the process in which Hage goes about attempting to convert these that raises a red flag about their scalability. In our data sample, about 50% of his zone entries were either turned over or lost (and potentially recovered) in the proceeding sequence…compared to only about 25% that resulted in him passing the puck to a teammate to extend the play. One other noteworthy piece about the data is that two-thirds of his three-line carries resulted in a turnover shortly after he crossed the line, while only about one-quarter of his one- and two-line carries suffered the same fate. Naturally, there are other circumstances that are more likely to be involved with the shorter carries as they may have been sudden change situations off of a steal or cross-ice, weakside passes from teammates, etc. that generally produce better outcomes anyhow. But the overall lack of vision and creative passing on these rushes is a concern. We see this match up with his primary assist sample as well: over one-third of his primary assists are rebound goals, but none of them have the characteristics of a pass-off-pads scenario. The scalability of a player skating down the length of the ice on the perimeter and trying to shoot to score is very low, and Hage doesn't have the ability to be a likely exception to that.

His shot release is fairly slow for a player of his skill level and his velocity is only above average or so. He is really good with his angle change shooting. This allowed him a lot of goals from the top of the circles and outside the dots this season. There's a lot of pull and drag action to freeze defenders and elude goalies. Still, the distance that a lot of these goals were scored from is a bit worrying. But we certainly don't want to dismiss all goals from distance as "junior goals", as some of them had positive timing and far-post or far hip placement. On the plus side, this is a player that showed a willingness to take pucks to the net off the rush and there is at least some consistency in his attack zone movement that sees him land at the far post. His finishing moves in close don't move the needle, unfortunately, but his give-and-go play in the house can be notably good. His rush play would probably be more effective if he would stop up in certain spots and demonstrate some tempo control, but he is decidedly not a start and stop player.

Michael certainly has the skating base to be effective in all facets. Quality posture and a fluid stride on a 6-foot frame. He has a lot to offer in his change-of-direction skating and edges. He leans off his center line well to offer some pressure on defenders and some puck protection ability on his outside hip. He still can get knocked off his skates a fair bit, but part of that might be his overall lack of engagement. As mentioned prior, he rarely takes a lot of heavy contact on rushes – and that's true – but part of is because he's on the outside a lot for a center. He rarely is first in line for loose change as he doesn't support the puck very well unless the play is clearly funnelling towards the net.

Defensively, he'll skate towards an already-marked player that's clearly not in his zone of control and will attack the wrong shoulder of a player well within his grasp and let him off the hook. There's just a lot of details missing from his game that add up pretty quick. His spatial awareness isn't super sharp either. Watching him attempt to negotiate zone exits via the pass is a real mixed bag and often results in some puzzlingly inaccurate passes. He just doesn't feel like a natural playmaker; we think he projects more as a streak-and-score winger by way of his style and thought process…but then we go back to his lack of high-end finishing ability and makes him tough to place. Multi-line puck carriers are worth their weight in gold, so it's important not to ignore that aspect. The technical skill here is worth a long look, even if it's a little unclear how it translates to the pro game right now. He's not a day 1 pick for us because of that.

"He's a tough evaluation. Not sure if his hockey sense is poor or if he is just still too green. I'm really struggling with him. He's too high on all the lists though in my opinion." – NHL Scout, March 2024

"I have Boisvert ahead of him because Hage is top six or bust and I'm leaning it will be bust. I think Boisvert is an absolute lock for bottom six. Hage is actually outside my top 35." – NHL Scout, May 2024

"He's categorically similar to Trevor Connelly, but a lesser version…he either wakes up and becomes a second liner or he completely fails out." – HP Scout, Michael Farkas

"There's some Brad Lambert in him with how good he's in transition" – HP Scout Jérôme Bérubé March 2024

"I empathize with Hage. My dad passed away at a young age as well, so I know it's a massive task for him to stay focused in a situation like that. Makes gauging his season extremely difficult." – HP Scout, Brad Allen, May 2024

"I first saw him in his OHL Draft year. Those are probably still my fave viewings I've had of him. Really talented player though." – HP Scout, Mark Edwards, December 2023

"I heard Rico Fata mentioned from three different scouts from three different teams. It blew me away. Basically the premise being his feet being faster than the brain could process." - HP Scout, Mark Edwards, March 2024

45	PLAYER	TEAM	LEAGUE	HEIGHT	WEIGHT	POS	GRADE
	HE, KEVIN	NIAGARA	OHL	5' 11.25"	181	LW	C+

NHLCS	CEILING	FLOOR	HOCKEY SENSE	COMPETE	SKILL	SKATE	MISC
NA-78	6	4	6	5	7	8	6

A high energy winger who propelled himself up the draft rankings with a strong second half of the season. A natural goal scorer, He potted 31 goals and 53 points in 64 games for the Niagara IceDogs this past season. While the scoring is great, He also displayed an energizer bunny like vigour on the ice with hits and hard forechecks and backchecks.

After scoring 21 goals as a rookie, He continued his scoring pace in Niagara for his sophomore season but that was not the only portion of his game that improved. At times last season, He was passive and not too aggressive, but by the end of the season He was stepping up to make hits and playing a much-improved game. We do want more consistency on the other side of the ice, but he does get back to the zone quickly and can use his speed defensively to break up plays and turn them into offensive opportunities the other way.

The speed in his game is an integral part of his success and is used to create strong offensive rushes. He is one of the best in the OHL's draft class in his ability to create offense on the rush.t. He does not have the most traditional release to his shot, but it is quick and effective with the potential to make him a goal scorer at the NHL level. He will need to make himself more versatile as an offensive player which with his physical ability he should be able to do. There is already the willingness to play in a more powerful way offensively, but he will need to be more consistent and not fall back on his more reliable finesse and quick shooting game and continue building upon the power game.

As a whole, He plays a hard and quick game that can translate well to the NHL in a middle six and secondary scoring position. He will need to work on being more discipline while staying aggressive. His speed and great release to his shot in addition to his effort level should help him in filling a role on the power play and in being a good rush attacker should he continue his progression as a scorer and an energetic forward.

"He isn't on my list." - NHL Scout, November 2023

"He hasn't shown me enough so far." - NHL Scout, November 2023

"Might be a late pick.. Poor kid is stuck in hell in Niagara." - NHL Scout, November 2023

"Playing much better. He was the best player on the ice by a mile when I saw him recently." - NHL Scout, December 2023

"He's a 5th to 7th round guy on my list." - NHL Scout, February 2024

"My early views of Kevin were very average. Some excellent flashes but I didn't feel like he ever put together a good full game. My last few viewings of him were as if I was watching a different player. He turned up his compete level to another level. He was the best player on the ice in my final viewing of him. I put on some video after that." - HP Scout, Mark Edwards, April 2024

"Inconsistent work ethic but he has some speed and is skilled. He grew on me late in the year as a player that has a chance. " - HP Scout, Mark Edwards, May 2024

13	PLAYER	TEAM	LEAGUE	HEIGHT	WEIGHT	POS	GRADE
	HELENIUS, KONSTA	JUKURIT	FIN	5' 11"	189	RC	A

NHLCS	CEILING	FLOOR	HOCKEY SENSE	COMPETE	SKILL	SKATE	MISC
INT-3	7	7	8	8	7	6	5

Konsta Helenius can be characterized as a natural playmaking centre who plays with an edge, while offering a good amount of agility and craftiness, but also suffers from inconsistency within his finishing ability. Helenius's biggest asset is his playmaking ability. His maturity was on display this season, which found him playing in Liiga where he accumulated 36 points in 51 regular season games, before stepping up in the playoffs and finishing point per game with 6 points in 5 games.

Konsta is a gifted passer, who can routinely make high end passes while at half and full speed. Much of his success as a playmaker is due to his ability to fluidly move through all three zones, while baiting a level of pressure or attention that he's able to handle, in order to open up options.

Helenius can see the ice very well. Both at even-strength, and on the powerplay, he looks to become the F1 carrying option before making backhand lateral passes, and crisp, accurate saucer passes that have the right trajectory in order to hit the tape. He's also effective at making himself an available passing option while keeping his hips open to set up the next pass; which further enhances his give and go sequences or sequences that require quick one touch passes while still in stride. Within his playmaking, there's a high level of deceptive look offs and skating fakes, to keep opponents guessing as he attempts to set up his teammates. He makes clean, hard passes under pressure and is able to use his agility and shiftiness to buy the extra second he needs to open up a passing lane in congested areas of the ice.

Despite being a gifted puck handler, Helenius can be largely ineffective at rapidly dragging his puck back into his frame before extending through his wrist shot, and this decreases his ability to suddenly change his shooting angle. If there was one reason why he didn't score as often off the rush as he should have been able to, it was due to this mechanical error. He would be overly reliant on two touching the puck into space and then snapping a shot without change in trajectory which would result in routine saves in high danger areas.

As a result of having poor shot quality at this time, Helenius is most likely going to rely on goals off of give and go sequences in transition where he can finish quick lateral passes or sneak back-door to finish point blank set-ups.

His slapshot fares better than his wrist shot at this time, and he will occasionally score from mid distance from the circles, but again the hallmark and foundation of his game is making his teammates around him better by using his advanced and technical playmaking ability; it's unlikely that he develops into a dual-threat finisher.

When evaluating his tool-kit, he's able to generate a decent amount of power in his first few steps by efficiently pushing out with his inside edges, and he's displayed dexterity when rotating through his upper half in order to gain momentum out of his first three steps. He's also quite fluid in his ability to shift his weight to avoid contact and rotate to square himself up to the play or to make a pass while keeping his momentum. We wouldn't label him as a separator off the rush, he rarely can blow past guys when rushing down a wing, but there's enough lateral agility and technical edgework found within his game to make him an evasive prospect when necessary - and considering that's he's not the biggest player - it most certainly will be necessary when looking to translate to the NHL.

Determining off the puck support is critical in evaluating a center's ability to translate from their draft season and into the NHL.. One of the major reasons why is due to the significance that puck support can have when determining a centers ability to control the middle portion of the ice for his team, and that's Helenius's bread and butter. His anticipation generates calculated positioning that keeps him above the puck on most sequences and it's led to continuous zone exits in each viewing. This gives him the natural tendency to be a third defenseman when his team needs him to be. A lot of young forwards are in a hurry to join an attack and generally over step their offensive limits in an effort to try and make something happen while exiting the zone, but Konsta is seemingly always in control, rarely putting himself out of position, that's complemented by his defensive awareness, when determining why he's above the puck as frequently as he is.

Although he's not a large center, he plays bigger than his size and comes with a natural strength that's surprising. Towards the playoffs in Liiga, the games demanded more physicality and speed out of him, yet he took shifts over as opposed to getting drowned out. In-fact, we would label Helenius as one of the more difficult players to play against. He routinely cross checks players out of their position, and has a gritty, determined side to his game that's complimentary to the rest of his skill-set. There's a fall back approach to his play style, and he refuses to be intimidated when matching up against much larger players than himself.

There's a technical, cerebral, well rounded two-way center that has the physical and mental tools needed for his game to translate, offering him a very high floor. Where his ceiling might fall short is within his lack of high end scoring upside and lack of dynamic skating ability. When you take his understanding of space, his balance between playing with poise and playing with urgency, his willingness to get the job done at the cost of comfort, and his innate ability to make his teammates around him better both on and off the puck, it forms a player that can contribute both in the regular seasons and in the playoffs. We think of Helenius as a player that fits the same mold as Nico Hischier, although we think his production falls more into the 60-65 point area.

" Super smart and very skilled. He's produced against men and he's just a really good player. You have him ranked properly." - NHL Scout, January 2024

" He's not explosive or dynamic enough to be a top 10 guy..maybe not even top 15." - NHL Scout, March 2024

" I think he'll stay in my top 20 but I can't warm up to him."- NHL Scout, April 2024

" He is a middle six guy. Not exactly an elite skater...and he's small." - NHL Scout, May 2024

He's like Finland version of Nico Hischier" - HP Scout Jérôme Bérubé (February 2024)

" Terrific defensive player, in one of the Liiga playoffs games that I saw he put on a clinic on how to play away from the puck. If he plays like that in the NHL he might win a few Selkes." - HP Scout Jérôme Bérubé (April 2024)

" The real stand out quality of his game for me is how nasty and combative he can be, he's smart but he's also mean at times, and that's going to pay dividends for his career." - HP Scout, Brad Allen

" Smart and skilled with compete mixed in. Didn't always play his best when a lot of scouts were watching." - HP Scout, Mark Edwards, May 2024

50	PLAYER	TEAM	LEAGUE	HEIGHT	WEIGHT	POS	GRADE
	HEMMING, EMIL	TPS	FIN	6' 01.25"	205	RW	C+
NHLCS	CEILING	FLOOR	HOCKEY SENSE	COMPETE	SKILL	SKATE	MISC
INT-6	6	4	6	5	7	5	6

Hemming played mostly in the Liiga this season after starting in the U20 league where he had 11 goals and 18 points in 13 games. In the Liiga he played 40 games and collected 7 goals and 11 points. He was a key member of the national

U18 team throughout the season, representing his country in 3 events (Hlinka-Gretzky Cup, November U18 Five Nations, and April U18 World Championship) amassing 23 points in 16 games in the process. He also was part of the U20 team for the World Junior Hockey Championships, but had a limited role there.

A good-sized winger who can be a weapon on the power play, every single one of his four goals at the U18 World Championship was from a one-timer from the left side of the ice. He's a shooter who enjoys the most success when paired with players who can set him up. However, he's too reliant on the power play. The aforementioned goals at the U18s were the only goals he scored in the whole tournament. He needs to be more of a threat to score at 5-on-5, which hasn't been the case this year. He also needs to play more inside, he finds himself too frequently on the perimeter.

His good shot equips him to score from distances in junior, but this would happen a lot less in Liiga and should continue to diminish even further in the NHL. Unless you're Alexander Ovechkin in his prime, shooting only from the outside is not a recipe for success in the NHL. If Hemming can shoot from the slot area, which he currently does not do enough of, this is where he will find more success. He's too reliant on those far-away shots and this won't help him despite his great velocity and quick release that we love. His shooting accuracy can be inconsistent. Despite taking a significant number of shots this season, his performance would vary, with a mix of high-end, impressive shots and some average ones. This inconsistency in his shot quality is something we are mindful of, as it highlights areas for improvement.

Hemming has good hands and is effective one-on-one. He can beat players with skilled dekes, especially in small-area plays such as in the slot or along the boards. However, he struggles more with his handling in transition and when making zone entries. In addition, his skating limits some of his one-on-one potential for the NHL. An average skater with average explosiveness and top speed, while he has progressed with his agility, deception and edgework, he won't be a huge factor in transition. He can beat players with his hands, but won't be a threat with his speed. If the pace of the game is quicker, it's going to be more challenging for him. The improvements we mentioned earlier are important because, while he won't be a threat off the rush with his speed, he can use these skills down low or along the boards. He can make quick changes of direction, alter skating routes, and use his deception skills to create time and space for himself to make plays.

He can pass the puck well enough, employing a decent level of creativity and vision. He's a shoot-first type of player, but sometimes we don't give enough credit to players of this genre for their playmaking. Hemming sees the ice well and can create chances for his teammates with his passing game. We also love his effort away from the puck, as he seems to understand how to play well and not be a liability. His reads, backcheck effort, and good stick make him a player that coaches can trust without the puck. He could be a power forward in the NHL because he's got the frame to do so, but he doesn't play like one. He doesn't have the physicality, nor does he use his frame well to protect the puck. He's also too passive on the ice, which has been a significant point of discussion among our scouts this year. While he has the physical frame to be more involved, he doesn't assert himself enough to do so. We would like to see more shifts where he takes control. Currently, he is not a play driver and lacks aggression on the ice. Despite his size, his perimeter-play tendencies negate the value of his frame, as we often see this more often out of players who are, say, 5'10", 170 pounds.

The more we watched, the more his projection shifted to a 3rd-line role– and that is if he adjusts his game. He can fit in as a 3rd-liner due to his play away from the puck and his ability to be a dual-threat skill player, which could make him a valuable complementary offensive player. However, he'll need to bring his intensity level up a notch or two or three. If he doesn't, he might never play full-time in the NHL. Our biggest complaints about his game this year have revolved around his lack of competitive drive. We often discuss the progression curve, and unfortunately, his is not particularly exciting. While he remains a decent prospect, we didn't see much progression in his game compared to the start of the season, aside from improvements in his edgework and agility on the ice.

"I've seen him ranked and mocked in the first round and I have to assume that they haven't seen him play a shift. Good player but first round? Let's get serious." – NHL Scout, May 2024

NR	PLAYER		TEAM	LEAGUE	HEIGHT	WEIGHT	POS	GRADE
	HERRINGTON, CAEDEN		HOLDERNESS	HIGH-NH	6' 1.5"	189	RD	NI
NHLCS	CEILING	FLOOR	HOCKEY SENSE	COMPETE	SKILL		SKATE	MISC
NA-120	5	4	5	5	5		6	6

In a weak year for the New England Prep School circuit, Caeden Herrington really stood out from the Holderness School blueline. With seven goals and 42 assists in 29 games, Herrington led all prep defensemen in points per game. He also got into 24 total games with the Green Bay Gamblers (USHL), eight of which were playoff tilts. His stat line (1+3=4) is modest, but so was his usage. He's expected to return to Green Bay next year.

Herrington is a smart, puck mover who does a nice job supporting the play. He constantly works to ensure proper spacing and gaps, while also providing intelligent partner support. There's a competitive edge to him and that can sometimes manifest itself physically near his own net – but he's not a killer. At 6'1", 189 pounds, Herrington is really good on his edges and gets a big plus for his lateral mobility. The rest of his skating package is teetering below average. His transition skating, in particular, leaves him susceptible to quick developing rushes. In USHL play, he played pretty cautious as to mitigate risk at best as possible. It ended up being rush opportunities that got the better of him than in-zone attacks. Caeden isn't the most efficient player we've seen. Doesn't feature an economy of movements - not only with his fidgety, shoulders-forward skating, but even with his wrist posture while holding his stick. That's easy enough to clean up.

In the meantime, he's an accurate passer who handles the puck well most of the time. Oddly, in our viewings, his second touch after receiving a pass or going back for a retrieval can sometimes get away from him for whatever reason. Otherwise, his good, but not great, stickhandling combined with his lateral movement could make him a threat at the attack line. He's quick to get point shots through, even if his shot is on the weaker side. Herrington could take a big jump if he could improve his first-step burst and develop the puck control window out away from his body (as opposed to the width, on the plane of the shoulders). Right now, what little true manipulative feints he has would be undone by his inability to capture the valuable ice behind his checker. He's a work in progress even as far as this draft class goes, but he looked the part for a healthy chunk of the USHL season, which is slightly promising.

NR	PLAYER		TEAM	LEAGUE	HEIGHT	WEIGHT	POS	GRADE
	HESLOP, JESSE		EVERETT	WHL	5' 10.5"	171	LW	NI
NHLCS	CEILING	FLOOR	HOCKEY SENSE	COMPETE	SKILL		SKATE	MISC
NA-136	6	4	8	4	6		4	4

The former 3rd round pick in the WHL bantam draft had a strong season for the Everett Silvertips with 19 goals and 54 points in 61 games. In the playoffs, Heslop often played with fellow draft eligible prospect Julius Miettinen and Vegas Golden Knights' draft pick Ben Hemmerling.

Heslop is a high IQ, playmaking winger. This season, he created most of his offense on the rush. Although he isn't a great straight-line skater in term of his posture, he combines good routes for puck acquisition with linear crossovers to carry in the neutral zone in control and with speed. When entering the offensive zone, that's where he shines. The timing of his passing is great, knowing when to move the puck quickly or when to hold it more to invite pressure and creating more options. He can make hook passes or slip passes under sticks. He also loves to cut diagonally to freeze defender and create more time and space. Although he owns great vision and look for the pass, in last resort when he can't find play, his great puck skills allow him to dangle defensemen and get closer to the net. He can score with accuracy in tight, but his shot isn't a threat from distance. Most of his goals form rush situations came from sprinting without the puck to score in tight around the net.

In the offensive zone, Heslop does a great job playing between checks. He loves to be high F3 and get lost when the puck is low in the offensive zone, and when the puck goes low-to-high, he slides downhill between coverage in the slot. He scored a few goals like this this season. He's not the fastest or strongest player, so his one-on-one situations need some work when battling for a 50/50 puck. When he has the puck in the offensive zone, his wall is good. His craftiness and deception allow him to create separation from defender and climb the wall to find passing options.

Defensively, he positions himself well and owns solid awareness, thanks to his hockey IQ. On the forecheck, he does a fine job when he's F3 because of his reads and angling skills. To be a more complete two-way player, Heslop with need to improve his one-on-one battles, his breakouts/zone exits skills and adding more pace without the puck to his game.

87	PLAYER	TEAM	LEAGUE	HEIGHT	WEIGHT	POS	GRADE
	HOLINKA, MIROSLAV	TRINEC JR	CZE JR	6' 01"	187	RC	C
NHLCS	CEILING	FLOOR	HOCKEY SENSE	COMPETE	SKILL	SKATE	MISC
INT-31	6	4	7	6	6	5	6

A late born 2005, Miroslav Holinka split time this season between HC Ocelari Trinec's U20 and top Czech league team. In U20, Holinka posted 41 points and 20 goals in 29 games in addition to 14 points in 15 playoff games while adding 3 points in 16 games in the top Czech league. Holinka was able to earn his call up due to his high intelligence and puck skills that he will be looking to translate to a smaller ice surface. Next season, Holinka will return to Czechia to play with HC Ocelari Trinec and try to stick with the professional club for the year.

The intelligence Holinka provides his team on the ice in the form of his craft two-way game shows up often in his defensive game with strong positioning and constant shoulder checks to know where his man is and being very active in coverage. He does not leave the zone early and supports his defensemen and wingers often in getting the puck out of the zone by finding holes as the puck begins to transition up ice. Offensively, his intelligence shows best down low where he can see the play and make passes with great vision to set his teammates up for good opportunities. However, while down low, he is not good physically and loses puck battles consistently along the boards. This art of his game will need significant improvement as the ice shrinks as he moves over to North America and the physical play only gets stronger.

Although he is a player who has offensive potential, he also has many translatable skills as a player that should the offensive talent not translate. He can still become a strong defensive forward at the NHL level with his deep forecheck that rushes defenders and quick hands that can be used to steal the puck from attackers. At the moment, Holinka uses his hands in both zones and has an impressive rush attack with finesse where he can move the puck outside to inside quickly around defenders. His skill is not game breaking, however combined with his vision he has the ability to be productive offensively, especially with his shot. Holinka has a good arsenal of shots with good weight behind them which include his one-timer on the power play and snap shot. He typically shoots from the outside but plays the middle of the ice as well, mostly looking for a pass option.

He does have an ok first step, but he does not possess great straightaway speed and does not move quickly laterally despite his edgework being fluid. Holinka has good balance and control of his feet to compliment a wide and powerful stance when protecting the puck down low in both zones.

It wouldn't hurt him to get him accustomed to the smaller ice surface as soon as he can to refine his skills with less space quickly in his development. The biggest want from his game is to improve his physical play and the smaller ice surface will promote more physical activity due to s lack of space compared to the larger ice surfaces in Europe.

43	PLAYER			TEAM	LEAGUE	HEIGHT	WEIGHT	POS	GRADE
	HOWE, TANNER			REGINA	WHL	5' 10"	184	LW	B
NHLCS	CEILING	FLOOR		HOCKEY SENSE	COMPETE	SKILL		SKATE	MISC
NA-41	5	7		7	8	5		5	4

As a late birthday, the former 4th round pick in the WHL bantam draft played his 3rd WHL season. He had a very good draft minus-1 season last year with 85 points in 67 games, although he did play on Connor Bedard's line for most of the season. This year, his production dropped a bit, but it was an even more impressive season, registering 77 points in 68 games, with 25 more points than the 2nd scorer on the team. Howe led his team in goals, assists, points, was the captain of his team and averaged around 20 minutes of ice-time per game, playing in all situations.

Howe is a great two-way forward who plays the right way. He was a driver in transition for his team, thanks to smart puck touches. He does a great job as a winger on the breakout to establish body position against pinching defensemen, then find his center or the weakside defenseman for a exit in control. Off the rush, he attacks the inside as a puck carrier, and fill lanes after his distribution. He gets behind defenseman, scoring many goals close to the net by winning his race.

In the offensive zone, Howe's wall play down low is efficient. He establishes body position to keep possession, look for inside plays, and his smart with his touches. He knows when the move the puck quickly versus when to hold it a little longer. Off the puck, he doesn't hesitate to be the net front player, creating havoc with good puck skills in tight on rebounds. On the man advantage, Howe run Regina's power play from his one-timer side half-wall. He was an efficient with quick passing, looking for seam pass, or to tag the bumper or net front-player. He owns a solid one-timer, scoring a few goals that way.

Defensively, Howe is a responsible player. On the forecheck, he's physical as F1 or F2, and he's smart as F3 to always stay above. He reloads quickly, often being the first player on the tracking and return to defensive zone for his team. In the defensive zone, he positions himself well and shows good awareness.

Overall, Howe's smart and high-compete two-way game projects really well at the next level. For an average size player, finding another gear in his skating would help his ultimate upside. Offensively, Howe doesn't possess high-end skills, but he's talented enough et smart in his puck touches to complement and play with offensive forward. His awareness off the puck, compete level and off the puck space creation are all assets that help a lot the player he plays with.

"Howe plays the right way. Smart two-way forward with high compete level, a forward that all coaches love to have on their team." - HP Scout, Tim Archambault, March 2024

"I like Howe, he's just small." - NHL Scout, April 2024

97	PLAYER	TEAM	LEAGUE	HEIGHT	WEIGHT	POS	GRADE
	HUMPHREYS, CHRISTIAN	USA U-18	NTDP	5' 10.5"	170	RC	C

NHLCS	CEILING	FLOOR	HOCKEY SENSE	COMPETE	SKILL	SKATE	MISC
NA-71	6	4	7	5	6	5	5

Highly intelligent, playmaking winger. Christian Humphreys is a subtle and understated player that seemed to lose his purpose a little bit after an impressive early start. He began the year centering Cole Eiserman and with six points in his first four games, that seemed like a fit. Humphreys really complemented Eiserman's simple grip-it-and-rip-it game.

After he was split up from Eiserman and dealt with a couple of injuries, he bounced around a bit...finding himself more at right wing. The purpose and drive in his game seemed to dwindle. Much later in the year, he seemed reluctant to shoot – he had just six shots on goal in his final seven USHL games. His first goal in the gold medal game vs. Canada will be credited as a goal from inside the house – the reality is, he lost it coming from behind the net, and it banked back to him and he tapped it in without taking any meaningful contact – his skates didn't even get above the goal line. Just not enough of his game was played in high rent areas, and that's been a real red flag. He doesn't need to be a killer, but he's smart enough to know that he needs to apply himself more in this regard if he wants to be a pro.

That's been the most frustrating aspect of Christian's play this year, we know that he knows better. He has one of the highest hockey IQ's on the NTDP. Ultimately, he "settles" for plays that are lower percentage to avoid the physical toll or to protect an injury or to just keep his nose clean. It's fairly obvious why that's a bad thing, so let's focus on why this can be a positive. His physical and technical development arcs, respectively, hint at a real steep grade. He's not as visually appealing as some of the other NTDP players, he doesn't work as hard, and he's not as big...but the reason why we'd take him is because we believe his development arcs are still at their early stages and have a lot of runway to go. He's not someone who gives the impression that he's a gym rat from a physique perspective and the flashes of technical ability give a lot of hope. Just looking at his shooting technique – it's also pretty low effort. There's no distinct hip drop or torque generated from rotation in his core. Again, not the best thing to read or watch...but he's still a productive player at this level and he's not working too hard to accomplish it. So, when we see him pull a defender's stick to him to expose his triangle and then slip past him on the rush or when we see him look off a downhill wrist shot to thread a diagonal dish to the far post for a tap-in, we see a big ramp on his technical development arc that hasn't been fully harnessed. A lot of that, too, can be weaponized and driven by just how smart he is as a player. He figures things out and he can be very slippery. We just have to make sure he isn't too smart for his own good and it ends up keeping him from applying himself to be better.

Going back, partially, to the physical arc – his skating needs improvement. It's probably not as bland as it sometimes looked later in the season, but it's a choppy stride that lacks good extension. There's a lot of upper body noise and counteractive movement associated with it, which could be a signal for a lack of core strength (not totally unexpected for an 18 year old, of course). Again though, there's potential. We look at his prudent start and stop game early in the season and his closing speed on loose pucks as markers that he can bring this along to be a positive trait in fairly short order. We'd be hopeful that more strength would naturally make him more comfortable about playing inside the dots. It's tough to find many goals from him driving the paint for a rebound or a tip – those don't get easier as a player goes up the ladder. We'd also want him to be cognizant of his ability to make himself small slipping up the boards after a deke, there's value in not losing that while also still being able to drive through it.

There is no better, more varied, or more creative passer among this NTDP's group of eligibles, nor is it a particularly close heat. His playmaking is not only impressive from a straightaway passing perspective, but it's also done with a lot of forethought to set up the pass receiver with better ice and a better situation. His understanding of area passing will make him a weapon on teams that lean heavily on weakside rotation plays. He has pre-pass deceptive maneuvers. He might even be better with head and shoulder feints than with his stick at this point which is a really promising sign. He exhibits a strong understanding of tempo control in the neutral zone and in attack zone regroup situations. He's also a good communicator on the ice and is constantly in the right position. Pucks tend to find him in any situation.

"Of all the middling NTDP forwards, this is my favourite because of his smarts and creative playmaking. If I take a chance on any of them, it's Humphreys." - HP Scout, Michael Farkas

46	PLAYER	TEAM	LEAGUE	HEIGHT	WEIGHT	POS	GRADE
	HUTSON, COLE	USA-U18	NTDP	5' 10.5"	165	LD	C+
NHLCS	CEILING	FLOOR	HOCKEY SENSE	COMPETE	SKILL	SKATE	MISC
NA-55	6	4	6	7	7	6	4

Cole Hutson easily led USNTDP's draft eligible D corps with just 12 points in 19 USHL games. For all intents and purposes, Hutson is the only defenseman of the 2024 NTDP draft group that has plus offensive skills at all. This was further evidenced by his 13 point performance at the U18 World Junior Championships, that figure was good for second best overall on the team and over twice that of the next d-man. He was named best defenseman in the tournament for his trouble. It's the second straight tournament where he was named to the all-tournament team. He had a bit of a slow start from a positive impact perspective this regular season, but started to pop towards the end of the year.

He's certainly a tremendous skater. As a 5'10" defenseman, if he wasn't a great skater, there probably isn't much of a conversation. His first-step explosiveness, razor-sharp edges, tight turning radius, and fluid stride make him extremely dangerous in any situation. Whether it's his four-way mobility in open ice eating up ground laterally or his ability to quickly turn against the grain to beat a defender to the inside, there isn't much he can't do with his footwork. He incorporated his footwork into his puck play much better in the second half of the season. This really comes into play with his shooting process. Not only can he manipulate defenders with his hands, but the ability to fully take advantage of the manipulative nature of the move with his feet creates more than just a shooting lane – it creates a bevy of new opportunities. This has allowed Hutson to work into the lower layers of the offensive zone and line up a higher quality shot or a cross-lane pass to an open teammate as defenders converge towards Hutson. This is possibly his greatest area of pro upside and most scalable trait, the work that he can do at the attack line could grow into legitimate point production at the NHL level.

His shot isn't bad either. Quick release and some good pop and placement on it. It's better than a lot of smaller defensemen of this type...not only that, he has a good selection of shots to choose from, which adds to the dynamic offensive package. His ability to skate the puck out of his own zone is a major plus. It, too, has a chance to be an asset at the NHL level. We'd feel more confident about his retrieval -> exit process if he was a little bit better with his zone exit passing. It's not a negative by any means, but it's not elite. Even adjusting for this being a weaker NTDP class, he can throw some pucks away looking for homerun passes. We'd love to see him lure a forechecker towards him and play off of that with a shorter pass and then have him jump up into an adjacent or far lane, for instance. Turning and throwing stretch passes up the ice doesn't maximize his best assets nearly enough and it has some application limitations at more structured higher levels. His short passing game is very accurate in all three zones, so maybe this is just technical experimentation on his part.

The inconsistent part of his game is certainly his defensive play. It's actually his technical defense that left us wanting a lot more. For a player that's really going to have to play the game on his toes and with plenty of compete, he looked pretty drowsy at times defensively this year. He leaves his feet a lot, which isn't generally a good idea to begin with, and it's made all the worse by canceling out his best quality in the process. But further, a lot of these types of plays really look like he's just going through the motions half-heartedly. A player goes down to block a pass and his head is up, there's stick action, there's an element of intentionality to expand the chance of success for this tactic – it's desperation. With Hutson, it almost looks like he's just taking a dive. Even the weight transfer and transition skating after a missed pokecheck is pretty lifeless – the in-play body language just seems off and almost exaggerated for effect. Now, maybe this is a player that's bored or frustrated with this level of play and he'll explode next season in a better environment – but we're not convinced Hutson is quite the caliber of player that can be put-off by his level of completion, if that's indeed part of the equation. There are just some inexplicably poor actions for a player with this skating base and this hockey sense, one example:

January game against Chicago, close game in the 3rd. Chicago recovers a puck in their own zone and skates back to maintain possession. They outlet to the top of the defensive zone on Hutson's side. Hutson comes down to gap up, but the play isn't ultimately going up his side, so he backs off. He only sees the back of his initial check, and there are three Chicago players with skates pointing north that could receive this puck in the interior. Hutson tracks all the way to the boards in the low NZ. The pass is made to the interior and it sparks a 2 on 4 scenario and Hutson works to recover into the middle – which he can easily do, especially against this non-threatening rush. As Chicago crosses center, the puck is kicked out to the left side away from Hutson. Hutson addresses the passer of the puck, who is his responsibility, and he should mark him as the play crosses the blueline – Hutson's over top of him at this point, so this is all standard stuff. But Hutson skates through that player, in an attempt to go after the puck carrier...so he also crosses in front of his partner (Skahan, who is in fine position). Then, realizing that doesn't make sense for anyone, he doubles back to his correct check. But in the meantime, Hutson's man got a free lane to the net and he's open. The pass attempt is dulled a bit by Skahan and it trickles towards the front of the net. Hutson continues to the corner, while Skahan goes behind the net...so, the puck just lies loose in front with neither d-man nearby and one of the two original Chicago rushers picks it up and easily scores from five feet. There's a number of opportunities, well within Hutson's skill set to prevent a shot there, much less a goal...but he just decided to do his own thing.

The defensive urgency, risk mitigation, and pokecheck timing really need work. Everything else, besides size, is there for him. So he's worth a look once he drops to a point where you are comfortable with his size/ defensive limitations. He's off to Boston University next year. The comparisons to brother Lane (MTL 2nd rd. 2022) are going to be unavoidable, but they aren't carbon copies of each other. Lane was much more dominant in his draft year and more competitive all over the ice. The thought with Lane was "if he was three inches taller, he'd be a top 3, 5, 10 pick" – and that's extremely high praise, but that's also not exactly the prevailing thought for Cole.

"He played a better later in the year but I'm not a big fan. He was only what I would call good in about 20% of my viewings." – HP Scout, Mark Edwards, May 2024

"Mixed reviews on our staff. Mike and I are the scouts that have him ranked lower." – HP Scout, Mark Edwards, June 2024

7	PLAYER		TEAM	LEAGUE	HEIGHT	WEIGHT	POS	GRADE
	IGINLA, TIJ		KELOWNA	WHL	6' 00"	191	LW	A
NHLCS	CEILING	FLOOR	HOCKEY SENSE	COMPETE	SKILL		SKATE	MISC
NA-9	8	8	7	8	8		6	6

If there was an award for the most-improved player in the 2024 NHL Draft, there's a good chance Iginla would win. After a rookie season in the WHL where he didn't get a ton of playing time, he was moved from Seattle to Kelowna and had a breakthrough year. He scored 47 goals in 64 games with the Rockets after only scoring 6 goals in 48 games in his rookie season. He also scored 8 goals in round 1 of the playoffs against the Wenatchee Wild.

It was not only in the stats department where we saw a big improvement from Iginla, we also saw it in his skill level. He made some massive improvements in terms of his stickhandling (his hands), he was much more comfortable handling the puck in small areas, and he's now one of the best in this draft class to handle the puck in tight spaces and through contact. This helps him both in his play along the wall and in his ability to get shots off quicker and from different angles. This is very important for him in terms of translating his goal-scoring abilities to the NHL.

Opposing goaltenders have a hard time tracking his shot; he reads their movements well and has strong accuracy in both his wrist shot and slapshot. He's got natural scoring instincts, in addition to a great work ethic that creates a lot of those goals. Then, he has a goal scorer's shot that will translate to the NHL because of both his ability to change angles and his lightning-quick release. He's a great forechecker who is very good at pressuring defensemen into making quick decisions, which can result in turnovers. Often this year we saw him get on the forecheck quickly and create turnovers either by stealing the puck or forcing the defenseman to make a bad pass.

We also saw him score goals by using his net presence and sheer tenacity; there's no quit in his game. He performed well in the bumper role on the power play with Kelowna this season, showcasing versatility, as he's also capable of playing the half-wall. He has demonstrated the ability to score goals in various ways – from distance, from the slot (in the bumper role), and by battling in front of the net.

When you combine a skill level like his with such a high compete level, more often than not, the outcome will be positive. One thing we highly value in a player is unwavering commitment to improvement. This drive is evident in elite players like Sidney Crosby, as well as in players like Brad Marchand and Zach Hyman, who initially weren't expected to reach their current level of success. It was their relentless work ethic that propelled them to exceed the initial expectations teams had of them, year after year.

Iginla has that; what he showed in terms of improvement this year compared to his rookie season shows us that he took things seriously in getting his game to another level. But we also see it on the ice and in the way he plays; he's relentless and plays the game the right way with great attention to detail in all three zones.

He's more of a shooter than a passer, but he does possess a good level of creativity. He can set up teammates with skillful passing plays on both his forehand and backhand. This year, he has incorporated more deception into his game, which keeps opposing defenses on their toes because he hides his intentions effectively. Deception can also prove useful in creating space for himself during-puck protection situations, with slight head and shoulder fakes. He's comfortable handling the puck on both sides of the stick blade. He's elusive on the ice, he has real good edgework, and he's tough to handle one-on-one because he's extremely tenacious on the ice and also changes directions quickly.

Since last year, Iginla's skating has improved; mostly he's stronger on his skates and has more power. By no means is he a great skater, but he can create enough distance between himself and his opponents, and he's tough to knock down. Off the rush, one thing he does well is to change his speed and his skating routes to fool defenders, giving them different looks. His play along the wall is another really solid part of his game; he's not a huge power forward like Cayden Lindstrom, but he's good at protecting the puck using his frame. He's also good at rotating his body to absorb hits, sometimes going for reverse hits to keep possession of the puck and giving himself an extra second or two to make a play. It's hard for opposing defensemen to get pucks away from him.

Another part of his game that we like is his 200-foot game. We mentioned earlier that he's excellent at creating turnovers on the forecheck, but he's also quite good with his stick to steal pucks in both the neutral and defensive zone. His value as a prospect increased due to his ability to play a strong 200-foot game and PK value. Over the past few years, especially during the NHL playoffs, we observed that the players who thrive the most are often those who possess a complete skillset without any glaring weaknesses, as opposed to flashy, one-dimensional forwards. The former aligns with Iginla's profile.

There was much debate this year about Iginla versus Catton, but as the year progressed, the more we saw that Iginla's game translates more effectively to the NHL compared to Catton's. There's a lot more physicality and pushback in Iginla's game. Both players struggled against Prince George in the playoffs, which was not surprising due to the Cougars being a powerhouse of a team. However, Catton was shut down with physicality (which could definitely re-occur in situations such as the NHL playoffs) whereas Iginla didn't play his best hockey in that series, but not because he couldn't handle the physicality. The physicality in the NHL won't be an issue for Iginla. We do think it will be for Catton, and his smaller frame.

Iginla's goal-scoring ability, 200-foot game and compete level made him an easy player for us to like this year. This was a strange draft year compared to last, and it was tougher to find guys that we really felt passionate about. Last year there were guys like Bedard, Carlsson, Simashev, But, Benson and others, but it was a different story this season. Iginla quickly became one of our favourites, however, and climbed our list as the year progressed. We think Iginla is a top-line, two-way forward who can score around 35 goals a season, and whose game is suited for the NHL playoffs.

"I didn't even like his game last season and now I think he's a first rounder." - NHL Scout, November 2023

"Awesome. That's my quote." - NHL Scout, December 2023

"Might be the hardest working player in the WHL." - NHL Scout, December 2023

"He's just a freaking hockey player, does everything well and he competes hard" - HP Scout Jérôme Bérubé, February 2024

"The more I watched him the more I thought back to the Seth Jarvis draft season. I think Jarvis was more dog on a bone relentless and slightly better playmaking ability than Iginla but not by much. They remind me of each other though. Iginla is bigger." - HP Scout, Mark Edwards, April 2024

"I mentioned Seth Jarvis to our scout Brad Allen about a month ago and he started laughing. He told me he had just mentioned Jarvis to another scout a day earlier." - HP Scout, Mark Edwards, May 2024

"Combine interviews were excellent. Scouts raved about him." - HP Scout, Mark Edwards, June 2024

NR	PLAYER	TEAM	LEAGUE	HEIGHT	WEIGHT	POS	GRADE
NR	JAMIESON, ERIC	EDMONTON	WHL	6' 02.5"	199	LD	NI

NHLCS	CEILING	FLOOR	HOCKEY SENSE	COMPETE	SKILL	SKATE	MISC
NA-84	4	5	3	8	4	5	6

A former 9th round pick in the WHL bantam draft, Jamieson is a player who's showing constant progress in his game. Undrafted in his first year of NHL draft eligibility last season, Jamieson played an important role for the Silvertips this season. Playing top 4 minutes, big PK minutes, an assistant captain on the team, Jamieson also scored 10 goals and 32 points.

Defensively, he's a really good shutdown defenseman in the WHL. He's mobile and athletic and tall, making him hard to beat off the rush. He uses the same stools in the defensive zone, killing a lot of play. He's physical down low, makes stops and box out hard in front of his crease.

With the puck, he improved a lot from last season. His transition and breakout abilities still need a lot of work and he uses his partner a lot, but it has improved from last season. Without the puck, he's active in the play, joining the rush and activating in the offensive when needed. He owns a really good shot from the point. It's hard, but he also does a good job of finding shooting lane and shooting with purpose.

73	PLAYER	TEAM	LEAGUE	HEIGHT	WEIGHT	POS	GRADE
	JECHO, ADAM	EDMONTON	WHL	6' 05"	201	RC	C

NHLCS	CEILING	FLOOR	HOCKEY SENSE	COMPETE	SKILL	SKATE	MISC
NA-22	5	4	4	4	5	5	8

The former 3rd overall pick in the CHL came with pretty big hype to Edmonton in the WHL after scoring 47 points (21 goals) in 37 games in U18 league in Finland. The 6'5" had a fine first season in North America with 47 points (23 goals) in 54 games. He represented Czechia at the U18 after the season, playing on their top line and top power play unit.

Offensively, Jecho's bread and butter is his shot. He owns a really good shot, as he can score from distance both with his wrist shot and one-timer. The Oil Kings and the Czechia team had many plays on the man advantage to exploit Jecho's release. Jecho is definitely a shoot first player, but he owns good puck skills and can make some solid passes on the rush when he has a bit of time and space. Overall, he needs to improve he first few steps, but he's a decent skater with strong top speed once he's started. That puck carrying ability makes him a solid transition and rush forward.

Without the puck, Jecho needs to improve his overall game. First, he was only 43% in the faceoff circle this season on 605 faceoffs taken. In the defensive zone, his awareness could be better. He's huge and can win battles, but he needs to show more consistency in this area, as well as playing more physical and being harder to play against.

Overall, Jecho has some pretty high upside with his huge frame, decent skating and very good shot. If he can put all of this together and improve the other part of his game, he can make some teams look bad on draft day and can become a pretty unique player. But as of right now, he needs to improve many areas of his game: Using his size more efficiently, like winning more battles and creating more offense from the offensive zone by establishing body position in 50/50 battles. He can play more physical and improve his overall two-way game.

"There are a lot of players in the WHL that I think are overrated but I like Jecho. He has some real upside." - NHL Scout, May 2024

"I know some scouts who have him in the first round, mid rounds and seventh round. It's all over the map." - HP Scout, Mark Edwards, May 2024

"He isn't lazy, but he doesn't have the drive I like to see either. I personally don't think he will play in the NHL based on his effort level so I have no interest at all." - HP Scout, Mark Edwards, May 2024

17	PLAYER	TEAM	LEAGUE	HEIGHT	WEIGHT	POS	GRADE
	JIRICEK, ADAM	PLZEN	CZECHIA	6' 02.5"	178	RD	A

NHLCS	CEILING	FLOOR	HOCKEY SENSE	COMPETE	SKILL	SKATE	MISC
NA-4	7	5	7	8	6	6	7

Adam is the younger brother of David, the 6th overall pick in the 2022 NHL Draft by the Columbus Blue Jackets. Adam made a big impression on us in last year's Under-18 World Hockey Championship, but this season, there were some notable ups and downs to his game. Unfortunately, in addition to this, his season ended due to a knee injury in his first game at the 2024 World Junior Hockey Championship in Sweden. We did see him plenty of times in the Czechia league, but also internationally in various U18 and U20 tournaments from August to December.

There are a lot of similarities between the two Jiricek brothers' games, but also some differences. Both have good frames to play this position. Adam is more physically raw, which explains some of his ups and downs in the Czechia league this season. They both have this great compete level and tenacity on the ice that makes them both tough to play against. Adam is a better skater and athlete with better recovery habits at the same age. They both can move pucks to contribute offensively, and David is the better shooter of the two. Both also injured their knee in the first game of their respective World Junior tournament that took place during their draft year, with the difference being that David was able to come back late in the year to play at the World Championship.

Adam Jiricek is a good-sized defenseman who we project as a two-way defenseman for the NHL who can play in a top-4 role. Data is missing from his profile due to his absence in the 2nd half, having missed three major scouting events: the U20 World Junior Hockey Championship during the holidays, the U18 Five Nations tournament in February and the World Under 18 Hockey Championship in April. He was not having a great year with his club team before his injury, but we were unable to assess his capacity to make notable improvements or turn things around in the 2nd half. We really believe that tracking the development curve of a player gives us a better picture when projecting them, and we are missing a lot of information with Jiricek. It's too much of a risk to rank him aggressively if the projection stays the same as it was in December.

We feel we might have overrated his offensive upside last season; with more viewings this year, we now feel as though it may be tough for him to become a PP1 guy due to his lack of shooting skills. His shot has only average velocity from the point, and he's not a threat to score from there as a result. He does move well laterally at the line to create shooting and passing lanes on the power play, moving pucks well enough and demonstrating some creativity, too, but he's far from being elite enough to compensate for his shot. He can help his team's transition game, however. He can rush pucks out of his zone and can pass at a good level. He does need to improve some of his decision-making and puck retrievals to take his game to another level, judging from his play in a tough Czechia league and the missing data and viewings we mentioned.

We like Adam's skating more than David's at the same age, but this was also an area that we possibly overrated. When playing against men, his stride didn't look as fluid, and his first three-step quickness was not as good as we projected. It is still going to be fine for the NHL when we project it long term, but not at the level we originally perceived it. We do think that once he adds more strength to his frame, his stride is going to be more powerful, and he'll be more explosive as a result.

We still like his potential, but feel he was not quite ready for the Czechia league. Had he played in the OHL (he was drafted by Brantford, 19th overall, in the CHL Import Draft last summer) his game could have shone more. Having said that, we still feel as though he was playing some good hockey with his club team just before he left in December, to the point where turning the corner in his season development seemed possible, but we will never have a definitive answer on that.

One of our favourite traits about him is what we call the "Jiricek Grit." Both he and his brother have this grit factor that matters a lot for us in terms of being able to project their defensive game for the NHL. They are physical, tough to play against, they make it tough for opposing players to manoeuvre in the offensive zone, they don't quit on plays, and they clear the front of the net well. Adam can defend with his physicality, but also has good footwork and a good gap. He challenges forwards on the ice that come to his side of the ice. He covers a good amount of ice with his size, skating and reach.

We think Jiricek projects as a good 2nd-pairing defenseman right now, but as previously alluded to, this projection is a bit tricky due to all the games he has missed. We originally thought he had first pairing potential, but what we saw until his injury brought our projection to #3 or #4 NHL defenseman. We think he's going to be able to bring some offense and play on PP2 with his puck-moving skills and good defensive value. NHL coaches will trust him to play heavy minutes due to his good athleticism and physicality.

"He's not always the smartest player on the ice but he doesn't have any huge weakness. I think he can be a middle paring guy." - NHL Scout, November 2023

"Tough to evaluate this year but guys know how good he is. He'll go high." - NHL Scout, January 2024

"I wish I saw more of him before he got hurt but I really like him." - NHL Scout, May 2024

"I think he has a really good well rounded game." - NHL Scout, May 2024

"He had a translator with him at the combine but he tried hard to speak English. Scouts really liked him." - Hp Scout Mark Edwards, June 2024

81	PLAYER	TEAM	LEAGUE	HEIGHT	WEIGHT	POS	GRADE
	JOHANSSON, LOKE	AIK JR	SWE JR	6' 03"	214	LD	C
NHLCS	CEILING	FLOOR	HOCKEY SENSE	COMPETE	SKILL	SKATE	MISC
INT-52	5	3	4	8	5	8	7

Loke Johansson is a large, hard-skating, heavy-hitting defenseman who plays a shutdown game successfully at both the J20 level and in the Allsvenskan league. At the J20 level, he had moderate production, putting up 13 points in 33 games, including 5 goals. At the Allsvenskan level, he was impressive in some appearances despite recording only 1 assist in 19 games.

Johansson's game starts with his mentality on the ice: to make life miserable for the opposition. His impressive toolkit, combined with his aggressive, tenacious approach, makes him a capable defender with a throwback element that's missing from many modern-day prospects. His defense begins with his skating base, allowing him to apply pressure rapidly when closing his gap off the rush or during man-to-man positional defense. He maintains good posture, can shift off his centerline quickly, and has a structurally sound stride. For a bigger player with a heavy frame, his crossover mechanics and edgework typically allow him to generate the necessary power to carry his frame and stop opposing teams' transitions before they begin.

He closes on players transitioning through the neutral zone using his impressive C-cuts and knows how to minimize risk by angling them into dead areas of the ice. One key element of his defensive game is his ability to end plays before they begin through his defensive anticipation.

Johansson doesn't just end plays by bodying players off pucks along the boards, aggressively cross-checking players out of the slot, or obtaining positioning by getting up and underneath forwards to take away their stick in high-danger areas. His stick instincts, stick timing, and ability to skate into passing lanes during the developing play make him well-rounded in his own zone.

Shutdown defensemen need to retrieve pucks and make a first pass, and this is where Johansson has been less consistent compared to his rush absorption, one-on-one coverage, and cycling defense. While you can count on him to finish a hard hit or make a well-timed cross-check that knocks a forward off balance as they receive a pass, he's not as reliable with his retrievals or outlet passes.

We wouldn't label his retrievals and outlet passes as poor, just inconsistent. Sometimes he uses his multi-directional pivoting base to make an advanced skating lane adjustment that allows him to suppress aggressive forechecks, giving him additional time and space to operate within a more comfortable exiting window. Other times, he fails to recognize the safer passing option, opting instead for passes directed more towards the middle of the ice. With some coaching, we believe this part of his game can be improved.

He's not a black hole from the offensive line either, but for the sake of brevity, let's just say he's not getting drafted for his offense. His game is predicated on a hard-hitting shutdown style. If Johansson can clean up his first pass and retrievals to be as reliable as his defensive stops, he has the potential to become an above-replacement-level, third-pairing defenseman responsible for insulating a more talented defensive partner. Most importantly, he brings a unique edge, packed into a powerful frame built for playoff hockey, and for these reasons, he made our list, albeit late. It's not easy for a young defenseman to stand out for the right reasons in the Allsvenskan, but he did just that in our viewings.

"I'll be surprised if he isn't drafted. He's physical, he's athletic, and he has already shown the ability to play at the Allsvenskan level." – HP Scout, Brad Allen

NR	PLAYER	TEAM	LEAGUE	HEIGHT	WEIGHT	POS	GRADE
	JOKINEN, MITJA	TPS JR.	FIN-JR	5' 09.75"	163	LD	C
NHLCS	CEILING	FLOOR	HOCKEY SENSE	COMPETE	SKILL	SKATE	MISC
INT-54	5	4	4	5	5	6	4

Jokinen spent this past season playing with TPS U20 team, finishing with a respectable stats line of 21 points in 41 games. He was also a regular on the national U18 team over the course of the season and had a decent performance in April to finish the year with 5 points in 5 games.

He's a smaller defenseman with solid skating skills, though not elite. His footwork and agility are good, and while his stride has decent power, his skating could become more explosive as he matures physically. There's some good potential with his offensive skills; he's a good stickhandler, unafraid to try things out offensively. There's some good creativity to his game as well, but some risks do come with this. He can fall victim to trying too much with the puck and doesn't complete enough simple, effective plays. Instead of making an easy pass in transition, too often he will try to beat an extra guy, losing the puck in the process. There's some risk associated with his defensive game as well. Given his size and frame, players typically need special skills to play full-time in the NHL. He's still developing physically, and while he may get stronger in the next few years, he'll likely remain undersized for the NHL. We wish he showed more physicality and pushback in his game, as these are crucial for defending at the NHL level. Unfortunately, he hasn't demonstrated enough of this in his play this season. His decision-making under pressure when retrieving pucks in his own zone has also been inconsistent.

To conclude, we like some of his skills (mostly with the puck on his stick) but our concerns about his size and lack of defending give us a hard time when ranking him on our list. For us, he looks like a good player that will make a career primarily in Europe.

NR	PLAYER	TEAM	LEAGUE	HEIGHT	WEIGHT	POS	GRADE
	JOSEPHSON, OLLIE	RED DEER	WHL	6' 00.25"	190	LC	C
NHLCS	CEILING	FLOOR	HOCKEY SENSE	COMPETE	SKILL	SKATE	MISC
NA-40	4	6	6	8	4	7	5

A former 5th overall draft pick in the WHL bantam draft, Josephson had a nice improvement in production, going from 19 points last year to 47 points this season. He started the season slowly with 9 points in his first 18 games., but then found his game with a 6 games points streak. He averaged more than 20 minutes multiple time season, playing in every situation for the Rebels. Josephson won two gold medals with team Canada this season (Ivan Hlinka and U18), playing as a defensive center and on the penalty kill.

AS shown by his role with team Canada, Josephson projects as a two-way center who can be trusted in defensive situations. He was a primary PK'er for his team this season, and was matched against top competitions every night, mostly playing alongside gritty Predators' prospect Kalan Lind. In the playoffs, he did a great job matching against top prospect Gavin McKenna, playing a huge role to help his team win the round against a talented Medicine Hat team. This season, he had an impressive 53% success in the faceoff circle on 1214 faceoffs taken. Josephson is a really good skater and uses his speed and skating to be involved all over the ice. He can close space early and finish contact as F2 or F3 on the forecheck, or can play a smart F3 role to stay above and cover for his defensemen. He tracks hard and smartly back to the defensive zone, and shows good awareness in his own-end.

Offensively, Josephson isn't a highly creative forward, but he's skilled and smart enough with the puck to be generate offense and be a chain connector for his linemates. His impact in transition is really good. In the defensive zone, he supports his defensemen and wingers well, helping to exit the zone in control. He's a strong puck carrier, and uses his speed to attack the middle ice. He kicks out on entries, drive the inside and create space for his teammates. On the man advantage, Josephson had the opportunity to run the strong-side half-wall for Red Deer.

Overall, Josephson's upside isn't the highest, but he has NHL upside with his skating, two-way game, PK abilities and transition impact.

14	PLAYER		TEAM	LEAGUE	HEIGHT	WEIGHT	POS	GRADE
	KAVAN, JAN		BRNO	CZE JR	6' 01"	176	G	C
NHLCS	CEILING	FLOOR	HOCKEY SENSE	COMPETE	SKILL		SKATE	MISC
INT-15	6	4	7	7	5		5	5

Jan Kavan is an advanced, positionally sound goaltender, with a controlled and poised game that helps him compensate for his lack of prototypical size. He rarely beats himself on a play and he remained very consistent throughout his +1 season. In-fact, when he was called up to play in Czechia Extraliga with the main club for a dozen games, he had some performances at that level that we've never seen from an 18 year old goalie before. He also helped his team reach the finals of the U20 playoffs, where he lost in 7 games to Ocelari Trinec.

Usually when an 18 year old goalie from a junior program gets called up to pro, they have difficulty adjusting not just to the speed of the plays that are generated around them, but also the amount of traffic that they need to see through in order to track the puck. Yet, these two primary areas are Kavan's bread and butter, and it's what allowed him to directly adapt to a superior level of play when transitioning from junior to pro hockey this past season.

Some goalies just seem to have an innate sixth sense on how various high-danger plays are going to unfold in-front of them. They can anticipate who's ultimately going to be the receiver off of a 3-on-2 rush sequence at speed, or recognize if a forward is bluffing, turning his shot into a shot-pass redirect instead. They know how to time their scanning to pick up on a backdoor play through traffic, and they know how to figure out the most threatening option during chaotic sequences that have resulted from a broken play. That's Kavan. Kavan just has a built in understanding of how to play the position that is both difficult to measure and is admittedly difficult to break down with words.

But, we're here to try. So, what we're trying to get across, is that goalies like Kavan who are very aware and intelligent, use their built in processing speed to calculate how to play their position. Jan's poise, depth management, and crease containment are a direct result of him having to build a game around his physical limitations and he's done that with his mind for the game.

He's also very good at finding pucks through traffic, and recognizing the initial shooting trajectory off of even high-end pro players at this stage in his development. Younger goalies usually get rattled a bit or turned when they are bumped or have multiple players crashing their net, but Kavan uses his poise to his advantage and remains very calm with players swarming his net area. Through his tracking, his advanced anticipation and his clean technique; it affords him rare rebound control at this stage. He's very smooth, and he's very efficient.

In terms of his physical gifts, his glove hand is his best one by far. In-fact, his glove hand is one of the best in this entire class. We've seen a lot of developing goalies drop pucks more often as a result of the modern glove having a stiffer webbing that's more difficult to break in. Yet, Kavan almost never has trouble controlling his rebounds on his glove side, it's been remarkably consistent. There are games where shots fired on his glove side look almost automatically caught, regardless of the threat.

When looking at his limitations, they are almost exclusively a result of his tool-kit and lack of high-end athleticism. We do feel that he does meet the minimum threshold for his size, from an athletic point of view or we wouldn't be talking about him, but it's still his weakest trait. His athletic plus traits are his glove as we mentioned but also his kicking reflexes, and he is a competitive goalie who does what he can on a given play to make up ground when he can't initially reach a puck. His competitiveness can help compensate for his tool-kit, at least to a degree.

When breaking down his athleticism further. One of his primary issues is that he has a tendency to lunge forward within his initial save-type, when pucks are in tight to him. On the one hand, this does occasionally allow him to get on top of rebounds or lose pucks quickly, but on the other hand, when he misidentifies an opponent's handling or shooting window, it can and has led him to being susceptible to shots that are low to the ice and directly targeted at his five hole, or on shots that require a full extension from him.

He's not long, so when he's forced to stretch out, he can miss shots at an easier rate than bigger goalies. In-fact the last goal of the season that was scored on him, was a direct result of a backhand shot by Miroslav Holinka (draft eligible) who out-waited him after carving through traffic.

Kavan is also susceptible to secondary shots in tight, aggressive cross crease cutting attempts, or on fast - low to high passing plays - that require explosive extensions due to how compact he stays and due to his overall lateral transition rates being above average but not high end, especially when factoring in that he has a smaller frame relative to the NHL standard goalie.

During his transitional butterfly, specifically when he's popping back up into a set position, he has a tendency to lean over the top of himself, inadvertently putting himself temporarily off balance. This is a result of not having his posterior chain fully developed yet, and is one of the reason's he can be susceptible to saves that require him to recover and transition out of his butterfly quickly, however this is correctable during his continued physical development.

His skating base can cause him to stay behind the play even though his mind is ahead of it at times. He's not a laterally explosive goalie, but his edgework and overall fluidity are at least decent and don't appear to be stoppers. We wish his T-push offs and micro-adjustments were more powerful and rapid, but they fall in the average category.

One interesting quality that he shares with Timofei Obvintsev is that he doesn't always drop to his butterfly for certain shots types that are labeled at the shoulder height or above. He's comfortable remaining upright. In Obvintsev's case, he's hyper athletic and very reflexive, and although Kavan is reflexive, we don't project him to be able to make these save types to the same extent if he theoretically makes it to the NHL.

Despite Kavan having more limited physical traits then we typically want to see, his curve improved throughout this season, showing that his adaptation acceleration under high pressure situations, such as when he was called up to

Extraliga. As an example, Jan had difficulty earlier in the season at timing when he should come back out of his RVH after integrating into his post which made him susceptible to low to high plays, this extended to the point where he wouldn't have an opportunity to square up correctly in the time frame needed to stop the initial shot correctly, but after getting called up to Extraliga and sticking there in January, this aspect of his game dramatically improved.

The point in the above breakdown is that when we have counted out this goalie, he's done nothing but improve on what we thought was a weakness. If a young goalie is going to be physically limited, they better have the mental attributes, and innate ability to play the position to make up for it. Kavan has that in spades.

There's actually some crossover to Carter George in the sense that they are similarly framed, exceptionally composed, and are mentally very consistent. We just feel George has shown better athleticism when evaluating them at the same age and faced a higher level of competition within their initial draft seasons.

That doesn't mean we don't have time for Kavan though. He's a unique goalie who might make it to the NHL, as most likely a one off. There's very few goalies that are his size with his athletic traits that play, but he has an outside but very real shot due to how he adapts to compensate. It might really come down to his growth rate within his skating foundation, and how much more powerful he can become when given more time to mature.

" I can't think of a goalie who has played better in Czechia Extraliga at the age of 18. He was unbelievable."- HP Scout, Brad Allen

" I can count on one hand the amount of times I've seen him let in a bad goal, and I've watched a lot of him." - HP Scout, Brad Allen

" This was an example of a goalie who forced my hand in a big way. I wanted to write him off since he's not my style of goalie. I typically like bigger, more athletically gifted goalies. If they are small I want them to be hyper-athletic like Saros and Wolf, but I can't deny that there's something not as measurable that he possesses, that is fundamental to the position. He is just a natural goalie and if he can improve his explosiveness, then he's got a shot." - HP Scout, Brad Allen

NR	PLAYER		TEAM	LEAGUE	HEIGHT	WEIGHT	POS	GRADE
	KEARSEY, MARCUS		CHARLOTTETOWN	QMJHL	5' 10.25"	173	LD	NI
NHLCS	CEILING	FLOOR	HOCKEY SENSE	COMPETE	SKILL		SKATE	MISC
NA-180	5	5	5	5	5		5	5

Marcus Kearsey is a left-handed mobile defenseman who was drafted by the Charlottetown Islanders in the 2nd round (32nd overall) of the 2022 QMJHL entry draft. Kearsey saw improvements in his production during his draft year as he was able to contribute 7 goals and 42 assists in 68 games this season which puts him second on the Islanders in the scoring department.

We like his skating a lot. He can move from side to side with agility which helps him with his gap control. He is also capable of working on his edges. The one downside to his skating is that his first couple of strides can be somewhat awkward and heavy, so it is very important for him to always have his feet moving to avoid getting left in the dust by opposing attackers, particularly while in transition.

On the offensive side of the puck, Kearsey is an effective powerplay quarterback as he can vary his approach on the attack and can adapt depending on the look that the defensive team is giving him. We like him a lot as a puck mover as he can use head fakes and fake passes to manipulate the defenders to create passing lanes for himself. One thing that would really help him however is to increase his shot power. As it stands right now his shot is a bit of a nonfactor from the point, he does get lucky from time to time on screens from the point but improving his power would make him even more dangerous and unpredictable in the offensive zone.

Defensively Kearsey is responsible and can be a pain to deal with in coverage. His good mobility in all four directions allows him to cover a lot of ground and we find that his gap control is good. He can make some errant passes on the breakout from time to time, but he is generally effective at finding the right options and delivering accurate passes to his teammates while leaving the defensive zone. He can use his great mobility to turn on a dime and shake his way out of trouble when he is retrieving pucks deep in the zone. Despite not being the biggest guy on the ice he can catch opposing players off guard with some big hits along the boards. That being said, it is a bit of a struggle for him to win 1 on 1 battle in the dirty areas of the ice.

Kearsey is an intriguing prospect for this year's draft as his toolkit is different from a lot of the other eligible QMJHL defensemen. Despite not having a cannon of a shot from the point, he can produce some offense from the point with his good puck-moving skills and his ability to manipulate opposing players. His defensive game is also on par, and he has been used in practically every situation at the junior level. The issue with him is that there are definitely doubts about how his game will project at the professional level. Teams at the NHL level tend to like the bigger mobile defenseman in this day and age. There are less and less defensemen under 6 feet getting drafted into the NHL, the average ones are getting ignored more and more on draft day. We feel Kearsey could be a great junior defenseman but it's unlikely that his game will translate to the NHL. He could hear his name late in the draft. It's somewhat similar to Pier-Olivier Roy of Victoriaville who was has been passed over in the 2022 & 2023 NHL Draft. A great junior defenseman with a high hockey IQ and passing skills but there's not enough there for the NHL. Kearsey is a better skater than Roy though which should get him drafted but the road to the NHL is going to be a long one.

NR	PLAYER		TEAM	LEAGUE	HEIGHT	WEIGHT	POS	GRADE
NR	KEMPF, NICHOLAS		USA-U18	NTDP	6' 02"	189	G	C
NHLCS	CEILING	FLOOR	HOCKEY SENSE	COMPETE	SKILL		SKATE	MISC
NA-4	5	4	5	5	7		7	6

Nicholas Kempf follows in the footsteps of recently drafted goalies Drew Commesso and Spencer Knight from the program, but unlike them, he had to do it on arguably one of the weaker USNTDP squads we've seen on the backend in recent years.

The stand-out quality to Kempf's game is his athletic base. He has slightly below average size at the position but his rate of recovery, split-save depth, overall extension rates, and reflexes make him very difficult to beat on shots that are lower to the ice. What's even more impressive is that he doesn't allow his athleticism to work against him. Goalies at this stage of their development who can move laterally rapidly have a tendency to over-rotate or lose their net, but Kempf's consistent at using his edgework to maintain his net. When evaluating the NHL today, the majority of goals are scored off of point blank re-directs, breakaways, high to low lateral backdoor passing plays, and off of lateral one timers/catch and release plays from the circles and in. Kempf's style of play and better qualities project to be able to counteract all these save types with the exception of the point blank redirects.

Kempf's set stance is very compact. He keeps his glove low but in an open, pronated position, but he has a tendency to slump or slouch at times which can give shooters more to look at when evaluating what's available upstairs. This point is emphasized because he lacks dexterity and overall rotation in his shoulders. So there's some issues with his posture which should be correctable to a degree, long term. Although his set stance makes him susceptible on high shots, it gives him distinct advantages on shots that are labeled for his five hole or on plays where a player is attempting to wrap the puck around him. Nicholas is also consistent at sealing his blocker and keeping his arm tight to his body while micro shuffling on shots that force him to laterally adjust. When forced to move, everything remains tight and sealed on most plays.

We mentioned how he keeps his glove both low and in a pronated position, and this allows him to cutdown on shots in a downward arch that are labeled either between his glove and his pad or nearer to the ice, but it also means that on high shots, there's a slight delay relative to a goalie who keeps his glove higher and in a neutral position like Carter George does, as just one example. When you factor in his lack of shoulder mobility with his lower pronated posture, it means he can be susceptible to having shots that are labeled both for his high glove and to the side of his head where he needs to rapidly contort his shoulder girdle. What's interesting to note, is that despite this limitation, he hasn't allowed many high glove goals in our viewings, instead he's had more difficulties on shots that are targeted for his low glove. This comes down to giving up too much room when it's a far side angle he needs to cut down, and mistiming how fast he needs to use his glove hand in general.

Although the above skill-set has some limitations he can heavily adapt it for the pro game still, however there's one major area that could keep him from playing full time at the NHL level and that's regarding his overall puck tracking. Nicholas can have difficulty evaluating both high danger passes and point shots when looking through traffic, and he can completely misread a shooter's intentions. This can leave him getting caught flat footed or puts him in a position where he enters his butterfly prematurely. This issue is compounded when factoring in that he's not a bigger goalie. Typically, the smaller the goalie, the more on point their tracking needs to be in order for them to have a chance to play long term. Unlike other areas of the game where you can improve technically, get significantly stronger, the game doesn't get slower and the players only get more deceptive the further a goalie progresses, so this limiting factor could be the difference between him becoming a full time NHL goalie or a fringe goalie.

There are aspects of Kempf that are impressive. He's not at the same athleticism as the top end goalies in this class but it's still a stand out trait and projects well for the NHL. He's competitive and doesn't give up on shots, and he's had some impressive performances that have showcased his potential. For us, we feel he's a draft but our ranking reflects that we feel there are several goalies with higher end starting potential, and we think there's considerable risk in the pick when evaluating how he reads certain plays.

"I understand why a team would draft Kempf, heck I would take him late but he will probably be gone by the time I would feel comfortable selecting him." - HP Scout, Brad Allen

"If he played bigger I'd be more interested. I wouldn't draft him as it is today." - NHL Scout, October 2023

"Constantly on his knees but I like him." - NHL Scout, May 2024

"He is very gifted but plays much smaller than his size. He seemed too eager to get small by dropping to his knees." - HP Scout, Mark Edwards, March 2024

NR	PLAYER		TEAM	LEAGUE	HEIGHT	WEIGHT	POS	GRADE
	KENNEDY, QUINN		RIMOUSKI	QMJHL	5'10"	171	LC	NI
NHLCS	CEILING	FLOOR	HOCKEY SENSE	COMPETE	SKILL		SKATE	MISC
NA-131	5	4	5	4	6		5	4

Kennedy was the 9th overall selection in the QMJHL Draft in 2022. After a rough rookie season, he was much better this year. He had some good moments but was quite inconsistent, and once again, he missed time due to injuries. After only scoring 2 goals and 5 points in 41 games in his rookie season, he bounced back with 21 goals and 45 points in 52 games this season. He battled an injury in December and January, only playing 7 games during those two months.

Before his injury in December, he was on fire with 23 points in his last 17 games, but he was never able to find that rhythm when he came back in late January.

One key thing for Kennedy will be to stay healthy and find more consistency in his game. The difference between his good and bad games was too big. He has the potential to be a very good player in the QMJHL, but the inconsistency has been problematic. He can be a dual-threat player offensively with his shooting ability, but he can also pass the puck at a good level. He's good in the offensive zone at finding soft ice and can be a threat from both faceoff circles for one-timers. He can also score from the point; he has a good shot and can score from distances. He scored 7 power-play goals this season, which is 33.3% of his total goals.

He's similar to Felix Lacerte of Shawinigan in the sense that we consider him a good junior player but not really a good NHL prospect. He lacks skating skills, off-the-rush value, and a two-way game. He can be a threat on the power play with his shooting skills, but 5-on-5 play in the NHL could be challenging for him due to his lack of size, athleticism, and tendency to play on the outside. We would like to see him compete harder on the ice and be tougher to play against.

Kennedy had some good moments this season and we think he'll be a good player for Rimouski in the next two seasons (they are hosting the Memorial Cup in 2025). However, we're not seeing enough to include him on our list. We could see him getting drafted in the later rounds, with a team betting on his skill level and hoping the rest of his game improves.

NR	PLAYER	TEAM	LEAGUE	HEIGHT	WEIGHT	POS	GRADE
	KENTA, ISOGAI	WENATCHEE	WHL	5' 11"	154	LW	NI
NHLCS	CEILING	FLOOR	HOCKEY SENSE	COMPETE	SKILL	SKATE	MISC
-	5	3	6	7	7	6	3

After a 39 points season in the USHL last year (where he won a Clark Cup, playoffs champion), the 19 years old forward exploded in the WHL this season with 88 points in 64 games. He continued his strong production in the playoffs with 8 points in 5 games. He played on the Wild top line, top power play unit and on the penalty kill.

Isogai shines in the offensive zone. He sprints to be first on puck, battles hard down low, and uses his shiftiness to win possession to extend offensive zone time for his team. Once the puck goes high in the zone, he drives inside, roll off defenseman to look for rebound in tight. His race to the net without the puck and how he battles inside in an area that will translate well at the next level. With the puck, he makes smart touches and has a solid wrist shot.

In transition, Isogai carries the puck with success. His acceleration can improve, but his top speed is solid, and combined with strong puck skills, he carries the puck inside. Off the rush, he's a deceptive player, as he can make play and shoot from distance as well.

On the man advantage, Isogai mostly played the half-wall on his one-timer side. His shooting arsenal was large. He loves to one-time puck, and he also likes to threaten the inside and use his wrist shot.

69	PLAYER	TEAM	LEAGUE	HEIGHT	WEIGHT	POS	GRADE
	KIVIHARJU, ARON	HIFK	FINLAND	5' 09.5"	184	LD	C
NHLCS	CEILING	FLOOR	HOCKEY SENSE	COMPETE	SKILL	SKATE	MISC
INT-8	6	3	8	5	6	5	5

Aron Kiviharju is a cerebral, undersized defenseman who uses advanced look-off's to set up the majority of his plays. At the age of 15 he was coveted as potentially the next Rasmus Dahlin, but after failing to grow and losing 2 years of his career recently to knee injuries, his projection has changed by many from a can't miss blue chip prospect to an undersized defender who's struggled just to stay in the lineup.

Kiviharju isn't large and he knows it. To counteract his physical limitations and average tool-kit, he makes sure that he's difficult to read. He doesn't telegraph his intentions on most play types, ranging from his breakout passes, to when he's quarterbacking a powerplay. He has advanced off-looks and understands how to use his body posture in combination with his playmaking to keep opposing defenses from taking his passing lanes from him. His precision playmaking extends through all three zones and it's the foundation of his game.

His best trait is his ability to recognize the skating trajectory and positioning of his teammates when he's not looking at them. Some players have better instincts than others for knowing the timing and trajectory of where their teammates will be in advance for a pass, and that's the defining quality of Kiviharju's game. He's a mental mapping machine, and can stretch the length of the ice.

His short area lateral playmaking game had made him efficient when running a powerplay from the backend as well. Due to his precision, the majority of his passes allow his shooters to operate properly within their wheelhouse and he very rarely forces unnecessary passes through heavy traffic that are likely to be intercepted.

Another quality that compliments his passing ability is how poised he is. Under heavy pressure during retrievals or when he's getting closed on at the offensive line, he's rarely rushed. He understands how to use feints to slow down faster players, and plays a mature, responsible game where he rarely throws pucks into bad areas of the ice or puts his teammates in bad positions when they are receiving passes.

Kiviharju's poise with the puck under pressure is based on his panic threshold. At the NHL level, you have split second reactions to plays happening on the ice, and we believe with Kiviharju's hockey sense he can come out a plus player at the highest pace of play due to his poise generating consistently good decisions on the ice. Furthermore, he has solid results in dynamic situations where he needed to adapt on the fly with a forecheck bearing down on him.

Defensively, he's out-thinking his opponents by trying to stay ahead of them. He's not an explosive skater and he's not a very powerful defender, so instead his defensive game is predicated off of good communication with his defensive partner, well timed positional switches, good stick timing and the understanding of how to cut out in-front of a pass and intercept the puck. We wish he had more of a multi-faceted defensive game, and we wish he operated with a higher motor, but there's no denying his efficient and cerebral game.

Some of you might be surprised by our ranking of Kiviharju, but it comes down to a philosophical approach of what we prefer in a defender. We naturally prefer bigger, meaner, and larger defenseman who can really skate, and that's the opposite of Kiviharju's game. If we rank a smaller defenseman high, it's because we feel they are dynamic enough offensively, which isn't the case with Kiviharju. He's a gifted playmaker, but he's not a great handler or shooter and lacks the skating needed to break down a line like Buium, Levshunov, Parekh or Dickinson as some examples. His tool-kit is weaker than we are comfortable with at this stage in his development, especially when factoring in his injury history and although he's very smart and we really appreciate that attribute, we feel there's too much risk involved in his game when looking at his development to rank him too high.

Small, puck moving defenseman are extremely rare at the NHL level, and are likely only going to be rarer in the coming years. Some of you might disagree with us, and that's perfectly fine, but we wanted to give our thought process as to why he's ranked lower than you might see elsewhere.

"He's unlikely to quarterback a powerplay at the NHL level. He's going to have to be insulated due to his play style and size and he's injury prone. That's not exactly a recipe for a defensive prospect that you wan to rank too high. I appreciate his sense for the game but with the knee injuries and the current skating base as a result of those injuries I think he's overrated." – HP Scout, Brad Allen

"We didn't leave him off our list entirely for a reason. He still has a chance to play meaningful minutes if he can stay healthy because he is a very smart defender who can really pass a puck." – HP Scout, Brad Allen

72	PLAYER		TEAM	LEAGUE	HEIGHT	WEIGHT	POS	GRADE
	KLEBER, ADAM		LINCOLN	USHL	6' 05.5"	215	RD	C
NHLCS	CEILING	FLOOR	HOCKEY SENSE	COMPETE	SKILL		SKATE	MISC
NA-34	6	4	5	6	4		7	7

Adam Kleber saw his production jump from just eight assists in 2022-23 up to 5+21=26 line in his second season with the Lincoln Stars (USHL). Though a fairly modest total league-wide, it was enough to lead the club's rearguards in points on one of the league's most anemic offenses. It's hard to dream up a stat line or…a stat…that would do Kleber's game justice.

Starting with the positive: His skating is much improved from a year ago, both in terms of the mechanics and the output. His lateral mobility creates a ranginess that is difficult for forwards to negotiate. The three-point flexion improvements are fuelling a more explosive and efficient stride. At the top end, he has really nice extension allowing him to get to a notable top speed when joining the rush. Having a skating base like this on a 6'5", 207 pound frame while also being a right-handed shot automatically puts him on the radar.

He's a rudimentary puck handler who lacks puck poise still. There are a lot of heavy puck touches in a small puck control window. His passing and pass catching under pressure is largely unimpressive, but when he has his feet moving and there's an obvious, direct pass that can be made, Kleber is capable. He puts pucks towards the net instead of fiddling around at the attack line, but he is generally not a threat to score from distance. There's some physicality mixed in there, but Adam doesn't seem naturally mean. He does understand what it means to focus on the chest of the opponent that's near the net and remove the opponent from that spot, certainly.

Watching Kleber this season is fascinating because no one can predict what you're going to get. We've tried to pin it down and find some pattern in the behaviour, but we just can't figure out the algorithm to his random stylings. Now, that's not to say that it's all bad. There are games where he sits back and manages the ice fairly well and gets pucks out and gets off the ice. Then there's a large number of games where he just sort of does his own thing all over the defensive and neutral zones. For starters, he's a very loose gap player. It's likely that he hasn't updated his play style to account for his improved skating, but he's going to want to. He allows some rubbish plays to fester for too long because of his spacing and gap management.

These situations, too, are where we question the natural toughness of this player. A lot of d-men of this supposed type would go and make a close off or a big hit…even if it's not the best play, it removes a threat that has or had the puck. Kleber is uneven with his physicality in this regard. Watching him deal with in-zone defense is really interesting because there are all kinds of things that can happen: He can mind the front of the net, picking up sticks, but ultimately being patient; he can play very physical and focus 100% of his attention on boxing out the man near the front, even if the play has switched sides and his partner wants to switch off with him; he could chase the cycle all the way up to the blueline and then park at the blueline and become the high forward for a while.

To use a truism, the good stuff is good and the bizarre stuff leaves his teammates scrambling to figure out what they should do next. His partner support is very wonky and oddly timed. For instance, we've seen sequences where the puck is dumped in and his partner goes to retrieve, so Kleber helps to pick F1 – which is perfect. Normally, after a stride or so, with the puck secured by the partner, you disengage, pivot, and widen out for a potential D-to-D pass. But we've seen Kleber continue to skate backwards just facing this F1, mirroring his movement, all the way back to his own end line, completely ignoring that his partner has already retrieved it and needs an outlet. Another truly bizarre thing that he does often is he just bats pucks with his hand into the middle of the rink. There was a late season game against Tri-City where a number of pucks were flipped out of the zone and under no real duress, he just batted them (already in the neutral zone) into the middle of the neutral zone. Of course, that's ok if a forechecker is right on you and it's a tough spot. But these were regular desperation flips by the opponent and he could have just put it down in front of him and played it…and he just batted every one of them into the middle of nowhere. Three of the four led to rush attempts for Tri-City, the other one was touched by a shrugging teammate for a hand pass whistle.

It's hard to say whether some of the mental processing that he undergoes can be smoothed out at this point. He doesn't calculate risk very well, and that's probably there to stay. But mechanically, there are some things that he can do to better his rush absorption techniques…for instance, he consistently extends his stick way out when defending the rush, but that declares his reach too soon and also leaves his triangle exposed too readily. With an elbow tuck and readiness to pivot skate, he can probably become a much more consistent rush defender and maybe disrupt more plays before they really begin. Pattern recognition in the defensive zone can probably help him there too. Right now, he's trying to do a little too much, while also playing way deep (usually) and he ends up screening his goalie a lot, he even crosses in front of his goalie as a shot is being released to address another player fairly regularly. It's just all very raw still, despite the amount of experience he has at this level. That said, he was playing for 14U and 15U AA teams as recently as 2021. So, the fact that he's playing in the Hlinka and World Jr. A Challenge tournaments three years later is nothing to sneeze at. Kleber still has a ways to go in terms of the structure of his game and his mental processing. If the technical skill set was more interesting, maybe we'd take a chance, but as it stands, another team will easily beat us to the punch.

"This is one where I might not see it right now, but in three years it all comes together for him… that said, there's more NHL-looking prospects available in the 2nd or 3rd rounds that I'd be much more comfortable with." HP Scout, Michael Farkas

	PLAYER	TEAM	LEAGUE	HEIGHT	WEIGHT	POS	GRADE
80	**KOIVU, AATOS**	TPS	FIN JR	6' 00.5"	170	RC	C

NHLCS	CEILING	FLOOR	HOCKEY SENSE	COMPETE	SKILL	SKATE	MISC
INT-27	5	4	6	5	5	6	5

Aatos Koivu, the son of former NHLer Saku Koivu, has experienced significant development over the past year, both physically and on the ice. He has noticeably grown stronger since last year; now listed at 6'00" and 165 pounds, compared to his previous listing of 5'10" and 126 pounds last season. He was a late bloomer who had never played internationally in big events for Finland until this year. Originally cut from the Hlinka Gretzky U18 team in the summer, he became the number one center for the U18 team at the Five Nations' Tournament in November.

Having begun the season in Finland's U18 league, he was called up to the U20 team after averaging over a point per game. There, he continued to maintain a similar ratio. He even had the opportunity to play some games in the Liiga. This progression exemplifies a great development curve. Aatos himself admitted that he initially expected to play the full season in the U18 league, with the NHL Draft not even on his radar at the start of the year.

Koivu is a smart center who plays solid hockey at both ends of the ice. The effort level that was a huge part of his father's game is also present in his. He's not as physical as his father was, but he works hard and doesn't quit on plays. Could the physicality come as he matures physically? It's possible, and this is not to say that he's a soft player, either. He just is not strong enough at the moment to really make a big physical impact, and tends to be on the wrong end of physical battles along the boards. Due to his lack of strength, he tends to stay on the perimeter; he will need to play more on the inside in order to enjoy more offensive success. Early on in the U20 league, he was having success in terms of speed, shooting and his play on the man-advantage. At some point teams did figure him out, and his production cooled off as a result. Some fatigue may have also come into play in terms of his production. He had 22 points in his first 15 games in the U20 league, ending the year with 9 points in his last 13. This is where he needs to add more dimension to his game, one of which is playing more inside, especially in the context of the North American style of play. This could become easier for him once he adds more strength to his frame, as he's currently quite slim.

Offensively, his best weapon is his shot, a big contrast from his father who probably wished he had his son's shooting skills. At the junior level and in international competitions, Aatos has demonstrated his shooting ability successfully. He has shown the ability to score from distance, often on the power play while playing from the Ovechkin spot, and was quite successful at this. He has a quick release, can pick corners with his shot and his velocity is considerably good. As of now, however, his shooting skills have been more noticeable than his passing skills. We wish we saw more projection with his playmaking but have yet to see significant high-end playmaking from him. Though this could develop over time, our observations this season suggest limited high-end playmaking from him, which impacts our NHL projection for him.

Another strong asset is his skating. While still physically weak, he does generate some real good speed. He can challenge defenders with his outside speed, good acceleration and agility on the ice. That acceleration enables him to create distance quickly to escape pressure. He's a good transition player because of that, and has good enough hands to beat players in the neutral zone and make good zone entries.

Koivu is a tough one to rank and to project because he's quite physically raw, and that affects some parts of his game. The exciting news is that there's been solid improvement from last year to now. Considering the development that is still left to do makes his profile intriguing. However, it also leaves us grappling with how much he'll improve over the next 2-3 years, which complicates his projection. His development curve from August 2023 to January 2024 was incredible, but since then, it appears to have plateaued. The latter part of the season combined with international events (February U18 Five Nations, April U18 World Championship) have tempered our enthusiasm when it comes to ranking him aggressively. While we still see potential in the player, we now view him more as a mid or late-round pick.

82	PLAYER			TEAM		LEAGUE	HEIGHT	WEIGHT	POS	GRADE
	KOL, TIMUR			OMSK		RUS JR	6' 03"	198	LD	C
NHLCS	CEILING	FLOOR		HOCKEY SENSE		COMPETE	SKILL		SKATE	MISC
INT-30	6	5		6		6	6		7	7

A large offensively inclined defenseman for Omskie Yastreby in the MHL, Timur Kol is a strong and reliable player who eats minutes and plays in all situations. Kol played at three different levels in Russia, all in Omsk, but finished the year with Omskie Yastreby in the MHL after stints in the VHL, Russia U18 and the KHL. In 14 games in the MHL Kol put up 8 points with an additional 5 points in 8 playoff games. The combination of size and production in addition to his soft defensive skills are consistently on display, no matter the situation or how big the game.

As a two-way defender who is more of an offensive threat at this stage in his development, Kol has a hard slap shot and loves to shoot from the point and by sneaking into the zone and shooting from the top of the circles. He has good accuracy and gets his shots on net in addition to having strong offensive instincts knowing when to pinch and when to pass or shoot. He has great vision from the point and often creates space for himself and teammates using his vision and his skating to force players out of position and then hit an open teammate with a set-up pass. He also uses his vision coming out of the zone, maybe his best attribute, where he makes great outlet passes setting up rush opportunities by scanning regularly while coming up ice in transition.

A big and physical defender, Kol is tough to play against for a number of reasons and we believe there is more to uncover defensively in his development. He covers space quickly and cuts off both passing and shooting lanes with long strides and a long reach that also help in his gap control. On the rush he uses his frame and reach to keep player to the outside and is very versatile in playing both sides of the ice with ease. We do want to see him be more aggressive with his size and become a bit faster as he gains even more strength and becomes even harder to knock off the puck.

With his size and offensive ability already intact, a defensive improvement would vault Kol even higher up draft boards, however currently he is not as defensively responsible as some other defensemen in this class. He does have the translatability and the intelligence as we often see him communicating with teammates in his own end and his strong transition up ice.

107	PLAYER	TEAM	LEAGUE	HEIGHT	WEIGHT	POS	GRADE
	KOROTKY MATVEI	SKA-1946 ST PBRG	RUS JR	6' 01"	198	RC	C
NHLCS	CEILING	FLOOR	HOCKEY SENSE	COMPETE	SKILL	SKATE	MISC
-	6	5	6	5	6	6	6

One of the latest 2005 births in the draft class, Korotky flies under the radar among Russian forwards in the 2024 NHL Draft. Putting up 38 points and 20 goals for SKA-1946 St. Petersburg in 51 MHL games this year and 14 points in 18 playoff games, Korotky provides a steady presence down the middle in either a scoring, power or shutdown role due to his versatility.

Although he seems to be top heavy at this time in his development, Korotky skates well and has a good stride and overall mobility that will only get better as he fills out more. He does not possess top level speed, but he is able to handle the puck well at his top speed and takes passes well in stride up the ice. Although more of a playmaker than a shooter, Korotky has a good shot with some power he will just need to work on his accuracy to improve his shot further. Korotky plays the offensive zone up the middle, in front of the net and down low which is where he is most comfortable and where he can create the most opportunities offensively. He is not a primary puck carrier into the zone, but he is good as a complimentary option on the rush and in the slot. He does bunch up with teammates at time and needs to work on being more consistent in puck battles, especially since he projects to be a power center at the NHL level.

In the defensive zone is where he is at his best, Korotky is typically the first man back and last to leave the defensive zone. He jumps on loose pucks defensively but needs to be more consistent in getting them out of his zone. He can do this by using his wingers more instead of trying to do it all himself. A very reliable defensive center, Korotky is good in his positioning off puck and clogs lanes not only in his own zone but on the backcheck as well. He is often blocking shots and getting himself and his stick into lanes to take away space from opposing forwards both five on five and on the penalty kill where he also shows his hustle.

Physically, Korotky will need to be more consistent as he is not the best in puck battles despite his size. He battles hard but he needs to show some more snarl and use his frame better by planting his feet more and gaining more lower body strength instead of trying to rely on his stick to win the battle. He does use his weight in body contact, although we would like to see him ramp it up physically at times and he likes to finish his checks high in the offensive zone and the neutral zone on the backcheck.

Korotky is a reliable center who is strong in all three zones and good on the draw with quick hands. We would like to see him progress more offensively next season with a power center style of play and get some more consistent time on the power play playing as a bumper as opposed to high on the outside.

75	PLAYER	TEAM	LEAGUE	HEIGHT	WEIGHT	POS	GRADE
	KOS, ONDREJ	ILVES JR.	FIN JR	6' 02.5"	176	LW	C

NHLCS	CEILING	FLOOR	HOCKEY SENSE	COMPETE	SKILL	SKATE	MISC
INT-26	5	5	6	7	5	7	5

Hard working, checking winger. Ondrej Kos followed the path of his brother Jakub (Fla 6th round, 2021) and left Czechia for the Finnish junior ranks for the last two seasons. Ondrej actually saw the majority of his abbreviated season up with KOOVEE in the Mestis League (second-tier Finnish pro). Despite being just 18 years old, Kos received a good deal of ice time on a fairly poor team. He had a 3+2=5 stat line in 14 tilts. At the U20 junior level with Ilves, he had three goals and no assists in eight contests. After missing the remainder of both seasons starting in late November, he did return to represent his home nation at the U18 World Championships – netting one goal.

His game isn't necessarily one that shows up in the box score, but he can still be an asset to a scoring line. His combination of compete level and skating permit him to be around the puck or supporting the play in all three zones. Already blessed with a long, powerful stride Kos has a well-rounded skating base on top of good mechanics. There really isn't a weakness to his skating. He has first step quickness, acceleration, maybe elite level top speed, smooth crossover-led turns, and he can set a wide A-frame for puck protection and tempo control purposes.

Further, his spatial awareness, hockey sense, and good defensive stick make him a demon on the forecheck. Ultimately, his forechecking ability may be his most transferable skill. It's really high end for a player of this experience level. He's a threat to get pucks himself as an F1 at the junior level. He patrols passing lanes, has a willingness to be physical and battle for contested pucks, and has enough technical skill to recover pucks and convert them into useful opportunities.

His game with the puck outside of forecheck recoveries is a little less convincing. Not because he's completely unskilled – Kos is a neat stickhandler, there are elements of deception in his game, he has a fairly wide puck control window, and the presence of mind to turn against pressure and try to hold pucks until a better situation arises. Not the softest hands around, he has some "heavy" touches mixed in there – it can force him to push pucks too far ahead when he's preparing for a shot, or he can tap it outside of his puck protection window when making sharp turns. We also notice the remarkably low conversion rates of his controlled zone entries. Because of his skating and pace, he authors a number of opportunities crossing the line with the puck – but too many of those plays end up failing shortly thereafter. There are a few very common threads in his neutral zone carrying ventures: one, he carries it wide up the boards, then does a tight Gretzky turn. He can make a short pass or play it back to an open point, this was his only consistent method of success in these situations. Other instances involved him turning towards the wall and holding it, ultimately losing it himself – as he scarcely has a way to get the puck from the boards to the interior by himself. Two, he carries it up the dots or wider and tries to make a pass in motion, usually a slip pass – almost all of these are not clean plays and often get turned over. Third, he gets a middle entry and fires a long, listless wrist shot towards the net from 55 feet out. It's not a pretty sight; about 2 out of 3 of his entries saw his team lose the puck in the immediate proceeding sequence.

That said, all hope is not lost. Part of what we like about what we see here is that he has the speed to push defenders back and get the line, but then incorporates a tempo control puck protection maneuver to buy some time for second wave offense. Right now, he's getting a little complex or fancy with those passes…and that's okay from a technical experimentation perspective. The foundation of something scalable is there. He rarely employs self-chip plays, which he almost certainly should be able to develop. We don't expect, however, him to be able to lead a rush and penetrate meaningful ice while holding the puck at the NHL level. His one-touch passing ability isn't very impressive and he doesn't quite anticipate passing lanes like a high-end playmaker. He's in a mode where he can identify a seam, take half a beat, and then make a pass. If he ever gets to a point, where through a turn, he can let go a cross-lane pass on the money – then we may see his zone entry conversion rates go up significantly. Right now, we don't get the sense that

that's going to mature to that level. He does show some in-stride shooting upside, which could provide some pop-gun offense off the rush in time. Kos gets shooting opportunities with his timing and ability to get open near the far post. He owns a nice cross-crease backhand finishing move – it has off-the-rush upside and net-front/rebound scoring upside. He has a strong stick, and he can get free in traffic to find loose pucks at very high level compared to his peers. That's ultimately where he's going to probably have to score from. Not that his shot is bad, but he's not an explosive, quick release shooter. He tries to rely on (over) holding pucks in his shooting process too, so he's a "timing" (against goalie movement) scorer, which is a good thing - but he needs to really have those types of chances jump off his blade with high-end push-pull wrist action and he's not there mechanically.

Right now, there's enough to like about his off the puck game to at least make him interesting. Forechecking, backchecking, net-front presence, board battles, there's a potential energy winger in here – We sometimes talk about giving a bit of a boost to players that we think can step up in the Stanley Cup Playoffs when called upon – Kos feels like he could be one of those guys.

NR	PLAYER		TEAM	LEAGUE	HEIGHT	WEIGHT	POS	GRADE
	LACERTE, FÉLIX		SHAWINIGAN	QMJHL	5' 09.75"	165	LW	NI
NHLCS	CEILING	FLOOR	HOCKEY SENSE	COMPETE	SKILL		SKATE	MISC
NA-133	5	4	6	4	6		5	4

Lacerte, drafted 22nd overall in the 2022 QMJHL Draft, has proven to be a standout player for Shawinigan over the past two seasons. In his rookie year, he scored 24 goals and had 52 points in 67 games, followed by an impressive 31 goals and 59 points in 51 games this season. He had the second-highest points-per-game average among U18 skaters in the league, trailing only Justin Poirier.

A good offensive player in minor hockey before his time in the QMJHL, Lacerte made a quick adjustment to major junior and performed well right off the bat. A smart player, he reads the play well and is good at finding soft ice in the offensive zone. An opportunistic scorer and good finisher, he has good hands and good shooting abilities. His quick release has helped him score a good portion of his goals. He can also score from various distances and is dangerous in the slot.

He's not huge, though, and that will diminish some of his offensive value at the next level. He's also not a gifted athlete, his athleticism is just okay and his skating is average for a player his size. He excels in the offensive zone, but he's not a game-breaking talent that will carry the puck; he'll need linemates to feed him in the offensive zone. His play away from the puck is also below-average; he is not very impactful in these situations.

He's a guy who can score lots of goals and is likely to score 40 or more in junior (he could even crack the 50 mark if all goes well), but he falls in the "good junior" category for us. His lack of size, speed, and compete level are reasons we believe that. He could surprise us at the pro level, but there's currently not enough to justify placing him on our list and seeing him as a bona fide future NHLer.

NR	PLAYER		TEAM	LEAGUE	HEIGHT	WEIGHT	POS	GRADE
	LAFOND, MAXIME		DRUMMONDVILLE	QMJHL	6' 04"	196	LC	NI
NHLCS	CEILING	FLOOR	HOCKEY SENSE	COMPETE	SKILL		SKATE	MISC
NA 162	5	4	5	5	4		5	7

A good-sized winger from Drummondville, Lafond played more of a depth role on this team for a second straight year. He finished with 23 points in 68 games after having 8 points in 60 games in his rookie season last year. He was a 3rd round pick by Drummondville in the 2022 QMJHL Draft.

His offensive game is a bit limited. He doesn't have a good shot, and it's something he should work on by improving both the velocity and release. Currently, he scores his goals around the net through deflections or rebounds, as he can't beat goaltenders from distances with his shot. His hands are just okay; he won't beat players one-on-one with them and his play in tight areas is not particularly strong. However, he's an underrated playmaker with decent vision and the ability to make creative passes in transition or in the offensive zone, setting up his teammates from his forehand or backhand.

He has a decent combination of size and skating and moves well enough for his size on the ice. As he adds strength to his frame, his stride could become more explosive. He's very raw and could be a player with a significant progression curve next season with more responsibilities and ice time. There's some physicality to his game as well; he can finish players with good hits here and there. While he can make an impact with his hits, he's not a mean player, or at least we haven't seen enough of that aspect this season.

We could see Lafond get selected late in the draft if teams are betting on his raw potential and size. His long playoff run in the QMJHL playoffs and his Memorial Cup experience probably benefit his chances of being seen more by NHL scouts.

111	PLAYER	TEAM	LEAGUE	HEIGHT	WEIGHT	POS	GRADE
	LAING, HUNTER	PRINCE GEORGE	WHL	6' 05.25"	205	RC	C
NHLCS	CEILING	FLOOR	HOCKEY SENSE	COMPETE	SKILL	SKATE	MISC
NA-86	6	4	6	6	5	4	8

The 6'6" forward played his 1st season in the WHL, scoring 25 points in 66 games for the Cougars. He mostly played in a 3rd line role on a deep Cougars' team, with 2nd power play unit in front of the net.

Offensively, Laing excels down low in the offensive zone. He's strong and protects the puck really well with his reach. He has underrated puck skills, as he can attack the net down low and take rebound in small areas. His vision is decent as well, finding inside play to F3 in the offensive zone. In transition, he uses his size well on breakouts wall play to connect the play on zone exits. His neutral zone transition needs work, as his ability to carry the puck is limited due to below average skating.

Defensively, Laing is a smart and responsible player. He works hard, makes defensive stops, and shows good awareness overall without the puck. He does a good F3 job on the forecheck, covering for his defensemen when needed, and scans in the defensive zone to cover his check. He's involved on the forecheck and tries to complete his hits, but sometimes is a bit late due to his poor skating.

It will be interesting to follow Laing's development in the next few seasons. His role should improve next season with some top forwards from Prince George graduating. He uses his size well to protect the puck, he has underrated puck skill and vision and is a smart player overall. His skating needs work and it's the most important part of his game he needs to develop to reach his upside.

NR	PLAYER	TEAM	LEAGUE	HEIGHT	WEIGHT	POS	GRADE
	L'ITALIEN, ELIOT	BLAINVILLE	QMJHL	6' 01"	187	LC	NI
NHLCS	CEILING	FLOOR	HOCKEY SENSE	COMPETE	SKILL	SKATE	MISC
NA -128	4	4	5	6	4	5	5

L'Italien was selected as the 8th overall pick in the 2022 QMJHL Draft. However, his numerous injuries since then have taken a toll on his development. Last season, he missed the entire second half, playing only 14 games and participating in the U17 Hockey Challenge. This season, he managed to play 46 games, but missed 22 due to various injuries.

Showing flashes at times during the season, he's a good skater with good size, which makes him intriguing for NHL teams. He has the speed to beat defenders wide, loves attacking defenders and tries to get around them with his outside speed. He can drive to the net with the puck, but needs to do it more often. Too often, we saw him opting to go behind the net rather than cutting towards it, attempting moves like wrap-arounds instead. It's tougher for him to try to go through the middle lanes because he has to use his hands more to dangle opponents, and his hands are below-average. Overall, his offensive skills are below average; he lacks stickhandling effectiveness despite his decent shot and vision. One of our primary issues this season was his limited involvement in games; in many of our viewings, he had too few puck touches. The amount of missed time since last season has put him at a developmental disadvantage compared to other players in the league. It's worth noting, however, that even in Midget AAA, he was never a player who had outstanding offensive upside. The questions about his offensive upside in general are warranted. We do appreciate his high compete level and ability to play sound hockey in all three zones, including the PK. He's also capable of playing a physical game, leveraging his projectable frame for the professional level. His primary challenge will be to improve his skills over the next few years in order to establish himself as a good prospect for the professional game.

L'Italien has some elements to his game that we like, but his lack of skills made him drop on our QMJHL (and overall) list during the year. We're not giving up hope, but we didn't see much improvement during the season that gave us enough to keep him on our list. If he goes undrafted, he's a player we will keep monitoring next season to see how his skills improve.

NR	PLAYER	TEAM	LEAGUE	HEIGHT	WEIGHT	POS	GRADE
	LAPOINTE, JEAN-FÉLIX	SHERBROOKE	QMJHL	6' 06"	196	LD	NI
NHLCS	CEILING	FLOOR	HOCKEY SENSE	COMPETE	SKILL	SKATE	MISC
-	4	4	4	5	4	5	7

Lapointe is a classic QMJHL late-bloomer type of defenseman with an interesting backstory. He played his first season with Sherbrooke this year as a 2005-born player. Last season, he played in the Quebec Collegial League. Instead of playing in the Midget AAA league before that, he went through the RSEQ program, as he was also playing high-level football in the Quebec school system at the same time. He also played (both sports) last season with his CÉGEP (Collège Champlain-Lennoxville) which at this level is almost unheard of.

He's one of those players that might get drafted based on his athletic abilities alone. It might not happen this season, as he's not well known, his game is very raw, and he also didn't exactly set the league on fire this season. As previously mentioned, he's a late-bloomer who started his QMJHL career in his 18-year-old season, but he still has decent tools to work with. Obviously, his size is one of them. While we felt he was a bit passive earlier in the season with his physicality, by the end of the season, he was meaner and tougher to play against. There's a lot of projection to be had in terms of his defensive game, but we feel that if there's nice progress over the next 2 seasons, the next level is within reach.

He's quick to cut time and space from puck-carriers, covering a good amount of ice with his reach and skating skills. He needs to get better in terms of reads and positioning, but that has a lot to do with his inexperience at the major junior level. His puck game is also just okay. He's not a future power-play guy in the NHL, but he's not awful, either. One thing to note: the quickness of his decision-making improved over the course of the season. Early on, he was slow when it came to moving pucks, but as the season progressed, he started to move them faster. His decision-making was not always on point either, and there's a lot of work that still needs to be done there (also, his passing accuracy). This goes back to him being really raw. His puck game is quite raw, and will need to continue to get better.

One key element when scouting defensemen that we watch out for is in regards to how they retrieve pucks. Basically, if you can't retrieve pucks, you can't play a regular role in the NHL. This was very up and down with him; he'll need to find more consistency.

There are some parallels that can be made between Lapointe and Chicago Blackhawks' defenseman Louis Crevier. Drafted by the Blackhawks in the 7th round in 2020 (in his second year of eligibility), Crevier did play some games in the NHL this season. Like Lapointe, he was a late-bloomer. While we feel Lapointe has better athleticism than Crevier, Crevier had a better hockey brain. We're unsure if Lapointe will get drafted this year; an NHL team will have to be willing to make a bit of a gamble based on his athletic abilities and hope for a good level of development and improvement to his overall skill level over the next two seasons in the QMJHL. He's a project, but he's huge and a good athlete, the rest of his game will just have to follow.

NR	PLAYER	TEAM	LEAGUE	HEIGHT	WEIGHT	POS	GRADE
	LARING, HUGO	FROLUNDA JR.	SWE JR	6' 01.75"	191	G	C
NHLCS	CEILING	FLOOR	HOCKEY SENSE	COMPETE	SKILL	SKATE	MISC
INT-7	6	3	4	7	7	5	6

Hugo Laring is a very raw, yet athletically gifted goalie who had a difficult season but still has shown considerable upside. He started the season poorly before finding another level to his play that peaked in his playoff performances. He presents one of the more bizarre and interesting goalie case studies this draft, as a direct result of not really having a full-time goalie coach, despite playing for one of the most famous organizations in Sweden. This was noticeable both on the ice and was also verified off the ice. Despite this, Laring has standout characteristics, which include not only his athleticism but also his competitiveness and aggressiveness.

Let's start with his lack of goaltending coaching and, as a result, his lack of technique in fundamental areas, then work towards why there's potential down the line.

From a philosophical perspective, we feel that most goalies are actually overtrained at this stage in their development. Back in the 90s, up until the mid-2000s, 17-18-year-old goalies relied more on their instincts and weren't all taught the same mechanics, which meant some of them had different styles of play and presented considerably different in net. Fast-forward to today's 17-18-year-old goalie, and they are basically all given the same techniques with subtle variation depending on their physical make-up. Goalies are technically refined at a young age, to the point where they don't ever get an opportunity to develop a base of instincts that would make them better as they turn pro. It's a difficult balancing act between blending the right amount of instinct with the right amount of technique in this age group.

In Laring's case, his technique falls behind the mark of where we generally feel comfortable at this stage in his development. It starts with his skating base and post-integration in an RVH position. Laring can fail to adequately use his edges properly along his post when in an RVH, meaning he can fail to push off properly, falling short of the transfer needed to get back out and in front of the puck on lateral passing setups or low-to-high setups from below the goal line. His micro shuffles from a set stance, his T-push offs from a relaxed stance, and his butterfly lateral transfer rates also need improvement so that he isn't as susceptible to high-danger shots off passing plays that force a positional transfer from him as they do currently.

Another area where he needs to rein in his technique is how often he over-rotates his positioning when he's transitioning between save types and sometimes fails to remain sealed. After making the first save, he has the reflexes and extension rates to get out in front of most rebounds, but when he's over-rotating, it takes away his advantages and takes him out of the play. When he's transferring through his butterfly, he can remain tall and large but then fail to seal off the necessary areas, taking away his butterfly height.

He can also remain stagnant and static in his butterfly after transferring into it. We want goalies to typically deploy what we call a transitional butterfly, where they enter their butterfly, and if the puck doesn't get through, then begin to immediately transfer back into a standing set position. Of course, there are specific plays in tight to the net where staying down to cover the lower part is the better play, but in Laring's case, when he loses pucks behind coverage, he has a tendency to evaluate where the puck might be while remaining seated.

We love aggressive goalies who are confident between the pipes, and Laring is that. In fact, he's arguably the most tenacious goalie that we've written about when looking to cut down on a high-danger angle. It's similar to Vladimir Nikitin's style of play in the BCHL, where they will travel well outside their blue paint in order to take away the net. It's a lot of fun to watch, and at times it really does give the shooter nothing to look at, but it's a balancing act that Laring has yet to become consistent at managing.

Laring can have difficulty recognizing potential backdoor setups and give-and-go sequences in tight to the net. Occasionally, he will aggressively cut down the initial angle but subsequently throw himself out of position if the potential shooting option decides to pass the puck off to a teammate that's open for an in-tight lateral setup or backdoor/redirect option. He needs to make sure he can counteract multi-option plays while still playing his position properly at a higher rate than he currently does. This means cutting down on his aggression when it's called for. Though, towards the end of the season, he was starting to show improvements in this area.

The good news is that despite these technical flaws, he can fix and modify them over time. We have evaluated tons of goalies who stay in their butterfly too long and have greatly improved their skating bases and learned how to keep everything tighter while heavily suppressing their aggression at the right times. We still want to illustrate these technical flaws, though, to emphasize the raw components of his game.

In terms of his plus components, his competitiveness can be seen with how willing he is to battle through shots, when he needs to fully extend through a save, or how willing he is to throw whatever limb is available to make the save while contorting his frame. Some goalies stay too confined within their games, and if they can't make the smooth or efficient save, they can look more flustered in chaotic moments, but Laring has a mentality of just getting the stop, no matter what it takes. This mentality bleeds into what we discussed earlier about relying more heavily on instincts, and in this regard, we welcome it.

His athleticism is multi-dimensional. He has excellent extension rates that allow him to enter a full post-to-post split. He has dexterous shoulders that allow him to elevate his frame on shots that are labeled near the top corners of the net, and he's reflexive to the point where he can rapidly shift into a different save type and make point-blank redirect saves as a result.

We have seen an impressive glove hand displayed by him as well. He can snag pucks that are lower to the ice and at difficult angles to catch. He can rapidly extend his glove, much like he can with his kicking rates, and with his blocker side, he's shown the ability to elevate it while remaining sealed so that he can absorb difficult shots. The hands and leg combination are dexterous and coordinated when taken as a whole.

In terms of his shooting evaluations, he grades out at a solid level. He can measure and recognize high-caliber shooters' sudden angle-shifting shots in tight to the net, and he's good at recognizing if a shot is labeled short or far-side, despite the shot distance. This was one of the reasons we felt he was as comfortable as he was at cutting down angles aggressively because even when closing the distance between himself and the shot, his initial evaluations of where they were labeled were consistently accurate.

Where Hugo can fall behind at times is through his lateral tracking,, especially if there's a lot of traffic in front of him. He can fail to match the speed of a lateral pass, fall behind the play, and as a result get beat on a shot that he would theoretically have given his athletic traits (when his skating base is holding). This was the most consistent and concerning issue that we evaluated right up until the end of the season. His athleticism and projection speak to a goalie who should be able to get ahead of the play on high-danger lateral setups at a solid rate as long as he continues to develop his skating base, but his delayed lateral tracking might fully stop that development.

As a whole, Laring has the size, athleticism, and mental makeup you want to see in a translatable NHL goalie base. His peak performances were at the end of the season, and his curve is in the right direction. He's raw, but he was also in a unique situation that is likely to improve next year. We think there's a lot of untapped potential despite him needing considerable time.

"Laring is a rare example of a goalie who is actually bigger than his current listing. I've stood next to him; he's 6'3", and there's lots of room to fill out." - HP Scout, Brad Allen

"He's a goalie who can make dynamic, highlight-reel saves but also beat himself out on the ice by not having the technique needed at this time." - HP Scout, Brad Allen

106	PLAYER	TEAM	LEAGUE	HEIGHT	WEIGHT	POS	GRADE
	LAVOIE, TOMAS	CAPE-BRETON	QMJHL	6' 03.5"	215	RD	C

NHLCS	CEILING	FLOOR	HOCKEY SENSE	COMPETE	SKILL	SKATE	MISC
NA-57	5	4	5	6	5	6	7

Lavoie was selected as the number 1 overall pick in the 2022 QMJHL Draft. Although he had a difficult first year in the league, he showed improvement in his second season. In the past season, he established himself as a dependable stay-at-home defenseman who can log a ton of ice time. He played in all situations and often played for over 25 minutes per game. He ended the year with 3 goals and 21 assists in 65 games and improved his +/- from -39 to +4 compared to the previous year.

Lavoie skates very well for a bigger player. His stride is very fluid, and he has some good straight-line speed. Moving laterally can sometimes be a problem for him as he can get burnt while in transition by quicker players and can have a hard time changing directions. Overall it's a good skating/size combo and he can work on the lateral agility and footwork to make it even better in the future.

Defensively, one of his biggest assets is his long reach as he quite frequently uses his reach to cut down passing lanes and can be tough to get past in 1 on 1 battles. We noticed that he added a bit more physicality to his game as the season progressed but still thought he could be a bit more tenacious along the walls and in front of the net. We would like to see more of a mean streak from him. He got beat far too often by smaller players particularly while trying to retrieve the puck down low. Also, when the other team gets settled in the defensive zone, we find that he can often get overly aggressive in pursuit of the puck which can lead to him being out of position. He is strong in puck retrievals, he used his big body and strong edgework to spin off of forecheckers and he has an accurate first pass which helps on his zone exits.

Lavoie does not seem to have much offensive upside as he tends to go for the safer low-risk plays and does not look very confident with the puck on his stick in the offensive zone. We have seen him make good plays when rushing the puck out of his zone and bringing the puck with success in the offensive zone but he rarely does it. We go back to his lack of confidence and opting to play a very simplistic puck game and cut down on turnover possibilities. One positive is that he has a cannon from the point, but he does not use it a ton and his play at the line is average. There was a game in Drummondville this season where he scored 2 goals and we thought this was going to be a turning point in his season offensively but we didn't see many games like this after.

With his combination of great size and good skating skills, Lavoie should definitely attract some NHL interest in June. Despite having a pretty high floor, we do not think that he has the upside to succeed in a top 4 role in the NHL but could definitely see him carve out a career as a bottom-pairing defender if everything goes right with his development.

"Vanilla is his middle name. Not always a bad thing though." - NHL Scout, November 2023

"Nobody on our staff likes this kid but I actually have time for him. He has some real upside." - NHL Scout, November 2023

"I kept expecting him to break out but it never happened. He is a late name for me." - NHL Scout, May 2024

"What does he do that gets him to the NHL is my question? Big and can skate but not much offense. Not physical and not hard to play against. He can move pucks when he has time and space but struggles mightily when he doesn't. A lot of hurdles to get over." - HP Scout, Mark Edwards, May 2024

9	PLAYER	TEAM	LEAGUE	HEIGHT	WEIGHT	POS	GRADE
	LEENDERS, RYERSON	MISSISSAUGA	OHL	6' 00.5"	165	G	C

NHLCS	CEILING	FLOOR	HOCKEY SENSE	COMPETE	SKILL	SKATE	MISC
NA-10	6	5	6	8	6	7	6

Ryserson Leenders is a well-rounded, competitive netminder who put together a quality season for Mississauga. Stylistically, he moves similarly to Alexander Georgiev when in his relaxed stance and when he's attempting to micro shuffle or move laterally. We also think there's going to be a lot of discussion surrounding George vs Leenders considering they both have similar stats, and are two of the top goalie prospects in the OHL this season. Here's our breakdown of Leenders game relative to George's, and where we think he has some advantages.

To start, Leender's relies more on his base instincts for the game and is more willing to break or free himself from his technique in order to make an exaggerated save on any given sequence, more so than George. George can choose to remain overly compact on certain save selections when he's dealing with high danger saves that are in tight to him, whereas Leenders embraces the concept of getting whatever limb he can, out in-front of the puck. Generally speaking, he can functionally break his technique when the play calls for it, at a higher rate.

We think it's important for Leenders to have this quality, since he doesn't read the game quite as well as George does, but he's a smart goalie in his own right. He recognizes the handedness of the shooters he's facing and plays the percentages correctly. He is aware of weak side or blind side passing set ups during both even strength and odd-man situations and he's attentive to back-door redirect plays in advance. He also fights through traffic, and like George sees through traffic relatively well.

Another commonality between the two of them is that they both have good glove-hands. One area to note with Leenders is that he's advanced at positioning his glove so that he can rotate through a shot that's labeled next to the side of his helmet. This specific area is targeted because it's harder for goalies to contort their shoulder posture and counteract the placement of these kinds of shots, but Leenders can extend his glove at uncomfortable vertical angles when the play calls for it. He's also capable of fantastic, point blank glove saves off of maintaining good glove posture when diving into a butterfly or kicking motion.

When evaluating his blocker-side, it grades out as a good to very good component of his game. He keeps his blocker positioned out in-front of him at the necessary range, and he understands how to rotate his frame through a shot that is labeled towards his blocker side so that he can continue to track it correctly on point of contact. He also recognizes how to modify his blocker saves relative to oncoming traffic. This means, that similarly to Carter George, he is largely successful at punching or deflecting pucks into dead areas of the ice, so they don't have to result in sporadic secondary or recovery saves as often.

Leenders presents a wider set stance and butterfly to the ice, which makes him considerably bigger looking than George at times, despite them having similarly listed heights. He has better kicking reflexes than George and we think he's actually just as good if not better at reactionary positional saves in tight to the net.

His weight transfers and ability to remain balanced, means that he's not scrambling to the degree we feel Carter George has to. Though we wouldn't label either as imbalanced goalies who cause chaos for themselves as a result of their skating bases very often. Their skating bases and transfer rates fall below Gardner's though. His curve also showed improvements in his skating base. In the first half of the season, Ryerson was caught in a seated RVH position when dealing with a low to high shot from below his goal line to out in-front of the slot or in the circles, too often. We have seen him remain stationary, without using his post to push off and square back up to the play. This is a technical fix, and he started correcting for it towards the end point of the season.

Leenders does have some difficulties in some areas of his game. Although he's an impressive athlete in his own right, when evaluating him next to other smaller goalies in this draft and others, he falls a bit behind them. He lacks Emil Vinni's explosive fast-twitch movement, and the extension rates and dynamism of Ivan Yunin, or the fluidity that's present in Evan Gardner. He's a well rounded athlete that grades above average everywhere, but he's not an exceptional one.

During lateral one-timer set ups from the circles during man advantages, or at even strength, on lateral passes that can result in a shot that requires a higher degree of extension, Leenders can have difficulty kicking out at a proper angle to take away short side options. This is due to failing to drive his pad parallel along the ice and instead remaining in a full butterfly with a partial extension. Part of this can be attributed to simple save selection, but the other part comes down to just not having extensions that are as powerful as he currently needs.

When evaluating his micro-adjustment and error correction skill-set, we saw a necessary improvement over the course of the season. At the beginning of the season we graded his transition between save types and overall fluidity as above average but not at a high enough level given his frame to feel overly comfortable. Yet, towards the end of the season, his transitions from a standing post integrated position to an aggressive push off that cuts down an initial shooting angle, into a lateral butterfly transfer before making an extended reactionary save, did improve significantly; as one example.

He's also displayed some unique techniques this past season. For instance, most goalies when they are seated and integrated into their post look to use their stick to counteract potential in tight lateral passes by keeping it low to the ice. However, by bringing their blocker and stick low to the ice it puts them off balance and off their centerline temporarily. To counteract this, Leenders doesn't bring his stick down to the ice on certain sequences, instead he holds his stick in mid-air and this allows him to remain on center so that he can laterally extend across the net faster when he's in a standing position while moving off his centerline.

One of the biggest areas of concern when looking at goalie prospects that are on the smaller side, such as Carter George, Evan Gardner, Ryerson Leenders, Jan Kavan, and in an extreme case such as Ilya Nabakov, is that they have to remain remarkably consistent in order to showcase starter potential. When looking at Leenders relative to the other goalies mentioned, we think there's an argument to be made that he's actually been more consistent than George, but not as consistent as Kavan or Nabokov, though they are also older goalies who you have to account for playing in very different environments, ranging from far weaker leagues, to very structures pro leagues. The stats back this statement up as well. Leenders allowed 5 goals or more in 9 regular season games, George allowed 5 goals or more in 13 regular season games.

Leenders showed an impressive development curve over the season and he's a battler. There were nights where without him in net, Mississauga would have been run over early and often. As a result of his impressive season and well rounded skill-set we found a spot in our ranking that reflects how we evaluated him relative to the other smaller goalies in this class.

"He was a goalie that took me time to get behind. He had a surge to start the year but there were also inconsistencies that hadn't been exploited yet. Towards the end of the season, his poor performances were few and far between, while his peak performances were more prominent, and that's what he needs in order to play, since he's not as talented as the top end that we have ranked." - HP Scout, Brad Allen

*"It's unbelievably hard for me to rank Leenders, George, Gardner, Kavan and Nabokov and get that order right. I sure tried, and time will tell but holy **** was it ever a battle and extremely difficult to gauge, due to differences in environment and playing styles." - HP Scout, Brad Allen*

"I like him. Played well in both my views so far. Moves well and was athletic...rebound control was good. Was able to recover and make some second saves as well...off to a good start." - HP Scout, Mark Edwards, October 2023

"Played great in my first viewing of him this season. Had a little blip but was solid almost all year long. I like his 'do anything to stop the puck' mentality he brings to the table and he isn't as cookie cutter as other goalies. He was much better in my views of him than George was in my viewings of him." - HP Scout, Mark Edwards, March 2024

34	PLAYER		TEAM	LEAGUE	HEIGHT	WEIGHT	POS	GRADE
	LETOURNEAU, DEAN		SAC	HIGH-ON	6' 06.5"	214	RC	B
NHLCS	CEILING	FLOOR	HOCKEY SENSE	COMPETE	SKILL		SKATE	MISC
NA-23	8	4	6	5	7		7	8

An imposing figure on the ice, St. Andrew's College center Dean Letourneau posted 127 points including 61 goals in just 56 games this season. He showed clutch ability in the playoffs with key goals for the Saints and will look to continue to showcase this ability next season. Letourneau will either join Sioux Falls in the USHL before heading to Boston College the following season or possibly head straight to BC if a spot opens up.

One of the easiest draft eligibles to notice on the ice due to his massive frame. As mentioned, Letourneau plays at the Canadian High School Prep level and this works against him despite the numbers, size and skill he displays on a consistent basis. At that level you not only need to stand out, but NHL Scouts also need players to go above and beyond expectations and Letourneau has done exactly that. At a towering 6'6 it is expected that he will fill out to around to 225-230lbs when he turns NHL ready and that is a lot to slow down when someone of that size has good mobility and will push to the middle. Once Letourneau gets to that weight, he will be extremely difficult to knock off the puck, he already is now, and his explosiveness up ice will improve in addition to his coordination.

Offensively he has clear talent as a point producer at his current level, but things will not come as easy for him as he continues to climb the ladder. Letourneau has continued to improve his offensive skills like his puck handling as the year progressed with a major change by the end of the year which helped in puck protection down low and on the rush with his finesse game. Letourneau has a quick and heavy release on his shot and is in no way afraid to shoot the puck. He developed a strong one timer that he uses effectively on the power play when he is working on the outside. He also excels as a playmaker with good vision and smart passing while making players around him better as a result. A physical aspect of the shooting and passing that will help translate him to the NHL is his long arms. Not only used in puck retrievals, but his long reach is also good for shooting and passing around defenders and gives him much more range with the puck than the average offensive forward. This will be a great benefit to him at the pro-level against bigger and smarter players as it gives him a layered offensive skill set with his reach, his skills shooting and passing in tight and his physical dominance down low and along the boards. This is all shown with a high level of confidence with the puck on his stick and how he is not just simply bullying kids in Canadian High School Prep hockey. Letourneau has the skills and athleticism to make the plays no one else is currently making at this level.

Letourneau's skating ability is much better than one might anticipate with good mobility, agility and speed, especially compared to other players his size. As he generates speed up ice, he becomes very difficult to stop as well as when he is down low cycling the puck with his physicality and speed. He has good explosiveness skating up ice and started to improve upon his puck handling with speed as the year went on. We would like to see him develop more of a mean streak on the ice, especially when barreling down on the rush and powering himself to the net. There are times where he can disengage without the puck on his stick, but this got better as the year went on.

The upside and the combination of size and skill are easy to rate highly. Knowing he is committed to his development and growth as a player as shown by his constant refining of his skills and not relying on his size make him even more attractive as a prospect. The NCAA path will give him the time he needs to refine some of his hockey sense and compete which at times can lack, but this pathway in his development will not rush him and give him all of the opportunity he needs to succeed in a successful college program. With so much potential, good long-term projection and a uniqueness not often found in players his age, Letourneau is a prospect that was on everyone's radar.

"High end skill but he plays a small man's game." – NHL Scout, October 2023

"Top 15 pick. Love his game." – NHL Scout, October 2023

"Looks like a mid to late rounder to me." – NHL Scout, October 2023

"He overpasses the puck. He needs to be more selfish." – NHL Scout, October 2023

"I love him. I have him as a top 20 pick already." – NHL Scout, November 2023

"He's huge and has a ton of skill. I've already seen him five times. I think he's a stud." – NHL Scout, November 2023

"Tough to figure out. He is obviously huge and has a ton of skill but he plays like he is a foot smaller than he is." – NHL Scout, November 2023

"I need players to get a minimum of two points per game in that league before I'll even consider going to see them and he is doing it. I haven't seen him yet though." – November 2023

"Not a fan...maybe a late pick." – NHL Scout, November 2023

"Seen him a few times. Good in some games...not good in others. Tough to figure out." – NHL Scout, November 2023

"I haven't seen him yet." – NHL Scout, December 2023

"I just saw him for the first time and he lost a battle to a 5'9"kid and it wasn't pretty. I'm going back to see him tomorrow and that will be his last chance. (Laughs)" – NHL Scout, December 2023

"He's way to easy to play against. I haven't seen him hit anyone with what I'd call a real hit in any of my games so far." – NHL Scout, December 2023

"He's going to be a nightmare to rank. He is 6'6" with skill and he can skate but he's dominating a garbage league. That coach doesn't make anyone better either." - NHL Scout, December 2023

"He played ok in the USHL. Nothing great but those games won't hurt him." - NHL Scout, January 2024

"I actually haven't seen him yet...not even on video." - NHL Scout, January 2024

"Heard he is going to the NCAA if one of the big three (players) leave (BC) So now that Smith just signed that opens a spot for him. If that happens than I think he's in trouble because I don't think he's ready for BC." - NHL Scout, May 2024

"He surprised me a bit. His combine interview was excellent. One of the best." - NHL Scout, June 2024

"Our Ottawa area scout, Connor Mulligan sent me a message about him a couple months ago. I've seen him now...big raw kid with skill. There are some things I don't like but they are fixable and there is some really big upside. I heard some NHL guys throwing around first round talk but he's new to me and I need to seem him more." - HP Scout, Mark Edwards, October 2023

"I've spoken to a ton of scouts about him. Most have him as a 'B' prospect with a few having him as an 'A' prospect and some others as a 4th to 7th round guy. It's a wide range. I even know one scout who doesn't have him as a draftable prospect." - HP Scout, Mark Edwards, December 2023

"The compete area is where there is some inconsistency. Don't get me wrong...this is not a lazy or soft player but he doesn't play with great pace all the time. I'd love to see him lean on some guys and drive to the net more often. I want to see him impose his will more often." - HP Scout, Mark Edwards, December 2023

"If I listed all the NHL Scout quotes in the book that included mentioning Mark Jankowski I'd have another fifteen quotes. He's the player that scares people off from drafting Letourneau too high." = HP Scout, Mark Edwards, December 2023

"A lot of scouts ranted to me about the prep league and all the failed picks coming from that league and I get it.... but I heard the same thing about the AJHL in Cale Makar's draft year. We ranked Makar high in early December. I had several scouts tell me we were crazy when I arrived in Bonnyville that year." - HP Scout, Mark Edwards, December 2023

"I'm told he's heading to BC in the fall." - HP Scout, Mark Edwards, May 2024

"I got really good feedback on his combine interviews. I always ask scouts who were some of their best interviews and his name came up several times." - HP Scout, Mark Edwards, June 2024

10	PLAYER	TEAM	LEAGUE	HEIGHT	WEIGHT	POS	GRADE
	LEVSHUNOV, ARTYOM	MICHIGAN ST	BIG 10	6' 01.75"	205	RD	A

NHLCS	CEILING	FLOOR	HOCKEY SENSE	COMPETE	SKILL	SKATE	MISC
NA-2	7	5	5	6	7	7	7

Artyom Levshunov is one of a number of players likely to go in the top half of the first round that has major and/or fundamental flaws but also huge upside. After a big D-1 season with Green Bay (USHL) in 2022-23, Levshunov – an October 2005 birthday – jumped to Michigan State University and played a prominent role as a freshman. He was second on his team in points with 35, first in plus/minus (+27), and second in penalty minutes (44) while playing all 38 games. He was named the Big Ten Defensive Player of the Year and was a Hobey Baker nominee. Unfortunately, due to circumstances, Belarus was not able to participate internationally once again, leaving evaluators with another single-venue season for the 6'2", 200+ pound rearguard.

He's a husky player who possesses explosive upside in all of his technical traits. He's a very good skater with a strong, extended stride. There's an element of first-step quickness that we like to see, but also smooth lateral ability. He really digs in to the ice, leveraging sturdy three-point flexion, to generate a lot of power with every stride that he's concentrating on. Not only does this provide value in his puck carrying ability and attack zone movements, but it also gives him a lot of maneuverability in his recovery skating – which he needs to utilize quite frequently. We like the overall skating package and four-way mobility that a player of this size possesses – he's very rangy. We'd like to see some improvement in his small-area footwork and some of his edgework. Levshunov has a tendency to take wide, circuitous turns at very inopportune times. Like most aspects of this player, he probably can physically do better than he shows, but either doesn't know any better or simply chooses not to do it any better. Depending on the game (or shift), his skating can look relatively dull because of his indecision, indiscretion, or lack of compete/focus. We've seen enough of him in green-lighted situations or select urgent instances to see that his skating has a lot of upside from a technical perspective and it's being graded as such.

Levshunov is a good stickhandler, again, from a technical perspective. Nothing about it is mind-blowing, but for a puck rushing defenseman, his ability to handle the puck well at speed is very useful. When he gets into a good glide, he can carve up some would-be defenders with some nifty, dynamic moves too. He has the reach and a good enough puck control window (though, a touch smaller than we'd like for a player of his size) to complete a lot of moves with success from this perspective. The combination of his long, swooping strides and reach allows him to really eat up useful ice – especially in 4 on 4 or man-advantage situations. However, where he falls short is the manipulative and deceptive setup process – which is on the mental arc. A good example of this is in the first round regional matchup vs. Western Michigan. Down 4 to 3 with a minute to go, Levshunov accepts a slow diagonal outlet pass on the weak side of his own zone. A WMU forechecker has a clear track over top of the puck with the necessary turn-and-go speed matching. Levshunov catches the puck at the dot line but his track is naturally carrying him to the outside - which is okay. But Levshunov makes no motion with his stick, shoulders, head, or eyes to the inside to do anything to break the stride of the forechecker at the onset of the rush. He just puts his head down and carries it up the wall as fast as he can. It worked at this level and because the player with the inside track didn't take the steps to close him off because he didn't realize how much support he had on his back. Also, there was oddly no defenseman (or cover) over the top to hold the blueline. Now, to Levshunov's credit once he starts to get into the lower layers of the offensive zone, he makes a push to "get corner" on his defender. Meaning, there's a pronounced movement to get his inside knee, hip, and shoulder in front of the space that otherwise would be occupied by the defender to allow the freedom of motion of his right side. Levshunov uses his reach and a hook pass to put the puck right on the tape of his man at the far post for a wide open tap in. This sequence is a really good microcosm of Artyom's game as a whole, where he can push the limits of the competition with his technical and physical traits, but there are limitations on its scalability because of the lacking mental contribution.

These aren't isolated incidents, there's a pattern of randomness to his game. He's unpredictable, but not in the desirable way. In a late season game against Ohio State, we see a categorically similar situation in terms of having of impending zone entry, time and space to manipulate the defense, and multiple passing/carrying options. Early 2nd period sudden change situation, the OSU point man bobbles the puck up high and only gets a piece of it before both defenders back off their attack line. Levshunov had already made an executive decision to chase the lo-hi pass out to the point, so he's – strangely - first on the puck that is just outside of his own blue line. He picks it up against a defense pair that is double stacked on the dot line with one of his men on the same-side boards at the center stripe. Levshunov's first stickhandle is smartly to the inside. This turns the skates of his defender and should have caused him some degree of discomfort. He has an MSU player sprinting up the weak side to join this rush. He has an entire lane (two lanes, really) to himself and is clear of any back pressure by over 30 feet. Levshunov handles the puck back outside – which can make sense because he has once again turned the skates of the defender – this time he turned the skates away from the wide-open sprinter coming up the weak side. Levshunov crosses center, he sees his primary defender's back now (as he's been corkscrewed by the stickhandling), and the secondary defender stacked up on the blue line. Instead of making the lateral or hook pass to the wide open player...he makes a 10 foot pass to the stationary and covered man that's been over the top of it from the get-go. The zone entry becomes bobbled and uncontrolled. It takes so long to untangle it, that all five Buckeye players are back in the defensive zone before the next pass can be attempted. It results in a turnover. It went from a full-on breakaway, to a potential 2 on 1, to a potential 3 on 2...and because Levshunov has little idea about what's happening outside of his direct line of vision, Sparty ends up without so much as a shot attempt.

What Levshunov does is play relentlessly downhill. More so than just winding rushes, the Belarusian speeds the game up with his stretch pass proclivity. Whether they are direct defense-splitting passes or indirect, Levshunov likes to recover the puck and get it immediately up the ice. This is where the majority of his assists came from this year – catching teams before they can setup their forecheck or finish their change. Like most things, when it works it looks great and when it doesn't it looks bad. The key is in the intentionality that he puts into these plays. Again here, we see a situation where a player isn't necessarily taking the time to evaluate the game with nearly as much care as necessary. He doesn't utilize his last-man-back surveying ability often enough to setup his teammates better. One thing that we'd expect from an elite defensive prospect is that he consistently improves the condition of the puck. Can he exhibit tempo control when his team needs to retain possession but also make a line change? Can he settle down a grenade from his partner and buy everyone time to reset their controlled breakout for timing purposes? Can he take a poorly managed play or a play that's tracking the wrong way and increase its odds of working out? As it stands now, we see a lot inconsistency at best.

The most disappointing parts about his transition game – which is his calling card – is that he is quick to make his problem also someone else's problem. This is a really interesting quirk to his game because he doesn't play with a lot of defensive urgency, but yet, he also has a low panic threshold. If he gets a tough pass from his partner, he'll blindly wing it in front of his own net to no one. If he loses control of the puck when attempting to exit the zone, instead of re-gathering it and making a secondary or safer play – he'll chop at the puck or try to pool cue it ahead and make the next player deal with it, or again, he'll just backhand it blindly away from himself and let the chips fall where they may.

Artyom is too willing to play pucks well away from his body without adjusting his feet and/or posture to improve the condition or potential of the puck or play. He's too often rushing puck decisions for a player of this skill level. We see this in the offensive zone even more often. He gets a lot of faux "possession" shot analytic credit because he's a volume shooter. He chucks a ton of pucks towards the net from the boards. Even if there are players wide open cruising down the slot, calling for pucks, he'll take it off the kick plate and send a mid-speed wrister at the net. His rushed wrist shots don't have a ton of zip on them and they aren't done with much intentionality, so he generated very few rebound assists compared to what his shooting volume might dictate. His one timer packs a really good punch though. That alone makes him a threat to score from distance. If he dug in, dropped his hip line more, and focused on his shooting from the point, he'd probably be able to boost his goal totals. It would need to come with a little better agility walking the line, but even if it compromised his release speed a tiny bit – it would be made up with any angle-change shooting that he could add to his game. Looking at his goal sample, it's pretty unimpressive. Ignoring the two long empty netters, there's also a few really tough goaltending errors in there. Having just four or so goals on the year wouldn't likely do his shooting prowess justice; but he's going to need a professional shooting technique and process to develop – and that should be fairly approachable with proper development because that's on the technical development arc.

His near-constant downhill style of play sees him step up a lot in the neutral zone. Early in games, he uses physicality to get himself into the game. It catches a lot of opponents off guard and leads to some good contact usually. Levshunov also consistently drives forward off of neutral zone faceoff losses. That style of "downhill" pressure is really difficult to anticipate, as it's so unusual. We'll give him credit for two reasons here: one, it's consistent with his mental process and two, it does sometimes force some tough decisions by his opponents. We're not sure how interested pro coaches will be in this approach, but that's not where he's playing right now. Loose pucks, particularly in the offensive zone, seem to be an automatic green light for him to pinch down on and try to make a play. It's not a 50/50-and-go deal, we have seen pucks that are 10/90 and he'll take a full-on stab at it rather than back off and try to absorb the next sequence. Given that this decision making and adaptive processing falls mostly on the mental development arc, we'd expect these issues to be far more difficult to iron out. He's very fundamentally unsound...whether he's the youngest player in this draft class or the oldest (he's an October 2005) or he's been in the U.S., Canada, or Europe, there's just no excusing some of his defensive play.

In a later season game against the University of Minnesota, there's a non-threatening attack under way for the Gophers and the puck is on the boards along with half their team. Levshunov is defending the net and he's standing in the mid-slot...there is no one remotely close to broaching his zone of control. The puck finds its way off the wall and gets to a flat-footed player approaching the faceoff dot. That Minnesota player is bracketed by a defenseman and a forward. Levshunov shades towards the biggest threat (the puck carrier), which is great. The bracketing players address the puck carrier, of course...so the most likely situation is that this puck is going to be jarred loose. And in fact, that puck does get knocked loose...and it would have come right to Levshunov and he could have cleanly exited out the weak side. However, Levshunov decides to turn his body around and attempt to hit that already-bracketed player with his backside. Now the puck traverses through that mess and the next puck touch is that same Minnesota player. It's alarming how many plays Levshunov allows to fester, continue, or succeed with his poor decisions and technique - especially his stick positioning and pokecheck timing/usage.

That's not to say that he's constantly cherry picking or generally out to lunch, but he's definitely a rover. There's potential for rush absorption improvement just on physical and technical traits alone. He has shown some box-out and wall-off capabilities already. There is a mean streak in there, but it's spotty. Like in board battles, he's rarely in there playing for keeps and loses more of them than a player of his size should. It's the glaring lack of detail in his game that's scary: randomly crossing in front of his goalie while a long shot is on the way, his stick positioning/triangle management, unkempt switches/pass offs defensively, spatial awareness and gap control, partner support, and the list goes on.

Physically, Levshunov is a horse already. He's a very imposing figure and appears to be fairly close to maximizing his current frame. That doesn't mean that he won't get any stronger or faster, but right now he's a player who is excelling – in part – because of his physical makeup, maturity, and strength. We don't project him to gain a ton more purely physical advantages as he moves up the ladder (compared to say an underdeveloped 17 year old player who may be dominating his age group, but without notable use of his physical traits/makeup).

The technical development arc, however, is where he likely has the most to gain. The core of skills that he possesses right now is already varied and impressive.. He'll need to be excellent technically if he wants to produce in the NHL and he has the potential for that. All that being said, with hockey sense and compete being our top two most important grades and those being Levshunov's biggest question marks, we might have him ranked slightly lower than some.

"Has similarities to Evan Bouchard...just a real messy player, but if he lands in a perfect situation, his head-manning could be useful too. Otherwise, this could be just a player that plays during his athletic prime and isn't a long-term value pick." HP Scout, Michael Farkas, January 2024

"I love him. I think he's a stud." - NHL Scout, November 2023

"I think he is overrated." - NHL Scout, November 2023

"He turned the puck over five or six times with and without pressure." - NHL Scout, December 2023

"I see him ranked second on lists and I ask myself what am I missing?" - NHL Scout, December 2023

"I haven't seen him play bad, but for every good play he made, he made an equally bad play." - NHL Scout, January 2024

"I really like his game a lot but I would agree with you that it seems like he is getting a little over hyped." - NHL Scout, January 2024

"Great skater, good shot...good puck skills...there is a lot to like. My top Dman." - NHL Scout, January 2024

"I like him but I'm not comfortable enough with his hockey sense right now to draft him in the top 10." - NHL Scout, January 2024

"He's 100% Evan Bouchard for me. A lazy defender. He's a one dimensional offensive player. By the way, I still really like Bouchard." NHL Scout, January 2024

"Did you see Bob McKenzie's scout quotes? They had this guy as the stud defender and big Silayev as the offensive guy. I don't get it. Did Bob mix up the quotes?." - NHL Scout, February 2024

"My list is going to be a nightmare to make and this guy is one of the many reasons why." - NHL Scout, April 2024

"Flashes of brilliance but I have seen some ugly shifts too." - NHL Scout, May 2024

"I have him ahead of Dickinson as my top Dman." - NHL Scout, May 2024

"In my last viewing of him he turned the puck over about six times. It was a trend in my views of him." - NHL Scout, May 2024

"I think he is the most overhyped player in this draft. It was Mews at the start of the year but people seemed to figure him out after Christmas." - NHL Scout, May 2024

"I see offense but I don't see this dynamic offense I've heard others rave about." - NHL Scout, May 2024

"I have him ahead of both Parekh and Dickinson and it wasn't a difficult decision for me." - NHL Scout, May 2024

"He is my top Dman and it wasn't really close." - NHL Scout, May 2024

"I watched all his points yesterday and asked myself how he is ranked second overall." - NHL Scout, May 2024

"I've seen him seven times and it's been a mixed bag. Some good, some bad, not much physical play. I'm glad we're not picking in the top 10." - NHL Scout, May 2024

"I've been trying to figure out how he can be number two overall on people's lists." - NHL Scout, June 2024

"I love the raw tools but our two most important traits are hockey sense and compete and he was inconsistent in both areas. Watching every single one of his points didn't get me out of my seat either." – HP Scout, Mark Edwards, May 2024

NR	PLAYER	TEAM	LEAGUE	HEIGHT	WEIGHT	POS	GRADE
	LEWIS, NATHAN	YOUNGSTOWN	USHL	6' 05"	209	RW	NI
NHLCS	CEILING	FLOOR	HOCKEY SENSE	COMPETE	SKILL	SKATE	MISC
NA-3	5	5	5	6	5	5	8

Nathan Lewis missed most of his third season in the USHL due to injury after his offseason trade from Madison to Youngstown. The 6'5" Lewis put up 8 goals and 7 assists for 15 points in 12 games.

Pucks jump off his blade from a shooting perspective, but he could stand to quicken his release still. He doesn't fool around with the puck very much, so the shot/pass decision comes quickly most of the time. His passing is wildly inconsistent still. Some games, he's able to navigate around players and put together some nice setups with one-touch playmaking…other games, he makes passes so conceptually poor that it's tough to reason what his intent even was. Lewis isn't a very dynamic puck handler, but he does boast a useful puck control window. This is particularly helpful for his work near the net, where he needs to manipulate lanes to keep plays alive or find rebound chances. He's no expert in front yet, and despite his frame, can be moved off his spot relatively easy still. But he goes to the net and the lowest lane of the offensive zone with a degree of enthusiasm. His is not a super high motor player, but he's a willing participant all over the ice. There's some urgency going for loose pucks or even attempting to help mitigate a threat on the backcheck.

His skating is above average, not for any explosive quality, but mostly for the surprising agility and small-area footwork that players at his size typically don't possess at this age. It's not the prettiest stride, but he gets around the rink well enough. The 2004 birthday was a rookie camp invite by the New York Rangers in the summer of 2023 and is off to Ohio State in fall. The long-term upside for his size, shot, and – maybe – attack-zone retrieval game might be tempting very late in the draft.

2	PLAYER	TEAM	LEAGUE	HEIGHT	WEIGHT	POS	GRADE
	LINDSTROM, CAYDEN	MEDICINE HAT	WHL	6' 03"	213	LC	A
NHLCS	CEILING	FLOOR	HOCKEY SENSE	COMPETE	SKILL	SKATE	MISC
NA-3	8	7	6	8	8	8	8

Lindstrom is the unicorn of this draft class at the forward position. He has tools that make him a very special talent that all NHL teams would want to add to their squad. He started his draft season with a very good performance at the Hlinka-Gretzky Cup, playing on Canada's 3rd line, where he showed his excellent skating skills and power game. Then, he started his WHL season on fire, and was one of the league's best players until mid-December. He injured his hand at the first practice after Christmas, an injury that required surgery. He also encountered back problems that didn't help him make a quick return to the ice. He only came back 3 months later for the start of the playoffs, where he played 4 of the 5 games against Red Deer (a series his team lost). He also withdrew from the U18 World Hockey Championship because he was not 100% healthy. This season overall, he still managed to score 27 goals and collect 46 points in 32 games. In the playoffs, he had 2 points in the 4 games he played in.

While his health status is a concern, so are all the games missed in the second half of the year. This is important data missing from his profile; his selection is a bit riskier than it would be if he didn't miss any games. However, it's really hard to find a player with his size, skating skills, hands and physicality. NHL teams will do their due diligence on him at the combine, but players like him don't wait to hear their name called for too long.

Lindstrom is a power center with elite athletic ability and one of the best pure athletes in this draft class. Not many players with his frame can skate like he does; think Quinton Byfield in 2020 who had the same combination of size and skating, but cases like these are rare. Adam Fantilli last season was another, but he's not a huge guy compared to Lindstrom or Byfield. Further to other comparisons made between Byfield and Lindstrom: while their athletic abilities are pretty similar, Byfield gets the edge in the skating department (mostly in his first three steps and better initial posture). Lindstrom, at the same age, gets the edge for top speed and acceleration. There's one thing to note about Lindstrom in terms of how violent of a skater he is. He's super aggressive on the ice, which was not something we could say about Byfield in his draft year. Cayden has acceleration, top speed, plus agility. With great size already, he still has added strength to obtain. When he fully matures, you'll see his stride become more powerful, which will make his overall skating really elite. He's not just a pure speed guy, either. He also changes skating routes and speeds, which makes him unpredictable during zone entries. Too many times we see top skaters (think Luke Misa) go full speed all the time, but pro teams and players adjust to this and it becomes a lot easier to counter. We also love Lindstron's energy level and stamina. He's a beast on the ice, and a future nightmare for opposing NHL defenses to deal with.

One element of his game we thought he really improved upon this season: his hand skills. He was really good at one-on-one play. He also had better success in terms of his dekes this season compared to last. This was vital in his development path towards that of a lethal scorer and one of the top prospects available in the 2024 NHL Draft. A lot of Lindstrom's success comes from his play in transition in the neutral zone, plus making good zone entries. Last year's stickhandling was up and down. This year, not only could he beat players with ease thanks to his great speed and power game, now his stickhandling is that much better. Yet another element to consider when defending against him; now he can beat opponents with more consistent speed, power game and hands.

A shoot-first type of player, he has fast hands, a quick release and his shot has great velocity. He can score from distance, but can also bulldoze his way to the net. For example, with Medicine Hat on the power play, he was the net-presence guy in front, with guys like Gavin McKenna and Andrew Basha creating plays from the half-wall or the point. At even-strength, he would never hesitate to take the puck to the net. He can create havoc at the front of the net on either special team. He often draws two players around him, which opens things up for his teammates. His mix of power, speed and reach is incredibly tough to handle for opposing defensemen trying to defend him one-on-one. When he can gain speed through the neutral zone, it's really challenging for any defenseman to stop him. He's dynamic in transition because of that speed and those quick hands. While he does protect the puck well, it could be better. He still needs to add strength to his frame; once he does, his puck-protection game will go to another level. He can still lose battles and needs to stay on his two skates more often. That added strength will improve his equilibrium on the ice in those tough battles along the boards.

While his hockey sense and playmaking are not his strongest assets, they do get a passing grade from us. He does need to slow down the play a bit more and work on improving his passing accuracy, but he always has good intentions with his pass attempts. He's creative enough with the puck; oddly enough, it's similar to that of Dmitri Simashev from last year's draft. This is not a huge deal for us, but he needs to improve his technical passing. All teams now have skills and development coaches that can work with players on things like this. If we had major issues with his passing skills or his hockey sense, we wouldn't rank him where we did.

One aspect of his game that we absolutely love is his physicality. One of the more physical players in this draft class, he is energetic with a mean streak, which is extremely rare to find in elite players. He's almost like an 80s roller derby player on the ice at times. A dominant player along the boards, he doesn't lose many physical confrontations with his combination of power and speed. He also has very good pushback and won't back down when challenged. There was a game earlier in the season where he was going at it with Carter Yakemchuk. It's worth noting that he should be a bit more disciplined in this area; in the playoffs, he took some bad penalties due to being overzealous with some hits. He plays right on the edge, sometimes going over that line, but that's what makes him a special player. We project him to be deadly in his prime come playoff time. Big, fast, athletic and powerful players can be unstoppable in the postseason.

To conclude with Lindstrom, we think he can be a good top line center or an excellent number 2 in the NHL. He could also move to the wing, but his tools are too good to not give him a very long look at center. With the time lost this season, his chances of playing in the NHL right away may have dwindled, but in the long term, we think he's going to be a very unique player in the NHL.

"I have questions with his hockey IQ." - NHL Scout, October 2023

"He isn't the smartest player I've ever watched but I do see the good things you pointed out." - NHL Scout, October 2023

"I haven't seen him yet." NHL Scout, October 2023

"Our west guy loves him...says he's a stud. Top guy on his list right now." -NHL Scout, October 2023

"He plays hard...that is a kid who will produce in the playoffs." - NHL Scout, December 2023

"His tools are really good. I wish his hockey sense was a bit better but I still have him in my top 5." NHL Scout, December 2023

"Big kids that play center that have his skill and play as hard as him don't come around too often. He is a top three pick all day long." - NHL Scout, December 2023

"He's not dumb but he's not a high end hockey sense guy either. He's going to be a power winger in the NHL who needs a center to let him shine...and he will." - NHL Scout, December 2023

"My only question is his health. He is till number two on my list though. - NHL Scout, March 2024

"So refreshing to see a player who is just a nasty SOB on the ice. You don't see them anymore...especial six foot four guys with skill." - NHL Scout, March 2024

"I know you have him second overall but I'm not that high on him. I heard he has issues with his back...did you know that?" -NHL Scout, May 2024

"He's injured all the time." - NHL Scout, May 2024

"You could make a case for about seven guys to go 2nd overall but he's my number two." - NHL Scout, May 2024

"If his injury checks out and I hear it will, he'll go very high." - NHL Scout, May 2024

"He is what he is...a six foot three power forward who is mean as f*** - sign me up." - NHL Scout, May 2024

"I love his game but don't think he's a center at the next level. Some do, I don't." - NHL Scout, May 2024

"I think you guys are the only list with him second overall. Love it." - NHL Scout, May 2024

"Can I just pass on putting someone at number two? I have Lindstrom but the injuries scare me a bit." - NHL Scout, May 2024

"I don't think he is a number two overall but I don't have anyone else I want to put at number two over him." - NHL Scout May 2024

"He is exactly what Chicago needs." - NHL Scout, May 2024

"Chris Kreider was mean. So is this kid." - NHL Scout, May 2024

"Unicorn power center with athletic tools like Lindstrom has don't wait too long to hear their name called in the draft" - HP Scout Jérôme Bérubé (December 2023)

"One of the biggest reasons he's as high as he is for us, is that not only is he talented, he's also ruthless at times and that's very hard to find down the middle." - HP Scout, Brad Allen (May 2024)

"I've seen his hockey sense questioned. He's not the smartest player in the draft, but he makes plays dumb hockey players simply can't make. He can also set up advanced plays at a higher level than some people realize." - HP Scout, Brad Allen (May 2024)

"He is big and skilled and plays with an edge. Some scouts told me they are worried about his hockey sense but I don't think it's even close to being a stopper. Is it high end? No but he isn't a dumb player and other stuff in his game is fantastic. I love that he's a mean SOB - hard to find those players these days." - HP Scout, Mark Edwards, December 2023

"He might not be all the way up at number two in previous seasons even as recently as last season but he's my number two overall this season." - HP Scout, Mark Edwards, May 2024

12	PLAYER	TEAM	LEAGUE	HEIGHT	WEIGHT	POS	GRADE
	LUCHANKO, JETT	GUELPH	OHL	5' 11"	187	RC	A
NHLCS	CEILING	FLOOR	HOCKEY SENSE	COMPETE	SKILL	SKATE	MISC
NA-20	7	7	8	7	7	8	6

Luchanko has been one of the more underrated players in this draft class all year long. He's an incredibly smart hockey player and one of the best hockey brains you will find in his draft class. This year with Guelph, Luchanko finished with over a point per game despite playing on a team with not much support around him. For example, they didn't win a game in February, and it's obvious that Luchanko would have had way better stats if he played on a team like London or Saginaw. After Guelph was eliminated from the postseason, he represented Canada at the U18 World Championship and played a key role in the team's gold medal victory. Centering the number-2 line between Tij Iginla and Ryder Ritchie, he may not have scored as much as others, but he made key plays at crucial moments throughout the tournament. Notably, his pass to Cole Beaudoin for the 4-3 goal in the final and his outstanding job checking James Hagens were particularly impressive.

The number one asset of Luchanko's game is his brain. He thinks the game at a very high level. Offensively, more often than not, he knows exactly what he's going to do on the ice before he even receives the puck. His processor is really fast, and that helps him in both his passing game in the offensive zone and in transition. He makes players around him better; his vision, ability to think at a high level, and ability to pass the puck on both his forehand and backhand are helpful in that regard. He's good at getting his passes or shots deflected by teammates around the net. He's good at moving pucks cross-ice to his teammates for one-timer scoring chances. He excels at finding the perfect time to make a pass while passing lanes open up, keeping that puck on his stick for that extra second. He hides his intentions well when in the playmaker role, with eyes in the back of his head. Even on off-days when he might not have the strongest game, he's going to make a pass that is going to break your jaw. Regarded as one of the best playmakers from this draft class, he finished tied for second in the OHL for assists on the power play, alongside OHL MVP Easton Cowan. To put his importance to the team into perspective, Guelph only ranked 14th in the OHL in terms of power-play efficiency.

As a shooter, Luchanko will need to improve his shot and add more regularity to his finishing abilities. He scored 20 goals this season, but only took 125 shots in 68 games. He'll need to increase his shot total next season to increase his potential as a dual threat on the ice. While his shot is decent, it doesn't suggest he'll be a high-end goal scorer at the NHL level. He's not likely to score often from long distances, so he'll need to position himself closer to the net to be effective. Additionally, as he gains more strength, he may be able to add some velocity to his shot. Working with a skilled coach in the NHL could further enhance his shot.

Luchanko is a good stickhandler who loves to rush the puck throughout the neutral zone and into the offensive zone. The more the season progressed, the more we saw him confidently challenge defenders one-on-one with his speed and hands. He possesses smooth hands and has emerged as a threat with his stickhandling skills in the OHL. He excels in tight spaces, demonstrating strong puck-control, particularly along the walls. His ability to control the puck in these situations has notably improved since last season and was one of the areas he progressed the most in.

As already one of the best defensive players in the OHL, he makes great reads to intercept passes in the neutral zone and also has a great active stick. His overall game has a lot of similarities to Nick Suzuki's (in terms of intelligence) but Luchanko is not as gifted a shooter. He's still going to make a very good PK player in the NHL. His smarts, the way he anticipates the play, his stick activation skills, his skating and his work ethic all put together provides him the ingredients to excel in this role at the NHL level.

His skating prowess stands out as another notable aspect of his game. With excellent acceleration and top speed, he demonstrates exceptional edgework and excels in changing directions with the puck. This contributes to his effective puck-protection abilities, despite not being particularly large. While he could enhance his physical power, his skating is already quite powerful. Once he adds more strength to his frame, you'll see his skating get even more explosive (plus, he'll be stronger on his skates). He demonstrated his great skating in transition to rush the puck into the offensive zone, plus to get back defensively and defend. He displays quick recovery and pursues the puck carrier with determination, also demonstrating tenacity and refusing to quit on any play. As he becomes physically stronger, his physical game is expected to improve, resulting in him winning more battles. There were instances during the season where fatigue seemed to affect him, leading to more mental mistakes. As he matures physically, these fatigue-related errors are likely to diminish. It's also worth noting that he's relatively young for this draft class, only turning 18 in mid to late August. This indicates that there's room for further development, which bodes well for his long-term potential and growth.

Luchanko is a player who our staff greatly appreciates. When a player possesses intelligence, skating, and a strong work ethic like his, they tend to rank quite highly on our list. The only aspects that prevent him from being placed even higher on our list are his shot and that he isn't a bigger kid.

"Might be the smartest player in this draft." - NHL Scout, December 2023."

"He's a great player but he is only 5'10" and he is a bit light. Not a great goal scorer but the rest of his game is exceptional." - NHL Scout, December 2023

"I can't think of a comparable for him but he plays the position the way it's supposed to be played." - NHL Scout, April 2024

"He isn't flashy but he doesn't cheat. He just plays the game the right way." - NHL Scout, April 2024

"If he was 6'2" he would be a top five pick. I think He'll still be a top 15 pick at 5'10.5" - NHL Scout, April 2024

"I actually saw him pretty late but it was worth the wait. I absolutely loved him in my first viewing and I haven't changed my mind." - NHL Scout, May 2024

"There is no weakness in his game other than his size." - NHL Scout, May 2024

"A poor man's Barzel. Matt was more arrogant though and wanted to show flash and show people up, I don't see that in Jett." - NHL Scout, May 2024

"No surprise, he was solid at the U18." - NHL Scout, May 2024

"He's got some Nick Suzuki in his game, just a fantastic hockey brain. He's faster than Suzuki but not as gifted as a scorer" - HP Scout Jérôme Bérubé, March 2024

"He was voted 2nd by the OHL coaches in the Western Conference for hardest worker, smarts and skating. He was also voted 3rd in that conference for shootout." - HP Scout Jérôme Bérubé, April 2024

"There's a lot of Suzuki comps that will get thrown around, so I'll go off the grid a bit and suggest there's a lot of Chandler Stephenson in his game." - HP Scout, Brad Allen, May 2024

"His incredible goal against North-Bay in late October highlights that there's way more talent there than some people might think, especially when you factor in his potential growth-rate." - HP Scout, Brad Allen, May 2024

"One of my personal faves in this draft class so far. Really smart player, skilled player. not a huge kid. Guelph isn't blessed with a ton of skilled players so he isn't surrounded by talent. He shows creativity and smarts all over the ice. I think he's just getting started." - HP Scout, Mark Edwards, December 2023

"It's pretty simple. He plays a pro game right now. He just needs time to gain strength. I have loved his game since my first viewing." - HP Scout, Mark Edwards, May 2024

"Reminded me of Mercer a bit (Devils) as far as the shot and playmaking. Both great playmakers in their draft years and shot was their biggest weakness. Luchanko is a much better skater and has a better overall 200 foot game at the same age though." - HP Scout, Mark Edwards, May 2024

"Great interviews at the combine." - HP Scout, June 2024

70	PLAYER	TEAM	LEAGUE	HEIGHT	WEIGHT	POS	GRADE
	MAISTRENKO, OLEG	CSKA	RUS JR	6' 01"	190	RC	C

NHLCS	CEILING	FLOOR	HOCKEY SENSE	COMPETE	SKILL	SKATE	MISC
-	6	4	7	9	6	5	7

Oleg Maistrenko is a violent, dual-threat power forward, whose consistency rates fluctuated throughout his second season of draft-eligibility. He captained Krasnaya while finishing with 44 points in 45 games at the MHL level, which was a massive jump from his first draft eligible season, where he only produced 13 points in 40 games. We felt that his play faltered a bit more in the second half due to conditioning issues and after he was injured for a brief period of time.

Maistrenko's defining feature is his ruthless aggression. We could go back and forth on who are the most physically gifted hitters in this class and who projects to hit the most, but the player that wanted to do the most damage was

Maistrenko. We've seen him annihilate goalies who are looking to play pucks, barrel over his own teammates, and decimate opposing players. He's a reckless – wrecking ball of a player and when he's using his aggression correctly it can really turn the momentum and tide of a game in his team's favour. He leads by example, putting his body on the line in each area of the ice.

What's unique about the psychological make-up of Maistrenko is that despite having vinegar for blood and seeing red often, he sees the ice at a surprising level. Usually tenacious power-forwards have difficulty recognizing when to slow down the play so that trailing options can get into position to receive passes, or they hurry a play using their frame that doesn't allow back-door entry points to materialize, but Oleg not only understands how to find trailing and backdoor options, you could make the argument that it's his best skill. He can execute dynamic, complexed passing plays that require a high level of precision and make them while under heavy pressure or while dealing with physicality.

Maistrenko combines his playmaking into his mindset for the better. When he's looking to initiate a direct cutting play towards the goal-line, he has the dexterity and the handling necessary to protect the puck before making reverse hook and no-look backhand passes back into the higher danger areas of the ice. What this means is that when he's charging through traffic on his way to the net, he can either cut across and cut through opposing sticks and hands of the defenseman, or he can slip around the net area and use the back of the net area to his advantage. When he merges the ability to get off his center line with his advanced handling and deceptive fakes, he can be an absolute handful for opposing teams to deal with.

This isn't a simple, cookie cutter power forward who thinks the game at a low or average level, instead he's difficult to predict and presents a ton of options from the entry point of the offensive blueline, right down through to the back of the net area.

Although we think Maistrenko's most successful area of translation comes from his playmaking upside and his physicality, he can also score in a number of ways. He can park net front and use his frame and aggression to find space to jam home rebounds. He has a knack for timing when he needs to skate by the crease area or slot area and redirect point shots. His shooting mechanics are impressive, and as a result he has shooting quality that can make him dangerous both in transition and from the left-circle, where he was deployed often on the powerplay. He has a soft catch and release and he has the ability to rapidly drag a puck, subsequently changing his shooting angles around triangles.

Off the puck, Maistrenko can do damage on the forecheck due to how tenacious he is. Yet, he has a natural affinity for the center position, which he also split time between playing. His ability to mentally map his teammates routes in advance generalizes to his ability to anticipate opposing routes, and as a result he can anticipate and get out in-front of passing options and break up plays in transition as they're unfolding. He's a capable shot blocker from the line, and his heavier set frame works to his advantage when absorbing pucks. Along the walls and during board battling sequences, he not only can win puck battles using his power and ferocity but he's also surprisingly nimble and creative as syncing his hands up with his edgework and pivots to find exit routes along the half-walls while still maintaining puck possession.

Where Maistrenko's game becomes less projectable is in transition when the pace of play ramps up. Which is the direct result of having difficulty with his first few strides out of the gate. Visually, when he's starting up, it looks like he's dragging a sled occasionally. Part of this can be attributed to ineffective push offs, which is a byproduct of his lack of fluidity and overall extension. The dexterity and coordination presented in his wrists and arms are not present within his overall frame, making him look rigid.

When you bulk up too much at his age, it limits his range of motion. This directly affects his torso and arm rotation. The more muscle a prospect has, usually they are less elastic, resulting in rigidity that doesn't allow them to manipulate their frame off their centerline as easily as it does for more fluid prospects. This is evident when watching him. Additionally, while it helps him absorb contact and stay up on his feet, his muscle mass hasn't helped him sit back further in his stride. The more stable a player is, theoretically, the easier it should be for that player to sit back and generate hip drive in most instances, but he has real difficulty with this mechanic.

We wouldn't label him as a bad skater but it's definitely the biggest area of improvement needed in order to picture him in an NHL line-up. Once he gets going, he can carry himself down a skating lane at a decent speed. It's not a separating speed but it projects to be passable.

He's going to have to mature within his play structure and recognize when he needs to conserve himself so he can become more efficient at conserving energy. He is also going to have become a more conditioned athlete to compensate for his skating. Games that required a lot of up and down transitional play made him effectively useless by the end of some shifts. We think that played a factor into why he was so inconsistent. When he could maintain his energy, he was effective, when he couldn't, then he had trouble impacting the game.

What's really unfortunate, is that due to how we project his skating going forward, it takes him out of the running as a center despite having a natural foundation for the position. He's instinctually a playmaker, who can make his teammates around him better. He's also very aware and responsible off the puck, showing an advanced understanding of how to support his teammates in both open ice and along the boards. There's an attention to detail on when he needs to switch with his defenseman and he has good anticipation in the neutral zone so that he can generate takeaways. He can control the middle of the ice, yet the transitional skating ability we believe will hold him back from developing into a theoretical two-way center.

The good news is that the offensive dimensions of Oleg's game should translate. The passing ability, sense for the game, and ability to handle the puck are all NHL caliber in a top-9 capacity. It's hard to find heavy hitting, big framed, powerful players who want to make a difference, and come with the right mental make up to do just that. He's also not one dimensional in terms of his off the puck play. He's willing to engage physically, his motor grades well overall, especially when considering the effects of his skating inefficiency on his conditioning at his age, and he can help his team defensively. As a result, we think there's an opportunity for Maistrenko to develop into a two-way, third line - power playmaker but he's going to have to dial up his consistency on a game to game basis in order for this projection to materialize.

" Maistrenko is my favourite under-the-radar player in this class. He's built for playoff hockey and he's a brilliant playmaker at times. If he can improve his acceleration, up his conditioning and consistency rates, then he could be a surprising compliment to a line. He's built for playoff hockey."
- HP Scout, Brad Allen

" I'm not as bullish on him as I was Nikita Grebenkin. They are completely different players, but Maistrenko is the dark horse Russian prospect for me this season." - HP Scout, Brad Allen

	PLAYER	TEAM	LEAGUE	HEIGHT	WEIGHT	POS	GRADE
NR	**MANNISTO, TOMMI**	**MICH ST**	**BIG 10**	**6' 00"**	**194**	**RW**	**NI**
NHLCS	CEILING	FLOOR	HOCKEY SENSE	COMPETE	SKILL	SKATE	MISC
-	4	4	5	7	4	8	6

Mannisto played his best hockey during the 2024 World Junior Hockey Championships in Sweden, scoring 3 goals in 7 games and playing with great energy all tournament long. Meanwhile, with Michigan State, he scored 1 goal in 29 games. This is his 3rd year of eligibility after being ignored in both the 2022 and 2023 NHL Drafts.

The best part about Mannisto's game is his skating. He's straight up one of the top skaters in this draft class, if not the best pure skater. He's a powerful athlete with great explosiveness. Lethal on the forecheck, he is incredibly quick to apply pressure and take advantage of turnovers in the neutral zone. He is also an asset on the PK thanks to his great speed and work ethic. Playing a physical game, he's never afraid to throw hits with his powerful frame and can make a solid impact. However, he's limited offensively, with average vision and below-average puck skills and hands. Despite this, he can create offense with his hustle and ability to drive the net, causing chaos in front. With three more years at Michigan State, he has time to improve his skills. If he does, he could carve out a depth role in the NHL, possibly as a 4th-line energy winger, thanks to his physicality and elite skating. His strong performance at the World Junior Hockey Championship might boost his draft stock, despite a less-than-fantastic freshman season at Michigan State.

92	PLAYER	TEAM	LEAGUE	HEIGHT	WEIGHT	POS	GRADE
	MARCHENKO, ARSENI	BEL U18	BEL JR.	6' 06"	207	RD	C
NHLCS	CEILING	FLOOR	HOCKEY SENSE	COMPETE	SKILL	SKATE	MISC
-	7	3	5	5	6	6	8

Arseni Marchenko is a defenseman we label as a unicorn, who is both incredibly raw but also intriguing due to his size, handedness, tool-kit and age. He's the youngest defenseman in the draft, yet despite his young age, he had enough maturity to captain the Belarus U18 squad, producing 31 points in 37 games, including 9 goals. In the playoffs his production dropped to 7 points in 13 games, including 4 goals. We had to weigh these performances more heavily then we typically wanted to, since Belarus is banned from international events.

Marchenko is a prospect that can have off nights. As an example, we watched him buckle under pressure when he faced the Kazakhstan U18 squad earlier in November, which turned out to be a surprisingly okay team at the U18's. It was the first time Marchenko ever went up against a squad that could really forecheck properly, since in the league that he plays in, there really isn't any sort of consistent pressure or structured forecheck. He didn't pass the test. He threw away pucks constantly and looked overwhelmed for the majority of the game. His execution rates in general throughout most of the season were very up and down, showing that he could botch simple exit passes or mishandle a puck without pressure at even moderate speed. This doesn't paint a great picture of a prospect you would be hammering the table to draft but it doesn't tell the entire story.

Arseni has his faults, but he also is in an environment that doesn't drive development. Diamonds are formed under pressure, and the quality of competition and lack of structure meant that Marchenko never really had to improve. Yet, despite his environment, we're writing him because he actually showed significant adaptation in the playoffs, and because when you factor in his potential growth rate, there's just too much there.

Typically, when you see a very raw, very large defenseman in a bad development league, the scouting instincts kick in and you think to yourself, "he's probably a shutdown defender who is stationary from the line", when you first lay eyes on him. That statement can be backed up time and time again, but it doesn't highlight Marchenko's game at all.

Instead, Marchenko's game has advanced offensive elements and he plays a modern style of defense, meaning that he initiates most plays by incorporating deception and feints within his first phase of operating with the puck. He can generate deception and feints at a high rate as the result of being a functionally coordinated athlete already.

This is exciting in it's own right, since as we mentioned earlier, his potential growth rate is bordering elite, as he's the youngest player in the draft and has an enormous frame that isn't even close to being filled out. He can handle a puck at a decent rate, his multi-directional skating is advanced in some areas, and he can think up creative and technical offensive plays.

Subsequently, he can make well-timed hesitation side stepping moves, effective pivoting feints that force opposing players into wrong skating lanes, or simple lateral cutbacks, where he combines his wingspan into his skating to rearrange his options. Some of his most surprising plays are the result of a three-zone dash, where he becomes the catalyst for breaking through layers of traffic before finding a high danger later passing set up. We've even seen him recognize that his trailing option wasn't in position for a backdoor set up yet, after he carved around the back of the net, so he hesitated before making a reverse no-look spinning lateral pass that hit directly on the tape. The pass wasn't put in the back of the net, but the advanced play burned its memory into our evaluation, because it wasn't the first or the last time we saw him make a surprising lateral set up that had us recognizing his untapped potential.

There's a raw base to work with within his shot as well. Right now, he has a very wide spectrum in terms of his mechanics. Sometimes, he just whiffs on routine wrist-shot from the line; other times he can make coordinated shots that feature a lateral drag into a double rock back to get it through a triangle. His catch and release can be surprisingly soft, and he has innate instincts for understanding how to drop through a one timer. His wheelhouse has let him down often this season but we really think it can get to a completely different level down the road, and that really goes for the rest of his game as well.

Defensively, we've seen him fail to identify very basic positioning, mismanage his gap, and get his wires crossed with a teammate that puts him in bad spots, but he can also rapidly C-cut and close on players, crushing them along the boards. We've seen him use his skating base to stay in-front of slippery forwards and his stick instincts are decent. We wish he was meaner, but we have seen him dominate physically which is going to be one of the most important elements of his game in order for him to have a chance to play.

Marchenko is a very rare player-type that played in a development league that makes his evaluation extremely difficult. We were left trying to figure out if this player can play hockey well enough at this stage in his development to actually matter, in a league that wouldn't answer all our questions.

Admittedly, we don't really have a definitive answer for describing what his projection actually is. He's not a dumb player, and he can recognize weakside options and evaluate when passing lanes are open. He does incorporate deception, and he can make advanced plays. He can also botch simple plays and fail to recognize his time and space. He's not an overly poised player. He also can lack the necessary pace and urgency you would typically want to see in a defensive prospect, especially one that needs to take advantage of his tool-kit. Yet, we did see some improvements in his game and there is significant, untapped potential.

His future will come down to his ability to handle pressure in a faster league, and if he can learn how to play with structure when asked to do so. If he can manage those two elements, then there's an outside shot he can play as a third pairing defenseman while bringing a truly unique package. Our ranking reflects the amount of variables that he needs to overcome and includes the uncertainty as a byproduct of the environment he played in.

"Here's the one off quote I use to describe one prospect in the Black Book each season and is it ever fitting.' Life is a box of chocolates, you never know what you're going to get.'" - HP Scout, Brad Allen

62	PLAYER	TEAM	LEAGUE	HEIGHT	WEIGHT	POS	GRADE
	MARQUES, MIGUEL	LETHBRIDGE	WHL	5' 10.25"	187	RW	C
NHLCS	CEILING	FLOOR	HOCKEY SENSE	COMPETE	SKILL	SKATE	MISC
NA-53	7	3	7	4	7	5	4

The former 10th overall in the WHL bantam draft improved a lot from last year. After scoring 20 points last season, Marques led his team in scoring with 74 points in 67 games this season.

Marques displays high-end offensive IQ with the puck. In transition, Margues' touches on the breakout are efficient, helping his team exiting the zone with control. His straight-line speed is average, but he's a good puck carrier because of his lower and upper separation. He can change direction quickly and deceptively using lateral weight shift to freeze defender, and he can build peed to exploit open space by using linear crossovers. Marques is very patient on entries, buying time to find the best play and inviting pressure to create open space for his teammates. Marques is dangerous offensively because of his dual-threat. When approaching scoring areas, Marques puts the puck on his hip pocket. Because of this great habit, he's always able to make plays in multiple directions. He's good at finding plays across the royal road with his passing. Although he's a pass first player, he has a good release of his shot, often dragging the puck from his hip pocket and changing the angle of the release point.

The offensive zone is where Marques is at his best. He climbs the offensive wall in control with poise, allowing his teammates to move off-puck to create confusion on the defensive team. Just like on the rush, he uses hip pocket deception to have options in many directions. The timing of his passing is great, making plays at the right time with shot assist to create grade-A scoring chances inside. Without the puck, he moves with purpose. When the puck is high, Marques loves to get lost down low, changing side behind the net to acquire the puck with time and space. He pre-scans well, making one-touch plays off the yellow wall when F3 is available. He can buy-time in space with decent body positioning and puck protection, although it's an area of his game that can find another level. On the power play, most of Lethbridge plays ran through Marques. He plays on his strong-side half-wall, which makes sense given how efficient he is when he plays with the puck on his hip pocket. He does a great job finding seam passes, as well as being a shooting threat with drag release.

Without the puck, Marques' defensive game will need to improve. He's a smart player positionally, but he needs to track harder and more constantly when returning to the defensive zone. He often looks to leave the zone early, which is a plus for creating offense, but a negative to cover the slot. It's a great strategy he needs to use as an offensive creator, but needs to find the right balance. In the offensive zone, he does a decent job pressuring the puck carrier to have offensive zone retrievals.

"Double thumbs down for me. No effort equals no interest." - NHL Scout, April 2024

"Not sure if there was anyone on the ice he didn't yell at. I think he had a bad day. (Laughs). I wouldn't draft him." - NHL Scout, May 2024

"He's in the Josh Ho-Sang, Ryan Merkley- Jake Virtanen group of prospects for me. Pass." - NHL Scout, May 2024

Of all players we have ever scouted at hockeyprospect.com, he might be the one with the widest range of opinions." - HP Scout Jérôme Bérubé (May 2024)

"In any given game, on any given play, you're looking at a top-6 forward." - HP Scout, Brad Allen , May 2024

"In any given game, on any given play, you're looking at a player who is never playing." - HP Scout, Brad Allen , May 2024

"My first viewing was as bad as it gets. He would've had to work at it to play worse in that game. Lazy play and turnovers were the order of the day. One of our scouts was a big fan and told me to watch him, so of course my first viewing was horrific. My second viewing was better...he flashed some skill. After that game the rest of my views were liker to the first viewing. I would not draft him." - HP Scout, Mark Edwards, March 2024

"Our scout Brad Allen loves him. I'll never let Brad forget it if he busts. I'll never hear the end of it from Brad if he hits." – HP Scout, Mark Edwards, May 2024

NR	PLAYER	TEAM	LEAGUE	HEIGHT	WEIGHT	POS	GRADE
	MARRELLI, FRANKIE	OTTAWA	OHL	5' 10.5"	187	LD	NI
NHLCS	CEILING	FLOOR	HOCKEY SENSE	COMPETE	SKILL	SKATE	MISC
NA-135	5	3	5	6	5	6	5

A former first round pick in the Ontario Hockey League draft, Frankie Marrelli has given the Ottawa 67's a burst of energy on the blue line since coming into the league. Marrelli put up 25 points in 60 games this season following that up with 3 points in 10 playoff games with the 67's and an invite to the U18's to represent Canada adding 2 points in his 7 games along with 29 penalty minutes.

Despite his smaller stature, Marrelli plays a decent game with some good defensive play and some physicality. He is more defensively inclined overall, however Marrelli does have bursts of offence that flash from time to time. He is not the fastest skater, but he does have good balance and control on his feet when skating up ice or when engaging physically along the boards. This lack of speed however hurts him in the coverage game at this level and without a big improvement it is hard to translate him to the next level with these lapses in coverage. He is a constant competitor out there and has a good amount of vinegar to his game when defending.

Offensively, he does not make the best passes in transition up ice or in the offensive zone and often simply passes back to whoever gave him the puck. This may not be a bad option as he has quite a poor shot and on the whole, does not offer much offensive upside at the OHL level let alone the NHL level. It is hard to see him putting up points against bigger, stronger and more intelligent players in addition to seeing him be able to carry the puck and make intelligence decisions with his lack of size and speed.

He does not have much special teams, more specifically penalty kill, projection despite his abilities as a defender who is not only willing but adept at blocking shots. This limits his projection and makes it tough to pin him into a line up especially on a team contending in the playoffs. He does have the physicality and the compete, but he does not have the skill, discipline or high intelligence to push himself or his team to the next level. His lack of size and skill is a stopper for us and despite a good defensive game, the offensive side is not there and keeps us in the position to wait and see for him to develop strength, size and skill.

54	PLAYER	TEAM	LEAGUE	HEIGHT	WEIGHT	POS	GRADE
	MARRELLI, LUCA	OSHAWA	OHL	6' 01.5"	185	RD	C+
NHLCS	CEILING	FLOOR	HOCKEY SENSE	COMPETE	SKILL	SKATE	MISC
NA-46	6	5	7	6	6	6	6

Luca Marrelli is an intelligent right-shot defenseman for the Oshawa Generals in the Ontario Hockey League. In 67 games for the Generals, Marrelli posted 57 points including 51 assists while chopping his penalty minutes in half from 32 the previous year to 16 in 2023/24. After a disappointing sophomore season, the late 2005 birth Marrelli followed it up with an outstanding third year in the league and vaulting himself up draft boards by displaying a plethora of skills to scouts all year in all three zones.

One of the biggest surprises this season for Marrelli was not only that he played power play minutes, but that he was their top power play defenseman and managed the point well with his vision. He saw open passing lanes throughout the offensive zone and knew when to shoot or pass from the point. We don't see Marrelli as even a second power play defenseman in the NHL, as it is extremely difficult to get power play minutes at the highest level. However, this did showcase some skills in the passing game, albeit with time and space he will not have at the NHL level.. On the penalty kill, we got to see some defending that can translate to the pro level with gap control, shot blocking, and, despite not having top speed, the ability to jump onto loose pucks and get them out of the zone. Often paired with fellow draft-eligible defenseman Ben Danford on the penalty kill, Marrelli and Danford made an exceptional pair that helped Oshawa become the second-best penalty-killing team in the regular season.

As a skater, Marrelli moves up the ice with both poise and confidence with the puck on his stick, keeping his head up and ready to make quick passes or accurate long stretch passes out of his own end. His backward skating is strong and fluid, which he uses to control gaps well both on the rush and in coverage in the defensive zone, where he also uses his edges to create space both forwards and backward. He uses his strong strides and fluid cuts to evade pressure well in the clogged-up neutral zone. It is not often you find Marrelli behind the play or out of position, and this is not just due to his intelligence but his skating as well. Marrelli will win puck battles in his own zone and does not overcommit on plays while still hustling hard to make plays in his own zone. Some improved speed would help him up ice, but overall, when it comes to Marrelli's skating, nothing jumps off the page as a red flag. In fact, with some more strength, Marrelli's skating game will be much stronger as he will be better equipped against bigger forwards. He will need this boost as his physicality, although not poor, needs to improve for play against bigger and stronger players. He is not scared to engage physically, which is a positive, but he will need more weight to throw around to continue his success.

Marrelli is one of the more underrated defensemen in transition as he makes highly intelligent plays up ice and out of his zone. He skates consistently with his head up and scans the forecheck effectively to set up his teammates for strong offensive opportunities. In the offensive zone, he has good instincts and tempo, timing pinches and passes with precision. He often makes the safe play and doesn't overdo anything offensively to avoid mistakes going the other way. His passing and shooting have greatly improved in both accuracy and power. He likely won't be a big offensive contributor at the NHL level, but with his offensive progression, he has shown us that he is not going to be an anchor offensively. Defensively, Marrelli is an excellent one-on-one defender against the cycle and on the rush. He uses good body positioning to keep the play in front of him and does not bite often on fakes made by forwards. Another skill of Marrelli's is his ability to get the puck out of the zone with both possession and in desperation. Marrelli is good at getting the puck high and out if there is no pass or carry option out of the zone, ensuring he does not ice the puck so his team gets a chance to change.

Marrelli has shown tremendous strides compared to his sophomore year. While considering that he should be a strong defenseman in his third year in the OHL, he shined in all areas of the game and played well in all situations. With his size and play, it is tough sometimes to see where he will translate into the NHL. He does not have the extremely high upside of a first-pair defenseman but shows better skill and intelligence projection than some third-pair projected defensemen. This puts him in the middle pair, and in our opinion, closer to the fourth spot than the third spot on the depth chart. There are translatable skills to the penalty kill and in his own zone which are tough to ignore, but we will need to see more offensive consistency next year to prove his development is on track. His vision and transitional play give us confidence that he will continue his development to the pro level.

"Good puck mover. Good mobility but I would want him to play a harder game. Too easy to play against." – NHL Scout, May 2024

"I don't hate him. I don't love him. He's fine. There are guys like him in the league." – NHL Scout, May 2024

"Played with Danford and was good…out played his partner." – HP Scout, Mark Edwards, October 2023

49	PLAYER		TEAM	LEAGUE	HEIGHT	WEIGHT	POS	GRADE
	MASSE, MAXIM		CHICOUTIMI	QMJHL	6' 02.25"	190	RW	C+
NHLCS	CEILING	FLOOR	HOCKEY SENSE	COMPETE	SKILL		SKATE	MISC
NA-30	7	4	7	6	7		5	6

Massé was the 3rd overall pick in the 2022 QMJHL Draft, and he won both the QMJHL and CHL Rookie of the Year awards. At the Hlinka Gretzky tournament in August, he scored 5 goals in 5 games. Although his 2023-2024 season had its share of ups and downs, he concluded it on a high note, showcasing strong performances in the latter half of the season and postseason.

The Rimouski native started turning things around in January. He had 34 points in 37 games at the end of the 2023 calendar year, but finished with 41 points in his last 30 regular season games. While the production was much better, his overall game saw significant improvements as well. He was better away from the puck; in some of our viewings he was really good at creating turnovers with a great active stick and good reads. He also became quite good at gaining inside leverage on players with his frame and active stick, which contributed to winning puck battles and creating turnovers.

He has good size, but we wouldn't categorize him as a physical player. While he does use his frame and stick to win puck battles, he's not a tenacious or physical power-forward who will throw tons of hits. Consistency remains a primary concern when it comes to him; despite his improved 2nd-half performance, his ups and downs continued. While some games showcased his great two-way abilities, others left us apprehensive about potentially overvaluing him.

Processing the game at a high level, Massé is a player who has good puck touches. Skilled on his backhand, he would use it to execute precise passes to his teammates. We saw lots of good one-touch passes as well, in both the offensive and neutral zones. He makes his linemates better thanks to his strong passing game, also using his frame and his long reach to extend play, making hook passes while in transition for example. In the latter part of the season, his ability to create offense with his playmaking down low improved. Offensively, he is a dual-threat: while his playmaking skills are solid (often underrated), he is recognized more for his shot. He is a threat in the offensive zone due to being able to score from distance with both his slapshot and wrist shot. He has higher efficiency with his wrist shot compared to his slapshot in terms of accuracy right now. His wrist shot has a quick release and impressive velocity, whereas there's less accuracy with his one-timer, but its velocity does increase. The best version of his one-timer is when he drops to one knee to slap pucks, similar to what Mike Cammalleri used to do in the NHL.

On the power play, he can play everywhere, demonstrating great versatility for his game to translate better to the NHL. He's often in the Ovechkin spot on the Saguenéens' power play, where he can one-time pucks but also pass to his teammates. As the season progressed, we started seeing real good chemistry between him and 16-year-old rookie Émile Guité on the power play. Both would try to set each other up from both the left and right-wing half-wall. Both players have this great dual-threat quality to their offensive game and are as good in the shooting department as they are playmakers. Massé can also be quite effective in front of the net and in the bumper role, which could end up being his role in the NHL. For example, playing for Canada at the Hlinka Gretzky Cup, he had his best success there, and he was also quite good at retrieving pucks in the slot and getting rebounds with his long stick and superior hockey sense to reach pucks before his opponents. We feel that this bumper/front-of-the-net role is what suits him the best for the pro game, but it's unlikely he'll ever play there with his QMJHL team. To play that role you need to really want it, as players are subjected to more physicality compared to playing on the perimeter. While he possesses the skills and size for this role, questions about his tenacity and grit level arise when it comes to him doing so consistently at the NHL level. He could also play on the other wing on the power play, or even the point, having demonstrated that he is a good puck-distributor on certain 4-on-3 or 5-on-3 sequences.

In the first half, conditioning seemed to be a concern for Massé. He would look tired on 20-25-second shifts. For someone with an average skating base, fatigue can highlight, even exacerbate certain things (especially skating being the weakest part of one's game, which it is for him). However, in the second half of the season, his energy levels seemed to improve, allowing him to maintain a better pace on the ice throughout games. Still, he's not a big factor in his team's transition game due to his skating, because he can't carry the puck up the ice with speed. Too often this year, he would get a breakaway chance that lasted all-too-briefly because an opponent would catch up before he could take advantage of a scoring chance.   He does make sharp turns and has decent athleticism traits, but lacks explosiveness with his skating. With time, we feel he's going to be able to add more power to his frame, adding more explosiveness to his stride as a result. Once he does, his skating will be fine; there are definitely worse skaters than him in the NHL. Tyson Foerster has still managed to score 20+ goals with the Philadelphia Flyers despite this being an issue for him.

We think Massé has top-9 potential for the NHL. His improvement level in the 2nd half of the season was noticeable and he re-established himself as a good prospect for this draft class. With his size, hockey sense, shooting and passing skills, there are a lot of good things going on with him for a team to invest in his potential. It's going to be interesting to see where he actually goes in the draft. Yes, the improvement level in the 2nd half was noticeable, but he might also have turned teams off in the 1st half. As we saw with Matthew Knies in 2021, it didn't matter how much better he got over time, he still dropped to the end of the 2nd round. We like the improvements Massé made, but his game is still inconsistent and he still lacks the big-time drive we saw from Knies in 2021 that made us believers. We had ranked Knies really high on our list back then, but are a bit more reserved with Massé's place on the list.

" I like a lot about his game but his skating might kill him when all is said and done." - NHL Scout, January 2024

" If he could just get his skating to be average I wouldn't have any issues taking him in the second round but his skating is below average in my opinion." - NHL Scout, January 2024

" I just down graded him. He is a mid rounder at best for me now. I can't get passed his poor skating." - NHL Scout, January 2024

" Power and explosiveness are solid but it's not translating to his skating." - NHL Scout, March 2024

" Can he improve his skating? If he can't than he won't play. I like his game other than that." - NHL Scout, May 2024

" He is easily my top player from the Q (MJHL) but his skating is an issue. It was exposed even more in Europe" - NHL Scout, May 2024

" Look at him during his shifts, the gas tank is empty after 20-25 seconds on the ice, how is the conditioning?" - NHL Scout (October 2023)

" People talk about his skating like it's bad, I don't have a problem with it. If Tyson Foerster is playing in the NHL I don't see why Massé skating is going to stop him from playing in the NHL." - NHL Scout, October 2023

" If I was someone in his entourage, I would make him watch Matthew Knies videos of how to play along the boards and around the net. I don't know if he's got that dawg in him though." -HP Scout Jérôme Bérubé (October 2023)

" Much better in the 2nd half but every time I want to move him up on my list I have a little voice in my head telling me not to do it. The lack of want is what is holding me back from putting him in my top-32" - HP Scout Jérôme Bérubé

" Masse was a tough evaluation for me. I like a lot of what he does but every time I started to get back on his bandwagon I'd get another viewing that backed me off a bit. Really weak draft class in the Q this year." - HP Scout, Mark Edwards, May 2024

83	PLAYER	TEAM	LEAGUE	HEIGHT	WEIGHT	POS	GRADE
	MATEIKO, ERIKS	SAINT JOHN	QMJHL	6' 05"	216	LW	C

NHLCS	CEILING	FLOOR	HOCKEY SENSE	COMPETE	SKILL	SKATE	MISC
NA-33	5	4	5	6	5	5	7

Mateiko is a Latvian prospect who played the past two seasons in the QMJHL with the Saint John Sea Dogs. He also played for his country in international competitions such as last year's U18 World Championship and this year's U20 World Junior Hockey Championship. He finished the year with 43 points in 49 games. His production decreased in the 2nd half of the season after he lost his centerman Peter Reynolds, who was traded to Halifax. In the first half, Mateiko was a point-per-game player with 30 points in his first 28 games. Post-trade, he had just 13 points in 21 games. Putting things further in perspective, the Sea Dogs were a bottom-3 team in the league (they won just 7 games in their last 35).

Mateiko's size alone (6'05", 210) makes him intriguing for the next level. Playing a good two-way game, he's nothing special offensively, but he gets into the areas that he needs to to score goals. A good front-of-the-net presence, Mateiko's tough to move, and makes it difficult for goaltenders to see the puck. He scored a lot of goals this season from two or three feet away. He was successful with Peter Reynolds in the first half of the season because he was good at getting open around the net and receiving passes from him. When Reynolds left, no one could replace him in that area.

Mateiko is not a play-driver. In junior, he's the 2nd-best player on a line. His uncoordinated hands, bumpy stickhandling and the fact that he won't beat players cleanly with just his hands will make him the 3rd-best player on a line at the pro level. His passing skills are only average. If his playmaking was graded higher, he would improve his chances of playing in the NHL (and also be ranked higher on our list). His transition game is below-average as far as the NHL is concerned. He's not the player you want to see carrying the puck through the neutral zone. He can make a pass just fine, but won't change the dynamic of his team's transition game. Offensively, he does his best work down low and in front of the net. He has an above-average shot, but this likely won't translate to the next level as a threat from long-distance. His bread and butter will remain his play around the net.

Other things he is good at: retrieving pucks, using his reach to dig them out of wall battles. He skates decently for a player of his size, however, his edgework and explosiveness will need some work (he can be slow in his starts). Once he gets going, he generates some interesting speed for a 6'05", 210-pound 18-year-old. His stride is a bit ugly, but he does move around at a decent level and has a lot of power. He also has good defensive habits, as he was used often on the Saint John PK unit during the year. With his reach and long stick, he demonstrated good anticipation, plus the ability to block passing lanes and create turnovers. Added experience in such a role could lead to him doing so again at the next level. Off the puck, he was good this year. The effort level is always there with him. He doesn't quit on backchecks and can be good in defensive puck-pursuit plays as well.

We think he can either be a decent AHL'er or have a nice career in Europe, but we're not sold on his NHL future. If he makes it he would be a depth forward. We think his lack of high-end skills is going to limit him in that regard.

NR	PLAYER	TEAM	LEAGUE	HEIGHT	WEIGHT	POS	GRADE
	MAYES, NATHAN	SPOKANE	WHL	6' 03.75"	194	LD	NI

NHLCS	CEILING	FLOOR	HOCKEY SENSE	COMPETE	SKILL	SKATE	MISC
NA-107	4	5	5	6	3	4	7

A former 3rd round pick in the WHL bantam draft, Mayes played his first season in the WHL this year. He was a ncie surprise for the Chiefs, playing in a top 4 for most of the season with good PK minutes.

Defensively, Mayes is overall steady. When defending the rush, he retrieves inside dots to keep the puck carrier on the outside. In the defensive zone, he shows good awareness overall. He's not overly mean as he doesn't chase huge hits, but he's physical when needed and makes stop down low. When defending the net front, he's aware of his check, looking to box out and tying his stick.

With the puck, Mayes plays a simple game. On breakout retrievals, he uses his size well to establish body position, shield the forechecker and find the next play. He relies on his partner a lot, but will make simple and smart touches. He's a surprised straight-line skater, and he loves to uses this tool to carry the puck when there's space. In the offensive zone, Mayes keeps it simple, moving the puck quickly and shooting when there's an open lane.

As a WHL rookie with his size, decent athleticism and IQ, Mayes was a strong defender for his team and has the upside to develop well in the future. To improve his stock as a prospect, adding a few dominant traits to his game would help him a lot.

NR	PLAYER	TEAM	LEAGUE	HEIGHT	WEIGHT	POS	GRADE
	MCINNIS, KEITH	BROOKS	BCHL	6' 01.25"	192	LD	NI

NHLCS	CEILING	FLOOR	HOCKEY SENSE	COMPETE	SKILL	SKATE	MISC
NA-213	4	4	4	6	4	4	6

McInnis had a rough 16-year-old season in the USHL, playing only 9 games due to shoulder injuries. This year, he was healthy, but it was evident that because of all the time he missed, his development path suffered as a result. After starting the year in the USHL with Waterloo, he played 24 games (only registering 2 assists) before leaving for the AJHL to play with Brooks after Christmas. He played 6 games in the AJHL until certain teams (including Brooks) left the AJHL to join the BCHL. In the AJHL/BCHL, he finished with 16 points in 26 games and 51 penalty minutes. We think the move back to Canadian Jr. A benefitted him; he got to play more minutes, got more puck touches and his confidence that he lost in the USHL slowly started coming back. He's committed to playing college hockey at North Dakota.

McInnis's skating shortcomings seem to affect both his offensive and defensive game. As far as recovery skating goes, if a turnover occurs and he gets caught in the offensive or neutral zone, it's tough for him to come back defensively. We wouldn't categorize him as a player with good athleticism; he seems quite average in that department. His skating stride is long and compact, but it lacks strength and doesn't have much explosiveness. Keeping in mind that this is a player who missed almost all of last season and had other injuries in minor hockey, it's likely that all this time away from hockey has derailed his development. He can't be an impact player rushing the puck from his zone because of the lack of speed. He has a good point shot, but struggles to get his shot on net; his shots get blocked often. He needs to work harder at finding better shooting lanes, needs to move more laterally, and needs to get his shot off faster. He also needs to improve his decision-making, as he struggled with his passing efficiency when he was forechecked hard and pressured to make plays.

We don't see his offensive game translating to the pro level, we think his defensive game is just okay, but he plays a very physical game. We do think his defensive game could translate if he can improve his skating skills and add more explosiveness. He's tough one-on-one, has good stick activation and takes his man out well. He's a big hitter, hitting hard, and forwards have to be aware of him on the ice. However, he still can get exposed when faced with fast players coming down his side of the ice. At this point, his potential looks quite limited, and this is a player who has had a hard time staying healthy. If he can play a few seasons without any injuries, he can work on improving his athleticism, skating and puck game. There could be something there in the end.

He's more likely to go undrafted at this point. If he does get drafted, it would be as a late pick. He's expected to play at North Dakota next season, but there's going to be some strong competition in terms of ice time with other freshmen defensemen coming in. The best long-term scenario would probably be for him to play another season in junior A, to continue to work on his game, and get as much ice time as possible. Ice time is exactly what he needs now; he might not get it at North Dakota next season. His case is similar to that of Charles-Alexis Legault a few years ago: a lengthy injury history led Legault to go undrafted in 2021, but he went back to play in the BCHL instead of college due to ice time being a factor. He then had a good 18-year-old season in the BCHL, and after playing one season at Quinnipiac, he was drafted in the NHL in his 3rd year of eligibility. With McInnis' injury story, what he needs most is the time and ability to work on his skills and overall game. He won't be able to get that right away in North Dakota. As the adage goes in scouting, it's not a sprint, it's a marathon.

NR	PLAYER	TEAM	LEAGUE	HEIGHT	WEIGHT	POS	GRADE
	MCISAAC, WILLIAM	SPOKANE	WHL	6' 03"	192	RD	NI
NHLCS	CEILING	FLOOR	HOCKEY SENSE	COMPETE	SKILL	SKATE	MISC
NA-93	5	4	3	6	5	7	7

For the 2nd season in a row, McIsaac played top 4 minutes for the Chiefs, often playing with Colorado Avalanche prospect Saige Weinstein. The former 2nd round pick had a decent season for Spokane with 27 points in 67 games.

McIsaac is a big right-handed defenseman with tools. Offensively, he owns a strong shot from the point and is active in the offensive zone, often looking to sneak back door as D2 when the defensive winger is puck watching. He has some flashes in transition with his good overall mobility, but his poise with the puck needs a lot of work. Being more patient with the puck would help him to exit the zone in control more often and would make his transition success much higher.

Defensively, it's pretty much the same. He can show some really positive sign as he can close play quickly with his size and mobility, and he can throw some pretty big hits as well. But overall, his defensive game needs refinement.

McIsaac has some pretty good upside with his toolbox, and if he can put it together, he could be a big contributor for the Chiefs down the road. Still, he overall game needs some refinement.

NR	PLAYER	TEAM	LEAGUE	HEIGHT	WEIGHT	POS	GRADE
	MCLAUGHLIN, FINN	FARGO	USHL	6' 01"	186	LD	NI
NHLCS	CEILING	FLOOR	HOCKEY SENSE	COMPETE	SKILL	SKATE	MISC
NA-132	5	4	4	6	4	6	6

Mobile defenseman. Finn McLaughlin has a unique skating stride. His skating is basically all hips. So he has a wide berth to him – wider than his vitals might indicate. He doesn't generate much power from this style of skating. The lack of drive through traditional three point flexion methods creates deficiencies in his explosiveness and, really, all the way through to his top speed. On the plus side, his edge work is very strong. Like almost every aspect of his game, his skating has a lot of room to grow and we're grading that as such, as it's the most projectable and has the highest likelihood of progressing meaningfully. The technical skill is much less of a certainty. He has a huge range of stickhandling maneuvers that he's willing to try (or not) depending on the game. Sometimes he's pulling pucks off walls and out of danger with some degree of aplomb…even going so far as to try to some moves in space on the rush and, rarer still, walking the offensive line. He can be a borderline overhandler in those instances, often exposing the puck to the interior of the ice before he's ready to make a play. Other games, he's very skittish with the puck, downright inefficient and thoughtless. One consistent thing is that we wished he had more puck poise. He can throw a lot of pucks away in the defensive zone in an unwarranted fashion. His stick comes up off the ice a good bit, so there's a lack of smoothness to his puck handles. There's a small bud of skill set potentially, but it's not close to interesting right now.

McLaughlin generally plays the game on his toes, but he's not tough to play against. In fact, the bit of grit in his game seemed to decay as the year wore on. His checks tend to slide through him. He's missing that defensive viscosity that we like to see. His gaps are really inconsistent – not just shift to shift or rush to rush – but within a single rush absorption sequence even. Finn will setup like he's going to step up and make a play, and then not process it fast enough and end up not speed matching properly. This miscalculation causes him to open his hips and have to play from behind a lot. That rushes his game and that leads to more frazzling and random decisions.

His game doesn't have a process. Every shift is brand new to him. As such, there's no real consistent progression to his game. Usually it's forwards that don't have a particular niche in their game, defensemen often figure it out first...but that's not the case here. In terms of player type or mold, he just isn't anything in particular yet. Not a ton of zip on pucks. Shot isn't a strength. He has taken up hardcore neutral zone surfing in Fargo (USHL), compared to what he was doing in Youngstown, and the results haven't been very pretty. The interesting thing is that his hippy skating and his occasional ability to quickly pull the puck away from trouble while still maintaining control could manifest as some escapability down the line, if crafted.

The troubling aspect is the hockey sense. As mentioned above, there's this feel that everything is new to him all the time. If he can ever find a way to develop some pattern recognition or even a process to his game, that might start to eat up his mental development arc a bit and give a better feel as to what he could become. Right now, this is a raw player that is notably unproductive at this level despite playing a prominent role as a D-1 player in the AJHL the year before. It's all too abstract now to reasonably use a draft pick here.

NR	PLAYER		TEAM	LEAGUE	HEIGHT	WEIGHT	POS	GRADE
	MCMORROW, BRENDAN		USA-U18	NTDP	5' 11.5"	175	LW	NI
NHLCS	CEILING	FLOOR	HOCKEY SENSE	COMPETE	SKILL		SKATE	MISC
NA-147	4	4	5	6	4		5	5

No frills, depth winger. Brendan McMorrow, like most USNTDP forwards this year, had been used up and down the lineup this season. He ended up way down the lineup to end the year at the U18 Worlds, but that was also some of his most inspiring work. He looked particularly dialled in throughout the tournament after a bit of up and down play in the dog days of the regular season. Just five goals and 11 assists in 27 USHL contests before being shutout in seven games at the U18 WJCs. Sort of an appropriate stat line for a fairly ubiquitous player. Average size, average skating, below average skill set, good compete level – there isn't a lot that stands about McMorrow. The biggest issue that we have with his game is: for a player that needs to be constantly punching up to find his way, he's very deferential in virtually all situations. There isn't a real "take charge" element to his game. If there's a loose puck and he and a teammate are near it, he'll defer or make a sheepish poke at it. He had just 32 shots on net in those 27 games; that's tied with physical defenseman Will Skahan, who played in less. If there's a chance to lean into an opponent and really take him out of the play, he'll stop short of that and just go for the tie. Part of that might be that he's pretty stiff from an athletic posture point of view. His small-area footwork doesn't do him any favors either. If the game is made up of a bunch of milliseconds, the best players tend to take those milliseconds from others to make room for themselves (deceptive maneuvers, puck protection techniques, etc.) – McMorrow is the type of player that they're taking those milliseconds from. We're not impressed enough with the DU commit's mental processor either. He's not ahead of the play, he's almost always chasing it. He's not dumb, but like his other traits – nothing pops. One thing that is a little unique about him is his desire to get deep hip drop action on his shot attempts in traffic, but that usually leaves rolling on the ice afterwards.

He's a short-shift worker bee with minimal technical skills and has a lot of trouble consistently gaining useful ice on opponents in any situation. Just doesn't really move the needle in any aspect.

NR	PLAYER	TEAM	LEAGUE	HEIGHT	WEIGHT	POS	GRADE
	MELOVSKY, MATYAS	BAIE-COMEAU	QMJHL	6' 01.75"	190	RC	C
NHLCS	CEILING	FLOOR	HOCKEY SENSE	COMPETE	SKILL	SKATE	MISC
NA-80	5	4	6	5	6	5	5

Melovsky just wrapped up his second season in the QMJHL with Baie-Comeau. He collected 60 points in 53 games, and also improved his goals' output from 6 last year to 18 this year. He was also a key player for Team Czechia at the U20 World Juniors with 11 points (10 assists) in 7 games, which was good for 3rd overall in tournament scoring. This is his 3rd year of eligibility for the NHL Draft, having been passed over in 2022 and 2023.

Melovsky is a smart center whose best quality is his playmaking. He loves to slow down the play and has good timing to find his open teammates with good passes. There's some good creativity to his game, even more so in power play situations where more space and time is available. Seen as a pass-first type of player, last year he was not shooting or getting into the tough areas of the ice often enough. He improved that this year, shooting the puck with more confidence and getting into traffic more frequently. His output (goals and points per game) improved this year, but this is also normal for a player under his circumstances (more experience, playing on the top team in the league) to improve on his past performance. These are factors we need to take into consideration when analyzing his play this year.

What is odd about his performance at the World Juniors was that it didn't carry over to his QMJHL play. He was good, but we couldn't call him a great or a dominant player in this league. At 19, and in his 3rd year of eligibility, this has us proceeding with caution as far as projecting him for the NHL. He's an average skater; his top speed and explosiveness leave a little to be desired, but he has decent edgework and the ability to change directions while in possession of the puck. He makes it difficult for opposing defenders to counter him off the rush. He's creative with his playmaking, but also with his skating route.

As he is a 2004-born player, the question we have is regarding how much he is going to be able to upgrade his skating compared to the other eligible draftees, most of whom were born in 2006. We also think he looks more like 6'00 rather than the 6'02 currently stated on the QMJHL website. For the record, he was listed at 6'00" and 183 pounds at the IIHF World Junior Hockey Championship in December.

While we would categorize Melovsky as a good junior player, he is more likely to have a good career in Europe or the AHL. There's just not enough there for us to project him for the NHL.

NR	PLAYER	TEAM	LEAGUE	HEIGHT	WEIGHT	POS	GRADE
	MERRILL, BEN	ST. SEB. SCHOOL	HIGH-MA	6' 03.25"	190	RC	NI
NHLCS	CEILING	FLOOR	HOCKEY SENSE	COMPETE	SKILL	SKATE	MISC
NA-127	6	3	5	4	6	5	7

Big, skilled forward. Ben Merrill had 24 points in 28 games at St. Sebastian's School in 2023-24. At 6'3", 190 pounds, Merrill stands out from a size perspective, but also from a reach perspective. He's a hulking player with surprising hand dexterity and an extremely wide puck control window. The toughest part about his game is the athleticism and skating package.

He's still growing into his frame and lacks any sort of dynamic or quick-twitch footwork. There's some decent top speed with his long stride. But he struggles with balance and leaning off his center line or even absorbing contact that he doesn't initiate. As a late 2005, who has yet to achieve this nor has really been challenged by a higher level of competition (two USHL games where he was scarcely used, notwithstanding), it's a real long shot for this to come together. He's going to Penticton in the BCHL next season before attending Harvard, that's probably the right, long-term development path. As for now, pucks really jump off his blade. He can make some neat area and saucer passes out of his quick hand movement – but he's not a natural playmaker. There is some jam to his game, especially near the net in the offensive zone. His defensive lies in his strong stick and reach combination, but he generally isn't digging in too hard on the backcheck.

It's a long range, longshot projection, but he could be a power winger that works the wall and the front of the net to some acclaim way down the road. He's at least a watchlist player, if not a very late pick.

88	PLAYER	TEAM	LEAGUE	HEIGHT	WEIGHT	POS	GRADE
	MEWS, HENRY	OTTAWA	OHL	6' 00.25"	189	RD	C
NHLCS	CEILING	FLOOR	HOCKEY SENSE	COMPETE	SKILL	SKATE	MISC
NA-37	6	4	5	4	6	7	5

High expectations come with being selected 7th overall by the Ottawa 67's. Mews however, has stagnated slightly in his development and major progression has not been seen in his game. Coming out of the Toronto Jr. Canadiens AAA program in the GTHL, there were high standards for Mews as an intelligent defender and effortless skater. Production wise, Mews posted 61 points in 65 games which included 15 goals. The production is good, however, with a below average compete level and trouble with the defensive and physical aspects of the game Mews doesn't project as well for the NHL level in our opinion..

Some consistency came from Henry Mews this season. Unfortunately, it was not the kind of consistency that moves you up our draft board. He displayed a lack of interest and effort a lot of the time during the season and did not like engaging in the physical aspect of the game. There were a number of times this season where it looked like Mews was the easy target of opposing teams after the whistle with no push back. He was constantly beat along the wall in our viewings and down low physically. He can sometimes win battles with his stick or by being first on the puck but, the wins are fewer than the losses defensively. Another defensive tendency from Mews is his problem chasing the play, especially on the cycle which continues to hurt his overall success in the defensive zone.

A positive in his defensive game is his active stick defensively to compensate for his seemingly unwillingness to play physically in his own end. He is better playing a zone coverage as opposed to a man where he will need to be a bit more physical as he has trouble clearing his net and bumping larger players off the puck with his poor body contact. However, as a zone defender it gives Mews the opportunity to use his stick more to break up plays and get into shooting and passing lanes.

Despite the fact that his strong skating should be an asset in man coverage because he can use his edgework and pivots to keep up with attacking forwards, he is better off in zone due to that lack of physicality. He does use his skating to his advantage in zone coverage by jumping to loose pucks at a good speed and carrying the puck out of the zone.

As a skater, Mews effortlessly pivots forwards to backwards and has strong edgework and crossovers while moving up ice with and without the puck. Mews has good speed and does not lose it with the puck on his stick and when carrying the puck out himself makes strong transitional plays. When Mews attempts to pass the puck out of the zone, he is often less effective and can make poor passes into coverage when pressured or when given time to overthink. An additional issue with these turnovers, is if they happen farther out of his own zone and even offensively, he does not have a high compete or effort level which leaves his teammates to clean up a lot of his mistakes. At the NHL level, mistakes and lapses in effort are amplified and would quickly become an issue should he not improve this part of his game. There are times when he waits too long before passing and allows the lanes to close up on him and then gets pressured into making a bad pass or skating himself into coverage. When he does not turn the puck over in transition, Mews makes hard and accurate passes, but he does not always lead his teammates into good offensive opportunities off his reads coming out of the zone.

On the power play he can create successful offensive chances with good vision from the point while up a man. He uses his speed well up ice when joining the rush and is an asset on the rush with his ability to score. Considering that Mews only switched from forward a few years ago, him being a more offensively inclined defender who can work a powerplay makes sense, However, we don't think he projects to become a power play specialist at the NHL level or much of a heavy offensive force. Where this leaves Mews is on the bottom pairing, but as someone who is not a power play guy or someone trustworthy enough to consistently work on the penalty kill, the projection gets weak.

When Mews is aggressive, he flashes NHL skills including his shot and his ability to execute under pressure and through traffic from the point, especially from the high slot. He does tend to get caught on pinches or by over thinking, and a fair amount of the time he leaves his teammates to clean up his mess with his lack of compete and effort on the backcheck after his mistakes.

With good endurance and conditioning, Mews has the ability to take long shifts and not get too winded or tired out on the ice even after an icing. He is a big minute muncher at the OHL level as a young defender and plays poised despite the mistakes in his game. One thing that was noticeable during the year was that opponents knew Mews was not a fan of playing a physical game, so he was targeted often when teams dumped the puck in.

Mews skating ability will be coveted by some on draft day, but, due to his liabilities in the defensive game and our projection for his offensive game, Mews is more of a 4th to 7th round pick for us.

"He is playing forward right now. That kinda backs up what I see in his game in the defensive game." - NHL Scout, December 2023

"Smallish and nothing special in his game. I give him props for his points but to me he is like an Erik Brannstrom...no defining quality in his game." - NHL Scout, April 2024

"He's closer to a 'C' rated player than 'A' rated player for me. I don't get this top 15 stuff I see out there." - HP Scout, Mark Edwards, October 2023

"I've seen a him a few times now. Really haven't changed my opinion of him. Moves pucks well, pretty smart player but he's 5'11" and doesn't defend overly well. I still don't see an overly dynamic player. He's not a bad player by any means though. There is some talent there but I just don't see this high end top 20 pick that I see ranked on a lot of lists. Most scouts I talk to have him as a 'B' rated player and other as a mid round guy." - HP Scout, Mark Edwards, December 2023

"I like the skating the puck through the neutral zone but I think he really struggles in the defensive game and I don't think he is dynamic enough offensively to offset those deficiencies. - HP Scout, Mark Edwards, May 2024

22	PLAYER	TEAM	LEAGUE	HEIGHT	WEIGHT	POS	GRADE
	MIETTINEN, JULIUS	EVERETT	WHL	6' 03"	201	LC	B

NHLCS	CEILING	FLOOR	HOCKEY SENSE	COMPETE	SKILL	SKATE	MISC
NA-18	6	8	6	8	5	4	8

The 6'3" Finnish two-way center had a strong first season in North America with 67 points in 66 games. His 31 goals rank 4th amongst 1st year NHL Draft eligible players from the WHL. Miettinen was a top 6 center for a strong Everett team, and played in every situation. He also had an impressive 55.1% on 1062 faceoffs.

Offensively, Miettinen generates a lot of offensive opportunities from the forecheck. As F1 on the forecheck, he does a great job initiating contacts to gain possession. On 50/50 pucks, he owns the lane between the defender and the puck to be first on it. He has an active stick, creating takeaways and change of possession. Once he gets the first touch, Miettinen loves to quickly attack before the other team set their defensive zone coverage. He establishes body position; his eyes are up and he's able to find open player inside the house. In offensive zone play, Miettinen wall work is a strength of his game. With good puck protection abilities and puck skills, he's an underrated playmaker to find open player inside dangerous scoring areas. With his strength, he's also able to attack the net down low by himself. He scored most of his goals around the net, and it's one of the reasons he was a good net front player on the man advantage for his team.

Miettinen's first few steps is an area of his game that needs work, but his speed is solid once he's in movement. His center routes allow him to cover a lot of ice and be a strong transition player. From the defensive zone, he supports his defensemen really well. He starts low, close to his defensemen to be a 5-foot pass middle pop option. If the D send to puck to the winger, Miettinen sprints the dot lane to be available. These great routes allow him to acquire pucks with speed and carry the puck in the middle ice. In connection with these routes, Miettinen loves to make the opposing defensemen collapse when he's on the rush. He attacks the middle, is patient with the puck, and once the Ds are close to him, he kicks out the puck to the wall with good timing. After his kickout, he sprints towards to dot and net as F2 to make the D back off and create space for the puck carrier. He's not overly creative on the rush, but he's a good chain connector and space creator for his linemates. He also has decent puck skills to attack weak defensive sticks, making quick one-on-one moves in the triangle or making hook pass on kickout plays.

The defensive side of the puck is a strength of Miettinen's game. As mentioned, he's a great F1 on the forecheck. But he also does a great job when F2 or F3, by reloading above the puck and showing strong angling skills. In his own-end, he defends well down low with his defensemen, with good defensive side positioning and box out abilities.

Miettinen isn't a flashy player, and he may not be one of the players with the higher-end upside in this draft, but with his size, IQ, two-way play, faceoffs skills, scoring touch around the net and underrated passing, he projects as a really useful and versatile player for a winning team at the next level that all coaches love to have on his team.

"I love Miettinen's game. He has the upside to be a strong, two-way top 9 center that every winning team has." - HP Scout, Tim Archambault, March 2024

"I actually like him but he has zero hands. Second rounder for me." - NHL Scout, March 2024

"I like him...he plays the right way but he isn't blessed with a lot of skill." - NHL Scout, May 2024

"I thought back in 2015 that Joel Eriksson EK was going to become a 3rd line center and my original projection of Miettinen was the same. Meanwhile, Eriksson EK has become a very good second-line center in the NHL and this gives me confidence that Miettinen can achieve this. Their games are quite

similar and I think the Finn has the upper hand with his skating and playmaking in the offensive zone."
-HP Scout Jérôme Bérubé (May 2024)

"There's so much depth to this player. He's crafty down-low, makes his teammates better, presents an untapped power game, and has transitional upside. I think he's just getting started." - HP Scout, Brad Allen (May 2024)

"Didn't produce in the playoffs as much as I would have liked, but he had 17 points over his last 10 regular season games, so the curve is still heading in the right direction." - HP Scout, Brad Allen (May 2024)

"Not quite as high on him as our other scouts because I don't think he is quite as skilled as they do, but I do like him. Good player who can play in multipley game situations." - HP Scout, Mark Edwards, May 2024

NR	PLAYER	TEAM	LEAGUE	HEIGHT	WEIGHT	POS	GRADE
	MILOTA, JAKUB	CAPE BRETON	QMJHL	6' 00.5"	170	G	NI

NHLCS	CEILING	FLOOR	HOCKEY SENSE	COMPETE	SKILL	SKATE	MISC
NA-18	4	4	5	6	5	5	4

Milota spent the past season with Cape Breton in the QMJHL, sharing the net with veteran Nicolas Ruccia. He played 33 games and posted good numbers: a .905 save percentage and a 2.82 goals-against average. During the playoffs, he was backup, and left the team after the second round to join the Czechia U18 team. He participated in the two main tournaments of the season for U18 players: the Hlinka-Gretzky Tournament in August and the U18 World Championship in April. He had a much better showing in August than in April, leading his team to the final against a strong Canadian team. However, in April, he delivered poor performances against Canada, Kazakhstan, and Slovakia in the quarterfinals.

He has average size for a goaltender, but decent athletic ability and a commendable work rate. He doesn't give up on pucks, demonstrating an impressive ability to rebound from rough or average games, as shown in his performance at the U18s, where he bounced back well after a tough game against Canada, delivering a solid performance against Sweden in the next game.

However, he needs to focus on improving his rebound-control, which was problematic during his performance at the U18 tournament. He also struggled during the season with tracking point shots and with plays originating from down low and along the goal line. His lack of height may have contributed to these struggles, as well as his tendency to play deep in his net. To address this, he needs to be more aggressive and challenge shooters. There's room for improvement in his skating skills and glove side, with his lateral movements being decent but not categorizing him as a goalie with exceptional athletic tools like Devon Levi.

At his size, he needs to be a high-end athlete and technical goaltender; he falls between average and above-average in those two areas. He does a good job with low shots, covering this part of the net well, and has quick legs. He is also one of the few goalies to be quite active with his stick in front of his net to block passes.

For us, he ranks as the third-best goalie from the QMJHL in the draft, behind St-Hilaire and Pelletier. However, we're unsure he'll be drafted. He didn't make our goalie list, as we view him more as a capable junior goalie who will likely have a professional career, in Europe rather than the NHL.

93	PLAYER	TEAM	LEAGUE	HEIGHT	WEIGHT	POS	GRADE
	MISA, LUKE	MISSISSAUGA	OHL	5' 10"	175	LC	C

NHLCS	CEILING	FLOOR	HOCKEY SENSE	COMPETE	SKILL	SKATE	MISC
NA-76	6	4	6	5	6	7	4

As a late 2005 born forward, Luke Misa has benefited from an extra year of development with the Mississauga Steelheads in the Ontario Hockey League. The older brother of the latest exceptional status player Michael Misa, Luke, like his brother is quick and skilled. Misa put up 81 points in 63 games this season, including 55 assists which was good for first place amongst draft eligible forwards and second only behind Zayne Parekh.

The best part of Misa's game is his intelligence. He has a great ability to scan the ice and make good plays offensively because he thinks ahead of the play and defensively he also uses his hockey IQ to break up plays coming back on the backcheck. Offensively, with the puck on his stick he is able to make quick decisions at high speeds and give teammates space with his offensive timing. With this, defenders it back more often and give him more space and time than he will get at the next level and with the threat of physical play involved and how he does not succeed with physical play it is tough to say how this will effect his offensive game.

Physicality was not Misa's strong suit this past season and is something he will need to improve to be able to have any type of success in the NHL. Although he did improve his play in the corners and against bigger bodies as the season went on, it was not at a rate that showed us it could be a consistent part of his game throughout the regular season and into the playoffs. His play in the playoffs was fairly underwhelming and for such a strong regular season we expected more after he made such a big jump production wise.

The offensive skills are there with regards to his playmaking, especially with speed, and his patience with the puck. He has a lot of talent with the puck on his stick in terms of control and creativity. The biggest downside of Misa's offensive game is his shot which lacks power and he is not deceptive as a shooter. This will need to drastically improve for him to have scoring success at the next level as teams will be able to take away his passing ability despite his intelligence if he is a one trick pony offensively at the next level with less space, time and against smarter and tougher players and systems.

Misa did not do much in his first two years in the Ontario Hockey League and now as a third-year player has taken off drastically in comparison to his previous years. If he was born a couple of months earlier, he would not be in the conversation he is in at this time. With all that being said, this year's improvements have been outstanding and are not something to brush away lightly as simply, some players take longer to develop than others. Ice time is certainly a factor as Misa received much more ice time this season than either of the previous two and took full advantage.

Misa might be able to develop into a middle six winger. He has the intelligence to be able to carve out a defensive role and use similar skills he uses for offense in the OHL, like his quick stick and speed. For this target, Misa will need to be better as a competitor and as a penalty killer, but it seems he will be getting more opportunity to become a penalty killer as his ice time while down a man should increase next season in Mississauga.

"What's the difference between him and Howe? I see Howe ranked in the first round on some lists and I prefer Misa. I'm not taking Misa until the 4th round though." - NHL Scout, December 2023

"I'm the scout on our staff who is highest on him. Smallish and late birthdate but he is racking up the points. Undersized guy with talent and he is playing some solid hockey. I don't have him ranked crazy high or anything though." - HP Scout, Mark Edwards, December 2023

NR	PLAYER	TEAM	LEAGUE	HEIGHT	WEIGHT	POS	GRADE
NR	**MISSKEY, NATE**	**VICTORIA**	**WHL**	**6' 03.25"**	**210**	**RD**	**C**
NHLCS	CEILING	FLOOR	HOCKEY SENSE	COMPETE	SKILL	SKATE	MISC
NA-89	5	5	5	5	4	4	5

After being undrafted in his first year of eligibility last season, The 6'3" right-handed defenseman sow huge improvements in his play this season. After posting 14 points in 2022/23, Misskey had 7 goals in 34 in 44 games this season. Misskey suffered an injury that held him out from early January to early march. Before his injury, he was 7th overall in scoring amongst WHL defensemen. Misskey averaged around 25 minutes of his ice time by game in all situations this season, second on his team behind Coyotes' draft pick Justin Kipkie.

In transition, Misskey is reliable with his puck moving. With decent mobility and puck skills, he does a good job moving the puck quickly with efficiency. Without making high-end plays, he makes good play most of the time and shows calmness and composure with the puck. He activates and join the attack smartly, filling lanes on the rush to be involved in the offense. He does a good job moving the puck in the neutral zone, but could add more deception in his game by having the puck more on his hip pocket rather than in front of him when carrying the puck. In the offensive zone, Misskey owns a good shot. He scored a few goals with nice release form distance. He's good at finding shooting lanes from the point as well. His average of 3.09 shots per game ranks 1st amongst all players from his team. On the power play, Victoria had movement between the high players to open shooting lanes, which fitted with Misskey shooting skills.

When defending the rush, Misskey does a gob job of retrieving inside dots and protecting the inside. With his decent mobility and size, he's a tough defenseman to beat one-one-one. Sometimes, his gap control can be a bit loose, giving too much space for the opposing players to enter the zone with control. In his own-end, Misskey is a good defender. He covers ice, he's physical down low and he boxes out in front of his net.

Overall, Misskey is a solid all-around defenseman. He's got size, decent mobility and skills, defends pretty well and can be physical. Like every player, he needs to improve some area of his game, but he has no huge, evident weaknesses. Although he solid all-around, if he can bring two assets/parts of his game from average/good to really good, it would really help him in term of projection and finding a definite role at the next level.

94	PLAYER	TEAM	LEAGUE	HEIGHT	WEIGHT	POS	GRADE
94	**MONTGOMERY, BLAKE**	**LINCOLN**	**USHL**	**6' 03.25"**	**180**	**LW**	**C**
NHLCS	CEILING	FLOOR	HOCKEY SENSE	COMPETE	SKILL	SKATE	MISC
NA-101	5	5	4	5	6	7	7

Blake Montgomery was a productive USHL rookie for Lincoln in 2023-24 with a team-best 22 goals, while his 43 points put him one off the team crown. Montgomery is a May 2005 birthday who was passed over in 2023 after a relatively unproductive season with Mount St. Charles Academy.

After trudging through lower line usage and a tough start, Montgomery became one of the lead catalysts for puck carrying and production down the stretch for the Stars. A wiry 6'3", 180 pounds, Blake has really improved his skating over the past 12 months. At the top end, he can blow past a large chunk of USHL participants.

He's competitive for loose pucks and flashes some punishing physicality. The overall athleticism looks fairly raw still. Even his skating stance is narrow and a bit wobbly. It's not terribly hard to knock him off balance still, as he's mostly arms and legs. We're grading his skating upwards though, given the mechanics and the perceived level that he's at on his physical development arc. He struggles with tempo control on the attack. When he's flying up the ice with the puck, he looks like a high-end prospect as he picks his way through traffic, but there are some blemishes when we break it down.

We like the speed differential dekes and the element of burgeoning puck protection maneuvers when he makes his cuts. On the flip side, is there really any noteworthy indication that there's skill chaining going on off these headlong rushes? It's not consistently there. If he was able to make cross net-line passes on the rush like this or if he had a consistently great shot or finishing ability in close, we're probably talking about a 1st round pick. But with these multi-line rushes, there's some tunnel vision that creeps in. Even at a slower pace, the playmaking doesn't look like it's going to hold up as it lacks creativity and quality seam recognition.

He can shoot with a lot of velocity, but it's sometimes hindered by general accuracy issues. Even with the shooting, he needs to be able to drop his shoulder and shoot against the grain at top speed if that's going to be his go-to move. Of minor note, he was 2nd in the USHL with five unassisted goals this season – he had a bit of a Michael Grabner-type streak in him for a while, where he was soliciting a lot of breakaways. The ordinary course (as it were) multi-line carrying is a plus, of course, but the next step in progression is getting some meaningful conversions out of that.

His defensive game is pretty spotty and this is where his mental processor really breaks down. If opponents cross in front of him out high, he has a tendency to freeze up trying to figure out what his next move is. Just getting to a contested spot or picking up a free puck that a teammate is also near sends him into a buffering state for a moment… usually in that time, someone else has made a decision, so it's a little more obvious what Blake should be doing. That's a concern and a hit to his upside. He should be able to cover up some of that with his skating and if he increased compete defensively. Consistent physicality wouldn't hurt his cause either, of course.

Given the questionable mental game and still iffy technical skills, or at least, application of those technical skills, we're not convinced this is going to be an impactful, offensive top-six winger.

NR	PLAYER	TEAM	LEAGUE	HEIGHT	WEIGHT	POS	GRADE
	MOORE, JAVON	MINNETONKA	HIGH-MN	6' 03"	190	LW	C

NHLCS	CEILING	FLOOR	HOCKEY SENSE	COMPETE	SKILL	SKATE	MISC
NA-47	5	4	5	5	6	6	7

Javon was one of the late 05' birthdates that chose to pass on junior hockey this season to return to High School to be on a stacked Minnetonka team to try to win a 2nd straight Class AA title and while they came up short on that goal by losing to Chanhassen in the sectional final, Moore had a bit of breakout season for the Skippers playing top minutes on a deep roster, registering 26 goals and 27 assists in 31 games. Despite being drafted in the 2nd Round of the 2022 USHL futures draft by Sioux Falls, Moore has only seen 5 games of junior hockey thus far which gave us a little pause on Javon for this year's draft. It's typically a challenge for players to come into the USHL late in the year and find their footing in junior hockey, so we don't want to put too much into his play in the 5 games he played with the Stampede this season but Javon struggled with the speed and physicality that the transition from MNHS to Tier 1 Junior hockey brings.

Moore was at his best this season when he played a straight line, north-south power forward game with speed. He needs to continue to develop his first step but his motor and top end speed is good and he has solid agility at high speed to jump in and out of lanes to get to the net. Moore has the ability to use his strong, athletic frame well down low and protect the puck while buying time for plays to present themselves. Moore excels along the walls to win battles and then showed good vision and playmaking ability to set up chances coming off the walls and to find guys with speed in the neutral zone in transition. Where he overreached at times offensively was trying to be something he isn't and taking on too much on his own with the puck, attempting high end skill plays and attempting to beat guys 1 v 1 with skill. Minnetonka was a dominate team throughout the MNHS season but one glaring aspect to Javon's game this season we saw in multiple live viewings, was when the bright lights were on, when they were playing other top teams like

Chanhassen, Wayzata or Edina, or in the Sectional final, Moore really struggled to generate offense and be effective in those games and it was largely because he tried to do too much and got away from the things he does well. The more of a power game Javon plays the more effective he was in creating offense, especially in tight checking games where there wasn't a lot of ice available.

Playing with more of an identity and consistency as well as continuing to develop his explosiveness with his feet will determine his pro ceiling in the next couple of years. Moore is committed to play for the University of Minnesota but will likely need a year of junior hockey before he is ready to make that step so he will likely play next year in Sioux Falls (USHL).

NR	PLAYER	TEAM	LEAGUE	HEIGHT	WEIGHT	POS	GRADE
	MORELLO, JONATHAN	ST MIKES	OJHL	6' 01.25"	178	LC	NI
NHLCS	CEILING	FLOOR	HOCKEY SENSE	COMPETE	SKILL	SKATE	MISC
NA-98	6	5	6	6	6	5	7

Jonathan Morello is a physically mature center for the St. Michael's Buzzers in the OJHL. He posted 57 points including 25 goals in 50 games played this season and followed that up with a productive post season scoring 21 points in 11 games, including 12 goals. He also represented Canada East at the World Junior A Challenge putting up a point per game in the tournament.

A trusted forward by coaches because of his ability to play in all situations, Morello plays an intelligent game positionally while backchecking hard and breaking up plays very well along the boards defensively with his strength. He plays with good pace offensively, varying his speed up ice and does not rush the play while he looks for the best pass options in the offensive zone. Morello is not much of a rush attacker due to his skating and inability to push to the middle consistently, despite his size. In addition, he does not use his strength and size offensively as much as we would like to see. He is good at a lot of his skills, but nothing pops out as great or excellent.

The stopper for Morello, however, is his skating. At the OJHL level he can be caught behind the play sometimes and loses inside body positioning in battles for the puck as he is slightly behind. His speed is not game breaking and he does not possess strong edgework. He will be attending Clarkson in the NCAA which will provide him with some extra development time to improve his skating and continue to build upon his other good attributes.

2	PLAYER	TEAM	LEAGUE	HEIGHT	WEIGHT	POS	GRADE
	MOYSEVICH, PAVEL	SKA ST. PTBRG	RUS	6' 04"	187	G	B
NHLCS	CEILING	FLOOR	HOCKEY SENSE	COMPETE	SKILL	SKATE	MISC
INT-4	7	6	7	6	7	6	7

Pavel Moysevich is a blocking style, technical goalie, and is one of the older and one of the larger goalies in this draft. He was also a goalie who never really got an opportunity to get situated for an extended period of time last season after playing for 4 different teams and moving from system to system. While in SKA's system, Pavel got an opportunity to finally situate himself, and he took advantage of it at the MHL, VHL and KHL levels, where he put together an exceptional season.

The first thing that stands out about Moysevich is how much room he takes up in his net. He's almost as wide as he is tall and when he's integrated into his post in his RVH, there's very little room for shooters to work with when evaluating their short-side options. In addition, for being such a large goalie, his transitional butterfly is impressive. He can seamlessly transition in and out of his butterfly without going off balance and he remains very tall within his butterfly.

The butterfly is the foundation for any modern day goalie, but for Pavel it really is his best quality. From a technical perspective, he's so good at timing when to actually drop through a shot regardless of distance, and into his butterfly. He keeps his arms flared outward in-front of him and on an angle so pucks can ramp up into his chest area so he can swallow the puck, and he's exceptional at sealing both his five-hole and potentially exposed areas under his arms, all while remaining extremely tall.

He can make difficult, high danger saves look relatively easy due to his butterfly mechanics, and he's exceptional at absorption pucks within his butterfly. His butterfly allows him to absorb initial shots at a high-rate, but it also does more than that for him. He has decent extension rates but they aren't his best trait, and they can leave him to shots lower to the ice since he has difficulty keeping his pad parallel when needing to suddenly kick out; so he looks to operate and function in his butterfly without fully extending as often as possible.

The same can be said about his general movement. His skating mechanics grade out well despite being one of the larger goalies. He can micro shuffle well for his size, and he can move laterally before collapsing into his butterfly to take away high danger shots. When you take these attributes into consideration, it showcases a goalie who actually plays up to his size, instead of shrinking in the net. He's big, but he actually looks big and plays big.

Typically, with bigger goalies, their reflexes and overall coordination haven't caught up with their frames yet in their initial draft year, but Moysevich is physically mature already, despite having a considerable amount of room left to fill out. We've watched him make beautiful point-blank saves in tight that require him to fully extend, and he can make sudden directional shifts that require him to reflexively kick out or sprawl.

One of his improved qualities from last season to this season is regarding his post to post transfer rates from a standing integrated position. Last year, he didn't have as much fluidity as he does now, and it means that he's been able to take advantage of his edgework and skill-set at a higher level. It also allowed him to stay in-front of lateral passing plays that required quick movement.

Despite being big, he doesn't hang back on his goal line or fail to cut down angles. He's functional with his depth and recognizes when he can cut down aggressively or when he needs to factor in a potential backdoor or weak side option. He rarely gets caught in between plays, and he was decisive in his decision making when evaluating his positioning relative to his net and the shooter. What this means, is that when he is focused and tracking well, he's staying ahead of the play and the shooter has very little to work with.

When evaluating his tracking in general, it's above average to very good. He's comfortable tracking from his set stance when looking around screens, and he has impressive instincts when he temporarily loses track of the puck. There's been several sequences where he gets momentarily screened but then immediately transitions into the higher danger angle, so there's an understanding of how to play the percentages correctly and maximizing his size, even when temporarily blind to the play or when he loses sight of the puck.

The most pressing issue for his translation can be seeing when he needs to make a sudden rotational save or a save that forces a very quick secondary reaction that forces a pad extension. He has a bigger frame to move and that means certain rebounds are harder for him to get to. If the rebound is on the same plane that the initial shot was from, then he's fine because he can rely on his extensions and lateral push offs, but if the rebound drops on a plane that requires an additional angular shift followed by a push-off, that's when he gets himself into trouble. The problem is that he does have a tendency to over rotate during the end phase of his butterfly when he's trying to absorb pucks, and it's one of the major areas he's going to have to improve long term. That said, we have seen season-to-season improvements dating back to last year, so that's a good step in the right direction.

We've also evaluated that he has had an opportunity to experiment with newer techniques that are being implemented in the game. As an example, due to his height, one of the only ways a lacrosse style goal has a chance of going in on him when he's already in position is directly past his ear. So one technique he's adopted is holding his glove to the side of his head, so that it gives him an opportunity to have the puck immediately get caught in his glove if the shot had perfect placement. It's interesting seeing these newer age goalies attempt to counteract shot selections that used to be less frequent but now are a general part of the game.

Overall, Moysevich presents one of the best, if not the best set stances in this year's class. He looks big, he plays big, and when we look at the goalies remaining in the Stanley Cup Playoffs, then look at him, we can't help but think he can't contend against them in the NHL one day. He is a modern-day prototype for the position, who is phenomenal at stopping mid to low danger shots of any variety. Where he has some difficulty is during scrambling sequences or on sequences that force him to make a recovery save that requires a full extension or an additional adjustment. We have seen an impressive growth curve already though, so we feel if given the right time to develop, then he has potential as a full time starter.

"He's one of the dark horse goalie prospects of this class (2023). He forced my hand.." - HP Scout, Brad Allen (May 2024)

"He reminds me a lot of Akira Schmid. Hard to replicate Schmid's development but they look really similar at the same age, though Schmid was internationally proven, where Moysevich isn't.)" - HP scout, Brad Allen (May 2024)

"He is a very sound goalie overall, that is one of the reasons that we put him in the top-two.." - HP Scout, Brad Allen

105	PLAYER	TEAM	LEAGUE	HEIGHT	WEIGHT	POS	GRADE
	MRSIC, TOMAS	MEDICINE HAT	WHL	5' 11.25"	170	LC	C

NHLCS	CEILING	FLOOR	HOCKEY SENSE	COMPETE	SKILL	SKATE	MISC
NA-64	7	3	7	5	7	5	5

With 23 points in his WHL rookie season, the former 8th overall pick in the WHL had a strong improvement with 62 points in 63 games this year. He had 34 points in 31 games in 2024, improving his production in the 2nd half of the season. Mrsic had a strong role with the Tigers, playing in their top 6, on the first power play unit and some PK time as well.

First of all, Mrsic is a shooter. He played on the top power play unit on his one-timer side, featuring 5 forwards with Tigers. His one-timer is dangerous. It's hard and pretty accurate for a one-timer, and most importantly, he's capable of one-timing from behind or in front of his body, even on hard or inaccurate passes. His upper and lower body separation allows him to catch & release puck with efficiency from that spot as well. At 5-on-5, he owns a strong wrist-shot. He scored many goals from distance on the rush and some beautiful catch & release shot in the offensive zone. On breakaways, he's able to deke goaltenders easily with strong puck skills and deceptiveness.

Mrsic is a shooter, but he can make plays as well. He connects plays well when needed, and shows decent playmaking with his touches in the offensive zone, often finding linemates in the Homeplate. Mrsic was also an impact transition driver for his team, carrying the puck, attacking the inside and creating on the rush.

In the playoffs, Mrsic showed his gritty side, completing many hits on the forecheck. His consistency in overall competitiveness could improve throughout the season, as well as his ability to win battle and protect the puck by establishing body position earlier.

Overall, Mrsic is a smart player with a great shot who impact the play in transition as well. He's got solid top speed, but his first few steps will need to improve. With a team that possess so much talent like the Tigers, Mrsic is a candidate to have a dominant season in the WHL next year.

33	PLAYER	TEAM	LEAGUE	HEIGHT	WEIGHT	POS	GRADE
	MUGGLI, LEON	ZUG	SWISS	6' 00.5"	177	LD	B

NHLCS	CEILING	FLOOR	HOCKEY SENSE	COMPETE	SKILL	SKATE	MISC
INT-11	6	6	6	7	5	6	6

Leon Muggli is a well rounded defenseman whose game is predicated on the idea that he's more than the sum of his parts. He's solid everywhere, without an inherent weakness, but his best quality might just be a byproduct of his moment to moment decisions, and his understanding of the ebbs and flows of the game. His maturity allowed him to play at the National league level for the entire season, where he produced 12 points in 42 games including 3 goals.

There's vinegar in Muggli's blood, and it allowed him to be an impact player despite his very young age, but it also made him overstep his positioning occasionally or make him prone to errant passes from time to time. Yet, we felt that his structure became more sound as the season progressed, and as he adapted to the overall pace of the National league, we saw his game grow with it.

He's a multi-faceted defender who is very difficult to play against, bringing a varied defensive game.

His defense starts with his ability to play heavy – his stick is heavy, there's heavy body contact with both his shoulders and his hips, and he comes up with a lot of pucks in 50/50 situations despite going up against much older and physically mature players. Muggli is not only strong for his age but also for his frame. He can really put some of his peers down in a hurry. While he's tough, he's rarely dirty about it and he doesn't spend a lot of time sequestered in the box for his efforts. He trusts his backwards skating and his anticipation to maintain a tight gap. In rush absorption situations, he's up on his toes almost every time and plays from the inside out, but very aggressively. He doesn't allow uninteresting plays to hang around. If he sees a potential weakness – whether it's a bobbled puck or he's identified that a weak player is leading the charge – he'll seek to stomp that play out and deny the entry full stop if he can. Leon does a really nice job with proper stick-led defending, but backs it with a physical element.

There's a decent level of skill displayed from him when he's defending without his frame as well. When he's out in the margins for a pin or other board play, he has the skills to pull the puck out of tie-ups and make a quick, technical play with the won puck. While he is a willing shot blocker, we like that he doesn't sell out for shot blocks that often and rarely leaves his feet.

Despite being overzealous at times with his physical game, he reduces his defensive risk by staying on balance. Players can get too caught up in the block attempt and expose their triangle or expose a passing lane that's way more threatening than the original shot, but Muggli exhibits a mature demeanor when it comes to his defensive work. He's not very fun to deal with near his net either. He understands and practices really good box-out principles. He really digs in and comes from up and underneath to gain some control over his check, while also keeping his stick free to take his man's stick off the ice. If the play heats up after the whistle, he's not backing down either.

Another reason Muggli is a successful defensive player and can activate with the puck is due to his solid skating foundation. Mechanically speaking, Leon has impressive hip rotation which gives him strong crossovers, and he's good at keeping off his center line when turning so that he can use his frame to propel himself forward out of turns without wasted energy. Although his legs wouldn't be labeled quick twitch, there's a lot of traction produced on the inside of his edges when heading in a straight line. That said, his explosiveness seems to be the result of how measured he is for a play. He has surprised us with just how fast he can go through the neutral zone or look to separate from an aggressive forechecker when he needs to. His skating projects to be able to handle elusive and agile skaters off the rush, and he can sync up his skating to the speed of the opposing players.

Muggli anticipates and processes the transitional play of the game better than most other draft eligible defenseman in this class after you get past the top end of this class. That's one of the hallmarks of this player, his mind allows him to put himself in proper positions quickly enough so that he's rarely caught behind the play. It's also one of the primary reasons he was able to stay up at the National League level over the entire season.

When evaluating his offensive game we feel that we should be giving him a bit of leeway. Stanislav Svozil was an example of a defenseman who stayed up at a pro level over his draft eligible season and his offense didn't get a chance to really take off until after he was drafted and started developing in the CHL. We aren't saying that Muggli is likely to replicate Svozil's offensive output and we don't project him to be a huge point contributor, but we do think there's a degree of untapped offense here much like there was in Svozil and a ton of other draft eligible defenseman who needed more time to mature their offense after playing in a solid pro league. He can skate, his handling has improved over the year, he can make high-end technical passes through traffic, and occasionally he flashes advanced offensive plays from the line, from time to time.

We think the role Leon Muggli will end up playing at the NHL level will be something similar to Nick Jensen's in Washington. We see him as a steady, well rounded, solid defenseman who can match up potentially in a top-4 capacity, move pucks, contribute defensively against larger forwards in playoff situations, all while chipping in offensively. He's smart, he's structured, and he's advanced for his age.

"Leon Muggli is the most underrated defensive player in this class. He's the perfect example of an under the radar prospect who lacks flash but makes up for it with substance." - HP Scout, Brad Allen

"One of the things I like about him is that he's not afraid, he's got some good pushback in his game" - HP Scout Jérôme Bérubé (December 2023)

"Most underrated defenseman in this draft? I think this kid has chance to play top-4 minutes in the NHL if everything goes right" - HP Scout Jérôme Bérubé (April 2024)

NR	PLAYER	TEAM	LEAGUE	HEIGHT	WEIGHT	POS	GRADE
	MUHONEN, NIILOPEKKA	KALPA JR.	FIN-JR	6' 04.25"	195	LD	NI
NHLCS	CEILING	FLOOR	HOCKEY SENSE	COMPETE	SKILL	SKATE	MISC
INT-32	4	5	5	5	4	6	7

Muhonen spent most of the season playing in Finland's U20 league with Kalpa, and he also had a 12-game stint in the Mestis league, Finland's second men's league. He represented Team Finland's U18 squad in various tournaments throughout the season. However, he was cut from the team before the April U18 World Hockey Championship.

Muhonen has the size and mobility coveted by NHL teams, standing at 6'4" and weighing 185 pounds. He moves well enough for his size, but has yet to adopt a more intense style of play. In many games this year, he appeared somewhat passive on the ice, showing hesitancy both in his physical play and with the puck, resulting in few impactful plays. His upside is rather limited, his puck skills are just okay, and his decision-making has been below-average this season.

His decision-making under pressure, particularly in puck-retrieval situations, was a disappointment this season and made us drop his name on our list as the year went on. His contribution to his team's transition game is minimal, as he rarely carries the puck out of his zone and his passing game is below-average. While his size and mobility may earn him the chance to hear his name called, there are few other aspects of his game that we find appealing. His upside is limited, with his best potential being that of a 3rd-pairing defenseman capable of solid defensive play and penalty killing. However, his puck skills, hands, and vision are below-average, and his offensive game is lacking. If he was a physical threat on the ice, he would be an easy player for us to like, but his game doesn't have a real mean streak. As mentioned before, we think there's a decent chance he gets drafted, but he's not someone we would draft based on our list.

65	PLAYER	TEAM	LEAGUE	HEIGHT	WEIGHT	POS	GRADE
	MUSTARD, JOHN	WATERLOO	USHL	6' 01"	186	LW	C

NHLCS	CEILING	FLOOR	HOCKEY SENSE	COMPETE	SKILL	SKATE	MISC
NA-27	7	6	5	6	7	6	6

Slippery, goal scoring winger. John Mustard burst onto the scene and became one of the bigger risers on the U.S. side of this draft class. A true USHL rookie after being an 8th round selection by Waterloo in the USHL Futures Draft from the North Jersey Avalanche, Mustard was one of just two rookies with 20 goals this year (he had 29). He missed the rookie points crown by one to Ben Kevan's (2025 draft eligible) 57. After he got his footing (just one point in his first four games), Mustard embarked on a 10-game point streak on his way to being one of the most consistent producers and shooters in the circuit. His 205 shots on goal placed him fifth in the entire league, his seven game winners ranked prominently as well.

By the end of the season, it was tough not to notice Mustard in games. Him revving up his headlong rushes with tremendous speed and spectacular moves to throw defenders and goalies into a panic became a staple of any Waterloo game. His puck transporting and multi-line carrying really blossomed in a hurry. Combined with his shooting prowess, Mustard could make something out of nothing on a team that wasn't exactly brimming with game breakers. His goal sample shows a good deal of variance. His shots are well-timed and accurate. He favors far post and against the grain shot placement – which we like – but he also features one-timers, rebound goals, and highlight reel skill chaining plays through defenses.

His edgework and speed make him a lot to handle for even veteran defensemen at this level. There was a lot of development in terms of his technical skill package and he got much more confident taking players on 1 on 1 by midseason. There is a lot of deception and slipperiness in his game. Not only with his stickhandling, but he exhibits head and shoulder feints that allowed him to beat defensemen clean at times. We have seen him look off passes and shots in odd-man situations as well, which is promising from the mental development arc perspective. He's not just overwhelming this level of play with his speed and hands, there's a scalable process to his puck carrying. That said, he may have gotten confident to a fault in this regard. What looked like more of a balanced attacker earlier in the year shaded heavily towards shooting/goal scoring by the end of the season. His playmaking prowess receded and we were left with just simple, open passes on the rush and nothing more – even when opportunities seemed to be looming. The seam recognition fell off. That's disappointing because we'd obviously prefer a player with a prominent "A" game and "B" game if possible. On the plus side, he has a quick release that gets really good velocity and accuracy off of either foot and there's some semblance of finishing moves in close that are still a work in progress.

Mustard can fly coming out of turns. His edges and acceleration are terrific. There's still some issues getting off of his center line and lowering his center of gravity. This is probably a core strength issue, at least in part. He's not hockey strong in general. On the backcheck, he matches speed by skating back with the play before pivoting to try to address what the opponent is doing, which is fairly unique for players of this type – it shows some discipline and pattern recognition mentally. Conversely, he doesn't own a lot of intentionality off the puck. Whether it's puck battles, stick positioning, even pass acceptance sometimes, there's some plays that he just whiffs on that made us wince. It would be really nice if more pucks "stuck" to him. Sometimes he has to double back to pick one up or his first touch is rotten, and it really dampens his retrieval process to a noteworthy degree. He's upright and a little stiff at times in his posture – and even that may be a contributing factor here. He looks thin and is easily knocked off the puck when guys can catch him – so chances are, he's low on his physical development arc still. His skating breaks down late in shifts with this posture and a shorter stride, so there isn't a lot of staying power if there's an extended shift situation.

The progression over the course of the year has been noteworthy. Going from a lesser-known prospect that was trying to find his way, then to being more of a support player offensively, to becoming one of the more dangerous rush players in the USHL is an impressive rookie season. We see upside remaining across all of his development arcs – physical, mental, and technical – and he just sneaks into this draft class by less than a month as an August 2006. While we're disappointed that he isn't showing more creative playmaking and his defensive technique is spotty at best, this is a player worth taking because there's a high ceiling backed by an appreciable floor.

6	PLAYER	TEAM	LEAGUE	HEIGHT	WEIGHT	POS	GRADE
	NABOKOV,ILYA	MAGNITOGORSK	RUS	6' 00"	179	G	C
NHLCS	CEILING	FLOOR	HOCKEY SENSE	COMPETE	SKILL	SKATE	MISC
INT -2	7	3	6	8	7	7	5

Ilya Nabokov is a small, hyper-athletic, and competitive goalie who made a very successful transition from the MHL within Magnitogorsk's system to the KHL this past season. To give you an understanding of the level of consistency he displayed, in the 43 games he played in the regular season, he had only 4 bad starts. He followed up his brilliant regular season with a playoff run for the ages, ultimately winning the Gagarin Cup.

Consistency rates are extremely important for smaller goalies since they have the lowest margin of error, and Nabokov's were the most impressive of any draft-eligible goalie. This is even more impressive when you consider that the most games he had played prior to this season totalled 36, and this was his first season of playing professional hockey.

The single most important determining factor for us when evaluating if a 5'11" goalie who isn't named Juuse Saros can actually play is for the exact same reason many of you know Saros's name in the first place, and that has to do with recovery rates. Goalies who are very small must be able to make micro-adjustments and secondary saves at an elite level, and we are here discussing this prospect and ranking this prospect as a direct result of Nabokov having exactly that.

We've manually tracked his micro-adjustment rates and have seen him make five adjustments in the span of three seconds. The smaller the goalie, the faster the error-correcting when attempting to identify the proper angle must occur. This is the fastest goalie in the draft at adjusting his positioning, and he has to be.

Elite recovery rates for a smaller goalie are predicated on the ability to make saves that larger goalies typically can't make or make at a slower speed. When Nabokov is fully extended with his chest hitting the ice or when he's fully extended out of his butterfly, he can still explode outward and cut down another angle. Typically, a goalie needs to transition between save types and get their skates back underneath them for an additional push-off after fully extending, but he doesn't. That's unique, and it helps him compensate for his extension rates in general.

Another unique quality of Ilya's game is regarding his stance. Due to his height, he has to primarily remain in a relaxed stance as opposed to a set stance when looking around a screen. What this means is that he should theoretically be at a disadvantage relative to a larger goalie who can look around a screen while already in his set stance since if he fails to track the puck correctly, he can still react quickly, while Ilya still has to move from his relaxed position to his set stance. Nabokov counteracts this, however, due to the sheer speed he can enter his set stance from a relaxed stance.

This is important for Nabokov. In order to minimize concerns with his size, he has to be able to get back out in front of the play even if he misreads it initially or when he is momentarily delayed. By having such a rapid descent into his set stance from his relaxed stance, it allows him to get set faster, at a higher rate, which in turn counteracts certain lateral passing setups, even if he falls behind on the initial read.

There is a limitation to this style of play, though. When a goalie rapidly transfers at too fast a rate, it can be more difficult to swallow and control rebounds depending on the shot type. That's why a lot of goalies have a middle phase between their relaxed and set stances when dropping through their butterfly, but Ilya doesn't do this as often. He can fail to time his butterfly, like Moysevich can, but again this comes down to a preference based on his stature and how aggressively he tries to cut away the lower part of the net.

Theoretically, one disadvantage that applies to Nabokov's set stance is that he has to present considerably wider. George can get away with standing as narrow in his set stance as he does since he's 6'1", but Nabokov is a true 5'11" goalie. This means that he's operating with his inside edge flatter to the ice than we would typically want to see since it usually takes some of the power away from the goalie when they have to transition laterally. However, Nabokov is so quick and explosive that it doesn't seem to affect him like it does for a lot of other goalies.

This is huge for his potential translation since he can present wide while still exploding laterally at an impressive rate. In general, when evaluating how he sets in net, he's closer to looking like Juuse Saros than, say, Dustin Wolf, who presents a much narrower stance. This gives Wolf a ton of lateral explosiveness and keeps his posture more upright, but it's more difficult to stay out in front of point-blank redirects.

This is where the wider stance of Nabokov comes into play. He's exceptional at finding pucks through traffic and although he's very small, his wider stance and ability to stay wide while still micro-adjusting make him adept at dealing with this shot type, which again theoretically should be a weakness, but it really isn't for him.

Ilya compensates for his lack of size by understanding how to operate within his frame to close secondary shooting angles after giving up rebounds. What this means is that when he closes down on shots that have the potential to elevate, he gets directly in front of the puck when he can because he knows that if he doesn't, then pucks can get elevated over him.

There are areas of improvement needed in order for him to translate his game successfully to the NHL, though. He can sometimes fail to seal with his blocker above his pad on short-area shots that target his blocker side. This leaves room for shooters to operate when suddenly adjusting their angle from the far side and shooting short side. He can get caught off guard during the shooting transition.

Another issue is that he can be late to swing from post to post when dealing with potential low-to-high danger passing options that start below his red line. The smaller the goalie, the faster they need to swing from post to post to fully integrate and to make sure they have time to explosively push off to the opposite side that they integrated from. If you look at Dustin Wolf's game, for instance, he looks to integrate before the opposing forward has finished wrapping around the back of his net with the puck. This allowed him to be in position in advance for these play types, whereas Nabokov has shown the tendency to either evenly match or fall behind the opponent who's swinging around the back of his net. Again, we want him ahead of his opponent on these play types.

Lastly, although he adapted very well to the overall speed of the KHL, he was susceptible to misinterpreting in tight lateral setups on the weak side, depending on the technical playmaking talent of the player he was evaluating.

There are very few NHL starters at Ilya's size. Wolf, who projects to be an exceptional starter, Levi, who also projects to be an exceptional starter, and Saros, who already is an exceptional starter, all are better at manipulating their bodies off of their centerline so that they can exaggerate their posture on higher shots or on shots that suddenly shift angles. They have a dexterity that Nabokov lacks to a degree, and even the slightest degree matters at their size. Perhaps the biggest concern has to do with his high-danger lateral pass tracking through traffic. He can be delayed at evaluating the endpoint of a lateral passing option that goes from strong to the weak side, and this didn't let up right through the playoffs. At the NHL level, he's going to be theoretically going up against not only the best playmakers in the world but also the trickiest—the type of players who can offset their playmaking timing, and that is a big area of concern.

Regardless of our numerous concerns, there is a legitimate argument to be made for Nabokov being the single most consistent goalie prospect in the last three years that's not named Dustin Wolf. He just put together one of the best goalie seasons in the history of the KHL, and he just turned 21 in March. Some of his play can counteract his height, and we think there's a legitimate shot that he can at least become a split starter in the NHL one day.

"I can't tell you if he's a special goalie who is undersized. We will only know that if he plays 120 games in the NHL and holds before having to adapt his game yet again when the players inevitably adapt theirs to his. What I can tell you, though, is that he had a special season." - HP Scout, Brad Allen

"I've watched a ton of games of Alexei Kolosov over the years and evaluated his curve over the span of the last four seasons, and I can tell you right now that I think Nabokov is the better goalie prospect of the two at the same age. He's dialled in more often, and he's a better athlete, and that's saying something because Kolosov is a heck of an athlete in his own right."

"You're hoping that Carter George and Ryerson Leenders get to the point where Nabokov is by the time they're 20. The primary reasons There is the the Russian factor but I leaned Nabokov. It's very tight between those 3 and Gardner for me." - HP Scout, Brad Allen

99	PLAYER	TEAM	LEAGUE	HEIGHT	WEIGHT	POS	GRADE
	NIEMINEN, DANIEL	PELICANS JR	FIN-JR	5' 11.25"	177	LD	C
NHLCS	CEILING	FLOOR	HOCKEY SENSE	COMPETE	SKILL	SKATE	MISC
INT-42	5	4	5	6	5	7	5

Nieminen is one of the more intriguing defensive prospects from Finland for this year's NHL Draft. He showcased his skills with the Pelicans U20 team this season, averaging just under a point per game with 29 points in 37 games, ranking 8th among defensemen in the league.

Despite his nice offensive numbers, we don't project him as an offensive defenseman if he were to make it to the NHL. We see him more as a two-way defenseman with good skating skills and compete. He's not huge, which does play against him, and nothing about his skillset stands out other than his skating. Defensemen like him need to find a more refined role in the NHL. Power play specialist? Great penalty-killer? Setting the tone with physicality? We think the lack of answers is a bit of an issue when projecting Nieminen in the NHL. We like him, but like many defensemen like him without a specialty have a tough time cracking the NHL. He's a solid skater whose footwork and on-ice agility we appreciate. He can surprise opponents with his hands, beating them one-on-one in transition or at the offensive line. He can defend with his feet, and there's some pushback to his game, which makes us like him even more. But we don't project him as a PP guy; he is definitely not a PP1 prospect and even PP2 is unlikely. We also don't see him as a shutdown guy due to his lack of size.

There's a significant chance he could end up being a solid NHL/AHL tweener or enjoy a successful career in Europe. As previously noted, his lack of specialty makes his projection challenging.

NR	PLAYER	TEAM	LEAGUE	HEIGHT	WEIGHT	POS	GRADE
	NÖRRINGER, VIKTOR	FRÖLUNDA HC J20	SWE JR	6' 03"	194	RW	NI

NHLCS	CEILING	FLOOR	HOCKEY SENSE	COMPETE	SKILL	SKATE	MISC
-	5	4	5	6	5	4	7

Nörringer is a big, competitive player with an outstanding shot. He competes hard and stands out with his physical presence on the ice. Nörringer's shot is a standout attribute, allowing him to score from various positions and making him a constant threat in the offensive zone. He uses his size effectively, both in protecting the puck and in battles along the boards. He plays on the inside and utilizes his size to excel in front of the net. He creates open space for his teammates but still has the ability to finish himself. Just don't expect too much in terms of playmaking.

This year, Nörringer has split his time between Frölunda's J18 and J20 teams, gaining valuable experience and showcasing his abilities at both levels.

However, there are areas for improvement in his game. His skating is one of the key development points. While he has the strength and determination, he needs to work on his skating and keep his feet moving consistently. This will help him become more agile and maintain his speed throughout the game, making him even more effective on both ends of the ice. He's had a spur of growth during the season which has made his stride look heavy.

Nörringer has the potential to elevate his game significantly. As he continues to refine these aspects, he will become a more complete player and could play an even bigger role in his team's success in the future. He could be an option late in the draft for a team that believe there's some untapped potential and he's also one of the youngest players in this draft class.

5	PLAYER	TEAM	LEAGUE	HEIGHT	WEIGHT	POS	GRADE
	OBVINTSEV, TIMOFEI	CSKA JR	RUS JR	6' 04"	176	G	C+

NHLCS	CEILING	FLOOR	HOCKEY SENSE	COMPETE	SKILL	SKATE	MISC
-	8	4	5	9	8	6	7

Timofei Obvintsev was in a difficult position while playing for CSKA due to a three goalie rotation for the majority of the year. This meant that he only played a handful of games by January, but due to a timely injury, he was elevated from a backup role to a starting role by February and that allowed him to showcase what we think is one of the more remarkable skill-sets out of any draft eligible goalie.

We bring up Timofei's impressive skill-set due to the fact that despite being 19 years of age, this is basically his rookie season in the MHL, having played just 6 games last year, which was his first year of eligibility. In addition, he's a unique goalie who relies heavily on his own instincts and plays a throwback, looser style of game that's not predicated as much on staying compact and sealed. On the one hand, that means he's technically raw, but on the other he makes saves to his own beat and has his own style. As an example, despite being a larger goalie, he has a tendency to make stand up saves a lot more frequently than most other draft eligible goalies.

It's a bit similar to how Georgiev operates between the pipes, where he is really one of the last hybrid goalies who blends in some stand-up. The difference is that Georgiev is 6'0 tall so having a bit of stand up in his game makes a lot of sense, whereas for Obvintsev, it's an aspect that will need to be slightly reigned in and refined. With that said, the reason he can get away with the style he plays is because he's one of the freakiest athletes out of any draft eligible goalies in some ways. Specifically when looking at his extension abilities.

We talk a lot about extension rates with goalies and that's because they are critical and Obvintsev has elite extensions and is the top goalie in this class when focusing on this quality. Other aspects of his athleticism also shine. He's excellent at transitioning between save types, had a rapid transitional butterfly, and is fleet of foot when needing to use his skating to either re-integrate or integrate from his post. He's as fluid if not more so than Saarinen, he has better and long extensions than Yunin, and he's almost as quick twitch and reflexive as Bilic. There's a rare blend of qualities when evaluating the overall tool-kit.

Like the rest of his game, his post integration is a bit unconventional as well. He can lose his net a bit more often than Moyseyvich or Zarubin, so to compensate he looks to use his extension length within his arms to find the posts when he has to rapidly transfer post to post, depending on the play. Furthermore, when he's attempting to read which post he needs to integrate with, he uses his arms to actually hold the center of the net, which tells you how long he can stretch out and how dextrous he is, since he can come close to touching both posts simultaneously while fully extending his frame. This technique allows him to maintain center when he thinks a low to high danger passing option from below the goal line is likely to hit a target within the high crease or middle of the slot.

When operating on down-low plays around his net area, he's also one of the more aggressive poke-checking goalies. He has an active stick and he uses it a lot to either disrupt shot attempts or deflect incoming passes. The more athletic the base, the easier it is for a goalie to extend out and use their length to their advantage, so his style is conducive with his tool-kit.

Another way he uses his extensions is to actually push off the post in combination with his edgework to come out through crescent push-offs that realign him with shots off of a sudden pass. Lastly, when he's in a RVH position, he has a tendency to overcommit on the player nearest to his short side post if they have the puck by completely pivoting and rotating his frame towards them, this theoretically means that he's more susceptible to sudden lateral passes since he has to complete a full rotation back towards his goal line in order to push across and stop the shot, but he can get away with this technique and projects to continue to get away with it at the NHL level because he's such a fluid and nimble goalie at his size. Most goalies need to transition in two motions, when pivoting back towards their goal line while in a RVH but Timofei doesn't and it really helps explain just how gifted he is.

Speaking of gifted, he has the best projectable blocker in this class. He has full range of motion and can make very dextrous blocker saves that are highlighted by windmill knockdown saves, to saves off of shots that require him to immediately throw his elbow into a position where it's directed towards the ceiling of the arena. When shots are high danger and in close quarters, he can go from a neutral blocker position into an elevated position at the top of his bar at an incredibly rare speed. He works this in combination with his active shoulders, which allows him to stay elevated. We rarely get this excited about a blocker side or the shoulder activity of a goalie, and the glove side is admittedly more important long term, but it's special.

Despite his impressive game, he is susceptible to shooters who can adjust their release by presenting short side before firing it far-side in high danger areas, and visa-versa. Another issue is that although we have seen him make outstanding glove saves, occasionally he will let in a soft goal, and it's usually low glove when this occurs. Like most younger goalies, he can have difficulty absorbing pucks into his butterfly at times, and this is usually a result of being too late to set up from his relaxed stance on in-coming shots, depending on the context of the play. This means that he can set too late on generic shots that then lead to problems that shouldn't be occurring. It's also means he can be late on some lateral set up plays. There's definitely a rawness to him, from a technical perspective, he's also busier, over-extending out of his net more and is therefore forced to scramble more often than both Moysevich and Zarubin. That said, he's also more athletically gifted than both as well.

Taken together, we consider Obvintsev to have arguably the highest ceiling out of any goalie in this class. But, he's a difficult evaluation due to how raw he is. His initial draft season was last year when he basically didn't play; so we're working from the thought process that we should treat this season as really his first full MHL year. When you look at his year on the whole, he was actually very consistent and had several stand out performances that flashed his enormous potential. If certain mechanical refinements to him are made, and his anticipation of the play and tracking can hold, then he's a bonafide starter.

"He's a mix between a Russian Brandon Bussi and Alexander Georgiev. In the case of Bussi they have different curves, but both of them are athletic, similarly sized, have their own styles and have raw elements to them. - HP Scout, Brad Allen

"Admittedly, this is my favourite goalie in this class. That doesn't mean he'll end up the best, but there's a bias here with me and I had to fight that bias. I think it comes down to the fact he's a breath of fresh air at the position, since he has some throwback in him by relying heavily on his instincts and less on some modern techniques. A ton of goalies look the same in net nowadays, but he doesn't, and that's where the bias comes in, so I had to fight hard here against it." - HP Scout, Brad Allen

"There's only one goalie who I would call a hybrid stand up goalie that's playing full time in the NHL and that's Georgiev. He's one of the strangest goalies to ever play the position but his hybrid style makes a ton of sense given his lack of height. I actually wish it was a style that was more common but it does require tremendous reflexes. If Obvintsev maintains the same style and makes it, he would be the first hybrid stand up goalie in the NHL that's over 6'1." - HP Scout, Brad Allen

"I'm a fan of goalies who don't play like goalie school robots. He fits." - HP Scout, Mark Edwards, May 2024

16	PLAYER	TEAM	LEAGUE	HEIGHT	WEIGHT	POS	GRADE
	BRANDSEGG NYGARD, MICHAEL	MORA	SWE 2	6' 00.75"	207	RW	A

NHLCS	CEILING	FLOOR	HOCKEY SENSE	COMPETE	SKILL	SKATE	MISC
INT-5	6	7	6	8	7	7	7

Michael Brandsegg Nygard is a fearless, high octane, power forward who is one of the most physically mature prospects available in this year's class. His structure and tool-kit allowed him to play full time at the Allsvenskan level, and he continued to elevate his game come playoff time, where he helped Mora reach the 2nd round, before getting an opportunity to play at the World Championships. When the quality of competition increased, his play increased. Nygard has that elusive "it" factor in his game at times. When he steps over the boards, the energy that's given off is of a player who wants to make an immediate impact. He has the ability to elevate his game at critical times, which can be seen in how he saved his best for last at the end of the season in the most important games of his young career.

Nygard's game is predicated around three main components. The first is his exceptional skating base, the second is his dextrous and manipulative handling, the third is his shooting ability.

Nygard is one of the more gifted skaters of the top end forwards in this class. There's some explosive skaters in this class that have power styles, but the separating factor for Nygard is how efficient and how smooth his stride is. He blends power with fluidity with exceptional edgework, and it gives him an alternate skating style depending on what the play calls for. For instance, in the neutral zone, despite being a well built and solid player, he's extremely elusive in tight spaces and can slip checks with the best of them. If he's looking to make a direct cut to the net though, that's when you see his evasiveness turns into a power skating style, where he can explode past opposing players and put opposing defense on their heels. There's a unique combination of power, posture, stride-depth, fluidity, balance, and effortlessness found within his skating game and he understands what the best modes of attack are when applying his skating base.

The expected style of play for driving and cutting with a player as athletically gifted and powerful as Nygard is usually to control possession on their backhand, then use their frame to counteract sticks while driving to the net. Michael can do that, but shows a far more advanced and enticing array of skills that he can operate while at high speeds.

It starts with his outside to inside maneuvers, where he leverages his multidirectional skating and small area unilateral moves that keep the defenseman from being able to knock him off the puck. This means that he can attack on unique angles while remaining on balance as effectively as he attacks in straight lines, and that opens up the entire ice surface in the offensive zone for him.

When he's dialled in and playing an aggressive, up tempo brand of hockey, he looks to attack the middle areas of the ice after developing space creation plays down low and around the boards. He can peel off pressure, and he can also rapidly pull the puck laterally across his frame to try and go against the grain of an incoming defender who is defending him on an angle. Nygard's space creation is a very important aspect of his game, since his most dangerous weapon is his shot and he needs to create room for himself in order to get it off his stick when driving the play.

Defensemen get burned consistently if they close in a straight line against him. Even if they are playing their position properly and cutting down on him at proper angles or on sweeping arcs that push him into the corners, his athleticism and handling combination can still mean that he can operate in a dead area of the ice, come out with the puck and generate another play. As a result of this, plays rarely die on his stick in positions of the ice where most players would get trapped or pinned.

Although Nygard is more of a streamlined thinker with how he functions offensively and lacks the necessary vision or two steps ahead thinking seeing in more gifted playmakers, the dynamic handling and skating combination still makes him difficult to counteract and it's difficult to anticipate exactly what he's going to do with the puck since he has so many options. Which brings us to our third component of his skill-set which is his shooting upside.

High volume shooters who are confident usually have overlapping traits. Arguably, the most significant overlapping trait you see from them is that they don't overthink the game. Meaning – there's an automated state – to the way they go about their business on the ice. That's not to be mistaken for a player who can't adapt on the fly or recognize his spacing so that he can get set for a high quality shot though. Which is exactly Nygard's most projectable offensive weapon. He needs very little time and space, in order to get off his fantastic slapshot and wrist-shot; he also has some of the best shot qualities featured in this class.

Like his shot quality, his ability to recognize a goalies transitions between movements gives him seam recognition that only true goal scorers possess. When you factor in how fast he can get his shot off his stick and that he understands proper spacing to receive short area passes both laterally and when becoming a developing drop option, it means that he can operate as a complimentary sniper when it's necessary.

Taken together, he's incredibly dangerous off the rush while maintaining possession, and he's equally as dangerous when becoming a potential passing option as a complement to a developing play.

On the forecheck and in the defensive zone, Nygard is a conditioned perpetual motion machine that understands advanced angling to limit retrieval attempts on the forecheck, or to barricade players into a small space during exit attempts. He's also physical by nature and is willing to mix it up after whistles. He presents good body language on the ice and has some fire in him.

Where Michael falls short in terms of talent is regarding his playmaking ability and at times, rush decision making. We've seen him make some high end passes, where he's read the defense properly, slowed down the play, shifted his passing lanes and made lateral or trailing passes that have resulted in impressive primary assists, but he's also prone to making errors under pressure.

However, he also demonstrated an impressive development curve over the course of this season. Earlier with Mora, we found Nygard was having difficulty adapting to the pro game. He was playing a junior style of hockey that was established on him, relying too heavily on his handling and over-extending his options as a result. As he adapted to the pro game though, Nygard started handling the puck in operating windows that allowed him to still find either passing or shooting options and as a result became a more efficient player. The points soon followed.

We don't think Nygard will end up one of the top point producers in this class, he lacks the creativity and level of hockey sense needed to project that but we think he has one of the highest floor and ceiling combinations in this class. It's easy to envision a 2nd line scoring role, where he's also featured on the powerplay. What makes his game so safe is that he has several fallback options when he isn't scoring. He's an exceptional forechecker, he's physical, and he can play in his own end of the ice as well. He also presents impressive transitional zone entry rates as the result of his speed. He's built for playoff hockey and he elevated his game when it mattered most this past season.

"Can't say he has ever blown me away but he's a good player." NHL Scout, January 2024

"I was frustrated with his play earlier on in the season. He was overhandling the puck and mistiming his passing options but he really impressed down the stretch and although there's no absolute guarantees in hockey, he's all but certain to play in at least a middle-6 role." - HP Scout, Brad Allen

"I'm a fan the player because of the way he plays the game but I'm probably not quite as high on him as our other scouts. - HP Scout, Mark Edwards, May 2024

32	PLAYER	TEAM	LEAGUE	HEIGHT	WEIGHT	POS	GRADE
	O'REILLY, SAM	LONDON	OHL	6' 00.25"	184	RW	B
NHLCS	CEILING	FLOOR	HOCKEY SENSE	COMPETE	SKILL	SKATE	MISC
NA-24	6	8	8	6	6	5	7

A versatile right shot forward for the London Knights in the Ontario Hockey League, Sam O'Reilly can play both center and the wing as a positionally sound player. After a five-game stint with London the year before, O'Reilly put up 20 goals and 56 points in a full 68 game season while contributing both five on five and on special teams. O'Reilly provides great adaptability and intelligence in all three zones and elevated his play when given the opportunity.

Sam O'Reilly is another example of a London Knights forwards pushing their way up the line up, and draft boards, as the season progressed. O'Reilly's biggest shining moment of his ability to take advantage of the opportunities given to him was during the World Juniors when London forwards Easton Cowan and Kasperi Halttunen were loaned and their ice time became available in London's top-six. During that time Sam O'Reily put up 12 points in 8 games and played some of his best stretch of hockey for the year when he was given the most opportunity.

O'Reilly plays a very patient game where he allows the play to develop itself and depending on the zone and what is in front of him, will make a calculated play to best create or prevent opportunities. In addition to his patience, he offers offensive deception to his game off the rush but he primarily creates offense from down low and on the cycle. He leads his teammates into good scoring opportunities and is opportunistic himself in tight and with the puck on his stick coming out of the cycle and pushing to the net.

O'Reilly is a responsible 200ft player who's best attribute is his responsibility both with the puck on his stick and without. He has strong positioning and is great at disrupting plays in his own end and being a frustrating penalty killer. He takes away time and space by not overcommitting and staying patient enough to take away shooting and passing lanes and quickly getting the puck out of the zone when it gets on his stick. On the forecheck, O'Reilly works hard and will aggressively finish his checks or work to limit space on the breakout. There is not much hesitation to jump into the dirty areas of the ice for O'Reilly.

The biggest weakness to his game is undoubtably his skating. There is room for improvement in his speed and edgework but with a good frame and the way he plays the game he does not need to develop into a speedster, he just needs to round out his skating which we already saw improvement in as the year went on. As his strength improves so will his skating, and he should be able to keep better balance when pressed physically by opposing defenders and improve his lateral movement coming into the zone to better evade defenders on the rush.

As a trustworthy player who plays in all situations and has some offensive upside, O'Reilly is someone who people should keep their eye on come draft day. Given his consistent playoff performance and his hard-working nature, O'Reilly has the potential to jump into a line-up and become a contributor.

"Not much there. Plays hard but not a tough kid or hard to play against. Good junior player." – NHL Scout, November 2023

"Smaller kid and skating is pretty average." – NHL Scout, November 2023

"Not a great skater and not overly big. Lacks high end skill. Just a good junior player for me." – NHL Scout, January 2024

"I have him and Vanacker back to back but I'm not telling you who is ahead." NHL Scout, January 2024

"I respect his game because he comes to play every night but he projects as 4th line NHLer to me. I'd take him in the 4th." – NHL Scout, May 2024

"What is all this first round conversation about? Holy Sh*t!!" NHL Scout, May 2024

"There's a kid who has grown on me. I really like him. He catches all parts of the game. Not amazing at anything but a really good work ethic. Clearly not a natural center but can fill in there if needed. He can play up and down a lineup." – NHL Scout, May 2024

"Plays hard...will play in the dirty areas. Not a high end skill guy but he can make some plays and score a little bit. He's a rookie so I want to give him his full season to see where he can get his game to." – HP Scout, Mark Edwards, December 2023

"Prior to December I had him as a 4th round type. As the year progressed he kept creeping up a little bit on my list. He's better than the sum of his parts - not an awesome skater or overly big and although he works his butt off he's not tough like his teammate McCue. His skill is good but not going to wow you. He is a player the Hunters love because he is smart and plays their system. He plays a strong defensive game. He brings value to his icetime. He forced me to keep moving him up my list every month with his continued improved play." – HP Scout, Mark Edwards, April 2024

NR	PLAYER	TEAM	LEAGUE	HEIGHT	WEIGHT	POS	GRADE
	O'SULLIVAN, ANDREW	KIMBALL UNION	HIGH-MA	5' 11"	165	RD	NI

NHLCS	CEILING	FLOOR	HOCKEY SENSE	COMPETE	SKILL	SKATE	MISC
-	6	4	6	7	5	6	7

Andrew O'Sullivan led Kimball Union Academy in assists this season with 47 in 34 games. Including forwards, that's top 10 in the nation at the prep school level among draft eligible players – and that's without accounting for the significant games played disadvantage that New England prep school has versus some other areas. In any case, O'Sullivan is a smart and engaged defender with a penchant for making clean outlet passes even if he's on his second or third look/route. A plus skater with really strong edges and a tight turning radius.

The Colgate commit doesn't possess high-end top speed, but the lateral mobility and edges more than make up for it. He plays the game on his toes and makes calculated attempts to shut down plays before they start. If he can't stop it on the first try, he quickly recovers and gets into good position to absorb the next sequence. Not a physical player by nature. He looks to try to use his skating and stick play to steal pucks, knowing that he'll get a second chance with his recovery process. And at his size, physicality might not produce the best outcome. His hockey sense and work rate combination is a big positive and nods at the idea that there's a lot of runway to go with him.

His puck handling is above average, and it's made all the better by his poise and vision. O'Sullivan really likes to make a sudden turn against the grain near the boards to elude defenders and forecheckers. There are still some puck control issues at times and he'll fan on some pucks that we'd expect a player of his caliber to connect on. But he does flash some useful, dynamic skill in space and that gives us some hope. The NEFPHL most valuable defenseman doesn't have pronounced shooting talent or a bias for shooting in general; he'd probably prefer to pass the puck into the net if possible. That said, he doesn't take advantage of his level of competition…he plays it straight up. We wager that he will end up looking better when the game gets more predictable at higher levels.

Even in his cup of coffee with Green Bay (USHL) late in the year, he looked extremely confident and comfortable in that environment. As a smart, sub-6' defenseman, he isn't terribly difficult to play against right now. His positioning and compete level are good enough where that can improve. He's expected to be a prime player for Green Bay next season. Andrew just makes the cut for this draft class by a month, and while he might not make our draft list this time around, he's certainly on the watch list.

9	PLAYER	TEAM	LEAGUE	HEIGHT	WEIGHT	POS	GRADE
	PAREKH, ZAYNE	SAGINAW	OHL	6' 00.25"	178	RD	A

NHLCS	CEILING	FLOOR	HOCKEY SENSE	COMPETE	SKILL	SKATE	MISC
NA-5	9	5	8	6	8	6	6

Zayne Parekh is a gifted offensive defenseman who displayed an impressive development curve this past season. His production was elite, with 96 points in 66 games, including 33 goals. His 1.45 PPG ranks among the top six all-time by a first-year eligible defender in the OHL, placing him in special company that includes the likes of Paul Coffey and Ryan Ellis.

Let's address his most glaring weaknesses first, starting with one that is no fault of his own. He is physically far more unpolished and underdeveloped than many other players. As a defender, this affects his ability to drive players wide during transitional defensive play and boxouts in front of his net.Along the wall, he can be physically overwhelmed, leading to turnovers. Currently, this limits his versatility as a defender.

Parekh needs to bulk up to improve his defensive play. However, what might be less evident is what he needs to do for his activation game to translate effectively. Zayne can be a rover on the ice, joining the rush as a fourth forward. The problem is that when he's handling the puck in high-danger areas off sequences where he becomes the drop option, he can get erased in traffic. Consequently, when the play heads the other way, he's late to re-establish the defensive side of the game.

Despite his limitations, he became far more willing to impose himself physically as the season progressed, showing a willingness to take a hit to make a play. Although there was a lack of general compete early on, his compete level improved significantly as he matured defensively over the season.

One note regarding his compete level is that because he skates in an upright posture, it can make him appear to be playing a more lackadaisical game than he actually is. His upright skating base can make him look disinterested because he doesn't seem to be in a "ready" position. This is something we actively discussed, acknowledging our bias towards a more active stance that suggests a player is ready at any given moment.

The second weakness is his own fault: he can lack a high pace of play or fail to match the urgency required in defensive assignments. This can result in him being late to coverage or failing to close a gap quickly enough, reminiscent of a prospect that admittedly burned us, Adam Boqvist. Boqvist, with his upright skating posture and finesse-oriented offensive style, hasn't translated well. However, there is a fundamental difference: Zayne has shown resilience and improvement in his positioning and willingness to maintain a better pace as the season progressed.

Zayne has been targeted more than any other player we've observed this season. He's been run over, cross-checked up high and through his back, blind-sided, and subjected to numerous slashes that visibly hurt him. Yet, he consistently stayed in games and continued to produce after getting hurt.

With his weaknesses addressed, let's discuss what makes him special. His remarkable playmaking can be characterized by his ability to pass the puck as if he had a bird's eye view of the rink. Off the ice, players often wish they could apply the perspective they gain from an elevated angle back onto the ice. In Parekh's case, this is a reality.

His breakouts are sophisticated. He usually won't defer to the easiest option directly in front of him that's uncovered or the tougher option of a covered weak-side lateral stretch pass. Instead, he chooses the option that produces the highest chance of a transitional advantage while still considering risk on most pass attempts.

There's poise in his play as he evaluates, but it's his ability to present hesitation passes timed properly that truly separates him. His exceptional production results from his precise playmaking windows, utilizing his hands and static postural fakes to buy time.

His decision-making extends from below the goal line to all three zones when he has the puck. His vision, spatial awareness, processing ability, tempo control, deception, and anticipation when seeing the ice unfold are graded from very good to excellent in most sequences. These skills give him a consistent outlet pass, the ability to make quick one-touch passes under heavy pressure, stretch passes through layered traffic, and no-look lateral passes that land directly on the tape after penetrating the offensive zone.

Parekh uses his adaptive thinking to control the rink's geography. If his shooting lane is blocked, he reconfigures it with advanced fakes and lateral agility. If pressured at the line, he uses his hands to protect the puck. If he messes up a play, he processes rapidly enough to find a new solution. His on-ice appraisal makes him difficult to contain and even more difficult to read.

This leads to his scoring rates. He arguably has the highest goal-scoring potential of any draft-eligible defender due to his excellent shooting mechanics, advanced understanding of timing and placement, and the combination of skills to regularly put himself in high-danger areas. This trait positively compares him to Adam Boqvist and makes him arguably the most talented shooter coming out of the OHL since Logan Mailloux and Boqvist.

Zayne Parekh is one of the most exciting dual-threat offensive defensemen we've seen in the OHL in a long time. His development curve is encouraging. He has improved his ability to manipulate himself off his centerline, paying dividends in his attempts to activate and defend at higher speeds. He's started to understand the importance of positional defense and recognizing when to stay in motion to avoid being caught puck-watching or flat-footed. He's been physically challenged by opposing teams and has held firm. For these reasons, we believe Zayne has the opportunity to develop into an offensive force. He may need a pairing built around him, presenting some risk, but not enough to warrant ranking him lower given his talent level

"He skates with a lack of awareness way too often and he'll get blown up in the NHL doing that and be out for months." - NHL Scout, December 2023

"I've never seen a prospect targeted more in a draft season than Parekh. Speaks to how opposing coaches view him as a threat when he's on the ice." - HP Scout, Brad Allen

"He's going to develop into what Adam Boqvist was supposed to become. He's a grittier, more determined version of Boqvist." - HP Scout, Brad Allen

"For me it is wide open at number two and Parekh is in that mix." NHL Scout, October 2023

"Parekh drives me crazy...not even in my top 20. He is way better than the little Dman in Windsor though." - NHL Scout, October 2023

"You just nailed it when you said he has an elite trait. That's it right there. He has two elite qualities that someone like a Henry Mews doesn't have." - NHL Scout, April 2024

"You can choose six foot two skill guy at Michigan State, monster Dman in Russia or maybe all around guy but probably not elite at anything in Dickinson or take Parekh? - NHL Scout, April 2024

"I like Parekh but it's not like he doesn't have his weaknesses too. Ranking these top Dmen is a bitch." - NHL Scout, May 2024

"When you talk just about puck moving he is in his own league." - NHL Scout, May 2024

"Skating is a good not great but it will improve with strength...the way he defends is a bit concerning because it's inconsistent." - NHL Scout, May 2024

"People compare him to Quinn Hughes and Hughes has been far from great in the playoff games I've watched him. I'm taking Dickinson over Parekh." - NHL Scout, May 2024

"It's a brutal top 10 after Celebrini but Parekh has some amazing attributes in his game." - NHL Scout, May 2024

"It's summer hockey but he didn't look like a first-rounder at the Hlinka Gretzky tournament, I have a real issue with his defensive game" - HP Scout Jérôme Bérubé (August 2023)

"Man, the improvement with his defensive game has been quite impressive this year, he's not far from being my top D in the draft which is hilarious thinking back what I thought of him after the Hlinka tournament" - HP Scout Jérôme Bérubé (February 2024)

"One thing that bothers me with him, is he has a heart but man does he need to be more aware on the ice because he can't get hit in the NHL like he does in the OHL because he won't have a long career" - HP Scout Jérôme Bérubé (April 2024)

"The safe pick is Dickinson, he is fantastic... but is he the best player in 5 years? Not for me." - NHL Scout, April 2024

"Who do you want in the playoffs? Parekh or Dickinson? That is where I struggle more when I'm ranking my top two Dmen." - NHL Scout, April 2024

"I'm not as high on him as others because to me he just plays rover, he doesn't defend." - HP Scout, Mark Edwards, October 2023

"I have a totally different opinion of his defensive game now than I did last season and earlier this season. I give him a ton of credit, he has really improved his defensive game and that is all I needed to see to jump on board. He is an elite puck mover. It's incredible to watch." - HP Scout, Mark Edwards, March 2024

"I had a scout say Zayne reminds him of Drysdale but I don't see that.." - HP Scout, Mark Edwards, March 2024

"It's so rare to see a player move the puck the way he does. I see so many passes in junior that miss their target. Zayne sees some plays even before I do and then hits the middle of the tape a high percentage of the time. Fun player to watch. It's rare that I change my mind this much about a player during his draft season but with his bigger effort defending, I give Zayne a ton of credit for improving his overall game. I wish he could avid some hits better though." - HP Scout, Mark Edwards, May 2024

"He just got destroyed again." (Text I sent to our scouts) - HP Scout, Mark Edwards, May 2024

20	PLAYER	TEAM	LEAGUE	HEIGHT	WEIGHT	POS	GRADE
	PARASCAK, TERIK	PRINCE GEORGE	WHL	5' 11.75"	179	RW	A

NHLCS	CEILING	FLOOR	HOCKEY SENSE	COMPETE	SKILL	SKATE	MISC
NA-15	7	5	9	8	7	5	6

As a first year WHL player after playing prep school U18 last season, the former 4th round pick in the WHL bantam draft was the surprise of the season early on. He started the year on fire with 29 points in the first 14 games. He had an outstanding draft season statistic wise with 43 goals and 105 points in 68 games, second behind Berkly Catton amongst U18 WHL forwards.

The number one reason why Parascak's offensive production is so good is because of his off-puck movement. In the offensive zone, Parascak is great at timing himself in good spot the get the puck. When he's F3, he plays between coverage and slide downhill with good timing. Down low, he does a good job of winning battles. He establishes body position and scans well, helping him to hold the puck and find passing options inside scoring areas. Where he's at his best is around the net. He is timing to get open is great, and he loves to roll-around or make quick change of direction around defender trying to box him out to always have his blade open for redirection or rebound. He mostly played the net front/goal line player on Prince George's top power play unit and did a great job, scoring 12 goals and 16 assists on the man advantage. He's a smart player, and he uses this hockey IQ to know when to make quick pass to the bumper or back door versus when to attack the net himself. His very good puck skills in tight allows him to be efficient when attacking the net. He's also able to exploit open space in coverage, popping between checks for quick shooting option when possible. Prince Geroge's power play finished 2nd overall in the WHL with 30.1%.

The transition game in an area Parascak will need to improve to bring his offensive to another level. Firstly, his skating in below average. Obviously, adding more explosiveness and speed would help him in puck carrying situations and would lead to more zone entries in his game. Once the zone entered on the rush, he does a good job. Off the puck, he works to sprint and beat his check to the net, scoring many goals that way this season. When he receives kickout passes on the wall, he's smart with his touches. His quick and accurate passing allows him to find open players on the rush. From the defensive, his wall work on breakouts is an area of his game that can improve. One place where he had success in transition was with his anticipation in defensive zone coverage. He knows when to get moving on potential change of possession. He also broke many high plays from the other team, giving him breakaways opportunities. With very good puck skill and accurate shooting skills, Parascak converted on many of these breakaway opportunities.

Defensively, Parascak is good two-way forward because of his hockey IQ and work rate. On the forecheck, he reads the play well which helps him in offensive zone puck retrievals. He tracks hard in return to defensive zone situations, and as mentioned, reads the play well in his own-end. Parascak was a trusted PK'er for his team and was used to defend late game leads/6-on-5 against situations.

Overall, it will be fascinating to see how Parascak's game will translate at the next level. The offensive production was elite this season. He has high-end hockey IQ, but most of his physical tools are around average (some below average, some above average). His overall hockey IQ, smart passing albitites to improve the condition of the puck, scoring touch inside the slot, to go along with his ability to do the dirty work down low and play a good two-way game makes him potentially a perfect complementary top 6 winger for skilled puck carrying forwards.

"I love everything about his game other than his skating. I have him in the 2nd round." – NHL Scout, January 2024

"He can't skate and he is about 165 pounds. I know you are a big fan but he's a third rounder at best for me." – NHL Scout, January 2024

"Love him. Smart, smart smart player who is skilled and can play with anybody." – NHL Scout, January 2024

"I know scouts who see a small scrawny kid who can't skate and they will regret not ranking him higher." – NHL Scout, April 2024

"Elite hockey sense." – NHL Scout, March 2024

"Really good grasp of where his game is now and what he needs to do going forward. Smart kid." – NHL Scout, June 2024

"I'm easily the scout on our staff that likes him the most. I'm basically the president of his fan club. The weakish skating and elite hockey sense reminds me of how I felt about Ryan O'Reilly. We ranked Ryan 21st overall in his draft year. Where is he ranked in a re-draft?" HP Scout, Mark Edwards, June 2024

"A little bit more of a quiet kid but good feedback from the Combine interviews." – HP Scout, Mark Edwards, June 2024

NR	PLAYER		TEAM	LEAGUE	HEIGHT	WEIGHT	POS	GRADE
	PARK, AIDEN		SHATTUCK	HIGH-MN	6' 00.75"	184	RC	C
NHLCS	CEILING	FLOOR	HOCKEY SENSE	COMPETE	SKILL		SKATE	MISC
NA-91	6	4	6	6	6		5	5

Aidan is coming off a highly productive season with the Shattuck St. Mary's Prep team, scoring 30 goals and 63 assists in 56 games. Aidan also saw 10 games with Green Bay, chipping in 3 goals and 2 assists for the Gamblers who drafted him 3rd Overall in the 2022 USHL Phase 1 draft.

Aidan is a strong and highly skilled offensive player that excels in creating offense in traffic. He has quick hands and good edgework that allow him to escape and make small plays in the crowd to create offense. His strength on the puck, paired with his edge work make him difficult to contain on an island because he can quickly spin off defenders on his back. The aspect of his skating that will hold him back at the upper levels if it doesn't improve is his straight-line skating explosiveness and overall speed. He is currently able to overcome some of this with the puck with his instincts, strength and quick hands as well as playing at the prep level but we saw the pace at the USHL level, especially in the playoffs be an issue at times, especially trying to get back into the play. As his competition gets bigger and stronger, improving his stride and gaining another gear will be required if he is to be an effective offensive producer at the professional level. Off the puck, Park does a good job in identifying lanes to the net to get passes, as well as finding the soft ice in the scoring areas. Park does a good job with his neutral zone routes and getting available for quick outlets on the breakouts as well. Park is able to think the game well and adapt to different situations quickly off the puck to get open.

One area of the game that we have seen significant improvement this year vs years past when it comes to Park is his play away from the puck. Not only has his overall compete and willingness to battle improved considerably but he has also improved his awareness and ability to read the play defensively. Park does a good job working to take away lanes both coming back on the backcheck as well as when hemmed in the defensive zone. Park has a lot of tools that will translate to the pro game down the road, how his skating develops over the next few years will determine a lot. Many players with his skill set have made the jump to be an effective offensive player at the next level, it just may take this player a bit longer to get there. Aidan is committed to the University of Michigan but will need some seasoning in the USHL before he is ready to make the jump to college so he will likely spend at least next season with Green Bay before heading to Ann Arbor.

NR	PLAYER		TEAM	LEAGUE	HEIGHT	WEIGHT	POS	GRADE
	PATTERSON, RILEY		BARRIE	OHL	5' 11.75"	192	RC	C
NHLCS	CEILING	FLOOR	HOCKEY SENSE	COMPETE	SKILL		SKATE	MISC
NA-61	6	5	6	5	6		6	6

It took some time for Riley Patterson to adjust in his rookie season in the OHL with the Barrie Colts, but after settling in, he showed scouts a lot of value as a potential secondary scorer at the pro-level. He was traded from Flint following his de-commitment from Michigan State and played in the OJHL with the North York Rangers last season. Patterson was given lots of praise from his new coach and general manager Marty Williamson, who said he saw lots of high-end skill from his new forward. As a rookie, Patterson posted 62 points in 68 gams including 29 goals, while proving to scouts that his coach was right about him as the season progressed.

A much more physical forward than expected, Patterson has the strength to hold off defenders while in possession of the puck with his core strength, his strength on his feet and balance to control the puck well on the cycle and down low despite his shorter stature, but low center of gravity stance. He throws his weight around well and is physically maturing well, while not compromising his skill set. Along the boards he battles hard for pucks and quickly jumps on loose pucks gaining inside body positioning and boxing out defenders no matter how much bigger than him they are. These abilities give him the opportunity to translate to the NHL in a third line secondary scorer type role of a quick and energetic forward who can chip in with some offense.

Patterson has a good IQ on the ice, knowing where he needs to be and covering off passing lanes. He was consistently engaged in the play by not just being aggressive and physical but disciplined and mentally tough as well. At the beginning of the year, Patterson would get pushed around, get frustrated by his lack of production and space and as a result did not produce a complete game. The turnaround for Patterson came a couple of months into the season after some inconsistent play to start the year and once he settled in, he displayed a lot of translatable intelligence and skills in his game.

The opportunity to kill penalties became an option for him as the season progressed in Barrie, as the Colts sold off a lot of veterans at the trade deadline. Short handed, he was a threat to score and took away space well from attacking forwards and blocking shots whether his team was down a man or not. On the forecheck, Patterson was a deep and aggressive attacker who disrupted play and caused turnovers from pressuring defensemen to make bad passes or stealing pucks himself with a quick stick. Patterson played the majority of the season on the wing and was a good defensive presence in addition to helping his team in high board battles to get the puck out of the zone in the same fashion that he gets to loose pucks offensively.

Rush attacks were hit and miss early on in the season as he would try but fail to push down the middle of the ice with the puck. As he settled in, Patterson displayed more patience and started creating more space by creating more outside to inside opportunities on the rush or off the cycle. This allowed him to find his teammates more consistently as he is more of a playmaker than a goal scorer even though he scored almost 30 goals as a rookie. The goals came as a result of his good shooting ability and his learned ability to find soft ice in the offensive zone and allow himself more time with the puck to pick his spot. The decision-making skills became much more prominent and much faster overall as he worked his way up Barrie's depth chart and his quick stickhandling skills on top of this made him more elusive and giving him more of an ability to make players miss.

Patterson battled through early adversity and showed what he can do when everything is not easy for him, like it seemed at times a year ago in the OJHL. He adapted to less time and space and having added responsibility on special teams and really stepping his game up on the penalty kill. Patterson should find his way onto a large number of draft boards as he continues to build upon his game in the OHL.

NR	PLAYER		TEAM	LEAGUE	HEIGHT	WEIGHT	POS	GRADE
NR	PEAPENBURG, MASON		CHIPPEWA	NAHL	6' 03.75"	186	RD	**NI**
NHLCS	CEILING	FLOOR	HOCKEY SENSE	COMPETE	SKILL		SKATE	MISC
NA-172	5	4	5	6	5		6	7

Peapenburg is a Wisconsin native that has seen his game take consistent developmental strides the last two years since being drafted in the 9th Round of the 2022 USHL Phase 1 draft by Des Moines. Mason played his High School hockey in Wisconsin for Notre Dame Academy, where he was part of an undefeated state championship team in 22/23. This season Peapenburg started the season well with Team Wisconsin U18, playing in the MN Elite League, where he started to gain some draft traction with NHL scouts with his play in that league, but Mason sustained a wrist injury 9 games in and missed the rest of the Elite League season. Peapenburg was planning on returning to Notre Dame Academy for his senior season this year but with not much development left at the Wisconsin High School level for him, Mason instead elected to make the jump to junior hockey for the Chippewa Steel (NAHL) where he was able to step right into the lineup and be a consistent player on the backend for the Steel. Mason also saw a two game call up to Des Moines (USHL) where he didn't look at all out of place with limited ice time.

Since being drafted by Des Moines, Peapenburg has added much needed strength to his 6'4" frame, with that added strength came a lot of coordination and explosiveness with his skating. There is still some work to be done with his lateral movements but his skating is trending in the right direction to be an added asset to go along with his size and range. Defensively, Peapenburg processes things at a quick rate where he is able to take away passing lanes well and quickly pick up his defensive assignments. Mason plays with high physicality and compete around his own net, he defends the crease area well, using his size to gain position and box out opponents for his goaltenders. The details and awareness in his defensive game give him a good platform to round out the rest of his game the next few years. His size and range allow him to keep opponents outside the dots and showed good defensive play on an island 1 v 1. Peapenburg projects as a defense first defenseman at the next level but he certainly can be effective with his puck touches. He is a high IQ player that shows good awareness and vision of the ice with the puck on his tape. In our viewings, Peapenburg moved pucks out of his own end consistently and made some good reads in the neutral zone to transition pucks quickly and create some scoring chances going the other way with his quick reads. We don't see Mason being a big end to end puck rusher but if his strength and explosiveness continue to progress, he should be able to transport pucks more effectively and gain zones with his feet as well. When it comes to creating offense or being a driver of offense from the back end, Mason's upside is limited with his current skill set. He doesn't possess the hands and puck skills to buy time for himself to create so he is forced to rely upon his ability to make quick reads and accurate passes to create chances. At the offensive blueline, Mason does a good job of getting shots through and does possess a pretty heavy release and shot from distance but he needs to learn to get himself into more situations to use it. There is time for him to develop some offensive skill but we don't see that being a staple of his game at the next level.

Peapenburg's progress in the last year saw him gain a lot of Division 1 interest and has recently committed to the University of Wisconsin to play his college hockey. Peapenburg will likely spend the next couple of years in Des Moines (USHL), rounding out the rest of his game before he is ready to step into the Badgers lineup.

NR	PLAYER			TEAM		LEAGUE	HEIGHT	WEIGHT	POS	GRADE
	PELLETIER, ZACH			GATINEAU		QMJHL	6' 03"	178	G	NI
NHLCS	CEILING	FLOOR		HOCKEY SENSE		COMPETE	SKILL		SKATE	MISC
NA-8	5	4		5		7	5		5	6

Pelletier is a good-sized goaltender who had an interesting rookie season in the QMJHL despite playing for one of the worst teams in the league. To their credit, after a horrible first half, they improved enough to qualify for the QMJHL playoffs. Pelletier finished the season with a 14-26 record, a 3.64 goals-against average and a .875 save percentage. However, we saw some good improvement during the season; before the Christmas break he was at .857 and improved to .891. We often talk about keeping track of players' curves to see signs of progression during a year: this was one example.

Pelletier was a second-round pick in the 2022 QMJHL Draft and established himself as a good number 1 goalie this season, even though his first few months in the league were not what we would call easy. He's got the size that NHL teams covet (6'03" and 178 pounds) and has a good, compact frame that is similar to Vegas' Adin Hill.

The good part about playing for a bad team is that you're getting to see a lot of pucks. The bad part about playing for a bad team is that you're getting to see a lot of pucks. Most of the time when scouting goaltenders, we prefer to see them playing for either average or bad teams. If a goaltender plays on a stacked team, it makes it difficult to get a good read on them. With Gatineau improving their play in the 2nd half of the season, it made it a bit easier for scouts to get a read on Pelletier. He covers a lot of his net, he looks big in his net and he's calm. He's not a great athlete, but he's usually square to shooters and gets hit by the puck a lot because of his big frame and sound positional game. He does get exposed a bit when he has to move laterally; teams have been successful when they make him move from side to side. He also had some trouble tracking pucks with heavy traffic in front of him and his rebound-control is another area we would like to see more consistency in. It can be quite good in certain games and let him down in others. He's still quite raw and has plenty of time to continue to work on his game and make improvements. He battles hard in his net, he doesn't quit on pucks and can make 2nd and 3rd saves thanks to his resiliency.

He, Samuel St-Hilaire and Jakub Milota are the best bets when it comes to QMJHL goalies getting drafted this season. He's younger and bigger than St-Hilaire, but he's not as gifted and talented as the Sherbrooke goaltender. He's raw and will have time to develop in the next 2 seasons on a Gatineau team that will slowly but surely start improving in the QMJHL. He didn't make our goalie list because we're not convinced we see an NHL goaltender; we see possibly a pro career that sees him going back and forth between the ECHL and AHL. Europe could be a good option for him at some point. His lack of athleticism played a big role in our projection and other goalies on our list were just above him on the technical side (and athleticism).

47	PLAYER	TEAM	LEAGUE	HEIGHT	WEIGHT	POS	GRADE
	PETTERSSON , LUCAS	MODO JR.	SWE-JR	5' 11.5"	173	LC	C+

NHLCS	CEILING	FLOOR	HOCKEY SENSE	COMPETE	SKILL	SKATE	MISC
INT-16	6	5	6	6	6	7	5

Pettersson emerged as one of the top scorers in Sweden's junior league, where he had 57 points in 44 games with his club team Modo Hockey. This placed him 10th in the league scoring race and 4th among U18 players, trailing only the trio from Orebro (Liam Danielsson, Melvin Fernstrom, and Alexander Zetterberg). He also made significant contributions to Sweden's U18 national team throughout the season, participating in various tournaments including: the Hlinka-Gretzky Cup, the Five Nations Tournament in November and February, the World Junior A Challenge, and the World Under 18 Hockey Championship. Across these competitions, he had 36 points in 27 games, the second-highest point total behind Alexander Zetterberg. Although he saw limited ice time in 5 games in the SHL, he is expected to have more opportunities at this level next year.

A versatile forward who can play at center and on the wing, we project him more as a winger for the NHL due to his lack of size to play down the middle. He has good skating abilities that he can use more efficiently on the wing to stretch the ice and challenge defenders with his outside speed. We like his pace and his ability to use his speed all over the ice. He's good at finding soft ice and supporting players in all three zones. He's dangerous on counter-attacks, and his effort level away from the puck is solid. When coupled with his speed, he becomes a player NHL teams could rely on in a two-way role. While we see him primarily as a 3rd-line player, there's potential for a middle-6 projection. He offers versatility, capable of playing all three forward positions. With a solid IQ and compete level and his strong skating abilities, he possesses the necessary tools for success.

However, inconsistency can be found in his game. We saw a good example of that at the recent U18 World Hockey Championship. Although he improved as the tournament progressed, slow starts and fluctuations in his play have raised some red flags for us. When he's not on, his game can fall off a cliff and render him completely ineffective for his team, as we saw early on at the U18s.

A dual threat offensively, he excels both as a shooter and a playmaker. There's a good level of creativity to his game, and he has demonstrated above-average stickhandling skills. His shooting skills are fine, but he's not a big-time shooter, either. At the NHL level, he'll need to focus more on playing inside to score goals, as he won't find the same success from distances as he did in junior hockey. Adding physical strength will be crucial, as he currently has a slight frame and will require time to add muscle mass.

He can be a valuable asset to a team's PK unit thanks to his strong work ethic and keen sense of anticipation, which are key for a successful penalty killer. He is not afraid to block shots and also takes important defensive faceoffs for both his club team and the U18 national team.

While his issues with consistency have brought us to be a tad less aggressive with his place in our rankings, overall, we think this is a good player that could become a versatile top-9 forward in the NHL if everything goes right with his development. However, it would be easier to justify a higher ranking, possibly even within our top 32, if he had better size, as he'll need to compete in the more demanding areas of the ice and currently needs to improve on what he has. We think he has a low chance of going late in round 1, but we think the chances are higher he'll hear his name in round 2.

86	PLAYER	TEAM	LEAGUE	HEIGHT	WEIGHT	POS	GRADE
	PIKKARAINEN, KASPER	TPS JR.	FIN-JR	6' 03"	197	RW	C
NHLCS	CEILING	FLOOR	HOCKEY SENSE	COMPETE	SKILL	SKATE	MISC
INT-24	5	4	6	6	5	5	6

Pikkarainen is a good-sized forward from Finland who played this past season with the TPS U20 team and also was a regular internationally with the U18 National team. He also played 5 games in the Liiga.

He projects more as a depth forward if he makes the NHL. With good size, he skates well enough for a player of his stature. He has okay hands and shooting skills and decent passing skills. He uses his frame well, along with his long reach, to protect the puck, and he is good on both the forecheck and the cycle. He was below a point per game in Finland's junior league, which doesn't bode well enough to be able to project him as an offensive player at the NHL level. We think one of the biggest hurdles to seeing his offensive game translate to the NHL is his lack of shooting abilities. His shot is only average in terms of release quickness and velocity. You simply don't see his shot leading to a lot of goals in the NHL. We do think his playmaking is a tad superior, which gives him a chance. He's also a solid player away from the puck. His effort level on backchecks and when supporting his defensemen down low is good. This enables him, along with his good active stick to block passing and shooting lanes, to kill penalties effectively. However, we would like to see more pushback. While he does have a good work ethic, if he could become tougher to play against, this would add more value to his game and long-term NHL potential. He did not push back consistently enough in our view.

If everything continues along his current development path, we see Pikkarainen as a depth forward in the NHL, because he can play well along the boards, has a decent hockey IQ, and his effort level is there. However, his other skills being pretty much average across the board leaves us with doubt, and we don't wish to rank him too high for those reasons. If he does not match our projection for the NHL, he can be a good player in the Liiga or elsewhere in Europe.

NR	PLAYER	TEAM	LEAGUE	HEIGHT	WEIGHT	POS	GRADE
	PIER BRUNET, SIMON	DRUMMONDVILLE	QMJHL	6' 01.75"	176	RD	NI
NHLCS	CEILING	FLOOR	HOCKEY SENSE	COMPETE	SKILL	SKATE	MISC
NA-185	3	4	4	7	4	6	6

Playing behind Komarov, Lamoureux and Diotte on the right side of the Drummondville Voltigeurs' defense, Brunet, in his second season with the team, took advantage of Lamoureux's injury to get himself more playing time in the postseason. He was originally drafted in the 5th round of the 2021 QMJHL Draft, out of the Gatineau midget program.

A defensive defenseman with limited upside for the next level, Brunet is an older player for this draft class (October 2005 birthday). Physically mature compared to many QMJHL players from this draft class, he plays a hard, physical game in his zone and has PK value. He makes it difficult for opponents with his physicality along the boards and his ability to clear out the front of the net. His defensive and physical game will translate to the pro game (ECHL/AHL). Not a creative player, his decision-making can be questionable, but he has a good point shot. He has great velocity with his slapshot, but needs to be more accurate with it, which would bring him more offensive success. He gets into trouble when pressured and forced to make quick decisions with the puck. He also struggles to defend against speedy wingers because he doesn't have the most fluid footwork (or overall skating skills).

We think this is a player who could see his productivity improve over the next two seasons once Komarov, Lamoureux and Diotte leave Drummondville. We think he has a chance to be a pro for the ECHL and AHL ranks, but we don't see a future NHL player in him, and this is why he's been left off our list.

NR	PLAYER	TEAM	LEAGUE	HEIGHT	WEIGHT	POS	GRADE
	PITNER, TORY	YOUNGSTOWN	USHL	6'00.5"	180	RD	C
NHLCS	CEILING	FLOOR	HOCKEY SENSE	COMPETE	SKILL	SKATE	MISC
NA-90	4	5	5	7	4	5	6

Tory Pitner got off to a torrid start in 2023-24, with 15 points in his first 15 games. However, Pitner would only add nine points the rest of the way. Point production isn't likely to be in the cards for Tory anyhow. He's not a very technically skilled player and his passing game is average. He lacks puck poise and vision in all three zones. While he is quick to get rid of the puck, he generally finds the exit in his own zone or pushes it towards the net in the offensive zone. While some of those pucks were being recovered and put into the net early in the season, that was more good circumstance than any sort of advanced playmaking or shooting process. He'll almost certainly be more of a support player as he moves up the ladder. This is actually fairly true of his defensive play as well. As a loose gap player that lacks strong anticipation ability, Pitner isn't a take-charge style of defenseman. In fairness to him, he was on one of the better defenses in the USHL. If he goes back to junior next year, maybe we'll see a bit different of a player. Further, while he does generally play with a loose gap, there is a pronounced physical element to his game – so he's inclined to try to close those gaps fairly quickly when the opportunity arises. Unfortunately, Pitner isn't the best skater. His edges and lateral mobility are up into plus territory and he pushes through with good foot churn and hip mobility. The first-step quickness and straight line speed don't move the needle very much. When he commits to hits, especially in the low neutral zone or high defensive zone, heads-up players can sometimes slip out of the way.

While he doesn't possess terribly interesting technical ability, he does try to cover for that with his compete level. He's a hard worker and well intentioned. There's even a little bit of defensive viscosity to his game, so he can gain some leverage on guys and hang in the battle.

Overall his game still lacks focus. His body movements are very busy but lack fluidity…not very efficient right now. If his mental processor was a bit quicker, it would be easier to see him as a third pairing defenseman. It would probably be best if he waited a year before going to college instead of having to punch up all over again. He has decent size, no fatal flaws, and a competitive spirit – add in the fact that he's right-handed, and there's an avenue for him to be a depth player down the line.

NR	PLAYER		TEAM	LEAGUE	HEIGHT	WEIGHT	POS	GRADE
	PITRE, KADEN		FLINT	OHL	5'11.25"	180	LC	NI

NHLCS	CEILING	FLOOR	HOCKEY SENSE	COMPETE	SKILL	SKATE	MISC
NA-144	5	5	5	4	6	4	6

Despite a productive season offensively with 30 points in 35 games in a shortened season for the younger brother of Anaheim Ducks draft pick Coulson Pitre, Kaden did not display the abilities that made him the 18th overall selection in the first round of the OHL draft. Kaden, like his brother Coulson, is a left-shot center who plays for the Flint Firebirds in the OHL.

Kaden Pitre was disengaged for the majority of viewings this season. He was able to out up a good number of points with Flint, who was one of the lower seeded teams in the OHL this past season, however he does not have the hockey IQ to be able to create offense himself as he is more of a complimentary player. Pitre got a lot of ice time with Flint's top players and was able to take advantage on the score sheet as a result. His best attribute offensively is his offensive positioning and board play on the cycle.

When it comes to compete, Pitre is one of the more disengaged players in this draft class. He was not active in the defensive zone and with the puck played with low effort and a slow pace. Pitre's skating is average at best with good balance but slow speed. He also displays some untranslatable skills offensively such as his preference to play along the outside as opposed to trying to drive the middle and push offence to the net. He plays better and with more confidence along the boards than he does inside the circles where he does not create space well or have the ability to play physically in front of the net.

NR	PLAYER		TEAM	LEAGUE	HEIGHT	WEIGHT	POS	GRADE
	PHILLIPS, OWEN		HALIFAX	QMJHL	5'11"	176	RD	C

NHLCS	CEILING	FLOOR	HOCKEY SENSE	COMPETE	SKILL	SKATE	MISC
-	5	4	6	6	5	6	6

Owen Phillips is a right-handed puck moving defenseman who was drafted by the Halifax Mooseheads with the 7th pick of the 2022 QMJHL entry draft. He has just finished his 2nd season with the Mooseheads in which he was able to contribute 4 goals and 15 assists for 19 points in 67 games this season.

Phillips is a good skater. Straight line speed is good, and he can definitely break away from people while handling the puck on the breakout. He has a nice fluid stride and does not seem to have any problems with changing directions. We would like to maybe see some more advanced edgework from him but other than that his skating is pretty solid.

He has never had an impressive output in the league, but we feel that the senses are there. He is very active in transition, is not scared to move the puck up the ice and can feather some nice passes when it is needed. We would like to see him maybe play with a little more confidence in the offensive zone instead of always electing for safer plays. His shot power could also improve as he is not really a threat to score from beyond the hashmarks.

Defensively, Phillips is a reliable player. He often makes good reads on breakouts, and he is very poised with the puck even when facing pressure. His skating allows him to get out of tough spots in the dirty areas while maintaining possession of the puck. We found that his gap control was a little off and that he has a bad habit of letting opposing forwards get too close to the net before challenging them, which has led to a couple goals against. The physicality is also not very much present, and we would like to see him be more tenacious in front of the net.

While it is clear that Phillips has not lived up to the hype of being a top 10 selection in the QMJHL, there are some parts of his game that could really interest NHL scouts. His calmness with the puck in the defensive zone along with his great decision making and smooth skating stride make him at least a slight bit intriguing. His lack of offensive production could partially be blamed on the fact that he has been on one of the better teams in the Q for the last two years and by consequence, has not gotten top line minutes or very many reps on the PP. It would not shock us to see him develop quite a bit with increased responsibility in the next couple of years. He could be worth a gamble for someone in the later rounds, even if that seems unlikely.

100	PLAYER	TEAM	LEAGUE	HEIGHT	WEIGHT	POS	GRADE
	PLANTE, MAX	USA-U18	NTDP	5' 11"	177	LW	C
NHLCS	CEILING	FLOOR	HOCKEY SENSE	COMPETE	SKILL	SKATE	MISC
NA-43	6	3	6	5	6	6	4

Max Plante played all three forward positions at various points this season, ending up on the right wing of the Cole Eiserman-Kamil Bednarik combination at the U18 Worlds. Plante's stat line pretty fairly represents his traits as a player: he led all USNTDP draft eligibles in assists with 23 in 25 games and was probably the second best draft eligible playmaker on the team (Christian Humphreys) throughout the year. He only amassed 32 shots on goal in those 25 contests too, which was more in line with the fourth line players on the team.

His shot isn't a bomb, but passable enough where it could have been used more. One of the more interesting quirks that we've noted about Plante is that he sort of abandons his playmaking nature when he's dealing with heavy traffic or contact. He doesn't play off of it very well and he develops a bit of tunnel vision or at least loses focus on where his teammates are. Plante becomes more individualistic and tries to stickhandle his way into lower density areas. He actually has a fair amount of skill to do that and there's a bit of deception and dynamic element to his game. He's especially good at getting d-men to turn their toes a bit and then attack their heels on the backside. The one caveat being – he favors shooting more when he's being contacted inside the house and the shot he gets off in those cases is surprisingly good and consistent.

Typically, when we see a player modify their game away from their strengths in traffic or with contact, it turns quickly into a red flag situation. In Plante's case, it's not a great advent, but it also forces him to up his pulse a bit and it creates some interesting looks. Frankly, this is one of the things that makes him more difficult to write off. His "A" game is being more of a perimeter playmaker. At 5'11", 170 pounds without outstanding skating or mental processing, that's not overly enticing. Another peculiar quirk about Plante regards his zone entries. We monitored his controlled zone entries over the course of the year at the USHL level specifically, and there were a lot of entries outside the dots and they were not successfully converted as often as we'd like to see (that is, ultimately, generating a scoring chance). Then at the U18 World Juniors, his conversion rates went way up – no matter the opponent. Even on rushes that began in the exterior, he was able to either work inside by himself or pass it to the inside. That's another feather in his cap and another one that gave him some more rope from our perspective.

The reason why we don't rate Plante as a better playmaker than Humprheys is the lack of variance and overall creativity in his process. Said in a different way: Plante isn't as much of a problem solver as Humphreys is. There's a lot of saucer passes across lanes with Plante and those are well done, there is some lo-hi passing sequences that show promise but there isn't a lot more that we see that's really scalable right now. He's pretty soft on his stick in general. Passes don't jump off of his blade. Even in sequences near the net, Plante won't fire a puck into it…he'll slide it in. And that's small potatoes in the grand scheme of things, but it's part of a longer list of traits that just show a lack of intentionality with what he does.

Watching him go for loose pucks, for instance, he's half a beat late making the commitment to it or he'll hesitate, back away, and then go for a puck or get to his route. Plante just bails on a lot of plays in general, even though it's subtle. He's easy to play against and easy to knock off pucks. Not only separated from pucks, but knocked off his feet entirely. For a player that doesn't play with a lot of pace nor does he have much pop to his acceleration, this is particularly problematic.

His skating stride isn't bad at all nor is his foot churn, it has fluidity and when he wants to, it can get to a decent top speed. He sits fairly high in his posture, which doesn't give off the notion that he's in a ready/athletic stance at any given time. That contributes to his lack of push back and does nothing for any head or shoulder feints that he may one day want to develop (they weren't present in our viewings).

Good hockey sense, but not great. The biggest issue is his adaptive processing. Max has a good idea in his head about how the game goes and he can execute in that space. But once things speed up or are materially altered from his vision, he gets bogged down in trying to figure out what to do next. This causes him to end up too close to a teammate or if the puck comes to him, he needs time to stop and re-survey the ice. Unfortunately, he isn't fast enough, skilled enough, or good enough at puck protection to make that happen, so it's a turnover. It's weird to say this for a skater instead of a goalie, but a lot of pucks get through him. Whether it's bad luck or not, pucks just find a way through areas between his body and stick more often than we care to see. It limits his forechecking and penalty killing effectiveness.

Plante has a decent skill level and we expect him to continue to be a productive playmaker as he moves up the ladder. However, this profile of player, that really lacks a hugely dynamic element, lacks fluid skill chaining, and isn't elite from a hockey sense or compete standpoint is not usually a player that plays in the NHL.

"He's not untalented, but to use a strange metaphor for a strange player: he's an ellipsis, when I want to draft exclamation points." - HP Scout, Michael Farkas

84	PLAYER		TEAM	LEAGUE	HEIGHT	WEIGHT	POS	GRADE
	POIRIER, JUSTIN		BAIE-COMEAU	QMJHL	5' 07.25"	185	RW	C
NHLCS	CEILING	FLOOR	HOCKEY SENSE	COMPETE	SKILL		SKATE	MISC
NA-82	6	3	4	6	7		4	3

Justin Poirier is a highly talented right winger who was drafted by the Baie-Comeau Drakkar with the 4th pick of the 2022 QMJHL entry draft. He has had a historic draft year, becoming the first player since Sidney Crosby in 2005 to score 50 goals at 17 years old. Despite producing at over a PPG pace with 51 goals and 31 assists in 68 games this season, Poirier has become one of the more polarizing prospects in this year's draft with the huge question marks how his game will translate at the pro level.

Poirier might be one of the best in the QMJHL at working on his edges. His impressive edgework and his great first steps allow him to blow past defenders while in transition. That being said, his straight-line speed is average which can be troublesome for him since he is a smaller player. Once opponents catch up to his fast starts, he can be rendered rather ineffective while in the offensive zone as his attempts to drive the middle of the ice are quickly thwarted. Improvements in straight line speed could go a long way in deciding if Poirier will be able to make an impact at the next level.

Offensively, we do not think we will surprise anyone by saying that he has an elite shot. His shot is very powerful, and he can pick the corners from almost anywhere in the offensive zone. We like that he is able to use a curl and drag move to change the angle on a lot of his shots which adds a bit of deception to an already lethal release. He is also able to unleash an accurate one timer which he uses a lot from the top of the left circle on the powerplay. Sometimes, we feel that he can get a little trigger happy and take shots from bad angles instead of trying to skate himself into a better position. That being said, there is no question that Poirier has a nose for the net, and he will almost always have a shot first mentality. On the other hand, his playmaking skills are definitely underwhelming. At times we find that he can even struggle to make simple break out passes while in transition and a lot of his passes in the offensive zone are easily deflected by opposing players. He will make the odd, impressive pass, showing that he does have some playmaking ability, but they are few and far between and that makes him a bit of a one-dimensional guy on the offense. While his scoring touch is borderline elite, we do have some questions as to if he will be able to do the same thing with bigger, smarter defenders.

Poirier tends to struggle quite a bit on the defensive side of the puck. Despite having an active stick that can lead to him breaking up a couple passing plays here and there, he lacks the physicality to be effective in one-on-one battles along the wall. He tends to skate away from the puck in the defensive zone and often won't go anywhere below the hashmarks even when his teammates need assistance down low. He will also frequently be too eager to jump into the transition game before making sure that the puck will not be turned over while leaving the zone, leading to odd man chances for the other team. He does not backcheck with any urgency and can often be seen gliding in pursuit of the puck carrier and being unsuccessful in preventing good shot opportunities. We do not think this is due to a lack of compete as he can surprise his opponents with solid body checks from time to time and he is often involved in scrums in front of the net. We think that his poor defense is simply the result of him thinking offense all the time, even while in his own defensive zone. This mindset has simply gotten him into tough spots on the defensive side of the puck one too many times.

Poirier is without a doubt one of the more interesting prospects eligible for this year's draft. Despite having an elite scoring touch for a junior player, we feel that there are simply far too many holes in the other facets of his game, particularly in the defensive zone. At his size, he would need to be an elite skater to have a better chance at success in the NHL and while his edgework is great, his straight-line speed is average. We think that it is likely that he falls into the category of players that are not getting consistent top six minutes at the pro level and that are not made to be playing in a bottom six role. With his elite shot and his accolades, we think an NHL organization will be willing to take a chance on him in the middle to late rounds of the draft.

"Not a draft for me." – NHL Scout, November 2023

"That kid is going to score 60 goals and he's going to get drafted in the 6th round" – NHL Scout (November 2023)

"Almost all the good small players in the NHL are great skaters and he's a below-average skater. Is he the exception to the rule?" – HP Scout Jérôme Bérubé (April 2024)

"Small and can't skate equals no draft for me. Are there outliers to every rule? Yes, but I'm not going use picks trying to find the needle in the haystack that hits." – HP Scout, Mark Edwards, December 2023

112	PLAYER	TEAM	LEAGUE	HEIGHT	WEIGHT	POS	GRADE
	PROCYSZYN, ETHAN	NORTH BAY	OHL	6' 02.25"	190	RC	C

NHLCS	CEILING	FLOOR	HOCKEY SENSE	COMPETE	SKILL	SKATE	MISC
NA-48	6	5	7	7	5	5	7

It wasn't the offensive productive season everyone was looking for from Ethan Procyszyn coming into his second year with the North Bay Battalion after being selected in the first round of the OHL draft in 2022. He put up 36 points in 62 games including 15 goals. However, Procyszyn had limited ice time on one of the top and oldest teams in the Eastern

Conference. He was limited to a more defensive role with some special teams time, but this did show us, even in a limited viewing, his translatable skills to the NHL.

The intelligence keeps him a step ahead of everyone, especially with his size and long strides, which help him keep pace despite his lack of quickness. When you add his willingness to battle along the boards in with his intelligence, especially in the defensive game, you get a bottom six forward who does flash some skill, but mainly plays a solid defensive and transitional game. He plays a strong perimeter game in all three zones and adds some strong abilities to plant himself in front of the net and cover the middle of the neutral zone on the backcheck. Along the wall, Procyszyn can muscle players off the puck and force inside body positioning to win puck battles even if he was second on the puck.

Offensively he does a great job in transition with the puck on his stick in the power game, pushing through defenders and maintaining control of the puck. He is great at controlling the puck on the cycle and on the rush, managing the puck well through contact with his strong skating stance. His hands are not quick and he has a small range with his stick handling, but he can use power moves even though he is better suited creating offense off the cycle and in tight. When in front of the net he can tip passes from the point and not get pushed around by defenders by planting his feet. He also has a strong finishing ability by getting off shots quickly and getting the puck up high in tight with defenders on top of him.

Another strong aspect of Procyszyn's game is his strength on the penalty kill, which should translate to the pro-level. He is patient and does not over commit positionally while being aggressive enough to jump on loose pucks and make puck carriers uncomfortable up high. Procyszyn finishes his checks and works hard on the forecheck cutting off lanes and pressuring defenders. The vision he possesses coming up ice and in the offensive zone are strong as well as his ability to win faceoffs making him a valuable asset as he rises to the professional ranks.

The value Procyszyn provides is as a defensive minded forward who could become a specialist on the penalty kill and is out on the ice in critical situations.

The versatility he provides with his ability to play center and wing is a valuable asset, especially come post season when an extra man who can take draws is important. With his ability to make plays offensively in the dirty areas, he can provide a physical game that would help a team both in the regular season and I the playoffs. He may transition to the wing as he begins his journey to the pro-level and this could allow him to play on the outside and down low more offensively in addition to having a net front presence and not force him back first on the back check. His high intelligence and compete are his strengths.

NR	PLAYER		TEAM	LEAGUE	HEIGHT	WEIGHT	POS	GRADE
NR	PROTAS, ILYA		DES MOINES	USHL	6' 03.5"	184	LW	NI
NHLCS	CEILING	FLOOR	HOCKEY SENSE	COMPETE	SKILL		SKATE	MISC
NA-49	6	4	5	5	5		4	7

Hulking, pass-first winger. Ilya Protas debuted in North America with the Des Moines Buccaneers (USHL) and produced a nice season after a slow start. Pointless and a minus-6 in his first six games, the Belarusian was nearly a point per game the rest of the way (which included a transition to the wing). The Buccaneers have one of the league's most anemic offenses and Protas found himself on the one line that was able to produce for most of the year. On a better team, he may not have been afforded such an opportunity.

At 6'4", 184 pounds, Protas looks pretty lean and strong on the ice, and he acts accordingly. While he did improve his willingness to make contact as the year progressed, his hits pack almost no punch at all. They are mostly just gliding hip bumps that knock him off stride just as much as his opponent. That really highlights one of the biggest flaws in Protas from a physical perspective, he has very poor balance. There is very little physical contact – even when expecting it – that he can withstand without hitting the deck. As such, not only is his physical game weak, but his puck protection and battle ability are severely compromised.

He has a rather long, hip-led stride, but his boots are still quite heavy. His skating is better than it was to start the year, but it's still below average. We like his crossover skating to pull through turns when he really engages his core and drives through his edges, but that doesn't happen nearly enough. There is no start and stop to his game, likely out of necessity.

Ilya's skill level doesn't move the needle, in part because he rarely has the puck on his stick. He throws a lot of pucks away, either because of a lack of confidence or a lack of puck poise. He tends to get rid of the puck in open ice without so much as a stickhandle sometimes. This method of play appears to be a lead cause in his passing accuracy issues. When he does hold onto it, the lack of puck control and one-on-one ability are concerning. On the plus side, his one-touch passing game improved due to just pure volume. When he really concentrates on what he's doing, those passes have a degree of scalability to them. His rarely-used shot does too. He owns a simple, torque-based wrist shot, but he can get a nice bit of power behind it. He only gets about a shot and a half on net per game, which is a very low figure considering his ice time. Even if the shot has some upside, it's going to be tough for it to translate if he can't win puck battles in tight areas. He's not overly coordinated still. A lot of his hands plays require his feet to stop...watching him try to flag down bouncing pucks causes him to lose focus on everything around him. He cannot skate through puck retrievals or loose puck situations, he can only glide into them – and that's a losing proposition. Despite having slightly above average hockey sense, again, the physical development arc is so raw that it compromises the output...as such, even his puck pursuit angles come up flat in forecheck and backcheck situations. Protas is fairly young for this draft class, he has height, and he's productive, so he'll likely go – but the physical and technical development arcs are still so raw and haven't shown enough signs of progression to be worthy of a selection for us.

"He improved over the course of the year, no question. But it's tough to see it right now. Worse than his brother was at the same time." HP Scout, Michael Farkas

109	PLAYER	TEAM	LEAGUE	HEIGHT	WEIGHT	POS	GRADE
	PRIDHAM, JACK	WEST KELOWNA	BCHL	6' 01"	177	RW	C

NHLCS	CEILING	FLOOR	HOCKEY SENSE	COMPETE	SKILL	SKATE	MISC
NA-65	7	4	6	6	6	7	7

A Boston University commit currently playing in the BCHL with the West Kelowna Warriors, Jack Pridham is a power forward who put up 23 goals and 48 points in his rookie season after a strong sophomore season with St. Andrew's College last season. Pridham also elevated his game in the BCHL post season for the Warriors, showing off his clutch abilities as a goal scorer.

As an active forward in all three zones, Pridham provides a deep and aggressive forecheck with the speed to be able to get back into his own zone swiftly on the back check. Pridham is able to use his speed to take away lanes quickly and fill gaps in order to pressure defenders to make a mistake. On the defensive side of the puck, he uses his speed in addition to his size and reach to cover a lot of space. This along with his strong positioning helps him to block shots by taking away both time and space.

On the offensive side of the puck, Pridham proves to be more of a perimeter scorer. He is more of a complimentary rush attacker and is the forward you would prefer not to have the puck entering the zone, but instead as more of an option for a one-timer or cross ice opportunity. Off the cycle is where more of his successful offense is recorded through goals in the slot and with his powerful shot or by setting up teammates in tight spaces.

Despite having a good shot, he does not use it as often as we would like for a goal scorer. This is a part of his game we hope to see develop. On the power play he is a good bumper player as a threat to score from the slot with a quick release on his one-timer while also being able to distribute the puck without delay to his teammates.

Body positioning is a strength of Pridham's game, as he uses his size to shield the puck along the boards and give himself space to maneuver offensively using his smooth skating to his advantage in tight spaces. Off the boards, Pridham will open up his body to receive the puck for better positioning and space which he uses well in the slot to get off his shot in high danger shooting areas. Another strength is that Pridham uses long reach to open himself up to puck receptions and to win puck battles offensively.

As Pridham develops and gains more weight, we expect his strength to increase and as a result this will improve a couple of components in his game. In his skating ability, which is already strong, he will become stronger on his feet and with his already sharp cuts will improve his elusiveness on the cycle and allow him better positioning, passing and shooting options off the cycle. His shot power should increase with his size, especially if he begins leaning into his shots more to add some additional variety as a shooter.

Despite Pridham being a goal scorer, he does fine as a playmaker. His ability to read play development offensively and in transition helps him make accurate cross ice passes. In addition, he makes a lot of passes through traffic up ice hitting his teammates in stride. He has good hands and can quickly evade defenders in tight however, he does not have the ability to consistently beat defenders on the rush.

Pridham is an active forechecker and is engaged overall on every shift. For a player of his size and power forward tendencies, he does not play as chippy or physical as we would want to see. He does engage in front of the net and along the wall but, not to the extent that would elevate his game. Pridham cannot rely solely on his goal scoring and skating to make the jump to the highest level, we would like to see him add a nastier side to his game. This is workable for how he plays the game, as he gets in deep and can get back into position quickly by finishing more of his checks and he can be more aggressive in his board battles so the opportunities for him are there.

The one issue is, again, he plays the perimeter too much and drives the net without the puck but seldom with it. His rush offense would improve greatly with some power move additions as he has the strength and footwork to be able to make pushes to the net with the puck and is better at making outside-inside moves in open space.

He looks to project as a third line forward at the NHL level who plays a strong checking role with scoring ability and a possible second power play option. There is work to be done on his end to fine tune and sharpen some edges to his game but, Pridham is worth a selection in the draft as he has potential, it's only a question of if he refines his game enough to reach it.

31	PLAYER	TEAM	LEAGUE	HEIGHT	WEIGHT	POS	GRADE
	PULKKINEN, JESSE	JYP	FIN	6' 06"	219	LD	B
NHLCS	CEILING	FLOOR	HOCKEY SENSE	COMPETE	SKILL	SKATE	MISC
INT-12	7	4	5	6	7	6	8

Jesse is a raw, towering offensive defenseman that falls into the "unicorn" category of prospect, or the ultra rare category that are one offs in their respective draft classes. He featured arguably the best development-curve out of any draft eligible player over the last two seasons, going from 4 points in 43 games at the U20 Sarju level in his initial draft eligible season to blowing past the U20 level this past year and ultimately ending up in Liiga, where he finished with 38 points in 25 combined regular season and playoff games in U20-Sarju, and 8 points in 29 Liiga games.

With a player that's extremely large, the first area we attempt to hone in on is the tool-kit. In Pulkkinen's case, his fluidity, coordination, dexterity, and peak-power output are further ahead in his physical development than most other players we've seen with his frame, at his age.

What makes Jesse even more interesting is that his physical growth rate is just beginning yet he's already displayed a rare level of natural athleticism. This results in an impressive start-up out of the gate given his size. When he pushes off, his shoulders are both elevated and pushed back, allowing for proper posture. He also featured three-point flexion and knows how to stay on the front of his skates when taking off. When skating in a straight line, there's a decent level of extension within his stride, though there's some room to grow there too. Perhaps the biggest area of note within his skating is regarding his inside and outside edges. He can pivot and shift his weight quickly, and this is very important to him specifically, since he needs to be able to keep up and then shutdown offensively gifted players off the puck.

Some larger defenseman who are still developing their coordination tend to shy away from attempting complicated offensive plays or dynamic plays that require a further range of refinement and control with the puck, yet Pulkkinen seems to carry a rare level of confidence and displays a high level of skill within his handling in each area of the ice.

When he's transitioning between his hands and his skating, he can generate both passing and shooting lane readjustments by incorporating pump fakes, off looks, exaggerated shot fakes, and lateral drag transfers. He can also offset his shot using his hands to rock the puck before transferring between different offensive skills. He has a multitude of ways of breaking down an opposing team from the line and this is further enhanced by his comfort that he's displayed on both operating on his forehand and his backhand.

In terms of his offensive tactics, he typically holds onto the puck to a fault both in his activation through the neutral zone and at the blueline. We like seeing defenseman display confidence and Pulkkinen does that, but he can fail to incorporate his teammates at the right time by over handling, and he can fail to reduce risk at the line by trying high risk plays that can result in odd-man rushes and breakaways going the other way. He systematically likes to break down the first layer by himself and consistently looks to use high slot pick and roll options while attempting to peel off of pressure. He can be overzealous, display tunnel vision, and fail to recognize the more efficient, safer, and smarter play.

This lack of proper puck management can be generalized to all three-zones. Although he's displayed advanced puck retrieving ability and at times can fire tape to tape weakside stretch passes through layers, he can also place himself and the puck in bad spots in his own end or operate with the puck in a window that takes away his breakout options.

There's risk presented within each area of the ice and it's due to this lack of understanding risk that we refer to him as an extremely raw and at times, unstructured defender.

Despite this criticism, Pulkkinen has shown marked improvements in critical areas of his game defensively. When we first evaluated him at the beginning of the season at the U20-level, he would get caught flat-footed and fail to match the urgency of the play, getting drowned out as a result. He didn't understand how to use his leverages to his advantage and he rarely defended on proper angles that would keep opposing players to the outside. Yet, when he moved up to the professional level, he applied his new found intensity on the defensive side of the puck. His motor improved, his pacing subsequently improved, and he became a much more assertive defenseman who started understanding how to close properly on opposing players more often.

As a result, his transitional defense started to hold more regularly and he became a stick pressing force in tight to the net. He projects to be able to box out players in the slot and crease area at a very high level, and he also projects to be able to dominate board battles down low once he physically finishes developing. It's not just because of his frame either, it's due to his hand speed and understanding of stick positioning.

Pulkkinen is a skating conundrum. On the one hand, he's a monster of a defender who's been gifted with a set of soft hands and a fluid skating base that merges with a take over mentality and a plus level skill-set in each area. He can look and operate like a dynamic 4th forward when activating into the rush on one sequence, yet on another look like a shutdown defenseman who uses his impressive tool-kit to overwhelm opposing forwards. He can score highlight reel goals on the backing of his impressive wrist-shot, stretch the length of the ice and fire technical passes, yet physically dominate. There is no other defenseman available in this class who can take over with a finesse oriented offense, before switching to a physically imposing shutdown style, or even a puck moving one when required.

On the other hand, you have a raw defender who largely stayed in an experimentation mode regardless of where he played. What this meant was that we saw a unique player, make truly rare plays that would blow you away and show a level of sophistication that displays a real sense for the game, but then we also watched a player who failed to understand risk at critical times in critical games, and a player who failed to understand how to optimize his play by incorporating his teammates at the rate you typically want to see at this stage in their development.

Regardless of his inefficient play at times and his occasional defensive lapses, Pulkkinen is a player who transformed his approach on the ice when he left the U20 circuit and joined Liiga. It's extremely rare to find a high caliber defenseman who can skate like he does, has the skill set that he possesses, all while consistently showing pacing improvements in his own end of the rink. If he can learn to leverage his offensive advantages by relying less on his 1-on-1 instincts and more on his adaptable vision, then he can be an indispensable defenseman on the ice, who's capable of taking games over, while displaying a considerable presence.

The on-ice mentality of this player really matters. Some of you are probably wondering what the delay is in Elmer Soderblom's development; as an example of a larger player like Pulkkinen needing time. For us, it comes down to recognizing how dominant a player can be with the gifts they possess and sometimes Soderblom doesn't recognize it. That's not the case here. Pulkkinen does and it's one of the reasons his development has accelerated to the point that it already has. It's also one of the primary reasons that we feel he can continue to refine his game into a truly unique top-4 defenseman at the NHL level. Our ranking tries to balance the potential of the player, while also recognizing that there are several variables that need to go right for him in order to successfully translate his game.

"He reminds me a bit of Ryan Sproul." – NHL Scout, December 2023

"He's one of the most unique players I've ever scouted. He can blow you away on one sequence and then leave you puzzled on the next, but I'm betting on him figuring things out once he's forced to play a more structured game." – HP Scout, Brad Allen

"If he never plays, it's going to be a result of him never understanding how to reduce his rate of risk with how he looks to generate plays." – HP Scout, Brad Allen

"My first ever viewing of him was not good. He made a ton of dumb mistakes. I was shocked when I watched three pro games as my next three viewings and he was like a different player. The gap between my positive views and poor views was large. Very high ceiling player who makes some jaw dropping great plays and than will mess up the simple stuff defending out of nowhere." – HP Scout, Mark Edwards, March 2024

"Combine interview feedback was just ok. Not anything that would hamper him being picked, but in a group where scouts raved about so many kids, his feedback just was just ok." – HP Scout, Mark Edwards, June 2024

NR	PLAYER	TEAM	LEAGUE	HEIGHT	WEIGHT	POS	GRADE
	RALPH, COLIN	SHATTUCK	HIGH-MN	6' 04"	216	LD	C
NHLCS	CEILING	FLOOR	HOCKEY SENSE	COMPETE	SKILL	SKATE	MISC
NA-30	6	5	5	5	5	6	7

Colin Ralph is a Maple Grove, MN native who has taken a rather unusual track thus far in his hockey career for someone from Minnesota. Ralph played his youth and bantam hockey in the Maple Grove, MN area but moved to the St. Louis area where he played for the CarShield U16 AAA team in 21-22 before moving to Shattuck St, Mary's for the last two years where he has been a staple on the blueline for the U18 Prep Team. Ralph put up good numbers from the back end this season with 8 goals and 58 assists in 57 games while getting a good amount of Power Play time throughout the season. Ralph was drafted by Dubuque in the 4th Round of the 2023 USHL Phase 2 Draft but decided to return to Shattuck this season. As a late 05' playing US Prep School and given his size, Ralph was able to dominate in a lot of the games we saw and while the Shattuck Prep team plays somewhat of an easy schedule, we did like Colin's game against some of the tougher opponents we saw him against such as Culver Academy and St. Andrews College. Ralph saw two games with Dubuque at the end of this season where we thought he acclimated himself well to the speed of the USHL and played an effective game by making quick reads and moving pucks quickly and accurately. Colin played with a good defensive gap in the neutral zone and used his reach well against the rush to disrupt plays.

Colin is a raw, rangy defenseman that is able to use his reach and good 4-way mobility to his advantage in defending the rush and take away time and space. While Colin has really good edges and mobility in his skating, he needs to continue to work on his straight-line speed and explosiveness. Where Colin sometimes struggled defensively in our views was using his size and frame effectively in 1 v 1 defensive situations when along the walls, in the corners or around his own net. At times we saw Colin struggle to contain skilled forwards when defending on an island due to his lack of body positioning or physicality in the hard areas of the ice. Colin uses his range well at the offensive blueline to keep pucks in the offensive zone, he is able to cover a lot of ice with his reach and mobility in order to keep plays alive in the offensive end. He possesses a quick release from the top of the zone that is able to get through to the net and the velocity on his release is a threat to score from range but he liked to shoot to generate chances more from the point than to score, which was a skill he excelled at in our viewings. While Colin doesn't project as a top PP guy at the next level, he did show the ability to use his mobility and puck skills to pull opponents and open up some lanes from the top of the zone. Colin is a long-term prospect for whichever team drafts him this June but his path going forward fits that plan well. Ralph will play next year for Dubuque (USHL) before playing his college hockey at St. Cloud State in 2025. It's hard to ignore some of the physical attributes Colin has that would translate well to the next level. Given Colin's range, mobility and athleticism, Colin projects as a primarily shutdown defenseman at the next level if he can continue to iron out some of the inefficient parts of his game in the next couple of years.

NR	PLAYER	TEAM	LEAGUE	HEIGHT	WEIGHT	POS	GRADE
	REBER, JAMIRO	HV-71 JR	SWE JR	5' 09.75"	168	LC	C
NHLCS	CEILING	FLOOR	HOCKEY SENSE	COMPETE	SKILL	SKATE	MISC
INT-115	5	3	6	5	5	7	4

Reber came over from Switzerland this season to play in Sweden's junior league with HV71. He had a decent season, averaging just under a point per game with 39 points in 46 games. He also played for the Swiss U18 National Team at various events during the year, for example, he made a good impression at the latest Hlinka Gretzky tournament in August.

Reber can play center and on the wing. He's a good skater with good agility and explosiveness. He's at his best in transition and off the rush. He can make defenders back down with his speed and has the speed to challenge them with his outside speed. He's not much of a shooter; he won't score much from distance. He needs to get closer to the net to score goals at even-strength. He'll need to get stronger to be able to insert himself in those spaces at the pro level. Physically immature, he's also one of the youngest in this draft class due to his September birthday.

Reber sees the ice well and is an above-average passer. Outside of his speed, his playmaking is his best quality. One issue we have with him is that he's not much of a factor offensively when cycling the puck in the offensive zone. His puck-protection is too weak, making it easy to take pucks away from him. That doesn't help us when trying to translate his game to the NHL, where there is a lot more a) physicality b) off-the-cycle play compared to the European game. However, he's a smart player. With his good hockey IQ, speed and anticipation, he has value defensively and on the PK.

There are some good qualities with this player, but we feel that his skill level is not high enough to compensate for some of his other flaws and the lack of NHL projectable's. We see him as a player who will have a better career in Europe than in the NHL. There are some similarities between his game and that of former Maple Leafs' draft pick and ex-QMJHLer Mikhail Abramov, who has not been able to establish himself as an important player in the American Hockey League over the last 3 seasons. We had more time for Abramov in his draft year than we do with Reber, but it's also a clear example that players of their shared caliber need to bring something special to the table to make it; we just don't see it with Reber.

NR	PLAYER	TEAM	LEAGUE	HEIGHT	WEIGHT	POS	GRADE
	REPCIK, PETER	DRUMMONDVILLE	QMJHL	5' 11.75"	184	LC	NI
NHLCS	CEILING	FLOOR	HOCKEY SENSE	COMPETE	SKILL	SKATE	MISC
NA-191	4	4	5	6	5	5	5

Repcik is a 3rd-year draft eligible who has had quite an eventful junior career since coming over from Slovakia. He first joined the Lethbridge Hurricanes of the WHL in 2021, was picked up off waivers by the Cape Breton Eagles of the QMJHL, then traded to the Charlottetown Islanders before being traded again last summer to the Drummondville Voltigeurs. He has been a standout performer for Team Slovakia at the last two World Junior Hockey Championships.

Playing a hard, honest game at both ends of the ice, he's the kind of player any coaches love to have on their team. He can play all three forward positions, but will likely be a winger at the pro level. He took fewer faceoffs in the second half of the season, as his efficiency decreased (well under 50%). He can be an asset on the PK unit. At the junior level, he can even be an asset on the power play with both his shot and play in front of the net. However, for the pro game, we think that his main assets will be his defensive game and compete level; we don't project him as an offensive player moving forward. He has a good shot, but the rest of his tools fall more on the average side, like his hands and vision. In addition, his skating is a bit weak, his speed is only average, his feet are a bit heavy, and he lacks explosiveness. We like the player, but he's also older and more physically mature than most of the other players in this draft. The growth in his game is a lot more advanced than others', which limits the room he still has for development to make further improvements over the next couple of years.

Repcik could end up becoming a good pro in the AHL or Europe, but for the NHL, it's a tough mountain to climb. However, he does have the work ethic to possibly overcome these hurdles. If he was a dominant player in the QMJHL, he would give us more reasons to put our trust in him. While this year was by far his best year in the league, it was only a good or slightly above-average performance, far from a great one.

51	PLAYER	TEAM	LEAGUE	HEIGHT	WEIGHT	POS	GRADE
	RITCHIE, RYDER	PRINCE ALBERT	WHL	6' 00.25"	177	RW	C+

NHLCS	CEILING	FLOOR	HOCKEY SENSE	COMPETE	SKILL	SKATE	MISC
NA-19	7	4	4	4	7	7	6

The former 1st round pick in the WHL bantam draft had a great rookie season last year with 55 points in 61 games, winning the rookie of the year in the WHL. This season, it was a year with up & down for Ritchie. He started the summer strongly, winning the gold at the Hlinka Gretzky Cup with 9 points in 5 games. He started the season fine in the Raiders with 23 points in his 1st 19 games. He struggled with only 9 points In the next 18 games, ultimately finishing the season with 44 points in 47 games. Going from 0.9 pts/game in his rookie season to 0.94 pts/game in his draft season was a bit underwhelming. He then had a strong playoff with 7 points in 5 games against a very good Saskatoon team, registering at least one point in each game of the series.

At the U18 tournament after the season, Ritchie won another gold medal with Canada. After a slow start in the tournament with below average puck management, Ritchie found his way back in Canada's top 6 and finished the event with 8 points in 7 games, 4th on the team. He stepped up in important moments, with two points in the semi-finals game and two points in the goal medal game, including a beautiful short-side snipe to open the scoring for Canada and helped them get back in the game against USA.

Offensively, Ritchie's strength is how dynamic he is in transition. With the puck, he's a dynamic skater, who explodes right away and uses linear crossovers to build great speed. He gets off the wall, attack the inside, and overall is one of the best skaters in the draft. He loves to swing in the neutral zone, build speed off-puck, and acquires it at top speed. He has quick puck skills, and can beat defender one-on-one, either with outside speed or with quick move in the triangle under the stick. He has a good wrist-shot that he can fire quickly, surprising the goaltender many times on his goals this season. On breakaways or in-tight around the net, he owns good poise to use his puck skills and beat goaltenders. Sometimes, his shot selection can improve. In terms of playmaking, Ritchie can make some great passes when he holds the puck and creates offensive advantages by beating defender before passing. We'd like to see him improve his quick/one-touch passing when needed.

In the offensive zone, the same skills show up. He's dynamic to climb the offensive wall and create from there. When he gets on the inside, his release is dangerous. On the man advantage, Ritchie run the PP from the half-wall, some games from his strong side and others from his one-timer side.

Defensively, Ritchie needs to improve his two-way play. Positively, he sprints hard with his speed on the forecheck and on the tracking and covers a lot of ice quickly. After that, Ritchie needs to generate more stops by creating contact (mostly using more stickcheck and stopping in battle when needed). He tends to turn too much in certain situations.

Overall, it will be interesting to see the development of Ritchie in the future. His overall production in the WHL regular season was under the expectations. There's no doubt that he has high upside with how dynamic he is in his skating and puck skills. If his puck management/decisions, two-way play and consistency can improve, he had the upside to explode and be a good offensive player from this draft.

"Selfish player." – NHL Scout, November 2023

"Skilled player who needs to learn how to work." – NHL Scout, January 2024

"I saw him recently...what a waste of time. No idea how he is ranked so high." – NHL Scout, April 2024

"Both Ritchie and Marques turn me off with their body language." - NHL Scout, April 2024

"He didn't get any better this year." - NHL Scout, April 2024

"I have him and Marques grouped together. Talented yeah, but I don't want either of them on my team." - NHL Scout, April 2024

"I see him ranked high and I don't get it. I do not see f***ing first rounder for him." - NHL Scout, May 2024

"Really good player. Great skill. He needs to mature his game a bit but he is really talented." - NHL Scout, May 2024

"He drove me crazy at the U18." - NHL Scout, May 2024

"I have never been a big fan and he didn't change my mind at the U18." - HP Scout, Mark Edwards, June 2024

41	PLAYER	TEAM	LEAGUE	HEIGHT	WEIGHT	POS	GRADE
	ROBERTS, COLTON	VANCOUVER	WHL	6' 03.75"	204	RD	B
NHLCS	CEILING	FLOOR	HOCKEY SENSE	COMPETE	SKILL	SKATE	MISC
NA-36	5	6	7	6	5	5	7

The 6'4" right-handed defenseman had a strong season for the Vancouver Giants with 7 goals and 27 points in 62 games, ranking 5th in points for U18 defenseman in the WHL. Roberts played in the Giants' top 4, averaging more than 21 minutes a night over the season. He played on both special units, including some times on the man advantage, either as the PP QB or on his one-timer half-wall.

Roberts moves the puck well with smooth puck skills and smart passing. On the defensive zone breakout retrievals, Roberts combines multiple variations of skills to be efficient. He has good pre-scanning habits, allowing him to move the puck quickly when possible. On 50/50 race retrievals, he does a great job using his size to control the area of puck, shield the opposing player and gain body positioning. He's able to lift his eyes and put the puck on his blade in a position to make and find the next play with ease. In neutral zone transition, Roberts is smooth, combined deception, smooth puck skills and decent edge work to invite pressure and move the puck. In the offensive zone, Roberts contributes positively to the offense. He can activate off the blueline with smart timing and shows good vision the find open forwards, just like he did on his assist at the CHL top prospects game. He owns a solid shot from the point that he can use smartly, shooting for open sticks or when there's a lot of traffic in front.

Defensively, Roberts does a good job being physical in the defensive zone without getting out of position. He hits/ immobilize opposing forwards down low and box out well in front of his net. His small aera footwork when defending against quick forwards and quick change of direction is an area he'll need to work on. When defending the rush, Roberts has good habits. He protects the inside well by retrieving inside dots, his posture and his stickwork are good. Tightening his gap, killing play earlier and more aggressively are areas he'll need to improve on to optimize his rush defense abilities.

Roberts plays a complete game with few glaring weaknesses, but no real high-end dominant strength either. His overall skating is smooth, but he definitely needs to add power in his skating movements. He moves the puck efficiently and can generate offense, he is physical and defends well. With his size, good IQ and all-around play, Roberts has strong changes of contributing in a bottom paring role eventually at the NHL level. To become a top 4 defenseman, Roberts will need to make sure one or two aspects of his game become dominant/higher than average to standout.

" Big defenseman who plays a complete game overall. If he can add layers to his game, I love his upside.". - HP Scout, Tim Archambault, February 2024

" I like him. Not crazy about his skating but otherwise he is a pretty solid player." - HP Scout, Mark Edwards, May 2024

NR	PLAYER		TEAM	LEAGUE	HEIGHT	WEIGHT	POS	GRADE
	ROED, NOLAN		WHITE BEAR LAKE	HIGH-MN	5' 10.5"	186	LC	C
NHLCS	CEILING	FLOOR	HOCKEY SENSE	COMPETE	SKILL		SKATE	MISC
NA-121	5	5	5	7	5		7	5

Nolan is the middle of three brothers from White Bear Lake, MN. Nolan's older brother Lleyton just finished his freshman year at Bemidji State. Nolan split his season between Tri-City (USHL) and White Bear Lake High School where he had a dominate season for the Bears, scoring 33 goals and 25 assists in 30 games. Nolan showed decent production with Tri-City as well, primarily playing middle six minutes, scoring 6 goals and 9 assists in 25 games. Roed showed the ability to elevate his game in the Clark Cup playoffs for Tri-City where he scored 4 goals and 2 assists in 6 games for the Storm. Roed's play translating well in junior and in the playoffs certainly helps his draft stock.

Roed doesn't have imposing size at around 5.10 but he is a strong player that wins battles by outworking opponents and utilizing leverage well to gain position on his opponents. Roed does a good job of getting over top of pucks and under sticks to win battles at both ends of the ice. Paired with his compete rate is an explosive skater that gets to a fast clip quickly and goes to the net hard consistently. While his speed allowed him to dominate games at the high school level, it was equally effective in the USHL this season. In many high school games, teams would key on Nolan, being one of the only big offensive threats on the roster and Roed was still often able to drive offense for his team. We saw Roed live a few time this year but his play in the Sectional Final vs Hill Murray stood out to us. Hill Murray is a very sound defensive team that did everything they could to contain Roed and he was still dominant in that game, lifting his team to a 3-0 win to get to the Minnesota State Tournament. What makes Roed an effective threat offensively is the speed in which he is able to make plays with the puck, he doesn't need to slow his pace to snap passes to teammates or attack lanes with the puck to drive the net. There were instances where some of the plays with the puck Roed made could best be categorized as high risk plays that might not fly at the upper levels, especially in the wrong areas of the ice, so he will need to learn to make the simple play rather than the high wire act he can sometimes default to. But it's better to have the skill to make those plays and have to learn to reign it in at times than not have it at all.

Nolan possesses a consistent work ethic at both ends and plays with a ton of energy, which allows him to positively affect games even if he doesn't end up on the score sheet. The speed he plays with opens up ice for his teammates and his ability to win pucks and create turnovers on the forecheck create possessions for his team. Roed is committed to St. Cloud St. to play his college hockey but will likely spend at least a year in junior hockey before heading to St. Cloud.

74	PLAYER		TEAM	LEAGUE	HEIGHT	WEIGHT	POS	GRADE
	RUOHONEN, HEIKKI		K-ESPOO JR.	FIN-JR	6' 01"	196	LC	C
NHLCS	CEILING	FLOOR	HOCKEY SENSE	COMPETE	SKILL		SKATE	MISC
INT-35	5	5	6	7	5		7	6

Ruohonen is a big-size center who played this past season with Kiekko-Espoo, where he had 47 points in 37 games. He finished first in points per game (1.27) among U18 players in the Finland junior league. He also played internationally during the season, saving his best performance for the U18 World Hockey Championship in April, as he recorded a point in each game. He was selected 1st overall in the USHL Draft (Phase-2) by Dubuque, and will play there next season before going to Harvard University in 2025-2026.

Despite how good his stats looked in Finland this year, as far as projecting him for the NHL, he's not a skilled offensive player. He doesn't have the talent to be a high point-producer, but does have good intangibles that could make him a 3rd or 4th liner in the NHL at some point. He lacks the stickhandling skills and hands of a top-6 forward in the NHL. However, we love the energy that he plays with. He has really strong physicality and is capable of dishing big hits along the wall and on the forecheck. He plays a North American game, and his game will look good on small ice. He is a good skater with a nice explosiveness within his stride. Strong on his skates and tough to knock down, he has good edgework, can abruptly change directions, and also uses his edges down low in puck-protection sequences, which makes it tough to counter him. Positionally, he's a center, but with his forechecking physical game we could see him move to the wing at the pro level. He's also not an overly creative player with the puck, which is another argument in favour of the wing. His faceoff prowess does add some value to him staying down the middle, however. Playing a simple but powerful north-south game, he's good at gaining inside leverage on players. He creates offensive chances with his net presence, plays down low, and plays off the rush with help from his speed and good shot.

While not necessarily a flashy player, NHL teams will love his intangibles, skating, physicality and the fact that he's coming to play in North America. His presence in the USHL next season followed by Harvard for up to 4 years gives him a maximum of 5 years of development, which a lot of teams are going to like. We think he's likely to go between rounds 3 and 5 at the draft, as a versatile forward who can play on a 4th (possibly 3rd) line in the NHL with penalty-killing value.

NR	PLAYER	TEAM	LEAGUE	HEIGHT	WEIGHT	POS	GRADE
	SAARELAINEN, JOONA	KALPA JR.	FIN-JR	5'09"	183	LC	NI
NHLCS	CEILING	FLOOR	HOCKEY SENSE	COMPETE	SKILL	SKATE	MISC
INT 49	4	4	5	6	5	5	4

Saarelainen had a solid season in the Finland junior league this year, with 36 points in 41 games. He also captained the national U18 team in various events throughout the season, including the Hlinka-Gretzky Cup in August.

He's an undersized center, but one with a very high compete level. He's strong on his skates, using his low center of gravity well. He does his best work down low and is strong on the puck. Those are not qualities you necessarily expect from a 5'09" center, but they are legit when it comes to Saarelainen. We like his stickhandling skills in traffic as well; he is effective down low and below the net. He's good in small areas. He likes to drive the net, winning puck battles in the corners and bringing the puck to the net. He's like a 5'09" power-forward on the ice with the way he plays.

However, how many 5'09" power-forwards are in the NHL? We love his game and the way he competes, but his game doesn't really translate to the NHL. If he was an explosive skater (he currently isn't), if his skill level was better (it's just okay), he would have better chances. There's also nothing that stands out with his offensive skillset. Much of his success is based on his compete level and ability to get inside despite his size. He does have a chance as a 4th-line energy player because of his work rate, bulldog mentality and penalty-killing potential, but despite all of this, it's far from being a sure thing.

We envision Saarelainen as a solid player in the Liiga in the future. While he may earn some NHL games by outworking his competition, we believe his long-term future lies in Europe rather than the NHL.

7	PLAYER	TEAM	LEAGUE	HEIGHT	WEIGHT	POS	GRADE
	SAARINEN, KIM	HPK JR.	FIN-JR	6' 04.25"	176	G	C

NHLCS	CEILING	FLOOR	HOCKEY SENSE	COMPETE	SKILL	SKATE	MISC
INT -3	7	4	7	6	6	5	6

Admittedly, there's some bias when determining Saarinen's game because we aren't big fans of his currant set stance and how he presents in net. He folds himself inwards and presents a narrower frame than he actually has. He's not a heavier set goalie, and there's a ton of room for him to fill out, so we had to take that into consideration. Due to his lack of physical development, he can also appear off balance, by leaning forward past his centerline. Despite how he appears in net, no one can take away his accolades this season.

His positioning is sound and he's one of the better goalies available in this class at recognizing when he needs to overlap with his post in order to take away short side shots in tight to his net. When breaking down his overlap technique, he uses a modified blocker down position where he leans over the top of his centerline and keeps the paddle flat to the ice with his blocker acting as the buffer between his five-hole. It's a unique technique that's specific to bigger goalies like himself but not one that can be used by smaller goalies. Lastly, we think he applies more unorthodox post integration and overlaps a bit differently than most other draft eligible goalies because he has difficulty with a standard RVH position at times, specifically on plays where he's getting cut on aggressively and he needs to transition from a set stance into the RVH on an angle. Part of this can be attributed to his skating base as well. His edgework allows him to hold the net but he has difficulty rotating his body through his skates depending on the play. To compensate, he cheats by not even attempting to go into a RVH position during post to post plays a lot of the time. He can get away with that at the U20-Sarju level, he won't be getting away with it once he hits Liiga full time in the coming seasons.

Despite having some difficulty with his post integration into a RVH, he's one of the more gifted goalies at moving off his centerline, and this further enhances his ability to lean into shots that are elevated and when you combine it with his positional awareness of when to overlap with his post, it projects him to be difficult to beat him specifically on sharper angle shots.

He's also projects to handle lateral in tight shots better than most other draft eligible goalies. He's athletically gifted, and he can transfer post to post rapidly and has come away with some very impressive saves off of his lateral transitions this season. One aspect of his lateral transfers when he goes from a set stance into either a butterfly or an extended save type, is that he knows how to match the immediacy of the shot. If the shot is coming off the stick in a hurry, he will extend explosively and break his technique in order to stay out-front of the puck.

Another strength of Saarinen's game is his rebound control for this age group. Typically, we don't mention rebound control if it's a weaker area since it's very common in goalies that are Saarinen's age, but we will bring it up here because it's ahead of a lot of other goalies in this class. This goes back to the ability to manipulate his centerline quickly. When he's actively engaging in his butterfly, he's rarely stiff or rigid and instead dynamically rolls into the shot so that he can absorb it easier. He's also very good at squeezing shots without them trickling out on point blank sequences, or at least in our viewings.

His centerline manipulation extends to how well he can see through or past screens. For a larger goalie, he can see around screens rapidly before transitioning his frame into the necessary space to block a shot that's labeled for the opposite side that he initially looked around the screen from.

Kim is consistent at sealing his blocker over his pad on shots targeted on his blocker side, even when fully extending. He has a good amount of hip dexterity as well, so when he is extending both his leg and arm fully, he can remain on balance. When he goes off balance, its usually the result of his skating base letting him down. It's not fair to say he's a bad skater, but more an uneven one. He can push off from a set stance or relaxed stance fluidly, which means on wider stretch passes or weak side passes he can go post to post but offensive plays that force him to move rapidly in a smaller area can throw him off balance. This comes down to his footwork within his micro-shuffling. He's a powerful goalie, but the skating base isn't nimble by any stretch and needs improvement.

Saarinen has a good sense of timing when he needs to drop from his relaxed tall stance when looking over a screen into his butterfly. He can be janky and unorthodox in some of his movements, such as when he's attempting to integrate rapidly into his posts, but when it comes to transitioning through his stances and through and backout of his butterfly, he's surprisingly fluid.

Like some other larger goalies who are first year eligible, Saarinen can be overly reliant on his size while failing to manage his depth correctly depending on the distance of the shot. On some of his worst goals against this season, he had a tendency to simply play too deep in his net, which caused shots to sail over him.

Another issue is one that he shares with Kempf, which is that his glove hand can be finicky and he was susceptible to glove shots that were targeted low. Unlike Kempf who had better success with high shots even though we think long term it projects to be one of his weaker links, Saarinen had difficulty with high shots as well. He has a tendency to reach for pucks on his glove side, as opposed to showing the necessary rotation at times. There were games where his glove would hold but there were too many viewings where pucks would pop out of his glove on what should have been a routine save. We would make an argument that his glove appears to project as slightly below average and it's one of the primary reasons we kept him a bit further back in our ranking, relative to what we feel is the top end of this class.

"He's not the most technical goalie but a whole lot of what he does can be modified and the base is impressive." - HP Scout, Brad Allen

"He grew on me as the season progressed and showed some better instincts that weren't present in my initial viewings. Speaking to growth, there's a ton of physical development left for him to do and that means there's more untapped potential here." - HP Scout, Brad Allen

35	PLAYER	TEAM	LEAGUE	HEIGHT	WEIGHT	POS	GRADE
	SAHLIN WALLENIUS, LEO	VAXJO JR.	SWE-JR	6' 00"	180	LD	B

NHLCS	CEILING	FLOOR	HOCKEY SENSE	COMPETE	SKILL	SKATE	MISC
INT-7	6	5	7	5	6	6	5

Leo Sahlin Wallenius paced his junior club in assists (31), points (42), and plus/minus (+20) in 43 games with the Växjö Lakers in Sweden's top U20 junior circuit. Sahlin Wallenius (LSW, going forward) is an extremely nimble defenseman who exhibits great skating, technical skills, and hockey sense. This is a player that plays the game enthusiastically on his toes. He has extremely quick feet, high-end foot churn, and can really dance around the ice.

Despite his agile footwork, we are a little troubled by his overall athleticism package. The hip mobility and churn aren't really there. He doesn't really get off his center line and drive through turns. Some skaters really dig into the ice and rev it up from a power perspective – getting a good deep knee bend, strong three-point flexion, and ultimately driving through an extended stride. LSW almost glides above the ice, so to speak. Now, maybe he'll add some flexibility and mobility, where warranted, as part of the strength development process to enhance his skating power. He's only listed at 5'11", 176 pounds right now – he looks quite thin on the ice still. And again, this isn't to say he isn't fast, he's fast. His foot work and churn are really good, the lateral mobility is excellent. But looking at it from the perspective of making quick escapes via swinging the net or even getting inside leverage on bigger pro opponents - what's going to happen near the paint when the line between successful defense and unsuccessful defense gets really thin. Also, even from a pass-catching perspective - really advanced puck catchers can sort of separate the top half of their body from the lower half as part of the in-stride pass-catching process and it creates a speed advantage. There isn't a lot of evidence that LSW has that going for him. What's more is that he also hasn't played any pro games in Sweden yet. Now, he is playing at the J20 level, so that's a bit of a step up, of course…but, also, about a quarter of that league is 2006 or 2007 births anyhow, so it's not as if he's punching up too much from that perspective.

Though it's easy to get caught up in his skating, LSW's best asset might be his hockey sense. This is a smart player who anticipates well all over the ice. Not only can he map out the game and execute, but he has a processor that allows him to problem solve on the fly. He plays a really competitive game, but has composure, puck poise, and a high panic threshold even when things get dicey. He mixes the right balance of holding the puck against pressure and pulling the rip cord to get the puck out of danger safely.

Defensively, he's really good in rush absorption situations. His gaps are consistent and well thought out. The timing with which he executes defensively is superb. LSW does like to try to play defense while going forward because he doesn't want to have to sit back on his heels and deal with the lowest layer of his defensive zone if he doesn't have to. He does it smartly, but whenever a player prefers to play defense like this, the misses can look really embarrassing. That said, he does a nice job of getting a piece of players physically if he fails with a pokecheck. His stick work is backed by his body and his triangle is seldom taken advantage of as a result. There's a willingness to box out and sort of pinball around (in a calculated manner) physically. A prime example of that was against Canada in the semis of the U18 World Juniors – he came out firing with a double-barrel in that one. There's still more that's in front of him that he can do to alleviate some concerns. In turn-and-go defense situations, he still needs to close off the lane to the net on the attacker. Good attackers are taking a proper arc towards the net and a good defender needs to make initial contact and then beat the attacker to a contested point on that arc. LSW doesn't consistently do that. And given that defense is the converse of offense, we see this demonstrated on his own rushes as well. He'll have a step on a defender, and the move should be to "get corner" on him to disable his hands and stick, while still keeping his own strong side free. But LSW can be escorted off his arc or not challenge for that ice meaningfully at all. But he shows a consistent willingness to compete, even if he's at a physical disadvantage and that's a good sign that he'll be able to adapt his way into something useful in time.

The ranking gets a little tricky when we have to factor in where he can be slotted in an NHL lineup. The difference in an opinion about which parts of his game are scalable will create a sizeable gap in where he's listed from scout to scout.

" Mid rounder." - NHL Scout, January 2024

" Just made it into my top 32." - NHL Scout, January 2024

" Another overrated player not even on my list." - NHL Scout, March 2024

" Good skater and has good skill but that league is so overrated I don't really like drafting players out of it." - NHL Scout, May 2024

" I don't know if he's on our list…if he is it's pretty late." - NHL Scout, June 2024

" His tool-kit terrifies me, but he did look better when I stood next to him and that helped ease my concerns a little bit." -HP Scout, Brad Allen (May 2024)

" He's one of the smartest players in this class." - HP Scout, Brad Allen (May 2024)

" I'm really impressed by this player. Wish he was a better athlete, but otherwise he offers a lot. I'd start looking at him in the middle part of the 1st round, personally." HP Scout, Michael Farkas

"One of our scouts will have bragging rights if he hits. The rest of us had him ranked much later."
- HP Scout, Mark Edwards, May 2024

85	PLAYER	TEAM	LEAGUE	HEIGHT	WEIGHT	POS	GRADE
	SATAN, MIROSLAV	BRATISLAVA JR.	SVK-JR	6'07"	190	LC	C

NHLCS	CEILING	FLOOR	HOCKEY SENSE	COMPETE	SKILL	SKATE	MISC
INT-51	6	4	5	5	5	6	8

Satan is the son of former NHLer Miroslav Satan, who currently serves as the head of Slovakia hockey. Satan Jr. played this past season in Slovakia's junior league, recording 30 points in 26 games. He was also drafted in the USHL by the Chicago Steel, providing him with an option to compete in a higher-level league if he chooses to pursue the NCAA route later on.

He's a long-term project due to his frame, currently listed at 6'07" and 190 pounds. He is expected to reach around 230 pounds in his 20s. While he didn't stand out as much of a prospect last year, he's slowly becoming more coordinated, showing glimpses of his potential. Skating is often challenging for players with such large frames, but Satan's is improving, with room for added explosiveness as he gains strength. He shows surprising agility for a 6'07" player, offering promise for his development. His strengths include his play in front of the net and along the wall, where his size makes him difficult to handle. While he's not yet a mean, punishing force on the ice, his imposing frame alone poses annoyances for opposing defenders in puck battles down low.

He could become, if everything goes well, a good player in playoff hockey that NHL teams want on their bottom 6. He's so raw that maybe there's more offense than we give him credit for. As of now, he has shown us that he can score goals from around the net, but we would like to see more playmaking out of him, which would help his projection. Given his size, raw potential, and bloodline, we expect him to hear his name in the mid or late rounds of the draft. A long-term project; the team that selects him will have to be patient with him. Opting to remain in Europe or pursuing the NCAA route would provide him with the best development path, allowing him time to maximize his potential.

6	PLAYER	TEAM	LEAGUE	HEIGHT	WEIGHT	POS	GRADE
	SENNECKE, BECKETT	OSHAWA	OHL	6'02.25"	177	RW	A

NHLCS	CEILING	FLOOR	HOCKEY SENSE	COMPETE	SKILL	SKATE	MISC
NA-13	9	7	8	6	8	7	6

Sennecke, selected 8th overall by Oshawa in the 2022 OHL Draft, has undergone significant growth since then (from 5'10" to 6'03"). While this is obviously a positive, it has also brought him challenges, resulting in some ups and downs in his performance. He has had to dedicate considerable effort to his physical strength, as he remains physically immature even today. Improving his overall athleticism has proven demanding as he grows.

He finished the year with 68 points in 63 games, which is a decent output. He finished strong, with 29 points in his last 21 games. In the playoffs, he improved even further with 22 points in 16 games. This was a significant change from the 39 points in 42 games he had until the start of February when he turned the corner.

Once he realized that playing good defense would lead to more offense, this seemed to be when it all clicked for him. His two-way game was always a work in progress, but once his off-the-puck game started being more noticeable, his production improved. We started seeing more effort from him away from the puck, such as when backchecking. He always had the anticipation to read plays well, or the ability to steal pucks with his long stick while backchecking, but could not do this efficiently or consistently if his effort level was absent. Once he started putting this into place, he saw his results improve, and there's nothing better for a player's psyche than when they make adjustments to their game and see results. Now that he has a better understanding of his off-the-puck game, he added another dimension to his game and long-term potential.

Offensively, Sennecke can be unpredictable on the ice, as he can create offense in different ways. He can be tough to defend because he's adept at changing directions quickly, using deception well in the process. He can also use different skating routes and is not afraid to cut inside with the puck. With the puck on his stick, he can be tricky to defend, as he's got very good puck poise and doesn't sell if he's going to shoot or pass the puck. Hiding his intentions well on the power play at the point or half wall, he incorporates hesitation moves to freeze his opponents for a fraction of a second, opening a shooting or passing lane in the process. He's good at extending his reach and swinging a pass to the other side of the ice. He's as good a shooter as he is a passer. He can beat you with his hands, his shot, his passing and his underdeveloped power game at the net. He's a creative player offensively, thinking the game quickly with one-touch passes on his forehand or backhand to create chances for his teammates. With the puck, he really likes to use the toe drag move one-on-one, changing the angle on his shot and making good use of his long reach when doing so. His reach is also useful in one-on-one play in tight spaces, as well as to help him deke out defensemen and go one-on-one with goaltenders. He can disguise his release well with poise. We really like his hands and his one-on-one abilities with the puck. He can make defensemen look silly on the ice, but we wouldn't categorize his shot as elite (simply above-average). His mix of quick hands, reach, size and potential speed makes his offensive package really intriguing; he's also one of the rawest players at the top of the draft. If he continues to improve without setbacks to his skillset or work ethic, you might have a heck of a player on your hands when he reaches physical maturity.

His skills and offensive abilities are evident, but he was hotly debated among our staff. While there's no denying his talent, his point-per-game ratio, whether just under or just over one, raised some questions for some of our scouts. Oshawa was not exactly a team brimming with offensive talent. He didn't regularly play with Ritchie until the end of the year, and found success with him and Roobroeck, particularly in the postseason. That line proved to be dynamite; Ritchie is undeniably talented, but Roobroeck doesn't stand out (aside from his size). Sennecke's absence due to injury during the series against North Bay, followed by missing the entire final, significantly affected their offensive momentum for Oshawa.

As mentioned, he's still quite immature physically. It shows when he protects the puck. He still doesn't win enough battles and can lose balance or simply get outmuscled on the ice. However, we saw positive improvements in his tenacity on the ice and overall strength since last year. The player-improvement curve for someone like Sennecke is very important; it helps us get a better read of his trajectory and long-term potential. He's far from a finished product, and this makes him an exciting prospect for NHL teams. His reach does help him now, but once he's physically stronger, the mix of his reach and projectable frame will make it quite difficult to take pucks away from him, thanks to his added ability to shield away from defenders.

While his skating has improved since last year, a lot of it has to do with his boost in physical strength. He's a bit more explosive now, which shows in his ability to challenge defenders wide. He has more value with his transitional game as well. His skating does expose his physical immaturity, as he lacks stamina and explosiveness late in his shifts. At the start of them, his skating looks fine and is even close to being well above-average. Adding strength to his frame will add more explosiveness, and his stamina will improve to perform better throughout those shifts.

His compete level and physicality were never poor but this area of his game also improved this season. He showed more physicality and effort level as the season progressed. As explained earlier, his overall game saw a boost in the last 20 games of the season. His compete level was even better in that last stretch; we had no complaints in the playoffs. We couldn't categorize him as elite in this category either, but from what we saw late in the year, it's not an issue. In the playoffs, we saw him engage more in physicality and scrums after the whistle. He was a focal point of the opposition's game plan in the first three rounds of the playoffs, and he performed admirably. For us, it's very encouraging for the future.

We think Sennecke will go high in the draft, a very real chance in the top 10, based on his skillset and the development rate we witnessed this season. When he's on his A game, he looks like a top-10, even top-5 pick in this draft. Obviously, certain teams might prefer to go with a center or defenseman high in the draft if they value drafting based on position. We think he has legit top-6 upside if his development goes well over the next 2-3 seasons. We don't expect him to be NHL-ready soon, but he might be worth the wait.

"Constantly on his ass. So weak." - NHL Scout, October 2023

"I like the skill but he is weak and his effort level is inconsistent." - NHL Scout, October 2023

"It would be nice if they would play him with some talent." - NHL Scout, October 2023

"He has elite puck skills." - NHL Scout, October 2023

"Really good skill. He can beat guys one one one and he can pass the puck too. Great vision." - NHL Scout, October 2023

"A bit lazy...not as high on him as you are." - NHL Scout, December 2023

"I love the deception in his game. Combine that skill and size and how much better his 200 foot game is compared to last year...the kid is a stud." - NHL Scout, December 2023

"My top player from the OHL." - NHL Scout, March 2024

"If he checks out for off ice stuff, he will be my top ranked player from the OHL." - NHL Scout, March 2024

"He is 6'3 now and not even close to filling out that frame. Imagine him in 5 years." - NHL Scout, May 2024

"Twitter got upset when he speared the kid. Scouts moved him up their lists." - NHL Scout, May 2024

"If he keeps improving at this rate he could be the second best player in this draft class in five years." - NHL Scout, May 2024

"I have him third in the OHL behind the two Dmen but ahead of Luchanko. They are all top 15 picks though." - NHL Scout, May 2024

"He has a motor now...he works and will take hits to make a play. With that size and skill he is a top 10 pick all day long." - NHL Scout, May 2024

"I'm not buying him. He took off when he got on Ritchie's line, not before. Now I'm hearing he's not doing any testing at the combine." - NHL Scout, May 2024

"Lanky...ton of room to grow. Really weak.Knocked off his feet with ease...reminded me of Julien in London last year when he was getting pushed around. With that said I'm a fan of Sennecke." - HP Scout, Mark Edwards October 2023

"One of my fave players in this class. Showed his raw talent early on and kept growing his game as the season went on. A few of our scouts took a bit longer to be sold on him but they were on *board by seasons end so I didn't need to have a big debate in the final meetings." - HP Scout, Mark Edwards, May 2024*

"He's not even close to reaching his ceiling yet. It was tight between him, Dickinson and Parekh as my top guy in the OHL. I really liked him last fall but he stepped up his game even more in the second half. He was blocking shots and playing a better 200 foot game. When I look ahead I see a high ceiling. He is 6'3" and should fill out to at least 200 pounds." - HP Scout, Mark Edwards, May 2024

NR	PLAYER	TEAM	LEAGUE	HEIGHT	WEIGHT	POS	GRADE
	SHAHAN, KADEN	SIOUX CITY	USHL	5' 10.75"	168	RW	NI
NHLCS	CEILING	FLOOR	HOCKEY SENSE	COMPETE	SKILL	SKATE	MISC
NA -115	4	4	4	8	4	5	4

Hard working, shooting winger. Kaden Shahan has come back with the same goal scoring exploits that he displayed as a USHL rookie in 2022-23. His 20 goal campaign failed to get him drafted the first time around, but with 39 goals in 2023-24, he might garner some attention. Ultimately, Shahan's game is extremely simple. He works hard and he shoots. Everything else involved in his game does little to help his cause.

The skating package is slightly above average overall, but the straight line skating and explosiveness is lesser than we'd expect from a player of this size and player type. That aspect of his skating is buoyed by his high work rate and foot churn. He's better on his edges and looks sharp working through turns. From a dead stop, though, it's pretty clunky mechanically. That can probably be smoothed out with some more core strength which would likely aid in some postural improvements.

He's not a smooth puckhandler in space. His hand speed is really weak compared to other players of his production level. Shahan works his way to the front of the net and down low with enthusiasm.

His shot power is above average, but nothing spectacular. He's able to find the upper corners of the net with a good deal of consistency. The accuracy and release are good enough. Accurate or not, it's difficult to look past the 24.5% shooting percentage (down from almost 36% with a month left in the season). His playmaking vision and passing ability are not at all interesting and have shown no obvious progression from last season. Naturally, for lower hockey sense players such as this one, there are defensive positioning concerns abound. Kaden is a work-a-day player that usually just skates at the puck carrier and tries to make a play. Sometimes he'll go for a hit, but he's not very hockey strong…his inability to get good leverage causes him to bounce off of a lot of would-be victims. He really doesn't show off a great understanding of off the puck movement in any zone. He'll get stuck flat footed for a beat or two sometimes trying to decode where he can get to to be open for a shooting attempt.

There's always some opportunities for players that can really work hard and with that added bonus that they'll go to the net and pot a couple. But this player doesn't seem worthy of being anything more than a watchlist player to maybe re-examine as an undrafted free agent down the road.

NR	PLAYER	TEAM	LEAGUE	HEIGHT	WEIGHT	POS	GRADE
	SHCHUCHINOV, ARTYOM	TRAK CHELYABINSK	RUS	5' 11"	154	LD	NI
NHLCS	CEILING	FLOOR	HOCKEY SENSE	COMPETE	SKILL	SKATE	MISC
-	4	4	6	5	5	5	3

Shchuchinov spent the past season in the KHL, playing in 54 games plus another 7 in the playoffs. On the surface, this sounds like good news but for him, he should have played another season in the MHL, which would have been more beneficial for his development. His ice time was an issue, playing 10 or more minutes in only 15 of the 61 games he played this season. He never played more than 13:06 in a single game.

He's an undersized defenseman who doesn't have a great toolkit. He's only 154 pounds, and was heavily physically challenged in the KHL when competing against grown men. He's a smart player, and this is why he was able to survive, but he was not good enough to really make an impact and we didn't see much improvement from the start of the year to the end of it. He can make a good first pass, but we don't project him as a power play guy. He's not a threat from the point, his shot is weak, and he's also not very creative with the puck. A defenseman of this size needs to be really good offensively to have their game translate to the NHL. At his size, we already know that defensively it's going to be challenging, but sometimes if his offense is really good, even elite, it can compensate for the lack of defense. We don't see this as being the case here.

Smaller defensemen need to specialize in something in order to have a chance to make it to the NHL, and Shchuchinov doesn't appear to have a real specialty. We think he will end up, over time, as a decent to good KHLer–we don't see an NHL future with this player.

48	PLAYER		TEAM	LEAGUE	HEIGHT	WEIGHT	POS	GRADE
	SHURAVIN, MATVEI		CSKA JR.	RUS JR	6' 03"	195	LD	C+
NHLCS	CEILING	FLOOR	HOCKEY SENSE	COMPETE	SKILL		SKATE	MISC
INT- 15	5	5	5	6	5		7	7

Shuravin is an intriguing defenseman from Russia who split the year in three leagues: the KHL (11 games), MHL (22 games) and VHL (5 games). He has a lanky frame and will need to get stronger physically to fill it out, but he's intriguing because of his good combination of size and skating, as well as his defensive game.

He's a good athlete with good skating skills who can defend well. He's a fluid skater with solid footwork; NHL teams covet defensemen like Shuravin who have both size and movement working in their favour. He covers a good amount of ice because of his good skating and athleticism, which gives him good value when combined with his overall defensive game. He can escape pressure and skate the puck out of his zone with ease thanks to his superior skating skills. Defensively he's good because of his mobility, reach and stick checks.

We have seen him have good sequences in some games (mostly MHL) where he showed some decent hands but overall it was very all over the place. His hands are very inconsistent at this stage in his development. He gets into trouble when rushing the puck in the neutral zone because his hands are below-average. He can't beat players with his hands alone, and will usually lose control of the puck when he attempts to do so. He can beat players if he gets past them with his skating skills, but his hands let him down in those situations. Also, when handling the puck in small areas, his lack of stickhandling skills hurts him.

Offensively limited (0 goals in 38 total games this season), his below-average hands really hurt his potential and his place on our list. The more we watched him this season, the more we started seeing his hands let him down. He was not fluid or even comfortable with the puck on his stick. He's one skill away from being a real solid defenseman in this draft class, but we think it will be a big detriment to his next-level potential. He doesn't have a big shot from the point and is not a threat from there due to his average shooting skills. He's also not someone who has a lot of creativity or vision, and we don't project him as a power play guy at the next level. He did however do an okay job of quarterback the power play in the MHL where he was able to show more handling and passing skills. Basically, he's a bit all over the place with his hands and puck skills depending on the league that he played in which makes him a tough one to project for the NHL.

As far as his energy level goes, we saw a different player in each league he played in. In the MHL, he was moving pucks better than he did in the KHL, but he was often too passive in the MHL. In the KHL or VHL, we saw a more physical game from him and he was much more tenacious. The latter version of Shuravin is the one we could see translating to the next level. This is something we see often with draft-eligible defensemen in Europe that move between pro and junior leagues. They tend to be more assertive when playing in the pro leagues compared to junior. We also need to see more consistency in his physicality. When he's physical, it does add another element to his defensive game.

If he can show more consistency in these areas, it would help his chances of playing on a 3rd pairing in the NHL. His size, skating skills, defensive game and physical game could lend themselves well to that role. However, we didn't see enough at this point to rank him aggressively due to his compete level (or lack thereof) in the MHL, where he played the most games this season. He also doesn't have any standout qualities, aside from his skating, that can compensate if he's too passive on the ice. In order for him to succeed in the NHL, he'll need to bring his effort and physicality consistently to become that stay-at-home, physical defenseman that NHL teams want.

NR	PLAYER	TEAM	LEAGUE	HEIGHT	WEIGHT	POS	GRADE
	SIKORA, PETR	TRINEC JR.	CZE JR	5' 11"	172	LC	C
NHLCS	CEILING	FLOOR	HOCKEY SENSE	COMPETE	SKILL	SKATE	MISC
INT-37	4	5	6	6	5	5	5

Sikora spent the past season in his home country, playing in the Czechia junior league (30 games) and in the men's league (22 games). He had a lot of success as a junior with 40 points in 30 games, but if he gets drafted, it will be mainly due to his play against men as well as his international performances; he was a good player for the Czechia U18 team all year long. Since 2019, only 5 players were drafted into the NHL from their play in the Czechia junior league alone. Those additional viewings were very important for Sikora this season.

A sound, smart two-way center, Sikora understands the game well, plays sound hockey away from the puck, and is usually on the right side of the puck when he has it. Offensively, his best assets are his playmaking and creativity; he's a good passer with good on-ice vision. We don't project him as a guy who will play on the power play in the NHL, but he can make good plays from the half-wall due to those assets. We also like his poise with the puck; he can slow down play and make the players around him better.

Where his projection gets tougher: he doesn't stand out in other areas of his game. An average-sized center with an average toolkit, his athleticism is also average, as is his skating (especially in terms of explosion, top speed and agility). He has value in the offensive zone with his playmaking, but that value decreases with his transition play due to the skating, coupled with the fact that his hands and one-on-one abilities do not make him an offensive threat. He also has an average shot, which limits his projection for the NHL as an offensive forward. We think he could become a good penalty-killer, as he has a good sense of anticipation and works hard.

If he can make improvements to his shot and speed, it would give him a chance of becoming a depth forward in the NHL with penalty-killing value. The more realistic projection for him is a future in the Czechia League, American Hockey League or somewhere else in Europe.

5	PLAYER	TEAM	LEAGUE	HEIGHT	WEIGHT	POS	GRADE
	SILAYEV, ANTON	NIZHNY NOVGOROD	RUS	6' 07"	211	LD	A

NHLCS	CEILING	FLOOR	HOCKEY SENSE	COMPETE	SKILL	SKATE	MISC
INT-I	7	9	6	8	5	8	9

Anton Silayev is one of the most unique shutdown defenseman we have ever scouted. We have never evaluated a 17 year old defenseman that has played extended minutes in a full-time, top-4 role at the KHL level before, and we have never seen a defenseman assert his game in his first year of eligibility at the KHL level like Silayev did this past season. His best performances were in the first third of the season and admittedly he underwhelmed a bit in the MHL playoffs, but when taken as a whole, he still had an incredibly successful season, while putting up 11 points in 63 games at the KHL level.

We think there's some similarities and differences between another shutdown defenseman that accelerated at the pro level in his initial draft seasons, and that's Moritz Seider. Like Silayev, Seider asserted his game early, had a fantastic tool-kit, showed a heady, smart, mature game; he backed down to no one, never looked intimidated and rarely was overwhelmed. The differences though lie specifically in the development curve offensively and as a result the offensive projection when determining Silayev drops below Seider's.

The single biggest difference offensively between Seider and Silayev is the finesse and overall puck skills between the two players and the offensive curve that Seider displayed by the end of his draft season, relative to Silayev's. Seider showed deft handling at the International level both against Junior players and at the end of the season at the World Championships, especially through the end phase of his passing plays.

Silayev is more rigid mechanically when transferring through his passing and his ability to rock back pucks and his ability to control pucks never hit a higher level from the start of the season, right through to the end of the season. That said, Silayev is significantly larger than Seider and that can result in a delay within his coordination. The rule of thumb is that the larger the player, the more time you need to allow that prospect time to develop his coordination, and in Silayev's case, it's possible and maybe you could even say likely, that his hands and puck control skill-set will continue to develop well past this season as he continues to mature into a young adult.

We don't want to give you the wrong idea though. Silayev is capable of handling the puck at his top speed at an okay rate already. He can effortlessly one touch a pass to his teammate that directly lands on the tape, and both his exit and retrieval rates within his playmaking skill-set already project to hold at an adequate level. Like Seider, he also thinks the game at a high level and can identify options under pressure and find weakside options in transition or back door options in the offensive end. He even got extended powerplay time at the KHL level in spurts this season, and showed a decent puck moving skill set that was predicated around his ability to pivot and find no-look lateral options.

Although Silayev's offensive potential is the talking point, it's never going to be the hallmark of his game. This player's bread and butter is his ability to force unrelenting pressure on opposing forwards when they cross the defensive-zone. His skating base for his size is both athletic and explosive, so when you combine it with his range, it means that players have to react very quickly to his defense. He's both a reactionary defender himself who can also anticipate swing passes below his goal-line at a high rate, but he's also a defenseman who forces opponents into errors. We wish he was more anticipatory than he is, but if you are going to be reactionary, bring a tool-kit to the table to work with, and he just happens to have one of the best in this class, or any class for that matter.

A lot of younger defenseman who are first year eligible have difficulty maintaining adequate posture when attempting to take away specific passing lanes while also simultaneously trying to stay in-front of their man, but Silayev is adept at keeping a lower center of gravity despite his enormous build, which is a testament to his skating base. There's depth within his skating and it allows him to make stick positional and body adjustments rapidly.

He's very aware as the result of keeping his head on a swivel, which allows him to monitor back door options and gives him the ability to recognize where he is positioned relative to his defense so that he can set up switches with them when needed. His awareness by using his head tracking extends to all three zones, which gives him the ability to assess his time and space but also track pucks through potential passing lanes.

Anton's a multifaceted defenseman, who doesn't just rely on wing-span and positioning. He's not physically developed and lacks pro strength but he understands how to leverage his frame to his advantage, even at this stage in his development. He knows how to properly board pin, and he knows how to use his frame to weigh heavy so that he forces opposing players to work out of corners, exhausting them in the process. We wish he would run through players more than he currently does but we think it will come in time once he physically matures. We also wish he was as ruthless as Stian Solberg or Lian Bichsel, but he makes up for his lack of a mean streak by still being hard to play against. He makes life difficult and that's what matters most.

He's also advanced at recognizing which lane an opposing skater is attempting to take when cutting away from the boards, and doesn't fall for deception easily. We've discussed this in other write ups but we will state it again. Defensemen that can force higher work rates on their opponents are very valuable in playoff series, since fatigue occurs at a higher rate due to the pace of play getting ramped up. Just through his innate play, he can force teams into making mistakes that he can then capitalize on due to their increased level of fatigue.

At the offensive line and into the neutral-zone, he's quick to anticipate the opposing teams transitional breakout routes, which allows him to take advantage of his rapid pivoting and turning ability, which then allows him to C-cut and close down his gap on proper angles, so that he can control the geography of the rink. We talk extensively about defenseman mitigating or reducing risk in a lot of our evaluations, and Silayev can do exactly that.

When projecting a player with tremendous shutdown capabilities, there's a process we undertake. These defensive attribute breakdowns hopefully show the reasoning behind why we value him. Silayev is going to be drafted based on the concept that he can eat minutes and swallow the ice surface faster than almost any other prospect we've seen. He's that extremely rare combination of a prospect who possesses elite recovery rates while having the transitional defense projected to be able to shutdown the likes of the Connor McDavids and the Nathan MacKinnon's of the hockey world. He projects to insulate a pairing better than any other prospect in this class, and that's why he's ranked as aggressively in our rankings as he is. The offensive touch that may or may not come is just an added bonus.

"Have you seen the big Russian yet? Holy Sh** what a player!" - NHL Scout, October 2023

"He will be one of the best shut down guys in the league in five years." - NHL Scout, November 2023

"Ranking the D has been difficult." - NHL Scout, December 2023

"He's played the right side a lot." - NHL Scout, January 2024

"He's a unicorn along with a few players in this draft." - NHL Scout, January 2024

"The way he skates and covers ice is like nothing I've seen." - NHL Scout, January 2024

"I saw a media guy say he's great on the powerplay but needs to fix his defensive game. I don't think these guys watch anything." - NHL Scout, March 2024

"All you need to do is watch the NHL playoffs and that will answer why a team drafted him so high." - NHL Scout, May 2024

"He set the U18 scoring record in Russia so he's doing something right." - NHL Scout, May 2024

"If he had very good puck skills and above average upside offensively he would be an easy 2nd overall on my list and would challenge Celebrini for 1st overall" - HP Scout Jérôme Bérubé, March 2024

"NHL Playoffs are such a good reminder of what matters in scouting, I had dropped him a bit on my list then I watched the NHL playoffs and asked myself why would I do that.... he's built for playoff hockey and he could be a game changer in the playoffs." - HP Scout Jérôme Bérube, May 2024

"I think there's another level to him offensively then we've seen from him this season. He was mishandling the puck more and making less dangerous offensive plays down the stretch, which speaks to fatigue for me and that makes a lot of sense when you factor in the sheer amount of games he played." - HP Scout, Brad Allen

"If you think our ranking of this player is too aggressive, please watch some playoff hockey and get back to us. These players are invaluable and they don't come around every-draft." - HP Scout, Brad Allen

"If you have been following us for a while than you know that we value Dmen that can shut down the opponents best players. We saw it in Schneider and Seider to name a couple. Add Silayev to that group. He's a unicorn. Really really tight between him and Buium for me. I was leaning Silayev for a while but PP guys are so tough to find...I go back and forth." - HP Scout, Mark Edwards, March 2024

58	PLAYER	TEAM	LEAGUE	HEIGHT	WEIGHT	POS	GRADE
	SKAHAN WIL	USA-U18	NTDP	6' 04"	211	LD	C

NHLCS	CEILING	FLOOR	HOCKEY SENSE	COMPETE	SKILL	SKATE	MISC
NA-56	4	5	5	7	3	7	8

Will Skahan is already a beast at 6'4", 209 pounds. He boasts just four goals and two assists in 24 USHL games this year on a defense that lacked a lot of offensive pop. He led all NTDP d-men by a mile at plus-17 despite his low production. His game is about as straightforward as anyone could expect.

He's a conservative defenseman that will finish hits with authority along the boards and is willing to battle in front of the net. He has some range to him that allows him to defend rushes well. He allows players to eat up his gap in rush absorption, especially around the middle layer of the defensive zone, and that's normally a tough spot for defensemen of this type...but Skahan opens his hips and has success with a lateral step and proper stick positioning to shut down these wide attempts with consistency. His reach and pokecheck impact is high end. The skating package is very good overall. He's a splendid athlete. His stride and his body posture atop that stride have a lot of upside, even though he's very advanced on his physical development arc – his father, Sean, has been a strength and conditioning coach for over 20 years. His weight transfers are really good, so he hits for keeps even against older players. It would be nice if he had more urgency getting back into position or back to his net after chasing some of these hits.

He's a calm player for how physical he is, and it's almost to a fault. If he's on the wrong side of a play, he doesn't fight too hard to get back into the right position...he tends to just glide into the play and try to find his way. We're going to need this to be a mauler at the next level for this to have any chance at success.

Naturally, when a player finds his way to just two assists in even a portion of a USHL season, that's not a ringing endorsement of his puck skills. And there's no sugarcoating it, Skahan is poor with the puck. There's no zip on his passes, there's no confidence in where they're going, he banks a lot of pucks up and out. Even when he's in the offensive zone, he just gets the puck and wrists it towards the net as quick as he can – even if he has 30 feet in front of him, he rarely takes a stride with it. The puck poise is about as low as it gets for a player in this book.

His puck skills and decision making (with and without the puck) need to improve. The latter showed some positive movement later in the season, the former did not. The decision making might be a mix of confidence and urgency, as he can't legitimately play any simpler than he already does, so it's not that. Tyler Kleven and Brady Cleveland were 2nd round picks in this vein, so we assume Skahan won't fall too far from that tree but that's too rich for our tastes.

" Much like Emery he is pretty limited with the puck on his stick but I did like that he was by far their most physical player. He's a 5th round type player for me" – NHL Scout, May 2024

NR	PLAYER		TEAM	LEAGUE	HEIGHT	WEIGHT	POS	GRADE
	SKINNARI, AXEL		ILVES JR.	FIN-JR	6' 01"	170	RW	NI
NHLCS	CEILING	FLOOR	HOCKEY SENSE	COMPETE	SKILL		SKATE	MISC
-	3	4	5	6	4		7	6

We noticed this player in November at the U20 tournament when he was playing for Team Finland. He had a great showing at this event, but unfortunately didn't make the cut for the World Junior Hockey Championships. He narrowly missed out on one of the final spots, given to another player who shares a similar style: Michigan State forward Tommi Mannisto. Skinnari is a 2004-born forward who made an impression on us because of his great speed and compete level. He split the past season between Finland's U20 junior league and the Liiga, where he played 23 games with HPK, recording 4 points total. While we don't think his skill level will translate to the NHL, we love his skating, net-driving ability and physicality. There's just not enough skill in his game for us to feel confident placing him on our list. We think he's going to become a very useful player in the Liiga.

NR	PLAYER		TEAM	LEAGUE	HEIGHT	WEIGHT	POS	GRADE
	SOINI, SEBASTIAN		ILVES JR.	FIN-JR	6' 02"	183	RD	NI
NHLCS	CEILING	FLOOR	HOCKEY SENSE	COMPETE	SKILL		SKATE	MISC
INT-17	4	4	4	6	4		8	7

Soini spent the majority of this past season playing for Koovee in the Mestis league, which is the 2nd-best professional league in Finland after Liiga. He also played 6 games with Ilves, and you can expect him to play full-time next season in the Liiga. As the adage goes, hindsight is 20/20, but in retrospect, it would have been beneficial for him to play at least a good chunk of the season playing in Finland's junior league. Against men, we didn't see him try too many things with the puck, he played a real safe game and seemed to focus on not making mistakes on the ice. In terms of his development, we would have liked to see him make more plays with the puck. Doing so would have made it easier for scouts to project his puck and offensive game. He was also cut from the national team before the U18 World Championships, which didn't help.

The first thing you notice with Soini is how solid his skating skills are. He's fluid and powerful on the ice for a player with his frame. He used his skating well to defend, he can be aggressive with his gaps, and he uses his good recovery skating when needed. He can also be elusive to skate himself out of trouble. He's a good athlete, and those are among his best traits as a prospect. He played his best hockey of the season at the February Five Nations U18 tournament, where he was able to put his skating skills on full display. He also demonstrated some good physicality in his zone. He's not a mean player, but he can finish hits and make it tough on opposing players coming to his side of the ice.

Our biggest problem with him has been his decision-making when pressured. He struggled to make quality decisions when retrieving pucks and trying to activate his team's transition game. One reason we think his offensive game is very limited is that he doesn't process the game well, which equals trouble for him when trying to make quick decisions with the puck. This will be an issue in the NHL, because defensemen are always pressured to make quick decisions by the opposition. We do like his point shot, which is either a good, hard slapshot or a quality wrister, but here again, he's slow when it comes to finding shooting lanes. We see his point shots getting blocked far too often. There's not much creativity on display when he has the puck on his stick, either.

If he could improve his decision-making and internal processor, he would have a chance as a 3rd-pairing defensive defenseman due to his skating, athletic ability and physicality. These are a lot of if's, however, and that's why we didn't rank him aggressively on our list.

24	PLAYER	TEAM	LEAGUE	HEIGHT	WEIGHT	POS	GRADE
	SOLBERG, STIAN	VALERENGA	NOR	6' 01.5"	205	LD	B
NHLCS	CEILING	FLOOR	HOCKEY SENSE	COMPETE	SKILL	SKATE	MISC
INT-20	6	6	5	9	5	8	6

Stian Solberg is a throwback, shutdown defenseman with some untapped offensive potential. Unlike most draft eligible defenders, Stian has honed his craft in Norway's top pro league, EliteHockey Ligaen. There, he produced 15 points in 42 regular season games, before ramping it up in the playoffs with 9 points in 17 games. He also represented Norway both at the U20 and World Championship level. His curve was impressive over the course of the season and it displayed the potential for him to modify himself into a two-way defenseman, if given the proper time to develop.

Solberg is the 80's era defender in this class that instills fear into opposing teams. He's incredibly tenacious and has the psychological profile that reminds us a bit of Lian Bichsel's. These players are extremely rare and difficult to acquire and we always take that into consideration during our evaluations. There's an effect that's generated through his physicality, and as a result the opposing team always has to be aware when he's out on the ice.

What we mean by the on ice effect, is the ability to generate intimidation through a defensive presence. Defensive presences can be generated through fantastic positioning and defensive structure too, such as the case with Chris Tanev or Jon Merrill as some examples, but we're referring to a presence that's generated primarily through forcing offensive errors as the direct result of not wanting to get hit.

We don't like seeing a prospect let up on a hit when it's a solid and legal one that they fail to deliver, but that's not the case here. This player forces his opponents to respect him when he's on the ice. We've seen him run players through the glass, smash players to the ice, compete at all costs to get inside on opponents during puck battles - whack, slash and disrupt opponents after whistles, and generally be a really difficult player to play against. This is relevant to his game since it gives him a very rare multi-dimensional approach that he can use to stay effective on the ice.

Intimidation is an incredibly important psychological component of hockey that has an increased value as teams continue to shrink down both at the defensive and forward positions. For some, this might be considered an old school type of thinking, and deemed completely unnecessary in an evaluation. Considering what we witness come playoff time year in and year out, we think it's invaluable. Highly skilled players must be suppressed on the ice and if a defenseman is capable of making them rush a play or force a mistake as a result of their ability to physically overwhelm them, it can change the complexion of a game.

He's also more than just an in-your-face defenseman. He's a gifted skater with exceptional posture who can distribute his weight evenly to spin off of pressure on a dime, while also being able to his crossovers mechanics to stay in-front of opposing forwards who are looking to carve east-west. When he does make mistakes, his ability to launch off his centerline and pivot quickly gives him rapid recovery ability. He projects to be able to use his skating base to stop faster players off the rush, and he's nimble enough to deal with evasive forwards who are difficult to target. This is a key component to his game considering how often he looks to throw his weight around.

Other areas of his defensive game that translate are his ability to positionally switch rapidly and cover his flank. He keeps his head on a swivel and recognizes when to scan the ice to take away back door passing plays. Further into the season, as he gained more confidence we watched him start to anticipate and intercept passes in advance that allowed him to generate transitional rush attempts more often than the earlier portions.

His transition game admittedly, is where he's still a work in progress but the curve is heading in the right direction. In the earlier portions of the season, Solberg would be prone to too many unforced errors when attempting to break out of his own zone. His retrieval rates were also inconsistent but towards the latter half of the season and throughout the playoffs, he started adjusting correctly to pressure. This was a direct result of starting to use hesitation feints, off-looks, and rely on his edgework to evade pressure and buy himself additional time and space so that he could operate in windows that he could play under.

His exit playmaking and retrievals aren't as clean as some of the top end defensive prospects in this class but we were starting to get more comfortable with the direction they're heading and he held at the World Championships level, which further enhances our confidence in them long term.

Another impressive area of his curve could be seen in his offensive game as well. During the beginning of the season and up to the U20's, Solberg was largely playing stationary from the line and failing to understand how to incorporate his skating or use his deception so that he could breakdown a line properly. Fast-forward to the end of the season, and continuing through the playoffs and World Championships, and we started evaluating a much more confident prospect in Stian, who started to understand how to take advantage of his athletic gifts from the line.

By the end of the season, he was making advanced and complexed offensive plays, such as laterally cutting back, using hesitation fakes in combination with his handling before finding off-look lateral options as one example. Another could be seen in how often he was willing to activate into the rush successfully where he could become the trailing option. He was threatening as a result of having impressive shooting mechanics and we've even seen him carve multiple times through the neutral zone and produce impressive end-to-end rushes. We feel at this point it's almost a disservice to simply refer to him as a shutdown defenseman, since it paints the wrong picture. There's untapped skill here and we started to see it surface and bubble.

Despite Solberg's flaws and lower ceiling relative to several other defensive prospects that we have scouted, you can't teach heart, passion, or genetics. Stian is a very good athlete, with a very strong skating base packed into a solid frame. He cares, he competes, and he's shown translatable defensive qualities. Some of his best work was done against his hardest competition and when he's playing up to his potential, he can move pucks and be an offensive threat from the line, he just needs to continue to develop in these areas so that they can become consistent enough to translate to the NHL. He's a unique and uncommon defenseman who is built for playoff hockey, and that was factored into our overall evaluation when ranking him.

"Terrible in December but I liked him leading up to that point." - NHL Scout, January 2024

" I was actually pretty high on him and liked him more than the forward (Brandsegg-Nygard) but the more I watched him the less I liked him. I have Brandsegg-Nygard way ahead of him now." NHL Scout,

"He's improved a lot. I had him as a mid rounder and I've moved him up to the 2nd round." - NHL scout, May 2024

"He'll go in the middle of the second round and that is probably around where he should go. I like him at that spot." - NHL Scout, May 2024

" I saw him mocked in the top 15 and I immediately closed up the mock." - NHL Scout, June 2024

" If he was around in the 3rd or 4th round we would take him for his physicality but not before then." - NHL Scout, June 2024

" My comparable for this kid is Alex Romanov" - HP Scout Jérôme Bérubé, September 2023

" This kid is going to do well in a playoff environment, he's built for playoff hockey" - HP Scout Jérôme Bérubé, April 2024

" He was great for Norway at the World Championships, he led the team in ice time (5th overall in ice time in the tournament after the preliminary round after Werenski, Josi & Hedman) and played in all situations" - HP Scout Jérôme Bérubé, May 2024

" He's my favourite defenseman in this class. I have loved him since the U18's last year. Such a unique blend of tenacity and athleticism." - HP Scout, Brad Allen

" Leon Muggli and Stian Solberg are the two most underrated defensive prospects in this class. You can't find players like Solberg if they can make it, and I really think Solberg showed he has the ability to make it by the end of the season." - HP Scout, Brad Allen

" A good athlete and I love the way he makes himself difficult to play against but he's not without limitations in his game. His World Junior wasn't good." - HP Scout, Mark Edwards, January 2024

" I like Solberg but I'm not nearly as high on him as some of our other scouts. His limited skill and inconsistent decision making are issues for me. I love Dmen that play hard and can defend but Solberg is still very raw in a few areas. He's a try hard guy, he's extremely physical but he's limited" - HP Scout, Mark Edwards, January 2024

" I just watched four more games because of the big gap in my ranking versus my scouts ranking. I don't recall having such a huge difference of opinion on a player with Brad and Jérôme. I didn't change my mind. Hockey sense and skill are limited in my opinion. He's somewhere around a mid second rounder for me but I caved to them on our list because they are so passionate about him. I did knock him back a bit on our list though." - HP Scout, Mark Edwards, June 2024

113	PLAYER	TEAM	LEAGUE	HEIGHT	WEIGHT	POS	GRADE
	SOLOVEY, JUSTIN	MUSKEGON	USHL	6' 02"	209	LW	C

NHLCS	CEILING	FLOOR	HOCKEY SENSE	COMPETE	SKILL	SKATE	MISC
-	5	4	6	6	6	4	8

Heavy, agitating winger. Justin Solovey has continued to get better and more noticeable in his time in the USHL. At this point, it's too much to ignore from a pro perspective. He makes his physical presence known on most shifts. He's also one of the leading purveyors of agita in the USHL. Solovey must be among the league leaders in post-whistle scrum participation – whether he creates them or ends them, he's always in it. His amplified toughness to play against has come on the back of improved athleticism and board play. Moreover, he protects the puck well and can work off the wall with regularity at this point. His puck control away from his body and reach are surprisingly good. Part and parcel with that, we noticed a marked improvement in puck poise – even when lined up on his off-wing. When he does lose the puck, he has a heavy stick to either get it back or disrupt a sudden change play against his club.

The skating power has improved at the top end. Solovey isn't a speedster by any means, but if he can keep up his cruising speed, his off the puck game becomes really effective. After he gets a few strides, especially out of crossover-driven net-swings, he can move well. We wish he was a lot more explosive in his first step out of a stop and go situation. The first three steps of his straight line skating are pretty ugly still, but the length of his stride helps to cover for that a bit. It still isn't where we'd like to see it though. If the small area footwork can improve, it's not hard to see him slotting into a depth role in the NHL down the line. Which isn't to sell some of his technical skill short, certainly.

Solovey can really shoot the puck. Terrific release, and it gets really noticeable when shooting off of a moving puck. He has registered some nod-inducing tallies this year right under the bar off of cross net line passes. He's finding soft areas to shoot from too. The Harvard commit is still finding the right balance between widening out for space purposes and cutting inside to support potential puck battles. That actually seems to be the case with a lot of Lumberjacks this year… a lot more wide tracking, so that may be baked into the plan. Still though, his hockey sense is a positive. We wish he passed the puck with some more zip and confidence, but that won't be his calling card anyhow.

Solovey is a big kid, he's really tough to play against, and he's one of the better hitting forwards in the USHL. Given his rate of progression combined with his level of production and his size, there's reason to give this player some rope to figure out what he can evolve into in the pro game eventually. Even if he just ends up being a rabble rouser down the line, he's a guy you want both when the chips are down (he had a 15+8=23 in 3rd periods alone this season; he led the team in playoff goals and points too) and during the dog days of the season.

"If I was looking for a long-term potential playoff player, I'd give Solovey a look…just keeps getting better without losing his edge." HP Scout, Michael Farkas

NR	PLAYER	TEAM	LEAGUE	HEIGHT	WEIGHT	POS	GRADE
	SMITH, GABE	MONCTON	QMJHL	6' 03.75"	208	LW	NI

NHLCS	CEILING	FLOOR	HOCKEY SENSE	COMPETE	SKILL	SKATE	MISC
NA-94	5	4	4	7	5	5	7

Gabe Smith is a hulking left winger who plays for the Moncton Wildcats in the QMJHL. He was drafted in the 2nd round (25th overall) by the Wildcats in the 2022 QMJHL entry draft. In his second season with the organization, Smith managed to put up 9 goals and 14 assists for 23 points in 54 regular season games. More production would've helped his draft stock, but with his combination of size and compete, some teams will find the young winger appealing in the later rounds of this upcoming NHL draft.

His skating has gotten a little bit better during this season but there are still massive strides that need to be taken in this area of his game. When he gets going, his speed is decent. His first three strides stick out as his biggest problem as they are very heavy and limits his ability to change directions. Edgework is also almost nonexistent and his crossovers when he performs tight turns are very slow and he does not generate a lot of speed off them. What we do like is that he rarely glides out there and his feet are always active, which is a good habit to have. We think that he can improve because while being heavy and slow, his stride is not badly mechanically flawed, and his issues are something that could be worked on.

There is not a lot of depth to Smith's offensive game. The only spot where he is effective is when he can get established in front of the opposing net. He's got decent hands which help him make plays from in tight and he can use his big frame to cause havoc in front of the goaltender. He can execute simple passes but does not seem to have very much creativity with the puck on his stick.

Defensively, he is strong along the walls and can be relentless on the forecheck. He never passes up the opportunity to deliver hits and can cause a lot of problems for opposing defenders with his long reach. He is an asset on the penalty kill as he is not afraid to block shots and can get in the way of passing lanes effectively. Where we think there is room to improve is on his defensive positioning. He can often be seen skating away from the puck and has trouble finding open ice to help on the breakout.

Because of his size at such a young age and his compete level, Smith will draw some attention from NHL teams in the later rounds of the draft. Because of a lack of offensive upside, we think that best case scenario for Smith is to carve out a decent career as a bottom six winger at the NHL level. To get there he needs to take big leaps when it comes to his skating and needs to clean up his positioning while in the defensive zone so he can become a trustworthy bottom six player. Because the physical traits are off the charts and he is one of the youngest players in the draft, we feel he could be worth the pick in the later rounds.

76	PLAYER	TEAM	LEAGUE	HEIGHT	WEIGHT	POS	GRADE
	SMITH, TARIN	EVERETT	WHL	6' 01.25"	187	LD	C

NHLCS	CEILING	FLOOR	HOCKEY SENSE	COMPETE	SKILL	SKATE	MISC
NA-38	6	4	4	5	6	4	6

After playing only eight games last season with the Silvertips due to an injury, the former WHL 1st rounder had a strong season with 8 goals and 44 points in 67 games. His 44 points and +26 rank 1st amongst U18 defensemen in the WHL. Of these 44 points, 16 came on man advantage. Smith averaged around 19 minutes a game in Silvertips' top 4, helping them finishing 4th overall on the WHL. He's a left-handed defenseman, but he played a lot on the right side this season with physical re-entry defenseman Eric Jamieson playing the left side.

Offensively, Smith shines in the offensive zone. He's confidant, activates and walks the blueline with ease. When playing on the right side, he loves to walk the blueline and attack the middle of the zone. He uses open hips moves to scan the offensive zone, and love to use deceptive lateral weight shift to freeze the defensive winger to find a play. When playing on the left side of the offensive blueline, he loves to fake D2D passes to open shooting lane. His shot is one of his best assets. It's hard, it gets through and can shot/pass for open sticks as well. When activating in the offensive zone, he loves to uses curl-and-drag release to change the angle of his shot. On breakout retrievals under pressure, Smith improved this season. He uses his size well to establish body position and control the area of the puck to find the next play. His decent mobility can help him in breakout situations as well. With more refinement in his retrievals, he'll be able to make more middle plays and increasing the exits in control for his team. In transition, as of right now, he's more efficient when carrying the puck to find control entries than when he moves the puck in the neutral zone. Overall, Smith is very talented and confidant with the puck, which is a plus in his game. Sometimes, his puck management could improve by forcing less play through multiple layers of pressure.

Defensively, Smith rush defending is inconsistent. Sometimes, he sets his gap well in the offensive zone, and combined with decent mobility and reach, it makes him hard to beat on the rush. Sometimes, his gaps are too loose, allowing the puck carrier to attack the middle or enter the zone in control. In his own-end, Smith does a good job battling down low. He's big and strong, and had some good work down low facing big forward Samuel Honzek in playoffs. In overall defensive zone awareness is an area of his game that needs to improve in the next years.

Smith's season was pretty impressive, especially after playing only eight games in the WHL last year. He has offensive upside with his shot, skills and confidence. His defensive game is a work in progress, but with his strength and decent mobility, he has tools to work with.

" Impressive skills and confidence in the offensive zone". Tim Archambault, April 2024

NR	PLAYER	TEAM	LEAGUE	HEIGHT	WEIGHT	POS	GRADE
	SMITHKNECHT, JACKSON	ROGERS	HIGH-MN	6'04.75"	182	LD	NI

NHLCS	CEILING	FLOOR	HOCKEY SENSE	COMPETE	SKILL	SKATE	MISC
NA-158	4	4	4	5	5	6	7

Jackson is a fairly late 06' born defenseman which makes him among a younger group of 06' draft eligible defenseman this year. Jackson is a big rangy defenseman out of Rogers HS in Minnesota. Jackson was drafted in the 7th Rd. of the 2022 USHL Phase 1 draft but has since seen his rights traded to Chicago (USHL) where he will likely play next season. Jackson first got on our draft radar early in the season while playing Elite League in Minnesota for Team SIT Financial where he played a simple but effective two-way game but we felt his draft stock cooled a bit throughout the High School season where he seemed to get away from some of the things he does well and tried to do too much offensively at times which lead to poor decision making and ill-advised turnovers. Initially, when watching Jackson, the first thing that stands out is his size and skating abilities which are easy to see translate to the next level. There is still a fair amount of filling out to do when it comes to Jackson's frame but he displays good mobility and separation ability for his size. When you combine his mobility and his range, Jackson was able to dominate his opponents defensively where he closed out time and space well.

Where Jackson struggled at times this season is where he tried to play above his abilities and do too much and in many of our viewings it was in big games against good teams that were able to take advantage of his mistakes. Jackson has good hands and shows the ability to transport pucks well through the neutral zone and into the offensive zone but that is where things tended to get off the rails and turnovers would occur. Jackson's decision making and vision lacked in order to create offensive from his zone entries, often he would attempt to go through both defenders, despite having options to kick out to the wings or find teammates streaking into the zone had he just displayed a bit more puck poise in those situations. Defensively, there is a lot of like about Jackson's game. He plays hard in the corners and around his net, does a good job making things hard on opponents in those areas. Jackson showed excellent ability to use his size to separate opponents from the puck in order to turn plays north quickly and showed and excellent stick to take away lanes and poke pucks off opponents sticks. Smithknecht makes quick reads and identifies pressure well which gives him added options with the puck in the defensive zone. There is a lot of like about the tools Smithknecht has for the next level, but they are raw tools and will need some time both to mature not only physically but regarding his decision making. If both of those things snap together in the next few years, it's easy to see Smithknecht contributing on the backend at the pro level someday.

Smithknecht is committed to Colorado College to play his NCAA hockey but will likely need at least 1 year in the USHL before heading to college. That long development path will be good for Jackson in order for his game to mature and for him to develop more of a consistent identity as a player.

NR	PLAYER		TEAM	LEAGUE	HEIGHT	WEIGHT	POS	GRADE
	SPELLACY, A.J		WINDSOR	OHL	6'02.25"	195	RW	C

NHLCS	CEILING	FLOOR	HOCKEY SENSE	COMPETE	SKILL	SKATE	MISC
NA-72	6	5	4	7	5	6	8

A.J. Spellacy is a large framed forward for the Windsor Spitfires in the OHL who put up 38 points in his sophomore season including 21 goals and 59 penalty minutes. Spellacy started off slow production wise but picked up the pace as the season went on when his ice time improved as the Spitfires traded off veterans. He effectively played a checking role early on in the year and later on when his team needed him to provide offense, he did not disappoint.

Spellacy has good skills as a skater with his speed being his best attribute along with his ability to keep himself balanced while taking contact from defenders. Spellacy uses his speed effectively in all three zones, but it is shown most on the backcheck and at chasing down dump in's. He is a relentless forechecker and body checks hard deep in the zone as an opposing force to defenders. With the puck on his stick he does lose some speed but he is not a primary option when entering the zone with the puck and instead works as a decent option to get a rebound or play a physical role down low or in front of the net.

As an offensive player, Spellacy needs to be much more consistent and provide more with and without the puck on his stick. He is always willing to grind things out offensively in the dirty areas and can push play to the front of the net, but he lacks consistency and the overall skill set to pull off these moves. His vision is not high level and he does not create plays with his passing or shooting. His offence is typically converted as the result of rebounds and good set ups from higher skilled teammates. His role at the NHL level would be a high energy bottom-six contributor with speed who plays hard on the cycle and on the outside of the offensive zone.

We love the combination of size and speed from Spellacy along with his proven effectiveness as an energy forward at the OHL level. His high compete, aggressiveness and his willingness to stand up for his teammates are coveted translatable skills to the professional level. Spellacy is always finishing his checks and is active defensively using his stick to break up plays. He also played more special teams as the year progressed and was an effective penalty killer for Windsor, something he may need to continue to implement into his game to make the next level as a serviceable forward.

As a more physically mature player, he is not expected to grow much more, but he is expected to put on some more weight with will make him more intimidating forward especially with his speed. He has the physical tools to be a speedy checking forward at the next level and with some added consistency be able to contribute some offense as well.

NR	PLAYER		TEAM	LEAGUE	HEIGHT	WEIGHT	POS	GRADE
	STEEN, NOAH		MORA	SWE-2	6'01"	187	LW	C

NHLCS	CEILING	FLOOR	HOCKEY SENSE	COMPETE	SKILL	SKATE	MISC
INT-43	4	5	6	7	5	7	6

A native of Norway, Steen is entering his third year of draft eligibility after being passed over in 2022 and 2023. He had a strong 19-year-old season in Sweden, splitting his time between the junior league and the Allsvenskan. Steen also played a big role on his team at the World Junior Hockey Championship and finished the season representing his country at the Men's World Hockey Championship. Notably, he scored 14 goals in the Allsvenskan, the highest total by an U20 player in the league this season. Steen often found himself playing alongside Michael Brandsegg-Nygard and Petter Vesterheim, both with his club team and internationally for Norway's national teams at both junior and senior levels.

His best traits as a player include his energy and compete level. He plays an intense game without being overly physical. He's quick on the forecheck, he's tenacious, and makes his way to the rough areas of the ice. He's quite good around the net, where he has scored a good portion of his goals this season. He's a fierce battler who is good at winning puck battles, digging pucks out of the corners, and driving them towards the net. In front of the net, he demonstrated some good hand-eye coordination to deflect point shots. We also saw his good anticipation come into play when he would quickly jump on rebounds in the slot. Another standout aspect of his game is his skating, as he consistently generates scoring opportunities with his speed. Showing explosiveness and impressive top-end speed, he uses these to create chances on turnovers and counterattacks. His combination of speed and anticipation adds to his skillset. He also showed that he has good hands on breakaway chances. Showcasing this ability one-on-one with goaltenders, he would use some good dekes, short hesitation fakes and deception skills on breakaways to freeze them. His ability to go forehand and backhand with ease helped him out in those situations as well. While he has good velocity on shots from in close, he lacks the threat of scoring from distance. Similarly, his playmaking skills are not exceptional; he can execute basic passes, but lacks the quick thinking and precision associated with high-end playmakers.

The main qualities of Steen's game lie in his willingness to play inside, compete level, skating and hands. As an older player, we would have liked to see more dynamic shooting and passing skills from him. He signed with Orebro in the SHL for next season, and we feel more secure in predicting that this will be where he continues his career, as a good player in Europe. However, he does have some intangibles that could make his game work in North America as well.

NR	PLAYER	TEAM	LEAGUE	HEIGHT	WEIGHT	POS	GRADE
	STERNER, KARL	FROLUNDA JR	SWE-JR	6' 03.25"	192	LW	NI
NHLCS	CEILING	FLOOR	HOCKEY SENSE	COMPETE	SKILL	SKATE	MISC
INT-106	6	4	4	4	6	5	6

Sterner is a good-sized forward from the Frolunda system. This season, he played in Sweden's junior league, where he had 34 points in 46 games. He also played for the U18 national team during the year.

Sterner is a frustrating player to scout. He's got tools that could translate to the next level, but other parts of his game are problematic. Let's start with the good. He's got the size that NHL teams covet, and his offensive talent is good overall due to his having a good shooting arsenal and hands. He's also a decent skater for his size; some mechanics need some refinement, but for his size and age, it's good enough. He can be an asset down low and in front of the net because of his frame and long reach. He can score goals in the slot, around the net and from the right faceoff circle on the power play.

Now for the problematic: he's very inconsistent in his playmaking and decision-making on the ice. He unfortunately also makes quite a few dumb plays with the puck on his stick, which leads us to rate him low in terms of hockey sense. He doesn't read the play well, he's slow at finding his teammates on the ice, and his passing efficiency is also quite average. He's quite inconsistent with his performances and is one of those players that is hard to get a read on. The skill level is there, but in some viewings, it's as though you're watching a player who could have a hard time making an impact in the SHL, let alone the NHL.

The biggest drawback for us has been his compete level. In some J20 games, he made no impact whatsoever and seemed flat-out uninterested. He also played in various tournaments with the national team this season, and didn't make much of an impact in any of these events. We have seen him capable of playing well in the past, with his good performance at last year's U17 Hockey Challenge for example, but this year, his international performances were all big disappointments and a good reason why he was cut from the U18 team in April.

It's tough to get behind a prospect that lacks consistency and compete level. However, we also know that the talent is there. There's always a chance that prospects like this flip a switch and come back strong the year after. We have seen it happen over the years: everything goes wrong during a player's draft year, only for them to turn it around the year after. It doesn't happen all the time though. We could see a team take him in the late rounds and hope their staff brings the best out of him.

56	PLAYER	TEAM	LEAGUE	HEIGHT	WEIGHT	POS	GRADE
	STIGA, TEDDY	USA-U18	NTDP	5'10"	178	LW	C+
NHLCS	CEILING	FLOOR	HOCKEY SENSE	COMPETE	SKILL	SKATE	MISC
NA-44	6	4	7	7	5	5	4

Smart, versatile forward. Teddy Stiga is probably the most improved USNTDP player of this group. He out-pointed all 2024 draft eligibles in USHL play with 38 points in 27 games; he also led all players in plus/minus. Certainly, a portion of those figures come from playing with the best play driver on the team, James Hagens (2025), quite a bit. But Stiga did show the ability to play with and complement a top end talent, which is a plus. In his relatively few opportunities at center, he tended to be less noticeable and his line was less successful in generating offense. That's ultimately where this player becomes tough to rank. Teddy, despite his improvements, doesn't give us a lot of confidence that he'll be a dynamic top-six talent…at least not as the best player on a line. The question then turns to: Can he be a support player on a skill line? There's a better chance of that, but there are still some hang-ups.

Looking at the two prime "output" technicals: shooting and passing – he doesn't jump off the page in either of those categories from a technical point of view. His shot is average at best. The release and velocity aren't overly threatening. In very specific cases, he can use his edges to move laterally to beat goalies wide when in close, but otherwise, he doesn't have a wide array of finishing moves. Where he might have some edge is with the timing of his shots. He has shown some ability to let shots go while goalies are in vulnerable spots from a movement perspective. His passes don't really jump off of his blade either. For as smart as he is, his puck poise and pass timing are strangely lacking. We'd like to see more consistently accurate passes. He doesn't even have a real calling card that he can go to in this regard either. Some players are better at lo-hi passing, some players can create lateral passing lanes with regularity, etc. but Stiga doesn't give off the feeling of having a particular specialty or "comfort" pass. He has the tendency to get a little antsy with the puck and throw them away too easily for what we'd expect from an upper echelon player.

The Boston College commit has really improved his skating since joining The Program. He's really good on his edges and incorporates his transition skating into his puck skills in an effective way. One of his best qualities in terms of puck transport is his ability to seamlessly turn and take passes. He'll turn and rotate his hips and core up the ice as he's receiving a zone exit pass to really put pressure on defensemen quickly in the neutral zone. While the first-step quickness is only okay and it's pretty choppy getting up to any sort of notable top speed, his overall mobility grades out nicely. He doesn't need to be a burner to be effective, we wouldn't expect him to be able to handle the puck very well at hyper speed anyway. The key is his small area footwork is very serviceable, he can move laterally very well, and his pivot skating is a plus too. These features grant him excellent angles in puck pursuit situations. If he can find a way to be stickier in those forecheck situations, that would add another important aspect to his game. That isn't to say that he's not a battler and doesn't win more than his share of puck battles – he does, especially for his size. But if he can dig in and leverage his lower center of gravity as an F1 or F2 forechecker and jam up some of his opponents with more consistency, it's a gateway to really having a "B" game that is pro scalable (or an "A" game if he doesn't develop enough skill to be useful on a scoring line).

At 5'10", 174 pounds and not brimming with elite athleticism, we're a little bit limited in where we can slot him into a lineup in some regard. While we are seeing more and more players in the 5'9", 5'10" area being able to hang on in depth line roles without being a killer (Colin Blackwell or Derek Ryan, for instance), it's not necessarily a widely accepted practice. The key will be keeping it positive. For instance, does he consistently improve the condition of the puck? As mentioned previously, he can make some fairly questionable passing decisions sometimes, opting for complicated or risky passes when easier options are there. Typically, smarter plays are very aware of their own limitations, but Stiga tries a lot of passes that just seem above his pay grade. Experimentation is something we look at as a positive, but he crosses the line in the wrong way often enough that it's noticeable. It was just enough to knock his IQ down to a 7, as opposed to an 8. There's a path for him though, and he has the intelligence and adaptive qualities that give him plenty of runway to figure it out in time. We're not projecting an impact, play-driving forward though, and he's ranked with that in mind.

"Good motor and skating improved." – NHL Scout, March 2024

"He's grown on my but he is still a mid to later round guy for me." – NHL Scout, April 2024

"He has some skill and he will go into traffic...skating looks better." – NHL Scout, May 2024

NR	PLAYER	TEAM	LEAGUE	HEIGHT	WEIGHT	POS	GRADE
	STOUT, JOHN	MINNETONKA	HIGH-MN	6' 00.75"	193	LD	NI
NHLCS	CEILING	FLOOR	HOCKEY SENSE	COMPETE	SKILL	SKATE	MISC
NA-165	5	4	6	6	5	7	6

Stout has anchored the back end for a stacked Minnetonka team the last two seasons. Stout was originally drafted in the 3rd Rd. 41st overall by Waterloo in the 2022 USHL Phase 1 Draft but saw his USHL rights get traded to Madison this year where he saw 18 games for the Capitols this spring. Stout showed a flawless transition to junior hockey, logging high minutes for the Capitols down the stretch. Stout plays a solid two-way game with a high compete and physicality factor in his own zone. Stout has decent size at 6'2" but it's development physically and from a strength factor already that is impressive. His physical conditioning and strength allow him to log reliable minutes on the back end with no fall off in his effectiveness and ability to impose his well defensively on his opponents. Stout didn't put-up eye-popping numbers this season for Minnetonka but found a way to find the score sheet a decent amount while not sacrificing anything on the defensive side of the puck, with 6 goals and 24 assists in 28 games.

Stout is a strong skater with good mobility and explosive crossovers that allows him to cover a lot of ice quickly when defending the rush. Stout isn't shy in his willingness to step up on opponents and deliver big hits in the open ice and he picks his spots well to do so without taking himself out of the play. On a number of viewings, Stout would quickly close on opponents at his own blueline, finish them along the wall and turn the puck north quickly in a flawless transition. He showed the ability to play the game one step ahead a lot whereas he is checking his opponent he is already thinking where he needs to go when he gets the puck.

Offensively, Stout possesses a heavy shot from the point, he has displayed the ability to hit a big one-timer from the flank as well as his quick release from the point carries some good velocity as well. While Stout certainly has good enough footwork to patrol the offensive blueline in order to open up lanes, his hands and puck skills are pretty average which will limit his ability to run a Power Play at he next level, but his shooting ability can certainly be an asset on the flank on the power play at the college and pro levels. Right now, we don't see Stout as much as a potential power play player at the next level but certainly has the physical tools and hockey sense to be a highly effective two-way defenseman that can play in all situations. Stout is an NHL draft prospect that doesn't have any aspect of his game that stands out as elite but doesn't have any glaring flaws in his game either.

While Stout certainly is physically ready to make the jump to college hockey next season, he is likely to spend next season in the USHL with Madison. A full year at the junior level in Madison where he will get coaching from former NHL player Tom Gilbert will get him ready to step right into college and be an effective defenseman in 25/26. Stout is committed to Minnesota - Duluth, which has churned out its fair share of NHL defenseman over the years, so we like the development path in front of Stout as well.

12	PLAYER	TEAM	LEAGUE	HEIGHT	WEIGHT	POS	GRADE
	ST-HILAIRE, SAMUEL	SHERBROOKE	QMJHL	6' 02.25"	185	G	C

NHLCS	CEILING	FLOOR	HOCKEY SENSE	COMPETE	SKILL	SKATE	MISC
NA-11	5	4	6	7	6	6	6

A 9th-round pick by Sherbrooke in the 2020 QMJHL Draft, St-Hilaire made his major junior debut at 18 last season. He may have been Sherbrooke's backup, but there were still some rumblings in the scouting community about him last season. This year, he was the clear-cut number 1 as Sherbrooke faced a rebuilding year. He also made Canada's World Junior team as its 3rd goalie, quite an ascension from someone who had only played 52 career QMJHL games at that time. When he left for the World Juniors, you could have made a case for him as the best goalie in the league with his 11-10 record, 2.29 goals against average and .920 save percentage. Sherbrooke was expected to be in the last third of the league standings, but thanks to his performances, they were in the top third instead.

After the World Juniors, he missed some significant time due to a knee injury. He only played 4 total games in the months of January and February. He also missed some postseason games against Drummondville, not playing in games 3, 4, 5 or 6. In the first two games of that series, he gave up 9 goals. However, without him, things would have been much worse. He made numerous highlight-reel saves in those two games to keep his team in it, at least until the 3rd period.

A good athlete, his ability to move from post to post was impressive this season. We like St-Hilaire's quickness in his crease and how well he moves laterally. We saw him make numerous highlight reel saves thanks to these abilities, his above-average extension rates and great anticipation. If we compare him to the other QMJHL goalie likely getting drafted (Zach Pelletier) we like St-Hilaire better because he is less raw technically and has better athleticism. One of St-Hilaire's strengths (lateral agility) is one of Pelletier's weaknesses. Not a huge goalie (listed at 6'02") but he has to work really hard to track the puck with heavy traffic in front of him, and that will only get worse at the next level, as players will be bigger than the ones in the QMJHL. Overall, his puck tracking is good, but the point shots with heavy traffic are more difficult. He does a good job covering the lower part of the net with his quick legs, and he uses his stick well to block lower shots or wrap-around attempts. We do think the big weakness in his game is his glove side; we've seen him get beat there too many times this season to not consider that this is an area we want to see improvement in. He does compete hard, there's no quit in him, and this has helped him make some high-end desperate saves this season.

The 19-year-old was passed over in the last two drafts. To put things in perspective, for the 2022 NHL Draft, he was not even playing major junior hockey. He was a 17-year-old in the Québec Midget AAA League. Last season, with more starts and more exposure, it's not crazy to think he could have been a late selection. We do think this year will be the right one for him, and we expect to see him get drafted somewhere between rounds 5 and 7. He took part in the Toronto Maple Leafs' rookie evaluation camp last July, as well as the Boston Bruins' rookie camp last September. Unless there's a huge surprise at his next NHL training camp, expect him back in the QMJHL for his last season in the league.

"This kid is getting drafted this year, good improvement from last year and looks like he's 6'02" now."
- NHL Scout (November 2023)

"Sherbrooke is doing well so far and it's basically because of him. He's not helping them getting a top pick in the QMJHL draft this season, they are supposed to be rebuilding and they are top-6 in the standing" - NHL Scout (November 2023)

26	PLAYER	TEAM	LEAGUE	HEIGHT	WEIGHT	POS	GRADE
	SURIN, YEGOR	YAROSLAVL JR	RUS JR	6' 01"	192	LC	B

NHLCS	CEILING	FLOOR	HOCKEY SENSE	COMPETE	SKILL	SKATE	MISC
INT-22	7	5	6	8	7	6	6

We first noticed Surin last year when scouting Dmitri Simashev and Daniil But on Loko's MHL team. In his second season in the MHL this year, he was over a point per game after a slow start to the season. He had 4 goals and 13 points in his first 15 games, but finished with 18 goals and 39 points in his last 27 games. He was great in the postseason, leading his team all the way to the final with 23 points in 19 games. One of the more tenacious players in this draft class, he doesn't back down from anyone, and hits like a truck. He had over 100 penalty minutes this season (2nd overall in the MHL) which is honestly a bit too much for a talented player like he is. He'll need to play a more disciplined game and spend less time in the box, but we love the bulldog mentality he plays with. He's right up there with Villeneuve and Beaudoin as the most physical forwards in this draft class.

We love this kind of player, and would have been more aggressive in ranking him if he was a more consistent playmaker. His pass efficiency had its share of ups and downs during the year, and sometimes he opted not to utilize his teammates and kept the puck for too long. We have seen his playmaking shine in some games, such as in the playoffs, but again, the lack of consistency explains his position on our list. It's also something whose progression we will monitor next season. We remember feeling the same way about JJ Peterka in his draft year, and two years later, he was fantastic at distributing the puck in his AHL rookie season.

Surin's goal-scoring potential isn't considered elite. While he possesses a quick release and impressive velocity on his wrist shot, there's some inconsistency in his shooting skills. At times, he can score high-end goals with his wrist shot, but in other games, it appears average. Although he has decent hands, he doesn't stand out as an elite player in terms of one-on-one skills and deke arsenal. One issue we observed is his tendency towards individual plays, sometimes trying to do too much on his own.

Surin is versatile, capable of playing every forward position. While he primarily played on the wing last year, this year saw him spending more time down the middle. However, considering his inconsistent playmaking skills, it's more likely he'll transition to a winger role at the NHL level unless there's significant improvement in this area.

A good skater with good agility and footwork, he can be deceptive at times one-on-one and fool opponents with his shoulder fakes and quick changes in direction. He's elusive, which helps him beat players one-on-one with his skating skills and low center of gravity. He can also beat opponents with his outside speed, or simply go through them. He's very hard to stop when he's going to the net with the puck.

Extremely tough to knock down, he's one of the more powerful pound-for-pound players in this draft class. Good at protecting the puck along the wall, he's not the biggest player (despite having grown from 5'10" last year to 6'01" this year) but wins a lot of battles against bigger defensemen. He does so by using his low center of gravity and his strong lower body. He has good off-the-puck habits, playing hard in all three zones, and his backchecking efforts are noticeable. He can be a factor away from the puck with his reads, effort level and physicality. He's good at tracking guys in the neutral zone, stopping rushes and creating turnovers.

His physicality remains the most interesting part of his game. Playing a hard, mean, borderline dirty physical game, opponents must constantly be alert (not to mention keep their heads up) and maintain an awareness of where he is on the ice. A furious forechecker, defensemen in puck-retrieval mode become targets for Surin's speed and force. He does, at times, take himself out of position going for big hits, but got better at regulating this as the season progressed. Plus, it's always better to deal with a player that appears to have too much energy compared to a passive, uneventful player.

To conclude, we see Surin as a top-9 forward, one that can move anywhere in the lineup thanks to his versatility and ability to play different styles. We think he could help on a PP2, and bring value to a penalty-killing unit due to his compete level and whatever-it-takes mentality that all coaches love to have on their team.

"Very easy to like him, one of the more tenacious, physical and borderline dirty players in this draft class" - HP Scout Jérôme Bérubé, April 2024

"His curve was impressive. He couldn't score or impact the game early, but then he started to get going and started looking like the top-9 power-forward we initially envisioned." - HP Scout, Brad Allen May 2024

"If he can learn to play in a structured environment and understand when and how to use his teammates better, then he's going to be invaluable to a team." - HP Scout, Brad Allen, May 2024

NR	PLAYER	TEAM	LEAGUE	HEIGHT	WEIGHT	POS	GRADE
	SWANSON, MAC	FARGO	USHL	5' 07.5"	167	LC	NI
NHLCS	CEILING	FLOOR	HOCKEY SENSE	COMPETE	SKILL	SKATE	MISC
NA-152	5	3	7	5	6	5	3

Mac Swanson led the USHL in assists this year with 51 and finished third in points at 77. He took home the league's Player of the Year award and was the Clark Cup MVP en route to a Fargo Force championship.

Swanson, as his assist totals dictate, is a very strong setup man. He's a natural playmaker that almost exclusively looks to pass his way out of a tight spot. He has quality seam recognition and can execute on it well. His best and most fluid work was probably at the World Jr. A Challenge. That gave us some confidence in his one-touch playmaking ability in the lower layers of the offensive zone. That trait, however, is one of the few really scalable things about his game in our eyes. We would have liked his next-level passing to be a little more prevalent in USHL play – and granted, that can be challenge at this level if players aren't in the right places and aren't thinking the game along with the primary playmaker. We suspect that he'll have a very productive collegiate career, as he'll have more weapons at his disposal. But it takes more than just a playmaking game from the wing to make a legit NHL prospect.

The skating is maybe the biggest stopper. The lack of launch fluidity is very evident. There just isn't explosiveness in his stride. In the event that he wins a puck battle and tries to turn and go with it, it takes a number of strides to really gain sufficient ground. There's some hitch steps in there even in no- and low-traffic areas. There's nothing about his skating package that really jumps off the page and that's a big problem at his size. The top speed is fine, the edges are good… but the smaller players that make it, generally have some quick-twitch element or a couple of elite pieces that allow them to survive. We see this as a big contributing factor in his ability to actually work back inside the rink. Watching his zone entries, he generally can't work back into the middle himself. He may well be able to pass it to the middle on the rush or with a Gretzky turn, but it was a rare sight to see him get from outside the dot line to inside the dot line. It looks like he uses a bit longer of a stick too, so there's an element there where he has to physically "catch up" to the puck if he makes certain dekes – and he's just unable to get to it. As such, he's more or less boxed out of the interior of the rink and there isn't a ton of fight by him to change that.

He owns a plus shot…it's a set-and-snap deal, so the shooting process takes a little while. His ideal shot is: pass catch, set, adjust hips, snap shot far-side high. And it's a good shot with accuracy and velocity. The time and the process need to quicken. We'd like to see what he can do with his shot in-stride. He cleaned up some rebounds with some low-angle put-aways that are a nice, but there wasn't a lot of rush shots overall and very few went in the net. Moreover, of the 31 goals Swanson nabbed this year (regular season and playoffs), six of them were empty netters – that's a sizeable chunk. The finishing moves near the net aren't overly sharp, as he just doesn't have the most dynamic hands. That's another element that would have been nice to see grow over the course of the year: adaptive handling. Swanson is a good stickhandler, he can control the puck fairly well, he skill chains together a quick move into a pass. But with so much of his puckhandling done on the outside of the rink, it's tough to see just how good he can be. The lack of technical experimentation in that regard was a little disappointing.

Now listed at 5'8", Swanson needs to have elite handling, processing, and skating to really be a player of interest – certainly, he would need at least 2 out of 3 of those. For our money, he isn't elite in any of those three categories. Now, that isn't to say that he's untalented by any means. But in terms of being a legitimate NHL prospect – he's not there in those areas for us. Moreover, he doesn't attempt to cover for any of those sub-elite qualities by being a high energy player either. His work rate is pretty average. He's not very detail-oriented at matching speed on the forecheck, he's more or less a zero defensively (despite a USHL-best plus-39, but no one hands out pluses for defensive plays, of course), and he struggles to really compete for loose pucks. Even if we breakdown his playmaking ability, it's very good...but it's not elite. We'd classify his seam recognition as "intermediate" before we'd say "advanced". He shows some propensity to push it further, as he's had some really nice looks this year in flashes. The key thing for Swanson is that he needs to be able to pass his way out of trouble almost every time. Without high-end skating, high-end adaptive handling, or even average puck protection, he needs an outlet and that outlet has to be elite because there's not a lot else that he can fall back on. Watching him in trouble, he misses about the same amount and same caliber of passes as the other "good" (categorically speaking) playmakers in this region. His puck poise, vision, and creativity aren't sublime – but they're very good.

NR	PLAYER	TEAM	LEAGUE	HEIGHT	WEIGHT	POS	GRADE
	TESTA, LUCA	BRANTFORD	OHL	6' 00.25"	182	LC	C

NHLCS	CEILING	FLOOR	HOCKEY SENSE	COMPETE	SKILL	SKATE	MISC
NA-143	6	4	6	4	6	6	6

Luca Testa is a left shot forward who came into the league as a centerman but played a lot of this season on the wing. A slightly underwhelming offensive season for Testa with 25 points in 48 games including 14 goals in an injury plagued season. After a disappointing rookie season, Testa did not help boost his draft stock with a rough regular season and then following that up by going pointless in the postseason while playing on the fourth line.

Despite the disappointing season production wise, Testa does have some good skills and tendencies that should not be overlooked. He is often playing in the dirty areas of the offensive zone with strong footing to plant himself in front of the net and in the cycle game while taking contact along the boards. When he is on, he shows a lot of aggression, is strong on the forecheck and often participates in the play physically which can cause disruptions for the opposing teams breakout. Testa can also backcheck hard and uses his strength well in puck battles.

When he is on offensively, Testa has good vision and can find his teammates well in transition and on the rush putting his teammates in a good position to score. There are moments where he can drive play offensively and play at a good pace pushing around defenders on the rush and can create shooting lanes for himself. Testa's downfalls offensively is his poor shot power and that he is hindered by his lack of speed which allows him to be caught by defenders at times and have his turnovers go the other way. He will also have mental lapses which take him out of position defensively which need to be remedied.

Testa did not consistently prove that he belongs on a draft board this season. Potential pops up in his game when he plays hard but considering that was few and far between during stretches in game, it is hard to commit to a draft selection without improvement. When he is competing, he is tough to play against, but when he is not competing he is hard to notice and can just be a body on the ice. The skill flashed during those bursts would also not give him a massive jump in the rankings which is why he has landed where he has.

NR	PLAYER	TEAM	LEAGUE	HEIGHT	WEIGHT	POS	GRADE
	THIBODEAU, CHRIS	KINGSTON	OHL	5' 09.25"	158	RC	NI
NHLCS	CEILING	FLOOR	HOCKEY SENSE	COMPETE	SKILL	SKATE	MISC
NA-151	5	4	6	6	5	6	4

As a late born 2005, Christopher Thibodeau gained an extra year of development in the OHL for the Kingston Frontenacs. This season he put up 60 points in 68 games which included 21 goals in his third year in the Ontario Hockey League.

Thibodeau, an undersized forward, is involved in every play and can show some offensive flair however, he typically does not drive play on his own and is either a secondary or third option on his line. As the season progressed, he began playing with some better linemates, including fellow 2024 Draft eligible forward Gabriel Frasca. This helped his production, but it also showed us that he was a bit behind the more skilled players and despite putting up the offensive numbers he did not show that he had the tools to succeed at the next level.

One example of this is his speed, as he does not possess the high speed you would expect a smaller player to possess in addition to his reaction time which is also slower. He is inconsistent, however present issues with pass reception and how he does not put his teammates is positions to succeed offensively does not give us a lot of confidence in him translating to the next level, where the pace of play is much faster. Another deterrent in his ability to move up to the next level would be that he takes a lot of contact and does not absorb contact well as a smaller player and naturally as he plays against players who are fully matured this will become an issue should he not build upon his low weight.

110	PLAYER	TEAM	LEAGUE	HEIGHT	WEIGHT	POS	GRADE
	THORPE, TYLER	VANCOUVER	WHL	6' 04"	209	RW	C
NHLCS	CEILING	FLOOR	HOCKEY SENSE	COMPETE	SKILL	SKATE	MISC
NA-111	6	4	5	7	4	4	6

After being undrafted last year, the 6'5" right winger progressed a lot. He went from 6 points in last year to 44 points and 23 goals in 51 games this season. Thorpe was an undrafted player in the WHL bantam draft. He had a huge growth spurt from bantam to junior and started the 2022/23 season in the BCHL. He signed with the Giants in October and starter his WHL in November 2022. After playing mostly in the bottom 6 in his first season, Thorpe had a good role for the Giants this year, playing in the top 6, on the man advantage and on the penalty kill.

Offensively, Thorpe has a really good shot, heavy and quick release. He scored multiple of his 5-on-5 goals from the high-slot because of his release. He did a good job as F3 in the offensive to play between checks and be open with timing to use his shot. His board play in the offensive zone is solid as he uses his frame and length to establish body position and protect the puck. Overall, he scans well to identify the next play, but he will have more success to find it by improving his puck handling in small area. In terms of net front play presence, he did a strong job as the net front player on Vancouver Giants' power play. He screes the goalie well, and scored some goals by using his size to find quick rebound. If he can dominate the net front play at 5-on-5, he should be an even better WHL goal scorer next season.

In transition, Thorpe uses his size well as a winger on the breakout, but his poise and execution can improve. His first few steps need a lot of work. Once he gets moving, Thorpe has pretty good top speed. We saw him get around defensemen on the rush this season, using his skating and reach to protect the puck. His puck skills in open ice are fine, allowing him to exploit open space.

Without the puck, Thorpe was trusted at even-strength and on the PK by his coaching staff to play in defensive missions. He has a real willingness to play physical, finishing his checks every possible opportunity he has, doing it smartly without putting himself out of the play. Because of his physical play and long reach, he was a strong forechecker for his team.

Thorpe's game is still really raw, and has a long way to go before impacting the game at the pro level. But with his growth spurt, the huge improvement he did in his game over the years, with some interesting tools to work with, there's still a lot of opportunities to improve and develop his game. He should be in a position to have a lot of success next season for the Giants. When you look at his statical profile, his size and traits his game, the late blooming aspect of his development, there's a lot of similarity to Justin Brazeau. If a team can be patient and invest in his development, there could be some rewards.

57	PLAYER	TEAM	LEAGUE	HEIGHT	WEIGHT	POS	GRADE
	TRAFF, HERMAN	HV71	SWE JR	6' 02.75"	216	RW	C+

NHLCS	CEILING	FLOOR	HOCKEY SENSE	COMPETE	SKILL	SKATE	MISC
INT-25	6	6	6	6	7	6	7

Traff is a Swedish power forward who spent the past season primarily with his junior club, HV71, but also played 10 SHL games and 8 Allsvenskans games. While he didn't dominate statistically with his junior club (21 points in 26 games) his on-ice performance suggests that he translates well to the next level. He also showed promising flashes when competing against men in both professional leagues. He also represented Sweden in various international tournaments (U19) in February and April. Traff's birthdate (December 31st, 2005) made him ineligible to play with the U18 team this season by just one day. Sometimes, players with late birthdays can go under the radar because they receive less exposure than those participating in U18 tournaments throughout the year.

With soft hands for a big player, he handles the puck well in tight spaces and also has real good agility to change directions quickly, which is quite impressive for a player of his size. He can create plays out of nothing from the wall thanks to this agility and his quick hands. He's got a long, powerful stride, and his skating is well above-average for a player his size. We often talk about the importance of size-skating combination, and Traff exemplifies this. Watching the NHL playoffs this year, we see how fast the game is, and how it's getting more difficult for players who lack speed to have success in the playoffs. This won't be an issue for Traff.

Traff's agility stands out in one-on-one confrontations, as well as in open ice, where his top speed and acceleration allow him to be effective while in transition, while rushing the puck, and while creating separation. His transitional game benefits from his ability to outpace opponents with his speed, use his hands skillfully, and leverage his long reach to shield the puck from opposing players. While he possesses a good shot, this season did not showcase it as an elite weapon that would translate into him becoming a high-end goal scorer at the next level. Some of the goals he scored demonstrated a promising shot, but it was inconsistent throughout the season. When he's on his game, he looks like a legit top-six scoring forward.

To maximize his offensive potential, he needs to improve the efficiency of his one-timer, particularly from the half-wall in the Ovechkin spot during power plays (as shown during his time in junior). Although he demonstrated the ability to score from distance, he appears more comfortable with his wrist or snap shot than with his slapshot (including one-timer).

He's a smart player with good vision and a good processor. He has good one-touch processing in the neutral zone. Offensively, he can be a dual threat thanks to his shooting and passing skills. He's got a very good projectable frame and could end up playing in a few years, at 6'03" and 220 pounds. He protects the puck well with his frame, reach, and adeptness at changing direction to make it challenging for opposing players to remove pucks from him. There's some physicality in his game, too. He's not a mean player, but he competes well. We like his effort on backchecks, where he has demonstrated being skillful at gaining inside leverage and stripping players of the puck with his excellent active stick.

His game projects as that of a good, two-way, top-9 forward in the NHL. If he can find more consistency with his shooting skills, he could even play a top-6 role. We think he's one of the more underrated players in this draft. Next season, he should play full-time in the SHL. If not, he should get loaned to a team in the Allsvenskans league. He would also be a strong candidate for Sweden's World Junior team.

NR	PLAYER	TEAM	LEAGUE	HEIGHT	WEIGHT	POS	GRADE
	ULJANSKIS, DARELS	AIK	SWE JR	6' 02"	194	LD	C

NHLCS	CEILING	FLOOR	HOCKEY SENSE	COMPETE	SKILL	SKATE	MISC
INT-40	6	5	5	6	6	5	6

A left shot and offensive-minded defenseman from Latvia playing in Sweden's J20 level, Darels Uljanskis is a threat to score from the point. He put up 12 points at the J18 level in a combined 11 games and 29 points in 45 games playing at the J20 level all with the AIK organization. Additionally, he put up three points in 2 playoff games and 3 points in 10 games in the U18 and U20 Championships while representing Latvia as one of their more trusted defenders.

As a smooth, but not fast skater, Ulkanskis's uses good footwork to keep up on the ice despite his slower pace. He walks the line well offensively and can use his deception and patience to shoot the puck through or around traffic and get the puck on target. There is also a good playmaking element to his game, although he is more of a shoot first defender as opposed to looking for the pass option. He can delay, making forwards bite and find a good shooting lane and has good accuracy in his shot placement which he likes to show off. He is a patient shooter and is strong on the power play with solid puck distribution and his mentioned love for shooting the puck. Uljanskis has the ability to utilize space well offensively and if given room to pinch in for an offensive chance, he does not hesitate to take it. He likes to activate on the rush when available and he makes strong and quick transitions up ice. However, he does not put himself out of position often but if he does, he is average at getting back and finding his coverage.

In coverage defensively, Uljanskis prioritizes the puck and not his man which can get him into trouble defensively. He is active and physical in his own end, but to take his defensive game to a more projectable level he will need to become more patient and use his mind more effectively in coverage as he can leave his man open in search of the puck. He can at times be too aggressive and try to do too much defensively however, he can cover himself with his reach and stick play. While he is off in his defensive coverage, Uljanskis does cover lanes effectively and can win puck battles along the boards with good strength.

Despite the slower speed, both forwards and backwards, Uljanskis does not give the puck away often and he seems to find forwards for decent breakouts even while under pressure. For a more offensive defenseman, he is good physically and his play in tight with the puck is good enough to translate to a smaller ice surface. In rush defense, he will use his stick more than his body to defend but can hold up against larger and stronger players which should hold up well when he makes the change to North American ice.

NR	PLAYER	TEAM	LEAGUE	HEIGHT	WEIGHT	POS	GRADE
	USTINKOV, DANIIL	ZURICH	SWISS	6' 00"	198	LD	C

NHLCS	CEILING	FLOOR	HOCKEY SENSE	COMPETE	SKILL	SKATE	MISC
INT-34	6	3	4	4	7	8	5

Puck rushing defenseman. Daniil Ustinkov spent most of the first half of the season in Switzerland's top pro league (NLA). After returning from a tough U20 World Junior Championships (where he was a team-worst minus-6), Ustinkov was optioned to the second-tier pro league in Switzerland (SL) for most of the second half of his season. He dabbled in a short playoff series at the U20 Swiss junior league before finishing off his time in the Swiss League (SL) and, finally, was a 20-minute defenseman at the U18 World Junior Championships – where he was once again a team-worst minus-7 with one assist in five games.

Overall, few draft eligible players can claim such a variety of venues. Though, the production wasn't quite what we'd like to see. Regular season and playoffs at the two pro levels in Switzerland, he tallied no goals and ten assists in 50 games. In fairness to Ustinkov, his ice time was very limited in NLA – which is to be expected for an August 2006 birthday. There's a perfectly reasonable explanation for all of his production values at every level this year, but we'll dig into why this issue may prevail as he continues his career later in the profile.

On the plus side, he's very technically skilled. His stickhandling is smooth and measured. His puck carrying upside is his calling card. He has consistent ability to make an opponent's F1 completely obsolete. With his excellent edge work and deceptive handling, he has some one-man breakouts that are reminiscent of Shayne Gostisbehere or Dmitry Orlov. His ability to exit from behind the net from a dead start or off of a D-to-D pass is probably the most scalable aspect of his technical skill offerings. There is also some upside for deceptive maneuvers at the top layer of the offensive zone. It's not quite as consistent as his exits, but there's obvious upside for it. Though, this is where Ustinkov is going to need to really be adaptable to smaller rinks when the time comes. Even at the junior level, we see him struggle a bit to get his checker's skates to turn and for Ustinkov to effectively attack their heels with enough explosiveness to convert the move.

Given his really strong skating base, it seems quite likely that he'll add some explosiveness as he gets more physically developed. Not that it's bad now, but given his elite edge work and skating mechanics, his acceleration and speed shouldn't be far behind. But it takes more than just excellent physical and technical traits to be effective in this manner at the NHL level. The mental processing needs to be sharp in order for these moves to work consistently and, more importantly, be converted into useful sequences. Ustinkov, as a fairly immature player, can go to the same well too many times and savvier opponents are getting a bead on it.

This is where we start to question the upside of the young defenseman – the mental processing level. In an element of fairness, let's take a sequence from a Swiss junior game where the game is much, much slower than NLA or tournament play. It's something that we see often in his game. It's the 2nd period of a quarterfinal playoff game at the Swiss U20 level. Puck comes diagonally out of the corner to Ustinkov at the left point. So all the skates turn up ice for the opponent Ustinkov is more than 10 feet inside the blueline, he has his partner (a right-handed shooter) to his right and an open left-handed shooting forward above the top of the circle – the latter would constitute an against-the-grain/weakside passing play. Ustinkov accepts the puck and pushes laterally to the left with it. A good move to further stretch out the defenders emerging from the opposite corner. He has successfully turned two high forwards' skates directly towards the side boards, away from the direction of where this pass should go. His partner (Gian Meier) has evened up with him, presented a target, and even splayed open his right hip because he knows there's an opportunity to flip the ice by directing this puck to the open winger at the top of the right circle. No pass. But a shoulder fake inside turned to an outside carry – so, this could be something good still. However, he's in the process of losing ground and now Ustinkov's heels are getting close to the blueline and he's now carried the disc outside the dot line. All the while, the fake wasn't sufficient to break the momentum that the checker was already carrying in the direction Ustinkov is trying to go. Now, the passing lane is covered, he's tracking backwards, and he's invited the speed of the checker into his lap. Daniil digs in and throws his shoulders well out in front of his knees to try to drive past this checker tight along the boards. Because his shoulders are so far forward, there is no puck protection mechanics in play, he doesn't have a good enough first-step, heel-to-toe launch to get by, and the puck is stripped clean and carried the other way. An unbalanced Ustinkov wipes out after the strip.

This is one example of a prevailing trait in his game and it gets to such an extreme, that it's to his detriment. In outlet situations, where he is more successful with individual moves, this lack of mental acuity manifests itself as poor pass timing and accuracy. He's a beat late to recognize the lanes that he's made available and for as technically skilled as he is, he throws some oddly inaccurate passes even in low pressure situations. In a similar vein, while he has an okay shot, his process for shooting is not good. He gets a lot of shots blocked because he fails to open up a lane or fails to recognize one. Or, as we detailed in the above sequence, he has a tendency to carry himself out of the play before throwing a puck towards the net – so his assist rates from rebound generation or deflectable pucks is very low. His head and shoulder feints aren't very effective right now. He doesn't sell them enough sometimes, but other times, he doesn't give them a chance to breathe. He can be so quick with the inside shoulder fake into an outside stickhandle, for instance, that he doesn't actually sell the opponent. Similarly, to a degree, on puck retrievals he tries to sell some pretty outlandish misdirection and it's just not believable at times.

He'll feel a player on his back and then take this wide arc towards the puck, wind up like he's taking a half slapper and then try to slip out the other way on his backhand. But that's not buying him the room that he thinks it is. One, the checker is going to take the correct shoulder more times than not, and two, if Ustinkov really did slap the puck away then there's nothing else for the checker to really do there but finish his hit. There's an element in Ustinkov's body language sometimes where he seems a little surprised that these misdirection retrievals don't work and that he still has a checker getting inside leverage on him.

There's reason to believe that he can improve on these because there are heavy elements of physical and technical development arc improvement involved with this process.

In order for Ustinkov to become a more legitimate prospect, his defensive game needs a complete overhaul. As it stands right now, there are almost no redeemable qualities about it. It's typical for draft eligible players to be missing pieces from their defensive game, but this has a lot of big time negatives on full display at every level right now. Not all of them are going to be imminently fixable either. For as terrific of a skater he is, his rush absorption and speed matching ability is poor. Between his lack of anticipation on how the rush is going to go combined with his puzzling lack of foot churn, he gets eaten alive on even rudimentary rush situations way too often. On top of that, his stick positioning and pokecheck timing are basically random. Further, his pokecheck process has almost no body backing and because of his low foot churn defensively, his recovery skating doesn't allow him to get a second chance at most plays. Usually with this player type, rush absorption is a plus – especially when there isn't anything complex, like criss-crosses or isolation plays – but not here. He's not hard to play against even against his peers. He shows limited concepts of boxing out, to the point that when he does engage, he'll pin as many sticks to the ice as he does lifting them off the rink. In board battles or cycle situations, he digs in on the wrong shoulder quite often, which usually allows for more sustained attack time against. For 6'0" and almost 200 pounds, he's easy to knock off his skates still. So, really all the elements of defensive play are lacking – the anticipation skills, the urgency, the compete level, the physicality, the technique, in-zone play, rush absorption, triangle management – it needs a lot of help. One thing that is a little unconventional to some defense coaches still, but might maximize Ustinkov's traits is allowing him to surf through the neutral zone. Instead of constantly putting this player on his heels, let him use his lateral skating ability to try to break the stride and momentum of rushes as they start. Even if this carries him to his off-side, if he makes a stop, he has the technical skill to possibly turn that into sudden change transition. Obviously, we're not going to be influencing ZSC head coach Marc Crawford, but this kind of tactic has helped players become better defensively overall because they apply pieces of the surfing concepts to ordinary rush defense – former Chicago Blackhawk Duncan Keith, is a success story in this regard.

This is a tough player to rank because his positive traits are really outstanding. The skating base and mechanics are very high end. If he was even a little bit better of a passer or shooter, his skill would probably grade up to an 8 because his hands are outstanding. On the flip side, his upside is likely stunted by his lackluster hockey sense. Ultimately, the poor spatial awareness, partner support, seam recognition coagulating with his lack of compete without the puck are enough to dissuade us from taking a gamble on the puck rushing upside.

"Multi-line puck carriers are worth their weight in gold to me, but too many of these rushes carry him into useless ice and he doesn't have the hockey sense to convert the passes enough. Probably not going to be worth the defensive headache." – HP Scout, Michael Farkas

NR	PLAYER	TEAM	LEAGUE	HEIGHT	WEIGHT	POS	GRADE
	VAISANEN, VEETI	KOOKOO	FIN	6' 00.5"	188	LD	C
NHLCS	CEILING	FLOOR	HOCKEY SENSE	COMPETE	SKILL	SKATE	MISC
INT-21	5	4	4	5	4	7	5

Vaisanen played 50 games in the Liiga as a 17-year-old with Kookoo, which can be rare for a defenseman in Finland. On the international stage, he missed the Hlinka-Gretzky Cup with an injury in August and was cut from the World Junior team in December. He played at the U20 Four Nations Tournament in November and the U18 World Hockey Championship in April.

A good skater from the back end, his ability to skate is his best asset. There's some good projection that can be made with his skating; his form is good and he has a powerful stride. At this point in his development, the quality of his skating is mainly useful in terms of his defensive game. He can keep up with speedy forwards, with good recovery skating to resume good positioning if he or a teammate gets caught or turns the puck over. He can be aggressive with his reads and gap control. A big difference between his first half and second half of the year was how much more comfortable he was at defending in the Liiga. He was more tenacious, won more battles and was more involved physically overall. In the first half, we had a really hard time projecting him for the NHL; we just didn't know what he was. That second half gave us a clearer picture of what he could become. His skating and defensive game are going to be his driving force.

The biggest hurdles between him and his NHL future remain his play with the puck, lack of creativity, lack of shooting skills and decision-making issues when pressured. We don't see much value with his play in the offensive zone. He had a hard time getting his shot through to the net all year; he's not a threat from the point because of his average shot and lack of creativity at the line. His puck game needs to be simple in order to be effective; when he tries to do too much, he gets into trouble. This season, we saw him make too many bad passes in the offensive zone. His decision-making under pressure, whether in his own zone or the offensive zone, tends to reveal a sense of panic. Too often this season, he has been prone to bad turnovers when retrieving pucks or attempting to move them out of his zone.

We view him as a defenseman with solid skating ability and defensive skills, although he needs to improve his puck-moving in order to succeed at the NHL level. While we appreciate his defending and tenacity, it doesn't quite match up to players like Stian Solberg, who has a similar profile but stronger physical game. However, Vaisainen doesn't have the same frame as Solberg. His physical game is decent, but nothing like the Norwegian defender's. He also doesn't have the ideal size to become a shutdown or stay-at-home defenseman (those types of defensemen should be at least 6'02"), but it's not impossible for him to play in the NHL. While it's not impossible for him to make it to the NHL, we see him as a mid to late-round draft pick and don't have a high willingness to select him.

	PLAYER	TEAM	LEAGUE	HEIGHT	WEIGHT	POS	GRADE
23	VANACKER, MAREK	BRANTFORD	OHL	6' 00.5"	175	LW	**B**

NHLCS	CEILING	FLOOR	HOCKEY SENSE	COMPETE	SKILL	SKATE	MISC
NA-17	7	5	7	7	7	6	6

Marek is another OHL forward who proved to get better as the season went on. Marek Vanacker stepped up for his team as the season progressed and became a primary all situations scorer for the Brantford Bulldogs, greatly improving upon his rookie season. Playing every regular season and playoff game for the Bulldogs, Vanacker put up 36 goals and 82 points for over a point a game in the regular season and continued his production in the playoffs with 7 points in 6 games with three goals. Vanacker has the ability as a scorer to break open a game and can turn the tide in his teams favour by creating offense with speed and awareness on the rush.

The goal scoring ability that was coveted from Vanacker coming out of AAA came to light this season, as he forced his way up Brantford's lineup and established himself as a fixture in the top-six forward group, as well as on the first power play unit. His value to his team cannot be underestimated as he, a 17-year-old, drove his team's offense at times this season. As a rush attacker, Vanacker uses his vision to create offense as well as a consistent ability to create offense up the middle with power and speed using his size to his advantage in addition to his quickness. Vanacker has good hands in front of the net and when passing, puts his teammates in good situations to score. His pace and high tempo are great assets to his offensive game and help him beat defenders on rush finesse and power moves in addition to his aggressive nature on the rush, especially in overtime. This also shows us how confident he is offensively and this translates to his teammates as a strong complementary player who can also lead offensively.

With the puck on his stick, Vanacker takes contact well and rarely loses the puck both on the cycle and in open ice. Sometimes he takes too much time too get his shot off, which he does lean into well to generate good shot power. He does separate himself from defenders to provide himself space and additional time. At higher levels this space and time will disappear, so getting his shot off quicker will be something to improve as his development continues. Luckily for Vanacker, should this develop nicely he will have an arsenal of tools to use offensively to score. His greatest scoring ability will presumably be his hands on the rush, as exemplified many times this season.

On the back check, Vanacker hustles to disrupt the opposing team and has the speed to cause some trouble. In his own zone he is active and reads plays well to cause turnovers by getting to opposing players quickly, taking away their space and rushing them into making poor decisions. Vanacker also uses and active stick to break up plays including cross ice passes o turn into offensive opportunities the other way with his speed and rush vision. He is also adept at getting the puck out of his zone by being first on pucks, again because of his speed and getting zone exits which are important for forwards to master while transitioning to the pro game.

As a special teams player Vanacker is a threat to score on the penalty kill, but is prone to some coverage mistakes while down a man. If he can clean this up, he could find himself as a secondary penalty kill forward with the ability to quickly take a turnover the other way shorthanded. Vanacker did continue his scoring tough on the penalty kill finishing tied for second in the league with 5 shorthanded goals.

On the power play, he is a Swiss Army Knife at the OHL level and can play as the bumper, out wide as a shooter or as a net front presence. While posting as the bumper Vanacker can get off his strong shot from a prime scoring area or make quick passes to set up teammates and have penalty killers commit to him to respect his scoring ability and free up other options when they make their move. As mentioned, he does take time getting off his shot but with the extra space the power play provides him it is not as much of an issue, and he can use a delay as an advantage for a teammate to cause a screen or be an option for a deflection or for a defender to screen his own goalie. The probability of Vanacker becoming a top power play forward is iffy, however he can provide a team with a good secondary option while up a man.

While not being the best skater overall, Vanacker does have good speed which he uses in all facets of his game, including puck retrievals. He has strong and quick strides that help him build up speed quickly linearly, but he will need to bulk up to improve his balance and edgework. Adding muscle mass will help him throw his weight around more, which he is already good at and help him as an offensive player on the cycle and give him more strength down low. His hands are good with space but like his shot when space begins to shrink, he bobbles the puck more in tight areas.

The offensive potential for Vanacker cannot be brushed aside. Vanacker has the potential to be a second line contributor or a third line secondary scorer who can contribute on the second power play unit. While there are some attributes Vanacker needs to work on, he has all the tools and confidence to be able to progress into a solid NHL winger who shoots to score. He'll miss a few months next fall recovering from surgery.

"He didn't play enough at the U18." - NHL Scout, May 2024

"Maybe more skilled than (Sam) O'Reilly but a little soft at times." - NHL Scout, May 2024

"No clue why he and Greentree couldn't get on the ice at the U18." - NHL Scout, May 2024

"Seen him twice so far...really good in one game, just ok in the other. He works hard and he can shoot a puck. I was surprised in my second viewing because he was so good in my first viewing. I'll be conservative and say he's a 'C+' so far but I can see him getting up to a 'B' (rated player)" - HP Scout, Mark Edwards, October 2023

"He was another player mentioned by several scouts as having very good combine interviews." - HP Scout, Mark Edwards, June 2024

NR	PLAYER	TEAM	LEAGUE	HEIGHT	WEIGHT	POS	GRADE
	VAN VLIET, LUCAS	USA-U18	NTDP	6' 01.5"	175	LC	C

NHLCS	CEILING	FLOOR	HOCKEY SENSE	COMPETE	SKILL	SKATE	MISC
NA-75	6	4	5	6	6	6	6

Two-way, goal scoring forward. Lucas Van Vliet had a rocky season and ultimately didn't ever really find strong footing in the USNTDP lineup – part of that was the nature of The Program this year and another part was his inconsistency and injury. Going 4+4=8 in 19 USHL games while getting shutout as a bottom line/extra forward at the U18 World Juniors may not look very impressive, but there's actually more to him than meets the boxscore. Of the forwards that generally played lower in the lineup this season, Van Vliet certainly flashes the most upside. He has some surprising hand quickness and dexterity and, with time, has one of the better wrist shots on the team. He doesn't have the quickest release but his ability to get his hands out away from his body and execute on his really nice push/pull mechanics creates a shot that a lot of goalies have trouble tracking at this level. Similarly, his stickhandling ability can be really high end, but there are some caveats. He is much better in second-chance situations, especially coming back up the ice than he is in on the initial rush. Part of that may be because of his lack of tempo control. Watching him carry the puck, in virtually any situation, there is strikingly little variance in his approach and technique. It has an effect of really narrowing his puck control window and he doesn't adapt his skating stance to call on a puck protection technique, this causes him to lose a lot of pucks as soon as a d-man matches his speed. However, when he recovers a puck and is carrying it back up the ice in the attacking zone, he has a lot more success. That's because his edges and burst coming through turns creates a speed differential situation that he can properly take advantage of. So, while his puck carrying and deking ability isn't very consistent right now, there is a lot of potential for it because the building blocks are in place.

As mentioned, Van Vliet has good edgework and can really surprise opponents with his burst coming off his edges, especially when he leans off his center line and really digs into the turn. He isn't super explosive from a pure first-step quickness point of view and his top speed is only above average generally, but overall the skating package is a plus on his 6'1" frame. Despite spending most of the year at center, he's not a natural playmaker. His short passing game is good, but his passing game breaks down a bit when it comes to conceptualizing and executing longer or more dangerous passes. He had three primary assists in USHL play this year: a 12-foot, adjacent lane pass in the NZ; an attempted slip saucer pass that hit off the thigh of a defenseman and went behind the net; and a 4-foot pass off of a forecheck steal on a 2 on 0. Either the pass was short and open, or it didn't really connect meaningfully. We think that his skill set in general would be better served on the wing anyhow. It might give him even more playmaking opportunities too because he won't have to manage so much ice. That said, he does come back defensively (which a player can do from the wing, of course) and supports the puck well. He goes into the corner and supports board battles. He isn't physical by nature, but he wouldn't classify as "timid". Good on draws.

It seems likely that Van Vliet will play for Dubuque next season before going to Michigan State the following fall. That's almost certainly for the best in his development. There's upside for him to have a 25+ goal season if he stays in the USHL, instead of being a depth player again at a higher level. He has a lot of good, not great, pieces to him and is said to be very coachable, so we'd expect a noteworthy jump in his D+1 season.

NR	PLAYER	TEAM	LEAGUE	HEIGHT	WEIGHT	POS	GRADE
	VAN VOLSEN, JACK	MISSISSAUGA	OHL	6' 01.25"	188	LC	NI
NHLCS	CEILING	FLOOR	HOCKEY SENSE	COMPETE	SKILL	SKATE	MISC
NA-164	5	5	5	4	6	5	6

Jack Van Volsen is a left shot forward for the Mississauga Steelheads in the Ontario Hockey League. Jack usually lines up as a center but can play wing as well for which he seems better suited. In 63 games he posted 20 goals and 32 points for a somewhat underwhelming year production wise, after being selected with the sixth overall selection in the 2022 OHL Draft. High selections lead to hopes of goal scoring force type players at the OHL level. He has scored goals at a decent pace for a second-year player, however, a lot of the other qualities of his game need refining.

A lot of the positives with Van Volsen like his defensive positioning are hindered by his poor skating ability. His edgework and poor first step hurt his ability to defend man-to-man, especially on the cycle. He will cut off opposing forwards, but with quick puck movement from the attacking team, he ends up behind the play enough to hurt his projectability moving to higher and more skilled levels. Physically, he has a good frame but he will need to improve his balance and edgework.

Offensively he shoots the puck very well when he has time, but as windows are taken away from him he rushes his shot resulting in more of a whipping motion which decreases his accuracy and power. His passing is also a weakness, as he misses big windows at the junior level that only shrink at the professional level.

All in all, what really stops Van Volsen is his skating and compete. Even if his skating was improved, his compete level lacks the consistency we like to see in players we would draft.

"I haven't seen anything so far that screams draft me. I'll keep him as a watch but not much there... disinterested at times, lack of effort at times." - HP Scout, Mark Edwards, October 2023

NR	PLAYER		TEAM	LEAGUE	HEIGHT	WEIGHT	POS	GRADE
	VEILLEUX, XAVIER		MUSKEGON	USHL	6' 00.25"	189	LD	NI
NHLCS	CEILING	FLOOR	HOCKEY SENSE	COMPETE	SKILL		SKATE	MISC
NA-74	5	6	5	6	4		4	6

Puck moving defenseman. Xavier Veilleux was Muskegon's (USHL) premier puck mover this season. Being behind one of the league's best forward corps paid dividends for Veilleux in terms of production. He led all draft eligible USHL defensemen in scoring. However, like a number of productive defensemen in the Lumberjacks' recent past, there aren't too many transferrable pro skills in his game. Good size at a shade over 6-foot and nearly 190 pounds, Veilleux has a labored skating stride. He's not explosive out of transition skating or turns. In turn, his recovery skating is also a weakness. This is really spotlighted on weakside rotation plays to his side of the ice. When he gets sucked into this type of play or an isolation play – and he is prone to do so – that unset meandering combined with his lack of burst creates an open window for the opposition in choice scoring areas. He deserves some credit for his net-front play. It's not consistent, but he shows some push back and toughness. Not nearly enough to be considered a bruiser by any means, but there's some thoughtfulness and desire in there at times...enough to move some weaker players off their spot. His overall defensive game lacks polish and urgency though. The rush absorptions are littered with irregularities – whether it's the initial gap, or the timing to turn and go transitionally with the attacker, or getting caught chasing his man all the way out to his own blueline, leaving the lower layer exposed – it's not done with any real process or consistency. His hockey sense doesn't grade particularly high, so it's unlikely that these reads will improve too much even with good help. If a coach can help him install some pattern recognition, it could allow a savvy partner to read off of him better down the line.

One of the more redeemable qualities about his hockey sense though is exhibited through his playmaking. To Veilleux's credit, it's almost hard to believe the level of complexity associated with some of his passes...even in his (comparatively smaller) assist sample, there are some really interesting plays being made. Typically, with this style of defenseman, we'd see more assists generated off of rebounds or off high-risk, "homerun" style passes. With Veilleux, there are more seam-splitting, second wave (even third wave) finds across multiple lanes. That, alone, gives us some degree of trust in his overall mental processing package. It's odd to see that level of guile not being applied without the puck in any obvious way. His D-to-D passing is crisp and accurate. Some of the zone exit passes can cross the line into dangerous for the receiving forward...that's a concern as the level of competition speeds up on him. It's unlikely that he'll be able to compensate for this with his puck carrying ability. While he's an okay or even above average puck handler in short spurts, his ability to cross lines with the puck is not a plus. He's not deceptive in space at all. Crossing his own line or the attack line with the puck on his stick is not a good omen for the forthcoming sequence. The lack of dynamic element to his game prevents him from opening up space for teammates and he has no ability to get the puck back into the interior once it's outside the dots. And on top of that, he's a very weak and very infrequent shooter. There's almost enough to his passing game and short-sequence puckhandling to bump his skill level up to a 5, but the puck carrier ability and shot kill it. If there was something convincingly more transferable, he'd get the bump.

If the transition game somehow becomes remarkably adept down the line, maybe there's a little something here. Otherwise, between his feet, his hockey IQ, and his lack of dynamic elements, there are just too many negative outs to have to overcome with this player for us.

108	PLAYER	TEAM	LEAGUE	HEIGHT	WEIGHT	POS	GRADE
	VESTERHEIM, PETTER	MORA IK	SWE	5'11"	172	LC	C

NHLCS	CEILING	FLOOR	HOCKEY SENSE	COMPETE	SKILL	SKATE	MISC
-	5	6	7	7	5	7	5

Petter Vesterheim is a high octane defensive center, who uses his skating and playmaking ability to general offensive plays. Vesterheim forms one third of a Norwegian draft-eligible trio on Mora that includes Michael Brandsegg Nygard, Noah Steen, and himself. He produced 17 points in 40 regular season games, and followed that up with 3 points in 12 playoff games. He also played for Norway at both the U20 and World Championship levels. One area that Vesterheim has relative to a lot of other draft eligible forwards, is that he has a lot of pro experience as the result of this being his second year of eligibility. He played regularly in the Allsvenskan, and that gives us a significant advantage when figuring out how his mature and already pro-style game can translate.

Vesterheim's game is established through his energy. It's an energy that's generated through his non-stop motor and mechanically efficient skating base. He uses that skating base to almost always be in motion and to pressure opposing puck carriers in each area of the ice. He can use his skating ability to engage and close rapidly on the backcheck, explode into space and get below coverage when receiving a pass off the rush, and he can rely on his skating ability to generate zone entries when he's carrying the puck.

Speaking of his skating, his top speed is very good, featuring proper mechanics and excellent posture, which he carries with him when attacking through high trafficked areas of the ice. In addition, his spatial awareness, timing, and deception come together with his puck handling, allowing him to maintain possession in high pressure situations, after defenses attempt to collapse on him.

His skating is part of the reason he's a multi-faceted, and well rounded player. Petter is also very efficient for a player who went from the Norwegian Junior circuit to the Allsvenskan and World Championships. His maturity away from the puck granted him penalty kill-time in critical situations and some of his better performances were actually in more structured environments, like the Allsvenskan, relative to J20.

The other reason he's a versatile winger is due to his competitive nature and natural ability to understand contact. What this means is that when he needs to apply his frame, despite not being a large player, he does it in a way that gives him advantageous positions.

For instance, if he's involved in wall battles, he's constantly looking to obtain inside positioning, or leveraging his frame to counteract larger players which forces their work rate to increase. This is a critical aspect of his game. The other aspect of his physical game that speaks volumes to his grit and determination is that he's not afraid to initiate against larger players so that he can fall back out of the contact while still potentially in possession of the puck.

Vesterheim Isn't someone we would label a gifted puck handler, he's more of an average to slightly above average handler, so the first phase deception, skating ability, spatial recognition and advanced physical game are the primary attributes that give him an ancillary skill-set to rely on.

He's also more of a primary playmaker than a shooter. Ironically, his best goal over the last couple of seasons came against men when he actually moved up in Allsvenskan, where he showed advanced footwork off the rush and rapidly changed his shooting angle from the far side to the short-side, which completely off-set the goalies timing, but this is more of an atypical play from him. Most of his goals will be net front after he uses his speed to bypass coverage.

What's more typical are adaptive playmaking sequences where he has showcased the ability to read and react to incoming pressure that gets the puck either moving up ice in the right direction in transition, or passes that further elongate the cycle. He's an advanced swing passer, and he can off look a high danger lateral option, which was showcased more prominently on the man advantage with Mora. There's a natural ability to see the ice, and he looks to use his teammates often, rarely forcing extended, low percentage plays.

He understands how to extend his operating windows as well. If he peels off of pressure and recognizes his space, he will take that space, but he doesn't rush his options when entering space. As an example, if a player is rushing to cover him, he knows that he can use that extra burst of speed against them, forcing a sudden directional shift out of that player that then gives Vesterheim an additional lane that otherwise wouldn't be there if he tried to rush the play.

The last quality that stands out is that despite not having a high end offensive skill-set, he's also not a streamlined player. There's some technical and advanced plays in his game, especially when he's incorporating his postural and passing fakes into his edgework so that he can bypass layers heading out of his end and into the neutral zone. He can surprise at times, and it's one of the reasons that he forced our hand and made us rank him again.

Petter Vesterheim is an athletically gifted, responsible defensive forward who can chip in on offense from time to time. These players sometimes have difficulty translating, since many of them can be deemed below replacement level, but we think Vesterheim has specific qualities that might make him an above replacement outlier in a 4th line role or if everything goes right, maybe even a 3rd line role.

Vesterheim makes up for lost value in his lack of scoring rates, with his high pressured pace of play, and the ability to reacquire pucks quickly. In his case, he's already an advanced penalty-killer who projects to be able to anticipate defensive coverage and generate short handed rush opportunities. He gains additional value due to his zone entry rate projection, and he has the energy that's needed in a depth role to give the top end players a boost when they are playing flat. For these reasons we felt the need to rank him, despite not having a ton of offensive upside.

"He's similar to Joel Kiviranta. They are similarly built and I think Vesterheim would be playing in a similar role, while potentially putting up similar production. I like Kiviranta for what he does, but admittedly, there's not many of his player type in the NHL, so despite liking Vesterheim's game, it's an uphill battle for him to make it." - HP Scout, Brad Allen (May 2023)

"I think he put together the type of season that should get him drafted just like I did last season. Admittedly, it comes down to if you feel Vesterheim can be above replacement level in a depth role and after watching a ton of playoff hockey, I think the answer is that he can." - HP Scout, Brad Allen (May 2024)

NR	PLAYER	TEAM	LEAGUE	HEIGHT	WEIGHT	POS	GRADE
	VESTERINEN, ROOPE	HPK JR.	FIN-JR	5' 09"	173	LW	NI
NHLCS	CEILING	FLOOR	HOCKEY SENSE	COMPETE	SKILL	SKATE	MISC
INT-89	4	4	5	5	5	5	4

We had high hopes for Vesterinen. To say he struggled this season would be an understatement. We liked his prior performance at the U17 Hockey Challenge, where he had 7 goals and 10 points in 7 games. He also played 8 games in the Liiga last season. At the junior level (the Finland U20 league) he scored 4 goals and recorded 14 points in 24 games. Fast-forward to this season: in 27 junior games, he had 5 goals and 6 assists. In international hockey, he was a non-factor for Finland with 6 points in 16 games. He also missed 3 months of hockey from October to January with a leg injury.

He's an undersized forward with some decent skills and a good compete level. He has struggled this season with his inside game; last year, he was scoring a lot around the net, but this year, he was a non-factor in many games we saw. He struggled all season long to establish his inside game. His skating didn't improve from last year, either; for a player of his stature, he needs to be more dynamic with his skating, and this is not the case with him. We think the will is there; he works hard, but his lack of size, skill level that is decent but nothing amazing, combined with his lack of speed makes it difficult for him to find success.

For smaller players to translate their game to the NHL, you need an elite/great asset, and we don't see it with Vesterinen. There are some decent qualities to his game, but not enough to think he can overcome his lack of size and speed to become an NHLer. For us, he looks like a player who will have a good career in the Liiga, but nothing more.

29	PLAYER	TEAM	LEAGUE	HEIGHT	WEIGHT	POS	GRADE
	VILLENEUVE, NATHAN	SUDBURY	OHL	5' 11"	193	LC	B
NHLCS	CEILING	FLOOR	HOCKEY SENSE	COMPETE	SKILL	SKATE	MISC
NA-60	6	8	8	8	5	7	6

Villeneuve was the 3rd overall pick in the 2022 OHL Draft and had an eventful second season in the OHL with the Sudbury Wolves, tallying 23 goals and 50 points in 56 games. However, he also received a 15-game suspension late in the year for violating the OHL Social Media Policy in a manner detrimental to the welfare of the League. Despite not always receiving regular top-6 ice time this season, he managed to produce just under a point per game. Initially, he had a slow start with 7 points in his first 17 games, but he finished strong with 43 points in his last 38 regular-season games. He's noted for his strong skating, high energy level, and mean streak, which is relatively rare in today's hockey.

Villeneuve is a versatile forward, as he can play all three forward positions, and has value on both the power play and penalty kill. He's not a high-end offensive or skilled player, but he brings an abrasive game that is tough to find and that will attract NHL teams. He's a player who will expand his value come playoff time in the NHL thanks to his grit. We think that, at his best, he could be a 3rd line player. We don't see top-6 upside within his game; his skill level is not high enough to project him high in an NHL lineup. For example, in transition, he's not the player you want with the puck; his stickhandling is too average, and he has difficulty consistently beating players one-on-one with his hands. His bread and butter in the NHL will be his play along the wall and in front of the net. This is how he's going to generate offense: by winning puck battles and bringing the puck to the net or slot area. His game thrives on physicality and pushbacks. Yes, he's an energy player, a trash talker, and annoying to play against, but he's also a willing fighter who will challenge opposing players all the time.

He's also a smart hockey player. We like his ability to get open in the offensive zone to receive passes. He anticipates the play well, which makes him a threat at 5-on-5, but also adds value to his potential as a penalty-killer. He's fearless, and loves to attack through the middle lane. He's anything but a perimeter player. He possesses an above-average shot with a good release and velocity. While he may not pose a significant threat from long distances, he can be dangerous from the slot area to the net. Throughout the season, he was often used in front of the net on the power play and could also perform well from the bumper position. However, it's unlikely that he'll secure a spot on the power play in the NHL (unless it's on PP2) in that front-of-the-net role.

His playmaking displayed some flashes of brilliance during the season, but it was inconsistent. We wished for more consistency in his passing game, as this would have boosted his spot in our rankings. In the playoffs, his passing game faltered. Comparatively, Ridley Greig stood out in his draft year due to his outstanding passing skills, which contributed to his high ranking on our list. We didn't see enough out of Villeneuve's playmaking to justify an aggressive ranking like Greig's.

A strong skater, he generates some good power within his first 2 or 3 strides. His stride is powerful and compact. He's tough to knock down; he is a physically powerful player who, as he continues to mature physically, will become increasingly difficult to handle along the boards. This enables him to keep up with anyone on the ice, both offensively and defensively, due to his strong skating. He competes hard, with one of the highest compete levels of any player in this draft class. When discussing compete level, it's not solely about a player's grit; observing Villeneuve away from the puck illustrates his commitment. His effort level on back checks is consistently high thanks to his excellent skating and physicality to disrupt puck-carriers. As mentioned earlier, he holds value as a penalty killer, thanks to his keen sense of anticipation and work ethic. He also possesses a good stick to break up plays and block passing lanes. Additionally, he's a good shot blocker, and these add even more dimensions to his contribution and effectiveness on the penalty kill.

We consider Villeneuve a safe pick in this draft. He's likely to be more appreciated by NHL teams than by the public discourse, similar to Easton Cowan of London last year, although they are different players. We believe there's a high likelihood that Villeneuve will develop into a dependable NHL player, although he may not be perceived as a sexy pick due to his lack of flashy offensive skills. However, this year's NHL postseason is sure to shed some light on why players like Villeneuve could hear their names called much earlier than what other public lists might suggest.

"I love him. Love how he plays." - NHL Scout, October

"Third round guy." - NHL Scout, May 2024

"I really like Nathan. He competes really hard and has some skill mixed in as well. Still think there is some limited upside but he might be a guy who can compliment some high end skilled players in the NHL. Need to see more to figure out if he can do more than just make the simple plays. I have him as a 'B' rated prospect right now and I'd guess he'll stay that way all year long." - HP Scout, Mark Edwards, October 2023

"Excellent interview feedback." - HP Scout, Mark Edwards, June 2024

13	PLAYER	TEAM	LEAGUE	HEIGHT	WEIGHT	POS	GRADE
	VINNI, EEMIL	JOKIPOJAT	FIN 2	6' 02.75"	187	G	C
NHLCS	CEILING	FLOOR	HOCKEY SENSE	COMPETE	SKILL	SKATE	MISC
INT-I	6	4	5	7	7	7	7

One of the difficulties when evaluating Emil Vinni is that he had an accelerated development curve. Very few goalies play full time in U20-Liiga at the age of 15, and it's the first time we've ever had to scout a first year eligible goalie in Finland who is playing as a full time starter in Mestis. To compound matters, Mestis is a slower league and there were a lot of games where he received a low shot volume, which makes our job even harder than it already is.

Vinni was a goalie who excelled at a young age due to his phenomenal quickness. He's one of the fastest and most explosive goalies in this class. Some goalies look like they are wearing weighted vests out on the ice at times, especially first year eligible goalies who lack strength and conditioning but Vinni is the exact opposite, he looks like he's going to take off on a rocket.

Typically, the more gifted the athlete, the more time needed for them to use it as a strength as opposed to allowing it to become a tool that's used against them. With Vinni's case, he fell into the camp much like Askarov has in the past, and Cossa for that matter, where he was his own worst enemy and essentially beating himself on the first shot as opposed to letting the shot come to him.

That's what we saw at the beginning of this season. He was over-active, he was over-committed and he was exaggerating his position and losing track of the puck too often. However, towards mid-December he started anchoring himself in the net at a more consistent rate and started taking advantage of his skill-set that allowed him to keep the puck out more often.

Having better crease containment is essential for Eemil's translation because he's a goalie that can fail to track property at the rate that's required at this stage in his development, when there's traffic. There's a concern with his tracking from a consistency perspective. We emphasize the word consistently because he certainly can read advanced plays and track them still or we wouldn't be talking about him. In-fact he's been impressive at reading point blank redirect plays and back door plays throughout the season. The game to game consistency has been the issue.

Despite the above concerns, this season he still showed much better scanning ability than last year and part of that can be attributed to learning when he can scan the ice when pucks are at dead angles relative to him. In-fact, you could make the argument that he looks to scan the ice and keep his head on a swivel constantly. It's good that's he's learning when he can evaluate the options presented on the ice at dead angles or when a player is rotating with the puck away from him so he can time his scans, but he's scanning so often in some games, that it leads us to believe that he just doesn't have a good "feel" or maybe the better word could be instinct for where the opposing players are positioned within his blind spots which is why he's looking around at options as often as he does.

Another quirk to his game is something he shared with Askarov in his draft year, and that's using a pulsing hand motion on shooters, usually in one-on-one situations. Askarov claimed to pulse so that he could maintain focus but Vinni appears to use it to confuse shooters. Either way, this made Askarov's glove overactive and it made it easier for gifted shooters to exploit his glove side, and it applies to Vinni as well, but unlike Askarov who specifically pulsed with his glove, Vinni does it with his blocker too. We don't like it and it's very likely to get removed once he comes over to North-America or at least toned down, much like it has in Askarov's case.

Despite the above shortcomings, he has a tremendous base to work with and that's because Eemil is a phenomenal athlete. It starts with the transitional save ability and reflexes. He can effortlessly move from a relaxed stance, into a set stance, into a lateral T-push off, into a butterfly, and back out of his butterfly, faster than almost any other goalie. He's incredibly fast, and this works in combination with his legs, where he can deal with point blank redirects and chaotic play in-front of him when he needs to rely more on his split second reaction time, as opposed to finding the angle in advance.

When projecting his high danger lateral save rates, they are up there near the top of this class, even when factoring in that he isn't overly long. This applies to him moving from his RVH position into a lateral transfer within his butterfly or into an extension as well.

When it comes to his RVH position, he looks to push off with his skates laces pressed into the post as opposed to the skate blade, which we feel gives him better explosiveness off of his post and lets him take advantage of his quickness. Another way he takes advantage of his agility is when he's looking to intercept potential passes while in the position, even when he reaches outward and goes off his own centerline, he's fluid and fast enough to compensate for the initial reach if the puck goes past him, forcing him to laterally extend to the opposite post.

One of the more unique aspects of his game is regarding his rebound control. He has a tendency to use his mask to deflect shots up high purposefully and when he's making kicking saves, sometimes he will purposely rotate his core and extend his stick to use his stick in combination with his leg to change the trajectory of the rebound. We like his butterfly. It's super explosive and because he's dextrous he can close everything off under his arms very quickly. This gives him an advantage when he's using he's reaching out in-front of him but then has to bring them down to his sides suddenly during deflections.

Another impressive aspect of Vinni's game is his glove side. He's able to stretch out to the limits of his frame at basically any angle, including on snots that are labeled for the sweet spot between his glove and his ear. On these shot types, he can move his shoulder into space and explode with his glove hand.

When looking at the weakness within his athleticism, really the only stand out issue isn't correctable and it's not his fault, it's just the nature of how he's built and that's regarding his extension rates. Some goalies that are 6'2" and under have the ability to fully extend within their hip line while maintaining balance, and Vinni isn't that goalie yet. When he's fully extending he has to usually fall forward into the play, and that leaves him rather susceptible.

He falls into the Devon Levi, Dustin Wolf, and Juuse Saros issue of not being very long, which puts him at a severe disadvantage when facing current net front monsters like Tom Wilson, past forwards like Wayne Simmonds, and future forwards such as Elmer Soderblom. The difference between the goalies mentioned above though, when contrasting them with Vinni, is that they are far more mentally dialled in and consistent on a game to game basis and that's really the biggest issue for us when projecting him.

He absolutely looks like a full time starter on any given save or game, but the mental consistency has never been there, and that's where his curve gets dangerous since that's been the case for the past 3 seasons now. When Vinni is dialled in and locked in on the play in-front of him, he can stand on his head, but once that first goal gets by him, the flood gates can sometimes open. Due to this danger, we feel he's under the mark needed to declare him a starter, but there's potential for a 1B split goalie if things go really well. He's competitive, he's a fantastic athlete, and he can skate, and that's a heck of a base, but mentally he's not at the starting level for us.

"He reminds me a lot of a 6'2" Askarov, and I was a massive Askarov fan in his initial draft season and still am. Askarov is a big goalie and was younger in his draft season, so my question that I've been asking throughout this season, is if a smaller version with worse extension rates can truly be an NHL starter? There's way more uncertainty here for me, when comparing him to Askarov and I tried to take that into consideration when finding a spot for him my ranking." - HP Scout, Brad Allen

"I like Vinni, but there's a subconscious bubbling for me, or a gut instinct where I just feel there's a bit too much missing for a full time starter when I watch him, but the gut can be your best friend or worst enemy depending on the player and this was admittedly a player I had a lot of trouble figuring out." - HP Scout, Brad Allen

"The last time I was high on a goalie with accelerated development at the age of 15 and 16 was Jakub Skarek. I think it's safe to say that didn't work out for me, so maybe that's why I'm hesitant." - HP Scout, Brad Allen

NR	PLAYER	TEAM	LEAGUE	HEIGHT	WEIGHT	POS	GRADE
	VIRGILIO, MATTHEW	SOO	OHL	5'11"	186	RD	NI
NHLCS	CEILING	FLOOR	HOCKEY SENSE	COMPETE	SKILL	SKATE	MISC
-	5	3	4	4	5	5	4

Matthew Virgilio is a right-shot defender for the Soo Greyhounds who checks in around 5'11 while weighing 186lbs however, watching him play you would guess he is a lot smaller than he is listed. His production was almost identical and arguably worse than his rookie year after putting up 15 points in both seasons while playing four more games this season. His biggest improvement was his +/- going from a -30 in his rookie year to +8 in his sophomore season while playing on a much better team this season.

As mentioned, his ability to play smaller than he is shows most prominently in his overall ability to take contact. He is often out muscled and pushed around by opposing forwards and does not do well in puck battles, especially against larger forwards. His decision making is not strong and will pass in his own zone and in outlet passes to covered teammates frequently regardless of if he is under pressure or not.

Virgilio will likely top out at the OHL level or USports. He already had a high hill to climb as a smaller defenseman and his lower hockey sense and compete are stoppers for us. They hurt his chances at becoming a late pick in the draft.

NR	PLAYER	TEAM	LEAGUE	HEIGHT	WEIGHT	POS	GRADE
	VORONIN, KUZMA	YOUNGSTOWN	USHL	5' 09.75"	157	LW	NI
NHLCS	CEILING	FLOOR	HOCKEY SENSE	COMPETE	SKILL	SKATE	MISC
NA-156	5	4	5	6	6	7	4

Kuzma Voronin burst onto the scene in 2022-23 with a short call up that saw him net four goals and five points in six games. This set expectations fairly high for 2023-24, but he ended up being more of a depth player than an impact scorer. With just 10 goals and 21 points in 52 games, it was a disappointing season for Voronin. He's a straight line player that gets to some really nice top speed at its high end. He's a bit of a wide-set skater, so his agility and small area footwork is worse than we'd expect for a player of his size. If he could develop his way into elite edge work, and implement some better puck protection mechanics, he'd likely win and keep more contested pucks. He's not a player that has one-touch playmaking, so if every puck he touches requires at least a couple of handles, there needs to be vast improvements in his retrieval process. Voronin flashes some individual skills and he has reasonably quick hands and deceptive maneuvers. Plus wrist shot, but needs to improve his ability to get shots through traffic. Not a player that can be counted on for anything besides rudimentary passing plays. He's a player that is willing to backcheck with his speed, but hasn't mastered the technical parts of defense. His weight transfer into hits and his ability to just gain inside leverage on opponents is pretty wonky and it leads to inconsistent results. His average anticipation and lacklustre risk mitigation process doesn't help his defensive acumen either.

One of the bigger drawbacks with Voronin is the profound lack of skill chaining. Even things that are taken for granted, like pass acceptance at speed and getting the puck smoothly to the outside hip…it's just not consistently there. So, the puck and play conditions need to be perfect for his game to really stand out and that's not a workable solution. Doesn't exhibit any sort of tempo control. Right now, there's a streak and shoot winger that has some pull away top speed but not much else.

60	PLAYER	TEAM	LEAGUE	HEIGHT	WEIGHT	POS	GRADE
	WALTON, KIERON	SUDBURY	OHL	6' 05.5"	211	LC	C
NHLCS	CEILING	FLOOR	HOCKEY SENSE	COMPETE	SKILL	SKATE	MISC
NA-117	7	3	6	4	7	6	8

A towering forward in this draft, Kieron Walton has a lot of potential with his large frame and surprising amount of skill he can display offensively. Walton put up 43 points in 65 games with 18 goals in his second year with the Sudbury Wolves, however going pointless in 9 playoff games. His production was great considering he did not consistently get a good amount of ice time throughout the year on a strong Sudbury team. He does have the frame, with plenty of room to fill out, and strong flashes of potential to make it as an NHL forward.

There were a lot of times during the season where Walton left us wanting more from him. During the season we saw two versions of Walton in viewings. When he was on his game, he was tough to play against and used his size to his advantage while adding more skill than expected. However, when he was off his game he would be tough to spot even with his large frame and seemed to be an afterthought at times.

His size alone is enough to put him on our radar, but it's also what he does with the puck that stands out to us. When he is on his game, he uses his hands to make plays happen offensively, coming off the cycle and on the rush. He has good vision in the passing game and uses his long reach to create more passing lanes and generate offense for his teammates and himself. He uses his surprisingly quick hands to create offense by drawing in defenders because of his size and creating space for scoring opportunities. His primary mode of creating offense is off the cycle down low, but he can create offense off the rush as well, using his power moves and ability to hold off defenders with strong balance to make pushes to the net. On the cycle, when he plants his feet, he is difficult to knock off the puck. He also has underrated patience with the puck, scanning the play well before making moves.

On the defensive side, Walton uses his best asset—his size and reach—to be an effective defender. Walton is good at breaking up plays with his stick and consistently disrupts play with an added intelligence to read the play on the defensive side. He is also consistent at finishing his checks, although the strength with which he finishes them needs more consistency. His skating, which can lag at times, is his biggest issue defensively. While he can read the play and at the junior level get away with having a long reach, this will need to be improved moving forward so he does not just rely on his size to make plays in the defensive zone and become a stationary presence at the highest level.

For a player of his size and stature, his skating is an area that does not raise too many red flags. He has good speed for a player of his size, and as mentioned, he is strong on his feet and uses this to cut off passing lanes for opponents on the backcheck. He will need to improve his first step and lateral movement, especially with the puck on his stick, to make the biggest impact on his development. He does have trouble breaking away from defenders in the offensive zone and getting caught by backcheckers heading up ice offensively. This was an issue at times throughout the year, as he would get stripped of the puck by a faster player, causing the puck to transition the other way. He shielded the puck better as the year went on, but this is something we will keep an eye on moving forward.

If Walton, moving forward, was able to add a finesse game to his rush attack or be more of a threat as a shooter, that would greatly improve his offensive output and force defenders to respect him more in the offensive zone. With that being said, he is still a strong contributor on the rush and off the cycle as a power forward and playmaker who has some creative elements to play with alongside his patience. He plays a heavily possession-based game offensively that translates to today's NHL, adding that to his size and his intelligence to process the game at a faster rate than he can skate, making him an attractive asset for us. Add in his hard and aggressive forecheck deep in the offensive zone to rush defenders, and Walton presents himself nicely as a player to add come draft day.

It is not hard to project Walton to the NHL with the size and skill we see from him. However, consistency will be the main thing in his way. Offensively, he is more of a playmaker than a shooter, although he does not have a poor shot; his playmaking skills are just more refined and consistent. Additionally, he needs to work on his consistency in using his size in all facets of his game and not rely on being bigger alone. His scoring was also inconsistent, as he scored in bunches often, which included a 17-game point streak. We would like to see his scoring come more consistently throughout the year as opposed to during stretches. He could probably blame this on playing time though. He will also need to up his compete level, as we found at times he would disappear and not be noticeable in almost any way despite standing out due to his size.

Walton's highest potential would be as a top-six forward; however, it is much more likely he would end up in a middle-six type of role for a team if he makes it. Consistency and compete level will need to be his two biggest focuses, along with his skating, heading into an important development year where he should get more ice time with Sudbury. His compete level is not low enough to be a stopper, but as mentioned, it needs improvement should he want to reach his full potential and make the pro-level. His tools and base development are already in place; it is now a case of how much work will go into his development moving forward.

"Not much to his game other than size." - NHL Scout, December 2023

"He actually has some talent but he plays a lazy game inside that huge frame." - NHL Scout, December 2023

"He's like 6'6" but he plays like he is 5'9". - NHL Scout, May 2024

"When I was watching him last year I thought he would be a second round pick this year. A year later and he's not on my list." - NHL Scout, May 2024

"Huge 6'6" kid who has kinda played like he's 5'6" so far in my views but not many views here so for sure not closing the door on him. If I had to grade him today it would be a 'C' but again I don't want to send to big a message on him yet because I'm kinda limited on where I'm at with him." - HP Scout, Mark Edwards, October 2023

"I was not a fan at all until later in the season. I started to realize he had much more skill than I thought. He got screwed in the icetime department so that hurts production. I wish he competed harder but it's hard to completely ignore 6'6" kids with skill." - HP Scout, Mark Edwards, May 2024

NR	PLAYER		TEAM	LEAGUE	HEIGHT	WEIGHT	POS	GRADE
	WARREN, KEEGAN		MONCTON	QMJHL	6' 01.75"	185	G	NI
NHLCS	CEILING	FLOOR	HOCKEY SENSE	COMPETE	SKILL		SKATE	MISC
NA-12	4	4	5	5	4		5	6

Warren is somewhat of a late-bloomer goaltender. The Newfoundland native was a 14th-round pick in the 2021 QMJHL Draft. This was his first season in the league after making the team out of training camp, but he also played a few games in the MJAHL, as the team started the season with 3 goaltenders on the roster. He comes from a hockey family. His dad played in the QMJHL with the Moncton Wildcats, and was drafted by Toronto in 1998.

To his credit, Warren has made huge strides since being drafted three years ago, going from a former 14th-rounder to the number one goaltender in the league. It's a great story, but as far as NHL potential, his athletic abilities are quite average and he's not particularly good in his crease in this aspect. Although he is listed at 6'02", he's not an imposing goaltender and can struggle with rebounds. His stance doesn't help him either; he needs to make himself look bigger. In addition, he encounters difficulties with point shots when there is heavy traffic in front of him.

On the positive side, he reads the play well when defending against east-west passes and gets across his crease fairly well in those situations. However, his technique is very raw. He still needs to work on his low coverage, improve his reflexes on low shots, and on plays coming from down low. One notable aspect of his game is his competitive spirit; he battles hard for loose pucks and rebounds near him.

Warren is not on our goalie list, although we think he's a great find by the Moncton scouting staff and will help them in the next two years.

NR	PLAYER		TEAM	LEAGUE	HEIGHT	WEIGHT	POS	GRADE
	WETSCH, CARSON		CALGARY	WHL	6' 00.5"	203	RW	C
NHLCS	CEILING	FLOOR	HOCKEY SENSE	COMPETE	SKILL		SKATE	MISC
NA-50	4	5	4	8	4		5	6

The former 12th overall in the WHL draft showed good improvement this season, going from 21 points in his rookie year to 50 points this season. The 6'2" right winger played Calgary's top 6, and saw ice-time in very situations like PP, PK, 6-on-5 for and against, etc. Before the season, Wetsch won a gold medal with team Canada at the Hlinka Gretzky tournament. After the season, he won another gold with Team Canada at the U18. He had a strong tournament, playing on Canada's identity line with Cole Beaudoin and Malcolm Spence, wearing an "A" on his jersey.

Wetsch is a north-south player who excels on the forecheck and in front of the net. He's a fine skater with good straight-line speed, so he's at his best on the forecheck when his team place pucks behind opposing defensemen, as he to play physical loves to finish his hits. He's strong physically, making contacts with authority to bring momentum to his team. Many of his goals/points came from his net front play, where he loves to screen the goaltender and establishing good body position for rebounds. He owns a decent shot as well that he likes to use in rush and offensive zone situations.

As of right now, Wetsch projects more as an energy 4th liner. For his offensive game to improve and translates at the next level, he'll need to improve his passing as a chain-connector for his linemates. In transition, improving his touches on breakout wall plays. In the offensive zone, improving his wall play down low to sustain puck possession and find the inside ice with his passing.

"Honest hard working player who lacks skill." - NHL Scout, December 2023

"I can find 30 better forwards for Team Canada." - NHL Scout, May 2024

"Kept him with a C grade but not a player I'm in a hurry to draft. Not enough in his toolbox for me." - HP Scout, Mark Edwards, May 2024

"I had a few scouts rave about his combine interview despite the fact that they don't have him ranked high. One thing they liked was his self evaluation." - HP Scout, Mark Edwards, June 2024

NR	PLAYER	TEAM	LEAGUE	HEIGHT	WEIGHT	POS	GRADE
	WHIPPLE, JOHN	USA U18	NTDP	6' 00.5"	192	LD	NI
NHLCS	CEILING	FLOOR	HOCKEY SENSE	COMPETE	SKILL	SKATE	MISC
NA-145	4	4	6	5	3	7	5

Mobile defenseman. John Whipple played down the lineup and in penalty kill situations all year for the USNTDP. As part of a defense that really struggled to find its offensive footing this year, Whipple produced a goal and three helpers in 27 USHL contests. With just rudimentary puck skills, Whipple doesn't project a high ceiling or a particularly high floor either. He's a weak handler with poor puck control. He has a weak shot too, in the rare event that he pulls the trigger. Even on the PK, it just felt like his unassisted clear rate would be very low end for a prospect at this level. It's one thing not to be a power play player – that's understandable – but his technical skill really needs to improve for him to be a legitimate NHL prospect. It's not like he's a 6'4" killer. He's 6-foot flat, maybe a touch taller and noticeably thin on the ice. To his credit, He does pursue some hits out there. He's knocked more than a few guys off their skates this year. On the flip side, he's very much a "fronter" of shots, not a crease battle guy – which is okay. He can use his skating to provide a physical edge, but he's not ready from a standing start. He overcompensates for his lack of ability to battle in-close by giving up even more leverage…he's on the ice a lot, and being on the ice isn't being in control. Shot blocking and passing lane blockades are altruistic, but he'd be a better player if he could do it on his feet instead of on the floor.

He has really good edge work and as he adds muscle, his whole skating package should round out nicely and allow him to play a little bit more explosively, if he chooses to. We're grading his skating in anticipation of that because it's mechanically good. We're also hopeful that will push him to play a more active style…more on his toes. Some of our viewings, it felt like this was a player that lacked confidence – and he almost certainly does with the puck on his stick. Though, as the year went on, our thought turned to him thinking that he can play the game in a rocking chair and be effective, but he's not in control enough or good enough to do that in our estimation. His deferential style leaves him vulnerable near his net, there's a bit of sluggishness filling in lanes near the attack line and providing puck/partner support in that way that just doesn't need to happen. He played the right side quite a bit this year, but that's not going to stick at a higher level. He has a hard enough time handling the puck on his forehand, asking him to do anything on his backhand is a mistake waiting to happen. When a player's best asset is his skating – and even that's not elite – it doesn't project very well to the pros.

61	PLAYER	TEAM	LEAGUE	HEIGHT	WEIGHT	POS	GRADE
	WOOLLEY, JARED	LONDON	OHL	6' 04.5"	207	LD	C

NHLCS	CEILING	FLOOR	HOCKEY SENSE	COMPETE	SKILL	SKATE	MISC
NA-73	7	5	6	7	6	5	7

Jared Woolley is a large and physically mature defenseman who split time between the GOJHL and the OHL this season with the St. Thomas Stars and London Knights respectively. Woolley put up over a point per game wit 21 points in 19 game in St. Thomas, tearing up the GOJHL before heading to London and putting up 5 points in 37 games. Don't let the points fool you, Wooley played well in London with limited ice time and offensive opportunities on a team stacked at his position. Woolley's play at the OHL level in his call up earned him a decent role with the Knights after the trade deadline and some injuries on the back end along with consistent play helped solidify his role with the team.

In his first stint with the Knight in the regular season, Woolley looked like he had played in the league before. He was very calm and poised and did not rush plays up ice with the puck, instead creating some strong breakouts with well read outlet passes. In viewings of his time in the GOJHL and watching his early stint with London, it was clear he was ready for a bigger role with the team and he proved to be a solid option in his limited minutes in all three zones despite being a primarily defensive defenseman in London. Woolley will take hits to make plays and does not rush plays up ice, instead making strong and accurate passes in and out of his own end. As a rush defender, Woolley positions himself well to box out players and is generally tough to beat but will need to be more consistent with his footwork as not only on the rush but in coverage he can get evaded by quick and craft forwards in tight.

Defensively in coverage, Wooley can take away time and space with a long reach and a long first stride to cover areas quickly with help him navigate play. Physically he is still learning to use his large frame to his advantage but when he does he is tough to beat, he pins forwards well along the boards and can clear the front of the net well even against older players in the league. He is able to get the puck out of his zone comfortably with his patience and ability to make good decisions with the puck under pressure and find forwards for offensive opportunities going the other way. On the offensive side of the puck, Woolley is confident enough to jump into the rush or jump into play in the offensive zone and let off a good hard shot on net. He reads the play very well.

The combination of size and poise on the back end alone make Woolley an attractive prospect, but when you add in his passing and physicality along with his offensive flashes he is a player we cannot leave off of our list. He is another in a long line of London Knights products to keep an eye on. He is someone we look forward to see progressing in a strong and professional environment to continue smoothing out the edges on his projectable game.

" No feet so no draft for me." - NHL Scout, January 2024

"He's ok. Maybe a late pick if we start running out of names. It might be that kind of draft again." - NHL Scout, March 2024

" I have time for him. Some parts of his game remind me a bit of Logan Mailloux. Wooley's skating is the big weakness but I think it has a legit chance of improving enough to not be a stopper. It's his short area quickness that is poor...otherwise it's not too bad. He has some smarts and knows how to get involved offensively. Don't be surprised if you see some crooked numbers beside his name as his icetime and PP opportunity increases in London." - HP Scout, Mark Edwards, March 2024

14	PLAYER	TEAM	LEAGUE	HEIGHT	WEIGHT	POS	GRADE
	YAKEMCHUK, CARTER	CALGARY	WHL	6' 02.75"	202	RD	A

NHLCS	CEILING	FLOOR	HOCKEY SENSE	COMPETE	SKILL	SKATE	MISC
NA-11	7	6	5	7	8	5	7

Yakemchuk completed his third season in the WHL, making him one of the older players eligible for this draft with his September 2005 birthday. Had he been born just two weeks earlier, he would have been eligible for the 2023 NHL Draft. Despite his team, the Hitmen, struggling and missing the playoffs, Yakemchuk had an impressive individual season. He ranked 5th in points (71) among defensemen and led the league in goals with 31.

An offensive defenseman with size and high skill level, he's also a tough player to play against. We've seen him challenge players in games, and he's one of those rare players who has this old-school, bring-the-pain mentality. This will get NHL teams excited about his game and potential. He does, however, have some drawbacks that prevent us from ranking him higher.

All season long, we have loved the skill level he has displayed; it's rare to see defensemen with his frame that have this. He is really confident with the puck on his stick, with soft hands for a big man. He's never afraid to use them when rushing the puck to beat opponents one-on-one in the neutral or offensive zone. His go-to move is the toe drag deke in transition, or in the offensive zone at the line. However, this makes him a risky player, prone to too many low-IQ plays on the ice. His play selection efficiency is low, and a potential nightmare for NHL coaches. We love his confidence he displays with the puck, but it sometimes leads to overconfidence, resulting in questionable decision-making. He tends to attempt high-risk, one-on-one plays excessively, which may not translate well to the professional level. This aspect of his game raises concerns about his hockey IQ and makes us hesitant to rank him higher.

His offensive abilities are a big draw for NHL teams. A right-handed defenseman with his size and skillset is highly sought after. This season, he led WHL defensemen with an impressive 275 shots on goal. His closest competitor, Luca Cagnoni, had 233 shots. On the power play this year, where he scored 10 goals, he had one mission: shoot the puck. Any time he had a chance, whether it was from the point or the half wall, he was getting it on net. His slapshot is powerful and he loves to one-time pucks from the left side of the ice. He's quite creative in the way he sets himself up for one-timing opportunities. We're not high on his IQ, but this is one area of his game we appreciate; how he creates room for himself and finds soft ice to receive passes for one-timers. He can also use his wrist shot efficiently, even becoming a bit unpredictable because the opposing player needs to know that he can fake it and go for a toe-drag move. He is also quite adept at changing the angles on his shots. There's a lot more diversity with his wrist shot than his slapshot, but his slapper is way more devastating when used in one-timer situations on the power play.

Much of his offensive success is based on his shooting. His passing and vision are decent to above-average if we would have to grade them, but he doesn't use them often enough as he's a shooter first and foremost. His ability to shoot the puck gives him PP1 potential in the NHL; we see him as moving to a more balanced, less selfish shot/pass approach in the professional ranks. While he occasionally rushes the puck too much, he's accurate with his passing from his own zone. Once in the NHL, he should rely more on his passing game, as he won't be able to use his junior-level skating to beat defenders off the rush as often.

When we talked about his low IQ for a player, his offensive aggressiveness, while it can be considered a strength, can sometimes lead to overcommitment and risky plays. He will often try to apply pressure by jumping into the play but he doesn't have the skating skills to be successful in his attempt. Also, if he does get caught, he doesn't have the skating or athleticism to get back. When he's down low in the offensive zone on the forecheck, he sometimes forgets that he's a defenseman. Post-forecheck attempt, he should think about getting back into position as soon as he can, but we've seen him reattempt to pursue the puck. If his opponents get the puck out quickly, it's a guaranteed odd-man rush if no one takes Yakemchuk's spot (which was too often the case). These are just a few examples of low-IQ plays that have bothered us this year.

His positional game in his end can also be problematic at times. His defensive game in general is a bit of a wild card. However, aside from being positionally erratic, he does a good job in his zone thanks to his pure physicality. It's not fun to play against him; he doesn't back down from anyone. During games against Medicine Hat in the first half, battles between him and Cayden Lindstrom were among the best we saw all year. It was really fun to see two very physical players going at it in front of the net and along the boards. Yakemchuk can be nasty at times, which explains the 120 penalty minutes he had this year. His old-timer mindset, physicality and mean streak on the ice have been well-noted by opponents and referees alike. He's also not afraid to use his stick to take the puck away from forwards, slashing them and crosschecking them along the way.

He does tend to struggle against quicker forwards off the rush; what he lacks in skating skills shows when he faces quick forwards. We believe his poor footwork and skating are going cause problems for him against top-line players in the NHL (think McDavid, MacKinnon and other high-end skaters). As a result, we can't project him as a 1st-pairing defenseman, and that has to be reflected in his ranking. When forced to use edgework and change directions too many times, we have seen him lose balance and lose strength on his skates, which can open things up offensively for the opposing team. When he can hit his top speed (for example, rushing pucks with a lot of space in front of him) his straight line speed looks more than fine, but his first three-step explosion is something that could stand to improve. His lateral agility and footwork are also among his weaknesses, and it shows when he gets into trouble with his rush defense game. Funnily enough, his defensive game is the complete opposite of Zayne Parekh's. Yakemchuk can be really good in his zone but struggles to defend against the rush, whereas Parekh struggles to use physicality in his zone, but his rush defense is quite good.

Yakemchuk was a player that bothered us. We tried to put him higher on our list, but it felt wrong every time we did. We appreciate his offensive skills from the blueline and his physicality, but the problematic nature of his decision-making and lack of good skating skills made us wonder. His skating issues position him more realistically as a #3 or #4 defenseman (with good PP value) on a good NHL team. For us, he can't be higher than this due to his lack of agility and overall footwork. Playing on a second pairing would shelter him more from some of the tougher matchups in the NHL.

"With the puck on the rush he is better than Parekh." – NHL Scout, October 2023

"Skating isn't great and he doesn't defend great." – NHL Scout, November 2023

"He's better with the puck than without the puck. Pivots will need to improve or he will struggle." – NHL Scout, December 2023

"He plays too much and I don't think he's getting pushed to play the game the right way. I have real issues with the coaching there." – NHL Scout, December 2023

"You have him ranked too late." – NHL Scout, January 2024

"Some of our staff think I'm crazy but I think he is a lazy player." – NHL Scout, April 2024

"He has a ton of risk in his game and he turns a lot of pucks over but his good is really good. Defensively I don't think he is bad, I just don't think it's always important to him because he is so focused on getting back up the ice." – NHL Scout, April 2024

"I don't like his skating but then I hear Evan Bouchard as the argument to that. My reply is he is not Bouchard on the powerplay." – NHL Scout, April 2024

"Terrible team and he finds a way to produce. The kid can play and is a top 12 pick." - NHL Scout, April 2024

"I have him and Greentree and Catton in the same area on my list. All three scare me a bit." - NHL Scout, May 2024

"I saw him mocked fourth overall to Columbus. Guess we won't get him. (laughs)." - NHL Scout, May 2024

"He's big and has a bomb for a shot and he is very skilled. He can skate the puck and beat guys one on one. I am not crazy about his skating and overall mobility though. Sometimes he tries to do too much. Kinda plays his own game on some shifts. Tough player to rank for me because of the high end talent mixed with some warts." - HP Scout, Mark Edwards, December 2023

"He kinda looks like he is playing his own game at times - as in without any structure. I have struggled to rank him all year. The tools are great minus the skating being a bit average but sometimes I'm left scratching my head at some decisions he makes." - HP Scout, Mark Edwards, May 2024

3	PLAYER	TEAM	LEAGUE	HEIGHT	WEIGHT	POS	GRADE
	YEGOROV, MIKHAIL	OMAHA	USHL	6' 05"	188	G	B

NHLCS	CEILING	FLOOR	HOCKEY SENSE	COMPETE	SKILL	SKATE	MISC
NA-1	8	5	6	8	7	5	7

Yegorov falls into a unique path when it comes to goaltending development. Last season he was developing in CSKA's program at the U17 level. It's very rare for a goalie to come over to North America without any MHL experience but that's exactly what Yegorov did, and to say it's a significant step up in competition to go from U17 Russian hockey to the USHL is a severe understatement. This is compounded further by the fact that Omaha was the worst team in the USHL. We don't need to break down Yegorov's teammates' goaltending numbers but let's just say they were significantly worse than his. There were many nights where he was facing forty or more shots and he was having to stand on his head in order for Omaha to even stay in the game. So his flat stats might not look good on paper but they certainly aren't reflective of his talent or level of play that he demonstrated throughout this season.

Mikhail falls into the modern goalie prototype that we tend to look for. He has the natural blend of athleticism and size, combined with what should become a solid skating foundation and a fundamentally sound set stance. His set stance is characterized by a sealed blocker that's kept completely tight to his side and a glove that's also kept very tight while facing slightly downwards. He's above average to very good in most areas. He's got an ideal frame, he's reflexive, he's explosive, and his extension rates are exceptional.

When entering his butterfly, he remains very tall, and just as importantly he keeps his butterfly wide. it's rarely narrow and this means he can take advantage of his height and overall frame each time that he enters it. Mechanically, one of his better traits is how often he maintains a technically refined butterfly, even during lateral movement within his crease.

One of the bigger improvements he's made throughout the season was his ability to hold a position on his inside edge when having to suddenly shift weight into the opposite direction from where he initially pushed off. Omaha was a terrible team defensively, and this meant that Mikhail had to do a lot of sudden adjustments that forced him to hold on an edge out of a laterally explosive push in order to counteract broken plays and regain his positioning, but once his edgework started to hold and he could re-square up at a higher rate, then he stopped swimming in his net as often.

Sometimes, during odd man rushes or developing plays where the end target was a weak side backdoor option, Yegorov would look to cheat by not squaring up entirely, instead remaining in a position that allowed him to use his edges to explode across on a singular plane in one motion, as opposed to fully squaring up and then having to use his small area skating to readjust on two separate planes. We think this is due to his hip dexterity falling a bit under.

When evaluating his athleticism relative to the other top end goalies, he falls a bit short of the top end of this class but he's still a very good athlete in his own right. He isn't as fluid or as explosive as Timofei Obvintsev and although Obvintsev is older, we don't think Yegorov will catch him at 19. The other goalies who are his age like Ivan Yunin and Eemil Vinni are much more dextrous and have a further range of mobility within their hip lines. This means that on shots that are against the grain in higher danger areas that force Yegorov to suddenly kick out his pads reflexively, he can be a little more susceptible then they are. It also affects his post integration and how he transitions between movements in and out of his posts in general. They can be fluid and very efficient whereas Yegorov looks more mechanical by nature. That said, Yegorov can explode from his RVH into a set standing position at the top of his crease effortlessly and he still projects to be able to deal with high danger lateral passes at a higher rate than most of the other draft eligible goalies.

One of the better ways we can summarize his movement between the pipes is that his large area skating, including T-push-offs, and push-offs from a seated back to a standing position are impressive; and that his small area micro-shuffles are also efficient. However, his small area skating game when it comes to integrating from a set position into a RVH is poorer, as is his ability to adjust to a different plane suddenly, when needing to re-open his hipline.

An area where he can continue to improve is regarding his tracking behind his own net and through traffic. He has a tendency to overcommit on a post too early when looking to transfer laterally when tracking players below his goal line and this leaves him susceptible to no-look reverse passes. Yegorov also lacks some instincts when it comes to moving into space to take away a shot through a screen. If he loses sight of the puck momentarily, he can fail to assess when he should move through a screen. Goalies like Zarubin and Yunin are much better trackers through traffic, and display better instincts on when they need to rotate from either the short side to far side or vice versa to take away a shot through a screen.

He can also be overzealous when entering his butterfly and drop too early, putting him in a position where he has to adjust rapidly while still down in his butterfly in order to make secondary saves. That said, he is very good at adjusting within his butterfly, and as stated earlier, we don't mind him being in his butterfly often with his style of play since technically speaking it's one of his best qualities.

There's also consistency issues with his glove hand when it comes to catching the puck. He has a tendency to knock pucks down within his glove while failing to actually hold onto the puck. The most concerning aspect of his game for us though comes down to his spatial awareness, relative to his own net, specifically on shots that are on sharper angles. Much like Yegor Yegorov last season, Mikhail has a tendency to overcommit in his standing overlap, while failing to square up on routine shots. Heavy repetition can improve this, and we were hoping to see marked improvements in this area over the course of the year, but by the end of the year we were still waiting. This is a basic instinct within a goalies game that must be present in order for a goalie to have any chance of developing to a starter at the NHL level, and it's worrisome to see his basic spatial ability falling short.

When evaluating Yegorov relative to the rest of what we consider to be a very strong and understated goalie class, the stand out quality within his game isn't a physical trait, it's a mental one, Omaha was under siege this season and he was arguably their most consistent player. There were performances where he was letting in more than 5 goals, but then put back in against the same team the next night and then stood on his head. That takes resolve and it shows that he can mentally recalibrate quickly. He's competitive and he rarely didn't show up, and on nights where he looked off, he battled, and that's a good sign of things to come.

"I thought he was going to run away with being ranked number 1 in our list after the first couple of viewings but then as we peeled back the layers, we became more worried about his overall translation. Theres still a lot to work with though." - HP Scout, Brad Allen

"I think it's better for a top goalie prospect to play on a bad team, then it is for a top goalie prospect to play on a good team. From a scouting perspective, it gives us a lot more to work with and from a development perspective, it lets the athlete know where he needs to improve faster." - HP Scout, Brad Allen

"I wish he stayed over in the MHL." - HP Scout, Brad Allen

8	PLAYER	TEAM	LEAGUE	HEIGHT	WEIGHT	POS	GRADE
	YUNIN, IVAN	OMSKIE	RUS JR	6' 02"	196	G	B

NHLCS	CEILING	FLOOR	HOCKEY SENSE	COMPETE	SKILL	SKATE	MISC
-	7	4	5	7	6	6	6

Ivan Yunin falls into the same territory as Yegor Yegorov last season. In other words, nightmare territory. This resulted from the fact that he was the backup for a top program in the MHL and was the youngest goalie on the team, which meant very limited starts, which in turn means we have to make our evaluation off of fewer games and look back to previous performances at a higher rate from when he was 16. In the case of Yunin, he played a grand total of 6 games this past season, and that makes our jobs more difficult. Despite this, Yunin presents a tremendous amount of potential.

This might come as a bit of a surprise to some of our readers, but we think pound for pound that this is one of the best pure athletes available in the draft. Yunin isn't as tall as HockeyProspect favourite, Adam Gajan but he's capable of laterally exploding into a fully extended split before stopping and then exploding laterally in the opposite direction through the same split. That requires freakish athleticism, edgework and a dextrous hip line, and that's exactly the base of Yunin's game.

Yunin is advanced at dealing with traffic. He actively pushes players in-front of him to give him additional room so that he can further rotate his body when looking around opponents, but when leaning off his centerline, he rarely over-extends himself which allows him to get positionally set in the time frame needed to evaluate the shot location through traffic. When needing to move into a shot around a screen, he's capable of adjusting his positioning with quick lateral shifts.

The lateral agility he displays when looking around screens applies to the rest of his game as well. Obvintsev and Vinni are the only two other goalies who show the lateral explosiveness that Yunin displays but he actually has better extension rates due to his dexterity and hip rotation then Vinnie. He's arguably the top in this class at micro adjustments, which as some of you who have read our previous work might be aware of, we weigh very heavily when determining a goalie ranking. His micro-adjustments are a result of his explosive transitional butterfly, advanced T-push offs, micro-shuffles, and elite reflexes. When you take into consideration what this means in terms of on ice performance, we're simply stating that he can adjust to a secondary shot faster than any other goalie in this class, and it projects to be NHL starter caliber.

One of the more unique aspects of Yunin's game is his ability to exit from a set stance overlap position when looking to stop shots on his short side or shots taken from more severe angles, and then rotate in one motion into an extension kicking save on the far side of the net. Most goalies need to readjust their hips so that they can push off on the secondary angle that allows the lateral transfer, Yunin's hips are so good though, that he can do this in one motion without the secondary adjustment, regardless of sometimes even overcommitting on the initial overlap. This means that on shots he misidentifies on his short side that then turn into high danger lateral passes, he has a distinct advantage relative to most other goalie prospects.

It's not just his raw athletic traits that make him appealing though, it's his evaluation and base instincts. In-fact his processing ability works in tandem with his athleticism when squaring up to a shooter. When Ivan has read the initial shot, he can exaggerate his glove or blocker side depending on the direction he thinks the shooter is most likely to release the puck on, which sometimes forces the shooter to pick the opposite side that Yunin presented the exaggerated posture on. Essentially what's occurring within his game, is that he's reading the intentions of the shooter in advance, and then baiting the opposing shooter into a shot selection that he prefers. This is a rare trait and speaks to how comfortable and confident Yunin can play the game, when he's on his game.

So what exactly are his limitations? To start, one of his bigger issues is also the most fixable and that's his rebound control. Athletic goalies have a tendency to be less reliant on absorbing the first shot at this stage in their development since they have an easier time making secondary saves after coughing up the rebound, and that's the case here as well. It extends to some technical aspects, such as timing how he drops through specific shots when transitioning from his relaxed stance, into his set stance and then finally into his butterfly. In addition, sometimes instead of trying to rotate his shoulders forward when in his butterfly so that he can absorb shots that are labeled for his chest, he remains stiff. This allows shots to bounce off of him without him being able to swallow them as often as we would have liked to see. These are very fixable issues though.

What's less fixable is regarding his size. This isn't a prototypical 6'3" plus goalie. He's probably closer to 6'1, and as a result of that he has to be pretty special in order for us to have him ranked high, but he is, and that's because the above traits we have written allow him to compensate for his lack of size to the degree necessary for us to still believe in potential starter upside.

Admittedly, one of the primary reasons we have him a bit further back despite his starting potential and fantastic athletic traits is due to his glove hand. We don't love having to deal with smaller game samples when it comes to goalies, especially if they are playing in the MHL because there's less high danger saves on average per game relative to a goalie playing in the CHL, and that means less saves where we can evaluate his glove hand and project it correctly. When evaluating what we had to work with, we found that his glove is a bit stiff and lacks upper rotation needed when catching shots labeled for the high glove occasionally. His glove is much better on shots targeted lower to the ice or at the mid level.

Another issue with his lack of games played is it gives us less of an evaluation to work with when evaluating how mentally consistent he is, which is an enormously important trait when determining how likely he is to hit as a prospect. Due to having a smaller sample of his glove and his consistent rates in general, we decided to keep him below Evan Gardner.

"Despite the small sample and relatively poor curve, he's still a very good goalie prospect with a lot of promise, especially if he can grow a bit more. He's currently 6'1". If he can continue to grow, then look out." - HP Scout, Brad Allen

"In terms of his style of play, he's a Russian Filip Gustavsson." - HP Scout, Brad Allen

1	PLAYER		TEAM	LEAGUE	HEIGHT	WEIGHT	POS	GRADE
	ZARUBIN, KIRILL		AKM TULA	RUS JR	6' 04"	179	G	B

NHLCS	CEILING	FLOOR	HOCKEY SENSE	COMPETE	SKILL	SKATE	MISC
-	7	5	8	7	6	6	6

Kirill Zarubin is a large, poised, blocking-style goalie with good but not exceptional athletic traits. He put together one of the most consistent seasons of any draft-eligible goalie. In fact, after Ilya Nabokov, you could argue that he was the most consistent goalie, presenting the most pro attributes we look for in a potential starter.

The best way to characterize Zarubin's game is that when he's on his game, he makes it look easy. The game doesn't seem too fast for him, he rarely rushes through his decisions on high-danger plays, and he always looks poised and in control. He lets the play come to him and rarely beats himself on the first goal.

Since we have two of our top-ranked goalies playing in the MHL, we'll do a contrast breakdown between them. Arguably the biggest difference between Obvintsev and Zarubin is how much more active Obvintsev is relative to Zarubin. Obvintsev's athleticism is almost always on display, whereas Zarubin brings it out when he needs it; there's very little wasted movement.

The reason we have Zarubin higher than Obvintsev is due to his tracking and overall reads. You almost never see this goalie scramble, and he very rarely misinterprets advanced passing plays. He's closer to Moysevich when it comes to his vision and initial reads. Another considerable difference in their tracking is that Obvintsev loses the puck below the goal line a lot more often than Zarubin does. Lastly, when it comes to identifying the end trajectory of a lateral drag around a triangle, Kirill is arguably one of the best in this class. He often makes difficult shots look easy to handle.

Another contrasting difference between Zarubin and Obvintsev is how often Zarubin seals everything off within his set stance and when he's laterally transferring. Obvintsev can be loose and keep his arms down when laterally shifting, whereas Zarubin keeps everything compact and tight. This applies to their butterfly as well. Zarubin has one of the best butterflies in the draft. Most goalies at this age now have an impressive butterfly mechanically, but Zarubin's is impressive not only because it can absorb a lot of shots but also because it forces opponents' shots wide. This is due to how wide Zarubin himself can maintain his butterfly. Some goalies have very good butterflies, but they are narrower and faster; Zarubin has the hip flexors needed to hold a butterfly that just takes up so much room.

Another one of Kirill's advantages is how he deals with opposing players who are cutting on him aggressively off the rush. He's adept at maintaining a standing overlap position that's square to the shooter as they skate closer to the net on him, which means he very rarely gets caught transitioning between a standing position and a seated one at a sharper angle. His overlap positioning blends into his overall positioning and spatial awareness. Zarubin is spatially aware and combines that with his impressive anticipation to get out in front of the play. When you look at his recovery rates, they are under some of the more athletically gifted goalies in this class, but he's very good at recognizing where the next shot is coming from and then using his larger frame to get back out in front of the puck. Some goalies tend to rely more on their extension rates when making recovery, secondary, or a string of saves together, but Zarubin is gifted at getting his whole frame back square to the puck.

The biggest setback to Zarubin's game is his overall athleticism. It isn't a below-average grade, and in some areas, it's actually a good to very good grade, but when comparing this toolkit to his mental game, it's the mental game that truly separates him. He does have good extension rates due to how long he is, and his reflexes are impressive, but he's not a very nimble or dexterous goalie. His lateral transfer rates should hold, but they are under some of the other top goalies in this class. He's also not as fluid as some of the other top goalies. He can be a bit robotic in his movements, but we don't think it's to a point where it will keep him from playing as a starter; it's just not his strength relative to the rest of his game.

When projecting why his athletic grade should hold for the NHL, some of it has to do with still being an impressive and coordinated skater. His edges hold well when he's moving from post to post rapidly, he can micro-shuffle rapidly, and he uses his edges to correctly form a standing overlap. He can weight-shift dynamically, and he developed a better level of crease containment after an initial push-off.

When projecting him, if he doesn't play, it will most likely be a result of his strength, conditioning, and physical development not being able to bring the fluidity between actual save types up enough; there's a distinction there, and we want to make sure it's properly mentioned.

What he is natural at is playing a poised, in-control, well-rounded game. He was exceptionally consistent, and he's very hard to beat on the first shot. His rate of recovery isn't close to goalies like Vinni, Yunin, and Obvintsev, but he also projects to be very good at controlling rebounds, which helps nullify that issue to a degree. We also don't want to give the wrong impression; he's more than capable of making beautiful and impressive saves at times, it's just not going to be his calling card or the reason we think so highly of him. We think highly of him because his mental foundation and frame are fantastic, and he showed what we believe is true starting potential. We're huge fans of hyper-athletic goalies, so the fact that he's ranked where he is, is a testament to the rest of his game and speaks to the physical growth rate we envision for him despite being one of the older first-year eligible goalies available.

"I think this is one of the deeper Russian goalie classes I can remember. There's just no outlier star-level goalie featured like in previous classes, but I'm a huge fan of a lot of these Russian kids." - HP Scout, Brad Allen

"It's concerning when your projection is out on a scouting island. I've never seen this goalie discussed or ranked anywhere. I think he's the best goalie in the draft, and I'd take him over any of the CHL goalies we have ranked." - HP Scout, Brad Allen

"Stylistically, he reminds me of a Russian Connor Hellebuyck. I'm not saying he's going to have the same career, but in terms of how he plays the game, they are similar." - HP Scout, Brad Allen

"Kirill Zarubin is better than Obvintsev and Yegorov now. If you give both of them 5 years, Obvintsev or Yegorov, or both, could catch up to him, if not surpass him, but it's unbelievably close. So I kept Zarubin ahead due to having to take in fewer variables within his development in order to play. I would be lying if I told you I didn't flip it throughout the season a half-dozen times. Welcome to the pain of goalie scouting." - HP Scout, Brad Allen

NR	PLAYER	TEAM	LEAGUE	HEIGHT	WEIGHT	POS	GRADE
	ZELLERS, WILLIAM	SHATTUCK	HIGH-MN	5' 10.25"	163	LW	C
NHLCS	CEILING	FLOOR	HOCKEY SENSE	COMPETE	SKILL	SKATE	MISC
NA-54	6	4	6	6	6	6	4

Will Zellers has been considered one of the top high school prospects of his age group in the US for a few years now. Zellers was selected 18th Overall in the 2nd Round of the 2022 USHL futures draft by Green Bay. For the last two seasons, Zellers has been a driving force on Shattuck St. Mary's U18 Prep team, bypassing the U16 team last year and playing up on the Prep team. Over the last two season's Zellers has registered 76 Goals and 84 Assists in 91 Games for the SSM U18 Prep team. Zellers was arguably the best forward for a struggling USA Team at the Hlinka Gretzky Cup last august, scoring 5 goals and 2 assists in 5 games. We most recently saw Zellers at the U18 Nationals in April where he was dominant, helping Shattuck capture the U18 National Championship with 9 goals and 5 assists in 6 games. While

Shattuck Prep doesn't always play the toughest schedule, we have had the opportunity to see Zellers vs his peers both in Minnesota District tryouts as well as USA Hockey National camps and he has been a stand out performer at each of these events vs his age group.

Zellers is a versatile forward and plays both down the middle and along the wall. Zellers showed good two-way hockey sense where he tracked back well to take away passing lanes and had good effort in applying back pressure and stripping pucks from opponents. Zellers played in all situations for Shattuck this season, his awareness and anticipation are an asset on the PK. One of the viewings of Zellers where he impressed the most was vs Edge School where he was dominant from start to finish, logging big minutes in all situations and creating scoring chances consistently. He was a dominant force in a game that Shattuck won handily. While there were very few games, we saw this season where Zellers was underwhelming, his performance at the Circle K and at USA Nationals certainly helped his draft stock for us. Zellers possesses good hands and hand eye coordination; he is able to quickly control bouncing pucks and errant passes with his head up and has the ability to see the ice and process situations quickly with the puck on his tape. In multiple views of Zellers this year we saw him use his hand eye coordination to control errant pucks with speed and continue to transport the puck up ice either with his skating for ability to make a quick read and tape to tape passes in transition. Like a lot of prospects his age, Zellers still has a bit of filling out to do with his frame but he is average size and once he adds some strength, he should gain a step with his skating as well as be able to be more effective down low and in the hard areas of the ice. Zellers ineffectiveness at times in these areas isn't from lack of effort or compete, just strength, which will come with time. Zellers has shown the ability to find the back of the net in multiple ways, his ability to find the soft ice and get available for quick shots between the dots is among the best we have seen in this age group, he is able to anticipate the play and the opponent's movements to get separation and in position for SOG. Shows a good nose for the net and willingness to go to the front of the net and take some punishment to score.

Zellers will be headed to Green Bay (USHL) next season before heading to the University of North Dakota in 2025. That career path going forward will give him the time needed to develop his body physically to get ready for pro hockey.

90	PLAYER	TEAM	LEAGUE	HEIGHT	WEIGHT	POS	GRADE
	ZETHER, SIMON	ROGLE	SWE	6' 03"	176	RC	C
NHLCS	CEILING	FLOOR	HOCKEY SENSE	COMPETE	SKILL	SKATE	MISC
INT-18	5	4	5	5	6	5	6

Zether started the year on a good note with the Rogle J20 team, with 27 points in his first 17 games. He earned a few callups and became a full-time SHL player by the end of November. However, he didn't get much ice time in the SHL, mostly playing under 10 minutes per game (for 6 games, he even received under 5 minutes of ice time).

Employing a pro-style game, he's got good size, making good use of his frame to win battles along the boards. He was also a dominant player along the boards at the junior level. It was a lot more difficult at the SHL level, but his frame and length will help him achieve proficiency at the pro level. He's not an aggressive physical player either, and we would like to see him be more engaged and more abrasive.

He needs to adapt his game to play more effectively in the high-pressure environments of higher leagues. While he found success in junior hockey by utilizing his shot and playing on the perimeter, he struggled to replicate this in the SHL. He was very successful on the perimeter and on the power play, where he had more time and space, but scored 0 goals in 42 games in the SHL. He showed a good shot (good velocity and accuracy) at the junior level, but was unable to find success with it at the pro level, where he would struggle to get his shot off quickly. That was the big difference between his junior and professional play: the lack of time he had to get his shot off.

His athleticism, particularly in his skating, is concerning. His stride lacks fluidity and power, indicating potential issues with agility and speed. While additional strength may improve his power on the ice, his overall athleticism remains limited. As a result, his projection to the NHL is risky, and he is more likely to become a solid player in the SHL rather than a full-time NHL player.

NR	PLAYER	TEAM	LEAGUE	HEIGHT	WEIGHT	POS	GRADE
	ZETTERBERG, ALEXANDER	OREBRO JR.	SWE-JR	5' 07"	158	RC	C
NHLCS	CEILING	FLOOR	HOCKEY SENSE	COMPETE	SKILL	SKATE	MISC
INT-30	6	3	6	5	6	5	3

Zetterberg is a tiny forward who, for the second consecutive year, had success with Orebro in the Swedish Junior League, collecting 58 points in 45 games, good for 8th overall in the league's scoring race. Additionally, he was a standout player internationally for Sweden, amassing 39 points in 24 games with the U18 team throughout the year. His strong performance at the U18 tournament was unfortunately cut short due to injury, resulting in a big offensive loss for Team Sweden.

The biggest problem for Zetterberg is obviously his size. At 5'07", you need to be a special player to play in the NHL. We don't think he's that kind of player, although he excels in power play situations. His smarts enable him to take full advantage of situations where he has additional time and space. His technical abilities are good; his passing and shooting allow him to be a dual threat offensively at this level, but in order for his shooting to translate to goals, he needs to get closer to the net. He can do so in power play situations (in Swedish junior hockey or in international competition) but it's going to be difficult to replicate that success at the pro level. His shot lacks the efficiency required at the pro level, particularly from distances, meaning he would have to play more on the inside, which presents difficulties given his size. While he has good puck skills, he struggles with less time and space, as shown in his less impressive 5-on-5 performances compared to his power play time internationally. In addition, his skating ability is not on par with that of other small players in the NHL, limiting his ability to compete at that level. Physically, he can be overmatched against more physical opponents, making a successful transition to the NHL unlikely.

We see parallels between him and Zion Nybeck from a few years ago. While some lists may have projected him (and Nybeck) as a first-round pick earlier in the year, ultimately, his chances of translating to the NHL are slim. We think he will find success in the Swedish Hockey League. This is why he ranks lower on our list. He's expected to join Boston University in the NCAA next season.

64	PLAYER	TEAM	LEAGUE	HEIGHT	WEIGHT	POS	GRADE
	ZIEMER, BRODIE	USA-U18	NTDP	5' 11"	196	RW	C
NHLCS	CEILING	FLOOR	HOCKEY SENSE	COMPETE	SKILL	SKATE	MISC
NA-59	5	5	6	8	5	4	5

Hard working, grinding winger. Brodie Ziemer captained the USNTDP U18 team this past season and put up respectable numbers – 24 points in 27 games in USHL play, followed by a 12-point effort in the U18. Though, it's unlikely that Ziemer will be much of a point producer at higher levels, he has some transferable pieces to his game that may be worthwhile. First is that he's a tremendous worker and an infectious leader. Some worker bees can wear down over the course of a season, but Ziemer actually seemed to improve his pace late in the season. His work rate does cover up some blemishes in his game, particularly in his skating. His stride is choppy and unbalanced with some upper body noise that drains its efficiency. His edges and turns are really not good; he struggles to lean off of his center line. There's a big lack of explosiveness and launch fluidity in his first step and out of pivots. These elements are particularly hurtful to sub-6-foot players that don't have a real hook from a technical skill perspective. As minor redemption, Ziemer does possess some really good straight line speed.

His puck handling ability is just okay. There are some good, quick handles mixed in to his game, but not a lot of deception or fluidity. Part of the lack of deception is that his puck control window is very small and almost entirely in front of his sternum. Without being crafty from the hip, it makes disguising shots pretty tough. Also, his lack of agility and explosiveness doesn't allow him to complete a lot of far-reaching maneuvers successfully. Watching him try to deceive defensemen on the rush, there's hardly a flinch from most of them. The only decent weapon he has in that scenario is a pull and drag shot. His shooting technique in space is good, but not great. The goal scoring scalability is limited by his shooting ability in contested situations. He already doesn't have a quick release or consistent release point… and part of that is his inability to get good body posture adjustments to get to his comfort spot, so it creates a lot of variance in his shot quality. He does adapt by driving the net regularly, where he has bagged his fair share of deflection goals. We'd also like him to iron out the bobbles that accompany his pass reception game and first touches. Another way that he could improve his scoring ability is with his routes. There are sequences where he's very poignant with where he wants to go, but then there are some sequences where he's very slow to process where he should be going. This applies to his passing game too. He has a few sneaky good assists mixed in there. Then there's also instances – like we referenced in the Austin Baker profile – where he throws an absolute no chance puck into double coverage without an immediate jump to correct the mistake. Without the skating to contribute meaningfully to the transition game, the routes and the puck decisions really need to be sharp and he's just not consistently there right now. There's upside to develop that because he's not a dumb player, but pace-read adjustments aren't a given either.

Brodie does play with genuine, physical enthusiasm. He delivered some pretty good hits along the boards this year at various levels of competition. One area where he could improve here is making more of those hits as close-off plays. A few too many of these hits resulted in him bouncing off of his opponent without gaining any territory. Part of that is the natural physical development of a teenage player, but there's also the slight, anticipatory adjustment in the skating route to facilitate that. But no one can knock his competitiveness and determination, so we suspect this will get cleaned up early on in his time with the Golden Gophers. This is a player that showed improvement over the year, but as a 5'11" player with skating issues and modest technical skill upside, there aren't a lot of "outs" where we'd feel good about investing a draft pick on him.

"The dark horse player on the program that actually has a chance to play." – HP Scout, Brad Allen

2025 NHL DRAFT TOP 32

RANK	LAST	FIRST	TEAM	LEAGUE	POS	HEIGHT	WEIGHT
1	Hagens	James	USA U18	NTDP	LC	5'10"	168
2	Frondell	Anton	Djurgardens Jr	SWEDEN-JR	LC	6'00"	179
3	Martone	Porter	Mississauga	OHL	RW	6'03"	170
4	Ryabkin	Ivan	Dynamo Moscow Jr	RUSSIA-JR	LC	6'00"	170
5	Schaefer	Matthew	Erie	OHL	LD	6'01"	161
6	Hensler	Logan	USA U18	NTDP	RD	6'02"	196
7	Misa	Michael	Saginaw	OHL	LC/LW	6'01"	174
8	O'Brien	Jake	Brantford	OHL	RC	6'00"	150
9	Desnoyers	Caleb	Moncton	QMJHL	LC	6'01"	163
10	Reschny	Cole	Victoria	WHL	LC	5'09"	161
11	Spence	Malcolm	Erie	OHL	LW	6'02"	192
12	McQueen	Roger	Brandon	WHL	RC	6'05"	190
13	Boumedienne	Sascha	Youngstown	USHL	LD	6'01"	183
14	Mrtka	Radim	Trinec Jr	CZECHIA-JR	RD	6'06"	198
15	Murtagh	Jack	USA U17	NTDP	LW	6'00"	185
16	Amico	Carter	USA U17	NTDP	RD	6'05"	205
17	Moore	William	USA U17	NTDP	LC	6'02"	161
18	Ihs Wozniak	Jakob	Lulea Jr	SWEDEN-JR	RW	6'03"	179
19	Mckinney	Cole	USA U17	NTDP	RC	6'00"	190
20	Guite	Émile	Chicoutimi	QMJHL	LW/RW	6'02"	164
21	Ravensbergen	Joshua	Prince George	WHL	G	6'04"	181
22	Trethewey	Charlie	USA U17	NTDP	RD	6'01"	190
23	Mooney	L.J	USA U17	NTDP	LW	5'07"	146
24	Potter	Cullen	USA U17	NTDP	LC	5'09"	161
25	Gastrin	Milton	Modo Jr	SWEDEN-JR	LC	6'02"	179
26	Ekberg	Filip	Almtuna Jr	SWEDEN-JR	LW	5'09"	163
27	Eklund	Victor	Djurgardens Jr	SWEDEN-JR	LW	5'11"	161
28	Gavin	Jordan	Tri-City	WHL	LW	5'11"	181
29	Radivojevic	Luka	Orebro Jr	SWEDEN-JR	RD	5'10"	165
30	Carbonneau	Justin	Blainville	QMJHL	RW	6'01"	189
31	Kindel	Benjamin	Calgary	WHL	RW	5'10"	165
32	Limatov	Kurban	Dynamo Moscow Jr	RUSSIA-JR	LD	6'04"	187
HM	Aitcheson	Kashawn	Barrie	OHL	LD	6'00"	172
HM	Annborn	Karl	HV 71 Jr	SWEDEN-JR	RD	6'00"	181
HM	Brzustewicz	Henry	London	OHL	RD	6'01"	198
HM	Fondrk	Conrad	USA U17	NTDP	LW	5'11"	174
HM	Hamilton	Reese	Calgary	WHL	LD	6'00"	160
HM	Kettles	Peyton	Swift Current	WHL	RD	6'04"	185
HM	Martin	Brady	Soo	OHL	RC/RW	6'00"	176
HM	Smith	Jackson	Tri-City	WHL	LD	6'03"	190

2025 NHL DRAFT PROSPECTS

1	PLAYER	TEAM	LEAGUE	HEIGHT	WEIGHT	POS	GRADE
	HAGENS, JAMES	USA-U18	NTDP	5'10"	168	LC	A
NHLCS	CEILING	FLOOR	HOCKEY SENSE	COMPETE	SKILL	SKATE	MISC
-	8	7	8	7	8	7	6

Hagens was the top player on the NTDP this season, even concluding the year by breaking Nikita Kucherov's record for most points at the World U18 Hockey Championships in April with 22 points in 7 games. He's an ultra-talented center with tons of smarts, vision and skills. He may be undersized, but his talent is too good to ignore at the top of this draft right now. We feel his potential is somewhere between that of Jack Hughes and Clayton Keller, two former great players from the NTDP. An offensive dual threat, he's a pass-first type of player with terrific on-ice vision and passing skills. He also can create on his own with his soft hands and shooting abilities. His play away from the puck is also underrated; he can kill penalties, he's not just an offensive dynamo. He was drafted by the London Knights in the OHL, but he's off to play college hockey for his NHL Draft year with Boston College next season.

2	PLAYER	TEAM	LEAGUE	HEIGHT	WEIGHT	POS	GRADE
	FRONDELL, ANTON	DJURGARDENS	SWE-JR.	6'00"	179	LC	A
NHLCS	CEILING	FLOOR	HOCKEY SENSE	COMPETE	SKILL	SKATE	MISC
-	8	7	8	7	8	6	6

Anton Frondell is currently Hagens's biggest competitor for the top spot in the 2025 NHL Draft class. Unfortunately, he was hurt and couldn't play in the World U18 Hockey Championship in April, but was the best player at the February U18 Five Nations tournament in Plymouth, even outplaying Hagens there. A power center, he is probably a tier below Leo Carlsson because he's not as physically imposing. He has improved his skating, and now has all the tools to become a number 1 center in the NHL: skills, hockey IQ and compete level. He's a gifted scorer with a borderline elite shot and can score all kinds of different ways. He protects the puck well, extending play with his good projectable frame. He also sees the ice well and his playmaking skills and creativity are both top-notch. He finished 3rd in points-per-game in Sweden's junior league for U18 players this season, and he's not far off from playing full-time in the Allsvenskan next season.

3	PLAYER	TEAM	LEAGUE	HEIGHT	WEIGHT	POS	GRADE
	MARTONE, PORTER	MISSISSAUGA	OHL	6'03"	170	RW	A
NHLCS	CEILING	FLOOR	HOCKEY SENSE	COMPETE	SKILL	SKATE	MISC
-	8	7	7	7	8	7	7

Martone is a power forward from the OHL who was in his second season with the Mississauga Steelheads, finishing the season with 33 goals and 71 points in 60 games. He was a standout performer at the World U18 Hockey Championship, playing with Gavin McKenna on Canada's top line. He finished with 17 points in 7 games, good for 3rd overall in scoring behind McKenna and Hagens. His puck skills are very impressive, and he can do some special things with the puck on his stick when you consider his size. He can be really flashy on the ice thanks to his above-average puck skills. However, he's got to work on his consistency in order to bring his A-game even further. He has also started adding more tenacity to his game this year, and his skating has continued to improve since we first saw him play in the OHL. He could get a look with Team Canada for the 2025 World Junior Hockey Championship.

4	PLAYER	TEAM	LEAGUE	HEIGHT	WEIGHT	POS	GRADE
	RYABKIN, IVAN	DYNAMO MOSCOW	RUS-JR	6'00"	170	LC	A
NHLCS	CEILING	FLOOR	HOCKEY SENSE	COMPETE	SKILL	SKATE	MISC
-	7	7	7	7	7	6	6

Ryabkin had a historical season in the Russian junior league, breaking the records for points and points per game in the MHL as a U17 player. He beat out both Matvei Michkov and Nikita Kucherov. He finished the year with 58 points in 44 games (2 points higher than Michkov, 4 higher than Kucherov) but it was his points-per-game ratio that was vastly superior to both (1.32 compared to 1.02 for Kucherov and 1.00 for Michkov). The young center has terrific hands that make him a dangerous player one-on-one. He has good vision, he likes to slow down play and control the tempo of the game with the puck on his stick. At times, he could stand to play with more pace, and we would like to see him add more explosiveness to his stride as well. This being said, he's a high-end talent for the 2025 NHL Draft. Next season is likely to be split between juniors and the KHL if he keeps progressing and dominating the MHL like he did last season. Dynamo Moscow did something similar this season with Igor Chernyshov.

5	PLAYER	TEAM	LEAGUE	HEIGHT	WEIGHT	POS	GRADE
	SCHAEFER, MATTHEW	ERIE	OHL	6'01"	161	LD	A
NHLCS	CEILING	FLOOR	HOCKEY SENSE	COMPETE	SKILL	SKATE	MISC
-	7	7	6	7	7	8	7

Schaefer was the top pick in the 2023 OHL Draft and had a good rookie season with Erie despite not being a high-point producer. He did well in international events such as the U17 Hockey Challenge in November and the World U18 Hockey Championship in April. He's a fantastic skater from the back end and a threat in transition due to his ability to rush the puck and move it quickly to his forwards. Thinking the game at a high level, he does fall victim to mental errors at times, but overall, there's a lot to like. He's a great athlete with a good toolkit, although we're still unsure how high his offensive upside is. His overall game and athletic tools will make him a very good defenseman long-term. It's worth mentioning that he's also extremely young for this draft class. If he was born 10 days later than he was, he would only be eligible for the 2026 NHL Draft. His profile looks a bit like what we saw from Sam Dickinson in his OHL rookie season.

6	PLAYER	TEAM	LEAGUE	HEIGHT	WEIGHT	POS	GRADE
	HENSLEY, LOGAN	USA-U18	NTDP	6'02"	196	RD	A
NHLCS	CEILING	FLOOR	HOCKEY SENSE	COMPETE	SKILL	SKATE	MISC
-	7	7	6	7	7	7	7

Hensler is an American defenseman that we have seen over the past two years with the NTDP program. He has made some nice progress over those last two seasons. He's a good-sized defenseman with strong skating skills and athletic abilities. Similar to Schaefer, we're unsure at this point how high will his offensive upside be, but there's a lot to like with this player. He's a very good passer, but we would like to see him be a tad more aggressive offensively at times when he has the puck on his stick. He moves well, and covers a lot of space on the ice with his skating and reach. He can also play a physical game along the boards and clear the front of his net, despite not having a mean streak in him per se. He has the potential to be a minutes-eater in the NHL that can play in all situations. He'll play in the NCAA in his draft year with the University of Wisconsin.

7	PLAYER	TEAM	LEAGUE	HEIGHT	WEIGHT	POS	GRADE
	MISA, MICHAEL	SAGINAW	OHL	6'01"	174	LW	A

NHLCS	CEILING	FLOOR	HOCKEY SENSE	COMPETE	SKILL		SKATE	MISC
-	8	6	6	6	7		7	7

Misa was the 1st overall pick in the 2022 OHL Draft by Saginaw after having received exceptional status to play major junior hockey as a 15-year-old. He had a solid first year in the league, but didn't make major strides in his second season. In fact, his points-per-game ratio decreased from 1.24 to 1.12 this season. In August at the Hlinka-Gretzky Cup, his performance did not blow us away. He does, despite this, remain a player with tons of potential and a great toolkit that can make his adaptation to the pro game a lot smoother: his well above-average athletic abilities and overall skill level. An effortless skater with a long stride and good top speed, he has a good projectable frame to go along with it, albeit still raw with lots of development time ahead. Next season, he will be the main guy offensively in Saginaw and he will see his responsibilities increase. We are looking at a big improvement with his production next season and possibly playing full time down the middle.

8	PLAYER	TEAM	LEAGUE	HEIGHT	WEIGHT	POS	GRADE
	O'BRIEN, JAKE	BRANTFORD	OHL	6'00"	150	RC	A

NHLCS	CEILING	FLOOR	HOCKEY SENSE	COMPETE	SKILL		SKATE	MISC
-	8	6	8	6	7		6	6

O'Brien was the most impressive rookie we saw in the OHL this season. There are not many players in the league who can pass the puck like he does. He has a great processor and thinks the game at a high level, making the linemates around him better thanks to his smart plays with the puck and elite vision. There's some Robert Thomas in the way that he plays; he could stand to shoot the puck more, but his passing game is exceptional. However, he'll need to add more mass to his frame and increase his physical strength. He also needs to increase his speed and add more explosiveness on the ice with his skating. If he can improve those two things without setbacks to his development next season, we think he's going to make a lot of noise in the OHL and be a popular name ahead of the 2025 NHL Draft.

9	PLAYER	TEAM	LEAGUE	HEIGHT	WEIGHT	POS	GRADE
	DESNOYERS, CALEB	MONCTON	QMJHL	6'01"	163	LC	A

NHLCS	CEILING	FLOOR	HOCKEY SENSE	COMPETE	SKILL		SKATE	MISC
-	7	7	7	6	7		6	6

Desnoyers is an ultra-smart center from the QMJHL who was the first overall pick in the 2023 QMJHL Draft. He was just under a point per game with the Moncton Wildcats this past season with 56 points in 60 games. He was also a standout performer at the U17 Hockey Challenge in November and took over for Roger McQueen in April after his injury and played well at 5 on 5 between Gavin McKenna and Porter Martone. A pass-first type of center, he sees the ice well and loves to feed his linemates passes in scoring areas. He makes the players around him better while playing a very mature game at both ends of the ice. A complete player who thinks the game at a high level, he needs to be just a bit more selfish and put more pucks on the net himself. There's not much missing to his game, aside from shooting the puck more and adding physical strength (as he's quite lanky). His brother Elliot was drafted by Philadelphia in 2020.

10	PLAYER		TEAM	LEAGUE	HEIGHT	WEIGHT	POS	GRADE
	RESCHNY, COLE		VICTORIA	WHL	5'09"	161	LC	A
NHLCS	CEILING	FLOOR	HOCKEY SENSE	COMPETE	SKILL		SKATE	MISC
-	7	6	7	6	7		6	5

Reschny was the 3rd overall pick in the 2022 WHL Bantam Draft and had a great rookie season, collecting 59 points in 61 games. He was also quite good at the U17 Hockey Challenge in November, where he had 8 points in 7 games. A smart player, Reschny was already playing in all kinds of situations for Victoria, regularly featured on the PK unit, which is rare for a 16-year-old rookie in major junior. We love his creativity and passing game. He makes the players around him better and has good one-on-one skills with his soft hands. He's not a huge player, and while he's a decent skater, we would like to see him improve his explosiveness to enhance his size/skating combination for his NHL Draft year. He's playing center now, but we could see him move to the wing due to his lack of size to play down the middle at the NHL level.

11	PLAYER		TEAM	LEAGUE	HEIGHT	WEIGHT	POS	GRADE
	SPENCE, MALCOLM		ERIE	OHL	6'02"	192	LW	A
NHLCS	CEILING	FLOOR	HOCKEY SENSE	COMPETE	SKILL		SKATE	MISC
-	6	6	7	8	7		7	7

The 2nd overall pick in the 2022 OHL Draft, this was Spence's second season in the OHL. He collected 19 goals and 62 points in 68 games and was a good performer for Canada at the Hlinka-Gretzky Cup in August (he scored the overtime goal in the final against Czechia). At the U18s in April, he was one of Canada's top players in the preliminary round, but his game cooled off a bit in the medal round. A two-way winger who can do about everything well, he has no major weakness to his game. We were really impressed with his defensive efforts this season. When you have his size, athleticism and two-way game, it bodes well for the future. He projects as a player who can play anywhere in a lineup and will be impactful on special teams. He might not be a high-end offensive player, but his overall game and smarts make him a very good player for the 2025 NHL Draft class.

12	PLAYER		TEAM	LEAGUE	HEIGHT	WEIGHT	POS	GRADE
	MCQUEEN, ROGER		BRANDON	WHL	6'05"	190	RC	A
NHLCS	CEILING	FLOOR	HOCKEY SENSE	COMPETE	SKILL		SKATE	MISC
-	7	6	6	7	7		5	7

The 4th overall pick in the 2021 WHL Bantam Draft, McQueen is a physical power forward who has progressed well since his WHL rookie season, going from 4 to 21 goals and from 14 to 51 points. His skating was one area that needed the most work, and we saw solid improvement in that category this season. He can keep up with the play better now, and his forecheck game has been bolstered by the improvement in his skating. He's still quite raw physically; the amount of development he has ahead of him makes him an intriguing prospect for the 2025 NHL Draft. He has a rare combination of size, physicality and skills that NHL teams search for. He has good hands; we like his vision and ability to attack the net with the puck. We expect big things out of him next season as he should continue to improve his offensive game and put up good numbers in his draft year.

13	PLAYER	TEAM	LEAGUE	HEIGHT	WEIGHT	POS	GRADE
	BOUMEDIENNE, SASCHA	YOUNGSTOWN	USHL	6'02"	183	LD	A
NHLCS	CEILING	FLOOR	HOCKEY SENSE	COMPETE	SKILL	SKATE	MISC
-	7	6	6	6	7	8	7

Originally from Sweden, Boumedienne has spent most of his youth in America, and now plays for Youngstown in the USHL. His father (Josef) was drafted by New Jersey in 1996 and has worked in both scouting and coaching with the Columbus Blue Jackets for the past 11 years. Sascha had a strong rookie year in the USHL, with 27 points in 49 games, good for 3rd overall in points for U18 defensemen. A great athlete, he has above-average skating skills, is a good puck-distributor, and has power play value as well. He needs to find more consistency with his decision-making on the ice, and to improve his defense. He has good size already, and we would like to see him use a bit more physicality in his own end. He's committed to playing college hockey at Boston University starting in the 2024-2025 season.

14	PLAYER	TEAM	LEAGUE	HEIGHT	WEIGHT	POS	GRADE
	MRTKA, RADIM	TRINEC	CZE-JR.	6'06"	198	RD	A
NHLCS	CEILING	FLOOR	HOCKEY SENSE	COMPETE	SKILL	SKATE	MISC
-	7	7	7	7	6	6	8

Mrtka is a hulking defenseman and played this past season in the Czechia junior league, but also internationally, for the U17 and U18 national teams. The first thing you notice about him is obviously his size, but he also has good puck poise and makes good decisions with the puck on his stick. He's still raw offensively, but he has a good point shot and can pass the puck well enough. He has decent to good mobility on the ice, still growing into his body, which means his coordination and explosiveness are still works-in-progress, but we saw positive improvements over the course of the season. From 6'04" at the beginning of the year to now 6'06", obviously NHL teams are excited about what he's going to look like on the ice when he's in his 20s. A smart defender, he has physicality and a very good stick to steal pucks from opponents. A very intriguing defenseman for the 2025 NHL Draft, and if he stays in Czechia next season, he should get a strong look to play in the men's league with HC Oceláři Třinec.

15	PLAYER	TEAM	LEAGUE	HEIGHT	WEIGHT	POS	GRADE
	MURTAGH, JACK	USA-U17	NTDP	6'00"	185	LW	A
NHLCS	CEILING	FLOOR	HOCKEY SENSE	COMPETE	SKILL	SKATE	MISC
-	6	7	7	7	6	7	6

Murtagh was one of the more impressive players on the U17 team this season, one that kept getting better as the season went on. This is a player who can play both down the middle and on the wing. He has good (but not great) skills, but what makes him intriguing is his non-stop motor, well-above-average skating skills and shooting abilities. He's a smart hockey player who brings value to this team both with and without the puck. He's similar to Malcolm Spence because of his excellent two-way game and ability to play anywhere in a lineup. He uses his acceleration well to create offensive chances off the rush, but also uses his speed to create turnovers with his backchecking efforts. He's a tenacious player along the wall and in front of the net. A good all-around player with a strong compete level, he's committed to Boston University starting in the 2025-2026 season.

16	PLAYER			TEAM	LEAGUE	HEIGHT	WEIGHT	POS	GRADE
	AMICO, CARTER			USA-U17	NTDP	6'05"	205	RD	A
NHLCS	CEILING	FLOOR		HOCKEY SENSE	COMPETE	SKILL		SKATE	MISC
-	7	6		6	7	6		7	8

Amico is one of the best pure athletes, not only for his NTDP team, but for the entire 2025 NHL Draft class. He's really raw, but his athleticism makes him the most intriguing player on the USA U17 team because of what could be his long-term potential. Already 6'05", he doesn't look like he's finished growing, and he should add at least 20-25 pounds to his frame before he's physically mature. He has good puck skills despite being widely inconsistent with his decision-making and play in his own zone. He's still scratching the surface of his on-ice talent; when you have his size, skating, physicality and puck skills, the combination is very intriguing. He still has much to learn, but if he can put everything together next season, he may become one of the more popular players in the 2025 class. He's committed to Boston University starting in 2025-2026.

17	PLAYER			TEAM	LEAGUE	HEIGHT	WEIGHT	POS	GRADE
	MOORE, WILLIAM			USA-U17	NTDP	6'02"	161	LC	A
NHLCS	CEILING	FLOOR		HOCKEY SENSE	COMPETE	SKILL		SKATE	MISC
-	7	6		6	6	6		6	7

Moore was a player who came to the program with a lot of hype. He could have played with the OHL's London Knights, but chose to go to the NTDP program instead. Drafted 18th overall by London in the 2023 OHL Draft, he was originally projected as a top-3 pick. He's a good-sized center who still needs to fill out physically. He has a good projectable frame with good hands and good shooting abilities. Still physically raw, the style that he wants to play can make it more evident when he gets outmuscled; he likes to slow down the play, but many of his projectable plays are from around the net or down low. What he lacks in physicality diminishes his efficiency in this area. We would also like to see him improve his consistency and on-ice explosiveness, and be tougher to play against. Moore committed in early June to play college hockey with Boston College in 2025-2026.

18	PLAYER			TEAM	LEAGUE	HEIGHT	WEIGHT	POS	GRADE
	ISH WOZNIAK, JAKOB			LULEA	SWE-JR.	6'03"	179	RW	A
NHLCS	CEILING	FLOOR		HOCKEY SENSE	COMPETE	SKILL		SKATE	MISC
-	7	6		6	6	7		6	7

Ihs-Wozniak is one of the top Swedes available for the 2025 Draft Class after Anton Frondell. He had an amazing season with his club team, collecting 50 points in 36 games, breaking the J20 Nationell record for most points by a U17 player (held most recently by Lucas Raymond). With great size already, he has soft hands and a great ability to shoot the puck. He's great on the power play and is a threat to score from the slot if he's used in the bumper role or from the half-wall on the left side. However, he's more of a complimentary scorer than the one who is running things on his line, and we would like to see more line-driving from him next season. If he can do that, you could see his name rise on draft lists. He was part of Team Sweden at the World Under 18 Hockey Championship in April, but didn't receive much ice time during this event. He could challenge for some playing time in the SHL next year, as he did play 2 games there this past season.

19	PLAYER		TEAM	LEAGUE	HEIGHT	WEIGHT	POS	GRADE
	MCKINNEY, COLE		USA-U17	NTDP	6'00"	190	RC	A
NHLCS	CEILING	FLOOR	HOCKEY SENSE	COMPETE	SKILL		SKATE	MISC
-	6	7	7	7	6		6	6

McKinney is a strong two-way center from the USNTDP's U17 team whose defensive game is quite advanced for his age. This will help him transition quicker as he moves to the next level. He can play in all situations and is the type of player coaches love to have on their team late in periods or games. A smart player, his off-the-puck game shines if you pay attention to the little details of the game. He's good in the faceoff circle, and has great value on the PK unit thanks to his anticipation and compete level. However, in order for us to place him higher on our list, we're going to need to see more upside. We have yet to be convinced that he's a true top-2 center when projecting him for the NHL. While he looks like a really safe pick right now, next season, we want to see him expand his offensive game. He's committed to playing at Michigan University once he's finished with the NTDP.

20	PLAYER		TEAM	LEAGUE	HEIGHT	WEIGHT	POS	GRADE
	GUITÉ, ÉMILE		CHICOUTIMI	QMJHL	6'01"	165	LW	A
NHLCS	CEILING	FLOOR	HOCKEY SENSE	COMPETE	SKILL		SKATE	MISC
-	8	5	8	7	7		5	6

Guité was named Rookie of the Year in the QMJHL this past season with 57 points in 61 games, playing for Chicoutimi, who selected Guité 2nd overall in the 2023 QMJHL Draft behind Caleb Desnoyers. A standout player in November at the U17 Hockey Challenge, he scored 7 goals and 10 points in 8 games, helping Canada White win the gold medal. The year prior, he won the Telus Cup with his midget team, amassing 13 points in 7 games and earning the MVP title of the tournament. He was also a great performer for Team Québec at the Canada Games, with 11 points in 6 games. Guité is deadly with the puck and has an elite hockey sense. He's a dual threat offensively: a sniper who also sees the ice well and makes precise passes. He's great on the power play from the right wing half-wall, where he's often set up for one-timers but can also set up his teammates, making him very unpredictable on the ice. Improvement in his skating will be the number one priority for his summer off-season training.

21	PLAYER		TEAM	LEAGUE	HEIGHT	WEIGHT	POS	GRADE
	RAVENSBERGEN, JOSHUA		PRINCE GEORGE	WHL	6'04"	181	G	A
NHLCS	CEILING	FLOOR	HOCKEY SENSE	COMPETE	SKILL		SKATE	MISC
-	8	6	6	7	7		7	8

This young goaltender was one of the best stories this year in the CHL. He came out of nowhere (having gone undrafted in the WHL Draft) only to become a vital part of the Prince George Cougars in addition to one of the top young goaltending prospects worldwide. He had a good rookie season with Prince George, but was even better in the playoffs, eventually losing against Portland in the league's semi-final. He had a great first half of the season, during which his save percentage was .934. His play to drop in the second half (.882 sv%) but he bounced back in the playoffs (.931 save percentage in the 12 games he played). He's a big, athletic goaltender who can make everything look easy. He also has the athleticism to make high-end saves when needed. We like the way he reads the play, in addition to his poise in his crease. In the series against Portland, he demonstrated a great ability to bounce back from weaker games, which is always a great sign for any goaltender.

22	PLAYER	TEAM	LEAGUE	HEIGHT	WEIGHT	POS	GRADE
	TRETHEWEY, CHARLIE	USA-U17	NTDP	6'01"	190	RD	B

NHLCS	CEILING	FLOOR	HOCKEY SENSE	COMPETE	SKILL	SKATE	MISC
-	6	6	6	6	6	6	6

Trethewey was tied for first in points among defensemen on the U17 team this year and made a huge splash in November at the U17 Hockey Challenge with 10 points in 7 games, which was good for first in points among defensemen and fourth overall for all skaters. He looked like a good offensive defenseman at this November tournament, but for the rest of the season, he was not a difference-maker on the scoresheet. If we have to project him, we're not sold on the idea that he's a PP1 guy at the NHL level. He still has a long way to go, however, and he's a very young player for this draft class with a lot of development time ahead to improve. His hockey IQ can appear problematic at times; he'll need to make better reads and decisions with the puck while under pressure. In addition, we would like to see him improve his skating; he's not the most fluid or explosive skater out there. However, we like his defending and his physicality in his own end.

23	PLAYER	TEAM	LEAGUE	HEIGHT	WEIGHT	POS	GRADE
	MOONEY, LJ	USA-U17	NTDP	5'07"	150	RW	B

NHLCS	CEILING	FLOOR	HOCKEY SENSE	COMPETE	SKILL	SKATE	MISC
-	8	5	7	7	8	8	4

Mooney had a strong first year with the NTDP program; he was the only player from the U17 team to graduate to the U18 team in the last stretch of the season and participate in the World Under 18 Hockey Championship. Mooney also has hockey lineage; Logan Cooley is his cousin. He's undersized, which will be a point of debate among NHL teams in his draft year, but his talent level is excellent. A great skater, he plays with pace and is a great stickhandler. He can make plays that will pull you out of your seat. There will be comparisons with Cole Caufield, but they're not the same type of player outside of their size. Mooney is a more well-rounded player at the same age, minus the elite scoring ability Caufield had at his age. We also very much like his compete level on the ice. He may be small, but he doesn't play afraid, and his energy level is always very good. He's a great athlete with a good work ethic whose size is the only real big question mark at this point. We like his game. Parallels can be made between his game and that of Dallas Stars rookie Logan Stankoven as well.

24	PLAYER	TEAM	LEAGUE	HEIGHT	WEIGHT	POS	GRADE
	POTTER, CULLEN	USA-U17	NTDP	5'09"	161	LW	B

NHLCS	CEILING	FLOOR	HOCKEY SENSE	COMPETE	SKILL	SKATE	MISC
-	6	6	5	7	6	9	5

Simply put, Potter is an elite skater. His skating abilities are off the charts. He reminds us a bit of Oliver Moore in the way he skates and plays. He's an elite transition player thanks to his speed and ability to make zone entries. He's also dynamic, taking advantage of turnovers in the neutral zone with his great speed. All this to say: his skating is a real advantage and factor in his efficiency on the ice. His skill level is above-average despite him not being a high-end offensive player. He plays at such a high speed that he doesn't really make his linemates better on the ice (similar to Oliver Moore once again). He needs to learn how to slow down the play a bit and adapt his speed to that of his teammates. He can't go 100 MPH all the time. An undersized player, he competes hard enough on the ice that it shouldn't be a huge concern if he can grow a bit and get physically stronger.

25	PLAYER	TEAM	LEAGUE	HEIGHT	WEIGHT	POS	GRADE
	GRASTIN, MILTON	MODO HOCKEY	SWE-JR.	6'02"	179	LC	B
NHLCS	CEILING	FLOOR	HOCKEY SENSE	COMPETE	SKILL	SKATE	MISC
-	6	6	6	6	6	6	6

Gastrin projects as a power center. Nothing stands out in his skillset, but he doesn't have any real weakness, either. He does everything well on the ice, is solid in all three zones, and has value on the PK unit and possibly a PP2. He's in the same mold as Julius Miettinen, eligible in 2024, or David Edstrom, who was the 32nd overall pick in the 2023 NHL Draft by Vegas. Gastrin brings a complete game down the middle: good size, skating and some skills. As he gets more development time next season, we're going to get a better picture of his offensive upside to see if it's more top-6 or 3rd-line. He was the captain of the Swedish U17 team last year and had 16 points in 41 games in his first season in Sweden's junior league with Modo Hockey.

26	PLAYER	TEAM	LEAGUE	HEIGHT	WEIGHT	POS	GRADE
	EKBERG, FILIP	ALMTUNA	SWE-JR.	5'09"	163	LW	B
NHLCS	CEILING	FLOOR	HOCKEY SENSE	COMPETE	SKILL	SKATE	MISC
-	7	5	6	6	7	6	5

Ekberg had just under a point per game in the Swedish junior league this season, with 29 points in 33 games, and was a good player for Sweden's U17 team this season. In 2022-2023 as a 15-year-old, he had 15 points in 20 games in J20. Unfortunately, it appears as though his progression curve fell a bit flat. We did expect a bit more out of him this season in J20 and internationally. He's on the small side, but has great offensive skills. Dynamic with the puck on his stick, the combination of his good skating and stickhandling skills makes him dangerous on the ice. He's as good a playmaker as he is a shooter on the ice. He's going to need to improve his play away from the puck and be tougher to play against in order to help his stock during his draft year

27	PLAYER	TEAM	LEAGUE	HEIGHT	WEIGHT	POS	GRADE
	EKLUND, VICTOR	DJURGARDENS	SWE-JR.	5'11"	161	RW	B
NHLCS	CEILING	FLOOR	HOCKEY SENSE	COMPETE	SKILL	SKATE	MISC
-	7	5	7	7	6	6	5

The younger brother of William Eklund (San Jose Sharks), Victor split this past season between the junior league and the Allsvenskan. A smart player with a similar playing style as his older brother, he's not the fastest, but sees the ice well and has great deception skills that make him a tougher player to counter because of his unpredictability on the ice. Again like his brother, he needs to continue to work on improving his shot so that he can be more of a threat shooting from distances. He'll also need to go into the rough areas of the ice to get his goals, which will be more difficult in the NHL. He will need to get stronger in order to be able to compete more in these situations. Despite his physical immaturity, he plays with really good energy on the ice, demonstrating some grit and playing a hard game. Even as the 2nd-youngest player on Team Sweden at the U18s in April, he was driving the play for his line at times, which is a good sign for the future.

28	PLAYER			TEAM	LEAGUE	HEIGHT	WEIGHT	POS	GRADE
	RADIVOJEVIC, LUKA			OREBRO	SWE-JR.	5'10"	161	RD	B
NHLCS	CEILING	FLOOR		HOCKEY SENSE	COMPETE	SKILL		SKATE	MISC
-	7	5		7	6	7		5	4

Luka had a really strong season in Sweden's junior league with 33 points in 43 games. He also played 6 games in the SHL. His point totals are the highest total for U17 defensemen in J20 history, breaking Erik Brannstrom's record. He also played internationally for Slovakia in big events such as the Hlinka Gretzky Cup and the U18 and U20 World Hockey Championships. An undersized, puck-moving defenseman, he's a smart player with good on-ice vision who can pass the puck really well. There's some power play value in his game, but we would like to see him improve his shot because at the moment he's more of a passer and not a huge threat with his point shot. His lack of size and strength can limit him in his zone when defending against bigger players, which could be problematic when projecting his game for the NHL. Defensemen like himself don't always pan out because of their lack of size and skating combination, and we will have a better idea of what he looks like next year after a good summer if he can improve his strength and quickness.

29	PLAYER			TEAM	LEAGUE	HEIGHT	WEIGHT	POS	GRADE
	GAVIN, JORDAN			TRI-CITY	WHL	5'11"	181	LW	B
NHLCS	CEILING	FLOOR		HOCKEY SENSE	COMPETE	SKILL		SKATE	MISC
-	7	6		7	5	7		5	5

Gavin was the 2nd overall selection in the 2021 WHL Bantam Draft behind Berkly Catton. This was his second season in the WHL. Despite slightly improving his numbers compared to his rookie year, he probably didn't make the huge progression we had hoped for. He finished the season with 23 goals and 68 points in 68 games. It's worth mentioning that his team was not very good (finishing second-to-last in the league) and he was not surrounded by really good offensive players. A smart winger who can pass the puck, his vision and creativity are his best assets. He has a decent shot with good hands, but he's not a high-end goal scorer. We would also like to see him improve his skating. An average skater for his size in terms of top speed and explosiveness, he does have good edgework to compensate for what he lacks. We would also love to see him engage more physically and be a tougher player to play against.

30	PLAYER			TEAM	LEAGUE	HEIGHT	WEIGHT	POS	GRADE
	KINDEL, BENJAMIN			CALGARY	WHL	5'10"	165	RW	B
NHLCS	CEILING	FLOOR		HOCKEY SENSE	COMPETE	SKILL		SKATE	MISC
-	7	5		8	7	7		6	5

Kindel was one of the top rookies in the WHL this past season, leading all U17 players not named Gavin McKenna in scoring (60 points in 68 games). He's more of a playmaker, as evidenced by 45 of his 60 points being assists. An ultra-intelligent player on the ice, Kindel makes the players around him better, and can score as well. He has an underrated shot and quick hands. Physically, he needs to get stronger, but we think his potential could be really good if he does. He's a decent skater, but he'll need to continue to work on his explosiveness and be stronger on his skates, especially in consideration of his size and physical rawness. Not only a talented player, Kindel also has a very good work ethic, and if he can put everything together, could become a very good small player for the NHL. Surprisingly, he was not chosen this past November for the U17 Hockey Challenge, but there's a good chance you'll see his name in the discussion for Canada U18 teams next season in August and April.

31	PLAYER	TEAM	LEAGUE	HEIGHT	WEIGHT	POS	GRADE
	CARBONNEAU, JUSTIN	BLAINVILLE	QMJHL	6'01"	189	RW	B

NHLCS	CEILING	FLOOR	HOCKEY SENSE	COMPETE	SKILL	SKATE	MISC
-	6	6	6	6	6	7	6

Carbonneau had a good first full season in the QMJHL, scoring 31 goals and 59 points in 68 games. He struggled early on (scoring only twice in his first 16 games), but soon found his confidence and started scoring at a very good rate, concluding the year with 29 goals in his last 52 games. With his size, reach, puck-protection game and skating, he does look like a pro prospect out there. His combination of size and skating is one that NHL teams love, in addition to the rest of his toolset. His shooting ability progressed well, and he was able to expand his playmaking which makes him a potential offensive dual threat. While he competes hard enough, he will need to improve his play in his zone. Next season, we will have a better read on his true potential and whether he projects as a top-6 forward or more of a third-liner.

32	PLAYER	TEAM	LEAGUE	HEIGHT	WEIGHT	POS	GRADE
	LIMATOV, KURBAN	DYNAMO MOSCOW	RUS-JR	6'04"	187	LD	B

NHLCS	CEILING	FLOOR	HOCKEY SENSE	COMPETE	SKILL	SKATE	MISC
-	6	6	6	7	6	7	7

Limatov is a big athletic Russian defenseman who played in the MHL as a 16-year-old this past season. We have seen Russia produce high-end athletic defensemen for the past two drafts (Simashev in 2023, Silayev in 2024); Limatov could potentially be the 2025 version. His play in the MHL saw its share of ups and downs this season, but he has the athletic tools to be an impact defender. Mostly, his decision-making was pretty inconsistent during the season and he might be a bit limited as far as being a PP1 guy in the NHL. He needs to learn to make better decisions while under pressure in his own end. A big defender, he moves well and makes life tougher for opposing forwards on the ice. He has the physicality and closes gaps quickly off the rush. He didn't play a lot with his team this season (in terms of ice time) and also missed some games due to injury at the beginning of the season. It took him a while to find his rhythm from there.

CREDITS

First off, I want to apologize for less NHL Scouts quotes in this years book. My in person viewings were limited in the second half of this season due to a family members illness and ultimately a death. This affected me getting as many quotes as I did in previous seasons. Things will be back to normal starting next seasons scouting schedule.

Next up - This will be the final year for our NHL Draft Black Book. We'll let you know later this summer what the 2025 publication will look like. The reason for the change is simply the time needed to create this book. It's a ridiculous amount of hours per day spanning over at least 10 weeks. 2024 is the start of year 20 for HockeyProspect.com - it's as good as time as any for a change in direction in our NHL Draft publication.

A big thanks to all our scouts who spend countless hours in the rinks and adding additional viewings through video.

While I have final say on our rankings for our top 45 players on our list. Jérôme took over final say on players 46 through to the end of our list 2 years ago. This doesn't translate to me leaving the meeting once we hit player 46 on our list. I still chime in and voice my opinion, but Jérôme has the opportunity to follow what **he** thinks is best after weighing the opinion of myself and our other scouts.

Once again a huge thank you to Katherine Kocur for her assistance with editing. She's been a huge hidden star behind the scenes for well over a decade We truly appreciate her. We give her very little time and she manages to work some miracles.

As always, I hope you enjoy our **2024 NHL Draft Black Book**. Please accept my gratitude for supporting our service again this season. Our costs are still high and we need people like you or HockeyProspect.com will disappear.

I know that everyone is still feeling the crunch of increased prices in all our daily lives. For that reason I decreased our membership pricing and it remains that way. . We simply can't do what we do, or survive without the continued support of people like you purchasing our memberships or books.

regards,
Mark Edwards
HockeyProspect.com

The scouts who made me look good again this year.

Jérôme Bérubé - Director of Scouting   J.Brad Johnston

Brad Allen - Cross Over Scout

Dusten Braaksma

Michael Farkas

Joel Collete

Tim Archambault

© HockeyProspect.com

Made in United States
North Haven, CT
25 July 2024

55393830R00170